Learning about Immigration Law

Third Edition

LEARNING ABOUT IMMIGRATION LAW

Third Edition

Constantinos E. Scaros

Australia • Brazil • Japan • Korea • Mexico • Singapore • Spain • United Kingdom • United States

Learning about Immigration Law
Third Edition
Constantinos E. Scaros

Career Education Strategic Business Unit Vice President: Dawn Gerrain

Managing Editor: Robert L. Serenka, Jr.

Acquisitions Editor: Shelley Esposito

Senior Product Manager: Melissa Riveglia

Director of Production: Wendy A. Troeger

Senior Content Project Manager: Betty L. Dickson

Technology Project Manager: Sandy Charette

Director of Marketing: Wendy Mapstone

Marketing Manager: Gerard McAvey

Cover Design: Rose Design

Cover Image: ©Getty Images ©Royalty-Free Corbis

Library of Congress Control Number: 2006013095

ISBN-13: 978-1-4180-3259-3

ISBN-10: 1-4180-3259-X

Delmar
Executive Woods
5 Maxwell Drive
Clifton Park, NY 12065
USA

Cengage Learning is a leading provider of customized learning solutions with office locations around the globe, including Singapore, the United Kingdom, Australia, Mexico, Brazil, and Japan. Locate your local office at **international.cengage.com/region**

Cengage Learning products are represented in Canada by Nelson Education, Ltd.

For your lifelong learning solutions, visit **www.cengage.com/delmar**

Visit our corporate website at **www.cengage.com**

Printed in the United States of America
2 3 4 5 6 7 11 10 09 08

To my father, Emmanuel C. Scaros, who first taught me about immigration law and professional integrity.

CONTENTS

FOREWORD

I am a lawyer, and I also teach and write about several types of law. A great deal of my work—both in teaching and practicing law—involves immigration. Having been an immigration lawyer for many years, I have learned some valuable things that I will share with you in this book.

Whatever your reason for wanting to learn about immigration law—whether you are an attorney, paralegal, or student or whether you wish to help yourself, a relative, friend, or neighbor with some aspect of immigration—you will find this book to be a valuable resource.

Constantinos E. Scaros

PREFACE

The last time I revised *Learning about Immigration Law* was when I wrote the second edition in 2000. At that time, the United States was a much different place than it is today. Since that time, many aspects of life in the United States have been affected significantly, not the least of which is immigration law.

At the time the second edition was published, there were already many immigration laws in place to safeguard our national security in the face of the growing threat of terrorism. In 1993, terrorists bombed New York City's World Trade Center—its two massive skyscrapers commonly known as the Twin Towers—resulting in property damage, bodily injury, and death. Fortunately, the Twin Towers were preserved, and the vast majority of employees, shoppers, commuters, and tourists in the area escaped unharmed. That act of terrorism was a prime factor that inspired some substantial changes to the immigration law that took effect in 1996. Sadly, this was not the last act of terrorism that the Twin Towers and the United States were to endure.

On September 11, 2001, a far more severe act of terrorism affected the Twin Towers, New York City, Washington, D.C., the rest of the United States, and the world. Terrorists crashed commercial airplanes into the Twin Towers, causing them to crumble to the ground and killing thousands of people in the process. Another airplane crashed into the Pentagon in Washington, D.C., and a third airplane (purportedly headed toward the White House or the U.S. Capitol) crashed in Pennsylvania. The heroic acts of a group of passengers on board—sacrificing their own lives—prevented the airplane from destroying its intended target (whatever that might have been).

The terrorists involved in these attacks were not citizens or residents of the United States. All fears and concerns about foreign terrorists circumventing our immigration laws and gaining access to our country grew exponentially following that infamous day—better known as 9/11.

This latest edition of *Learning about Immigration Law,* third edition, addresses the changes that have taken place to immigration law since 9/11: formal laws, policies, and procedures, as well as general attitudes about U.S. immigration.

The aftermath of 9/11 is a time in which our activities such as boarding an airplane, entering a federal building, or visiting certain countries abroad have been met with heightened scrutiny. Similarly, the thousands of decent, law-abiding people throughout the world whose dream it is to visit, study or work in, or move to the United States have a more difficult time in doing so because of the horrible acts of a few. Nonetheless, their opportunities for legal entry into the United States have not been lost.

The third edition will point out how, even after 9/11, that dream still can become a reality.

WHY *LEARNING ABOUT IMMIGRATION LAW* IS USEFUL

This book is designed for anyone interested in learning about immigration law: legal professionals, law students, historians, sociologists, or anyone else interested in this fascinating subject.

Immigration is featured in the news on an almost daily basis. But news stories usually are not written by lawyers and may lack the legal accuracy and completeness that is necessary to master the subject matter. On the other hand, many lawyers who do write about immigration tend to be overly technical and may confuse or alienate the reader. That's why this book is different. It is based on simple language, common sense, and plenty of examples.

Rather than serve as a manual, this book is a readable guide that directs the reader through the whole story of immigration, step by step, era by era. It explains not only the *what*, but also the *why*.

A WALK THROUGH THE THIRD EDITION

Chapter 1 introduces the reader to the basics of immigration law and provides a brief but necessary review of U.S. history.

Chapter 2 is all about nonimmigrants—those people who want to come to the United States temporarily. Chapters 3, 4, and 5 deal with immigrants—those people who want to come here permanently.

Chapter 6 is devoted to the greatest immigrant dream of all—U.S. citizenship.

Chapter 7 is about inadmissibility and removal—conditions that prohibit certain people from entering or remaining in the United States.

Chapter 8 is about refugees and asylum—conditions that are exceptions to the general rule and provide a safe haven in the United States for some.

Chapter 9 provides some valuable tips for the immigration legal professional.

Famous U.S. Immigrant profiles are provided in each chapter.

Review Questions and Hypotheticals at the end of each chapter are designed to test your knowledge about immigration laws.

The Appendices provide a guide to U.S. citizenship preparation and a vast array of immigration forms. The Glossary includes some of the most important immigration terms.

SUPPLEMENTAL TEACHING MATERIALS

- The *Instructor's Manual with Test Bank* is available online at *http://www.paralegal.delmar.cengage.com* in the Instructor's Lounge under Resource. Written by the author of the text, the *Instructor's Manual* contains suggested syllabi, lecture notes, answers to the text questions, useful Web sites, and a test bank.

- Online Companion™—The *Online Companion*™ Web site can be found at *http://www.paralegal.delmar.cengage.com* in the Resource section of the Web site. The *Online Companion*™ contains the following:
  - Chapter Summary
  - Trivia
  - Internet Resources
  - Appendices
- **Web page**—Come visit our Web site at *http://www.paralegal.delmar.cengage.com*, where you will find valuable information specific to this book such as hot links and sample materials to download, as well as other Delmar Paralegal products.
- **Westlaw®**—West's online computerized legal research system offers students "hands-on" experience with a system commonly used in law offices. Qualified adopters can receive ten free hours of Westlaw®. Westlaw® can be accessed with Macintosh and IBM PC and compatibles. A modem is required.

ACKNOWLEDGMENTS

While the list of those whom I should thank is far too numerous, I'll mention some of the more essential ones here.

To my parents, the rest of my family, and my friends—for all of whom I am grateful.

To my students.

To everyone involved at Delmar Cengage Learning.

To the reviewers who provided valuable comments:

Barry Chaifetz
New York Career Institute
New York, NY

Adria-Ann McMurray
San Francisco State University
San Francisco, CA

Colleen Reid
Lansing Community College
Lansing, MI

George Salis
Keiser College
Lakeland, FL

I hope that you enjoy the book and that I have made it easy for you to use. I would be very happy to hear your feedback or to answer any questions that you might have. Please feel free to contact me through Delmar Cengage Learning.

Constantinos E. Scaros
November 2005

About the Author

Constantinos E. Scaros is an attorney and a college educator in New York City. He has practiced, taught, and written and lectured about immigration law for several years. He has written several books about law and other topics.

INTRODUCTION

Immigration law is a subject with which many people, including legal professionals, are not familiar. It can be difficult to learn depending on where you are looking for guidance and information. Some of the laws are not easy to read and understand, and other sources are often outdated and obsolete. Also, depending on whom you ask for help, there is a good chance that you will be given the wrong information.

Now, the good news: I wrote this book in order to make it easy for you to learn about immigration law. There is no need to use complex words or ideas. The key to learning is clear language, common sense, and plenty of examples. If you read all of the examples provided in this book, you will find that you will learn a great deal about the immigration field.

Immigration law is shaped by our country's history, so many of the lessons in this book will be easy for you to remember and apply as you can relate them to things that you already know. Immigration policy is directly related to current events. Much of what you will learn simply will make sense, so there is not much need to do a lot of memorizing. Unfamiliar terms are defined in the glossary as well as in the text. A U.S. citizenship preparation guide is included in the Appendix so that you can see what people must learn in order to become citizens; it is a good source for someone to study for the American citizenship exam.

From this book, you will learn the underlying policies and basics of immigration law. Also included are review questions for classroom instruction that will ensure that you have mastered the concepts of each chapter.

You will also learn valuable tips about how to use your knowledge to become a successful immigration attorney or paralegal and how to help a neighbor, friend, or relative who may have some immigration questions. Many of the necessary forms are provided in Appendix B, along with instructions for duplicating, completing, and filing these forms.

By the time you have finished reading this book, you will have gained a great deal of knowledge in one of the most highly specialized areas of law. You will probably be surprised at how easy you will find the whole experience to be!

CHAPTER 1

Immigration Law and Policy

Chapter Objectives

After completing this chapter, you should know:

- The story of United States immigration from early times to the present
- The basics of our American system of government
- The ever-changing immigration law
- Some common immigration definitions

The United States is often referred to as "a nation of immigrants." Although it is the world's foremost military, economic, and political superpower, the United States is a relatively young nation (barely over 200 years old). It was founded by immigrants and through its first two centuries has been settled by immigrants consistently.

To this day people from all over the world flock to the United States in order to visit, do business, and settle. Accordingly, immigration continues to flourish, and the opportunities for immigration lawyers and paralegals continue to grow.

In this book you will learn about the basic principles of immigration law. You will learn how the immigration process works and how to help various clients, Americans and non-Americans alike, who need your help.

AN OVERVIEW OF AMERICAN IMMIGRATION

Let's begin by examining the concept of immigration: Why do people want to come to the United States, and how do Americans feel about that? Have the average American's views changed toward immigrants over the last 100 years? What about over the last 50, or 20, or 5?

The Principle of "Overloading the Boat"

American policy and attitude—both official and unofficial—toward immigration often changes based on need and on the principle that is often referred to as "overloading the boat." The "boat" principle is as follows:

Suppose that you are on a cruise; your cruise ship is an average-sized boat—not too big, not too small. It is quite comfortable, and you are having a great time. As the boat continues sailing at sea, the captain notices what appears to be a drastic emergency. Hundreds of people are floating in the sea, some with life preservers, some barely able to stay afloat. A very large boat, much larger than the one you are traveling on, can be seen in the distance. It is rapidly sinking, and the people in the water apparently jumped ship to save their own lives. But if they are not rescued fast, then surely they will drown.

Let's make the situation a bit more dramatic. Suppose that neither ship's communications radio works. In other words, nobody ashore can be informed that the large ship is sinking or that its passengers are in trouble. If you and your cruise mates do not save them, they will not survive.

Your first instinct is to save all of those helpless people. To bring them aboard your own ship and rescue them. However, you realize that there are hundreds of people in the water. If you load all of them onto your own boat, it will sink. Accordingly, not only would you have failed to save those people's lives, but you and your shipmates would also have drowned in the process.

That is the concept of "overloading the boat," a theory often applied to immigration policy.

The Immigration Door

Now, instead of a boat, picture the United States as being entered into, the drowning passengers being those who wish to enter. We, the people of the United States, are in charge of monitoring the door.

On the one hand, we can open the door completely and let everyone in. Very simply, whoever wants to come to the United States will be free to do so. The problem is that millions upon millions of people will take us up on our offer. As a result, our vast resources of land, food, shelter, jobs, and goods will run out. Millions of people, including those born and raised in the United States, may become homeless, unemployed, and may starve to death. Before we examine the other options at this "immigration door," let's look at why so many people choose to come to the United States in the first place.

The Land of Freedom and Opportunity

It is often said that Americans take two things for granted: The American dollar and American citizenship. The dollar is our means of buying goods and services in the United States. But in other countries, the dollar is looked upon as a valuable stock because more often than not it becomes more valuable as another country's currency value decreases.

For instance, suppose that someone uses British pounds or Japanese yen to buy United States dollars. If, over a period of months or years, the dollar becomes more valuable while these foreign currencies devalue, then that person may sell them and receive more money than he or she invested originally.

Like the dollar, American citizenship is a treasure coveted by many around the world. But why? That is an interesting question—and one that makes us think that how we perceive ourselves is often very different from what others think about us. Have you ever thought of yourself as poor or if not poor, then at least in need of more money than you have? In some region of the world right now, there is probably someone, or a few people, who think that you and all other Americans are "filthy rich."

These people think that when your car runs out of gas or gets a little scratch on the fender that you simply leave it on the side of the road and walk into a car dealership to buy a new one. Even if they realized that your lifestyle is not quite that extravagant, in reality, you are very rich when compared to people in some other places around the world.

Next, think about your rights. Have you ever felt discriminated against? Powerless? Did you ever think about not voting because "all politicians are the same" and "things are never going to get better?" If so, then think about this: In the United States at least you have the right to seek change. You may criticize your local politicians, your state's governor, and even the president of the United States. In fact, you may write a letter to the newspaper or even your own book to express your opinion. In many countries, though, that is not the case. If you dared to express your opinion, you suffer various consequences from being denied a job, to imprisonment, and even death.

Have you ever been involved in a legal proceeding and thought that our system of justice is unfair? In some other countries, there is no organized system of justice. In fact, you may not even have a right to a trial or to legal representation. If you are subjected to cruel and unusual punishment, no one will lift a finger to help you.

What about the best restaurants, schools, or doctors? They are very expensive in the United States, right? Only the very rich can afford them. At least, for the most part, Americans have access to some form of food, education, or health care. In other nations, people may starve to death, never have the opportunity to learn how to read or write, and die because they cannot afford any medical attention.

Why Some Stay While Others Go If you've heard the song "Should I Stay or Should I Go," then you might agree that it can be applied to the dilemma that immigrants often face: Should they stay in their beloved homeland or go to seek a better life elsewhere?

Keep in mind that these examples, in which other countries are depicted as lacking freedom and opportunity whereas the United States provides all of that, are not representative of the entire world. In fact, there are many places around the world that Americans may consider to offer an even better quality of life than here at home.

Allow me to share a personal experience with you, one that can be applied to immigration on a worldwide level. I was born and raised in the United States, and that is where I live. But as I write these very words, I am vacationing in Greece—the country from which both of my parents hail. I have visited many places here—including the famous islands of Corfu and Rhodes, and will visit the island of Nisyros (where my parents were born) shortly.

Nisyros is a tiny island compared to the other two. Yet, when I meet Greek Americans in the United States, I am surprised as to how many I meet from Nisyros! It would be like you traveling to Australia and running into large numbers of Americans not from New York, Los Angeles, or Chicago but from a place called Tiny Town, Colorado (yes, that really is the name of a town).

Why do I not run into more people from Corfu and Rhodes? Because there is more opportunity for people there. Nisyros is a small, dry island. It has beautiful blue water and fresh air. But there's not much chance to grow any produce there or find gainful employment. That's why people from Nisyros tend to immigrate to the United States (or elsewhere) in greater percentages than people from Corfu, Rhodes, or other places where more opportunity exists.

In any event, another often-used expression is true: With all its flaws, the United States continues to be the most popular country in which to live. Sometimes persons born and raised in the United States take this country for granted and do not understand why millions of people risk their lives to try and settle here. But, in reality, the conditions that exist in some other parts of the world are so bad that their residents genuinely consider the United States to be their last, best hope on Earth.

Back to the Immigration Door

These are some of the reasons why so many people would like to enter the United States through the "immigration door." If we leave the door wide open, there is a great risk that there will not be enough resources for all of us (those of us already here and those coming in through the door). As a result, many people will suffer the consequences.

What if we decided to close the door completely? We could take the simple approach and say: "We have enough people here. Nobody else may come in." Let's consider some of the problems with that notion.

First, we would be shutting the door on ourselves. We would be rushing in to get inside the door and then slamming it behind us, shutting out people with an incredibly wide range of talent, character, and ability. Granted, there are those on the outside trying to get in who are thieves, drug dealers, rapists, murderers, and terrorists. But most will be kind, supportive, decent human beings. Among them will be some brilliant scientists, talented musicians, gifted athletes, and others who can contribute to the greatness of the United States. By completely shutting the door, we may shut out crime and immorality, but we will also shut out hope, genius, and compassion.

Finally, what about people in special circumstances such as the man whose life is in danger because he spoke out against a political leader in his country? What about the woman whose husband is a U.S. citizen and she wants to come here and live with him? Do we shut the door on them, too?

We are faced with a dilemma with no clear answers. Our answer, therefore, is a compromise. We keep the door neither wide open nor completely closed.

THE CHANGING STAGES OF THE IMMIGRATION DOOR

In the early days of our nation, we kept the door open much wider. At times, we kept it completely wide open. We were a young nation and wanted to become big and strong. Immigrants provided the labor necessary to build our country—our homes, our schools, our roads.

After awhile, things changed. Criminals fled from justice in their own countries and escaped to the United States. Many committed crimes here, too. That's when the door began to shut a little bit—to exclude known criminals.

Next, some people with dangerous, contagious diseases came here and, unfortunately, spread the diseases here as well. So the door began to shut on those who were afflicted by such diseases.

A larger problem developed as immigrants—who were delighted to have any job at all—worked for much cheaper wages than did Americans. The result? Americans could not get a job.

xenophobia
The fear of strangers or people from another country.

Add overpopulation and **xenophobia** (fear of strangers) to the mix, and that's when the movement began to shut the door completely, or at least to close it more significantly.

The attack on 9/11 certainly did not help matters. When the story unfolded that the terrorists involved came to the United States and attended flight school here—thus having been trained by the country they then attacked—the xenophobia became worse.

The debate continues. It is unlikely that the door will be completely open or shut anytime soon. However, the debate will decide to what degree the door will remain open (or shut, depending on one's perspective). As you continue to read this book and learn about immigration law, keep the concepts of "overloading the boat" and "the immigration door" in mind, because they will shed light on your questions and concerns.

Immigration Fraud

As people throughout the world remain interested in coming to the United States, it makes sense that a lot of them will do just about anything to get here, including using fraudulent means.

Such methods may include the use of false documents, misrepresentation of identity or status, or other types of fraud. For example, Eric wants to come to the United States, so he creates a fraudulent U.S. passport that identifies him as a U.S. citizen, or Ella presents a fake letter of admission to a U.S. university in order to get "inside the door."

These types of fraudulent acts may indirectly impact everyone who has a legal right to be in the United States. A person who enters with fake documents and has no legal right to be here is one more person who is filling an apartment that you want or one more person who may take away a job from you or a seat on the bus. The person may be one more person living on public assistance or otherwise abusing the resources of this country. That person is illegally sharing the rights and privileges of U.S. citizens and all noncitizens who are in the United States legally.

Accordingly, our government has methods by which to combat immigration fraud. Unfortunately, the methods are not 100 percent foolproof. But while some people may think of crafty ways to evade the immigration process, there are government agents in place whose primary purpose is to prevent such fraud. We will discuss some ways by which these agents foil many fraudulent attempts.

A REVIEW OF OUR AMERICAN SYSTEM OF GOVERNMENT

Let's take a look at our U.S. system of government. This is essential for those of you who have grown up outside of the United States and even more essential for those of you who have lived here your entire life! We Americans are taught about our government at a very early age, and then we tend to forget about it. But our system of government is not something that we ought to forget or take for granted, not if we are going to be successful in immigration law.

Our Two-Tier, Three-Branch System of Government

The U.S. government is a two-tier, three-branch democratic republic. It is not only a democracy, in which the people rule and govern, but also a republic, in which elected representatives rather than every single American create, execute, and enforce laws and policies.

THE TWO TIERS OF GOVERNMENT

The two tiers are:

1. The Federal Government
2. The fifty individual State Governments

In order to better understand and appreciate this two tier system, let's take a look at what is often a great starting point in learning about many things—American history.

Before emerging into a vast fifty-state nation, the United States consisted of thirteen small colonies that—for the most part—wanted to be self-governing. The colonies were first united under the Articles of Confederation, which didn't work very well. After a few years under that system, our current government was developed, as set forth in a document known as the **United States Constitution.** The Constitution was a compromise between the desires of the states to govern themselves and their practical understanding that in order to remain free and strong that they must be united.

United States Constitution The document on which our two-tier, three-branch system of government was founded.

The Constitution allows the individual states to remain self-governing to a certain extent. It also provides for a higher authority, known as the federal government, to maintain power over all of the states in certain, limited areas. This is the United States two-tier system of government: Federal and State.

Where State and Federal Interests Conflict Because federal and state laws are created separately and by different legislative (lawmaking) bodies, it is possible that they may conflict. What happens if a state law conflicts with a federal law? The Constitution proclaims itself to be. "the Supreme Law of the Land . . . Laws of any State to the Contrary notwithstanding . . ." This statement, commonly known as the Supremacy Clause, declares that the Constitution (which is federal law) is superior to state law.

Therefore, if a state law contradicts a federal law, the federal law takes precedence. But if a state law, though different from a federal law, does not conflict with the federal law, then both may happily coexist.

For example, if a federal law was passed that does not allow the sale of cigarettes to anyone under the age of 18 and Montana passes a state law that allows the sale of cigarettes to anyone 17 or older, then the Montana law would be unconstitutional because it would conflict with federal law. If Montana then changed its law to make 18 the minimum age to purchase cigarettes, then its law would be valid because it would be consistent with federal law. Moreover, if Montana changed its law and made the minimum age 19, that law would be fine as well. Why? Because even though it would be different from the federal law (minimum age of 19 instead of 18), it would still satisfy the federal law's requirement that no one under the age of 18 would be allowed to buy cigarettes.

How the Two-Tier System of Government Affects Immigration

Immigration law is a federal law. If a person from another country wishes to visit or settle in any of the fifty states, then that person is subject to federal immigration law.

Any conflicting state law would be invalid. For instance, suppose that Alex, a citizen of a foreign country, decides to visit Wyoming and would like to teach school there. If Alex meets Wyoming's requirements for teaching in that state but immigration law (which is federal) prohibits Alex from working anywhere in the United States, then Alex would not be permitted to teach in Wyoming (or in any other state, for that matter).

Accordingly, persons from foreign countries are subject to United States federal laws as well as the laws of the state in which they live or visit. In any event, because immigration law is federal, most of the law that you will encounter in this book will be federal law.

THE THREE BRANCHES OF GOVERNMENT

The three branches of the federal government are:

1. Legislative Branch
2. Executive Branch
3. Judicial Branch

legislative branch The branch of government responsible for enforcing the law.

executive branch The branch of government that executes the law.

judicial branch The branch of government responsible for enforcing the law.

Senate Along with the House of Representatives, a body of legislators that comprises the United States Congress, that is, the legislative branch.

House of Representatives Along with the Senate, a body of legislators that comprises the United States Congress, that is, the legislative branch.

Immigration and Nationality Act of 1990 (INA) The United States immigration law, as established by Congress.

The **legislative branch** creates the law, which is then executed (put into effect) by the **executive branch** and enforced by the **judicial branch.**

1. The Legislative Branch

The laws by which we live—how old we must be to vote, how fast we may drive on the highway, our right to a fair trial, and so forth—are created by the legislature. On the federal level, the legislature is the United States Congress, which is made up of two houses: the **Senate** and the **House of Representatives.** Moreover, each state has its own legislature that creates laws specifically for that state.

2. The Executive Branch

Once the laws are created, the executive branch executes them. In other words, the executive branch is like the "manager" of the country. On the federal level, the head of this branch, or chief executive, is the president of the United States. In each state, the chief executive is that state's governor. Various administrative agencies are part of the executive branch both on the federal and state levels.

3. The Judicial Branch

The judicial branch is comprised of federal and state courts and is the branch that enforces the laws (that are made by the legislature and carried out by the executive branch). Typically, judicial matters begin at the trial level and, if necessary, are appealed to higher courts.

Now that we have reviewed a little bit about the U.S. legal system, let's take a look at how it applies to immigration:

THE INA

In our two-tier, three-branch system of government, the **Immigration and Nationality Act of 1990 (INA)** sets forth immigration law and policy. The INA is the U.S. (federal) immigration law created by Congress. Specifically, it is Title 8 of the United States Code. (At times, immigration law is cited in INA format; at other times, it is cited as Code.

In its role as the federal legislature, Congress has the power to create law and to delegate authority to the other branches of government. Accordingly, the INA is carried out either by Congress or by another branch, in whole or in part, to which Congress has granted such authority. For the most part, enforcement of immigration law has been delegated by Congress to the executive branch. In other words, Congress makes the law (the INA), and the executive branch carries it out. When a person is subject to or elects to undergo immigration proceedings, his case or matter will be handled within the executive branch, as set forth by the INA.

THE EFFECTS OF 9/11: THE DHS REPLACES THE INS

As we discussed earlier in this book, the **9/11** attack has changed many aspects of our lives, including immigration law. Prior to 9/11, the INA was largely enforced by the **Immigration and Naturalization Service (INS).** The INS was an agency of the executive branch and handled immigration matters in most instances.

Following 9/11, one of the reactions was: "What went wrong?" Why were foreign terrorists able to infiltrate our country and wreak such havoc, and what could we do to prevent that from happening again?

In 2002, in order to maximize our national security, President George W. Bush established a new government agency, the **Department of Homeland Security (DHS).** Shortly thereafter, immigration matters once handled by the INS were placed under the authority of DHS "subagencies," called bureaus.

Services and benefits (such as obtaining permission to visit the United States or to gain U.S. citizenship) are handled by the **Bureau of Citizenship and Immigration Services (BCIS).** Matters dealing with immigration investigations and illegal aliens now fall under the **Bureau of Immigration and Customs Enforcement (BICE).** Finally, aspects of border patrol and inspections fall under the **Bureau of Customs and Border Protection (BCBP).**

The rationale behind these administrative changes was that because the INS was too big and bureaucratic that it was easier for dangerous terrorists to slip through the cracks, yet cumbersome for law-abiding people whose reasons for being here were benign. By creating subagencies, each with its own purpose, the hope was to make legal immigration more accessible, prevent illegal immigration, and protect our nation and its people from terrorist attacks.

Are all these multi-lettered agencies confusing you—BCIS, BICE, and so forth? Do you feel like you're swimming in a bowl of alphabet soup? To make things easier, we will refer to the DHS and its subagencies collectively as "DHS." Brace yourself, because there's more. But don't worry, after a short while, you'll get the hang of it and they'll roll off your tongue just like ABC, NBC, or CBS.

THE BIA

When someone loses a court case at trial, he or she may choose to appeal the decision to a higher court. Angry vows such as "I'll take this all the way to the Supreme Court if I have to" are not uncommon. The point is that there is an appeals process; just because you lose the first time doesn't mean that you don't get to present your case to a higher court.

Similarly, appeals about immigration matters are handled by the **Board of Immigration Appeals (BIA).** The BIA decisions are reported (formally published) so that they can be used as precedent in future matters. Nonetheless, if you are looking at a BIA decision, don't assume that it is still good law. The BIA may have issued a more recent decision that overturns the older one. This leads us to this very important point: The law is always subject to change.

THE EVER-CHANGING IMMIGRATION LAW

Like many other laws, the INA has (at least partially) changed quite often. In fact, while this book is very current in terms of having been updated after 9/11, it is, like anything else, current as of the time of its writing. Immigration laws, forms, filing fees, and other procedures change from time to time, and it is important for you to be aware of the changes.

A mistake in understanding the law or the necessary procedure may cause significant delay. Even though the new subagencies under the DHS were created to establish more efficiency, there are still thousands upon thousands of applications in the pipeline.

9/11
September 11, 2001. The day on which terrorists flew airplanes into New York City's World Trade Center and the Pentagon Building in Washington, D.C., killing thousands. A third airplane, purportedly headed toward Washington, D.C., was thwarted in its attempt by passengers; the plane crashed in Pennsylvania, killing all on board.

Immigration and Naturalization Service (INS)
Formerly the administrative agency under the United States executive branch that was primarily responsible for executing the INA. The INS has been replaced by the Department of Homeland Security (DHS) and its subagencies.

Department of Homeland Security (DHS)
In order to maximize our national security, President George W. Bush established a new government agency, the Department of Homeland Security. Includes three subagencies, called bureaus, that now handle immigration matters once handle by INS. The three bureaus are the BCBP, BCIS, and BICE.

Bureau of Citizenship and Immigration Services (BCIS)
This is the DHS subagency responsible for immigration services and benefits, such as obtaining permission to visit the United States or to gain U.S. citizenship.

Bureau of Immigration and Customs Enforcement (BICE)
This is the DHS subagency responsible for dealing with immigration investigations and illegal aliens.

Bureau of Customs and Border Protection (BCBP)
This is the DHS subagency responsible for aspects of border patrol and inspections.

Board of Immigration Appeals (BIA)
The court of appeals within the administrative branch of immigration law. Decisions from the lower immigration court are appealed to the BIA.

For example, if you file an application for your client to obtain permission to enter the United States as a college student and if you are unaware of the necessary requirements or even if you submit an incorrect filing fee, it may result in months of delay! If your client does not meet the requirements to study in the United States altogether, the delay was a waste of time (during which your client might have made the necessary changes to fulfill the requirements or to decide to go to college in another country).

The best way to make sure that you are aware of the correct law or procedure is to ask. One way of finding out is through the DHS's Web site http://www.dhs.gov or through http://www.immigration.gov. Another way is through an organization called the American Immigration Lawyers Association (AILA), whose Web site is http://www.aila.org.

Specific Changes—The 1996 Amendments

The last major change to the INA was in 1990. Since then, there have been some minor changes from time to time. However, in 1996, a series of changes took place that were considerably more significant: the 1996 Amendments.

Specifically, three Congressional acts comprise what are collectively referred to as the 1996 Amendments:

1. The Illegal Immigration Reform and Immigrant Responsibility Act of 1996 (IIRAIRA)
2. The Anti-terrorism and Effective Death Penalty Act of 1996 (AEDPA)
3. The Personal Responsibility and Work Opportunity Reconciliation Act (PRAWORA)

illegal alien
An alien in the United States who either entered illegally or became illegal because his or her lawful status expired.

The 1996 Amendments impose various restrictions on many aspects of the INA, including increased criminal penalties for fraud, significant hurdles for **illegal aliens,** and fewer opportunities to avoid removal.

Where applicable, we will discuss these amendments as they apply to the various types of immigration law.

The 1996 Amendments after 9/11

Many people believe that immigration law has changed significantly since 9/11. Actually, as already discussed, an administrative restructuring has taken place (the DHS and its subagencies having been created and the INS having been eliminated). However, major changes to the INA (such as in 1990 and, to a lesser extent, in 1996 [the Amendments]) have yet to be made.

It is very likely that, given the relatively new status of the DHS and its subagencies, and continued public concern about terrorism and immigration in general, more changes to the INA are in progress.

Now that we have learned a little bit about how our government works in terms of immigration, let's take a look at some basic definitions of some of the more commonly used terms in immigration law so that you can better understand them.

alien
A person in the United States who is not a U.S. citizen.

with inspection
The process of an alien being lawfully admitted into the United States.

without inspection
The act of an alien entering the United States without being lawfully admitted.

DEFINITIONS

1. Aliens

A person who is not a United States citizen is an **alien.** Those aliens who enter the United States **with inspection** (official approval) are legal aliens. Those who enter **without inspection** or who entered with inspection but whose time limit to remain in the United States has expired are illegal aliens.

First, in immigration law, it is important to get comfortable with the word "alien." Generally, when a person thinks of an "alien," other definitions may come to mind. For immigration purposes, an alien is a human being, specifically a human being who is in the United States but is not a U.S. citizen. Until and unless the legal terminology changes, it is important for you to know what aliens are.

LEGAL ALIENS

Legal aliens are aliens who are in the United States legally. In other words, if a person is an alien and has a legal right to be in the United States, then that person is a **legal alien.**

legal alien
An alien who is legally in the United States.

Our country officially welcomes multitudes of legal aliens each year. Foreign government officials, athletes, entertainers, scientists, students, and people from all walks of life are aliens. If they entered and remain in the United States lawfully, they are legal.

ILLEGAL ALIENS

Illegal aliens are persons who are in the United States illegally. This happens in one of two ways: either the person was an illegal alien to begin with or the person became illegal by failing to comply with the immigration law.

For example, suppose Mark is in a country that adjoins the United States, namely Canada or Mexico. Mark pays Wayne, a U.S. citizen, $1,000 so that Wayne will let Mark hide in the trunk of Wayne's car as Wayne drives across the foreign country's border back into the United States. If Wayne and Mark make it into the United States without being caught, then Mark would be an illegal alien who entered without inspection.

Suppose that Cara enters the United States as a visitor. She flies into JFK Airport in New York City and enters with inspection. She is permitted to visit the United States for six months. But when the six months expire, Cara is now an illegal alien—one who entered lawfully but now remains unlawfully.

When people think about illegal aliens, they often think of "border jumpers" like Mark. However, the vast majority of illegal aliens are more like Cara—aliens who entered lawfully but have stayed beyond their legally allotted time.

Quite often, when people talk about protecting our country against illegal immigration, they point to strict border patrol as the solution. Granted, stricter border patrol will prevent border jumpers from Canada and Mexico from entering. However, it will not solve the problem entirely, since the vast majority of illegal aliens flew here from some other country, were officially "welcomed" by our government, and then overstayed their welcome.

2. Emigrants, Immigrants, and Nonimmigrants

A person who leaves a country intending to abandon his or her residence there is an **emigrant.** A person who settles into another country, intending to become a permanent resident there is an **immigrant.** A person who goes to another country but does not intend to permanently settle there is a **nonimmigrant.**

emigrant
A person who leaves his or her country with the intent to permanently settle in another country.

immigrant
A person who has arrived into another country with the intent to permanently settle there.

nonimmigrant
A person who is in another country without the intent to permanently settle there.

For example, suppose that Linda is a citizen of Brazil and that she is legally eligible to settle in the United States permanently. If Linda indeed leaves Brazil and moves to the United States, she will have emigrated from Brazil and immigrated to the United States. In other words, she is a Brazilian emigrant and a U.S. immigrant.

Instead, suppose that Linda has no intention of leaving Brazil permanently. Rather, she wants to visit the United States in December to spend the holidays with her family and then return to Brazil in January. In that case, Linda would be a nonimmigrant alien in the United States. Because Linda has no intention of abandoning her residence in Brazil, she is neither an emigrant of Brazil nor a U.S. immigrant.

3. A Word about Citizenship

Throughout the book, "American citizens" and "American citizenship" are interchangeable with "U.S. citizen" and "U.S. citizenship," respectively. So, when we say "American" citizen we are referring only to a citizen of the United States; not one of another American country (such as Canada, or Argentina, which are in North and South American, respectively).

We will discuss citizenship in much greater detail in Chapter 6.

4. Visas

A **visa** is an official approval permitting a person to enter the United States as an immigrant or nonimmigrant. Generally, visas are divided into two categories: nonimmigrant

visa
Written official approval permitting a person to enter the United States as an immigrant or nonimmigrant.

consulate
A branch of the U.S. embassy that typically grants visas to eligible persons who want to travel to the United States.

embassy
The residence and place of business of an ambassador. An embassy, or where applicable through its consulate, typically grants visas to eligible persons who want to travel to the United States.

visas and immigrant visas. Visas are granted by the U.S. government, generally the U.S. Consulate in the foreign country. (A **consulate** is a branch of the U.S. **Embassy.** The United States has embassies in many countries throughout the world.)

In an earlier example, we discussed that Cara entered the United States with inspection. In the previous example, we spoke about Linda either settling in the United States permanently or visiting this country for about one month. In each of those situations and in all instances of aliens entering the United States according to the immigration laws, an alien must be granted a visa.

Thus, if Linda would like to visit her family in the United States, then a nonimmigrant visa is granted based on an alien's intent not to immigrate, and she must be granted a nonimmigrant visa from the U.S. Consulate in Brazil. (See Chapter 3.) Instead, if Linda seeks to immigrate to the United States, then she must be granted an immigrant visa.

More definitions will follow throughout the book, as well as in the Glossary. But now you've got a good sense of what immigration law is about, and that is an important foundation. The next section deals with ways by which you can study each area in greater detail and the sources of law from which immigration policies are made.

IMMIGRATION LAW—SOURCES AND RESEARCH

1. The United States Constitution

As we discussed earlier in the chapter, the Constitution is the supreme law of the United States. Accordingly, all other law must stem from the Constitution. It created the three branches of government which, in turn, create, execute, and enforce the various immigration laws.

2. Statutes

statute
A law created by the legislative branch of government.

A **statute** is a law passed by the legislature that either commands that something be done or prohibits something. Statutes can be found in both annotated (with references to case law) and nonannotated form. Because immigration law is federal law, the statute with which you will become most familiar can be found in Title 8 of the United States Code (U.S.C.). Title 8 is entitled "Aliens and Nationality" and is, in fact, the INA. The statutes are categorized by broad subject areas: General Provisions, Immigration Selection System, Admission Qualifications for Aliens, and so forth.

In order to research immigration law, you should also become familiar with the Code of Federal Regulations (C.F.R.) and the Federal Register. The C.F.R. is the collection of rules published by the departments of the executive branch of the federal government, and the Federal Register updates the C.F.R. through legal notices. These sources may be found at a law library or through the U.S. government printing office online at www.access.gpo.gov.

3. Case Law

opinion
A judicial decision about a case.

When a court issues a decision about a case, it creates an **opinion.** An opinion is the court's written explanation of which laws it applied to the facts of the case and why, its reasoning, and its conclusion. The immigration law cases about which you will read are often brought by the government (DHS) or against the government. You will see INS in many of the immigration case headings, which stands for the defunct Immigration and Naturalization Service agency. Though the agency no longer exists, the law of court cases in which it was involved is still important.

4. Administrative Decisions

Decisions of the BIA, which is an administrative body, provide useful information about immigration law. Studying BIA decisions carefully will help you to gain a sound understanding of current trends in immigration law.

Black Letter law
A clearly measurable law, such as "The maximum speed limit is 55 miles per hour."

5. Case Law versus Black Letter Law

Some statutes are exact, whereas others are not. Exact laws are often referred to as **"Black Letter" laws** because they are followed to the exact black (print) letter of the law as it is printed on a page. An example of Black Letter law is: "A person must be at least 18 years old in order to vote in an election." This law is easy to follow because if a person is 18 or older, then he or she may vote. Persons who are even one day shy of their eighteenth birthday may not vote.

However, other laws are not quite so exact. For instance, a law that reads "aliens with extraordinary ability may be granted permanent resident status" may be difficult to interpret. What constitutes "extraordinary ability"? One way to figure it out is to read case law. If you read several cases about people who applied for entry into the United States on the basis of extraordinary ability and who were admitted as legal aliens, then you will have a better understanding of what the statute means. Reading **case law** is reading how the courts have interpreted the words of the statute in the past, so that you can get an idea of how the next court might interpret the same statute.

case law
Law determined by judicial decisions.

IMMIGRATION FORMS

In Appendix B you will find some of the most common forms used in immigration matters. While most forms are created by the BCIS or other DHS subagency, some are issued by non-DHS subagencies (such as the Internal Revenue Service).

As with all other aspects of immigration law and procedure, forms are subject to change. As of this writing, the forms in the Appendix are current. However, you should recognize that they are subject to change. A great way to make sure that you have the correct form is to obtain them directly from the DHS Web site.

The forms at the end of this book are organized by chapter and reflect the types of matters discussed in each particular chapter.

REVIEW QUESTIONS AND HYPOTHETICALS

Each chapter ends with a series of review questions and hypotheticals that are designed to test your knowledge about immigration law.

FAMOUS U.S. IMMIGRANTS

Could he become our first foreign-born president?

ARNOLD SCHWARZENEGGER

Arnold Schwarzenegger was famous as a bodybuilder and then even more famous as an actor. But when he was elected governor of California in 2003, his fame reached new heights. His natural charisma and wide-scale popularity caused many of his supporters to push him to run for president. The only catch? He was not born in the United States.

Schwarzenegger was born in Austria in 1947. He immigrated to the United States in 1968 and became a U.S. citizen in 1983. As a U.S. citizen, he is qualified to serve as governor of any state. According to the U.S. Constitution, in order to be president, he must have been born in the United States.

Will the "Governator" (as he is affectionately known, combining the words "Governor" and "Terminator"—one of his most famous film roles) become so popular as to spark a national movement to change the Constitution so that he can run for president? Probably not. But his success story is a classic example of an immigrant that experienced the American Dream.

CONCLUSION

So now we've begun our journey: learning about immigration law. If you approach everything one step at a time, you will see how much quicker and easier the whole experience will be than you ever imagined.

Always look at the big picture. Keep the main ideas of immigration law in mind: that the United States is like a sold-out concert or ball game—more fans want to attend than there are seats to hold them. Immigration law is federal, which means that it is the same in every state. Immigration law changes from time to time, so it is important to be alert for any updates.

Now that you've gotten a basic overview of immigration law, let's turn to Chapter 2 and discuss our first type of immigration category—nonimmigrants.

KEY TERMS

9/11
alien
Black Letter law
Board of Immigration Appeals (BIA)
Bureau of Citizenship and Immigration Services (BCIS)
Bureau of Customs and Border Protection (BCBP)
Bureau of Immigration and Customs Enforcement (BICE)
case law
consulate
Department of Homeland Security (DHS)
embassy
emigrant
executive branch
House of Representatives
illegal alien
immigrant
Immigration and Nationality Act of 1990 (INA)
Immigration and Naturalization Service (INS)
judicial branch
legal alien
legislative branch
nonimmigrant
opinion
Senate
statute
United States Constitution
visa
with inspection
without inspection
xenophobia

REVIEW QUESTIONS

1. What is the two-tier, three-branch system of government of the United States?
2. What is meant by the Supremacy Clause? Can you give an example of when it would apply?
3. What is the INA, and in what year was the major portion of the INA enacted?
4. What is an alien? What is the difference between a legal alien and an illegal alien? What are the two main types of illegal aliens?
5. What is the difference between an immigrant and a nonimmigrant?
6. What are the two houses of Congress?
7. Which is the highest court in the United States?
8. Explain the theory of "overloading the boat."
9. What are some of the advantages found in the United States that may not exist in some other countries?
10. What is xenophobia?

11. Administrative agencies are part of which branch of government?
12. What is the BCIS, and what is its role in the immigration process?

HYPOTHETICALS

1. If the federal government passed a law that all persons living in the United States must attend school until they are at least 16 years old but New Jersey passed a law allowing a person to drop out of school once they became 15, which law would prevail? Why?
2. Consider the preceding example, but suppose that New Jersey required their students to remain in school until they reached the age of 17. What would be the effect of both the federal and New Jersey laws in that case?
3. Suppose a person is involved in a federal lawsuit. In what court would he normally bring the lawsuit? If he loses the lawsuit, may he appeal the case? What is the highest court to which he may appeal?
4. Suppose that Claudia lives in Uganda but wants to live in the United States permanently. She is given permission to legally do so. Meanwhile, Ramon, who lives in Portugal, wants to visit the United States during the summer and then to return to Portugal. Finally, Niles, a citizen and resident of the United States, wishes to permanently settle in England, from where his ancestors hail. In what way are each of these people emigrants, immigrants, or nonimmigrants?
5. Suppose that an immigration law is passed that declares that an illegal alien who commits a crime in the United States will be punished twice as severely as a legal alien who commits the same crime. What branch of government would have passed that law? What branch would enforce it? If an illegal alien is affected by this law and his or her attorney wants to have the law reversed, to what branch of government would the attorney argue to determine whether this law should remain in effect?

CHAPTER 2

NONIMMIGRANTS

CHAPTER OBJECTIVES

After completing this chapter, you should know:

- What it really means to be a nonimmigrant
- How to qualify for a nonimmigrant visa
- The various types of nonimmigrant visas
- Some special options for academic students

This chapter is designed to familiarize you with the basic principles of nonimmigrant visas. Each nonimmigrant visa comes with a different set of privileges, such as the right to study at a U.S. educational institution. Along with the privileges come several responsibilities, such as the obligation to stay in school in good academic standing (that is, regarding student visas).

Each nonimmigrant visa has a different time limit and different rules about extending it. Nonimmigrant visas are referred to by letter—such as a "K" visa. Generally, the letter corresponds to the subsection of the INA that deals with nonimmigrant visas.

In this chapter we will continue to discuss immigration policy and we will look at the different types of nonimmigrant visas. You can find some immigration forms regarding nonimmigrant visas in Appendix B, as well as explanations and advice about filling them out correctly.

QUALIFYING FOR A NONIMMIGRANT VISA

As discussed in Chapter 1, a nonimmigrant is an alien who enters the United States on a temporary basis. The actual time period may vary, but the stay is not intended to be permanent. In order to be a legal nonimmigrant, an alien must be granted a nonimmigrant visa.

Generally, a nonimmigrant visa is easier to obtain than an immigrant visa. There is less of a gain, so the stakes are not as high. In fact, most legal aliens are nonimmigrants rather than immigrants. This makes sense because the United States grants less with nonimmigrant than immigrant status. It is often easier to obtain something of less value than something of greater value.

However, this is not to suggest that nonimmigrant visas are granted automatically; there are a number of reasons why a nonimmigrant visa would be denied. Besides the obvious concern of national security, there is also caution about nonimmigrants who have no terrorist intentions but would nonetheless hamper the legal system by remaining unlawfully.

For example, if Daniel wants to settle in the United States but does not qualify for an immigrant visa, he might apply for a nonimmigrant one. If Daniel's secret plan is to stay beyond his allotted time, then he would be a classic example of an alien who entered the United States legally but became illegal once he remained here beyond his allotted time. The DHS wants to make sure that nonimmigrants remain in the United States only as long as their visa allows them to do so.

As we read through each type of nonimmigrant visa, pay attention to the type of person who qualifies for each type of visa (professional status, purpose for visit, etc.). By recognizing that certain types of statuses are more common than others (for example, visitors are more common than foreign government officials), you may begin to sense that some visas are more commonly issued than others.

A VISAS: ACCREDITED FOREIGN GOVERNMENT REPRESENTATIVES

Persons who are accredited by foreign governments to serve as representatives of those governments in the United States as ambassadors, public ministers, or career diplomatic or consular officers may enter the United States on an "A" visa.

B VISAS: VISITORS

Nonimmigrants who wish to visit the United States for pleasure or for certain business purposes may receive a "B" visa. These visas have a time limit but are renewable.

A person who is granted a visitor's visa must demonstrate that he or she does not intend to immigrate to the United States. Moreover, the alien must show that he or she will leave the United States once the allotted visiting time has expired. One way by which the alien may show this is to provide evidence of strong ties to the home country. For example, the alien who produces bank statements that show substantial money in the home country can make the argument that the visit to the United States is temporary because he or she would not leave all of that money behind. The same holds true if the alien owns a business or substantial property in the home country.

Another strong indicator that visiting aliens are likely to return to their countries is family. To the extent that aliens have family members back home or lack of family in the United States, the consulate may consider this to be a significant factor in granting a visitor's visa.

For instance, suppose that Anna, a citizen and resident of Italy, wishes to visit her uncle in the United States. However, Anna's husband, children, parents, and siblings all live in Italy. The consulate may determine that it is unlikely that Anna's potential desire to immigrate to the United States would outweigh her desire to be with her family. Accordingly, ties to family may be a strong factor in persuading the consulate to grant Anna a visitor's visa.

Another bit of evidence of the likelihood to return to the home country is a return travel ticket. If Anna applies for a visitor's visa that allows her to visit the United States for six months and she buys a return airplane ticket to Italy in advance, this strengthens the evidence of her intent to return to Italy in a timely manner.

Financial support while in the United States is another important factor. For reasons that we will explore later on, the DHS has a strong interest in preventing **visitors** from obtaining employment in the United States or from being financially supported by our federal or state governments.

visitor
An alien who may enter the United States as a nonimmigrant in order to visit the United States for a specific period of time for purposes of either business or pleasure.

Accordingly, an alien who shows evidence of financial support while in the United States either independently or through a third party is more likely to be granted a visitor's visa. But the alien should demonstrate financial ties to his or her home country as evidence that he or she would be likely to return home. That means the alien should show substantial money at home and enough money by which to live while visiting here.

C VISAS: VISITORS IN TRANSIT

Visitors in transit, such as persons changing airplanes in the United States, may receive a special limited time visa for that purpose, known as a "C" visa. For example, it might apply to an alien who wants to fly from Australia to Mexico. There are no direct flights—in which case the alien first must fly to the United States and then take another flight to Mexico.

D VISAS: CREW MEMBERS

Aliens defined by the INA as "crewmen" are person who work on vessels. This type of visa applies when such vessels are docked in the United States. The "D" visa permits the crew member to lawfully remain in the United States for the duration of the visa. Generally, the visa is granted in connection with the typical duties that a crew member might undertake while the vessel is docked. For example, the visa does not authorize the crew member to remain in the United States once the vessel departs or to take a different job on dry land.

E VISAS: TREATY TRADERS AND INVESTORS

There are certain treaties (agreements) between the United States and other countries throughout the world regarding trade, commerce, and navigation or investment in such goods and services. People who enter the United States to engage in such trade are **treaty traders.**

treaty trader
An alien who may enter the United States as a nonimmigrant in order to engage in trade of commerce or navigation based on treaties between the United States and their country.

treaty investor
An alien who may enter the United States as a nonimmigrant in order to invest money in goods and services involved in the trade or commerce of navigation based on treaties between the United States and their country.

A **treaty investor** invests money in such a treaty venture. Both treaty traders and treaty investors may enter the United States by using an "E" visa. Those individuals' families may enter the United States on such a visa as well. For both treaty traders and investors, the effort (whether trade or money) must be "substantial."

The treaty trader or investor must qualify as an owner or "key employee." The treaty investor or trader should not be a blue-collar laborer. The line between laborer and owner, however, is not a clear one. This is an example of a non-Black Letter law. If you research the topic online, using LEXIS, WESTLAW, or other legal research sources, you can find ample cases dealing with the topic and determine what standards the INA, DHS, BIA, and the federal courts have applied.

F VISAS: ACADEMIC STUDENTS

"F" visas are issued to academic students. Because this is a broad topic, we will discuss it later on in the chapter.

G AND N VISAS: CERTAIN FOREIGN GOVERNMENT REPRESENTATIVES

A special nonimmigrant visa is available to certain foreign government representatives if these governments are members of certain international organizations that enjoy particular types of privileges and immunities. Such persons and their staffs and families may be entitled to enter the United States under the "G" visa and their family members under the "N" visa.

These visas generally are renewable. Also, the visa holder may often be able to gain additional (different) immigration status. This type of visa is a prime example that everyone, whether an ordinary civilian or a foreign government representative, is subject to the INA.

H VISAS: TEMPORARY WORKERS—REGISTERED NURSES AND PROFESSIONALS

One of the most sought after nonimmigrant visas is the "H" visa. It is generally available for some registered nurses and for "professionals"—persons who have obtained at least a baccalaureate (bachelor's) degree or who have certain relevant work experience.

The "H" visa is issued to qualified aliens who will be performing their jobs in the United States based on their education and professional experience. Since this is a work-related visa, the INA requires that the alien receive prevailing wages and that the job will not have an adverse effect on U.S. workers. (We will discuss these concepts when we cover academic students and when we talk about work-related immigrant visas).

Two vital advantages that this visa provides are: (1) it is typically issued for three years and is renewable and (2) the visa holder may seek and obtain different immigration status—such as becoming an immigrant.

Accordingly, registered nurses and persons who hold a bachelor's degree or who have significant professional experience may obtain an "H" visa. As long as they retain that job in good standing, they are typically allowed to remain in the United States for the duration of the visa. Because three years is a comparatively long duration for a nonimmigrant visa and because the visa is both renewable and opens a window of opportunity to gain immigrant status, the H visa remains very much in demand. It is important for legal professionals to be aware of this visa, because it often may be the answer to the client's immigration concerns.

I VISAS: FOREIGN MEDIA REPRESENTATIVES

Members of the media (newspapers, magazines, radio, television, film, or other information medium) of a foreign country and their families may be eligible for an "I" visa. Holders of this visa may enter the United States to take part in activities related to their media status.

For instance, suppose that Cassandra is a member of the foreign press and wants to come to the United States to cover the president's State of the Union address. She is a typical candidate likely to receive such a visa.

The "I" visa is specifically granted to members of the media profession, which does not make it as common as some of the visas that cover a broader range of people.

J AND Q VISAS: EXCHANGE VISITORS

People who are students, professors, or other scholars may enter the United States as **exchange visitors** on a "J" visa in order to teach or learn in a particular academic course or program similar to the course of study that they have undertaken in their own country. You are probably familiar with the term "foreign exchange student." That is a prime example of a "J" visa holder. The "Q" visa is similar and applies to specific international exchange programs.

exchange visitor
An alien who enters the United States as a nonimmigrant in order to teach or learn in a particular academic course or program similar to the course of study in the alien's own country.

For instance, if an exchange student or professor is admitted to Harvard University to learn or teach for a summer session, then the visa generally would be valid for that period of time and may be renewed, as appropriate.

These visas are designed to promote international cultural exchange, so that others may learn things about our culture while teaching us about theirs.

K VISAS: FIANCÉS AND FIANCÉES OF U.S. CITIZENS

Persons who are engaged to be married to U.S. citizens may obtain a limited time "K" visa to enter the United States in order to marry the citizen. If the alien does not marry the citizen within the time set forth in the statute, the alien must leave the United

States. Generally, extensions are not available for this type of visa, so a case of "getting cold feet at the altar" and postponing the wedding may have immigration consequences. Note that a *fiancé* (one "e") is a male engaged person and a *fiancée* (two "e's") is a female engaged person.

In Chapter 3, we will discuss marriage as it relates to immigration in greater detail.

K-3 AND V: THE LIFE VISAS

The Legal Immigration Family Equity Act of 2000 (LIFE) amended the INA by creating additional nonimmigrant visa categories specifically for aliens who are waiting to become immigrants.

The "K-3" visa is for certain family members (spouses, children) of U.S. citizens and the "V" visa is for certain family members of U.S. immigrants who are not citizens.

These visas allow the family members, subject to fulfilling all of the eligibility conditions, to be in the United States while their paperwork to become immigrants is pending. The purpose of the LIFE Act is to keep families together rather than living apart in separate countries because of immigration backlog. Keep the LIFE Act in mind when we discuss immigrants in Chapter 3.

L VISAS: INTRACOMPANY TRANSFEREES

Persons who work for a foreign company that has affiliated sites in the United States may be eligible for an "L" visa. Such persons must have worked for the parent company for a certain period of time and must possess special skills necessary for employment in the U.S. affiliate. If such applicants qualify, then they may be admitted to the United States on the "L" visa and eventually may apply to become immigrants. This is an excellent way for aliens to be eligible to come to the United States, provided they qualify.

For example, suppose that Honda, a Japanese automobile manufacturer, decides to open a new factory in El Paso, Texas. Willie, a resident and citizen of Japan, has worked for Honda in Japan for ten years. He is a top-level sales director and an expert in marketing research. Honda would like to send Willie to the United States to be the Executive Director of Marketing and Sales in Texas. In addition to Willie's sales and marketing experience, he is fluent in Japanese, English, and Spanish, and he knows a great deal about American consumers, particularly concerning the automobile industry. In short, Willie would be ideal for the position.

In that case, Honda may petition for Willie to enter the United States as an **intracompany transferee.** Because Willie possesses the skills necessary for the position, has worked for Honda for many years, and will be working for a branch of Honda (the parent company) in the United States, he is qualified to obtain an "L" visa.

intracompany transferee An alien who enters the United States as a nonimmigrant because he works for a foreign company which has (or will open) affiliated sites in the United States and who will work at one or more of those affiliated sites.

The visa will be granted for a certain period of time (for example, one year) and may be renewed (for example, a second year). It is important to note that if the alien's intracompany transferee status ends, so does his right to remain in the United States under that type of visa. If General Motors offers Willie a similar job with a much better salary and benefits, Willie will not be able to quit his job with Honda and remain an intracompany transferee. Thus, to legally remain in the United States, Willie would need to obtain some other type of visa. In Chapter 4, we discuss the circumstances under which a person in Willie's position might be granted permission to work for General Motors and under what terms General Motors might be permitted to hire him.

M VISAS: VOCATIONAL STUDENTS

Unlike academic students, vocational students are those who undergo a nonacademic course of study. Persons studying or training to become auto mechanics, locksmiths, or plumbers fall into this category.

The "M" visa is available to such prospective students and possibly to some of their family members. Generally, "M" visas are issued for the duration of the student's course of study.

Although academic students are subject to certain employment restrictions, vocational students are often permitted to work while learning their trade, provided that the work is related to their course of study.

N VISAS

"N" visas were discussed along with "G" visas, earlier in the chapter.

O AND P VISAS: ALIENS WITH EXTRAORDINARY ABILITY OR INTERNATIONAL RECOGNITION

Certain aliens who are outstanding in their field, whether performers, artists, professionals, or scholars, or who are internationally recognized in their field may obtain an "O" (extraordinary ability) or "P" (international recognition) visa and enter the United States in order to engage in an activity related to their status as such.

You probably know many such visa holders: Actors and actresses, athletes, and religious leaders are some prime examples. Even though they are worldwide celebrities, they remain subject to the U.S. immigration laws. Of course, because they have much to offer to the United States (in terms of their ability), they remain more likely to obtain a visa than the average nonimmigrant.

Extraordinary versus Internationally Renowned

There are some differences between those who qualify for **extraordinary ability** and those who qualify for international recognition visas. In many cases, a person will be both. For instance, the tennis player Roger Federer has both extraordinary ability (as of this writing, he is one of the top tennis players in the world) and international recognition (he has multitudes of fans in countries around the world). However, there are situations when an alien may be classified on one, but not both of these areas (but one is all that the alien will need).

extraordinary ability
A person who is uniquely outstanding in a particular field.

For example, a doctor who is the top cancer researcher in the world probably does not have the same type of international recognition that Yao Ming (the Chinese basketball player) or Luciano Pavarotti (the opera singer) have. The outstanding doctor probably is far from being internationally recognized.

Conversely, someone who is an average musician might have achieved overnight success with a couple of hit songs and is now internationally recognized.

Keep in mind that an "O" or "P" visa holder will be admitted to the United States in connection with his or her extraordinary ability or recognition. In other words, an actress who enters the United States on this type of visa in order to star in a film will be admitted for that purpose. Once filming is over, she would have to leave the United States (unless she receives an extension or is admitted under some other type of visa).

Q VISAS

"Q" visas were discussed along with "J" visas, earlier in the chapter.

R VISAS: RELIGIOUS WORKERS

Persons who have been authorized by their respective religions to perform specific religious functions (such as conducting religious services) may be eligible to enter the United States on an "R" visa, provided that they have performed such functions

religious workers
An alien who enters the United States either as a nonimmigrant or an immigrant, who is permitted to enter based on the religious work he or she has done in his own country and such work which he or she plans to do in the United States.

for a certain period of time and are entering the United States solely to perform such functions.

"R" visas are issued for a specific time period and may be renewed. Under the Constitution, no particular religion is officially endorsed or given more credibility than another. While it is not relevant that DHS would support a particular religion, it is important that DHS is satisfied that the alien actually does.

Take Hal, an alien, who is a minister of religion X. It does not matter whether DHS believes in the principles of religion X. It only matters whether DHS is satisfied that Hal truly believes in those principles and is not merely pretending to in order to gain admission to the United States.

Again, it is important to understand that many people would do almost anything to come to the United States. Keeping that in mind, it does not seem too far-fetched that a person would pretend to hold a particular religious belief in order to be admitted under an "R" visa. Accordingly, it is important that the alien establish evidence of having been a religious worker who has performed religious functions for a sufficient period of time.

TN VISAS: NORTH AMERICAN FREE TRADE AGREEMENT (NAFTA)

Under the North American Free Trade Agreement (NAFTA), citizens of Canada and Mexico who wish to enter the United States as nonimmigrants may be able to do so more quickly than aliens from non-North American foreign countries. Aliens who qualify for this "TN" visa include various types of business professionals (business visitors, treaty traders and investors, and other professionals).

V VISAS

"V" visas were discussed along with "K-3" visas, earlier in the chapter.

ACADEMIC STUDENTS

Persons who wish to undertake a full-time academic course of study in the United States, such as high school, college, or graduate school, may enter on an "F" visa.

Duration of Status

Persons granted a student visa are generally admitted for the proposed duration of status as a student. Students may change educational levels and enroll in more advanced educational programs.

For instance, suppose that Emily has graduated from a high school in her country and would like to go to college in the United States. She applies to Columbia University and is accepted. She wishes to earn a BA (Bachelor of Arts) degree in history. Typically, it takes a full-time student four years to complete that degree. Accordingly, it is likely that Emily will be granted a student visa that ultimately will permit her to remain in the United States as a full-time student for four years.

If after four years Emily wishes to continue her education, she may be granted further time in which to complete her advanced degree. For example, if Emily is accepted to law school, the DHS may grant her an additional three years to earn her law degree, which is the normal time in which a full-time student normally earns that type of degree.

But if Emily did not plan to study at Columbia and merely wanted to gain entry into the United States, quit college after her first two weeks, and remained here illegally, she would be the primary reason that obtaining a student visa is not quite as simple as asking for one.

Full-Time Status

An alien who is admitted to the United States on a student visa must enroll as a full-time student. Full-time status is determined by undertaking a particular courseload. This requirement is helpful in preventing a person from merely enrolling in one course every semester in order to maintain "F" visa status. Under that scenario, a person conceivably could remain in college for twenty years!

Generally, a person who falls out of full-time status or who is academically disqualified will no longer be a student visa holder in good standing and may be required to leave the United States. There might be an exception to the rule only under extreme conditions. So slacking off can get a student kicked out of college and the United States.

If Emily is staying with her aunt while studying at Columbia and the aunt becomes very sick, Emily may have to take time off from school to take care of her. Emily might try to do everything, and her grades might suffer as a result. In that case, Emily would have to provide evidence of what happened in order to maintain her student visa status. Such extreme cases are taken into consideration, but there is a keen eye watching for abuse of the student visa privilege.

On-Campus Employment

Student visa holders are generally not permitted to work while in the United States, even with the astronomical cost of tuition! But a student may work on campus for a limited number of hours per week, provided that the position will not displace a U.S. resident. When school is not in session (i.e., in between semesters), the student may increase his or her work hours.

Note that one of the main reasons that a student visa holder is not permitted to work is to prevent those whose main purpose is to work in the United States from coming here on the pretense that they want to go to school. Remember, the demand of those who want to attend college (whether residents or nonresidents of the United States) exceeds the supply (the number of seats available). So, it is important that the seats go to the ones who really want them.

Off-Campus Employment

Although persons holding student visas generally are not permitted to work off-campus, exceptions are made if: (1) the student has been in good standing for a specific time period; (2) the prospective employer has not successfully recruited U.S. workers for the position in a specific time period; (3) the employer will pay the student the prevailing wage; and (4) the student will not work more hours per week than permitted for on-campus employment.

Off-campus employment is employment at a site that is not on the school or college campus nor is affiliated with the school or college. The requirements for student visa holders to work off campus are stricter than for such students to work on campus.

Students in Good Standing for a Specific Time Period Generally, a student who applies for off-campus employment must be in good academic standing for a specific time period, as established by the INA. The time period normally would be substantial, such as one year. This would allow the DHS to examine the viability of the student's status in order to determine whether the student is in fact complying with INA requirements.

Unsuccessful Recruitment of U.S. Workers As we discussed earlier, there is a need to protect U.S. workers from being displaced by nonimmigrant aliens. One way to demonstrate that is for the employer to attest that he or she has unsuccessfully tried to recruit a U.S. worker for the position for a specific period of time. Actually, this requirement is directed by the U.S. Department of Labor (also part of the executive branch of government).

Prevailing Wage Another key requirement for off-campus employment is that the student/employee must be paid the **prevailing wage** normally paid for such a job. That requirement is important to both protect U.S. workers and prevent student visa holders from being exploited.

prevailing wage
The wage which the U.S. Department of Labor determines to be the competitive rate in a particular occupation.

For instance, if the prevailing wage for a particular job is $12 per hour and a student visa holder was paid $6 per hour, then U.S. workers would not be hired (because they can't live on $6 per hour, and the employer would rather pay $6 than $12), and foreign students would be taken advantage of (working at a rate lower than the industry standard).

Limited Work Hours Again, limited work hours protects U.S. workers and also prevents those whose real goal it is to work in the United States from obtaining student visas as a convenient way in. The maximum number of work hours, whatever it may be, applies equally to off-campus and on-campus employment.

Curricular Practical Training

In order to assist alien students who might benefit from hands-on training in their field of study, the INA allows these students to work in their field for a limited time while in school. This is known as **curricular practical training.** The student may take part in such training only if the school requires an internship or other such field experience and, at times, if such employment is not available in that student's home country. If that is the case, then the school may authorize the training and keep immigration officials abreast of the situation.

curricular practical training
Permission for alien nonimmigrant students who have not yet completed their course of study to work in a certain capacity and for a certain period of time.

Students who receive practical training for the maximum allotted time are not eligible for such training after graduation. Examples of students who may be required to accumulate practical training hours are nursing students and teaching students.

Postcompletion Practical Training

Based on the same concept as curricular practical training, the INA also allows alien students to receive their practical training for a limited time after completing their studies. This is known as **postcompletion practical training.** Students are eligible for such training only once, and any time spent in curricular practical training generally is deducted from the allotted time.

postcompletion practical training
Permission for alien nonimmigrant students who have completed their course of study to work in a certain capacity and for a certain period of time.

For a student to qualify, the school must make a recommendation to DHS, which must then grant approval. Postcompletion practical training occurs after completion of the course of study (as opposed to curricular practical training, which occurs during the course of study).

If the student visa holder (e.g., a nursing student) was allowed a maximum of one year of practical training time and used up to two months for curricular practical training, the student (now a nurse) would be eligible to use ten months (one year minus two months) for the postcompletion practical training.

Violation of Student Status

As we discussed, an "F" visa holder is granted student visa status for the anticipated duration of the academic program, with a reasonable extension for postcompletion practical training. A person who withdraws from the academic program loses "F" visa status.

The 1996 Amendments to the INA, in an effort to curb abuse of the "F" visa program, imposed stricter sanctions on those who fall out of "F" status. Moreover, consular officers abroad are increasingly skeptical of granting immigration benefits to someone who violated "F" status.

For these reasons, it is imperative that "F" visa holders commit to completing their course of study.

FAMOUS U.S. IMMIGRANTS

Bet you didn't think you'd see *her* in this book!

PAMELA ANDERSON

What in the world is Pamela Anderson doing in a book about immigration law? She's an immigrant; that's what. A Canadian international celebrity who immigrated to the United States, she eventually became a U.S. citizen in 2004.

Anderson's rise to superstardom resulted from her role in the worldwide hit television show *Baywatch*. In addition to her television performances, Anderson has appeared in numerous films and has done extensive modeling. She is also a well-known animal rights activist.

CONCLUSION

Well, we're all done learning about nonimmigrant visas. While we didn't cover every sentence of the INA, we certainly touched on the most important points.

Don't be intimidated by all of the different letters representing the different types of visas. Time, focus, and repetition will help you to become familiar with these. Besides, some nonimmigrant visas are far less common than others. It is more likely that you will encounter nonimmigrant issues involving academic students than those involving crew members. That does not mean that you shouldn't learn about all the visas discussed in this chapter, just that some are more common than others.

Keep in mind how nonimmigrant visas apply to the concepts of overloading the boat and the immigration door.

In the next chapter, we will begin discussing some types of immigrant visas.

KEY TERMS

curricular practical training
exchange visitor
extraordinary ability
intracompany transferee
postcompletion practical training
prevailing wage
religious worker
treaty investor
treaty trader
visitor

REVIEW QUESTIONS

1. Give some examples of evidence that an alien visitor may use to demonstrate his or her intent not to immigrate to the United States.
2. What is an exchange visitor? Give an example.
3. What is an intracompany transferee? Give an example.
4. What is a treaty investor? How can you know if your client qualifies for that status?

5. What is an alien of extraordinary ability? Give examples of how such an alien may or may not have international recognition.
6. What evidence must an alien establish in order to gain a visa as a nonimmigrant religious worker?
7. What are the privileges of a student visa? What are some obligations that student visa holders must fulfill?
8. How might a person who has graduated from college with a student visa extend his or her stay for another few months or a year without changing status?
9. What type of employment may nonimmigrant academic students seek?
10. What are some of the policy reasons for denying nonimmigrant students the right to work?
11. What is the main difference between an academic student and a vocational student?
12. Give an example of when an alien would want to obtain a fiancé/fiancée visa but not an immigrant visa.

HYPOTHETICALS

1. Abed has been in the United States on a student visa for three years. He would like to change his status from nonimmigrant student to immigrant. Abed tells you that he was arrested for possession of marijuana when he first came to the United States, was fined $100, and has not been in any trouble with the law ever since. His application includes the question: "Have you ever been arrested?" Abed does not want to disclose his arrest and subsequent conviction. What is the best course for Abed to take and why?
2. Wendy and Jackie do not know each other, but they have a few things in common. They are both citizens and residents of Iceland and wish to visit the United States during the summer. Wendy is married and has three children. They all live together in a large home. She also has a steady, full-time job. Jackie, on the other hand, is single with no children, has a part-time job, and a one-year lease on an apartment. What type of factors would be examined to determine whether Wendy or Jackie would be issued a nonimmigrant visa? Who has the better chance to get one? Why?
3. Gunther wishes to enter the United States for the first time in his life. He would like to take two courses in international politics at Georgetown University. Although Gunther is a professional fisherman in his country, he has always enjoyed studying world history and politics and would love to learn about these topics from the American point of view. What type of nonimmigrant visa is Gunther likely to obtain?
4. Hondo owns a restaurant in Boston. Ranjin, a visiting alien student, wishes to work in Hondo's restaurant. Under what conditions would Ranjin be able to work?

   A. Part-time in the restaurant if he was a music major in college?
   B. Part-time in the restaurant if he majored in restaurant management?
   C. Full-time in the restaurant?

CHAPTER 3

IMMIGRANTS: RELATIVE-BASED

CHAPTER OBJECTIVES

After completing this chapter, you should know:

- What a Legal Permanent Resident is
- What a Green Card is
- Who may qualify for relative-based immigration
- How a "child" is different from a "son" and a "daughter"

In Chapter 2, we discussed the various types of nonimmigrants, aliens whose status indicates that they do not intend to settle in the United States permanently. In this chapter, we will begin to talk about those aliens who do want to settle here. They are immigrants.

LEGAL PERMANENT RESIDENT (LPR) STATUS

In order to be a legal alien, a U.S. immigrant (just as a nonimmigrant) must obtain a visa. An immigrant visa holder is known as a **Legal Permanent Resident (LPR).** LPR status is commonly referred to as obtaining a "green card."

Legal Permanent Resident (LPR)
A legal U.S. immigrant who is not a U.S. citizen.

The Green Card

A **green card,** officially known as an **Alien Registration Card,** is a wallet-sized card that identified an alien's LPR status. Actually, LPR status occurs when there is an official approval of the immigrant visa (and, where applicable, official entry into the United States). The green card is merely a confirmation of the official approval. Thus, although many aspiring immigrants might ask "how can I get my green card," the actual LPR status occurs when the DHS has officially granted the status.

green card
Formally, an Alien Registration Card, which identifies an alien's LPR status.

Alien Registration Card
A card which identifies an alien's LPR status; informally known as a green card.

An analogy is getting a driver's license. The right to drive is determined by the Department of Motor Vehicles of the particular state. The actual driver's license is an ID card confirming that right.

One more thing about the green card: It is not green. Originally, "green cards" actually were green in color. But in order to prevent counterfeiting (such as with paper money), the color of the card is changed from time to time. Nonetheless, the nickname "green card" has remained in use, even though it has been many years since the card actually was that color.

Let's take a look at the types of relatives that might qualify for a "green card" (i.e., LPR status). These are aliens eligible for relative-based immigration. We will discuss other types of immigrants in Chapters 4 and 5.

TYPES OF RELATIVES

immediate relative
For immigration purposes, a spouse, parent, or child of a U.S. citizen.

For immigration purposes, relatives may be classified as three types:

1. **Immediate relatives,** who are eligible for relative-based immigration

2. Relatives subject to numerical limitations, who are eligible for relative-based immigration
3. All other relatives, who are neither 1 nor 2 and, thus, who do not qualify for relative-based immigration

Essentially, only aliens in the first two categories—immediate relatives and relatives subject to numerical limitations—are eligible for relative-based immigration. What is the difference between these two types of eligible relatives?

IMMEDIATE RELATIVES

Immediate relatives are spouses, parents, or "children" of U.S. citizens. They are not subject to numerical limitations, which means that there are no limits on the number of these relatives who are allowed to become LPRs.

Do you remember when we discussed the "immigration door" and said that it remains open, but only to a certain extent? That's because if there were millions upon millions of U.S. citizens' relatives who wanted to come through the door, our government might say: "There are far too many of you out there; not all of you can come in." But such limitations do not apply to immediate relatives. Accordingly, the spouses, parents, and children of U.S. citizens may become immigrants in unlimited numbers (provided they are not disqualified for any other reason, such as being criminals).

1. Spouses of U.S. Citizens

Spouses of U.S. citizens are categorized as immediate relatives. At first glance, marrying a U.S. citizen may seem like the easiest way to become an LPR. Marriage is a relationship that can be achieved by choice: You can't decide who your mother or father is, but you can make someone your husband or wife with just a short trip to the altar. It might seem easy, but it's not.

As easy as marrying a U.S. citizen in order to achieve LPR status may appear, this approach is loaded with potential problems. On the one hand, Congress strongly favors family unity and wants to keep couples together. On the other hand, Congress is very aware of marriage fraud and wants to make sure that couples do not decide to get married for the primary purpose of the alien spouse gaining LPR status as a result.

Accordingly, if a U.S. citizen and an alien decide to get married and would choose to be married regardless of immigration reasons, then the INA strongly favors family unity. But if the couple wants to get married specifically so that the alien will become an LPR, the INA prohibits this. Many people try to pretend that they are getting married because they are in love, while their real reason is to gain the immigration benefit. This is known as **immigration marriage fraud,** which is a federal crime, and both parties taking part in such fraud are subject to enormously heavy fines and extremely long prison sentences.

immigration marriage fraud
The act of an alien and a citizen entering into a marriage for the primary purpose of benefiting the alien's immigration status.

The Immigration Marriage Fraud Amendments

As a method to combat immigration marriage fraud, Congress passed the **Immigration Marriage Fraud amendments,** which grant some alien spouses a two-year conditional LPR status. This conditional status will be reviewed by DHS two years after the conditional status is first granted. At that point, the authenticity of the marriage is again reviewed. This applies to aliens married to citizens for less than three years.

Immigration Marriage Fraud amendments
A set of laws established as a method to combat immigration marriage fraud.

For example, suppose that Edward is an alien who marries Laurie, a U.S. citizen. They married because they fell in love and decided to spend the rest of their lives together, although they are happy with the "bonus" that the immigration laws will permit Edward to become a U.S. citizen as a result.

Now let's look at this through the DHS's eyes. Edward and Laurie know the real reason they got married—but how can the DHS be certain? When Edward and Laurie are interviewed by the DHS and say "but we really do love each other," surely that alone can't be enough. Otherwise, everyone would do that and immigration marriage fraud would be rampant. Edward and Laurie would have to prove that their marriage is real, an inconvenience to them, considering they really are in love and got married for that reason.

But what if Edward and Laurie were perpetuating a fraud? What if Edward paid Laurie $50,000 so that she would marry him, and once he became an LPR, they would get a divorce? That would mean Edward would stay in this country forever! That's one less slot available for someone else, one less job, one less apartment, or one less seat on the bus. All because Edward got to stay here under false pretenses!

Accordingly, there are several methods in place to combat such fraud. One of them is the conditional two-year status. Edward would be granted temporary two-year LPR status. After two years, he and Laurie would have to return to DHS for another interview in order to prove that they really are a couple.

During this interview, DHS will look for clues that might determine whether or not Edward and Laurie are a real couple. They might interview them separately, asking them questions about what they had for dinner last night, how they spent last weekend, and to describe all of their living room furniture. They might ask each of them to take out their house key and hold the two keys together to see if they are identical. Those are just two of thousands of questions that trained DHS agents ask to sniff out immigration fraud.

If Edward and Laurie are, in fact, a married couple, then they have nothing to worry about. The truth will be self-evident. But if Laurie got her $50,000 from Edward and then they went their separate ways, only to reunite two years later just for this second interview, then there is a good chance that DHS will pick up on this. At that point, Edward and Laurie may both find themselves on the way to jail for many, many years. Upon Edward's release (since he is an alien), he probably will be promptly booted out of the United States forever.

Again, aliens who are married to citizens for three years or longer do not have to go through the conditional two-year status; three years is a period long enough to satisfy DHS concerns that the couple genuinely is married.

Genuine Marriages That Go Sour What if a couple entered into a marriage for bona fide reasons (such as being in love and wanting to be together), the alien spouse received the two-year conditional status, and then before the two years was up, the marriage was annulled or the couple got a divorce for reasons that have nothing to do with immigration?

Let's look at Edward and Laurie again. What if they were thrilled about the concept of being married and then just a short while after Edward received his two-year status, he and Laurie began to argue every day and decided to split up? What would happen two years later when Edward would return for his second interview and state that he and Laurie are now divorced. How would he prove to DHS that the marriage had been genuine to begin with?

As divorce rates in the United States are disturbingly high, that scenario is not far-fetched. But the good news is that Edward still has a chance to obtain permanent relative-based immigration. If an alien and a citizen choose to get a divorce for reasons that have nothing to do with immigration, the alien may still be able to receive permanent LPR status by proving that the marriage was legitimate. This is a difficult but not impossible process.

How would a couple, whether or not they are still married, prove to DHS two years later that their marriage was legitimate to begin with? Here are some ways:

1. Wedding photos and video
2. Bank accounts and utility bills in both of their names at the same address
3. Children that are products of the marriage
4. Affidavits (sworn written statements) from friends, neighbors, employers, relatives, and so forth that attest to the legitimacy of the marriage

The stronger the evidence, the better the chance of proving that the marriage is real.

Hardship Waivers There is another possibility: The couple is having severe marital problems but has not divorced, and the alien is caught between a rock and a hard place.

For example, Bill is a U.S. citizen who travels to China and meets Mei. The two become engaged and return to the United States to be married. Shortly after their marriage, Mei is granted two-year conditional LPR status. Mei has left her family, friends, and every other aspect of her life in China to start a new life in the United States with her husband Bill.

Several months later, Bill's personality changes for the worse. He becomes verbally and physically abusive, and he batters Mei at least once per week. Moreover, he leaves the house for days at a time, and leaves Mei with no money for food or other needs. Bill clearly has become an abusive husband, and Mei wants out of the marriage badly. But does this mean she will lose her immigration rights and have to leave the United States?

In that case, the U.S. Attorney General (or designee) has the authority to remove the conditional status and make Mei's LPR status permanent, even before the two years is up. Mei would have to prove "extreme hardship" (not a "black letter" law term, but one whose standards can be better understood by studying various cases on the topic).

Ethical Considerations Perhaps in no other area of immigration law is there more of a chance for fraud than with marriage-based LPR status. Chapter 9 considers some of the day-to-day problems in practicing immigration law and will address some of the tricky issues about what to do when faced with clients whose case seems to be riddled with fraud.

2. Parents of U.S. Citizens

Parents of U.S. citizens are immediate relatives and eligible to become LPRs if their son or daughter is a U.S. citizen who is at least 21 years old.

As we will learn in Chapter 6, one way to become a U.S. citizen is to be born in the United States. Thus, children born in the United States, even to alien parents, are (with rare exception; see Chapter 6) U.S. citizens. But their parents may become U.S. citizens only once their sons or daughters become 21 themselves.

As discussed earlier, the United States continues to be the country to which most people from around the world want to immigrate. If parents of U.S. citizens were allowed to become LPRs regardless of their sons' or daughters' ages, then can you imagine how many aliens would rush to the United States to have children here?

Not only would aliens rush to the United States in order to get pregnant, but also pregnant women (and expecting couples) would make sure to rush here before the baby's due date! Naturally, there are millions of people all over the world who have absolutely no desire even to visit the United States, let alone settle here.

Nonetheless, there are countless stories of people who literally have risked life and limb in order to come here—even as illegal aliens who would have to spend much of their time in hiding. In light of that, having a baby to gain U.S. citizenship does not seem too high a price to pay.

Accordingly, the immigration laws are designed to protect against the "baby-for citizenship" strategy. If an alien gives birth to a baby in the United States, then the alien has to wait 21 years in order for her adult son or daughter to sponsor her for LPR status.

For example, suppose that Donna, a pregnant alien, travels to the United States on a visitor's visa. While here, Donna gives birth to a baby girl, whom she names Vanessa. Vanessa is a U.S. citizen automatically. Nonetheless, once Donna's allotted time (as per her visa) has expired, she must leave the United States. What would happen to Baby Vanessa? Vanessa is a U.S. citizen and thus would have every right to stay here. Donna might choose to leave her here (but in whose care) or take her with her when she returns to her country. Should Donna remain here beyond her allotted time, then she would be an illegal alien.

The Effects of 9/11

Prior to 9/11 and certainly since then, there is growing concern about illegal aliens in the United States. Some members of Congress, reflecting growing public opinion, have proposed that children born in the United States to one or two illegal alien parents should not be U.S. citizens. Returning to the preceding example, if Donna's visa had expired and then she gave birth to Vanessa in the United States, Vanessa would be a U.S. citizen nonetheless (even though her mother would have been an illegal alien at the time). But many people want to change that law. Such a change would mean that Baby Vanessa would be illegal, too, and then both she and her mother would have to leave the country.

3. Children of U.S. Citizens

The INA defines "children" as unmarried, minor offspring. Children are distinguished from "sons and daughters" to indicate the INA's special elements of a "**child**" for immigration purposes. Thus, children of U.S. citizens are considered immediate relatives (whereas "**sons** and **daughters**" are not).

child
For immigration purposes, unmarried minor (under 21 years old) offspring.

son
For immigration purposes, a male offspring who is married, at least 21 years old, or both.

daughter
For immigration purposes, a female offspring who is married, at least 21 years old, or both.

This definition of "child" is another example of how certain words in the English language have multiple meanings, depending on the context and circumstances. For instance, in most circles, you would be considered your parents' "child," even if you are over 21 and even if you are married. This is not so in immigration law.

For example, Anthony and Brenda are U.S. citizens and have five offspring: Carlos, who is 15 and single; Danielle, who is 19 and married; Elaine, who is 22 and single; Frank, who is 24 and married; and Georgia, who is 20 and single. Which of these people are considered "children" under immigration law? Only Carlos and Georgia are "children." The others are not "children" because they are either over 21 (Elaine), or married (Danielle), or both (Frank). Therefore, Danielle, Elaine, and Frank are not "children." They are sons and daughters. Carlos and Georgia are "children" whether they are Anthony and Brenda's natural (biological) or legally adopted children.

Legitimated and Adopted Children

Alien children born out of wedlock to U.S. citizens are their natural children but have special immigration problems. If they are legitimated by the U.S. citizen, then they can qualify for relative LPR status. However, legitimated means more than just being recognized as someone's offspring. The parents have to formally legitimize the child by getting married or by formally adopting the child. In turn, adopted children of U.S. citizens are immediate relatives as well.

RELATIVES SUBJECT TO NUMERICAL LIMITATIONS

Certain persons who do not qualify as immediate relatives may gain LPR status nonetheless as a result of their being related to U.S. citizens or LPRs. These people may gain visas that are granted by order of preference and are subject to **numerical limitations.** A numerical limitation is the limit on the number of visas available, as set forth by immigration law. These preferences, based on type of family relation, are often dependent—in terms of the number of available visas—based on the previous category or preference.

numerical limitations
Restrictions in the number of applications made to DHS during a particular period of time, often creating long waiting lists for applicants.

There are four preferences: Unmarried sons and daughters of U.S. citizens; spouses, children, and unmarried sons and daughters of LPRs; married sons and daughters of U.S. citizens; and brothers and sisters of U.S. citizens.

FIRST PREFERENCE: UNMARRIED SONS AND DAUGHTERS OF U.S. CITIZENS

There are two types of sons and daughters (remember, these are not "children"): married and unmarried. Unmarried sons and daughters (21 years or older) of U.S. citizens are the first preference category. Those sons and daughters of U.S. citizens who are unmarried qualify for the first preference of the relative immigrant visas that are subject to numerical limitations. Thus, while immediate relatives have no waiting list at all, unmarried sons and daughters are first in line on the waiting list.

For example, Roger is a U.S. citizen who has an unmarried 24-year-old daughter named Grace. Because she is 21 or older, she is not Roger's "child" for immigration purposes; she is Roger's "daughter." Because she is single, Grace is considered Roger's unmarried daughter and thus qualifies for a first preference visa.

SECOND PREFERENCE: SPOUSES, CHILDREN, AND UNMARRIED SONS AND DAUGHTERS OF LPRS

Persons who are married to LPRs (Note: not U.S. citizens) qualify under the second preference. Also in this category are any unmarried offspring (any age) of LPRs.

Pay careful attention to this preference category: It is the only one in which the family relationship is to an LPR, not to a citizen. Therefore, spouses and children of LPRs qualify for the second preference, whereas spouses and children of U.S. citizens are immediate relatives. Also, unmarried sons and daughters are in the second preference category (unlike unmarried sons and daughters of U.S. citizens, who are first preference). Remember, "sons and daughters" are the opposite of "children." Children are unmarried and under 21; sons and daughters are 21 or older, or married, or both. If this seems a little confusing at first, here's an example to help you along.

For example, suppose that Angelo is an LPR who lives in the United States. Angelo's wife, Bianca, and their two daughters, Lisa (21) and Stella (20), want to become LPRs as well. Lisa is single, but Stella is married. Accordingly, Bianca (an LPR's spouse) and Lisa (an LPR's unmarried daughter) qualify under the second preference. But Stella (an LPR's married daughter) does not. Keep in mind that for the second preference, Stella and Lisa's ages do not matter (as both children and sons and daughters are accounted for), although their marital status does matter.

THIRD PREFERENCE: MARRIED SONS AND DAUGHTERS OF U.S. CITIZENS

The married offspring of U.S. citizens qualify for the third preference. Again, for immigration purposes, a "son" or "daughter" (as opposed to a child) means that the individual in question is married.

Suppose that Finola is a U.S. citizen. Her sons, Jaco and Tao, who are residents of foreign countries, are both married. Jaco is 25, and Tao is 19. If Jaco and Tao both want to become LPRs through their being related to their mother, then both would qualify as third preference relatives. Had Tao been single, he would have been a "child" (single and under 21) and would have been an immediate relative. Had Jaco been single, he would have been an unmarried son (over 21) and thus a first preference relative.

FOURTH PREFERENCE: BROTHERS AND SISTERS OF U.S. CITIZENS

Brothers and sisters of U.S. citizens qualify under the fourth preference, provided that the citizen is at least 21 years old. (If you recall, a citizen also must be at least 21 years old in order to petition for his or her parent to become an LPR.)

This particular restriction makes sense if you consider the desire to keep an eye on the "immigration door." For instance, if this law were not in place, then the same problem of women running to the United States to give birth might just be rampant.

To illustrate, take Valerie, an alien from Australia who is visiting the United States. While here, Valerie gives birth to a son, Michael. Michael automatically is born a U.S. citizen. Valerie has another son, Victor, who was born in Australia.

If Victor wants to become an LPR based on his brother, Michael, being a U.S. citizen, then Victor will have to wait until Michael becomes 21. This 21-year wait might curtail Valerie's motivation to come to the United States to give birth to Michael, knowing it would take at least 21 years before her other son, Victor, could benefit from that. But if no such age restriction were in place, then Valerie might think it was a clever idea to rush here, give birth, and ensure LPR status for any other children that she might have.

NUMERICAL LIMITATIONS ON CERTAIN COUNTRIES

In addition to the numerical limitations placed on preference category relatives, there are other limitations based on aliens' native countries. The immigration places a maximum percentage of annual visa allotment on any one country. For instance, suppose that 10,000 immigrant visas were granted last year and that the maximum allotment for any single country is 7 percent. Let's suppose that there were 800 citizens of Germany who had applied for LPR status in the United States. Under the immigration law, only 700 of those visas could be granted (because 700 is 7 percent of 10,000). The remaining 100 Germans would have to wait.

Accordingly, aliens from some countries must wait for many years before they can obtain U.S. immigrant visas. When discussing practicing immigration law later in this book, this issue will be addressed, specifically immigration issues based on the country from which the client hails.

PRIORITY DATES

LPR status begins with an official application. A **priority date** is the date when the application is received. Therefore, the actual processing time is more important than the date itself.

priority date
A date used to measure when an approved application to DHS has been received.

The processing time depends on how long the list of applications is. For example, if Uma is a married daughter of a U.S. citizen, she may apply for her LPR status as a third preference relative. If DHS receives her application on February 7, 2004, then that is Uma's priority date.

A year later, Uma wonders what's going on with her application. She finds out that DHS is now issuing visas with priority dates going back to 2001. Thus, Uma realizes she still has a long time to wait.

Ironically, if the fourth preference line is shorter, then the priority dates for fourth preference relatives might move along faster, and some fourth preference relatives actually might get their visas faster than Uma! How can that be? Consider this:

If you walk into a diner to eat dinner, you can get a table right away without a reservation (i.e., an early "priority date," let's say). But a fancy restaurant might require an hour's wait for a table (a later priority date). But if the diner is packed with a long line of people ahead of you, it is possible that it could take you *two* hours to get a table, versus the one hour's required wait at the other restaurant. Unlikely, but possible.

The Life Act

In Chapter 2, we listed the K-3 and V visas as nonimmigrant visas. Technically, that is exactly what they are. But, practically, they are only available to relatives of U.S. citizens or LPRs who are awaiting relative-based LPR status. Rather than force those relatives to live apart from their citizen or LPR family members, the Legal Immigration and Family Equity Act of 2000 (LIFE) allows those relatives who are eligible to receive these nonimmigrant visas in the meantime.

FAMOUS U.S. IMMIGRANTS

An elder statesman

HENRY KISSINGER

Henry Kissinger was born in Germany in 1923. He and his family (who were Jewish) moved to the United States in 1938 to avoid Adolf Hitler's persecution, and he became a citizen in 1943.

Kissinger is best known for having served as National Security Advisor and Secretary of State under President Richard Nixon, during the turbulent years of the Vietnam War, the Cold War, and fragile dialogue with China. Kissinger stayed on as Secretary of State under President Gerald Ford and continued to advise future presidents.

Though Kissinger was a very controversial figure, drawing criticism from liberals and conservatives alike, he always has had the reputation of possessing a brilliant mind. As a result, he remains one of America's most respected "elder statesmen" in terms of foreign affairs.

CONCLUSION

We have covered all of the types of aliens who may gain relative-based immigration. All other types of relatives are not eligible.

Be aware that some eligible relatives are closer to the front of the waiting line than others. Keep that in mind, since some aliens may maximize their opportunities once some circumstances around them change. For instance, unmarried sons or daughters of LPRs are only second preference relatives, whereas unmarried sons or daughters of citizens are first preference. Accordingly, LPR parents who become citizens not only benefit themselves in terms of immigration status, but also some of their relatives as well.

Chapter 9 will discuss some valuable resources for becoming highly skilled in practical immigration matters. Such skills will help you to recognize all roads to immigration that your client might have available and to place your client on the best path.

In the next chapter we will continue discussing ways by which aliens may gain LPR status, specifically employment-based immigration.

KEY TERMS

Alien Registration Card
child
daughter
green card
immediate relative
immigration marriage fraud
Immigration Marriage Fraud amendments
Legal Permanent Resident (LPR)
numerical limitations
priority date
son

REVIEW QUESTIONS

1. What is a Legal Permanent Resident (LPR)?
2. What is the purpose of a green card? Why is it called a "green card"?

3. What is the difference between a green card and a visa?
4. For immigration purposes, what type of aliens are considered immediate relatives?
5. What are the Immigration Marriage Fraud amendments?
6. What is "conditional" LPR status?
7. If a person is granted conditional LPR status because he married a U.S. citizen, what happens if the couple divorces after one year?
8. What are some ways by which to prove a bona fide marriage?
9. For immigration purposes, what type of aliens are considered children?
10. How can the parent of a minor child U.S. citizen become an LPR?
11. How can a child be "legitimated" for immigration purposes?
12. What is the importance of requiring U.S. citizen sons and daughters to at least be 21 years old before they can petition for their parents to become LPRs?

HYPOTHETICALS

1. Rebecca is a U.S. citizen. She has three daughters living overseas. Angela, who is 16 and single; Carmen, who is 20 and married; and Jessica, who is 22 and single. May Rebecca file a relative petition (for LPR status) for each of them? If so, under what relative category would each daughter be classified?
2. Henry is an LPR. His mother, Clara, and his brother Paul (Clara's son) want to become LPRs, too. What are Paul's chances of becoming an LPR if Henry refuses to become a U.S. citizen or Clara refuses to become an LPR?
3. James and Joanne come to your law firm with a problem: James is a U.S. citizen who fell in love with Joanne, an alien, while vacationing overseas. The two had a whirlwind romance and married only three months after their first date. They returned to the United States, and James filed a relative petition for his new wife. Six months have passed since James filed the petition. Now, the couple is approaching their first wedding anniversary, and they no longer want to be married to each other. They realize that the marriage is over, but that they did not enter into it for immigration purposes. You are convinced that they married out of love. Joanne is afraid that her LPR status will not become permanent, and James is very supportive of her immigration situation. If they get a divorce, they do not want to hide that from DHS. How should you proceed?
4. Christina, a citizen and resident of Austria, just married Carlos, a U.S. citizen. Christina has a 14-year-old daughter, Katia, from a previous marriage. Katia is a citizen and resident of Austria, too. Christina's family owns a restaurant in a tiny Austrian village. However, her parents are too old to operate it, and the other relatives are too inexperienced. She is the family's only hope to make the business survive. Christina wants to remain in Austria until the restaurant is running smoothly but would like Katia to become an LPR and live with her stepfather Carlos in the United States until Christina is ready to join them. May Carlos petition for Katia to obtain LPR status? What steps must he take in order for that to happen?
5. Cynthia was born and raised in Peru. Her only family member in the United States is her cousin George, who is a U.S. citizen. George's mother is Monica. Monica's brother is Angelo, who is Cynthia's father. Monica and Angelo were also born and raised in Peru and, like Cynthia, have never been to the United States. Under what circumstances involving George, Monica, and Angelo may Cynthia eventually become an LPR through a relative petition?

CHAPTER 4

IMMIGRANTS: EMPLOYMENT-BASED

CHAPTER OBJECTIVES

After completing this chapter, you should know:

- Why there is a fear of permitting aliens to work in the United States
- How some aliens may qualify for employment-based immigration
- The types of visas held by foreign-born athletes and movie stars
- The impact of illegal alien employees

In Chapter 3 we discussed how aliens may become LPRs because of their being related to U.S. citizens or LPRs. In this chapter we will take a look at another way to obtain LPR status: through employment sponsorship.

Generally, U.S. employers may petition for aliens to become their employees (and gain LPR status as a result) provided that the alien is qualified for the position; that there is no U.S. citizen ready, willing, and able to assume that position; that the employer pays the alien employee prevailing wages; and that other standards that demonstrate the employer's need are met. In some instances, the alien first must be granted **labor certification** (approval by the Department of Labor of the state in which the alien seeks to work and then by the U.S. Department of Labor). In all instances, approval must be granted by DHS. In order to better understand some of the reasons why this process is what it is, let's revisit our discussion about the history of immigration in the United States, as well as the principle of "overloading the boat."

labor certification
Approval by the U.S. Department of Labor to permit an alien to become a LPR through employment-based immigration. The alien then must apply to DHS to become a LPR.

EMPLOYMENT IMMIGRATION AND "OVERLOADING THE BOAT"

As discussed previously, the United States was once a young nation in need of laborers to help build it up. Quite often, those laborers were aliens. As our industrial and technological bases grew, so did our population. Accordingly, there came a point when it was no longer necessary to obtain workers from foreign countries, because we had plenty of bodies right here at home.

With so many aliens coming here to work, it made it difficult for our own rapidly growing population to find jobs. Clearly, something had to be done.

If we look at the "immigration door" that lets in aliens, we see that it is neither completely open nor completely shut when applied to workers. If it were completely open, then any alien who wished to work in the United States simply could walk right in. If it were completely shut, then no alien could come in. Instead, the door is open, but only to a certain extent. Aliens may qualify to come here to work, both as immigrants and nonimmigrants. But they must meet certain standards before they are allowed in. Therefore, these aliens are taken "aboard the boat," with a cautious eye to not "overloading the boat."

QUALIFICATION FOR THE POSITION

Typically, an alien must have a specific job in order to apply for employment-based immigration. The alien may not be granted immigration status simply because of a desire to work in the United States; there must be a particular job to go along with the desire!

Once the alien indeed has a firm offer, then the alien must prove that he or she is qualified to do the job. This can be proven by presenting evidence that the alien possesses the necessary education, training, and experience for the job. Typically, school and college letters or transcripts, letters from former or current employers, awards or achievements, and other relevant documents are instrumental in demonstrating such qualifications.

THE EMPLOYER'S NEEDS MUST BE GENUINE

The employer must demonstrate that the job requirements are genuine (i.e., that the job is not for the purpose of helping the employee gain LPR status). Moreover, the qualifications for the job must be necessary, not tailor-made for a particular alien applicant.

In other words, let's say that Alonzo is an alien who is in the United States visiting his uncle Nelson. Nelson's good friend and neighbor, Clark, owns a restaurant nearby. Alonzo would like to become an LPR, and his uncle Nelson wants to help him out. So, Nelson asks Clark for a favor to sponsor Alonzo through employment-based immigration.

Clark really does not need extra help in the restaurant but agrees to take Alonzo on, especially after Nelson agrees to help pay Alonzo's salary (off the record, making it look like Clark is really paying the entire salary). Alonzo has some experience as a waiter, and so Clark would hire him as one. Alonzo happens to speak five languages: English, Spanish, French, Italian, and German. As a boy, he swept the floors at an international language school in his native country and became friends with the professors there. That's how he picked up those languages.

Clark indicates that: (1) he really needs a waiter and (2) that the waiter must speak English, Spanish, French, Italian, and German (which is not really necessary).

Clearly, this is an example of what an employer is not allowed to do: to create a job and specific job requirements for the purpose of assisting an alien to gain LPR status. In other words, neither Clark's needs nor the position requirements are genuine.

As both the state (in which Clark's restaurant is) and the U.S. Department of Labor will have to review the petition, it is likely that they will catch on that a waiter really does not have to speak five languages and deny the petition.

THERE IS NO U.S. CITIZEN OR LPR READY, WILLING, AND ABLE TO FILL THAT POSITION, AND PREVAILING WAGES ARE PAID

For many of the employment-based categories that exist, it is necessary for the sponsoring employer to show that there is no U.S. citizen or LPR qualified and willing to undertake the job opening that the alien seeks. Moreover, the employer must pay the prevailing wages that the job usually demands.

Suppose that Alex is an alien who is a skilled wood craftsman. Feldman is the owner of Feldman's Fine Furniture, a successful furniture store that specializes in fine wood furniture and cabinetry. Feldman is looking for a skilled craftsman for his store. That type of job usually pays around $35,000 per year.

Max, a U.S. citizen, is interested in the job. Both Max and Alex apply for the position. Max, an experienced craftsman himself, knows that the pay ought to be around $35,000 per year, and that's what he expects to be paid.

Alex, on the other hand, comes from a very poor country, where the lifestyle is much different than it is here. The average salary in his country is about $5,000 per year. People usually own no more than one pair of shoes and two pairs of pants. Only the rich have televisions or telephones, and many families often have to share one bathroom. For these reasons, Alex is not used to much, and he is not asking for much. Alex would be thrilled to do the job for $10,000 per year.

If there were no laws restricting Feldman's ability to hire whomever he wanted to hire, then if both Alex and Max were equally qualified, Feldman surely would hire Alex and would pay him a lot less than he would have paid Max! Feldman would be happy, and so would Alex. But Max would not be happy. That's why these laws are in place—to protect U.S. citizens and LPRs from not losing out on jobs.

The U.S. people have an interest in protecting themselves and their ability to find a job in their home country. This is why Congress creates laws that help to safeguard their interests.

Moreover, paying an alien, like Alex, less than half of the prevailing wage would be taking advantage of him. It would be an exploitation of the fact that he is easy to please.

For these reasons, the immigration law demands that an alien will be eligible for a job in the United States only if there is no U.S. citizen or LPR ready, willing, and able to accept the position and as long as the alien is paid the prevailing wages.

THE DEPARTMENT OF LABOR

Keep in mind that with all the examples we have examined thus far that each petition for employment-based immigration must pass through the U.S. Department of Labor first. This is known as labor certification. The next section examines the various preferences (categories) of employment-based immigration. Some of the preferences will not require the U.S. Department of Labor to become involved. In any case, all employment-based immigration must be approved by DHS.

FIRST PREFERENCE—PRIORITY WORKERS

1. Persons of extraordinary ability in the sciences, arts, education, business, or athletics
2. Outstanding professors and researchers
3. Certain multinational executives and managers

priority workers
For immigration purposes, persons of extraordinary ability in the sciences, arts, education, business, or athletics; outstanding professors and researchers; or certain multinational managers and executives.

These types of workers are considered **priority workers** and are granted immigration visas of the first preference.

Priority workers do not need to first gain approval from the U.S. Department of Labor. Moreover, their sponsoring employers do not have to demonstrate that there is no U.S. citizen ready, willing, and able to fill the job in question. There are three types of priority (first preference) workers.

1. Persons of extraordinary ability in the sciences, arts, education, business, or athletics

When we discussed nonimmigrant visas (see Chapter 2), we referred to "extraordinary ability" as being "outstanding." This standard remains consistent with employment-based immigrant visas, too.

A person of extraordinary ability in the sciences, arts, education, business, or athletics is typically someone who has truly made an outstanding contribution to one or more of these fields. Generally, such a person will have at least one of these qualifications: National or international fame, universally-renowned status within his or her field, numerous published works in his or her field, and other similar achievements consistent with truly extraordinary ability.

For example, Thomas is an accomplished musician in his country. He has performed in live concerts for the past three years and has recorded an album that sold a few thousand copies. Generally, would this person qualify as an alien of extraordinary ability in the musical arts? No, he would qualify if he was perhaps Paul McCartney (the ex-Beatles member and world-famous solo musician). Typically, that is the type of caliber meant by extraordinary.

2. Outstanding Professors and Researchers
"Outstanding" is a category that is similar to extraordinary. For immigration purposes, outstanding professors typically are those who are internationally recognized and who have made significant contributions to their field through research, publications, or other efforts. Like aliens of extraordinary ability, outstanding professors are first preference workers.

3. Certain Multinational Executives and Managers
Top-level executives and managers of multinational companies may be considered first preference workers, depending on the length and nature of their work. The concept of this visa is similar to the one regarding intracompany transferees (see Chapter 2). The difference is that the priority immigrant visa is available only to very high-level employees.

SECOND PREFERENCE

Professionals holding advanced degrees or persons of **exceptional ability** in the sciences, arts, or business qualify for the second preference. Unlike priority workers, approval in this category is first granted by the U.S. Department of Labor.

exceptional ability
For immigration purposes, a person who has achieved excellence in a particular field but is not uniquely outstanding.

advanced degree
For immigration purposes, an academic degree beyond the baccalaureate.

baccalaureate
A bachelor's degree.

1. Advanced Degrees
Generally, a degree beyond a baccalaureate or its equivalent is considered to be an **advanced degree.** A **baccalaureate,** more commonly referred to as a bachelor's degree, typically is achieved after four years of college education. Other countries' educational systems may vary from ours, and so there are degrees that are not quite the same as a baccalaureate but are considered to be its equivalent.

An advanced degree is a degree gained beyond the baccalaureate, such as a master's degree or a doctorate. Examples are: MBA (Master of Business Administration), JD (Juris Doctor, which is a law degree), MD (Medical Doctor), and PhD (Doctor of Philosophy).

Accordingly, aliens holding advanced degrees are in the second preference category.

2. Exceptional Ability
Previously, we discussed extraordinary ability. Now we are talking about exceptional ability. What's the difference?

On first impression, it would seem that the two are synonymous. Logically it seems difficult to tell them apart. In searching for the correct answer, keep in mind that words often have different meanings depending on their context. Just as "child" means something different for immigration purposes than it does for everyday use, so do the words "extraordinary" and "exceptional."

While there is no exact definition in the INA for either word, the first rule of thumb is that "extraordinary" is a higher standard than "exceptional." The tricky part is where to draw the line.

Typically, a person with exceptional ability is someone who has achieved excellence in a particular field but is not uniquely outstanding. For example, let's go back to the earlier example with Thomas the musician. Suppose that Thomas did record a couple of albums and each sold tens of thousands of copies. Also suppose that Thomas has performed in six cities in his country over the past two years in arenas with seats of at least 1,000 and that each concert was sold out.

In that case, Thomas might be considered to be a person of exceptional ability, though not extraordinary ability like Paul McCartney. On the other hand, a local musician who has not recorded any albums and plays a couple of nights per week to a small audience probably would be neither extraordinary nor exceptional.

Although determining the standard is not an exact science, looking at past decisions by the BIA will help you to understand the guidelines better.

THIRD PREFERENCE

Skilled workers in short supply, persons holding baccalaureate degrees, and other workers in short supply qualify for the third preference. As with the second preference, approval must be granted first by the U.S. Department of Labor and then by DHS.

1. Skilled Workers in Short Supply

For immigration purposes, a "skilled worker" is one who has at least two years of training or experience in the field of the particular offered position. Keep in mind that skilled workers under this category must be in short supply—positions for which it generally will be difficult to find U.S. workers qualified and willing to do the job.

2. Persons Holding Baccalaureate Degrees

As discussed earlier, a baccalaureate degree is a college diploma more commonly known as a bachelor's degree and one that usually takes a student four years to earn. Persons holding baccalaureate degrees or their equivalents (a similar degree from a foreign country) are third preference workers.

3. Other Workers in Short Supply

"Other workers" generally means unskilled workers. More specially, "other workers" means workers who do not have at least two years of training or experience for the job that they seek to fill. There will be more aliens who fill the "other workers" category than any other category, which makes both the waiting list and waiting period quite long.

Again, it is important to point out the "short supply" aspect of this category. Some jobs need to be filled, and workers for those jobs are in short supply. In other jobs, however, the supply exceeds the demand. Therefore, the type of job applied for plays a great role in determining the likelihood of gaining employment-based immigration.

FOURTH PREFERENCE—CERTAIN SPECIAL IMMIGRANTS

Special immigrants such as religious workers, former employees of the U.S. government, or employees of international organizations qualify for the fourth preference. (There are other types of special immigrants, but those types are very rare.)

1. Religious Workers

Religious workers who are members of a recognized bona fide religion may qualify. Chapter 2 discussed religious workers for nonimmigrant purposes and covered the difference between the validity of a religion (which is subjective and determined by each individual, not by the INA) and the validity of a person's belief in a particular religion (which is required by the INA and determined by the DHS).

2. Former Employees of the U.S. Government

A person who has worked for the U.S. government may qualify under this category. If a person has allowed his or her LPR status to lapse, then that person may be eligible to regain that status through this category.

3. Employees of International Organizations

Persons who are employed by international organizations, such as the World Bank or the United Nations, may qualify under this preference.

Keep in mind that there is no need to go through the U.S. Department of Labor for fourth preference employment-based immigration.

FIFTH PREFERENCE—EMPLOYMENT CREATION VISAS

Persons who invest one million dollars in an enterprise that will create at least ten U.S. jobs qualify for the fifth preference. At times, the minimum amount may be reduced to as little as $500,000 or increased to as much as $3 million, depending on the location and the rate of unemployment.

"Can I buy my green card?" This is a question that you, as an immigration legal professional, may be asked quite often. The answer is no. However, it is not quite that simple.

Direct payment of money or other value to obtain a green card is against the law. Unfortunately, that and many other illegal acts involving immigration actually occur. But paying a government employee for a green card is like paying a U.S. Customs officer to allow drugs to be smuggled into the United States. Obviously, these acts have no proper place in immigration law and practice.

However, there is a legal way by which an investment can be made that will lead to a green card (i.e., LPR status). The money invested must be a substantial amount that will open a business or other venture and that will create at least ten full-time jobs.

The focus is on investment and job creation. It is not "buying" a green card. Rather, a substantial financial investment is often a good indicator of a person's intent to permanently settle here. Also, it is in our national interest for an investor to create at least ten full-time jobs for U.S. citizens or LPRs.

If we apply the "overloading the boat" principle to this type of visa, we wind up with just one more person being let into the United States, but at least ten more jobs are created for our workers. Moreover, the venture might improve the overall economy of the surrounding area by providing a service and by requiring the services of neighboring businesses. That is a long-term benefit for everyone.

THE IMPACT OF ILLEGAL ALIEN EMPLOYEES

Logically, many people who are willing to sponsor alien employees know the employees ahead of time. For instance, if Carl owns a restaurant in Denver, he is unlikely to learn that Stavros, a citizen of Greece who lives there, is a great waiter. It is even less likely that Carl would contact Stavros and say to him: "I want to help you to become an LPR. Even though I've never met you, I want to go through all the trouble of sponsoring you."

A far more likely scenario might be that Stavros is an illegal alien who is already working in Carl's restaurant. Because Carl recognizes that Stavros is doing an excellent job and because he likes Stavros personally, he is willing to help him to become an LPR. In that case, would Carl and/or Stavros get in trouble if they move forward with a petition for LPR status? Would that reveal Stavros' illegal status and land both of them in jail?

Technically, it is illegal to hire illegal aliens, and Carl could get into trouble. Stavros, upon being discovered, might wind up in jail or be removed from the United States. Then why have you heard that "restaurants are full of illegal aliens working in the kitchen?" Because with limited resources, immigration officials are busiest trying to capture terrorist aliens or to close down huge factories that employ many illegal aliens. Carl and Stavros are not exactly high on DHS radar. Jail would not be likely for either of them. Stavros might be required to leave the United States, and Carl might have to pay a fine. Nonetheless, both Carl and Stavros could face legal problems.

However, all of this does not mean that there aren't legal aliens who would attempt to gain LPR status through employment-based immigration. These could involve various types of legal nonimmigrants currently in the United States and people who are currently abroad. Surely, it is unlikely that Carl would contact Stavros in Greece and go to all that trouble to hire him to be a waiter (which is a job that is in demand and not particularly difficult to fill).

Instead, suppose that Carl owned a Greek restaurant and that a friend of Carl's told him that there is this excellent chef living in Greece named Stavros. In fact, Carl may have heard the story about Stavros' cooking from many people. In that case, Carl might be willing to go out on a limb and sponsor Stavros for LPR status, even though he has never met him.

Famous U.S. Immigrants

A history-making immigrant

MADELEINE ALBRIGHT

Madeleine Albright served as Secretary of State under President Bill Clinton. She is best known for becoming the first woman to serve in that capacity, but not many people realized that she is also an immigrant. Like one of her predecessors, Henry Kissinger (see Chapter 3), Albright was a foreign-born secretary of state.

Albright was born in Prague, Czechoslovakia (now the Czech Republic) in 1937 and moved with her family to the United States in 1948 after the communists had assumed power there. She became a U.S. citizen in 1957.

She continues to comment on numerous issues in foreign affairs, and she continues to be respected both nationally and internationally.

CONCLUSION

We have now covered employment-based immigration, which is an essential part of LPR status overall. In many instances, it is the best approach to take, especially when aliens are not closely related to U.S. citizens or LPRs.

Employment is one of the prime examples of why the United States is concerned about "overloading the boat." Again, remember this, and it will help you to better understand why some immigration laws are what they are.

Chapters 3 and 4, which deal with relative and employment-based immigration, respectively, cover the vast majority of immigration eligibility. Chances are that most LPRs that you might encounter will have gained LPR status by one of those two methods.

In Chapter 5 we will examine some other ways by which aliens may become LPRs.

KEY TERMS

advanced degree
baccalaureate
exceptional ability
labor certification
priority worker

REVIEW QUESTIONS

1. What is meant by labor certification?
2. When hiring an alien, what are some of the steps that an employer must take in order to satisfy the U.S. Department of Labor?
3. For immigration purposes, what type of aliens are considered to be priority workers?
4. What is an employment creation visa? What are the criteria for getting one?

5. What are some reasons why the laws require specific criteria before labor certification is granted?
6. What are some of the risks and consequences of employers and employees engaging in employment of illegal aliens?
7. What is a good method by which to distinguish between "extraordinary ability" and "exceptional ability"?
8. For immigration purposes, what is an advanced degree?
9. What is the difference between being outstanding in a particular academic or vocational field and being internationally recognized in that field? Give examples of each.
10. Which preference workers first must satisfy the U.S. Department of Labor's requirements before gaining employment-based immigration?
11. What type of workers may gain employment-based immigration through the fourth preference?
12. For immigration purposes, what constitutes a skilled worker?

HYPOTHETICALS

1. The *New York Times* wants to hire Graham for its Washington, D.C. bureau because of Graham's specialty in international politics and economics. Graham is an alien and wishes to gain LPR status through employment-based immigration.

   In which preference category would Graham most likely be classified if:

   A. He has an internationally syndicated weekly political talk show seen on television in over twenty countries.
   B. He holds a PhD in political science.
   C. He holds a baccalaureate in economics.

2. Franz is from Germany and has lived there his whole life. A couple of years ago, he was involved in a serious automobile accident that left him hospitalized for several weeks. He wasn't getting much better until his sister brought him a pet goldfish in a small bowl. As soon as Franz began to stare at the goldfish, he started to feel better. For several nights, he would dream that the goldfish spoke to him in a human voice and gave him advice about healing and about life in general.

   Within days, Franz made a full recovery. He continued to have this dream and became convinced that fish are God's personal messengers to humans. As a result, he explained this to several of his friends, many of whom were very moved by his story. As a result, Franz started the Church of Aquatic Spirituality (CAS), whose mission was to understand God by observing fish.

   The CAS grew in popularity in Germany, and now Franz wants to establish the same church here in the United States. He comes to you for advice. Though you do not believe in the premise of his religion (that fish are God's messengers to humans), you are convinced that Franz really does believe this himself. You choose to help him.

   What type of preference category is most suitable for Franz? What are some of the obstacles he might face in his attempt to gain LPR status?

3. Salvador is a citizen and resident of Mexico. He has traveled to the United States as a visitor, primarily traveling to the cities and towns along the Gulf Coast. In Mexico, Salvador is a successful businessman, owning several travel agencies and a luxury hotel in Acapulco.

Salvador believes that there is much unchartered territory along the Gulf Coast that would be an ideal location for a new resort hotel. Currently, Salvador is in the United States on a business visa and is interested in purchasing some land along the Gulf Coast on which to build his enterprise.

Salvador has no formal education, no relatives in the United States, and no offers of employment. However, he has a vision of transforming an otherwise undeveloped portion of the Gulf Coast and the financial resources to accomplish his goal.

Salvador comes to you for help. Under what category would Salvador best fit in order to gain LPR status, and what additional information do you need to know in order to determine if he qualifies?

CHAPTER 5

OTHER TYPES OF LPR STATUS

CHAPTER OBJECTIVES

After completing this chapter, you should know:

- How some aliens may become immigrants by winning a lottery
- Special privileges for aliens who have lived here since before 1972
- The past and possible future of the immigration amnesty law
- How some legal and illegal aliens may become immigrants

In Chapters 3 and 4, we discussed the two most common methods by which to obtain LPR status: relative and employment-based immigration. However, there are more ways by which a person can become an LPR. In this chapter we will discuss these alternative approaches as well as how many aliens may adjust from one immigration status to another.

DIVERSITY IMMIGRANTS

The DHS establishes diversity immigrant visas for persons who are from countries that have been adversely affected by immigration capability. This concept is very similar to affirmative action. A quick review of U.S. history will help to illustrate this point.

Affirmative action is a policy to give preferential treatment to individuals belonging to historically underrepresented groups. A good way to explain this is to begin with the phrase: "The United States is run by white males." That point of view is based on the notion that in earlier years there were various reasons, including direct laws, that benefited white males to the detriment of nonwhites (persons of color) and women, among others. For example, neither nonwhites nor women had the right to vote at one point in time. As our laws became more consistent regarding race and gender, the opportunities increased for more and more groups of people.

However, those historically underrepresented groups continued to lag behind. It is as if you are about to run in a race that is twenty blocks long. As the race begins, a group of people hold you back, and then they let you go once your opponent has ran about ten blocks ahead of you. Now the only way you can win the race is to run twice as fast as your opponent. Even if you run one and one-half times faster, your opponent will still win. Why? Because you were held back.

But if some group witnessed this injustice of you having been held back, then they might give you a ride in their car for about ten blocks, so that you can catch up to your opponent and then it will be a fair race. That's exactly what affirmative action is: giving someone a boost to make up for having held back that person in the past.

Some argue that affirmative action is a great way to level the playing field—to give historically underrepresented groups a chance to compete in today's world. Others believe that while past discrimination against such groups was unjustifiable indeed, continued discrimination based on factors such as race and gender—even with noble intentions of equity in mind—only add to the problem. Accordingly, the debate about the merits of affirmative action continues.

diversity-based immigration
A process providing immigrant visas for persons from countries that have been adversely affected in the immigration process.

In any event, we can liken affirmative action to **diversity-based immigration.** For a variety of reasons, aliens from some countries have immigrated to the United States with much greater frequency than those from other countries. Accordingly, aliens from those "historically underrepresented countries" are eligible for diversity-based immigration. Essentially, this is "affirmative action" immigration.

The Lottery

lottery
An actual lottery by which aliens eligible for diversity immigration may receive LPR status if their names are selected from the drawing.

Commonly, diversity immigration is known as "the **lottery.**" In fact, the process very much resembles a typical lottery drawing. Any alien who is eligible for diversity-based immigration (an alien from a historically underrepresented country) may send in some basic information (name, address, date of birth, etc.) to DHS. A lottery-type drawing is then held, and those aliens whose entries are selected become eligible for LPR status.

Generally, the immigration lottery is no different from any other lottery in the sense that:

(1) The chances to win are very slim.
(2) The effort is very minimal.

If you purchased a state-operated lottery ticket for one dollar, your effort would be minimal (both in terms of time and money). Then again, your chances to win would be minimal, too. It is the same with the immigration lottery. All it takes is filling out some basic information on a postcard and sending it in—nothing to get your hopes too high, but nothing to lose either.

Of course, a lot of people in the United States who enroll in the lottery are illegal aliens (if they are here and not citizens or LPRs already, then chances are that they are here illegally). A good question that they often ask is: "But if I try to enter the lottery, won't they find out that I'm an illegal alien and catch me?" Again, the answer is more practical than technical here.

The DHS simply does not have anywhere close to the number of resources it would need to be able to capture illegal aliens in this manner. Typically, DHS agents do not make "random arrests" of illegal aliens. Accordingly, the DHS does not make a practice of inviting aliens to enroll in the lottery and then tracking down the illegal ones and saying: "Aha, gotcha!"

REGISTRY

registry
For immigration purposes, a status which provides for legal or illegal aliens to become LPRs because they have continuously resided in the United States since before 1972.

Another way to gain LPR status is through **registry.** Persons who have resided in the United States continuously, legally or illegally, since before 1972 qualify for LPR status.

Some aliens know about this and may ask: "I have lived here for a long time. May I get my green card because I've been here for so long?" If "so long" means before 1972, then the answer is yes (subject to other criteria).

In order for an alien to qualify for registry, the alien must demonstrate that he or she:

1. Entered the United States since before 1972;
2. Has resided here continuously since that time;
3. Is a person of good moral character; and
4. Is not otherwise ineligible for U.S. citizenship

1. Entered the United States Since before 1972

The words "since before 1972" mean exactly that. Because "1972" began on January 1, 1972, that means any alien who seeks LPR status through registry must have entered the United States on or before December 31, 1971.

Why 1972 in particular? What's so special about that year? Think back to the "immigration door" and to "overloading the boat." On the one hand, there could have been no law about registry at all—the logic being that aliens who are here for a very long time would assimilate into U.S. culture anyway.

Prior to the Immigration Reform and Control Act of 1986, the registry date was June 10, 1948. If a person was applying for registry in 1985, that person would have to show that he or she had been in the United States for at least 27 years (since 1948). Now, an alien needs to be here even longer (since January 1, 1972).

It is possible that aliens who have been here for over thirty years probably have children born in the United States, jobs (albeit illegally), and other aspects of their lives that arguably would make it unduly burdensome for them to leave.

That's why closing the immigration door completely and not letting them in would seem overly harsh. On the other hand, if the registry date were to change each year (for example, it changes to 1973 next year, 1974 the following year, etc.), then it would be an incentive for aliens to remain here illegally until their registry date comes up. In effect, it would be like telling aliens: "If you are here illegally, make sure to stay well hidden until your registry date comes up. Then, you can come out of the woodwork and become an LPR!"

Accordingly, the 1972 date might seem arbitrary. But it is one of the many compromises that the INA provides in opening the door just enough or in loading—but not overloading—the boat. As the immigration law changes from time to time, keep an eye on the registry date. It might change sooner than you expect.

2. Has Resided Here Continuously Since That Time

Residence in the United States must be continuous since before January 1, 1972. In other words, suppose that Jack, an alien, entered the United States in 1971, lived here for 10 years, moved to another country for eight months, and then moved back to the United States. Jack would not be eligible for registry because he did not continuously reside in the United States since before 1972.

3. Is a Person of Good Moral Character

Aliens applying for LPR status through registry must demonstrate that they are of good moral character. Quite often, this means that they must have led a clean, crime-free life while here in the United States. Also, it helps their case a great deal if they have had nothing to do with anti-American organizations, for example.

4. Is Not Otherwise Admissible

Aliens seeking LPR status through registry should be otherwise admissible. There are exceptions to immigration qualifications that would render an alien inadmissible even if he or she has fulfilled all of the necessary requirements. For instance, suppose that there are two aliens—Tom and Samantha—who are seeking to become LPRs. Samantha is the sister of a U.S. citizen and thus eligible under the fourth preference of relative-based immigration (see Chapter 3). A few weeks before her priority date is about to be current, Samantha is arrested for armed robbery. She is tried and convicted. Accordingly, she is no longer eligible for LPR status.

Tom has lived in the United States since 1970. He seeks LPR status through registry. If Tom, like Samantha, was convicted of a felony prior to gaining LPR status, then he would be denied LPR status as well.

Accordingly, registry aliens, like all other aliens, must be "otherwise admissible."

AMNESTY

Aliens who have resided in the United States continuously before 1982—legally or illegally—were for some time also eligible to obtain LPR status. However, that is no longer the case. That **amnesty** law applied for a limited time only, and persons who did not take advantage of it in time no longer have that option available to them.

You might be wondering: If this is no longer current law, why learn about it? The concept of amnesty is an important one to understand. There is a movement at this time to create a new amnesty law.

amnesty
The process by which legal or illegal aliens were permitted to become LPRs if they arrived in the United States before 1982. This provision of the INA has expired.

The amnesty law mentioned previously was signed into law by President Ronald Reagan in 1986. Many aliens often referred to it as "the Reagan Law." At that time, the federal government began to get much stricter on employers who hired illegal aliens. That's why President Reagan approved the law, in order to buffer some of the negative impact that the tough hiring standards would have on the economy.

For example, suppose that you owned a restaurant in the United States and that there was no law preventing you from hiring illegal aliens. Of course, if they ever got caught, they would have to leave the United States. But nothing would happen to you. No risks are involved. Yet, the rewards would be huge: hard-working, dedicated, grateful employees eager to do a great job for very little money. What could be better than that from a business perspective?

Suppose further that you have a staff of thirty employees and that twenty-four of them are illegal aliens. Now the immigration law changes, and it is a serious federal crime for you to employ illegal aliens. You have to let them go. But think about how that would devastate your business. How can you lose twenty-four out of thirty workers in one day? That's 80 percent of your workforce!

The effect on your livelihood could be catastrophic. What if your restaurant was the only one within an industrial complex where hundreds of people worked and depended on your restaurant for their meals? If you had to close down, that would affect them as well.

What about the workers themselves? If they suddenly were fired, they would lose their source of income on the spot. This would affect their buying power. They would not be able to buy food, clothing, or other goods. That would affect supermarkets, department stores, and various other retail businesses. That's just from your business. What about everyone else's? Do you see now what effect such a law would have without a buffer?

Accordingly, the "buffer" was the law that granted amnesty to illegal aliens who had been in the United States continuously since 1982. Aliens had a specific amount of time in which to go through the legal process of becoming LPRs. In that way, the employers would not have to fire them.

However, that law no longer exists! Therefore, if a client asks you: "I've been in the United States since 1982; may I get my green card?" The correct response should be: "No, not based on that reason alone. That law no longer exists. But if you've been here since before 1972, then you should apply on that basis."

Amnesty after 9/11

President Reagan heard some criticism for the amnesty bill that he signed into law in 1986. Almost twenty years later, President George W. Bush heard even stronger criticism for proposing a similar plan.

It would seem quite improbable that, so soon after 9/11, a president who appears to stand very strongly against terrorism would be so agreeable to giving illegal aliens a chance to become LPRs. "That's rewarding them for illegal behavior and sending a message that it's okay to break the law!" That's what a lot of angry protesters shout. But the proposal involves aliens who are highly unlikely to be terrorists, and future laws—much tougher on aliens trying to enter illegally at the borders—would accompany it.

Supporters of the proposal believe that it will help the economy in the long run and account for the illegals who are here now (and apparently in hiding, thus statistically invisible). They say that the type of illegal aliens who pose a physical threat to our country are not the ones who would benefit from this law. It will benefit those whose dream is to come here and work—to earn a piece of the American dream. Then they would pay taxes, just like U.S. citizens and LPRs.

The debate is a controversial one and sure to continue for years to come. Currently, no new amnesty law exists. But in this world of ever-changing laws, keep your eye on it; it may change very soon.

ASYLUM

Chapter 8 discusses asylum in greater detail. **Asylum** is a status granted to certain aliens who have established that they have a well-founded fear of persecution in their own country or in the country in which they were living immediately prior to coming to the United States. Those aliens who are granted asylum are known as **asylees** and usually are permitted to become LPRs one year after having been granted asylum.

asylum
A process available to aliens who qualify as refugees, permitting such aliens to lawfully remain in the United States and to become LPRs.

asylees
A person who has been granted asylum.

ADJUSTMENT OF STATUS

Certain nonimmigrants who are in the United States either legally or illegally may adjust their status to become LPRs. They may also change their status to another nonimmigrant status, but that is different from adjustment. Adjustment of status involves changing from nonimmigrant to immigrant status only.

Aliens who have been granted asylum may become LPRs after one year. Those aliens adjust their status from asylees to LPRs. The main feature of adjusting one's status is that it does away with the need to leave the United States only to return again.

For instance, Alvin is an asylee in the United States, and one year has passed since he was granted asylum. He now wants to become an LPR. Rather than having to leave the country to go to a consulate abroad, only to obtain his visa and reenter the United States, Alvin might be able to adjust his status and not have to leave the United States to do so.

But adjustment does not apply only to asylees. Consider the following examples.

Marcia comes to the United States on a student visa in order to go to college. She meets a U.S. citizen, Tom, there. They fall in love and get married. Marcia is now eligible to become an LPR because she is the spouse of a U.S. citizen (see Chapter 3).

Consider the same example, but with a twist. Let's say that Marcia dropped out of college and got a full-time job. She would be out of student status, and with no other lawful status, she would be an illegal alien. Marcia then meets Tom, and they get married. Again, she would be eligible for LPR status as the spouse of a U.S. citizen.

In both scenarios, Marcia would have to go through some procedure in order to become an LPR. However, the laws are a little different depending on whether the alien in question is legal or illegal.

In the first case, Marcia is a legal nonimmigrant seeking to become an LPR. She either may leave the United States and obtain an immigrant visa from a U.S. consulate abroad or adjust her status to LPR while remaining in the United States. Because she is here legally, she has the option to obtain her LPR visa abroad or adjust her status here. Why would she bother going abroad when she simply can adjust her status right here in the United States. Two main reasons are: First, maybe she wants to go abroad anyway (to marry Tom at a wedding in her home country, for instance). Second, it might be cheaper (the adjustment of status process can be expensive).

In any event, most aliens who have the option usually prefer to adjust their status in the United States rather than to obtain an immigrant visa abroad.

In the second case, in which Marcia would have become an illegal alien, her only option would be to adjust her status here. Many people would do just about anything to marry a U.S. citizen, including pretending that the marriage is real (i.e., not for immigration purposes) and thus risking spending many years in jail if they're caught (see Chapter 3).

Minimum Adjustment of Status Requirements

There are certain requirements that must be fulfilled in order to adjust one's status. The alien must demonstrate that he or she: (1) has applied for adjustment of status; (2) is eligible to receive an immigrant visa and is admissible to the United States as a permanent resident; and (3) that an immigrant visa is immediately available to him or her at the time that the application is filed.

Adjustment of Status for Legal Aliens

admission
For immigration purposes, physical presence and freedom from official restraint in the United States.

parole
Permission granted to an alien who is found to be excludable to leave the United States border without being placed in custody, with the promise that he will be present at his removal hearing.

Persons who enter the United States lawfully (i.e., with the knowledge and consent of U.S. immigration officials) have been inspected and **admitted** or **paroled.** Either an alien was inspected by an immigration officer and admitted into the United States or is inspected and allowed into the United States for further inspection, but not officially admitted (thus, paroled).

A person can demonstrate that he or she was "inspected and admitted" by showing the I-94 form, which is an entry stamp placed in the alien's passport and serves as proof of inspection.

Then, if the alien wants to apply for adjustment of status (i.e., to change from nonimmigrant status to immigrant status or to another nonimmigrant category), a visa must be available immediately for the immigrant. That would be possible if:

1. The alien is an immediate relative of a U.S. citizen (spouse, parent, or child; see Chapter 3) and that U.S. citizen petitions that alien for LPR status; or
2. The alien's priority date for gaining LPR status is current.

For example, if an alien would have to wait two years for his or her priority date to be current, then he or she cannot simply say: "Oh, in that case, I'll just adjust my status right now and get my visa tomorrow."

Adjustment of Status for Illegal Aliens

entry with inspection
Applies to aliens who entered the United States with DHS knowledge.

entry without inspection
Applies to aliens who entered the United States without DHS knowledge. Such aliens are also referred to as "border jumpers."

There are two types of illegal aliens: those who **entered with inspection** and those who **entered without inspection** (i.e., "border jumpers"). The 1996 Amendments to the INA made it increasingly difficult for illegal aliens to adjust their status. Prior to the 1996 Amendments, it might have been possible for an alien who violated his or her legal status to adjust nonetheless. However, under the new law, this may be possible only if the alien is an immediate relative and was lawfully admitted into the United States.

For example, suppose that Rachel came to the United States three years ago on a visitor's visa. When her term of stay expired six months later, Rachel did not leave the United States. At that point, she became an illegal alien and decided to apply for a job. Rachel's prospective employer agreed to sponsor Rachel for employment-based LPR status. Rachel's application has now been approved.

Under the old law (prior to the 1996 Amendments), Rachel would have been eligible to adjust her status at this point. However, subject to the 1996 Amendments, Rachel is not eligible to adjust her status because she failed to maintain her lawful status.

Suppose instead that Rachel did not seek to gain her LPR status through employment. Rather, she met a U.S. citizen, George, fell in love, and married him. As the spouse of a U.S. citizen, Rachel is an immediate relative and thus qualifies to adjust her status even though she is an illegal alien.

However, if Rachel originally came to the United States through Canada or Mexico, hiding out in the trunk of a car, she would be a "border jumper" or, in more formal terms, an alien who entered the United States without inspection. In that case, she would not be able to adjust her status even though she married George.

In that case, Rachel's best alternative would be to leave the country and obtain a visa from abroad and then return to the United States. But the 1996 Amendments have made the penalty so strict for border jumpers that she might have to wait ten years before being admitted! That's how strict the 1996 Amendments are.

FAMOUS U.S. IMMIGRANTS

Hakeem the American dream

HAKEEM OLAJUWON

Hakeem Olajuwon (born "Akeem" Olajuwon but later changed his first name's spelling for religious reasons) was born in Nigeria in 1963 and immigrated to the United States, where eventually he became a citizen in 1993.

Often called "Hakeem the Dream," Olajuwon arguably was one of the greatest professional basketball players ever. He was the center for the Houston Rockets and led them to two National Basketball Association (NBA) championships in 1994 and 1995.

In his long and illustrious career, Olajuwon managed to be one of the top ten NBA players ever in points, steals, and blocked shots, and eleventh in rebounds. To date, he is the only NBA player ever to achieve that status in all four categories!

CONCLUSION

This chapter deals with some issues that go beyond the law and are at the core of everyday social and political debate.

First, there's the immigration lottery, which is based on the model of affirmative action. Is it important for all countries throughout the world to be represented equally in terms of immigration to the United States? Is the United States a country that happens to let in some people from other countries, or is our country's goal to be an international melting pot? These are fundamental questions that Americans discuss and debate almost every day, in private and public settings alike.

Next, there are illegal aliens. There is a lot of talk about capturing all illegal aliens and sending them back to their own countries. But what would that do to the economy as a whole if so many workers that drive our country's engine behind the scenes are removed from the steering wheel? This, too, is a fundamental question that continues to be debated very intensely, especially in the post-9/11 era in which we live.

These are just two reasons why this chapter is particularly relevant not only in terms of law, but also in terms of modern history and politics, too.

We have covered all of the typical ways by which an alien can gain LPR status. Some smaller categories for becoming an LPR were not covered. Examples of these are former diplomats, some foreign medical graduates, and others. These categories are rather rare, and it is unlikely that you would encounter aliens in these situations. If you would like to find out more about these categories, consult the INA.

Now that we are done learning about nonimmigrants and immigrants, we take it to the next step in Chapter 6: American citizenship.

KEY TERMS

admission
amnesty
asylee
asylum
diversity-based immigration
entry with inspection
entry without inspection
lottery
parole
registry

REVIEW QUESTIONS

1. What is the immigration lottery?
2. What is affirmative action, and how is diversity-based immigration similar to it?
3. What is registry?
4. What was the immigration amnesty law?
5. Why was the amnesty law considered to be helpful to the economy?
6. If the amnesty law is now obsolete, then why is it important to learn about it?
7. What is adjustment of status?
8. Compare and contrast the options of adjusting status in the United States versus obtaining an immigrant visa abroad.
9. May illegal aliens adjust their status?
10. May all legal aliens adjust their status?
11. If Congress were to discontinue the adjustment of status option, what impact might that have on aliens seeking LPR status?
12. Which immigration law is sometimes referred to as "the Reagan Law"?

HYPOTHETICALS

1. Robert, Stanley, and Thomas are brothers who are in the United States illegally. All three have heard that they can get their green cards because they have lived in the United States "for a long time." They have worked here for many years and have paid their income taxes. Robert has been here since 1985, Stanley since 1980, and Thomas since 1970. Thomas and Stanley are both married, but their wives are illegal aliens. Robert is not married. None of them have relatives here, and all three are self-employed (with no potential job offers elsewhere). Under what laws, if any, may any of the three brothers gain LPR status?
2. Paulina is an illegal alien currently in the United States. She has no means of obtaining her LPR status through any of the traditional ways. She has heard about the immigration lottery and would like you to help her fill out the "application." How difficult of a process is it?
3. Esonia came to the United States on a student visa. She met and began to date Alan, a U.S. citizen. The couple fell in love and after about two years of being together decided to marry. Esonia's student visa is still valid, but now she wants to become an LPR. Alan and Esonia approach you for advice. What are Esonia's options? What are the advantages and disadvantages of each option?

4. Using the same facts as stated in #3, assume that Esonia really is an illegal alien. Does this change the advice that you would give her about LPR status? How so?

5. Oscar, an alien, has just been offered a position to be a full professor at Yale University. Oscar had received a temporary nonimmigrant visa to teach at Yale as a visiting professor. After one semester, Oscar's department chairperson was so impressed with Oscar's teaching style that she offered him a full-time professorship. Your law firm is contacted by Yale to handle the matter. After studying the current processing times, you determine that even if all goes well it would take at least two years for Oscar to receive his LPR status. Under what circumstances would Oscar qualify for an adjustment of status?

CHAPTER 6

AMERICAN CITIZENSHIP

CHAPTER OBJECTIVES

After completing this chapter, you should know:

- The benefits of becoming a U.S. citizen
- Why new U.S. citizens must speak, read, and write basic English
- Why only those born in the United States may become president
- How some people may lose their U.S. citizenship

Unlike LPRs, U.S. citizens enjoy full Constitutional protection, the right to vote, the right to hold most political offices, and generally cannot be barred or expelled from the United States. For these and other rights, citizens also bear responsibilities, such as the duty to serve on a jury or in the military, if needed.

Earlier on we discussed how natural-born Americans often do not realize the true value of U.S. citizenship. But from an alien's point of view, citizenship often is a very important dream. In this chapter we will look at the ways in which U.S. citizenship is inherent or otherwise may be gained.

SOME BENEFITS OF CITIZENSHIP

The U.S. Constitution is the document on which our nation is founded (see Chapter 1). It outlines our two-tier, three-branch system of government, which is based on human and civil rights guaranteed for all citizens. While LPRs and other noncitizen aliens enjoy some aspects of Constitutional protection, U.S. citizens are its fullest beneficiaries.

The Right to Vote

Unlike LPRs and other aliens, U.S. citizens enjoy the right to vote. Again, this is a right that many Americans take for granted because they are generally among the world's most politically inactive people. Some argue that "it doesn't make a difference," while others contend that the only reason it doesn't make a difference is because not enough people vote.

Elections Since 2000 Interestingly, the political climate in the United States has been highly charged since the year 2000, which is quite an unusual phenomenon. Part of the interest was due to the prediction that the presidential election that year between incumbent Vice President Al Gore and Texas Governor George W. Bush would be very close. To call the election "close" was an understatement. The election was so close that it led to a remarkable string of recounts and lawsuits. Eventually, the United States Supreme Court intervened and put an end to the recounts. Bush had been declared the winner on Election Day and after the recounts, and so his supporters felt that he deserved the win.

Gore's supporters felt that the Supreme Court stopped the recount process prematurely and were confident that another recount would have determined that Gore was the winner (eventually, an unofficial recount conducted afterward by members of prominent media organizations found that Bush actually won by an even slightly higher margin than the previous recount).

In any event, with an election that close, it makes sense that one side would walk away elated and the other side dejected. It would be no different if it was the seventh game of the World Series and one team won it by a single run in the bottom of the 14th inning! (For those of you who know baseball, that's about as close as you can get.)

Then came 9/11: The political climate in the United States intensified. The average American, oblivious to terms such as Al Qaeda and the Taliban, suddenly became glued to the television to absorb up-to-the-minute information. This intensity was evident at the polls as more voters participated in the 2004 presidential election. This time, the candidates were incumbent President Bush versus Massachusetts Senator John Kerry. This unusually heated campaign resulted in a close election once again (though not as close as in 2000), with Bush winning a second term.

Perhaps now more than ever, Americans appreciate the right to vote. Our one-person, one-vote system is cherished particularly by aliens who do not have such a privilege in their home countries.

Political Office

U.S. citizens are not only permitted to vote in elections, but they are also eligible to be the candidates in them. Generally, U.S. citizens may run for any political office, but only **natural-born citizens** may become president of the United States.

natural-born citizen
Persons born in the United States or, in many cases, its territories and are subject to the jurisdiction of the United States.

naturalized citizen
An alien who has become a U.S. citizen through the process of naturalization (i.e., by the DHS, in compliance with the INA).

Why do you suppose that is the case? Why can a **naturalized citizen** (one who became a citizen through immigration) become mayor of a city or governor of a state (as recently demonstrated by Arnold Schwarzenegger—the Austrian-born U.S. citizen who became governor of California) but cannot become president?

The president of the United States, who is our nation's chief executive, is also our commander-in-chief over all of the military. As such, he is our leader—over both domestic and foreign policy. The president's decision about foreign policy should be rooted in what is best for the United States, without any personal favoritism toward a particular country due to an ancestral bond.

For example, suppose that Ryan is an immigrant from Ireland who has become a U.S. citizen and now wants to run for president. Suppose that he wins the election and a few months later the United States is involved in mediating a political dispute between Ireland and another country. There is a point of view that suggests because Ryan was born and raised in Ireland that he may be more inclined to favor Ireland in the dispute. Such favoritism may not necessarily be in the best interests of the United States.

Of course, that argument is not perfect. First, Ryan may be an open-minded leader who is not swayed by sentimental ties. Second, even if he were born in the United States, Ryan may have had ties to Ireland for some other reason. Maybe his parents are from there, or maybe he vacationed there in the past and loved it there. Maybe he is trying to gain the support of Irish-Americans.

Nonetheless, the general assumption that the president should be American-born endures, as does that law, which is set forth in the United States Constitution.

The Arnold Factor Let's turn again to Arnold Schwarzenegger. His meteoric rise to political stardom, inspired a movement to change the Constitution and allow naturalized citizens to run for president, too. Perhaps that will be possible some day. For the time being, only natural-born citizens may become president, and that is one of the very few differences between natural-born and naturalized citizens.

Increased Immigration Benefits for Relatives

As discussed in Chapter 4, aliens may become LPRs based on being relatives of U.S. citizens or LPRs. However, relatives of citizens enjoy greater advantages.

Spouses, parents, and children of U.S. citizens are immediate relatives and thus are not subject to numerical limitations in gaining LPR status. Practically speaking, this generally results in gaining LPR status much faster.

Next, unmarried sons and daughters receive a higher immigration preference if their parents are citizens instead of LPRs. Again, this often means a faster priority date.

Finally, a U.S. citizen may petition for his or her married son, married daughter, brother, or sister to become an LPR. But an LPR may not petition for those relatives at all.

For these reasons, LPRs who choose to become U.S. citizens may not only increase their own immigration benefits, but also those of their relatives.

Benefits and privileges often have obligations attached to them. That is the case with U.S. citizenship as well.

SOME OBLIGATIONS OF CITIZENSHIP

Although U.S. citizenship arguably is the most enviable status that an alien can hope to achieve, there are some things that a U.S. citizen is required to do, whereas an alien is not. In his inaugural address in 1961, President John F. Kennedy said: "Ask not what your country can do for you, ask what you can do for your country." That quote is relevant to learning about the privileges ("what your country can do for you") as well as the obligations ("what you can do for your country") of U.S. citizenship.

Jury Duty

U.S. citizens are obligated to serve on juries in courts of law, if called upon to do so. In order to better understand the concept of jury duty, let's take a quick look at our legal system.

We are a free nation and are restricted only by the laws that we create for our benefit as a whole. A person who breaks the law may be sued by an individual or group or may be prosecuted by the government (representing the people) for having committed a crime.

In either case, the person is entitled to a jury trial at which he or she must be proven liable (or guilty, in a criminal trial) before the court can determine the consequences (such as compensation or imprisonment). This determination of liability/guilt may be determined by a judge, but most often is determined by a jury.

A jury is selected by attorneys from both sides and is designed to be made up of a person's peers. People from all walks of life are chosen. There is no specific requirement to balance race, gender, religion, or other such factor. The goal is to select a neutral, nonbiased jury—one that will not have a predetermined notion of the outcome but instead is willing to listen to both sides and then render a reasoned decision.

Juries are chosen from pools of official government lists, such as lists of registered voters. A person may be chosen for jury duty at any time. Often, some who are chosen grumble at the chore. Nonetheless, it is a civic duty that is essential to our system of justice.

Accordingly, serving on a jury is an obligation that any U.S. citizen may be called upon to fulfill.

Military Service

U.S. citizens are obligated to serve in the U.S. armed forces if called upon to do so. For most of the twentieth century, the U.S. military operated a draft. In other words, male U.S. citizens were obligated to serve in the military.

In 1973, President Richard Nixon repealed the draft. Since that time, the United States has operated with a volunteer military. There is a Selective Service system, which means that young men are required to register in the event that there would be a draft in the future due to a change in legislation or some military emergency. Nonetheless, actual service in the armed forces at this time is not required.

Actually, LPRs are required to register with the Selective Service as well.

The Draft in the Post-9/11 Era In the aftermath of 9/11, President Bush pledged not to relent in fighting the war on terror. As part of that war, our troops were used in military battles in Afghanistan and Iraq. The newly-established democracy in Iraq has been riddled with insurgents seeking to subvert it. Some opponents of our involvement have criticized the president for not sending enough troops. Accordingly, there was concern that the president would reinstate the draft. Both he and almost all of the members of Congress have vowed that they will not do so.

Technically, any U.S. citizen can be asked to serve at any time. Accordingly, this is another call to service that U.S. citizens are obligated to undertake if so required.

Interestingly, LPRs who enlist in the military voluntarily during wartime or during other periods of heightened tensions regarding foreign affairs might be on the fast track to gaining U.S. citizenship. This trade-off allows those LPRs to gain citizenship faster, all the while bolstering our military personnel.

NATURAL-BORN VERSUS NATURALIZED CITIZENS

As discussed earlier, there are two types of U.S. citizens: those who are born citizens and those who become citizens.

Natural-Born Citizens—Citizenship by Birth

Persons born in the United States or, in many cases, its territories and who are subject to the jurisdiction of the United States automatically qualify as U.S. citizens. Also, persons born outside the United States to a parent who is a U.S. citizen also qualify (though the citizen parent must formally complete the necessary paperwork to make it official).

Persons born in the United States or its territories are automatically U.S. citizens. Some very rare exceptions exist to this almost universal rule. These exceptions include children born on public foreign vessels in U.S. waters and children born to alien enemies in hostile occupation in the United States.

For example, suppose that William's parents are aliens, and he is born on a public foreign ship in U.S. waters near New York harbor. William would not be considered a U.S. citizen. Consider Ramona, who is an international terrorist now captured and serving a sentence in a U.S. prison. Prior to her last entry into the United States, Ramona became pregnant by a countryman of hers. If Ramona gives birth to a baby girl while in prison, that little girl would not be a U.S. citizen.

Barring these highly unusual types of circumstances, persons born in the United States or its territories are U.S. citizens.

Citizenship by Naturalization

Aliens who are 18 years or older may become citizens by naturalization or, if under 18 at the time, by the naturalization of a parent. Some of the requirements follow.

1. **Naturalization after LPR Status**

Persons who have been LPRs for at least five years may apply for naturalization. However, persons who are married to LPRs may become citizens three years after becoming LPRs if they became LPRs as a result of the marriage.

In other words, suppose that Ron has been an LPR for five years. Now he may apply for naturalization. Next, suppose that Kathy married Stan, a U.S. citizen, a few years ago. Stan sponsored her for LPR status, and she has been an LPR for three years. Kathy now may apply for citizenship.

However, if Kathy had obtained her LPR status through some other means (e.g., through employment-based immigration), then she must wait another two years (five years in total) before she can become a citizen. The three-year "shortcut" is available to spouses of citizens and only if the marriage was the basis of the LPR status.

2. Continuous Residence and Physical Presence

Persons applying for naturalization must have resided in the United States continuously for a specific time prior to the application and must have been physically present here for a specific period of time (not necessarily as long as the continuous residence). Why do you suppose that these conditions are required?

Think about the "immigration door" and "overloading the boat" again. There is "limited seating" in the United States. While the immigration door is not completely closed, it is open only to a certain extent. So the precious space is reserved for those who really want to be here.

There are a great many benefits to being an LPR. For one thing, LPRs are allowed to work in the United States legally or to study here. Those are two highly-coveted goals for many people throughout the world. Others want the status in order to be able to help their relatives (see Chapter 3) or to receive various government benefits. Keeping that in mind, can you imagine what would happen if someone obtained LPR status but did not want to live here? That person would take a "seat" away from someone who really does want to be here.

For that reason, it is necessary for the LPR to show that he or she has resided in the United States and has been physically present here for a certain time period.

3. Good Moral Character

Persons applying for naturalization (citizenship) must be found by DHS to be of good moral character. Factors determining moral character include: (1) no criminal background; (2) no habitual drunkenness; and (3) no adultery, among other factors.

Why do you suppose that good moral character is required in order to become a citizen but is not a continuous requirement for those who already are citizens? In other words, if Al is an alien who has committed adultery, that might prevent him from becoming a citizen. But Bob, who was born in the United States, commits adultery on a regular basis. Why doesn't Bob lose his citizenship?

The answer is similar to other circumstances in general: Quite often, gaining a particular status is harder than losing it. More specifically, what would happen to Bob (who was born and raised in the U.S.) if he were to lose his U.S. citizenship? Would he have to leave the United States? If so, then where would he go? He cannot be sent back to his native country because the United States is his native country!

U.S. citizens are almost completely invulnerable to losing their citizenship. However, in order to obtain citizenship in the first place, aliens must prove that they are of good moral character.

4. English Literacy

Citizenship applicants must be able to speak, read, and write basic English. DHS officers ask applicants a few questions regarding basic U.S. history as well.

Although the United States is a culturally diverse nation, its predominant language is English. Accordingly, persons who choose to become U.S. citizens are expected to be capable of communicating in the English language. Moreover, prospective citizens are expected to know a bit about U.S. history. Typical questions that aliens are asked include the president, members of Congress and the Supreme Court, and the U.S. flag.

Typically, the DHS creates a list of commonly asked questions and provides this to the general public. Accordingly, aliens may obtain this list and study for their citizenship interview. There is an entire section in the back of this book devoted to the citizenship examination.

5. Allegiance to the United States and the U.S. Constitution

Aliens applying for citizenship must take an oath of allegiance to the United States and to the U.S. Constitution.

In effect, when aliens become U.S. citizens, they adopt the United States as their primary country. As U.S. citizenship is a privilege sought by millions of people throughout the world, the United States wants allegiance in return. U.S. citizens are expected to agree with the principles set forth in the Constitution and to embrace our form of government.

Obviously, it is possible for a person to swear falsely that he or she supports the Constitution when that is not the case. But any statement made regarding immigration matters that is later discovered to be false might result in the revocation of any rights that were granted as a result of the statement.

For example, suppose that Nathan applies for U.S. citizenship. Nathan is an anarchist, which means that he does not believe in organized government at all! He wants to live in the United States because his siblings are here, but he does not like our system of government at all. He thinks that our Constitution is one big mistake. Of course, if he said all of that, then there is a good chance that he would not be granted U.S. citizenship. So Nathan decided to lie—to make false statements in order to gain citizenship.

If Nathan then joins an organization called the International Anarchy Alliance—which is devoted to peaceful philosophical discussions on the ills of organized governments—then his citizenship application might be rejected. Even without examining the substantive nature of that organization, Nathan has already lied on his citizenship application: He says that he supports the U.S. government, though his actions say otherwise. That's why it's not as easy as saying anything because actions to the contrary may come back to haunt you.

But what if Nathan became a citizen and joined that organization afterward? Would he lose his citizenship?

CITIZENSHIP FOR PERSONS UNDER 18 WHEN A PARENT IS NATURALIZED

Persons who are under 18 years of age at the time when at least one of their parents are naturalized may become naturalized as well at that time. For instance, suppose that Nancy is 15 years old and that her mother, Betty, is about to become a U.S. citizen. When Betty becomes a citizen, Nancy can become one as well.

LOSS OF AMERICAN CITIZENSHIP: DENATURALIZATION AND EXPATRIATION

There is a possibility that someone might lose his or her U.S. citizenship. Although that is quite uncommon, it is possible nonetheless. Even more uncommon, but also possible, is that natural-born U.S. citizens might lose their citizenship! If you were born and raised in the United States, it is possible that even you might lose your U.S. citizenship.

Denaturalization

Natural-born citizens cannot be "denaturalized"; only naturalized citizens can have their naturalization revoked. Although it is the exception rather than the rule, naturalized citizens may be denaturalized under certain circumstances. Such exceptions include cases of concealment of material fact, willful misrepresentation, and illegal procurement of naturalization. Moreover, residence in a foreign country within one year after naturalization is presumed to contradict the essence of becoming a U.S. citizen, which is to live in the United States. Therefore, this may also result in **denaturalization.** These are among the most common reasons that may cause a person to lose his or her citizenship.

denaturalization
The process by which a naturalization citizen loses his or her U.S. citizenship.

1. Concealment of Material Fact

If a citizen gained naturalization but concealed a material fact in the process, then he or she may be denaturalized as a result. For example, if the citizen was a member of a terrorist group whose goals were to subvert the U.S. government, that would constitute a "material fact," especially because allegiance to the United States is essential to gaining U.S. citizenship. Accordingly, concealment of this or of another material fact may result in revocation of naturalization.

2. Willful Misrepresentation

Instead of concealing a material fact, suppose instead that an alien lies on his or her naturalization application. For instance, Brian applies for citizenship and claims that he has never been arrested. In fact, Brian was arrested for disturbing the peace five years earlier. It was a minor offense and one that might not invalidate his application. But the fact that Brian lied probably would be considered worse than the actual arrest and would be enough to deny his application.

3. Illegal Procurement of Naturalization

If an alien has unlawfully procured or attempted to procure naturalization for himself or herself or for another person, this may result in denaturalization. Consider Helen who is a naturalized citizen. She sets up a "service" whereby she helps naturalization applicants use false information and fraudulent documents to become citizens. If Helen and/or any of her "clients" are caught, they may be denaturalized.

4. Residence in a Foreign Country within One Year of Naturalization

A U.S. citizen, whether natural-born or naturalized, may live outside the United States for as long as he wants, even forever. However, during the first year of naturalization, a citizen may not reside outside of the United States.

Choosing to become a U.S. citizen implies that a person selects the United States as his or her primary country—first and foremost above all others. Therefore, choosing to move to another country within such a short time period after naturalization might suggest that the person became a U.S. citizen only to receive the benefits of citizenship without actually having made a commitment to the United States. If that were the case, then it would deprive another person of a "precious seat" in the United States because someone wanted to "use" the United States for its resources.

Accordingly, persons who have become naturalized should stay in the United States for at least one year after such naturalization, lest they risk losing it.

Expatriation

expatriation
The process by which both natural-born and naturalized citizens lose their U.S. citizenship.

Denaturalization may only happen to naturalized citizens, not natural-born ones. However, both naturalized and natural-born citizens may lose their citizenship through **expatriation.** Expatriation involves actions that, expressly or implicitly, suggest a person is giving up his or her U.S. citizenship. Such actions include: gaining naturalization in a foreign country; allegiance to or military service in a foreign country; foreign government employment; formal renunciation of U.S. citizenship; or acts of treason.

1. Gaining Naturalization in a Foreign Country

U.S. citizens who become citizens of other countries may risk losing their U.S. citizenship. Americans are expected to remain loyal to the United States—not to seek citizenship elsewhere.

dual citizenship
Simultaneously holding citizenship in two countries.

Keep in mind that there is such a concept as **dual citizenship.** Citizens of some countries enjoy a special status that allows them to retain that citizenship and to be a U.S. citizen simultaneously.

The concept of dual citizenship aside, anyone who becomes a citizen of another country—whether naturalized or born here—risks losing U.S. citizenship.

2. Allegiance to or Military Service in a Foreign Country

A U.S. citizen who pledges allegiance to a foreign country or serves in that country's armed forces may be expatriated.

Clearly, if someone serves in another country's military, that act is evident. But "pledging allegiance" is a bit vaguer than serving in the armed forces. For example, consider the presidential election of 2004. The 2004 election was a close one, in which incumbent President George W. Bush won reelection against the challenger, Massachusetts Senator John Kerry. The election was a close one: Understandably, Bush supporters were elated whereas Kerry supporters were devastated. Some Kerry supporters vowed to move to Canada in protest, proclaiming that they could no longer live in the United States.

Certainly, those words, taken in context, easily could be construed as temporary feelings of frustration, not an overt act to pledge allegiance to another country. Suppose that Charlie, a devout Kerry supporter, was one of those people. If Charlie said: "I don't want to be a part of this country anymore; I'm moving to Canada," mere words probably are not enough to get him expatriated.

However, if Charlie actually did move to Canada and decided to join their military, then the chances of his expatriation would increase significantly.

3. Foreign Government Employment

Let's continue considering Charlie for a moment. Suppose that he has no problem with the United States but would like to move to Australia because he likes it there. Having vacationed there the previous summer, Charlie made some contacts and decided to get a job teaching for a private college there. Charlie could live there as long as he wants—even permanently—and not lose his U.S. citizenship. However, if Charlie decided to work for a public college (i.e., government-owned), then he would be working for a foreign government and could be subject to expatriation.

4. Formal Renunciation of U.S. Citizenship

A U.S. citizen may be expatriated if he or she formally renounces his or her U.S. citizenship. For instance, if Stella tells her friends: "I no longer want to be a U.S. citizen," that probably would not be formal enough. However, writing a formal letter to a government official declaring that intention might be sufficient grounds for expatriation.

5. Acts of Treason

Treason is the attempt to overthrow or actual overthrowing of the government or betraying one's country into the hands of a foreign enemy. If a U.S. citizen commits treason, then he or she might be expatriated.

treason
The act or overthrowing (or attempting to overthrow) the government or betraying the country into the hands of the enemy.

Treason usually involves some type of overt act. It goes beyond mere words. After all, as a nation that prides itself on various rights guaranteed by the Constitution, the United States permits freedom of speech at almost any time and in almost any place or manner. Accordingly, citizens may criticize the government and the country virtually at will. But any actual attempts by a citizen to commit treason for which there is apparent ability and intent to carry it forth may result in expatriation.

Treason in the Post-9/11 Era In the aftermath of 9/11, treason is a word that is far more common than it was beforehand. While most of those considered to be terrorists or otherwise enemies of the United States are not U.S. citizens, there are some who are. Various federal laws, such as the Patriot Act, have been promulgated in an attempt to prevent future terrorist attacks. While proponents of such laws applaud them, opponents argue that they curb many of our civil liberties. The debate continues. In any event, Americans found guilty of treason may very well wind up losing their citizenship.

Voluntary Expatriation

Losing one's U.S. citizenship by expatriation is not an easy task. It is not one that usually happens by accident. But if someone chooses to be expatriated (i.e., to lose his or her U.S. citizenship) that can be arranged rather easily.

People in some countries do not have a choice. They must remain citizens of their country and must physically stay there. That's why some people literally risk life and limb in order to escape. This is not so in the United States. In effect, U.S. policy can be summed up as: "If you'd like to be part of us, we'd love to have you (we just have to check you out first to make sure that you're all right). But if you don't want to be here, we're not going to stop you."

FAMOUS U.S. IMMIGRANTS

One of our newest celebrity citizens

JANE SEYMOUR

Jane Seymour was born in England in 1951 and has been known for her acting by American audiences for decades. But only recently, in 2005, did she become a U.S. citizen.

Her performance in a television remake of *East of Eden* won her acclaim, leading to a few film roles. But she is perhaps best known for her role in the television series *Dr. Quinn, Medicine Woman.*

Seymour remains a versatile television and film actress and is known for her unique beauty: Her left eye is brown, and her right eye is green.

CONCLUSION

Let's take a look at some of the benefits that citizens enjoy, while LPRs do not.

Benefit	Citizen	LPR
Voting in an election	Yes	No
Running for political office	Yes*	No
Moving to a foreign country permanently	Yes	No
Receiving Social Security benefits while living abroad	Yes	No
Petitioning for parents, spouses, and children to become LPRs as immediate relatives	Yes	No
Petitioning for brothers and sisters to become LPRs	Yes	No
Petitioning for married sons and daughters to become LPRs	Yes	No
Enjoying full Constitutional protection	Yes	No

*Naturalized citizens may not become president of the United States.

U.S. citizenship is something truly special. That's why some people literally will risk life and limb to gain it. That's why gaining it is so special that it takes a lot more than to simply apply for it.

Appendix A about U.S. citizenship is a special one, too. It deals with the basic tenets of our very unique country and system of government. It is something that all Americans—whether natural-born or not—should know.

Finally, consider the English literacy requirement. The United States, being the truly diverse nation that it is, is home to more languages and cultures than any other country on earth. But the United States' main language is English. It is important to know English in order to be able to function capably in U.S. society. That's why it is so important for aspiring citizens to improve on their English skills.

In Chapter 7 we will discuss what happens to those who violate their immigration status and immigration laws.

KEY TERMS

denaturalization
dual citizenship
expatriation
natural-born citizen
naturalized citizen
treason

REVIEW QUESTIONS

1. What are some rights and obligations connected with U.S. citizenship?
2. What is the difference between a natural-born and a naturalized citizen?
3. What are some criteria necessary to gaining naturalization?
4. What is revocation of naturalization? What type of citizens may be denaturalized? Under what circumstances?
5. What is expatriation? What type of citizens may become expatriated?
6. What are some differences between a citizen and an LPR?
7. Why is it important for naturalized citizens to be able to read, write, and speak English?
8. Why is it important for naturalized citizens to pledge allegiance to the U.S. Constitution?
9. Why are naturalized citizens not eligible to become president of the United States?
10. What immigration status must each alien obtain prior to becoming a U.S. citizen?
11. For naturalization purposes, what is the difference between "physical presence" and "continuous residence" in the United States?
12. What are some acts that, although not crimes, are considered immoral acts and may cause denial of naturalization?

HYPOTHETICALS

1. Jackson is an LPR who wishes to become a U.S. citizen. He asks you to prepare his application for naturalization. Jackson knows that a person must have been an LPR for a specific period of time prior to applying for citizenship, but he is not sure if he has waited long enough. From the time Jackson became an LPR, how many years must he wait to apply for citizenship if:

   A. He obtained LPR status through employment-based immigration
   B. He obtained LPR status through registry
   C. He obtained LPR status by marrying a U.S. citizen

2. Kim is a natural-born U.S. citizen who recently traveled to Germany. She was drawn to the people, the landscape, the way of life. Being a professional photographer, Kim took many photographs in all of the German cities and towns that she visited. Her photos were so impressive that she received several offers to work there.

   Kim returns to the United States, seriously thinking about the job offers. She comes to your law firm and tells you about the proposals. She is interested in moving to Germany but does not want to jeopardize her U.S. citizenship in any way.

   How (if at all) would her U.S. citizenship be affected if she:

   A. Becomes a photographer for a privately-owned German fashion magazine
   B. She becomes an official photographer for the German army
   C. She becomes the mayor of a small German town
   D. She becomes the photographer for a privately-owned German political magazine whose aim is to sabotage and overthrow all democratic governments, including the U.S. government
   E. She decides not to work in Germany at all but to live there in retirement for the next 50 years

3. Georgia, a native of Bulgaria, has just become a U.S. citizen. For various reasons, she wishes to travel to Bulgaria for a long visit. Primarily, she would like to take care of her grandmother, who lives there and is in failing health. Secondly, she has inherited a plot of land there and is thinking of developing it. She is not sure whether she would like to build a small house or a mid-size hotel. Since you were the person who helped Georgia to gain her citizenship, she tells you about the proposed trip. How (if at all) may the length and nature of her trip affect her U.S. citizenship?

4. Yung has been an LPR for twelve years and has resided in the United States during that entire period of time. Yung is concerned that the immigration laws may hurt him eventually in terms of certain benefits that he receives now as an LPR. Accordingly, he is interested in becoming a U.S. citizen.

   You explain to him that as part of the process he will sit for a naturalization interview, during which he may be asked to read, write, and speak simple English, as well as to demonstrate his knowledge of basic U.S. history. Yung becomes upset, stating that he has worked very hard in the United States, pays taxes every year, and has been a model resident. He is afraid that his English is not good enough to succeed in the interview but that he deserves to be a citizen nonetheless.

   A. How would you explain to him the importance of being literate in English?
   B. How would you suggest that he improve his English literacy between now and the day of his interview?

5. Ricardo calls your office during the weekend and leaves a message on your voice mail stating the following:

   A. He has been an LPR for over five years
   B. He is anxious to become a U.S. citizen
   C. During the last five years, he has "gone back" to his native country of Argentina for some "trips."

   Are the length of his trips important in determining his application for naturalization? What two factors are most important regarding the length of his trips?

CHAPTER 7

Inadmissibility and Removal

Chapter Objectives

After completing this chapter, you should know:

- Why some aliens are not allowed to enter the United States
- Why some aliens are removed from the United States
- Severe removal penalties for some illegal aliens
- Exceptions to being removed from the United States

We began learning about immigration law by discussing the principle of "overloading the boat" and about how the "immigration door" leading into the United States is partially open—allowing some inside while keeping others out. Now, suppose that an alien who does not qualify to be here shows up at our borders or is discovered already inside. Now what?

In this chapter we will examine some of the more common reasons for excluding certain people and the process of dealing with aliens who may not legally remain here, either as nonimmigrants or as immigrants.

INADMISSIBILITY

Persons may be rendered **inadmissible**—not permitted to enter the United States—for various reasons that are criminal, security, and/or health-related. Inadmissible aliens were referred to as being **excludable** prior to the 1996 Amendments. Moreover, admission was identified as entry with inspection.

inadmissible
Denial of an alien to enter the United States at the point of DHS inspection. Formerly called exclusion.

excludable
Denial of an alien to enter the United States at the point of DHS inspection. Now called inadmissibility.

Admission means physical presence in the United States and freedom from official restraint. Therefore, a person actually may be present in the United States without having gained admission. The alien who arrives at the border and is inadmissible must leave the United States either immediately or within a prescribed time period.

One reason why the alien might be inadmissible is that his or her visa might be denied at the border. For example, Jones, a citizen of New Zealand, is granted a visa to visit the United States. He boards an airplane in New Zealand and flies here. Once he arrives here, DHS officials examine his visa and his circumstances and conclude that he is ineligible to visit the United States. Perhaps they discover something that the Consulate in New Zealand had overlooked, or maybe Jones tells them: "I'm so excited to be here. I'm going to look for a job tomorrow." (Visitors are supposed to be here temporarily, not to find jobs and overstay their allotted time.) So what happens to Jones?

Jones is inadmissible and will not be able to remain in the United States. One solution would be for Jones to board the next plane back to New Zealand. But that might not be a viable option for numerous reasons. For one thing, there might not be a plane leaving that day. Next, Jones may not have the money immediately on hand to buy a return ticket. Finally, Jones may have a return ticket, but it may not be the type that can be changed (to a different flight date and time). For these and other reasons, the notion of Jones instantly boarding another plane to leave the United States might not be a realistic possibility.

removal hearing
A formal hearing to determine whether an alien should be inadmissible or removed. Formerly called exclusion hearing (to determine inadmissibility) or deportation hearing (to determine removability).

Accordingly, Jones would have to remain in the United States for a specific amount of time. He would either be detained by DHS or permitted to remain in the United States on his own. In both cases, however, Jones would be given a date on which there would be a **removal hearing**, at which time an immigration judge would determine whether or not Jones would be removed—that is, required to leave the United States.

If Jones was permitted to remain in the United States on his own, this is known as parole. The word "parole" usually is associated with criminal law and involves the temporary release of a criminal from jail. Here, the person who is temporarily released is the inadmissible alien—not necessarily a "criminal" in terms of having robbed a bank or mugged a person—though the circumstances involve the same concept of temporary release.

In any event, Jones is not deemed to have been admitted into the United States because admission involves physical presence and freedom from official restraint. In this case, his pending removal hearing amounts to "official restraint."

The 1996 Amendments have curbed parole significantly. Instead, aliens may be subjected to expedited removal proceedings, which occur often at the point of entry.

An alien ordered removed usually is sent to a country determined by the immigration judge, not by the alien. Typically, it would be the country where the alien is a citizen or resident or the country from which the alien departed immediately before arriving in the United States (if different).

GROUNDS FOR INADMISSIBILITY

There are several reasons why an alien might be rendered inadmissible.

1. Health-Related Grounds

Persons who have either a communicable disease (as defined by the U.S. Department of Health and Human Services) or a physical or mental disorder (currently, or, if in the past, when there is a likelihood of recurrence) that may pose a threat to the welfare of others are inadmissible. Moreover, persons defined as either drug addicts or drug abusers (again, by the U.S. Department of Health and Human Services) are also inadmissible.

If we consider why aliens might be inadmissible because of health-related grounds, we probably will realize the following: First, the United States has an interest in protecting the health and safety of its citizens and residents. Second, a citizen or alien generally would not be required to leave the United States based on health-related reasons, though an alien who is not lawfully admitted might be turned away. This is another example of how U.S. citizens and other aliens enjoy rights superior to those of other persons.

In any event, the INA continues to render aliens inadmissible for health-related reasons. The 1996 Amendments added as inadmissible immigrants who have not received appropriate vaccinations for those diseases that can be prevented by vaccination. Such diseases include: mumps, measles, polio, and tetanus. People who are HIV-positive or who have communicable venereal diseases are inadmissible as well, as are drug abusers.

2. Criminal and Related Grounds

Aliens may be rendered inadmissible based on various crimes. Such crimes typically are "of moral turpitude." For instance, riding a motorcycle without a helmet technically may be a crime, but not one considered to be "immoral" by society. Aliens who have committed various crimes involving "controlled substances" are inadmissible, too.

Prior to 1990, "criminal" activity included being a homosexual, and numerous homosexual aliens were rendered inadmissible (which was called "excludable" then) on that ground alone. The 1990 changes to the INA removed homosexuality as a ground for inadmissibility.

In terms of the "immigration door," the United States is interested in keeping criminals—even former criminals—locked outside.

3. Security and Related Grounds

Aliens who are likely to engage in criminal activity (i.e., future criminals, as opposed to past or present criminals), particularly terrorism, espionage, or sabotage, or aliens who are members or former members of Nazi, Communist, or other totalitarian parties who are likely to disrupt U.S. foreign policy are inadmissible.

Take note of the specific reference to "Nazis" and "Communists." They, as specific groups, were considered the greatest threats to U.S. security in the past. But now, in the post-9/11 age, with the Soviet Union long-collapsed and with the Nazis even-longer defeated, future changes to the INA will focus on other enemy groups.

Whether an alien is likely or not to engage in such activity is determined by the "reasonable belief" of the consular officer or Attorney General (or designee). The Attorney General's office, in turn, grants this decision-making discretion to the DHS.

The decision to render potentially dangerous people inadmissible is consistent with the U.S. government's interest in protecting our country against foreign enemies.

4. Public Charge

An alien who is likely to become a public charge is inadmissible. Again, the "likelihood" may be determined by the consulate abroad or by DHS. The national interest in not admitting aliens likely to become public charges stems from priority of public assistance granted to U.S. citizens and LPRs. The United States was founded as a country that would guarantee certain liberties. In order to preserve such liberties, it was decided that our government would play a limited role.

Accordingly, although the government does not completely remove itself from assisting those in need, its resources are limited, as are its public assistance services. Any dollars spent to assist other aliens financially would become unavailable for U.S. citizens and LPRs who face similar needs. That's why the government is adamant about not admitting potential public charges into the United States.

5. Unqualified Workers

Certain aliens qualify either as immigrants or nonimmigrants based on the work that they intend to undertake in the United States (see Chapter 4). But if the Attorney General (or designee) determines that the alien is unqualified to do the work in question, then the alien would be rendered inadmissible.

For example, suppose that Raimondo was approved to enter the United States via employment-based immigration as an advanced degree holder (Second Preference; see Chapter 4). Raimondo's "advanced degree" was accepted as the equivalent of a U.S. master's degree at the Consulate in Raimondo's native country. But the DHS official who inspected him here determined that the degree is not at all equivalent—not even to a bachelor's. Accordingly, Raimondo would not be admitted into the United States.

6. Illegal Entrants and Immigration Violators

Illegal entrants are border-jumpers. Other immigration violators are those who entered legally and remained unlawfully (such as, students who stayed here illegally once they were done with school). Both types are inadmissible.

7. Documentation Problems

Aliens who do not possess the necessary documents to enter the United States, such as a valid visa and a passport, are inadmissible. The same holds true for aliens who present fraudulent documentation.

8. Ineligible for Citizenship

Aliens who are permanently ineligible for citizenship are inadmissible. As discussed in Chapter 6, aliens who have had criminal convictions or committed other acts of moral turpitude would be ineligible for citizenship. If those aliens committed those acts before being admitted into the United States and DHS found that out, then those aliens would be inadmissible.

9. Aliens Previously Removed

If an alien remains in the United States unlawfully for 180 days but less than one year (whether the alien entered without admission or was admitted and his or her lawful term of stay expired subsequently), the alien is, upon leaving the United States voluntarily, barred from returning for a period of three years from the alien's date of departure. If the alien in that situation unlawfully remains here for over one year, the time for which the alien is barred from returning after departure is ten years.

The preceding section, which became law as part of the 1996 Amendments, is arguably the most significant change to immigration law in decades!

This law effectively makes life extremely difficult for illegal aliens, and that's exactly why it was designed—to curb illegal immigration drastically.

For example, suppose that Frank hides on a ship that is sailing from Europe to the United States. Once the ship docks in New York's harbor, Frank finds a job working illegally. Seven months later, Frank is discovered by DHS and removed (back to his native country). A few months later, Frank tries to return to the United States through perfectly legal means. He can't! He has to wait three years from his removal date before being eligible to return because he had been in the United States illegally for over 180 days but less than one year.

Suppose instead that Frank had never been removed the first time. Suppose that he arrived originally not as a stowaway, but as a legal visitor. But when his visitor's visa expired, Frank did not leave. Instead, he stayed here for an additional two years illegally. But he was never discovered and thus never removed.

Meanwhile, a U.S. employer became interested in hiring Frank, and now Frank is set to leave the United States in order to go back to the Consulate in his home country where an immigrant visa is waiting for him! But there's one catch: Because he was here illegally for one year or more, Frank must wait ten years before being allowed to return!

This presents quite a problem for illegal aliens. On the one hand, if they come out of hiding and leave the United States, then they won't be able to return for at least three years, if not ten! On the other hand, if they remain in the United States, they do so illegally—always looking over their shoulders and afraid to be seen. The moral of this story is do not stay in the United States illegally.

10. Other Factors

Practicing **bigamists, polygamists,** guardians required to accompany aliens ordered removed, international child abductors, unlawful voters, and former citizens who renounced their U.S. citizenship in order to avoid taxation are also inadmissible. Here are some examples:

bigamist
For immigration purposes, a person who is married to more than one person at the same time. (*NOTE:* Typically, a person married to more than two people at the same time is a polygamist, although in immigration law, such person is also referred to as a bigamist.)

polygamist
A person who is married to two or more people at the same time; for immigration purposes, such person is a bigamist (which traditionally means a person married to two people at the same time).

David is married to both Carol and Edna at the same time. As such, he is a polygamist and thus is inadmissible.

Margaret is an alien who is ordered to be removed. Because Margaret is sick and elderly, her nurse, Joanne, is required to be with her at all times. Joanne, who is also an alien, is on her way to the United States specifically to care for Margaret. When she gets here, she discovers that she is inadmissible.

Fred is an alien who has abducted a child and has taken that child outside the United States. Generally, Fred is inadmissible. Depending on the nature of the abduction and surrounding circumstances, Fred may be inadmissible permanently or, at the very least, until he returns the child.

Clara was in the United States in 2004 as a visitor. Caught up in the political hype of the presidential election, she voted—illegally since only U.S. citizens are eligible to vote. She left the United States a couple of months later, and her act of voting illegally was discovered subsequently. Now when she tries to return to the United States, again as a visitor, she is rendered inadmissible.

Suppose that Robyn is a U.S. citizen who owns a business in Chicago. During one year, Robyn was faced with paying an enormous amount of money in taxes. She figured out a loophole in the tax law by which she could save a lot of money in taxes if she renounced her U.S. citizenship. She did so, sold her business, and moved to Argentina. Two years later, she wanted to come back to the United States as a visitor.

However, because she had renounced her U.S. citizenship in order to avoid taxation, Robyn is inadmissible.

Waiver

There are some instances when an inadmissible alien may be granted a **waiver.** That means although the alien may be inadmissible on the ground of, for example, being a smuggler, that ground may be removed in some cases so that the alien would not be removed. Generally, waivers are granted based on the level of hardship (the standard is usually "extreme hardship") to the alien if the waiver were not granted and whether the alien is a close relative (i.e., spouse, child, son, or daughter) of a U.S. citizen.

waiver
A form of discretionary relief, whereby a condition requiring an alien to be removed or to face another penalty is removed.

REMOVAL

Aliens may be removed—ousted from the United States—for a variety of criminal or immoral acts committed before or after entry. Aliens who are inadmissible may be removed, too. Aliens may be removed for various reasons, including but not limited to some of the reasons that are grounds for inadmissibility.

Prior to the 1996 Amendments, the word used to describe **removal** was **deportation.**

removal
Expulsion from the United States as ordered by the immigration court. Formerly called deportation.

deportation
Old term referring to expulsion from the United States as ordered by the immigration court. Now called removal.

1. Inadmissible Aliens or Immigration Violators

Aliens who are inadmissible at the time of entry or time of adjustment of status, who violate their status or condition of entry, or who otherwise are present in the United States in violation of law are removable.

An alien who was inadmissible at the time of entry is removable. This means that even though the alien's inadmissibility was not detected at the time of entry, a subsequent discovery of the alien's inadmissibility would render the alien removable at that point.

For example, suppose that Jeremy enters the United States illegally through Canada. He would have been inadmissible at the time had he been caught. Jeremy is discovered now; because he was inadmissible when he entered (albeit undetected), he may be removed now as a result.

If an alien was inadmissible at the point of his or her adjustment of status but for some reason DHS did not detect the inadmissibility, the alien is removable upon subsequent discovery. For instance, suppose that Jeremy (from the preceding example) had entered the United States as a visitor legally but then remained beyond his allotted time. If one year later he attempted to adjust his status through some other means and DHS did not detect that he had been here illegally for some time, then Jeremy may be ordered removed upon the discovery. Of course, Jeremy could also be removed if DHS discovered that he had remained unlawfully even if he had not tried to adjust his status.

Aliens who are present in the United States in violation of the provisions of the INA or any other U.S. law are removable.

2. Criminal Offenses

As with inadmissibility, aliens who have been convicted of various types of crimes are subject to removal. Generally, such provisions include crimes of moral turpitude, drug and firearm offenses, and domestic violence.

3. Failure to Register and Falsification of Documents

Aliens who have failed to register properly (including being fingerprinted and recording their addresses, where applicable) and aliens who have falsified their visas or other DHS-related documents are subject to removal.

The registration requirement applies to aliens who have already entered the United States, while the documentation condition applies at any point in time. If the alien attempted to enter, reenter, or remain in the United States by using a false document, then that alien may be removed. Then again, if the false document had been detected during the alien's attempted entry, that alien most likely would have been found inadmissible on the spot.

4. **Security and Related Grounds**

As is the case with inadmissibility, aliens who have engaged in terrorist activity or other activity that would tend to endanger public safety or national security are subject to removal. Also included in this category are people who participated in the Nazi genocide. In removal cases, the government has the burden of proving its case by clear, convincing, and unequivocal evidence that does not leave the issue in doubt. The longer the events in question took place, the more difficult it might be for the government to prove its case.

5. **Public Charge**

Generally, aliens who have become public charges within a certain time period since having entered the United States may be removed. The time period is set forth in the INA—five years. Thus, if Jade is lawfully admitted into the United States today and becomes a public charge after seven years, she may not be removed on that ground (since she became a public charge after the time period set forth in the INA.

6. **Unlawful Voters**

Aliens who have voted unlawfully are subject to removal. The same holds true for aliens at the point of entry; they're inadmissible. Both of these provisions are recent additions to the INA. Why do you suppose that Congress would make such laws?

Keep in mind that although many Americans take voting for granted, it is a right and a privilege of our system of government and is reserved only for U.S. citizens. Voting by noncitizens, whether legal or illegal, is not only against the law, but also may alter the outcome of an election. Accordingly, in order to ensure a lawful election process, Congress has added unlawful voting as a ground for removal.

Removal Hearing

An alien subject to removal is granted a removal hearing. At the hearing, an immigration judge will determine whether the alien is removable. If so, the person may be removed, removal may be canceled, the person may voluntarily depart the United States within a specific time period, or other relief may be sought. Aliens ordered removed may appeal the decision to the Board of Immigration Appeals (BIA). The BIA is an appeals board that is part of the U.S. Department of Justice (see Chapter 1).

Unlike U.S. citizens, aliens subject to removal do not have a right to an attorney. Accordingly, while an immigration judge may advise the client to seek legal representation, the government is not obligated to provide or to pay for such representation.

Aliens who are convicted of aggravated felonies (i.e., particularly serious crimes) typically are subject to expedited removal proceedings. These proceedings usually take place during, not after, the alien's incarceration.

Aliens Ordered Removed

Aliens who are ordered removed generally are directed to leave the United States at a particular place and time. In many cases, the removal may have serious consequences for the alien, such as leaving behind a family, friends, home, and livelihood. Removed aliens are barred from returning for a specific amount of time. However, there might be other options available to aliens subject to removal.

Relief from Removal

discretionary relief
Relief that may be granted to aliens at the discretion of the DHS, BIA, or federal court under the judicial system.

There are several alternatives to removal. Some may apply to all aliens in general, not just to those found to be removable. Some of these are discussed in Chapter 8.

Appeals and Judicial Administrative Relief Aliens who have been ordered removed may bring a motion to reopen or to reconsider the decision of the immigration judge. A motion to reopen is made in order to seek **discretionary relief,** particularly when it was not available during the hearing. A motion to reconsider usually is made when there is additional evidence to the matter at hand.

For example, suppose that Kambro, an alien, was charged with voting fraudulently in an election. At his removal hearing, the judge ordered him removed. If Kambro moves for discretionary relief on the grounds that his family cannot return with him to his home country and has no way of surviving here without him, that might require a motion to reopen in order to seek discretionary relief.

On the other hand, if Kambro is able to provide evidence that he in fact did not vote in any election, then that would require a motion to reconsider the additional evidence.

Also, an alien may appeal the order of removal to a higher court, namely the BIA. If the BIA affirms (sustains) the removal order, then the alien may appeal to a federal court of appeals.

Discretionary Relief Suppose that in the preceding example the judge grants Kambro discretionary relief. The most common types of such relief are voluntary departure, cancellation, withholding, or stay of removal.

Voluntary Departure **Voluntary departure** is an option that allows the alien to leave the United States voluntarily at his or her own expense. Here's the trade-off: By being removed by the government, the alien gets a free ride out of the country. But by voluntarily departing, the alien has to pay his or her own way. Why would the alien choose to do that? Because by leaving voluntarily, there is no stigma of removal on the alien's record, affording the alien the opportunity to reenter at a later time without much difficulty.

voluntary departure
A process permitting an alien ordered removed to leave the United States voluntarily, at his or her own expense, thus avoiding some of the consequences of removal.

Think of voluntary departure as an investment: Pay for your trip out of the United States now and hold on to your ability to return without problems (by qualifying for some type of legal status). But if you opt for the free escort out of the United States, your status of having been removed will make it much more difficult for you to return in the future.

Cancellation of Removal In some cases, aliens may be granted a waiver to remain in the United States even though there were sufficient grounds for removal. This **cancellation of removal** may be available to aliens who have continuously resided in the United States for ten or more years, are of good moral character, and whose removal would be an extreme hardship to any of the alien's family members who are U.S. citizens.

cancellation of removal
A term in the INA essentially replacing suspension of deportation, although some of the requirements may differ.

Consider the following example of extreme hardship. Alexia is an alien who has resided in the United States continuously for twelve years and is of good moral character. Her son, Andro, was born in the United States and is thus a U.S. citizen. Andro is seven years old. Andro has a rare medical condition for which treatment is readily available in the United States, though not in Alexia's home country. The treatment allows Andro to lead a healthy, normal life; without the treatment, he would be very ill. In fact, the treatment has worked so well that the doctors are convinced by the time Andro is an adult that he will no longer need the treatment at all!

If Alexia were to be removed now, then either Andro would have to return with her to her home country and not continue to receive medical treatment, or he would have to stay here without his mother (because she is his only living relative).

Alexia would be a prime candidate for cancellation of removal. She would have to demonstrate continuous residence by providing various types of evidence: bank accounts, employment records, school records, utility bills, and so forth.

Withholding of Removal **Withholding of removal** sometimes is granted if the alien's life might be in danger if he or she leaves the United States. See Chapter 8—though those circumstances deal with a broader range of aliens, not just those ordered removed.

withholding of removal
A waiver of removal typically granted to aliens seeking asylum.

stay of removal
A temporary waiver of removal granted to aliens who have secured some other method of remaining in the United States lawfully.

Stay of Removal **Stay of removal** really is not a full-fledged waiver. Rather, it is a temporary condition usually granted because an appeal is pending or because the alien has secured an alternative lawful method for remaining in the United States.

For instance, Kyle was ordered removed but has just proposed marriage to his longtime girlfriend Ariana—who is a U.S. citizen. By marrying a U.S. citizen, Kyle may become an LPR (see Chapter 3). In that case, Kyle might be granted a stay of removal pending his marriage and application for LPR status. Of course, Kyle and Ariana will have to prove that their marriage is real—especially since they got engaged after Kyle was ordered removed! But even though their battle might be an uphill one, it is not impossible for them to prove their case.

FAMOUS U.S. IMMIGRANTS

America's lovable hero is from England?

BOB HOPE

Many young Americans have not even heard of Bob Hope. After all, he died only recently at the ripe old age of 100! His peak of stardom probably ranged from the 1930s through the 1950s, when even many of today's senior citizens had yet to be born!

But Hope is one of the most famous and accomplished American entertainers of all time. He was a big name in radio, television, film, and in entertaining U.S. troops on foreign soil during wartime. Because he was known for being such an American patriot, many people do not realize that he was not born in the United States.

Hope was born in England in 1903 and immigrated to the United States as a child. In fact, he became a U.S. citizen in 1908 at age five. Thus, he lived most of his life here. He is one of the most famous and most patriotic immigrants ever to become a U.S. citizen.

Hope died in 2003, a few weeks after his 100th birthday, having spent most of his life (almost 70 years) in show business.

CONCLUSION

These are the general principles that apply to inadmissibility and removal. Keep in mind that there may be some other rare circumstances that apply to each and that the laws may change. Nonetheless, these broad, basic concepts provide a solid foundation from which to continue learning about this specific area of immigration.

In our post-9/11 world, many Americans relish the idea of capturing and removing all illegal aliens. Realistically, that task is quite difficult. That may be the reason that both major political parties (Democrats and Republicans) have not quite sunk their teeth into this issue with much commitment.

To some Americans, the words "illegal alien" conjure images of a terrorist seeking to blow up a large building. To other Americans, an "illegal alien" could be their neighbor, coworker, or relative—a decent, honest person who simply wants to live in this country just as much as those fortunate enough to have been born here. Of course, there are many in between, not quite as horrible as the first or as wonderful as the second.

The immigration laws regarding inadmissibility and removal, along with the DHS's methods of implementing them, are the centerpiece of limiting U.S. immigration to legal aliens only.

In Chapter 8 we will discuss some special categories by which certain aliens—based on their unique circumstances—may be admitted or may remain in the United States lawfully.

KEY TERMS

bigamist
cancellation of removal
deportation
discretionary relief
excludable
inadmissible
polygamist
removal
removal hearing
stay of removal
voluntary departure
waiver
withholding of removal

REVIEW QUESTIONS

1. What is inadmissibility? Under what conditions is an alien inadmissible?
2. For immigration purposes, what is meant by parole?
3. What is removal? Under what conditions is an alien removable?
4. What is the main difference between inadmissibility and removability?
5. What is voluntary departure? Why might some aliens choose voluntary departure instead of removal?
6. What is the rationale for the creation of inadmissibility and removal laws that apply to unlawful voters?
7. Why is someone inadmissible or removable if he or she is likely to be a public charge?
8. Why is someone inadmissible or removable if he or she is likely to be a member of the Nazi or Communist parties?
9. Why is someone inadmissible or removable if he or she suffers from communicable diseases?
10. Give an example of how someone might be inadmissible based on false documentation.
11. What are the legal options for an alien who has been ordered removed?
12. Give an example of how—for immigration purposes—someone who is physically present in the United States actually has not been admitted into the United States.

HYPOTHETICALS

1. Gaetano is an alien who came to the United States on a student visa in order to attend college. His wife, Concetta, lawfully accompanied him on a visa granted to spouses of nonimmigrant students.

   After one semester in college, Gaetano dropped out and started doing odd jobs for various employers. Eventually, he realized that he could not obtain full-time employment, mainly because he had no legal authorization to work in the United States. Accordingly, Gaetano opened his own business.

After ten years of living in the United States, Concetta decided to take a trip overseas to see her family. Meanwhile, Gaetano remained in the United States. Concetta obtained a visitor's visa in order to return to the United States but was questioned at the airport upon her arrival. The immigration officers discovered that she had violated her immigration status when she remained in the United States for all these years even though her husband had dropped out of college.

What type of consequences might Gaetano and Concetta face? Are their immigration violations different? How so?

2. Lee and Sandra both are aliens who came to the United States on visitor's visas about fifteen years ago. They did not know each other at the time. Shortly after their arrival, they met and began spending time together. When their allowable visiting time expired, they failed to leave the United States. Eventually, they moved into a small apartment together in Brooklyn, New York, and had two children out of wedlock: Clara and Michael, who are 10 and 8 years old, respectively.

   About two years ago, Lee abandoned Sandra and the children. Sandra has no idea where Lee is. She imagines that he returned to his native country. A few weeks after Lee left his family, Sandra was discovered by DHS agents while she worked illegally as a cook in a diner. She was found to be removable.

   Sandra attempted to represent herself at her removal hearing and filed an application requesting a cancellation of removal. Do you think that she will qualify? Why or why not?

3. Maria arrived in the United States on a nonimmigrant exchange visa. She was going to teach one course in world religions at Boston University. When Maria's plane landed, the DHS officers determined that her passport was fraudulent. Maria admitted that she did not go to retrieve her passport from an official government office in her country but that she honestly believed that her passport was genuine. What immigration consequences might Maria face?

4. Consider the same facts in Hypothetical #3, but suppose that DHS did not discover that Maria's passport was fraudulent until after she had already entered the United States. DHS made the discovery several months later when Maria attempted to renew her status as an exchange visitor. Would that change Maria's immigration situation? How so?

5. Carlton has been ordered removed and seeks your legal services. After reviewing his file, you conclude that his removal is very likely. Carlton explains to you that he has virtually no money and that he can only pay you a minimal fee.

   Carlton also tells you that he has no money to buy a ticket to leave the United States. Therefore, he thinks that if he is ordered removed at least he will not have to worry about buying a ticket out of the country. Carlton's friend is willing to lend him the money for a ticket, but Carlton does not want to add financial debt to his list of problems.

   If you represent Carlton at his removal hearing, assuming that voluntary departure is a viable option, what advice would you give Carlton about the advantages of voluntary departure instead of removal?

CHAPTER 8

REFUGEES AND ASYLUM

CHAPTER OBJECTIVES

After completing this chapter, you should know:

- The benefits of being a refugee
- The benefits of gaining asylum
- The benefits of Temporary Protected Status
- Frivolous claims that abuse benefits granted under the law

We have learned about some of the ways by which aliens can come to the United States, discussed various types of nonimmigrant and immigrant categories, and talked about what can happen to an alien who is not qualified to enter or remain in the United States. All of these concepts are general rules, and sometimes there are exceptions to them.

In this chapter we will discuss some of these exceptions. We will talk about aliens who may be permitted to stay in the United States even though they have no lawful basis for doing so! Specifically, these aliens are **refugees** or asylees, and the categories that permit them to stay in the United States are refugee status or asylum.

refugee
A person outside his or her native country or country where he or she last resided who is unable or unwilling to return there because of persecution or a well-founded fear of persecution.

REFUGEES

Refugees are persons outside their native country or country where they last resided who are unable or unwilling to return there because of persecution or a **well-founded fear of persecution.** The phrase a "well-founded fear of persecution" is the basis for granting refugee status or asylum. Generally, such well-founded fear must be on account of race, religion, nationality, membership in a particular social group, or political opinion. Actual persecution is sufficient for this status as well.

well-founded fear of persecution
Along with actual persecution, the basis for granting refugee status or asylum. Generally, the alien must have a well-founded fear of persecution based on race, religion, nationality, membership in a particular social group, or political opinion.

Many who have always lived in the United States take some of our liberties for granted. Here, we are not persecuted. Is there racism in the United States? Are people sometimes treated rudely because of their religion or nationality? Sadly, the answer is yes. But these victims are not tortured, imprisoned, or executed because of these factors. To the extent that such discrimination exists here, it is illegal. The Constitution forbids it, and so whoever practices it risks violating federal law.

However, in other countries such persecution is very real. Those who have a well-founded fear of it might be eligible for refugee status.

The next question is: Exactly what constitutes a "well-founded" fear? This is a perfect example of broad (even somewhat vague) legal terminology that is often determined by case law and other interpretations, since this is not black letter law (as evidence of actual persecution).

Race, Religion, or Nationality

Some countries throughout the world are harshly divided on the basis of race, religion, and/or nationality. Violence often breaks out as a result. In the Middle East, such violence has been rampant for thousands of years. This is just one of many examples that exist. Accordingly, it is quite conceivable that a member of a particular race, religion, or nationality might be a target in certain countries or, in particular, certain regions of certain countries.

Social Group Membership and Political Opinion

Similarly, many countries are bitterly divided based on certain social groups and political opinion. By comparison, that is hardly a problem in the United States. Members of the Elks Club usually do not attack the Veterans Administration, or vice versa. Democrats and Republicans might engage in some heated debates, but they work together, socialize together, and live together.

But in other countries, one's membership in a social group and/or political opinion could result in dangerous, even fatal consequences.

Aliens who have established a well-founded fear of persecution may be admitted as refugees, though such admission is subject to numerical limitations. Aliens who are admitted as refugees typically may adjust their status to LPR after one year.

ASYLUM

Refugees present in the United States or those who have arrived at its borders may apply for asylum. In other words, refugees may seek refugee status at any point once they are outside their native country or country where they last resided, whereas they must be inside the United States or at its borders in order to seek asylum. This is the principle difference between seeking refugee status and asylum. So, why bother to seek asylum? Because, unlike refugee status, asylum is not restricted by numerical limitations! In other words, asylum seekers cannot be told: "You have to wait until a slot becomes available for you."

Just "Plain Old" Asylum

You may have heard the term "political asylum." Perhaps, the word was used to refer to someone who sought (or was granted) asylum based on political opinion or affiliation. But for immigration purposes, the official term is "asylum" without adding the word "political" (or any other word) to it.

Timely Filing

The U.S. government is concerned about filing asylum applications in a timely manner. Specifically, aliens must file their applications within one year of being in the United States. Why do you suppose that is the case?

For example, let's take Farid. He was a former government official in his country—former because his party lost the recent elections. Now, the new party is in charge, and Farid, seeing no future for himself in his country, leaves and comes to the United States illegally.

Realistically, Farid is not in any danger in his own country. The new party is trying to reach out to Farid's party in order to unite the nation. But after a couple of years in the United States, Farid has learned that asylum is an easy ticket to LPR status! At that point, Farid would not be able to apply for asylum because it would be too late.

As Farid's claim would be frivolous, it is more likely that frivolous claims would tend to be made later than genuine ones. After all, if Farid was in real danger, he might have come forward earlier. At least that is what the government believes to be the case. That is why the one-year time limit is in place, the general notion being that those with genuine claims would not delay.

On the other hand, suppose that Farid's claim is genuine and that he does have a well-founded fear of persecution. Suppose that his political party did not lose an election; rather, they were ousted in a military coup. Suppose that the new dictatorship is imprisoning, torturing, and assassinating members of Farid's party. Further, suppose that once Farid flees to the United States, he realizes that there are loyalists to the new dictatorship in the United States seeking to kill members of Farid's party—a foreign quarrel right here on U.S. soil! This is another reason why the immigration door has to be monitored closely.

In any event, Farid goes into hiding until he believes that his enemies have stopped looking for him. That's when he comes out of hiding—two years later—and applies for asylum. In that case, Farid can claim that there were extreme circumstances for his delay. If he can prove his case, then it is likely that he will be granted asylum despite the delay.

FRAUD AND FRIVOLOUS CLAIMS

Refugee and asylee status ranks high along with marriage as a great way to gain LPR status. That is why Congress and DHS are concerned with stamping out fraud and frivolous claims. Otherwise, imagine how many aliens might say: "If I go back to my country, I'll be killed, so please grant me asylum and let me stay here forever!" If all of them were merely taken at their word, then the "boat" would be "overloaded" in no time.

Accordingly, mere words will not substantiate such a claim. Rather, convincing evidence—such as eyewitness testimony, connection to a particular group, or evidence of family members similarly persecuted—will be necessary to support the claim. Aliens from a particular country that is in turmoil or who belong to a particularly persecuted group might be given the benefit of the doubt.

It is understandable that some aliens might have difficulty proving their case—they simply cannot go back into their countries, where their lives are in danger, and obtain the evidence that they need. However, it is also understandable that DHS would be adamant about the evidence being convincing rather than tenuous.

In fact, as a method to curb frivolous claims, recent amendments to the immigration law will ban some aliens from the United States for life if they submit frivolous asylum claims.

For instance, suppose that Yung is from a foreign country and came to the United States as a visitor nine months ago and overstayed, so he is now here illegally. He applies for asylum, claiming that his country's government has ordered him to be executed. DHS officials investigate the story and determine that he is a scammer whose claims have no basis. In fact, a couple of years ago, he claimed to be someone else from an entirely different country with a similar story!

Yung probably will be banned from the United States for life! If ten years from now, he married a U.S. citizen, was a prime candidate for employment-based immigration, or had a genuine asylum claim, DHS effectively would say: "Sorry, you're banned for life!"

That's how serious Congress and DHS take frivolous asylum claims. There are far too many people with genuine claims and far too few spaces to be wasted on those who lie.

ADJUSTMENT OF STATUS FOR REFUGEES AND ASYLEES

Refugees and asylees who have been granted that status may adjust their status to LPR after one year. Logically, there would be no other alternative. After all, if they are granted this status permanently, then they are not nonimmigrants. They cannot be considered illegal aliens because they were granted official status (refugee status or asylum) by the U.S. government. Thus, by default, they would have to be classified as legal immigrants, which is why they may adjust their status to LPR.

TEMPORARY PROTECTED STATUS (TPS)

Temporary Protected Status (TPS)
A provision permitting aliens to enter or remain in the United States because their countries are in the middle of war, political turmoil, or environmental disaster. (Distinguish from asylum.)

Temporary Protected Status (TPS) may be granted to persons whose countries are in the middle of war, other political turmoil, or environmental disaster (such as a flood or an earthquake).

TPS differs from refugee status or asylum in two ways. First, TPS need not apply to an alien's specific, personal persecution or fear thereof. Second, TPS is not permanent and might be removed once the adverse condition has been terminated.

For example, Jonas was governor of a large region in his native country. Five years ago, he was ousted from power through a military coup and thrown in jail for his political views. Jonas managed to escape from jail and fled to the United States, where he has been granted asylum.

Meanwhile, there was such turmoil in Jonas' country that another citizen of that country (but one not involved in politics), Kevan, was granted TPS. Last year, the United States led an international coalition that established democracy in that country. The results have been spectacular, and the danger appears to have been removed. Kevan, who was granted TPS, must leave the United States now, since the dangerous condition has been removed. Jonas, however, is now an asylee (i.e., an asylum-seeker who has been granted asylum) and does not have to leave.

FAMOUS U.S. IMMIGRANTS

In the spotlight, on and off the court

MARTINA NAVRATILOVA

Martina Navratilova was born in Revnice, Czechoslovakia (now the Czech Republic) in 1956. She was one of the greatest women tennis players of all time, having won 18 Grand Slam tennis singles titles, nine of them the prestigious Wimbledon championship.

But that's not the only reason she grabbed headlines in the 1970s and 1980s. In the fall of 1975, while not yet 19 years old, Navratilova decided to defect (leave her country in order to immigrate) to the United States. That move was politically humiliating to communist Czechoslovakia and the entire communist superpower, the Soviet Union.

In 1981, Navratilova became a U.S. citizen. Since then, she has remained active and outspoken on a number of matters. She has been a staunch animal rights activist and is an advocate of various other causes.

CONCLUSION

These are exceptions to the traditional rules of inadmissibility and removal. Keep in mind that is exactly what they are—exceptions. That means they are rare; far fewer people apply for refugee status and asylum than are granted either status.

At times, the notions of "overloading the boat" and the "immigration door" appear to indicate that the United States is rather harsh when it comes to immigration and that it is an anti-immigration society. The concepts of refugee status, asylum, and TPS help to provide a more balanced view. The United States will open its doors to aliens who truly need a safe haven, and it is another reason why it is the country to which more people want to immigrate than any other country in the world.

Now that we have covered all of the basics of immigration law, let's turn to Chapter 9 and look at some practical tips for immigration legal professionals.

KEY TERMS

refugee
Temporary Protected Status (TPS)
well-founded fear of persecution

REVIEW QUESTIONS

1. What is a refugee?
2. What are the standards that constitute a well-founded fear of persecution?
3. What is asylum? What types of aliens are eligible for asylum?
4. What is TPS? How does it differ from asylum?
5. How does adjustment of status apply to refugees and asylees?
6. Why does adjustment of status seem to be the logical continuation of asylum?
7. Why is there a likely chance of fraudulent claims for refugee status and asylum?
8. Give an example of political persecution that may exist in some foreign countries.
9. Give an example of religious persecution that may exist in some foreign countries.
10. How are some types of racial and ethnic discrimination that exist in some foreign countries different from such discrimination in the United States?
11. Give examples of the type of evidence that would support an application for asylum.
12. Give an example of an actual or hypothetical international issue that may warrant TPS or asylum.

HYPOTHETICALS

1. Edward lives in a small country in Africa that recently has been subjected to severe environmental changes. Combinations of massive flooding and severe storms have forced Edward and many of his friends to flee their homes.

   Would Edward be more likely to be granted TPS than asylum? Why or why not?

2. Frank is an alien who came to the United States several years ago as a nonimmigrant visitor. His visa expired, but Frank remained in the United States illegally. He began to work for himself and has earned a great deal of money over the years. Recently, DHS discovered that Frank is an illegal alien and has rendered him removable. His removal hearing is in two months.

   Frank comes to your office and tells you that he has heard wonderful things about applying for asylum. He says that he doesn't have much basis to prove his case but is confident that all DHS has to do is listen to him and they'll grant asylum without much of an argument.

   What would you say to Frank to explain what he has to do to prove that he is entitled to asylum?

3. Ana was born and raised in a small country in South America. Her country is in the middle of a civil war. Both she and her family have lived in a quiet, farming community. They have never been involved in local or national politics. Also, they are not in any particular danger based on their race, nationality, or religion. However, Ana fears for her life because there is a great deal of fighting in the streets. She is afraid that she might be caught in the crossfire.

   Is there any way by which Ana will be allowed to come to the United States based on the danger surrounding her in her own country? Under what category would she most likely be classified?

4. John is an alien currently living in the United States. A few years ago John was an elected official in his country's government. His political party was the only ruling party at the time, and the country was a military dictatorship that was allied with the United States. One day, rebel troops ousted John's government, and he fled the country. John arrived in Canada by airplane and then entered the United States illegally from the Canadian border.

   The rebel troops are still in power. John comes to you seeking asylum. Do you think that he qualifies for asylum?

5. Use the same facts from Hypothetical #4, suppose that the rebel troops have been ousted from power now, after having been in power for five years. John's government is back in control. In that case, do you think that John qualifies for asylum in the United States?

CHAPTER 9

TIPS FOR THE IMMIGRATION LEGAL PROFESSIONAL

CHAPTER OBJECTIVES

After completing this chapter, you should know:

- What legal ethics are
- Why a legal professional must keep client information confidential
- Why a legal professional must be competent in his or her work
- Some valuable tips for immigration legal professionals

We spent most of this book discussing immigration law and policy and we learned about the history of immigration in the United States. Now it's time to take our skills and knowledge and put them to practice.

People who read this book do so for various reasons. Many of you are current (or aspiring) legal professionals, and you want to learn about immigration law in order to work in that field. You will find this chapter helpful; it is filled with tips about how to be a successful immigration legal professional.

ETHICS

Ethics are a set of values about what is good, right, and just. Who decides what these values are? The best answer is: society as a whole.

ethics
A set of values about what is good, right, and just. Various professions, including law, have their own set of ethical codes.

Society often is divided on certain notions of values, morality, and so forth. For instance, abortion is one of those very divisive issues. Abortion is the medical termination of a pregnancy, and many people in society believe that it is a pregnant woman's right to choose whether or not she wants to have the baby or to terminate the pregnancy. There are many other people in society who believe that a fetus (an unborn baby) is a human life as any other person, so having an abortion is like committing murder. On the issue of abortion, society remains strongly divided.

There are other issues about which society remains divided: premarital sex, gay marriage, prayer in schools, and so forth.

But there are many issues that are settled. For instance, society as a whole believes that murder, rape, and robbery (among other acts) are just plain "wrong" and thus should be against the law. Of course, there might be a handful of murderers, rapists, and robbers who disagree. (There is no one issue about which 100 percent of society agrees.) But society as a whole typically includes the overwhelming majority of people.

Ethics are a set of values that are rules rather than laws. A law (see Chapter 1) is made by the legislative branch of government—whether federal, state, or local. On the other hand, a rule is something that a particular organization establishes as a requirement but is not something that renders behavior legal or illegal.

For example, Amber is a student at Hoover College. Amber is 22 years old and about to graduate. Although Amber is legally old enough to drink alcoholic beverages, Hoover forbids drinking on campus. After her final exam, Amber opened a bottle of wine in the Student Lounge and shared it with some of her friends. Campus security reported Amber to the Dean of Students, who is about to hold a hearing to determine whether Amber will be allowed to graduate! This is a prime example of something (drinking) that while not against the law is against the rules of Hoover College.

Of course, certain acts might be violations of both rule and law. For instance, if Amber set the college library on fire, that would be against the law and, most probably, against Hoover's rules as well.

Nonetheless, ethics are a code of conduct to which members of a particular organization are expected to adhere.

LEGAL ETHICS

Legal ethics are a set of ethics about the legal profession. The American Bar Association (ABA) is the country's leading bar association and its most influential one. State bar associations and other legal professional organizations model their ethical codes on the ABA.

MAY NONATTORNEY LEGAL PROFESSIONALS GIVE LEGAL ADVICE?

nonattorney
A legal professional who is not an attorney (lawyer). One type of nonattorney is a paralegal.

Paralegal
A type of nonattorney. Paralegals arguably are more formally recognized than any other type of nonattorney.

Whether or not **nonattorney** legal professionals may give legal advice is one of the most commonly-asked questions involving the legal profession. Let's start with the ABA's definition of legal assistants and **paralegals.** The ABA defines a paralegal as follows:

A legal assistant or paralegal is a person, qualified by education, training or work experience, who is employed or retained by a lawyer, law office, corporation, governmental agency or other entity and who performs specifically delegated substantive legal work for which a lawyer is responsible.

The ABA's definition seems to outline the following requirements:

1. **A paralegal must have received the requisite education, training, or work experience in order to be considered a paralegal.** In other words, that statement implies that a person who has absolutely no legal education, training, or work experience cannot proclaim himself or herself to be a paralegal.
2. **A paralegal must be employed or retained by a lawyer, law office, corporation, governmental agency, or other entity.** At first glance, this statement might seem to require that a paralegal must work for an attorney or other legal organization. But the words "or retained" and "or other entity" seem to broaden the category to the point of almost no boundaries.
3. **A paralegal must perform specifically delegated substantive work.** This implies that a paralegal may not engage in independent decision-making regarding legal matters. Also, it means that the paralegal performs substantive legal work. In other words, answering phones and making appointments in a law office does not render one a paralegal.
4. **A lawyer is responsible for the paralegal's work.** This statement requires all work done by paralegals to be an attorney's responsibility. In other words, if Susan needs some legal work done and hires Maggie, a paralegal, to do it, an attorney must be responsible for it. In turn, that implies that an attorney ought to supervise at least the final product, if not the work at various increments along the way.

Do Immigration Nonattorney Legal Professionals Violate the ABA Rules?

Contrary to the ABA's definition of paralegals, there are, in fact, immigration nonattorney legal professionals who work independently of attorneys and for whose work attorneys are not responsible.

Does that behavior contradict the ABA rules?

First, the ABA defines a "legal assistant" and a "paralegal." But there is no official definition of those words. Arguably, the ABA's definition is prestigious and widely accepted. But the terms "legal assistant" and "paralegal" are used to describe a far broader spectrum of particular jobs than, say, the term "doctor," "lawyer," or "police officer."

Second, the ABA rules are not federal, state, or local law. But because the ABA is an organization on which state bar associations model their rules, it behooves attorneys to follow its rules faithfully, lest they risk being sanctioned. But nonattorney legal professionals have nothing to lose; if they're not part of this prestigious "club," there is not much risk of them being kicked out.

Finally, many immigration nonattorney professionals refer to themselves as "consultants," thus continuing to provide legal services independently, while not calling themselves "legal assistants" or "paralegals." Technically, they are not specifically violating any ABA rules—even if they are not bound initially by the ABA.

Laws That Prohibit Nonattorney Legal Professionals from Giving Legal Advice

Laws, as opposed to rules set by certain organizations, must be followed. If you don't obey a certain rule, you can always resign from the organization. But you are not allowed to disregard a certain law just because you feel like it. Accordingly, any laws that prohibit nonattorney legal professionals from giving legal advice must be followed. At this point in time, such laws are quite rare. In other words, many nonattorney legal professionals remain free to give legal advice, even though various legal organizations are fighting to prevent that.

What Is the Big Deal about Nonattorneys Giving Legal Advice?

Suppose that Carson, a nonattorney legal professional, is upset about anyone who tries to prevent him from giving legal advice professionally: "I think those lawyers just don't want me to take away their business! That's what this is all about!" While that may be true to some extent, there's a lot more to it.

For one thing, lawyers undergo specific training that allows them to practice law. If Carson simply said: "Hey, let me open up a legal consulting firm and give legal advice, that's a good way to make money," who is to say that Carson knows what he's talking about?

Next, lawyers are licensed to practice law. If they violate certain standards, they can be banned from practicing law temporarily or even permanently! Lawyers have a lot to lose if they do not do their job correctly. But Carson has nothing to lose, that is, except some clients.

Additionally, DHS itself permits nonattorneys to represent clients on immigration matters, as set forth in Form G-28 (see Appendix B). Because many aliens have little or no money and cannot afford an attorney and because the U.S. government does not provide attorneys for them free of charge (as it does for U.S. citizens), organizations that use immigration nonattorney legal professionals at a reduced (or deferred) cost exist, and many of them are officially recognized as such.

Of course, this does not mean that DHS thinks it is all right for simply anyone to perform such services. The nonattorney should be a competent legal professional.

Finally, can you imagine what it would be like if members of other professions faced the same problem? What if someone with no medical experience decided to perform surgery at a much lower cost than doctors? How would people be able to trust the professional services that they receive?

There is no absolute answer to this question. However, prudent judgment would indicate that those immigration paralegals who work under the supervision of an attorney maximize their chances of performing a quality service—one that is fully approved by the law and by bar associations and, ultimately, one that will be appreciated by the clients whom they serve.

COMPETENCE

Legal professionals, whether attorneys or nonattorneys, have an obligation to their clients to perform their professional services in a competent manner. In the preceding example, Carson decided he wanted to provide professional legal services and charge for them, without having any background in the law whatsoever! That is not "right" which is why it is considered to be unethical.

But what if Carson was a paralegal or an attorney but never had experience in immigration law? Should he open up an office and start undertaking immigration cases? That, too, is unethical. All legal professionals should not undertake any task unless they have sufficient experience in handling that task competently.

Therefore, if immigration law is new to you, work closely with an experienced immigration professional before making any decisions on your own. Remember, you owe a responsibility to your client to provide excellent service.

ZEALOUS REPRESENTATION

zealous representation within the bounds of the law
An ethical rule by which attorneys and other legal professionals must use their best efforts to represent their clients within the bounds of the law in order to achieve the best possible result.

Legal professionals are bound to represent their clients zealously. This is known as **zealous representation within the bounds of the law.** Consider this example. You are a paralegal who works for an immigration law firm. Part of your job is to conduct legal research to try and help two clients who were ordered removed and are now appealing their decision to the BIA (see Chapter 7).

One client is Zach, and the other client is Moore. You met with both of them, and you know their stories very well. You happen to like Zach and think that he is a good, decent man who would be a great asset to this country if he were allowed to remain. But you think that Moore is a schemer and an opportunist, someone whom the United States would be better off without!

You are bound by the code of ethics to do your best for both clients! You must represent Moore just as zealously as you do Zach. You are not permitted to work extremely hard to help Zach but work incompetently for Moore's case because you really don't care what happens to Moore. If you really don't want to help Moore at all, then tell your supervisor. Of course, by doing so, you risk causing problems for the firm—who had agreed to represent Moore in the first place. But that is a decision that you, as a legal professional, will have to make.

CONFIDENTIALITY

confidentiality
The requirement that a lawyer, or anyone working for a lawyer, not disclose information received from a client.

Another important aspect of being a legal professional is respecting **confidentiality.** Information that clients give to attorneys and other legal professionals is to be kept confidential. There are exceptions, however, if the client is about to commit a crime.

For example, suppose that you are working on Edwina's application for adjustment of status. Edwina is a neighbor of yours, and the whole neighborhood knows her. Last month, Edwina had a big party at her house to celebrate her 30th birthday. She invited you and a lot of other people that you and Edwina know in common. While preparing her paperwork, you look at her birth certificate and realize that she is not 30 years old after all—she is 40! You are surprised not only because she looks younger than her actual age, but also because only last month she told you and a whole bunch of other people that she is 30!

However, as a legal professional, you must keep that information confidential. As much as the temptation might be there, you must not tell anyone—such as another neighbor, a friend, or even Edwina's husband—this secret that you just discovered.

The reason you must keep this information confidential is because Edwina confided in you in connection with a legal matter (her adjustment of status). If the circumstances were different, if she didn't need your legal advice at all but at the party took you aside and said: "Guess what, I'm really 40, but don't tell anyone," then if you betray that secret, you might become known as a gossip who can't be trusted. But you will not have violated any legal ethical rule because Edwina did not tell you her true age in connection with any legal matter.

Committing Future Crimes Exception

Considering the preceding example, suppose that while you are completing Edwina's application she tells you that she is planning to smuggle drugs into the United States and sell them here. This is a prime example of a "future crime." Accordingly, not only are you not bound to keep this a secret, but as a responsible legal professional you are also bound to disclose the information.

RESISTING THE TEMPTATION TO PERPETUATE IMMIGRATION FRAUD

Throughout this book, multiple possibilities of immigration fraud were presented. Such fraud could involve information and/or documentation. Circumstances particularly likely to involve fraud are the marriage of a U.S. citizen to an alien and a well founded fear of persecution.

As an immigration legal professional, you might encounter alien clients who have entered into a marriage primarily for immigration purposes. As discussed in Chapter 3, that is against the law. If your client confides in you that the marriage is fraudulent, do yourself a favor and don't take the case! The same holds true for aliens who fabricate a well-founded fear of persecution in order to gain asylum without deserving it.

Sometimes it might be tempting to overlook these things and keep the client anyway. After all, you will make money, and you will help another human being become very happy by gaining LPR status. You might say: "After all, this client didn't commit murder; he or she simply told a little lie in order to stay in this country. Where's the harm in that?"

The harm in that is threefold: legal, ethical, and logical. First, as discussed before, the penalties for immigration fraud are very severe in terms of fines and imprisonment. Your career and life might be ruined if you go along with a hoax to defraud the U.S. government.

Second, it is unethical for a legal professional to engage in fraudulent behavior. Besides losing your fortune (by paying incredibly heavy fines) and freedom (by being locked in jail), you can lose your license to practice law (if you have one) and your job.

Finally, if you think about it logically, you should not help aliens in that situation. Remember, the United States has "limited seating available." Logically, shouldn't those seats go to those who deserve them? Those who have complied with the immigration laws? By allowing someone to cheat their way to LPR status, you are denying that opportunity to someone who honestly deserves it.

Accordingly, make a commitment to yourself, to the legal profession, and to your country: Do not take part in anything fraudulent or otherwise underhanded. There are plenty of honest clients whom you can make very happy and from whom you can earn money representing. You don't need to perpetuate immigration fraud.

LEARN A FOREIGN LANGUAGE

There's an old saying: "The person who knows only one language is blind in both eyes. The person who knows two languages can see with both eyes. And the person who knows three languages can see with both eyes." Let's take that saying a step further: The more languages that a person speaks, the more immigration clients that person can attract!

Growing up in the United States—the country to which most people want to immigrate—certainly has its advantages. But one huge disadvantage is that Americans often tend to isolate themselves from the rest of the world. They grow up speaking only English, not learning any foreign languages.

Learning a foreign language or two opens your eyes to a whole new world. It can do wonders for your immigration law career. Aliens from other countries who don't speak English often seek the comfort and familiarity of a legal professional who speaks their language.

Of course, it is not necessary for you to learn a foreign language. There are many immigration legal professionals who are very successful and happy with their careers and all they speak is English. But knowing an extra language can't hurt and it certainly can help.

GET ALL THE HELP YOU CAN GET

If you're worried about doing a good job as an immigration legal professional, here are some words of encouragement: There is plenty of help out there. Here are some examples.

Bar Associations

As discussed earlier in this chapter, the ABA and state bar associations are here to help. You can join them even if you are not an attorney. They want you to do a good job just as much as you do. They can provide you with helpful information about how to succeed as a legal professional in immigration and in other legal fields. The ABA's Web site is http://www.abanet.org. You can find the Web sites for each state's bar association very easily through the Internet.

American Immigration Lawyers Associations (AILA)

The American Immigration Lawyers Association is ideal to help you with just about any immigration question that you might have. It is a group of dedicated and experienced professionals who provide their guidance and advice. The Web site is http://www.aila.org.

Books, Books, Books

In addition to this book, there are plenty of other books that are helpful in that capacity. First and foremost, keep a copy of the INA at hand. Second, other immigration books are helpful, too. You can obtain many of these books from the ABA, other bar associations, and from AILA.

Internships

What better way to learn about immigration law than to work with a good immigration lawyer or other legal professional? It's not as easy to get a job as simply wishing for one. But what about an internship? Why not provide your services to a law firm free of charge for a few hours per week. If you can devote even five hours per week to this task, you can learn a great deal in that short time. The law firm would be thrilled to have you if you do a good job.

Internships are a great way to learn almost anything, including immigration law.

FAMOUS U.S. IMMIGRANTS

Luuucy, I'm a citizen!

DESI ARNAZ

Desi Arnaz, who was born in Cuba in 1917, is best known for his role as Ricky Ricardo in television's best known comedy of all time, *I Love Lucy.* But there's a lot more to this Cuban-born actor than meets the eye.

Arnaz not only starred in *I Love Lucy* with his real-life wife, Lucille Ball, but he also produced the show. In fact, he developed the multiple camera system that revolutionized situation comedies and has been used ever since.

Arnaz appeared in several movies, was a singer and a band leader, and in 1943, he became a U.S. citizen. Having divorced Lucille Ball in 1960, he remarried and then spent most of his remaining years away from the public eye. He died in 1986, but his legend lives on, mostly in reruns of *I Love Lucy.*

CONCLUSION

These are just some tips to help you get started. If you follow them carefully and faithfully, you will be well on your way to being a first-rate immigration legal professional—someone who will be an asset to the profession, make a lot of people happy, have a lot of clients, and help fill the United States with good aliens and immigrants that will make this an even greater country than it is right now.

Most of all, don't forget to keep your eye on the law! You never know when it's going to change. Consult the INA and visit the AILA and DHS (and its subagencies) Web sites.

Finally, always maintain your professional integrity and high code of ethics. Unfortunately, there are some "bad apples" in the legal profession who tarnish the good name of all legal professionals in the public's eyes. Happily, there are a lot of good, honest, and competent legal professionals. The more of them that there are, the more they can help achieve and maintain integrity across the profession.

KEY TERMS

confidentiality
ethics
nonattorney
paralegal
zealous representation within the bounds of the law

REVIEW QUESTIONS

1. What are ethics?
2. What is the difference between a rule and a law?
3. What is the ABA?
4. May a paralegal give legal advice?
5. Must a paralegal be supervised by an attorney?
6. What is a G-28 form?
7. What does it mean to represent a client zealously?
8. When may you reveal a client's confidential information?
9. What are the two most common instances when immigration fraud is likely?
10. Why is it useful to speak a foreign language if you are an immigration legal professional?
11. What is AILA?
12. Why might an internship help you get started in your immigration law career?

HYPOTHETICALS

1. You just got a job as a paralegal working for Simspon & Cunningham, a large immigration law firm in your city. Your supervisor is George Windell, an attorney. George is out to lunch when Alfredo, a potential client, walks in. Alfredo begins to tell you about his immigration problem. He is considering whether or not to obtain employment-based immigration or to ask his brother, a U.S. citizen, to petition for his LPR status. He asks you: "What should I do?" George will be back to the office in half an hour. What should you tell George?
2. You are an immigration attorney and your good friend, Samantha, owns a coffee shop. Samantha just hired Jack to work for her part-time as an evening manager. Jack is a student at a nearby college studying business management, and this position is perfect for him (and legal, too; see Chapter 2). Samantha tells Jack about you, and he has some immigration questions.

   Jack comes to your office and wonders how he can become a U.S. citizen one day. He is worried that he might be rejected because he was fired from two other jobs for stealing and both of his former employers reported the matter to the police. There was no proof of the theft, so Jack was never convicted.

   You are worried that Jack might steal from Samantha, too. You are tempted to tell her about Jack's past. What should you do?
3. You have been handling immigration cases for about one year now—mostly simple matters such as relative petitions. Now you are offered the chance to represent a very wealthy person who is applying for political asylum. This potential client, Ivan, is a bestselling author in his country but is on the run because he wrote a highly controversial book criticizing his country's corrupt government. The government officials are out to get him, and he is hiding in the United States.

   Ivan heard about you through a mutual friend. He is willing to pay you a lot of money to represent him. But you have never worked on an asylum case in your life. What should you do?

4. Samir and his wife Elba own a deli near your office. You stop in there to get a sandwich almost every day. They are pleasant, friendly people and make tasty sandwiches. One day, Samir comes to your office alone. He brings along a young woman named Aida and introduces her as his friend's daughter. Samir explains that Elba is pregnant and wants to stop working in the deli, and Samir wants to sponsor Aida to take Elba's job. After reviewing Aida's credentials, you conclude that she is an excellent candidate for employment-based immigration. Nonetheless, you realize that the process is complicated and you will have to work very hard to get her approved.

   As they leave your office, you watch them from the window. When they cross the street, they begin to kiss each other passionately! You conclude that they are lovers, having an affair. "Poor Elba!" you exclaim. "I can't believe Samir is cheating on her!" You are disgusted with Samir and feel sorry for Elba. You believe that the more you help Aida, the worse it will be for Elba. You don't think you can give this case the attention it deserves, especially since you really don't want Aida's claim to succeed. What should you do?

5. You just finished studying immigration law in school and are looking for your first job as an immigration paralegal. In the meantime, you work a full-time job in a department store and spend about five hours per week acting in a local community theater as a hobby. There is an immigration law firm in your neighborhood, but you don't think that they are hiring. The department store job pays the bills, and the acting is fun. But your dream is to work in immigration law, and there don't seem to be too many opportunities at the moment. What can you do to get your foot in the door at the law firm without jeopardizing your income?

AFTERWORD

We have spent a lot of time discussing the concerns, much of them well-founded, about illegal immigration in the United States. The worst example is illegal aliens who wish to cause harm to the our nation.

So I think it is only fitting that we close our discussion with arguably the most wonderful example of U.S. immigration: The application for posthumous citizenship.

Noncitizens may enlist in the U.S. military; some of those who die during military service may have their wish granted in death—to become U.S. citizens. *To become American citizens!* That is the ultimate display of patriotism.

These veterans' family members do not receive any type of financial or other benefit as a result of this honorary citizenship. This process is purely done to honor those men and women who honored our country by fighting and dying for it.

Truly, they deserve to be referred to by us as "fellow Americans."

Constantinos E. Scaros

APPENDIX A

UNITED STATES CITIZENSHIP PREPARATION

AMERICAN HISTORY

Here are some basic facts about U.S. history. Of course, there's a lot more to U.S. History than what is written here. But this is the information that DHS focuses on when conducting a naturalization (citizenship) interview. Accordingly, this is what an alien applying for citizenship must learn.

There are **Practice Questions** at the end of each section. These questions are the type asked by DHS officials during the interview.

SETTLEMENT IN THE UNITED STATES

People from various countries wanted to leave those countries and settle in a new place, mainly so they could enjoy religious freedom. These settlers, known as **Pilgrims,** arrived in this "New World," which is now the United States.

The first group of settlers came here on a ship called the **Mayflower.** When they arrived, they found that there were people already here. Those people were known as **American Indians** and are now also referred to as **Native Americans.**

These settlers, thankful for their religious freedom, celebrated what has become the first U.S. holiday—**Thanksgiving Day,** which is typically observed each year by Americans on the last Thursday in November.

Eventually, various European countries started sending some of their people to this New World. Those people, because they formed groups known as **colonies,** were called **colonists. England (part of Great Britain)** had sent groups of people who eventually formed **Thirteen Colonies.**

These original thirteen colonies were:

1. **Connecticut**
2. **Delaware**
3. **Georgia**
4. **Maryland**
5. **Massachusetts**
6. **New Hampshire**
7. **New Jersey**
8. **New York**
9. **North Carolina**
10. **Pennsylvania**
11. **Rhode Island**
12. **South Carolina**
13. **Virginia**

In time, the colonists began to feel that they were not experiencing as much freedom as they had anticipated. One colonist, **Patrick Henry,** best captured the colonial thinking when he said: **"Give me liberty or give me death."**

Then the colonists decided to gain their independence from England. **Thomas Jefferson,** a colonist, was the main writer of the **Declaration of Independence,** a document whose basic belief is that **"All men (human beings) are created equal."** This document was signed and adopted on **July 4, 1776,** a holiday that continues to be celebrated each year, known as **The Fourth of July** or **Independence Day.**

Then the colonists fought the **Revolutionary War** against England. During the war, **Francis Scott Key** wrote **"The Star Spangled Banner,"** which has become our **national anthem.**

Practice Questions

1. Q: What day is Independence Day?
   A: July 4.
2. Q: What country did we fight in the Revolutionary War?
   A: England (part of Great Britain).
3. Q: When is Thanksgiving Day usually celebrated?
   A: Each year on the last Thursday in November.
4. Q: What are the original thirteen colonies (states)?
   A: Connecticut, Delaware, Georgia, Maryland, Massachusetts, New Hampshire, New Jersey, New York, North Carolina, Pennsylvania, Rhode Island, South Carolina, and Virginia.
5. Q: Who said "Give me liberty or give me death?"
   A: Patrick Henry.
6. Q: Why did the Pilgrims come to America?
   A: To enjoy religious freedom.
7. Q: What was the first holiday celebrated by American colonists?
   A: Thanksgiving Day.
8. Q: Who was the main writer of the Declaration of Independence?
   A: Thomas Jefferson.
9. Q: What is the basic belief stated in the Declaration of Independence?
   A: That all men (human beings) are created equal.
10. Q: What is the U.S. national anthem, and who wrote it?
    A: "The Star Spangled Banner," written by Francis Scott Key.
11. Q: Who helped the Pilgrims in America?
    A: The American Indians (Native Americans).
12. Q: What is the name of the ship that brought the Pilgrims to America?
    A: The Mayflower.

THE AMERICAN FLAG

Our national anthem refers to the **American flag.** The colors of the U.S. flag are **red, white, and blue.** There are also **red and white stripes. Thirteen** of them represent each of the **original thirteen colonies.** In the upper left-hand corner of the flag, there are **white stars,** representing each **state.** Originally, there were **thirteen stars,** representing each of the **thirteen colonies.** Each time a new state was added to the United States, a new star was added to the flag. Today there are **fifty states in the United States, so there are fifty stars.**

Practice Questions

1. Q: What are the colors of the American flag?
   A: Red, white, and blue.

2. Q: How many stripes are on the U.S. flag?
   A: Thirteen.
3. Q: What do the stripes represent?
   A: One stripe for each of the original thirteen colonies.
4. Q: What color are the stripes?
   A: Red and white.
5. Q: How many stars are on the flag?
   A: 50.
6. Q: What do the stars represent?
   A: One star for each of the 50 states.
7. Q: What color are the stars?
   A: White.

THE UNITED STATES GOVERNMENT

Once independence from England was gained, there was a need to establish a formal government. The original thirteen colonies became **states.**

In 1787, after much discussion and debate, the thirteen states agreed to adopt the **United States Constitution as the supreme law of the land.** Through this form of government, the United States became known as a **democratic republic.** The **Constitution** may be **changed** by an **amendment.** Currently, there are **27 Amendments** to the **Constitution.**

The Constitution contains a set of rights that are guaranteed to everyone in the United States. These rights are known as **The Bill of Rights,** which are **the first ten amendments of the Constitution. Three such rights include the freedom of speech (First Amendment), the right to bear arms, and the right to a trial by jury (in most cases).**

The introduction to the Constitution is called the **Preamble.** The Constitution created **two tiers of government, federal and state, and three branches: Legislative, Executive, and Judicial. The federal branches have the following powers and obligations.**

The Legislative Branch

The **legislative branch** is **Congress,** which **makes the laws.** Congress is **elected** by the **people.** In order to **vote,** a person must be a **U.S. citizen and at least 18 years old. Federal elections** are held in **November.** Congress is made up of the **Senate** and the **House of Representatives.** There are **two senators from each state, which equals 100 senators** in total. **Senators** are elected for **six years,** and there is **no limit** to how many times they may be **elected.** The **number of representatives** from each state depends on that state's **population.**

There are **435 representatives. Representatives** are elected for **two years,** and there is **no limit** to how many times they may be **elected.**

Congress meets in the U.S. Capitol (building) in Washington, D.C., which is our nation's capital. Congress has the **power** to **declare war. Congress** also proposes **bills** and presents them to the **President** to sign into **law.**

The Executive Branch

The **executive branch** is made up of the **President** and the **Cabinet,** which is a special **group** that **advises** the President. The executive branch **executes** (carries out) the law.

The **President** is the **leader** of the **executive branch,** the **commander-in-chief of the U.S. military,** and **signs congressional bills** into law. The **President lives in the White House, at 1600 Pennsylvania Avenue, in Washington, D.C.**

The **President** is elected by the **people** and is elected for **four years.** The **President may serve a total of two terms (eight years) in office.** The **President** is **inaugurated** (takes office) in **January.** If the **President dies while in office, the Vice President becomes President.**

If **both the President and the Vice President die in office, the Speaker (leader) of the House of Representatives becomes President.** The **first president** of the United States (and, thus, the **first commander-in-chief of the U.S. military**) was **George Washington.** He is called the **"Father of our country."**

The Judicial Branch

The **judicial branch interprets the laws.** The **top level of the judicial branch is the United States Supreme Court,** which is the **highest court in the United States.** It is made up of **nine judges** called **justices.** They are appointed by the **President.**

State and Local Government

Each state has its own government, and there are local governments. The **head** of the state government is the **governor,** who lives and works in the state's **capital.** Typically, the **head** of a **city** or **town** government is called a **mayor.**

Practice Questions

1. Q: How many branches are there in the U.S. government?
   A: Three: legislative, executive, and judicial (judiciary).
2. Q: What is the legislative branch?
   A: Congress.
3. Q: What is the supreme law of the land in the United States?
   A: The United States Constitution.
4. Q: What do we call a change to the Constitution?
   A: An amendment.
5. Q: What is the Bill of Rights?
   A: The first ten amendments of the Constitution.
6. Q: Name 3 rights or freedoms guaranteed by the Bill of Rights.
   A: Freedom of speech, the right to bear arms, and the right to a trial by jury in most cases.
7. Q: What is the minimum voting age?
   A: Eighteen.
8. Q: What type of government does the United States have?
   A: A democratic republic.
9. Q: When was the Constitution adopted?
   A: 1787.
10. Q: What is the introduction to the Constitution called?
    A: The Preamble.
11. Q: What is the function of the legislative branch?
    A: To make the law.
12. Q: What are the two houses (parts) of Congress?
    A: The Senate and the House of Representatives.
13. Q: Who elects members of Congress?
    A: The people.
14. Q: How many senators are there in Congress?
    A: 100, two from each state.

15. Q: For how long do we elect each senator?
    A: Six years.

16. Q: How many representatives are there in Congress?
    A: 435.

17. Q: For how long do we elect each representative?
    A: Two years.

18. Q: Who has the power to declare war?
    A: Congress.

19. Q: Who signs bills into law?
    A: The President.

20. Q: How many times may a senator or representative be elected?
    A: There is no limit.

21. Q: Where does Congress meet?
    A: The U.S. Capitol.

22. Q: Who is the President of the United States now?
    A: **Subject to change. Learn and remember.**

23. Q: Who is the Vice President of the United States now?
    A: **Subject to change. Learn and remember.**

24. Q: Who was the first president of the United States?
    A: George Washington.

25. Q: Who becomes president if the president dies?
    A: The vice president.

26. Q: Who becomes president if both the president and vice president die?
    A: The Speaker (leader) of the House of Representatives.

27. Q: How many terms may a president serve?
    A: Two terms (eight years).

28. Q: What is the executive branch?
    A: The President and the Cabinet.

29. Q: What is the cabinet?
    A: The special group that advises the president.

30. Q: What is the White House?
    A: The president's official home.

31. Q: Where is the White House located?
    A: At 1600 Pennsylvania Avenue, Washington, D.C.

32. Q: Who is the commander-in-chief of the U.S. military?
    A: The president.

33. Q: Who was the military's first commander-in-chief?
    A: George Washington.

34. Q: In what month do we vote for the president?
    A: November.

35. Q: In what month is the new president inaugurated?
    A: January.

36. Q: Name at least one requirement a person must meet to become president.
    A: The person must be at least 35 years old.

37. Q: What is the top level of the judicial (judiciary) branch?
    A: The United States Supreme Court.

38. Q: What are the duties of the judicial branch?
    A: To interpret laws.

39. Q: Who is the Chief Justice of the Supreme Court?
    A: **Subject to change. Learn and remember.**

40. Q: Who selects the Supreme Court justices?
    A: They are appointed by the president.

41. Q: How many Supreme Court justices are there?
    A: Nine.

42. Q: What is the capital of the state in which you live?
    A: **Learn and remember.**

43. Q: Who is the current governor of your state?
    A: **Subject to change. Learn and remember.**

44. Q: Who is the head of your local government?
    A: **Subject to change. Learn and remember.**

45. Q: What is the head executive of the state government called?
    A: The governor.

46. Q: What is the head of a city or town government called?
    A: The mayor.

OTHER EVENTS IN UNITED STATES HISTORY

The United States has grown into a country of fifty states. The **49th and 50th states are Alaska and Hawaii.** Currently, the **two main political parties in the United States are the Democratic party and the Republican party.**

One of our **most important presidents was Abraham Lincoln.** He was **President during the Civil War,** in the **1860s.** At that point, states in the **South seceded (separated from) the United States and formed the Confederate States.** In the **Civil War, the Northern states fought against the Southern states.** The **main issue** was **slavery.** The **North** was **against slavery;** the **South** was **for slavery. Lincoln** wrote the **Emancipation Proclamation,** declaring that **all slaves will be free.**

Although the slaves (who were mostly blacks, now called African-Americans) were freed, many of their **civil rights** (rights guaranteed to all Americans under the Constitution) were being violated. **Dr. Martin Luther King, Jr.** was a powerful **civil rights leader during the 1960s.**

In the early 1940s **during World War II,** the **United Nations** was formed. The United Nations is an organization made up of **many nations throughout the world, including the United States.** The **main purposes of the United Nations are to resolve political problems and provide economic aid throughout the world. During World War II, the United States fought against Germany, Italy, and Japan.**

Practice Questions

1. Q: What are the two major political parties in the United States?
   A: The Democratic party and the Republican party.

2. Q: Which countries were our enemies during World War II?
   A: Germany, Italy, and Japan.

3. Q: What are the 49th and 50th states?
   A: Alaska and Hawaii.

4. Q: Who was the President during the Civil War?
   A: Abraham Lincoln.

5. Q: What is the Emancipation Proclamation?
   A: An executive document, written by President Lincoln, that freed all slaves.

6. Q: What is the main purpose of the United Nations?
   A: To resolve political problems and to provide economic aid throughout the world.

UNITED STATES CITIZENSHIP

One of the most important rights granted to U.S. citizens is the right to vote. A person may become a naturalized citizen through DHS. The main form used to gain naturalization is the N-400. It is important for aliens wishing to become U.S. citizens to learn about U.S. history so they can understand our system of government and our way of life.

Practice Questions

1. Q: Name one benefit of being a U.S. citizen.
   A: The right to vote.

2. Q: What DHS form is used to apply for citizenship?
   A: The N-400.

3. Q: A U.S. citizen must have allegiance to what country, first and foremost?
   A: The United States

4. Q: Why is it important for naturalized citizens to know about U.S. history?
   A: To understand our system of government and our way of life.

APPENDIX B

IMMIGRATION FORMS

This section includes some of the more common immigration forms. The forms are divided into different categories—each form belonging in the category most appropriate to its purpose.

As you read through the forms, please keep the following in mind:

1. **FORMS CHANGE:** As of this writing, the forms included here are 100 percent up-to-date. They may remain unchanged for years to come, or they may change tomorrow! That's just how the law works. Therefore, before you attempt to use any of the forms to assist a client, please consult with DHS (you may do so through its Web site) to make sure that you are using only the most up-to-date forms.

Form Information

Many of the forms have information in the bottom right-hand corner, indicating the form number, when the form was created or revised, and whether a previous version of the form may be used.

For example, the form used by LPRs to apply for citizenship is called the Application for Naturalization (it is one of the forms that you will find in this appendix). The bottom right-hand corner of that form contains the following information:

Form N-400 (Rev. 07/23/02) N

N-400 is the name of the form. It was revised last on July 23, 2002. The "N" means that NO previous versions of the form may be used. If the form contained a "Y," for "YES," then that would mean that previous versions may be used.

Of course, if the form changes and the new form also contains an "N," then the existing form would be obsolete. You wouldn't know that by holding the old form in your hand! That's why it is vital that you check to make sure the forms you have are up to date each time that you intend to use them.

Interestingly, this latest version of the N-400 was revised shortly before the INS was dismantled and replaced by the DHS and its subagencies. Because the substance of the form did not change, DHS has yet to revise it. Accordingly, the form makes reference to INS, not DHS. Newer forms usually contain the name of the specific DHS subagency—usually the Bureau of Citizenship and Immigration Services (BCIS).

2. **MAKE SURE THAT YOU HAVE ALL OF THE FORMS THAT YOU WILL NEED:** The forms contained in this section are not necessarily *all* the forms that you will need to complete a specific immigration matter. Always make sure that you have the *complete* checklist on hand (available through DHS).

3. **ADDITIONAL VERSIONS OF FORMS:** Variations of certain forms are provided. For instance, the form G-325B (included in this appendix) is for military personnel only, who want to become LPRs. Most applicants use the G-325A (also included).

FORMS FOR GENERAL PURPOSES

G-28: Notice of Entry of Appearance as Attorney or Representative

The G-28 is the most widely-used form by legal professionals, so let's begin with that one. It is the form that attorneys and other legal professionals must use when representing clients on immigration matters. An original is submitted with the immigration application at the onset, and the legal professional submits copies of the original in subsequent correspondence.

So, if Jenna is an attorney who files an application for Samantha to obtain LPR status, Jenna will file an original G-28 with Samantha's application and then enclose a copy of it anytime when she writes to DHS regarding that matter. Of course, for all other matters relating to Samantha or to other clients, Jenna would file a new G-28.

Notice that there are categories that nonattorneys may complete, evidence that immigration is one of the few legal fields in which nonattorneys are authorized to represent clients.

AR-11: Aliens' Change of Address Card

Aliens, (i.e., noncitizens), whether nonimmigrants or immigrants, must submit this form to DHS within 10 days of changing their address. This allows DHS to maintain better records regarding aliens' whereabouts.

U.S. Department of Justice
Immigration and Naturalization Service

Notice of Entry of Appearance as Attorney or Representative

Appearances - An appearance shall be filed on this form by the attorney or representative appearing in each case. Thereafter, substitution may be permitted upon the written withdrawal of the attorney or representative of record or upon notification of the new attorney or representative. When an appearance is made by a person acting in a representative capacity, his personal appearance or signature shall constitute a representation that under the provisions of this chapter he is authorized and qualified to represent. Further proof of authority to act in a representative capacity may be required. **Availability of Records** - During the time a case is pending, and except as otherwise provided in 8 CFR 103.2(b), a party to a proceeding or his attorney or representative shall be permitted to examine the record of proceeding in a Service office. He may, in conformity with 8 CFR 103.10, obtain copies of Service records or information therefrom and copies of documents or transcripts of evidence furnished by him. Upon request, he/she may, in addition, be loaned a copy of the testimony and exhibits contained in the record of proceeding upon giving his/her receipt for such copies and pledging that it will be surrendered upon final disposition of the case or upon demand. If extra copies of exhibits do not exist, they shall not be furnished free on loan; however, they shall be made available for copying or purchase of copies as provided in 8 CFR 103.10.

In re:	Date:
	File No.

I hereby enter my appearance as attorney for (or representative of), and at the request of the following named person(s):

Name:	☐ Petitioner ☐ Beneficiary	☐ Applicant		
Address: (Apt. No.) (Number & Street)	(City)	(State)	(Zip Code)	
Name:	☐ Petitioner ☐ Beneficiary	☐ Applicant		
Address: (Apt. No.) (Number & Street)	(City)	(State)	(Zip Code)	

Check Applicable Item(s) below:

☐ 1. I am an attorney and a member in good standing of the bar of the Supreme Court of the United States or of the highest court of the following State, territory, insular possession, or District of Columbia

______________ ______________ and am not under a court or administrative agency
Name of Court
order suspending, enjoining, restraining, disbarring, or otherwise restricting me in practicing law.

☐ 2. I am an accredited representative of the following named religious, charitable, social service, or similar organization established in the United States and which is so recognized by the Board:

☐ 3. I am associated with ______________
the attorney of record previously filed a notice of appearance in this case and my appearance is at his request. (*If you check this item, also check item 1 or 2 whichever is appropriate.*)

☐ 4. Others (Explain Fully.)

SIGNATURE	COMPLETE ADDRESS
NAME (Type or Print)	TELEPHONE NUMBER

PURSUANT TO THE PRIVACY ACT OF 1974, I HEREBY CONSENT TO THE DISCLOSURE TO THE FOLLOWING NAMED ATTORNEY OR REPRESENTATIVE OF ANY RECORD PERTAINING TO ME WHICH APPEARS IN ANY IMMIGRATION AND NATURALIZATION SERVICE SYSTEM OF RECORDS:

____
(Name of Attorney or Representative)

THE ABOVE CONSENT TO DISCLOSURE IS IN CONNECTION WITH THE FOLLOWING MATTER:

Name of Person Consenting	Signature of Person Consenting	Date

(NOTE: Execution of this box is required under the Privacy Act of 1974 where the person being represented is a citizen of the United States or an alien lawfully admitted for permanent residence.)

This form may not be used to request records under the Freedom of Information Act or the Privacy Act. The manner of requesting such records is contained in 8CFR 103.10 and 103.20 Et.SEQ.

Form G-28 (09/26/00)Y

OMB No. 1615-0007; Expires 08/31/08

Department of Homeland Security
U.S. Citizenship and Immigration Services

AR-11, Alien's Change of Address Card

Name (Last in CAPS) (First Name) (Middle Name)	I am in the United States as a: ☐ Visitor ☐ Permanent Resident ☐ Student ☐ Other ______ (Specify)
Country of Citizenship — Date of Birth (mm/dd/yyyy)	Copy Number From Alien Card A
Present Address (Street or Rural Route) (City or Post Office)	(State) (Zip Code)
(If the above address is temporary) I expect to remain there ______ Years ______ Months	
Last Address (Street or Rural Route) (City or Post Office)	(State) (Zip Code)
I work for or attend school at: (Employer's Name or Name of School)	
(Street Address or Rural Route) (City or Post Office)	(State) (Zip Code)
Port of Entry Into U.S. — Date of Entry Into U.S. (mm/dd/yyyy)	If not a Permanent Resident, my stay in the U.S. expires on: (Date - mm/dd/yyyy)
Signature — Date (mm/dd/yyyy)	

Form AR-11 (Rev. 01/20/06) Y

AR-11, Alien's Change of Address Card

This card is to be used by all aliens to report a change of address within ten days of such change.
The collection of this information is required by Section 265 of the Immigration and Nationality Act (8 U.S.C. 1305). The data is used by U.S. Citizenship and Immigration Services for statistical and record purposes and may be furnished to Federal, State, local and foreign law enforcement officials. Failure to report a change of address is punishable by fine or imprisonment and/or removal.

ADVISORY: This card is not evidence of identity, age or status claimed.

Public Reporting Burden. Under the Paperwork Reduction Act, an agency may not conduct or sponsor an information collection and a person is not required to respond to an information collection unless it displays a currently valid OMB control number. We try to create forms and instructions that are accurate, can be easily understood and that impose the least possible burden on you to provide us with information. Often this is difficult because some immigration laws are very complex. This collection of information is estimated to average five minutes per response, including the time for reviewing instructions, searching existing data sources, gathering and maintaining the data needed, and completing and reviewing the collection of information. Send comments regarding this burden estimate or any other aspect of this collection of information, including reducing this burden to: U.S. Citizenship and Immigration Services, Regulatory Management Division, 111 Massachusetts Ave. N.W., Washington, D.C. 20529. **Do not mail your completed form to this Washington, D.C. address.**

Mail Your Form to the Address Shown Below:

	For commercial overnight or fast freight
Department of Homeland Security U.S. Citizenship and Immigration Services Change of Address P.O. Box 7134 London, KY 40742-7134	**Department of Homeland Security** U.S. Citizenship and Immigration Services Change of Address 1084-I South Laurel Road London, KY 40742-7134

FORMS FOR NONIMMIGRANTS

The forms contained in this section pertain to various nonimmigrant matters.

I-538: Certification by Designated School

This form must be completed by aliens seeking student status, as well as by an official from the school in question.

I-129: Petition for a Nonimmigrant Worker

A nonimmigrant worker is an alien who is permitted to work in the United States despite not being an immigrant. In Chapter 2 we discussed various types of nonimmigrant workers, including treaty traders, religious workers, and intracompany transferees (among others).

This form is a long one, as there are many types of nonimmigrant visas available that have to do with employment.

I-765: Application for Employment Authorization

This form allows aliens who are in the United States temporarily to receive an Employment Authorization Document (EAD), allowing them to work during all or part of their stay. This form is the one used by students who seek practical training or other employment and is used by other nonimmigrants who are not covered by the I-129 form.

I-129F: Petition for Alien Fiancé(e)

This form must be completed by U.S. citizens seeking to obtain a nonimmigrant visa for their alien fiancés or fiancées. As we discussed in Chapter 2, aliens may obtain this type of visa to enter the United States in order to marry a U.S. citizen. Of course, this is allowed by DHS only if the marriage is a genuine one (i.e., not for immigration purposes).

I-539: Application to Extend/Change Nonimmigrant Status

Nonimmigrants who wish to extend their status or change to another nonimmigrant status use this form. This is *not* the form to use when adjusting from a nonimmigrant to an immigrant status. (That form, the I-485, is covered later in this appendix.)

U.S. Department of Justice
Immigration and Naturalization Service

OMB Approval No. 1115-0060

Certification by Designated School

SECTION A. This section must be completed by the student, as appropriate. *(Please print or type):*

1. Name: *(Family in CAPS)* *(First)* *(Middle)*	2. Date of birth:
3. Student admission number:	4. Date first granted F-1 or M-1 status:
5. Level of education being sought:	6. Student's major field of study:

7. Describe the proposed employment for practical training:

Beginning date: ____________ Ending date: ____________ Number of hours per week: ________

8. List all periods of previously authorized employment for practical training:

A. Curricular or work/study:	B. Post completion of studies

Signature of student: ______________________ Date: ____________

SECTION B. This section must be completed by the designated school official (DSO) of the school the student is attending or was last authorized to attend:

9. I hereby certify that:

The student named above:

☐ Is taking a full course of study at this school, and the expected date of completion is: ____________

☐ Is taking less than a full course of study at this school because: ____________

☐ Completed the course of study at this school on (date): ____________

☐ Did not complete the course of study. Terminated attendance on (date): ____________

Check one:

☐ A. The employment is for practical training in the student's field of study. The student has been in the educational program for at least nine (9) months, is in good academic standing, and is eligible for the requested practical training in accordance with INS regulations at 8 CFR 214.2(f)(10). The training that the student will participate in is an integral part of an established curriculum.

☐ B. The employment is for an internship with a recognized international organization and is within the scope of the organization's sponsorship. The student is in good academic standing.

10. Name and title of DSO:	Signature:	Date:
11. Name of school:	School file number:	Telephone Number:

For Official Use Only
Microfilm Index Number:

(See instructions on reverse)

Form I-538 (Rev. 08/12/02)Y

Instructions

A student seeking authorization for off-campus employment (F-1 only) or practical training (F-1 and M-1) must submit as supporting documentation to Form I-765, Application for Employment Authorization, a certification by the designated school official (DSO) of the school the student is attending or was last authorized to attend.

Certification by the DSO is required of all students (F-1 and M-1) seeking authorization for employment off campus or practical training, including required or optional curricular practical training.

The DSO must certify on Form I-538 that the proposed employment is directly related to the student's field of study.

Where to Submit Certification.
A copy of the DSO's certification must be mailed to: ACS Students/Schools (STSC) Section, P.O. Box 170, London, KY 40741. Overnight carrier deliveries must be sent to: ACS - INS, INS Students/Schools (STSC) Section, 1084 South Laurel Road, London, KY 40744.

All students requesting school certification must complete questions 1 through 6. Students requesting a recommendation for practical training must complete questions 7 and 8. Answers to questions 7 through 9 may be continued on this page, if needed.

Since the I-538 is used by the DSO for certification purposes, no fee is required for the submission of this form.

NOTE: M-1 students seeking extensions of stay must file a completed Form I-539, Application to Extend/Change Nonimmigrant Status, supported by a current Form I-20M-N, as appropriate. The I-539 application must be submitted to the INS service center that has jurisdiction over the student's residence.

Reporting Burden.
An agency may not conduct or sponsor an information collection and a person is not required to respond to an information collection unless it contains a currently valid OMB control number. The public reporting burden for this collection of information is estimated to average 4 minutes per response, including the time for reviewing instructions, searching existing data sources, gathering and maintaining the data needed, and completing and reviewing the collection of information. Send comments regarding this burden estimate or any other aspect of this collection of information, including suggestions for reducing this burden, to: U.S. Department of Justice, Immigration and Naturalization Service, HQPDI, 425 I Street N.W., Room 4034, Washington, DC 20536; OMB No. 1115-0060.
DO NOT MAIL YOUR COMPLETED CERTIFICATION TO THIS ADDRESS.

Comments: ______________________________

Form I-538 (08/12/02)Y Page 2

Department of Homeland Security
U.S. Citizenship and Immigration Services

OMB No. 1615-0009; Expires 05/31/08

Instructions for Completing

Form I-129

OMB No. 1615-0009; Expires 05/31/08

Department of Homeland Security
U.S. Citizenship and Immigration Services

Form I-129, Petition for a Nonimmigrant Worker

NOTE: You may file Form I-129 electronically. Go to our internet website at **www.uscis.gov** and follow the detailed instructions on e-filing.

Instructions

Please read these instructions carefully to properly complete this form. If you need more space to complete an answer, use a separate sheet (s) of paper. Write your name and Alien Registration Number (A #), if any, at the top of each sheet and indicate the number of the item to which the answer refers. NOTE: The U.S. Citizenship and Immigration Services (USCIS) is comprised of offices of the former Immigration and Naturalization Service (INS).

Purpose of This Form.

This form is used by an employer to petition the U.S. Citizenship and Immigration Services (USCIS) for an alien to come as a nonimmigrant to the United States temporarily to perform services or labor, or to receive training, as an:

- **H-1B,** specialty occupations; an alien coming to perform services of an exceptional nature relating to a project administered by the U.S. Department of Defense; a fashion model who has national and international acclaim; an alien coming in accordance with a trade agreement with Chile or Singapore.
- **H-2A,** agricultural worker.
- **H-2B,** temporary nonagricultural worker.
- **H-3,** trainee.
- **L-1,** intracompany transferee.
- **O-1,** alien of extraordinary ability in arts, science, education, business or athletics.
- **O-2,** accompanying alien who is coming to the United States to assist in the artistic or athletic performance of an O-1 artist or athlete.
- **P-1,** internationally recognized athlete/entertainment group.
- **P-1S,** essential support personnel for a P-1.
- **P-2,** artist or entertainer in reciprocal exchange program.
- **P-2S,** essential support personnel for a P-2.
- **P-3,** artist/entertainer coming to the United States to perform, teach or coach under a program that is culturally unique.
- **P-3S,** essential support personnel for a P-3.
- **Q-1,** alien coming temporarily to participate in an international cultural exchange program.

This form is used also by an employer to request an extension of stay or change of status for the following nonimmigrants:

- **E-1,** treaty trader.
- **E-2,** treaty investor.
- **Free Trade Nonimmigrants, H-1B1s and TNs.**
- **R-1,** religious worker.

NOTE: A petition is not required to apply for an E-1, E-2 or R-1 nonimmigrant visa or admission as a TN nonimmigrant from Canada or Mexico. A petition is also not required for an H-1B1 Free Trade Nonimmigrant from Chile or Singapore. These persons may apply directly to a U.S. consulate or embassy abroad.

A petition is required only to apply for a change or extension of stay in such status.

NOTE: The Form I-129 consists of a basic petition, individual supplements relating to specific classifications, and for H-1B petitions, the H-1B Data Collection and Filing Fee Exemption Supplement with its particular instructions (formerly issued separately as Form I-129W).

The following Table of Contents will help you locate information on the form and each supplement:

Table of Contents. Page

Who May File.

General. A U.S. employer may file this form and applicable supplements to classify an alien in any nonimmigrant classification listed in **Part 1** and **Part 2** of these instructions. A foreign employer may file for certain classifications as indicated in the specific instructions.

Agents. A U.S. individual or company in business as an agent may file for types of workers who are traditionally self-employed or who traditionally use an agent to arrange short-term employment with numerous employers. A petition filed by an agent must include a complete itinerary of services or engagements, including dates, names and addresses of the actual employers, and the locations where the services will be performed. A petition filed by a United States agent must guarantee the wages and other terms and conditions of employment by contractual agreement with the beneficiary or beneficiaries of the petition. The agent/employer must also provide an itinerary of definite employment and information on any other services planned for the period of time requested.

Including more than one alien in a petition. Multiple aliens who will seek admission in H-2A, H-2B, H-3, P-1, P-2, P-3, O-2 or Q-1 classification may be included on the same petition provided:

- They will all be employed for the same period of time;
- They will all perform the same services, receive the same training or participate in the same international cultural exchange program; and
- If the petition is for aliens seeking H-2A classification, they will apply for a visa at the same consulate or, if visa exempt, will apply for admission at the same port-of-entry.

NOTE: If the employer includes more than one alien on the petition (other than those seeking H-2A classification) and needs to request USCIS to notify more than one consulate or embassy concerning the processing, the employer should file a Form I-824, Application for Action on an Approved Application or Petition, with appropriate fee, for each embassy or consulate that must be notified.

Multiple locations. A petition for alien(s) to perform services or labor or receive training in more than one location must include an itinerary with the dates and locations where the services or training will take place.

Unnamed aliens. All aliens in a petition for an extension of stay or change of status must be named in the petition. All aliens included in any other petition must be named, except:

- An H-2A petition for more than one worker may include unnamed aliens if they are unnamed on the labor certification;
- An H-2B petition for more than one worker may include unnamed aliens in emergent situations where it is established on the petition that the names cannot be provided due to circumstances that cannot be anticipated or controlled.

Where some or all of the aliens are not named, specify the total number of unnamed aliens and total number of aliens in the petition. Where the aliens must be named, petitions naming subsequent beneficiaries may be filed later with a copy of the same labor certification. Each petition must reference all previously filed petitions using that certification.

General Filing Instructions.

Complete the basic form and any relating supplement. Please answer all questions by typing or clearly printing in black ink. Indicate that an item is not applicable with "N/A."

If you need extra space to answer any item, attach a sheet(s) of paper with your name and your Alien Registration Number (A#), if any, and indicate the number of the item to which the answer refers. You must file your petition with the required initial evidence. The petition must be properly signed and filed with the proper fee.

NOTE: Submit the petition and all supporting documentation in duplicate if you checked block "a" in Question 5 of Part 2 of the form.

Classification - Initial Evidence.

These instructions are divided into two parts.

- The first part includes classifications requiring a petition for an initial visa or entry and any extension of stay or change of status.
- The second part includes classifications requiring only a petition for a extension of stay or change of status.

1. Petition always required.

The following classifications always require a petition.

A petition for new or concurrent employment or for an extension where there is a change in previously approved employment must be filed with the initial evidence listed below, and with the initial evidence required by the separate instructions for a change of status or extension of stay.

However, a petition for an extension based on unchanged, previously approved employment should only be filed with the initial evidence required in the separate extension of stay instructions.

H-1B.

An H-1B is an alien coming temporarily to perform services in a specialty occupation.

Write **H-1B1** in the classification requested block.

A specialty occupation is one that requires the theoretical and practical application of a body of highly specialized knowledge to fully perform the occupation and requires the attainment of a bachelor's or higher degree in a specific specialty, or its equivalent, as a minimum for entry into the occupation in the United States.

The petition must be filed by the U.S. employer and must be filed with:

- Evidence that a labor condition application has been filed with the U.S. Department of Labor;
- Evidence showing that the proposed employment qualifies as a specialty occupation;
- Evidence showing that the alien has the required degree by submitting either:
  - -- A copy of the person's U.S. baccalaureate or higher degree as required by the specialty occupation;
  - -- A copy of a foreign degree and evidence that it is equivalent to the U.S. degree; or
  - -- Evidence of education and experience that is equivalent to the required U.S. degree.
- A copy of any required license or other official permission to practice the occupation in the state of intended employment; and
- A copy of any written contract between you and the alien or a summary of the terms of the oral agreement under which the alien will be employed.

An H-1B is also an alien coming to perform services of an exceptional nature relating to a cooperative research and development project administered by the U.S. Department of Defense (DOD).

Write **H-1B2** in the classification requested block.

A U.S. employer may file the petition. The petition must be filed with:

- A description of the proposed employment;
- Evidence that the services and project meet the above conditions;
- A statement listing the names of all aliens who are not permanent residents, and who are or have been employed on the project within the past year, along with their dates of employment; and
- Evidence that the beneficiary holds a baccalaureate or higher degree in the field of employment.

An H-1B is also a fashion model, who has national or international acclaim and recognition, coming to be employed in a position requiring such a level of acclaim and recognition.

Write **H-1B3** in the classification requested block.

A U.S. employer or agent or foreign employer may file the petition.

On October 21, 1998, Congress enacted the American Competitiveness and Workforce Improvement Act ("ACWIA"), Public Law 105-277, that modified the H-1B nonimmigrant program. On December 8, 2004, Congress enacted the H-1B Visa Reform Act of 2004.

Because of these two Acts, an H-1B or H-1B1 Free Trade Nonimmigrant petitioner must complete the H-1B supplement form which is part of this petition. The supplement is used to collect additional information about the H-1B nonimmigrant worker and the H-1B petitioner (U.S. employer). It will also be used to determine whether the H-1B or H-1B1 Free Trade Nonimmigrant petitioner is exempt from the additional ACWIA filing fee and, if not exempt, the appropriate fee. (The supplement was formerly issued separately as Form I-129W).

The H-1B Visa Reform Act of 2004 also imposed an additional fee of **$500.00** for certain H or L petitions. On or after **March 8, 2005**, a U.S. employer seeking initial approval of H-1B or L nonimmigrant status for a beneficiary, or seeking approval to employ an H-1B or L nonimmigrant currently working for another U.S. employer, must submit this additional **$500.00** fee. **There are no exemptions from this fee**. This form will serve as the vehicle for collection of the **$500.00** fee.

H-1B and H-1B1 Data Collection and Filing Fee Exemption.

Who is required to file? A U.S. employer seeking to classify an alien as an H-1B or H-1B1 Free Trade Nonimmigrant nonimmigrant worker must file this supplement concurrently with Form I-129 and the appropriate fee. (See **"Fee"** for additional information regarding the appropriate fee.)

Completing Part A of the Supplement Form.

All U.S. employers seeking to classify an alien as an H-1B or H-1B1 Free Trade Nonimmigrant nonimmigrant worker must complete **Part A** of the supplement form. An employer must answer all of the questions in the "Employer Information" Section.

- **H-1B Dependent employer.** An "H-1B dependent employer" means an employer that:
  - -- Has 25 or fewer full-time equivalent employees who are employed in the United States and employs more than seven H-1B nonimmigrants;
  - -- Has at least 26 but not more than 50 full-time equivalent employees who are employed in the United States and employs more than 12 H-1B nonimmigrants; or
  - -- Has at least 51 full-time equivalent employees who are employed in the United States and employs H-1B nonimmigrant in a number that is equal to at least 15 percent of the number of such full-time equivalent employees.
- **Willful Violators.** A willful violator is an employer whom the Secretary of Labor has found, after notice and opportunity for a hearing, to have willfully failed to meet a condition of the labor condition application described in section 212(n) of the Immigration and Nationality Act.
- **Exempt H-1B nonimmigrant.** An "exempt H-1B nonimmigrant" means an H-1B who:
  - -- Receives wages (including cash bonuses and similar compensation) at an annual rate equal to at least $60,000; or
  - -- Has attained a master's degree or higher (or its equivalent) in a specialty related to the intended employment.
- **Highest education level.** Place an "X" in the appropriate box of **Part A, Number 3** ("**a**" through "**i**") of the supplement form that is most closely related to the highest formal education level attained by the beneficiary. **DO NOT** consider work experience in determining the beneficiary's equivalency.
- **Major/Primary field of study.** Use the beneficiary's degree transcripts to determine the primary field of study. Once the beneficiary's major is determined, fill in the boxes with one character per box. Thirty (30) characters maximum. **Do not** consider work experience to determine the beneficiary's major education level.
- **Master's or higher degree from a U.S. institution of higher education.** Indicate whether or not the beneficiary has earned a master's or higher degree from a U.S. institution of higher education, as defined in 20 U.S. C. section 1001(a).
- **Rate of pay per year.** The "rate of pay" is the salary or wages paid to the beneficiary. Salary or wages must be expressed in an annual full-time amount and do not include non-cash compensation or benefits. For example, an H-1B worker is to be paid $6,500 per month for a four-month period including a health benefits package and transportation. The yearly rate of pay if he or she were working for a full year would be 12 times the monthly rate or $78,000. This amount does not include health benefits or transportation costs. The figure $78,000 should be entered on this form as the rate of pay.
- **LCA Code.** The LCA Code is a three-digit occupational group for professional, technical, and managerial occupations and fashion models that can be obtained from Appendix 2 of the Dictionary of Occupational Titles printed on Department of Labor ETA Form 9035, Labor Condition Application for H-1B Nonimmigrant.
- **NAICS Code.** The North American Industry Classification System (NAICS) code can be obtained from the Department of Commerce, U.S. Census Bureau **(www.census.gov/epcd/www/naics.htm)**. Enter the code from left to right, one digit in each of the six boxes. If you use a code with less than six digits, enter the code left to right and then add zeros in the remaining unoccupied boxes.

  For example the code sequences 33466 would be entered as:

3	3	4	6	6	0

  The code sequences 5133 would be entered as:

5	1	3	3	0	0

Completing Part B of the Supplemental Form.

A U.S. employer seeking an exemption from the **$1,500.00** or **$750.00** filing fee must complete Part B. A U.S. employer is exempt from payment of the additional **$1,500.00** or **$750.00** filing fee if:

- The employer is an institution of higher education as defined in the Higher Education Act of 1965, section 101 (a), 20 U.S.C. section 1001 (a); or
- The employer is a nonprofit organization or entity related to, or affiliated with an institution of higher education. Institutions of higher education are defined in the Higher Education Act of 1965, section 101(a), 20 U.S.C., section 1001(a). Such a nonprofit organization or entity includes but is not limited to hospitals and medical research institutions. "Related to" or "affiliated with" means the entity is:

  (a) Connected or associated with the institution of higher education through shared ownership or control by a board or federation operated by the institution of higher education, or

  (b) Attached to the institution of higher education as a member, branch, cooperative or subsidiary.

  "Nonprofit organization or entity" means the organization or entity is **(a)** defined as a tax exempt organization under the Internal Revenue Code of 1986, section 501(c)(3), (c)(4), or (c)(6), and **(b)** has been approved as a tax exempt organization for research or educational purposes by the Internal Revenue Service; or

- The employer is a nonprofit research organization or governmental research organization that is primarily engaged in basic research and/or applied research. "Nonprofit organization or entity" means the organization or entity is:
  - **(a)** Defined as a tax exempt organization under the Internal Revenue Code of 1986, section 501(c)(3), (c)(4), or (c)(6); 26 U.S.C. 501(c)(3), (c)(4), or (c)(6), and
  - **(b)** Has been approved as a tax exempt organization for research or educational purposes by the Internal Revenue Service.

  A government research organization is a U.S. Federal government entity whose primary mission is the performance or promotion of basic research and/or applied research; or
- This petition is the second or subsequent request for an extension of stay filed by the employer regardless of when the first extension of stay was filed or whether the **$1,500.00** or **$750.00** filing fee was paid on the initial petition or the first extension of stay; or
- This petition is an amended petition that does not contain any requests for extension of stay filed by the employer; or
- This petition is to correct a USCIS error; or
- The employer is a primary or secondary education institute; or
- The employer is a nonprofit entity which engages in an established curriculum-related clinical training or students register at the institution.

What evidence is required under Part B?

U.S. employers claiming exemption from payment of the **$1,500.00** or **$750.00** filing fee on the basis of status as **(a)** a nonprofit organization or entity related to, or affiliated with an institution of higher education, or **(b)** as a nonprofit research organization must submit evidence of tax exempt status under the Internal Revenue Code of 1986, section 501(c)(3), (4), or (6), 26 U.S.C. 501(c)(3), (c)(4), or (c)(6); or

All other U.S. employers claiming exemption from payment of the **$1,500.00** or **$750.00** filing fee must submit a statement describing why the organization or entity is exempt.

Completing Part C of the Supplemental Form.

All U.S. employers must complete **Part C** even if they are not claiming the fee exemption in **Part B**.

H-2A.

An H-2A is an alien coming temporarily to engage in temporary or seasonal agricultural employment.

Write **H-2A** in the classification block on the petition.

The petition must be filed by a U.S. employer or an association of U.S. agricultural producers named as a joint employer on the certification. The petition must be submitted with:

- A single valid temporary agricultural labor certification or, if U.S. workers do not appear at the work-site, a copy of the U.S. Department of Labor's denial of a certification and appeal, and evidence showing that qualified domestic labor is unavailable; and
- Copies of evidence showing that each named alien met the minimum job requirements stated in the certification at time the application was filed.

H-2B.

An H-2B is an alien coming temporarily to engage in non-agricultural employment that is seasonal, intermittent, to meet a peak load need, or a one-time occurrence.

Write **H-2B** in the classification block on the petition.

The petition must be filed by a U.S. employer with either:

- A temporary labor certification from the U.S. Department of Labor, or the Governor of Guam if the proposed employment is solely in Guam, stating that qualified U.S. workers are not available and that employment of the alien will not adversely affect the wages and working conditions of similarly employed U.S. workers; or
- A notice from such authority that the temporary labor certification cannot be made, along with evidence of the unavailability of U.S. workers and of the prevailing wage rate for the occupation in the United States, and evidence overcoming each reason why the certification was not granted; and
- Copies of evidence, such as employment letters and training certificates, showing that each named alien met the minimum job requirements stated in the certification at the time the application was filed.

NOTE: Employers filing H-2B petitions for employment to commence on or after October 1, 2005 must submit an additional fee of **$150.00**. The Save Our Small and Seasonal Businesses Act of 2005 authorized this **$150.00** Fraud Prevention and Detection Fee.

NOTE: For additional information see the U.S. Department of Labor Internet website at **www.ows.doleta.gov/foreign**.

H-3. (Two types)

An H-3 is an alien coming temporarily to participate in a special education training program in the education of children with physical, mental or emotional disabilities.

Write **H-3** in the classification block on the petition.

Custodial care of the children must be incidental to the training program. The petition must be filed by the U.S. employer with:

- A description of the training, staff and facilities, evidence that the program meets the above conditions, and details of the alien's participation in the program; and
- Evidence showing that the alien is nearing completion of a baccalaureate degree in special education, or already holds such a degree or has extensive prior training and experience in teaching children with physical, mental or emotional disabilities.

An H-3 is also an alien coming temporarily to receive training from an employer in any field other than graduate education or training.

Write **H-3** in the classification block on the petition.

The petition must be filed by the U.S. employer with:

- A detailed description of the structured training program, including the number of classroom hours per week and the number of hours of on-the-job training per week;
- A summary of the prior training and experience of each alien in the petition; and
- An explanation stating why the training is required, whether similar training is available in the alien's country, how the training will benefit the alien in pursuing a career abroad, and why the petitioner will incur the cost of providing the training without significant productive labor.

L-1A.

Write **L-1A** in the classification requested block on the petition.

An L-1A is an alien coming temporarily to perform services in a managerial or executive capacity for the same corporation or firm, or for the branch, subsidiary or affiliate of the employer who employed him or her abroad for one continuous year within the three-year period (six months within the previous three years if the employer is eligible and has filed for a blanket L-1 approval and meets the requirements for expedited processing), immediately preceding the filing of the petition, in an executive, managerial or specialized knowledge capacity.

L-1B.

Write **L-1B** in the classification requested block on the petition.

An L-1B is an alien coming temporarily to perform services that entail specialized knowledge for the same corporation or firm, or for the branch, subsidiary or affiliate of the employer that employed him or her abroad for one continuous year within the three-year period (six months within the previous three years if the employer is eligible and has filed for a blanket L-1 approval and meets the requirements for expedited processing), immediately preceding the filing of the petition, in an executive, managerial or specialized knowledge capacity. Specialized knowledge is special knowledge of the employer's product or its application in international markets or an advanced level of the knowledge of the employer's processes and procedures.

L Petition Requirements.

A U.S. employer or foreign employer must file the petition, but a foreign employer must have a legal business entity in the United States. The petition must be submitted with:

- Evidence of the qualifying relationship between the United States and foreign employer, based on ownership and control, such as an annual report, articles of incorporation, financial statements or copies of stock certificates;
- A letter from the alien's foreign qualifying employer detailing his or her dates of employment, job duties, qualifications and salary; and
- A description of the proposed job duties and qualifications, and evidence showing that the proposed employment is in an executive, managerial or specialized knowledge capacity.

If the alien is coming to the United States to open a new office, also file the petition with copies of evidence showing that the business entity is located in the United States; and

- Already has sufficient premises to house the new office;
- Has or upon establishment will have the qualifying relationship to the foreign employer; and
- Has the financial ability to remunerate the alien and to begin doing business in the United States, including evidence about the size of the U.S. investment, the organizational structure of both firms, the financial size and condition of the foreign employer, and if the alien is coming as an L-1 manager or executive to open a new office, such evidence must establish that the intended U.S. operation will support the executive or managerial position within one year.

Blanket L Petition.

An L blanket petition simplifies the process of later filing for individual L-1A workers and L-1B workers who are specialized knowledge professionals employed in positions requiring the theoretical and practical application of a body of highly specialized knowledge to fully perform the occupation and requiring also completion of a specific course of education, culminating in a baccalaureate degree in a specific occupational specialty.

A blanket L petition must be filed by a U.S. employer who will be the single representative between USCIS and the qualifying organizations.

Write **LZ** in the classification requested block. Do not name an individual employee. File the petition with copies of evidence showing that:

- You and your branches, subsidiaries and affiliates are engaged in commercial trade or services;
- You have an office in the United States that has been doing business for one year or more;
- You have three or more domestic and foreign branches, subsidiaries or affiliates; and
- You and your qualifying organizations have obtained approved petitions for at least ten "L" managers, executives or specialized knowledge professionals during the previous 12 months or have U.S. subsidiaries or affiliates with combined annual sales of at least 25 million dollars; or
- You have a U.S. work force of at least 1,000 employees.

After approval of a blanket petition, you may file for individual employees to enter as an L-1A alien or L-1B specialized knowledge professional under the blanket petition. If the alien is outside the United States, file Form I-129S, Nonimmigrant Petition Based on Blanket L Petition. If the alien is already in the United States, file the Form I-129 to request a change of status based on this blanket petition. The petition must be submitted with:

- A copy of the USCIS approval notice for the blanket petition;
- A letter from the alien's foreign qualifying employer detailing his or her dates of employment, job duties, qualifications and salary for the three previous years; and
- If the alien is a specialized knowledge professional, a copy of a U.S. degree or a foreign degree equivalent to a U.S. degree.

O-1A.

An O-1A is an alien coming temporarily who has extraordinary ability in the sciences, education, business or athletics (not including the arts, motion picture or television industry).

Write **O-1A** in the classification block on the petition. The petition must be submitted with:

- A written consultation from a peer group or labor management organization with expertise in the field. If the above item cannot be obtained, the consultation can be from a person of your (the employer's) choosing with expertise in the alien's area of ability (see **General Evidence**);
- A copy of any written contract between you (the employer) and the alien or a summary of the terms of the oral agreement under which the alien will be employed;
- An explanation of the nature of the events or activities, the beginning and ending dates for the events or activities, and a copy of any itinerary for the events and activities.
- Evidence of the alien's extraordinary ability, such as receipt of major awards or prizes, major published material by the alien or relating to the alien's work, evidence of the alien's contributions to the field, evidence of the alien's original scholarly work or contributions to the field, evidence of the alien's high salary within the field, evidence that the alien participated on a panel, judging the work of others in the field, or evidence of the alien's prior employment in one or more critical capacities.

NOTE: If the preceding forms of evidence do not readily apply to the alien's field of endeavor, you may submit other comparable evidence.

O-1B.

An O-1B is an alien coming temporarily who has extraordinary ability in the arts or extraordinary achievement in the motion picture or television industry.

Write **O-1B** in the classification block on the petition. The petition must be submitted with:

- A written consultation from a peer group or a person of your (the employer's) choosing with expertise in the alien's area of ability (see **General Evidence**). If the petition is based on the alien's extraordinary achievement in the motion picture or television industry, separate consultations are required from the relevant labor and management organizations;
- A copy of any written contract between you (the employer) and the alien or a summary of the terms of the oral agreement under which the alien will be employed;
- Evidence that the alien has received or been nominated for significant national or international awards or prizes in the field, such as an Academy Award, Emmy, Grammy or Director's Guild Award, or at least three of the following:
  - -- Evidence that the alien has performed or will perform as a lead or starring participant in productions or events that have a distinguished reputation;
  - -- Evidence that the alien has achieved national or international recognition for achievements in the field;
  - -- Evidence that the alien has a record of major commercial or critically acclaimed successes, as evidenced by ratings, box office receipts, etc.;

-- Evidence that the alien has received significant recognition from organizations, critics, government agencies or other recognized experts;

-- Evidence that the alien commands or will command a high salary or other remuneration for services in relation to others in the field; or

-- Evidence that the alien has performed in a lead or starring role for organizations that have a distinguished reputation.

NOTE: If the preceding forms of evidence do not readily apply to the alien's field of endeavor, you may submit other comparable evidence.

O-2.

An O-2 is an alien coming temporarily, solely as an essential and integral part of the artistic or athletic performance of an O-1 artist or athlete because he or she performs support services that are essential to the successful performance of the O-1. No test of the U.S. labor market is required.

Write **O-2** in the classification block on the petition.

This form must be filed in conjunction with an O-1 petition and submitted with:

- A written consultation (see **General Evidence**);
  - -- If it is for support of an athlete or an alien with extraordinary ability in the arts, the consultation must be from an appropriate labor organization; or
  - -- If it is for support of an alien with extraordinary achievement in motion pictures or television, the consultation must be from an appropriate labor organization and management organization.
- Evidence of the current essentiality, skills and experience of the O-2 with the O-1. In the case of a specific motion picture or television production, the evidence must establish that significant production has taken place outside the United States and that the continuing participation of the alien is essential to the successful completion of the production.

P-1A.

A P-1A is an alien coming temporarily, to perform at a specific athletic competition as an individual or as part of a group or team participating at an internationally recognized level of performance.

Write **P-1A** in the classification block on the petition. The petition must be submitted with:

- A written consultation (see **General Evidence**) with an appropriate labor organization;
- A copy of the contract with a major U.S. sports league or team or a contract in an individual sport commensurate with national or international recognition in the sport, if such contracts are normally utilized in the sport;
- Evidence of at least two of the following:
  - -- Substantial participation in a prior season with a major U.S. sports league;
  - -- Participation in international competition with a national team;
  - -- Substantial participation in a prior season for a U.S. college or university in intercollegiate competition;
  - -- A written statement from an official of a major U.S. sports league or official of the governing body for a sport that details how the alien or team is internationally recognized;
  - -- That the individual or team is ranked, if the sport has international rankings; or
  - -- That the alien or team has received a significant honor or award in the sport.

P-1B.

A P-1B is an alien entertainer coming temporarily to perform as a member of a foreign-based entertainment group, that has been recognized internationally as outstanding in the discipline for a substantial period of time, and who has had a sustained relationship (ordinarily for at least one year) with the group.

Write **P-1B** in the classification block on the petition. The petition must be submitted with:

- A written consultation (see **General Evidence**) from an appropriate labor organization;
- Evidence that the alien or group is internationally recognized in the discipline as demonstrated by the submission of evidence of the group's receipt or nomination for significant international awards or prizes for outstanding achievement, or evidence of at least three of the following:
  - -- The alien or group has performed or will perform as a starring or leading group in productions or events with a distinguished reputation;
  - -- The alien or group has achieved international recognition and acclaim for outstanding achievement in the field;
  - -- The alien or group has a record of major commercial or critically acclaimed success;

- -- The alien or group has received significant recognition for achievements from critics, organizations, government agencies or other recognized experts in the field; or
- -- The alien or group commands a high salary or other substantial remuneration for services, compared to other similarly situated in the field.

NOTE:

- By filing for a P-1 group, the petitioner certifies that the group has been established and performing regularly for a period of at least one year, and that at least 75 percent of the members of the group have been performing with the group for at least one year. This one-year period requirement does not apply to circus groups coming to perform with nationally recognized circuses.
- Use the "Supplementary Information" form to request a waiver of:
  - -- The one-year relationship requirement and the international recognition requirement based on emergent circumstances, or
  - -- The international recognition requirement because the group has been recognized nationally as outstanding in its discipline for a substantial period of time.

P-2.

A P-2 is an alien coming temporarily to perform as an artist or entertainer, individually or as part of a group, under a reciprocal exchange program between an organization in the United States and an organization in another country.

Write **P-2** in the classification block on the petition.

The petition must be filed by the sponsoring organization or U.S. employer with:

- A written consultation (see **General Evidence**) from an appropriate labor organization;
- A copy of the reciprocal exchange program;
- A statement from the sponsoring organization describing the reciprocal agreement as it relates to the petition;
- Evidence that the alien and the U.S. artist or group have comparable skills and that the terms of employment are similar; and
- Evidence that an appropriate labor organization in the United States was involved in negotiating or concurred with the exchange.

P-3.

A P-3 is an alien coming temporarily to perform, teach or coach, individually or as part of a group, in the arts or entertainment fields in a program that is culturally unique.

Write **P-3** in the classification block on the petition. The petition must be submitted with:

A written consultation (see **General Evidence**) from an appropriate labor organization;

Evidence that all performances will be culturally unique; and **either**

Affidavits, testimonials or letters from recognized experts attesting to the authenticity of the alien's or group's skills in presenting, coaching or teaching art forms; **or**

Documentation that the performance of the alien or group is culturally unique as evidenced by actual reviews in newspapers, journals or other published material.

Essential Support Personnel.

Accompanying support personnel are highly skilled aliens coming temporarily as an essential and integral part of the competition or performance of a principal P-1, P-2 or P-3, or because they perform support services that are essential to the successful performance or services of the principal P-1, P-2 or P-3. The accompanying personnel must have prior experience or critical skills with the principal P-1, P-2 or P-3. The petition must be filed in conjunction with a principal P-1, P-2 or P-3 petition.

Write **P-1S, P-2S** or **P-3S** as appropriate in the classification block on the petition.

The petition must be submitted with:

- A written consultation (see **General Evidence**) from an appropriate labor organization;
- A statement describing the alien's critical skills and prior experience with the principal P-1, P-2 or P-3;
- Statements or affidavits from persons with first hand knowledge that the alien has had substantial experience performing the critical skills and essential support services for the principal P-1, P-2 or P-3;
- A copy of any written contract between the employer and the alien or a summary of the terms of the oral agreement under which the alien will be employed.

Q-1.

A Q-1 is an alien coming temporarily to participate in an international cultural exchange program for sharing the attitude, customs, history, heritage, philosophy and/or traditions of the alien's country of nationality.

The culture sharing must take place in a school, museum, business or other establishment where the public, or a segment of the public sharing a common cultural interest, is exposed to aspects of a foreign culture as part of a structured program.

The work component of the program may not be independent of the cultural component, but must serve as the vehichle to achieve the objectives of the cultural component. An employer (U.S. or foreign firm, corporation, non-profit organization, or other legal entity) or its designated agent may file the petition. If a designated agent is filing the petition, that agent must be employed by the qualified employer on a permanent basis in an executive or managerial capacity and must be either a U.S. citizen or lawful permanent resident. Write **Q-1** in the classification block on the petition.

The petition must be submitted with evidence showing that the employer:

- Maintains an established international cultural exchange program;
- Has designated a qualified employee to administer the program and serve as liaison with USCIS;
- Is actively doing business in the United States;
- Will offer the alien wages and working conditions comparable to those accorded local domestic workers similarly employed;
- Has the financial ability to remunerate the participant(s).

To illustrate an established international cultural exchange program, submit program documentation, such as catalogs, brochures or other types of material.

To demonstrate financial ability to remunerate the participant (s), submit your organization's most recent annual report, business income tax return or other form of certified accountant's report.

However, if the proposed dates of employment are within 15 months of the approval of a prior Q-1 petition filed by you for the same international cultural exchange program, and that earlier petition was filed with the above evidence of the program, you may submit a copy of the approval notice for that prior petition in lieu of the evidence about the program required above.

2. Petition only required for an alien in the U.S. to change status or extend stay.

The following classifications listed in this **Section 2** do not require a petition for new employment if the alien is outside the United States. The alien should instead contact a U.S. embassy or consulate for information about a visa or admission.

Use this Form I-129 when the beneficiary is physically present in the United States and a change of status, concurrent employment, or an extension of stay is needed. Note, however, that the beneficiary must maintain legal status in the United States to remain eligible for the benefit sought.

Change of Status: A petition for change of status to one of the classifications described in this Section must be submitted with the initial evidence detailed below and with the initial evidence required by the separate instructions for all petitions involving change of status.

Extension of Stay: A petition for an extension of stay must be filed with the initial evidence listed below and with the initial evidence required by the separate instructions for all petitions for extension. However, a petition for an extension based on unchanged, previously approved employment need only be filed with the initial evidence required by the separate extension of stay instructions.

E-1.

An E-1 is a national of a country with which the United States maintains a qualifying treaty, who is coming to the United States to carry on substantial trade principally between the United States and the alien's country of nationality.

Qualifying trade involves the commercial exchange of goods or services in the international market place. Substantial trade is an amount of trade sufficient to ensure continuous flow of international trade items between the United States and the treaty country. Principal trade exists when over 50 percent of the E-1's total volume of international trade is conducted between United States and the treaty country.

E-2.

An E-2 is a national of a country with which the United States maintains a qualifying treaty, who is coming to the United States to develop and direct the operations of an enterprise in which he or she has invested or is actively in the process of investing a substantial amount of capital.

An E-2 must demonstrate possession and control of funds and the ability to develop and direct the investment enterprise. Capital in the process of being invested or that has been invested must be placed at risk and irrevocably committed to the enterprise. The enterprise must be a real, active, and operating commercial or entrepreneurial undertaking, which produces services or goods for profit. The investment must be substantial and the enterprise must be more than marginal.

E-1 or E-2.

An employee of an **E-1** or an **E-2** who possesses the same nationality may respectively be classified as E-1 or E-2. The employee must principally and primarily perform executive or supervisory duties or possess special qualifications that are essential to the successful or efficient operation of the enterprise.

E Petition Requirements.

The petition must be filed with evidence of:

- Ownership and Nationality, including but not limited to lists of investors with current status and nationality, stock certificates, certificate of ownership issued by the commercial section of a foreign embassy and reports from a certified personal accountant;

- Substantial Trade (E-1), including but not limited to copies of three or more of the following: bills of lading, customs receipts, letter of credit, trade brochures, purchase orders, insurance papers, documenting commodities imported, carrier inventories and/or sales contracts;
- Substantial Investment (E-2), including but not limited to copies of partnership agreements (with a statement on proportionate ownership), articles of incorporation, payments for the rental of business premises or office equipment, business licenses, stock certificates, office inventories (goods and equipment purchased for the business), insurance appraisals, annual reports, net worth statements from certified professional accountants, advertising invoices, business bank accounts containing funds for routine operations, funds held in escrow; or
- Executive or Supervisory Duties, or Special Qualifications Essential to the Enterprise (E-1 Employee or E-2 Employee), including but not limited to certificates, diplomas or transcripts, letters from employers describing job titles, duties, operators' manuals, and the required level of education and knowledge.

R-1.

An R-1 is an alien who for at least two years has been a member of a religious denomination having a bona fide nonprofit, religious organization in the United States, coming temporarily to work solely:

- As a minister of that denomination;
- In a professional capacity in a religious vocation or occupation for that organization; or
- In a religious vocation or, occupation for the organization or its nonprofit affiliate.

Write **R-1** in the classification block on the petition.

The petition must be filed by a U.S. employer with the following documentation:

- A copy of the tax-exempt certificate showing the religious organization, and any affiliate that will employ the person, is a bona fide nonprofit religious organization in the United States and is exempt from taxation in accordance with section 501(c)(3) of the Internal Revenue Code of 1986 relating to religious organizations, or documents as is required by the Internal Revenue Service to establish eligibility for this tax exempt status.
- A letter or letters from the authorizing official of the religious denomination or organization that will be employing the alien or engaging the alien's services in the United States establishing that:
  - -- If the alien's religious membership was maintained in whole or in part outside the United States, the foreign and U.S. religious organizations belong to the same denomination;
  - -- Immediately prior to the filing of the petition or application for admission to the United States, the alien has been a member in the religious denomination for at least two years;
- As appropriate:
  - -- If the alien is a minister, he or she is authorized to conduct religious worship services for that denomination and to perform other duties usually performed by members of the clergy of that denomination, including a detailed description of those duties;
  - -- If the alien is a religious professional, he or she has at least a U.S. baccalaureate degree or its foreign equivalent and that at least such a degree is required for entry into the religious profession; or
  - -- If the alien is to work in another religious vocation or occupation, he or she is qualified in the religious vocation or occupation.
- The arrangements made, if any, for remuneration for services rendered by the alien, the amount and source of any salary, a description of any other types of remuneration to be received, and a statement whether such remuneration shall be in exchange for services rendered;
- The name and location of the specific organizational unit of the religious organization for which the alien will be providing services within the United States; and
- If the alien is to work in a non-ministerial and non-professional capacity for a bona fide organization that is affiliated with a religious denomination, evidence of the existence of the affiliation.

Change of Status.

In addition to the initial evidence for the classification you are requesting, a petition requesting a change of status for an alien in the United States must be submitted with a copy of the employee's(s) Form I-94, Nonimmigrant Arrival/Departure Record.

NOTE: Family members should use Form I-539, Application to Change/Extend Nonimmigrant Status, to apply for a change of status.

A nonimmigrant, who must have a passport to be admitted, must keep that passport valid during his or her entire stay. If a required passport is not valid, include a full explanation with your petition.

The following nonimmigrants are **not eligible** to change status:

- An alien admitted under a visa waiver program;
- An alien in transit (C) or in transit without a visa (TWOV);
- A crewman (D);

- A fiancé(e) (K-1) or his or her dependent (K-2);
- A J-1 exchange visitor whose status was for the purpose of receiving graduate medical training (unless a waiver has been granted under section 214(l) of the Immigration and Nationality Act);
- A J-1 exchange visitor subject to the foreign residence requirement who has not received a waiver of that requirement; and
- An M-1 student to an H classification, if training received as an M-1 helped him or her qualify for H classification.

Change of status to Free Trade nonimmigrants.

A Free Trade Nonimmigrant is a citizen of Canada or Mexico coming to the United States as a TN or a citizen from Chile or Singapore coming to the U.S. as an H-1B1 Free Trade Nonimmigrant temporarily under the provisions of a Free Trade Agreement. A qualified employer may file this Form I-129 for a citizen of one of the above countries if that citizen has already been admitted to the United States in a nonimmigrant category eligible for change of status. Along with the Form I-129 and related supplement (Nonimmigrant classification based on a Free Trade Agreement Supplement), petitioners for Chile or Singapore H-1B1 nonimmigrants must also file the H-1Band H-1B1 Data Collection and Filing Fee Exemption Supplement to ensure accurate fee and data collection.

NOTE: Canadian or Mexican TN nonimmigrants can be petitioned for by either a U.S. employer or a foreign employer. However, for Chile or Singapore H-1B1 nonimmigrants, the petitioner must be a U.S. employer.

In addition to the required information noted above under **"Change of Status,"** submit the following:

- A letter from the employer stating the activity to be engaged in, the anticipated length of stay and the arrangements for remuneration;
- Evidence that the alien meets the educational and/or licensing requirements for the profession or occupation (including, for citizens of Chile, the post-secondary certificate for Agricultural Managers and Physical Therapists that is accepted by the U.S. Department of State if the citizen of Chile is receiving a nonimmigrant free trade visa overseas);
- For citizens of Chile and Singapore, a U.S. Department of Labor issued certified labor condition application.

Extension of Stay.

Extension of stay for all except Free Trade nonimmigrants.

A petition requesting an extension of stay for an employee in the United States must be filed with a copy of the employee's Form 1-94, Nonimmigrant Arrival/Departure Record, and a letter from the petitioner explaining the reasons for the extension. Consult the regulations relative to the specific nonimmigrant classification sought.

NOTE: Family members should use Form I- 539 to file for an extension of stay.

A nonimmigrant, who must have a passport to be admitted, must keep that passport valid during his or her entire stay. If a required passport is not valid, include a full explanation with your petition. Where there has been a change in the circumstances of employment, submit also the evidence required for a new petition.

Where there has been no change in the circumstances of employment, file your petition with the appropriate supplement and with your letter describing the continuing employment, and:

- If the petition is for H-1B status, submit an approved labor condition application for the specialty occupation valid for the period of time requested.
- If the petition is for H-2A status, submit a labor certification valid for the dates of the extension, unless it is based on a continuation of employment authorized by the approval of a previous petition filed with a certification, and the extension will last no longer than the previously authorized employment and no longer than two weeks.
- If the petition is for H-2B status, submit a labor certification valid for the dates of the extension.

Extension of Free Trade stay.

NOTE: Canadian or Mexican TN nonimmigrants can be petitioned for by either a U.S. employer or a foreign employer. However, for Chile or Singapore H-1B1 nonimmigrants, the petitioner must be a U.S. employer.

An employer requesting an extension of stay for an alien with a nonimmigrant classification based on a Free Trade Agreement should follow the above instructions. Submit with your extension request:

-- A letter describing the continuing employment,

-- The newly requested length of stay,

-- Continued valid licensing if required by the profession and/or the State, and

-- In the case of a Chile or Singapore H-1B1 Free Trade Nonimmigrant, a currently valid labor condition attestation.

Along with the Form I-129 and related supplement (Nonimmigrant classification based on a Free Trade Agreement Supplement), petitioners for Chile or Singapore H-1B1 nonimmigrants must also file the H-1B Data Collection and Filing Fee Exemptions Supplement to ensure accurate fee and data collection.

If the extension is for a Chile or Singapore H-1B1 Free Trade Nonimmigrant and it is the sixth consecutive extension request for that person, a statement to that effect must be provided.

Form I-129 Instructions (Rev. 04/01/06)Y Page 12

General Evidence.

Written consultation. Noted classifications require a written consultation with a recognized peer group, union and/or management organization regarding the nature of the work to be done and the alien's qualifications, before the petition may be approved.
To obtain timely adjudication of a petition, you should obtain a written advisory opinion from an appropriate peer group, union and/or management organization and submit it with the petition.

If you file a petition without the advisory opinion, you should send a copy of the petition and all supporting documents to the appropriate organization when you file the petition with USCIS, and name that organization in the petition.

Explain to the organization that USCIS will contact them for an advisory opinion. If an accepted organization does not issue an advisory opinion within a given time period, a decision will be made based upon the evidence of record.

If you do not know the name of an appropriate organization with which to consult, please indicate so on the petition. However, be advised that a petition filed without the actual advisory opinion will require substantially longer processing time.

Translations. Any foreign language document must be accompanied by a full English translation that the translator has certified as complete and correct, and by the translator's certification that he or she is competent to translate the foreign language into English.

Copies. If these instructions state that a copy of a document may be filed with this petition and you choose to send us the original, we may keep that original for our records.

Liability for Return Transportation.

The Immigration and Nationality Act makes a petitioner liable for the reasonable cost of return transportation for an H-1B, H-2B, O and P alien who is dismissed before the end of the authorized employment.

When to File.

Generally, a Form I-129 petition may not be filed more than six months prior to the date employment is scheduled to begin. Petitioners should review the appropriate regulatory provisions in 8 CFR which relate to the nonimmigrant classification sought.

File the petition as soon as possible before the proposed employment begins or before an extension of stay will be required. If the petition is not submitted at least 45 days before the employment begins, petition processing and subsequent visa issuance may not be completed before the alien's services are required or previous employment authorization ends.

Where to File.

Mail your Form I-129 to the following address (unless the beneficiary is seeking **L-1** admission under the North American Free Trade Agreement.) See instructions below.

USCIS Vermont Service Center
75 Lower Welden Street
St. Albans, VT 05479

If the alien is seeking admission as an **L-1** under NAFTA, the petion should be filed in person at the port of entry upon arrival in the United States.

Fee.

The basc fee for this petition is **$190.00**.

A U.S. employer filing a **$190.00** form I-129 for an H-1B nonimmigrant or for a Chile or Singapore H-1B1 Free Trade Nonimmigrant must submit the **$190.00** petition filing fee and, unless exempt under Part B of the H-1B Data Collection and Filing Fee Exemption Supplement, an additional fee of either **$1,500.00** or **$750.00**.

A U.S. employer with a total of 25 or less full-time equivalent employees in the United States (including any affiliate or subsidiary of the employer) is only obligated to pay the **$750.00** fee.

A U.S. employer filing a Form I-129 who is required to pay the additional fee may make the payment in the form of a single check or money order for the total amount due or as two checks or money orders, one for the additional fee and one for the petition fee.

NOTE: H-1B and L-1 petitioners required to pay the **$500.00** Fraud Prevention and Detection Fee mandated by the H-1B Visa Reform Act of 2004 must submit a check or money order separate from the additional fee and petition fee. Petitioners for Chile or Singapore H-1B1 Free Trade Nonnimmigrants do not have to pay this fee.

NOTE: Employers filing H-2B petitions for employment to commence on or after October 1, 2005 must submit an additional fee of **$150.00**. The Save Our Small and Seasonal Businesses Act of 2005 authorized this **$150.00** Fraud Prevention and Detection Fee.

The fee must be submitted in the exact amount. It cannot be refunded. **Do not mail cash.** All checks and money orders must be drawn on a bank or other institution located in the United States and must be payable in U.S. currency. The check or money order must be made payable to the **Department of Homeland Security**, except that:

- If you live in Guam and are filing this petition there, make your check or money order payable to the "Treasurer, Guam."

- If you live in the U.S. Virgin Islands and are filing this petition there, make your check or money order payable to the "Commissioner of Finance of the Virgin Islands."

When preparing the check or money order, spell out Department of Homeland Security. Do not use the initials "DHS" or "USDHS."

Checks are accepted, subject to collection. An uncollected check will render the petition and any document issued invalid. A charge of $30.00 will be imposed if a check in payment of a fee is not honored by the bank on which it is drawn.

How to check if the fee is correct. The fee on this form is current as of the publication date appearing in the lower right corner of this page. However, because USCIS fees change periodically, you can verify if the fee is correct by following one of the steps below.

- Visit our website at **www.usics.gov** and scroll down to "Forms and E-Filing" to check the appropriate fee, or
- Review the Fee Schedule included in your form package, if you called us to request the form, or
- Telephone our National Customer Service Center at **1-800-375-5283** and ask for the fee information.

Processing Information.

Any petition that is not signed or accompanied by the correct fee, will be rejected with a notice that the petition is deficient. You may correct the deficiency and resubmit the petition. A petition is not considered properly filed until accepted by USCIS.

Initial processing. Once a petition has been accepted, it will be checked for completeness, including submission of the required initial evidence. If you do not completely fill out the form, or file it without required initial evidence, you will not establish a basis for eligibility and we may deny your petition.

Requests for more information or interview. We may request more information or evidence, or we may request that you appear at a USCIS office for an interview. We may also request that you submit the originals of any copy. We will return these originals when they are no longer required.

Penalties.

If you knowingly and willfully falsify or conceal a material fact or submit a false document with this petition, we will deny the petition and may deny any other immigration benefit.

In addition, you will face severe penalties provided by law and may be subject to criminal prosecution.

Decision. The decision on a petition involves separate determinations of whether you have established that the alien is eligible for the requested classification based on the proposed employment, and whether he or she is eligible for any requested change of status or extension of stay. You will be notified of the decision in writing.

Privacy Act Notice.

We ask for the information on this form and associated evidence to determine if you have established eligibility for the immigration benefit you are seeking. Our legal right to ask for this information is in 8 U.S.C. 1154, 1184 and 1258. We may provide this information to other government agencies. Failure to provide this information and any requested evidence may delay a final decision or result in denial of your petition.

Information and Forms.

To order USCIS forms, call our to toll-free forms line at **1-800-870-3676**. You can also get USCIS forms and information on immigration laws, regulations and procedures by telephoning our National Customer Service Center at **1-800-375-5283** or visiting our internet website at **www.uscis.gov**.

Use InfoPass for Appointments.

As an alternative to waiting in line for assistance at your local USCIS office, you can now schedule an appointment through our internet-based system, **InfoPass**. To access the system, visit our website at **www.uscis.gov**. Use the **InfoPass** appointment scheduler and follow the screen prompts to set up your appointment. **InfoPass** generates an electronic appointment notice that appears on the screen. Print the notice and take it with you to your appointment. The notice gives the time and date of your appointment, along with the address of the USCIS office.

Paperwork Reduction Act Notice.

We try to create forms and instructions that are accurate, can be easily understood and that impose the least possible burden on you to provide us with information. Often this is difficult because some immigration laws are very complex.

The estimated average time to complete and file this petition is as follows: (1) 60 minutes to learn about the law and form; (2) 60 minutes to complete the form; and (3) 45 minutes to assemble and file the petition; for a total estimated average of 2 hours and 45 minutes per petition.

If you have comments regarding the accuracy of this estimate or suggestions for making this form simpler, you can write to the U.S. Citizenship and Immigration Services, Regulatory Management Division, 111 Massachusetts Avenue, N.W., Washington, D.C. 20529; OMB No. 1615-0009. **Do not mail your petition to this Washington, D. C. address.**

OMB No.1615-0009; Expires 05/31/08

Department of Homeland Security
U.S. Citizenship and Immigration Services

I-129, Petition for a Nonimmigrant Worker

START HERE - Please type or print in black ink.

Part 1. Information about the employer filing this petition. *If the employer is an individual, complete* ***Number 1.*** *Organizations should complete* ***Number 2.***

1. Family Name *(Last Name)* Given Name *(First Name)*

Full Middle Name Telephone No. w/Area Code ( )

2. Company or Organization Name Telephone No. w/Area Code ( )

Mailing Address: *(Street Number and Name)* Suite #

C/O: *(In Care Of)*

City State/Province

Country Zip/Postal Code E-Mail Address *(If Any)*

Federal Employer Identification # U.S. Social Security # Individual Tax #

Part 2. Information about this petition. *(See instructions for fee information.)*

1. **Requested Nonimmigrant Classification.** *(Write classification symbol):*
2. **Basis for Classification** *(Check one):*
   - **a.** ☐ New employment (including new employer filing H-1B extension).
   - **b.** ☐ Continuation of previously approved employment without change with the same employer.
   - **c.** ☐ Change in previously approved employment.
   - **d.** ☐ New concurrent employment.
   - **e.** ☐ Change of employer.
   - **f.** ☐ Amended petition.
3. If you checked **Box 2b, 2c, 2d, 2e,** or **2f**, give the petition receipt number.
4. **Prior Petition.** If the beneficiary is in the U.S. as a nonimmigrant and is applying to change and/or extend his or her status, give the prior petition or application receipt #:
5. **Requested Action.** *(Check one):*
   - **a.** ☐ Notify the office in **Part 4** so the person(s) can obtain a visa or be admitted. (**NOTE:** *a petition is not required for an E-1, E-2 or R visa*).
   - **b.** ☐ Change the person(s)' status and extend their stay since the person(s) are all now in the U.S. in another status *(see instructions for limitations)*. This is available only where you check "New Employment" in **Item 2**, above.
   - **c.** ☐ Extend the stay of the person(s) since they now hold this status.
   - **d.** ☐ Amend the stay of the person(s) since they now hold this status.
   - **e.** ☐ Extend the status of a nonimmigrant classification based on a Free Trade Agreement. *(See Free Trade Supplement for TN and H1B1 to Form I-129).*
   - **f.** ☐ Change status to a nonimmigrant classification based on a Free Trade Agreement. *(See Free Trade Supplement for TN and H1B1 to Form I-129).*
6. **Total number of workers in petition** *(See instructions relating to when more than one worker can be included):*

For USCIS Use Only

Returned	Receipt
Date	
Date	
Resubmitted	
Date	
Date	
Reloc Sent	
Date	
Date	
Reloc Rec'd	
Date	
Date	
☐ Petitioner Interviewed on ______	
☐ Beneficiary Interviewed on ______	

Class: ______
# of Workers: ______
Priority Number: ______
Validity Dates: ______
From: ______
To: ______

☐ **Classification Approved**
☐ Consulate/POE/PFI Notified
At ______
☐ Extension Granted
☐ COS/Extension Granted

Partial Approval ***(explain)***

Action Block

To Be Completed by *Attorney or Representative*, if any.
☐ Fill in box if G-28 is attached to represent the applicant.

ATTY State License #

Part 3. Information about the person(s) you are filing for. *Complete the blocks below. Use the continuation sheet to name each person included in this petition.*

1. If an Entertainment Group, Give the Group Name

Family Name *(Last Name)* | Given Name *(First Name)* | Full Middle Name

All Other Names Used *(include maiden name and names from all previous marriages)*

Date of Birth *(mm/dd/yyyy)* | U.S. Social Security # *(if any)* | A # *(if any)*

Country of Birth | Province of Birth | Country of Citizenship

2. If in the United States, Complete the Following:

Date of Last Arrival *(mm/dd/yyyy)* | I-94 # *(Arrival/Departure Document)* | Current Nonimmigrant Status

Date Status Expires *(mm/dd/yyyy)* | Passport Number | Date Passport Issued *(mm/dd/yyyy)* | Date Passport Expires *(mm/dd/yyyy)*

Current U.S. Address

Part 4. Processing Information.

1. If the person named in **Part 3** is outside the United States or a requested extension of stay or change of status cannot be granted, give the U.S. consulate or inspection facility you want notified if this petition is approved.

Type of Office *(Check one)*: ☐ Consulate ☐ Pre-flight inspection ☐ Port of Entry

Office Address *(City)* | U.S. State or Foreign Country

Person's Foreign Address

2. Does each person in this petition have a valid passport?

☐ Not required to have passport ☐ No - explain on separate paper ☐ Yes

3. Are you filing any other petitions with this one? ☐ No ☐ Yes - How many?

4. Are applications for replacement/initial I-94s being filed with this petition? ☐ No ☐ Yes - How many?

5. Are applications by dependents being filed with this petition? ☐ No ☐ Yes - How many?

6. Is any person in this petition in removal proceedings? ☐ No ☐ Yes - explain on separate paper

Form I-129 (Rev. 04/01/06)Y Page 2

Part 4. Processing Information. *(Continued)*

7. Have you ever filed an immigrant petition for any person in this petition? ☐ No ☐ Yes - explain on separate paper

8. If you indicated you were filing a new petition in **Part 2**, within the past seven years has any person in this petition:

a. Ever been given the classification you are now requesting? ☐ No ☐ Yes - explain on separate paper

b. Ever been denied the classification you are now requesting? ☐ No ☐ Yes - explain on separate paper

9. Have you ever previously filed a petition for this person? ☐ No ☐ Yes - explain on separate paper

10. If you are filing for an entertainment group, has any person in this petition not been with the group for at least one year? ☐ No ☐ Yes - explain on separate paper

Part 5. Basic information about the proposed employment and employer. *Attach the supplement relating to the classification you are requesting.*

1. Job Title

2. Nontechnical Job Description

3. LCA Case Number

4. NAICS Code

5. Address where the person(s) will work if different from address in **Part 1**. *(Street number and name, city/town, state, zip code)*

6. Is this a full-time position?

☐ No - Hours per week: ☐ Yes - Wages per week or per year:

7. Other Compensation *(Explain)*

8. Dates of intended employment *(mm/dd/yyyy)*:

From: To:

9. Type of Petitioner - *Check one*:

☐ U.S. citizen or permanent resident ☐ Organization ☐ Other - explain on separate paper

10. Type of Business

11. Year Established

12. Current Number of Employees

13. Gross Annual Income

14. Net Annual Income

Part 6. Signature. *Read the information on penalties in the instructions before completing this section.*

I certify, under penalty of perjury under the laws of the United States of America, that this petition and the evidence submitted with it is all true and correct. If filing this on behalf of an organization, I certify that I am empowered to do so by that organization. If this petition is to extend a prior petition, I certify that the proposed employment is under the same terms and conditions as stated in the prior approved petition. I authorize the release of any information from my records, or from the petitioning organization's records that U.S. Citizenship and Immigration Services needs to determine eligibility for the benefit being sought.

Signature	**Daytime Phone Number** *(Area/Country Code)*
	( )
Print Name	**Date** *(mm/dd/yyyy)*

NOTE: If you do not completely fill out this form and the required supplement, or fail to submit required documents listed in the instructions, the person(s) filed for may not be found eligible for the requested benefit and this petition may be denied.

Part 7. Signature of person preparing form, if other than above.

I declare that I prepared this petition at the request of the above person and it is based on all information of which I have any knowledge.

Signature	**Daytime Phone Number** *(Area/Country Code)*
	( )
Print Name	**Date** *(mm/dd/yyyy)*

Firm Name and Address

OMB No.1615-0009; Expires 05/31/08

Department of Homeland Security
U.S. Citizenship and Immigration Services

E Classification Supplement to Form I-129

1. Name of person or organization filing petition:

2. Name of person you are filing for:

3. Classification sought *(Check one)*:

☐ E-1 Treaty trader ☐ E-2 Treaty investor

4. Name of country signatory to treaty with U.S.:

Section 1. Information about the employer outside the United States (if any)

Employer's Name

Total Number of Employees

Employer's Address *(Street number and name, city/town, state/province, zip/postal code)*

Principal Product, Merchandise or Service

Employee's Position - Title, duties and number of years employed

Section 2. Additional information about the U.S. Employer

1. The U.S. company is to the company outside the United States *(Check one)*:

☐ Parent ☐ Branch ☐ Subsidiary ☐ Affiliate ☐ Joint Venture

2. Date and Place of Incorporation or Establishment in the United States

3. Nationality of Ownership *(Individual or Corporate)*

Name *(First/Middle/Last)*	Nationality	Immigration Status	% Ownership

4. Assets

5. Net Worth

6. Total Annual Income

7. Staff in the United States

a. How many executive and/or managerial employees does petitioner have who are nationals of the treaty country in either E or L status?

b. How many specialized qualifications or knowledge persons does the petitioner have who are nationals of the treaty country in either E or L status?

c. Provide the total number of employees in executive or managerial positions in the United States.

d. Provide the total number of specialized qualifications or knowledge persons positions in the United States.

8. Total number of employees the alien would supervise; or describe the nature of the specialized skills essential to the U.S. company.

Section 3. Complete if filing for an E-1 Treaty Trader

1. Total Annual Gross Trade/Business of the U.S. company

2. For Year Ending *(yyyy)*

3. Percent of total gross trade between the United States and the country of which the treaty trader organization is a national.

Section 4. Complete if filing for an E-2 Treaty Investor

Total Investment: Cash

Equipment

Other

Inventory

Premises

Total

OMB No.1615-0009; Expires 05/31/08

Department of Homeland Security
U.S. Citizenship and Immigration Services

Nonimmigrant Classification Based on Free Trade Agreement-Supplement to Form I-129

1. Name of person or organization filing petition:

2. Name of person you are filing for:

3. Employer is a *(Check one)*:

☐ U.S. Employer ☐ Foreign Employer

4. If Foreign Employer, name the foreign country.

Section 1. Information about requested extension or change *(See instructions attached to this form.)*

1. This is a request for an extension of Free Trade status based on *(Check one)*:

- **a.** ☐ Free Trade, Canada (TN)
- **b.** ☐ Free Trade, Chile (H1B1)
- **c.** ☐ Free Trade, Mexico (TN)
- **d.** ☐ Free Trade, Singapore (H1B1)
- **e.** ☐ Free Trade, Other
- **f.** ☐ I am an H-1B1 Free Trade Nonimmigrant from Chile or Singapore and this is my sixth consecutive request for an extension.

Or

2. This is a request for a change of nonimmigrant status to *(Check one)*:

- **a.** ☐ Free Trade, Canada (TN)
- **b.** ☐ Free Trade, Chile (H1B1)
- **c.** ☐ Free Trade, Mexico (TN)
- **d.** ☐ Free Trade, Singapore (H1B1)
- **e.** ☐ Free Trade, Other
- **f.** ☐ I am an H-1B1 Free Trade Nonimmigrant from Chile or Singapore and this is my first request for a change of status to H-1B1 within the past six years.

Part 2. Signature. *Read the information on penalties in the instructions before completing this section.*

I certify, under penalty of perjury under the laws of the United States of America, that this petition and the evidence submitted with it is all true and correct. If filing this on behalf of an organization, I certify that I am empowered to do so by that organization. If this petition is to extend a prior petition, I certify that the proposed employment is under the same terms and conditions as stated in the prior approved petition. I authorize the release of any information from my records, or from the petitioning organization's records, that the U.S. Citizenship and Immigration Services needs to determine eligibility for the benefit being sought.

Signature	**Daytime Phone Number** *(Area/Country Code)*
	( )
Print Name	**Date** *(mm/dd/yyyy)*

NOTE: If you do not completely fill out this form and the required supplement, or fail to submit required documents listed in the instructions, the person(s) filed for may not be found eligible for the requested benefit and this petition may be denied.

Part 3. Signature of person preparing form, if other than above.

I declare that I prepared this petition at the request of the above person and it is based on all information of which I have any knowledge.

Signature	**Daytime Phone Number** *(Area/Country Code)*
	( )
Print Name	**Date** *(mm/dd/yyyy)*

Firm Name and Address

OMB No.1615-0009; Expires 05/31/08

Department of Homeland Security
U.S. Citizenship and Immigration Services

H Classification Supplement to Form I-129

1. Name of person or organization filing petition:

2. Name of person or total number of workers or trainees you are filing for:

3. List the alien's and any dependent family member's prior periods of stay in H classification in the United States for the last six years. Be sure to list only those periods in which the alien and/or family members were actually in the United States in an H classification. **NOTE:** Submit photocopies of Forms I-94, I-797 and/or other USCIS issued documents noting these periods of stay in the H classification. If more space is needed, attach an additional sheet(s). (If applying for H-2A/H-2B classification skip this item.)

Subject's Name	Period of Stay *(mm/dd/yyyy)*	Subject's Name	Period of Stay *(mm/dd/yyyy)*
	From: To:		From: To:
	From: To:		From: To:

4. Classification sought *(Check one)*:

- ☐ H-1B1 Specialty occupation
- ☐ H-1B2 Exceptional services relating to a cooperative research and development project administered by the U.S. Department of Defense (DOD)
- ☐ H-1B3 Fashion model of national or international acclaim
- ☐ H-2A Agricultural worker
- ☐ H-2B Non-agricultural worker
- ☐ H-3 Trainee
- ☐ H-3 Special education exchange visitor program

Section 1. Complete this section if filing for H-1B classification.

1. Describe the proposed duties

2. Alien's present occupation and summary of prior work experience

Statement for H-1B specialty occupations only:

By filing this petition, I agree to the terms of the labor condition application for the duration of the alien's authorized period of stay for H-1B employment.

Petitioner's Signature	**Print or Type Name**	**Date** *(mm/dd/yyyy)*

Statement for H-1B specialty occupations and U.S. Department of Defense projects:

As an authorized official of the employer, I certify that the employer will be liable for the reasonable costs of return transportation of the alien abroad if the alien is dismissed from employment by the employer before the end of the period of authorized stay.

Signature of Authorized Official of Employer	**Print or Type Name**	**Date** *(mm/dd/yyyy)*

Statement for H-1B U.S. Department of Defense projects only:

I certify that the alien will be working on a cooperative research and development project or a co-production project under a reciprocal government-to-government agreement administered by the U.S. Department of Defense.

DOD Project Manager's Signature	**Print or Type Name**	**Date** *(mm/dd/yyyy)*

Section 2. Complete this section if filing for H-2A or H-2B classification.

1. Employment is: *(Check one)*

a. ☐ Seasonal **c.** ☐ Intermittent

b. ☐ Peakload **d.** ☐ One-time occurence

2. Temporary need is: *(Check one)*

a. ☐ Unpredictable **c.** ☐ Recurrent annually

b. ☐ Periodic

3. Explain your temporary need for the alien's services *(attach a separate sheet(s) paper if additional space is needed).*

Section 3. Complete this section if filing for H-2A classification.

The petitioner and each employer consent to allow government access to the site where the labor is being performed for the purpose of determining compliance with H-2A requirements. The petitioner further agrees to notify USCIS in the manner and within the time frame specified if an H-2A worker absconds, or if the authorized employment ends more than five days before the relating certification document expires, and pay liquidated damages of ten dollars ($10.00) for each instance where it cannot demonstrate compliance with this notification requirement. The petitioner agrees also to pay liquidated damages of two hundred dollars ($200.00) for each instance where it cannot be demonstrated that the H-2A worker either departed the United States or obtained authorized status during the period of admission or within five days of early termination, whichever comes first.

The petitioner must execute **Part A**. If the petitioner is the employer's agent, the employer must execute **Part B**. If there are joint employers, they must each execute **Part C**.

Part A. Petitioner:

By filing this petition, I agree to the conditions of H-2A employment and agree to the notice requirements and limited liabilities defined in 8 CFR 214.2(h)(3)(vi).

Petitioner's Signature	**Print or Type Name**	**Date** *(mm/dd/yyyy)*

Part B. Employer who is not the petitioner:

I certify that I have authorized the party filing this petition to act as my agent in this regard. I assume full responsibility for all representations made by this agent on my behalf and agree to the conditions of H-2A eligibility.

Employer's Signature	**Print or Type Name**	**Date** *(mm/dd/yyyy)*

Part C. Joint Employers:

I agree to the conditions of H-2A eligibility.

Joint Employer's Signature(s)	Print or Type Name	Date *(mm/dd/yyyy)*

Joint Employer's Signature(s)	Print or Type Name	Date *(mm/dd/yyyy)*

Joint Employer's Signature(s)	Print or Type Name	Date *(mm/dd/yyyy)*

Joint Employer's Signature(s)	Print or Type Name	Date *(mm/dd/yyyy)*

Section 4. Complete this section if filing for H-3 classification.

1. If you answer "yes" to any of the following questions, attach a full explanation.

a. Is the training you intend to provide, or similar training, available in the alien's country? ☐ No ☐ Yes

b. Will the training benefit the alien in pursuing a career abroad? ☐ No ☐ Yes

c. Does the training involve productive employment incidental to training? ☐ No ☐ Yes

d. Does the alien already have skills related to the training? ☐ No ☐ Yes

e. Is this training an effort to overcome a labor shortage? ☐ No ☐ Yes

f. Do you intend to employ the alien abroad at the end of this training? ☐ No ☐ Yes

2. If you do not intend to employ this person abroad at the end of this training, explain why you wish to incur the cost of providing this training and your expected return from this training.

OMB No.1615-0009; Expires 05/31/08

Department of Homeland Security
U.S. Citizenship and Immigration Services

H-1B Data Collection and Filing Fee Exemption Supplement

Petitioner's Name [ ]

Part A. General Information.

1. **Employer Information** - *(check all items that apply)*
   a. Is the petitioner a dependent employer? ☐ No ☐ Yes
   b. Has the petitioner ever been found to be a willful violator? ☐ No ☐ Yes
   c. Is the beneficiary an exempt H-1B nonimmigrant? ☐ No ☐ Yes
      1. If yes, is it because the beneficiary's annual rate of pay is equal to at least $60,000? ☐ No ☐ Yes
      2. Or is it because the beneficiary has a master's or higher degree in a speciality related to the employment? ☐ No ☐ Yes

2. Beneficiary' s Last Name | First Name | Middle Name
   Attention To or In Care Of | Current Residential Address - Street | Apt. #
   City | State | Zip/Postal Code
   U.S. Social Security # *(If Any)* | I-94 # *(Arrival/Departure Document)* | Previous Receipt # *(If Any)*

3. **Beneficiary's Highest Level of Education.** Please check one box below.
   ☐ NO DIPLOMA
   ☐ HIGH SCHOOL GRADUATE - high school DIPLOMA or the equivalent (example: GED)
   ☐ Some college credit, but less than one year
   ☐ One or more years of college, no degree
   ☐ Associate's degree *(for example: AA, AS)*
   ☐ Bachelor's degree *(for example: BA, AB, BS)*
   ☐ Master's degree *(for example: MA, MS, MEng, MEd, MSW, MBA)*
   ☐ Professional degree *(for example: MD, DDS, DVM, LLB, JD)*
   ☐ Doctorate degree *(for example: PhD, EdD)*

4. Major/Primary Field of Study.

5. Has the beneficiary of this petition earned a master's or higher degree from a U.S. institution of higher education as defined in 20 U.S.C. section 1001(a)?
   ☐ No ☐ Yes (If "Yes" provide the following information):
   Name of the U.S. institution of higher education | Date Degree Awarded | Type of U.S. Degree
   Address of the U.S. institution of higher education

6. Rate of Pay Per Year.
7. LCA Code.
8. NAICS Code.

Part B. Fee Exemption and/or Determination

In order for USCIS to determine if you must pay the additional $1,500 or $750 fee, please answer all of the following questions:

1. ☐ Yes ☐ No Are you an institution of higher education as defined in the Higher Education Act of 1965, section 101 (a), 20 U.S.C. section 1001(a)?

2. ☐ Yes ☐ No Are you a nonprofit organization or entity related to or affiliated with an institution of higher education, as such institutions of higher education are defined in the Higher Education Act of 1965, section 101 (a), 20 U.S.C. section 1001(a)?

3. ☐ Yes ☐ No Are you a nonprofit research organization or a governmental research organization, as defined in 8 CFR 214.2(h)(19)(iii)(C)?

4. ☐ Yes ☐ No Is this the second or subsequent request for an extension of stay that you have filed for this alien?

5. ☐ Yes ☐ No Is this an amended petition that does not contain any request for extensions of stay?

6. ☐ Yes ☐ No Are you filing this petition in order to correct a USCIS error?

7. ☐ Yes ☐ No Is the petitioner a primary or secondary education institution?

8. ☐ Yes ☐ No Is the petitioner a non-profit entity that engages in an established curriculum-related clinical training of students registered at such an institution?

If you answered "Yes" to any of the questions above, you are ONLY required to submit the fee for your H-1B Form I-129 petition, which is $185. If you answered "No" to all questions, please answer Question 9.

9. ☐ Yes ☐ No Do you currently employ a total of no more than 25 full-time equivalent employees in the United States, including any affiliate or subsidiary of your company?

If you answered "Yes" to Question 9 above, then you are required to pay an additional fee of $750. If you answered "No", then you are required to pay an additional fee of $1,500.

NOTE: On or after March 8, 2005, a U.S. employer seeking initial approval of H-1B or L nonimmigrant status for a beneficiary, or seeking approval to employ an H-1B or L nonimmigrant currently working for another U.S. employer, must submit an additional $500 fee. This additional $500 Fraud Prevention and Detection fee was mandated by the provisions of the H-1B Visa Reform Act of 2004. **There is no exemption from this fee.**

Part C. Numerical Limitation Exemption Information.

1. ☐ Yes ☐ No Are you an institution of higher education as defined in the Higher Education Act of 1965, section 101 (a), 20 U.S.C. section 1001(a)?

2. ☐ Yes ☐ No Are you a nonprofit organization or entity related to or affiliated with an institution of higher education, as such institutions of higher education are defined in the Higher Education Act of 1965, section 101 (a), 20 U.S.C. section 1001(a)?

3. ☐ Yes ☐ No Are you a nonprofit research organization or a governmental research organization, as defined in 8 CFR 214.2(h)(19)(iii)(C)?

4. ☐ Yes ☐ No Is the beneficiary of this petition a J-1 nonimmigrant alien who received a waiver of the two-year foreign residency requirement described in section 214 (l)(1)(B) or (C) of the Act?

5. ☐ Yes ☐ No Has the beneficiary of this petition been previously granted status as an H-1B nonimmigrant in the past 6 years and not left the United States for more than one year after attaining such status?

6. ☐ Yes ☐ No If the petition is to request a change of employer, did the beneficiary previously work as an H-1B for an institution of higher education, an entity related to or affiliated with an institution of higher education, or a nonprofit research organization or governmental research institution defined in questions 1, 2 and 3 of Part C of this form?

7. ☐ Yes ☐ No Has the beneficiary of this petition earned a master's or higher degree from a U.S. institution of higher education, as defined in the Higher Education Act of 1965, section 101(a), 20 U.S.C. section 1001(a)?

I certify under penalty of perjury, under the laws of the United States of America, that this attachment and the evidence submitted with it is true and correct. If filing this on behalf of an organization or entity, I certify that I am empowered to do so by that organization or entity. I authorize the release of any information from my records, or from the petitioning organization or entity's records, that U.S. Citizenship and Immigration Services may need to determine eligibility for the exemption being sought.

Certification.

Signature	**Print Name**

Title	**Date** *(mm/dd/yyyy)*

Form I-129 H-1B Data Collection Supplement (Rev. 04/01/06)Y Page 11

OMB No.1615-0009; Expires 05/31/08

Department of Homeland Security
U.S. Citizenship and Immigration Services

L Classification Supplement to Form I-129

1. Name of person or organization filing petition:

2. Name of person you are filing for:

3. This petition is *(Check one)*:

a. ☐ An individual petition **b.** ☐ A blanket petition

Section 1. Complete this section if filing for an individual petition.

1. Classification sought *(Check one):*

a. ☐ L-1A manager or executive **b.** ☐ L-1B specialized knowledge

2. List the alien's and any dependent family member's prior periods of stay in an H or L classification in the United States for the last seven years. Be sure to list only those periods in which the alien and/or family members were actually in the U.S. in an H or L classification. **NOTE:** Submit photocopies of Forms I-94, I-797 and/or other USCIS issued documents noting these periods of stay in the H or L classification. If more space is needed, attach an additional sheet(s).

Subject's Name	Period of Stay *(mm/dd/yyyy)*	
	From:	To:
	From:	To:
	From:	To:
	From:	To:
	From:	To:

3. Name of employer abroad

4. Address of employer abroad *(Street number and name, city/town, state/province, zip/postal code)*

5. Dates of alien's employment with this employer. Explain any interruptions in employment.

Dates of Employment *(mm/dd/yyyy)*		Explanation of Interruptions
From:	To:	
From:	To:	
From:	To:	

6. Description of the alien's duties for the past three years.

7. Description of the alien's proposed duties in the United States.

8. Summary of the alien's education and work experience.

1. Name of person or organization filing petition:

2. Name of person you are filing for:

Section 1. Complete this section if filing for an individual petition. *(Continued)*

9. The U.S. company is to the company abroad: *(Check one)*

a. ☐ Parent **b.** ☐ Branch **c.** ☐ Subsidiary **d.** ☐ Affiliate **e.** ☐ Joint Venture

10. Describe the stock ownership and managerial control of each company. Provide the U.S. Tax Code Number for each company.

Company stock ownership and managerial control of each company	U.S. Tax Code Number

11. Do the companies currently have the same qualifying relationship as they did during the one-year period of the alien's employment with the company abroad? ☐ Yes ☐ No *(Attach explanation)*

12. Is the alien coming to the United States to open a new office? ☐ Yes *(Attach explanation)* ☐ No

13. If you are seeking L-1B specialized knowledge status for an individual, answer the following question:

Will the beneficiary be stationed primarily offsite (at the worksite of an employer other than the petitioner or its affiliate, subsidiary, or parent)? ☐ Yes ☐ No

If you answered "Yes" to the preceding question, describe how and by whom the beneficiary's work will be controlled and supervised. Include a description of the amount of time each supervisor is expected to control and supervise the work. Use an attachment if needed.

If you answered "Yes" to the preceding question, also describe the reasons why placement at another worksite outside the petitioner, subsidiary or parent is needed. Include a description of how the beneficiary's duties at another worksite relate to the need for the specialized knowledge he or she possesses. Use an attachment if needed.

Section 2. Complete this section if filing a blanket petition.

List all U.S. and foreign parent, branches, subsidiaries and affiliates included in this petition. *(Attach a separate sheet(s) of paper if additional space is needed.)*

Name and Address	Relationship

Section 3. Fraud Prevention and Detection Fee.

As of **March 8, 2005**, a U.S. employer seeking initial approval of L nonimmigrant status for a beneficiary, or seeking approval to employ an L nonimmigrant currently working for another U.S. employer, must submit an additional **$500.00** fee. This additional **$500.00** Fraud Prevention and Detection fee was mandated by the provisions of the H-1B Visa Reform Act of 2004. **There is no exemption from this fee**. You must include payment of this **$500.00** fee with your submission of this form. Failure to submit the fee when required will result in rejection or denial of your submission.

OMB No.1615-0009; Expires 05/31/08

Department of Homeland Security
U.S. Citizenship and Immigration Services

O and P Classifications Supplement to Form I-129

1. Name of person or organization filing petition:

2. Name of person or group or total number of workers you are filing for:

3. Classification sought *(Check one)*:

a. ☐ O-1A Alien of extraordinary ability in sciences, education, business or athletics (not including the arts, motion picture or television industry.)

b. ☐ O-1B Alien of extraordinary ability in the arts or extraordinary achievement in the motion picture or television industry.

c. ☐ O-2 Accompanying alien who is coming to the U.S. to assist in the performance of the O-1.

d. ☐ P-1 Athletic/Entertainment group.

e. ☐ P-1S Essential Support Personnel for P-1.

f. ☐ P-2 Artist or entertainer for reciprocal exchange program.

g. ☐ P-2S Essential Support Personnel for P-2.

h. ☐ P-3 Artist/Entertainer coming to the United States to perform, teach or coach under a program that is culturally unique.

i. ☐ P-3S Essential Support Personnel for P-3.

4. Explain the nature of the event

5. Describe the duties to be performed

6. If filing for an O-2 or P support alien, list dates of the alien's prior experience with the O-1 or P alien

7. Have you obtained the required written consultation(s)? ☐ Yes - Attached ☐ No - Copy of request attached

If not, give the following information about the organization(s) to which you have sent a duplicate of this petition.

O-1 Extraordinary Ability

Name of Recognized Peer Group | Daytime Telephone # *(Area/Country Code)* ( )

Complete Address | Date Sent *(mm/dd/yyyy)*

O-1 Extraordinary achievement in motion pictures or television

Name of Labor Organization | Daytime Telephone # *(Area/Country Code)* ( )

Complete Address | Date Sent *(mm/dd/yyyy)*

Name of Management Organization | Daytime Telephone # *(Area/Country Code)* ( )

Complete Address | Date sent *(mm/dd/yyyy)*

O-2 or P alien

Name of Labor Organization | Daytime Telephone # *(Area/Country Code)* ( )

Complete Address | Date Sent *(mm/dd/yyyy)*

OMB No.1615-0009; Expires 05/31/08

Department of Homeland Security
U.S. Citizenship and Immigration Services

Q-1 and R-1 Classifications Supplement to Form I-129

1. Name of person or organization filing petition:

2. Name of person you are filing for:

Section 1. Complete this section if you are filing for a Q-1 international cultural exchange alien.

I hereby certify that the participant(s) in the international cultural exchange program:

- Is at least 18 years of age,
- Is qualified to perform the service or labor or receive the type of training stated in the petition,
- Has the ability to communicate effectively about the cultural attributes of his or her country of nationality to the American public, and
- Has resided and been physically present outside the United States for the immediate prior year, if he or she was previously admitted as a Q-1.

I also certify that I will offer the alien(s) the same wages and working conditions comparable to those accorded local domestic workers similarly employed.

Petitioner's signature **Date** *(mm/dd/yyyy)*

Section 2. Complete this section if you are filing for an R-1 religious worker.

1. List the alien's and any dependent family member's prior periods of stay in R classification in the United States for the last six years. Be sure to list only those periods in which the alien and/or family members were actually in the United States in an R classification. **NOTE:** Submit photocopies of Forms I-94, I-797 and/or other USCIS issued documents noting these periods of stay in the R classification. If more space is needed, attach an additional sheet(s).

Subject's Name	Period of Stay *(mm/dd/yyyy)*	Subject's Name	Period of Stay *(mm/dd/yyyy)*
	From: To:		From: To:
	From: To:		From: To:
	From: To:		From: To:

2. Describe the alien's proposed duties in the United States.

3. Describe the alien's qualifications for the vocation or occupation.

4. Description of the relationship between the religious organization in the United States and the organization abroad of which the alien was a member.

Attachment - 1

Attach to Form I-129 when more than one person is included in the petition. *(List each person separately. Do not include the person you named on the Form I-129.)*

Family Name *(Last Name)*	Given Name *(First Name)*	Full Middle Name	Date of Birth *mm/dd/yyyy*
Country of Birth	Country of Citizenship	U.S. Social Security # *(if any)*	A # *(if any)*

IF IN THE U.S.

Date of Arrival *(mm/dd/yyyy)*	I-94 # (Arrival/Departure Document)	Current Nonimmigrant Status	Date Status Expires *(mm/dd/yyyy)*
Country Where Passport Issued	Date Passport Expires *(mm/dd/yyyy)*	Date Started With Group *(mm/dd/yyyy)*	

Family Name *(Last Name)*	Given Name *(First Name)*	Full Middle Name	Date of Birth *mm/dd/yyyy*
Country of Birth	Country of Citizenship	U.S. Social Security # *(if any)*	A # *(if any)*

IF IN THE U.S.

Date of Arrival *(mm/dd/yyyy)*	I-94 # (Arrival/Departure Document)	Current Nonimmigrant Status	Date Status Expires *(mm/dd/yyyy)*
Country Where Passport Issued	Date Passport Expires *(mm/dd/yyyy)*	Date Started With Group *(mm/dd/yyyy)*	

Family Name *(Last Name)*	Given Name *(First Name)*	Full Middle Name	Date of Birth *mm/dd/yyyy*
Country of Birth	Country of Citizenship	U.S. Social Security # *(if any)*	A # *(if any)*

IF IN THE U.S.

Date of Arrival *(mm/dd/yyyy)*	I-94 # (Arrival/Departure Document)	Current Nonimmigrant Status	Date Status Expires *(mm/dd/yyyy)*
Country Where Passport Issued	Date Passport Expires *(mm/dd/yyyy)*	Date Started With Group *(mm/dd/yyyy)*	

Family Name *(Last Name)*	Given Name *(First Name)*	Full Middle Name	Date of Birth *mm/dd/yyyy*
Country of Birth	Country of Citizenship	U.S. Social Security # *(if any)*	A # *(if any)*

IF IN THE U.S.

Date of Arrival *(mm/dd/yyyy)*	I-94 # (Arrival/Departure Document)	Current Nonimmigrant Status	Date Status Expires *(mm/dd/yyyy)*
Country Where Passport Issued	Date Passport Expires *(mm/dd/yyyy)*	Date Started With Group *(mm/dd/yyyy)*	

Form I-129 Attachment - 1 (Rev. 04/01/06)Y Page 16

Attachment - 1

Attach to Form I-129 when more than one person is included in the petition. *(List each person separately. Do not include the person you named on the Form I-129.)*

Family Name *(Last Name)* | Given Name *(First Name)* | Full Middle Name | Date of Birth *mm/dd/yyyy*

Country of Birth | Country of Citizenship | U.S. Social Security # *(if any)* | A # *(if any)*

IF IN THE U.S.

Date of Arrival *(mm/dd/yyyy)* | I-94 # (Arrival/Departure Document) | Current Nonimmigrant Status | Date Status Expires *(mm/dd/yyyy)*

Country Where Passport Issued | Date Passport Expires *(mm/dd/yyyy)* | Date Started With Group *(mm/dd/yyyy)*

Family Name *(Last Name)* | Given Name *(First Name)* | Full Middle Name | Date of Birth *mm/dd/yyyy*

Country of Birth | Country of Citizenship | U.S. Social Security # *(if any)* | A # *(if any)*

IF IN THE U.S.

Date of Arrival *(mm/dd/yyyy)* | I-94 # (Arrival/Departure Document) | Current Nonimmigrant Status | Date Status Expires *(mm/dd/yyyy)*

Country Where Passport Issued | Date Passport Expires *(mm/dd/yyyy)* | Date Started With Group *(mm/dd/yyyy)*

Family Name *(Last Name)* | Given Name *(First Name)* | Full Middle Name | Date of Birth *mm/dd/yyyy*

Country of Birth | Country of Citizenship | U.S. Social Security # *(if any)* | A # *(if any)*

IF IN THE U.S.

Date of Arrival *(mm/dd/yyyy)* | I-94 # (Arrival/Departure Document) | Current Nonimmigrant Status | Date Status Expires *(mm/dd/yyyy)*

Country Where Passport Issued | Date Passport Expires *(mm/dd/yyyy)* | Date Started With Group *(mm/dd/yyyy)*

Family Name *(Last Name)* | Given Name *(First Name)* | Full Middle Name | Date of Birth *mm/dd/yyyy*

Country of Birth | Country of Citizenship | U.S. Social Security # *(if any)* | A # *(if any)*

IF IN THE U.S.

Date of Arrival *(mm/dd/yyyy)* | I-94 # (Arrival/Departure Document) | Current Nonimmigrant Status | Date Status Expires *(mm/dd/yyyy)*

Country Where Passport Issued | Date Passport Expires *(mm/dd/yyyy)* | Date Started With Group *(mm/dd/yyyy)*

EFFECTIVE APRIL 1, 2005
DIRECT MAIL INSTRUCTIONS FOR PERSONS FILING FORM I-765

If you live in one of these states or territories, please read this notice to determine your filing location: ALASKA, CALIFORNIA, IDAHO, IOWA, KANSAS, MARYLAND, MISSOURI, MONTANA, NEBRASKA, NEW MEXICO, OKLAHOMA, OREGON, TEXAS, AND WASHINGTON

AS PREVIOUSLY PUBLISHED AND REMAINS IN EFFECT - EFFECTIVE DECEMBER 1, 2004
DIRECT MAIL INSTRUCTIONS FOR PERSONS FILING FORM I-765

If you live in one of these states or territories, please read this notice to determine your filing location:

ALABAMA, ARIZONA, ARKANSAS, COLORADO, CONNECTICUT, DELAWARE, FLORIDA, GEORGIA, HAWAII, ILLINOIS, INDIANA, KENTUCKY, LOUISIANA, MAINE, MASSACHUSETTS, MICHIGAN, MINNESOTA, MISSISSIPPI, NEVADA, NEW HAMPSHIRE, NEW JERSEY, NEW YORK, NORTH CAROLINA, NORTH DAKOTA, OHIO, PENNSYLVANIA, RHODE ISLAND, SOUTH CAROLINA, SOUTH DAKOTA, TENNESSEE, UTAH, VERMONT, VIRGINIA, WEST VIRGINIA, WISCONSIN, WYOMING AS WELL AS THE DISTRICT OF COLUMBIA, GUAM, PUERTO RICO, AND THE VIRGINIA ISLANDS OF THE UNITED STATES.

The mailing address has changed for certain applicants living in the locations above, and filing under certain categories - please review the list below to determine if you should use this direct mail address.

This affects aliens residing in the locations above who are filing Form I-765, seeking employment authorization under 8 CFR 274a.12 in the following categories:

- (a)(10) - Aliens granted Withholding of Removal;
- (c)(9) - Aliens filing a family-based application for adjustment of status (Form I-485) who are presently required to file with the USCIS local office having jurisdiction over their place of residence;
- (c)(10) - Aliens applying for suspension of deportation or cancellation of removal, except those applying for NACARA 203 relief;
- (c)(11) - Aliens who are paroled into the United States temporarily for emergency reasons or the public interest;
- (c)(14) - Aliens granted deferred action, except those aliens who have been granted deferred action based upon (1) an approved Form I-360 (as a battered spouse or child of a U.S. citizen or lawful permanent resident), (2) a pending bona fide application for T nonimmigrant status, or (3) U nonimmigrant status interim relief;
- (c)(16) - Aliens who are filing for creation of record of lawful admission for permanent residence under section 249 of the Act; and
- (c)(18) - Aliens granted an Order of Supervision (except for those individuals affected by the recent U.S. Supreme Court decision, Clark v. Martinez 125 S. Ct. 716 (i.e. Mariel Cubans));

These aliens must submit their Form I-765 and all supporting evidence to the Chicago Lockbox Facility listed below.

The Direct Mail address for the aliens mentioned above seeking employment authorization is:

U.S. Citizenship and Immigration Services
P.O. Box 805887
Chicago, IL 60680-4120

Or, for non-United States Postal Service (USPS) deliveries (e.g. private couriers):

U.S. Citizenship and Immigration Services
Attn.: FBASI
427 S. LaSalle - 3rd Floor
Chicago, IL 60605-1098

Department of Homeland Security
U.S. Citizenship and Immigration Services

OMB No. 1615-0040; Expires 08/31/08

Application for Employment Authorization

OMB No. 1615-0040; Expires 08/31/08

Department of Homeland Security
U.S. Citizenship and Immigration Services

I-765, Application for Employment Authorization

Instructions

U.S. Citizenship and Immigration Services (USCIS) recommends that you retain a copy of your completed application for your records. NOTE: USCIS is comprised of offices of the former Immigration and Naturalization Service (INS).

Index

Part 1. General.

Purpose of the Application. Certain aliens who are temporarily in the United States may file a Form I-765, Application for Employment Authorization, to request an Employment Authorization Document (EAD). Other aliens who are authorized to work in the United States without restrictions should also use this form to apply to USCIS for a document evidencing such authorization. Please review **Part 2: Eligibility Categories** to determine whether you should use this form.

If you are a Lawful Permanent Resident, a Conditional Resident, or a nonimmigrant authorized to be employed with a specific employer under 8 CFR 274a.12(b), please do **not** use this form.

Definitions

Employment Authorization Document (EAD): Form I-688, Form I-688A, Form I-688B, Form I-766, or any successor document issued by USCIS as evidence that the holder is authorized to work in the United States.

Renewal EAD: an EAD issued to an eligible applicant at or after the expiration of a previous EAD issued under the same category.

Replacement EAD: an EAD issued to an eligible applicant when the previously issued EAD has been lost, stolen, mutilated, or contains erroneous information, such as a misspelled name.

Interim EAD: an EAD issued to an eligible applicant when USCIS has failed to adjudicate an application within 90 days of receipt of a properly filed EAD application or within 30 days of a properly filed initial EAD application based on an asylum application filed on or after January 4, 1995. The interim EAD will be granted for a period not to exceed 240 days and is subject to the conditions noted on the document.

Part 2. Eligibility Categories.

The USCIS adjudicates a request for employment authorization by determining whether an applicant has submitted the required information and documentation, and whether the applicant is eligible. In order to determine your eligibility, you must identify the category in which you are eligible and fill in that category in **Question 16** on the Form I-765. Enter only **one** of the following category numbers on the application form. For example, if you are a refugee applying for an EAD, you should write **"(a)(3)"** at **Question 16**.

For easier reference, the categories are subdivided as follows:

Asylee/Refugee Categories.

Refugee--(a)(3). File your EAD application with either a copy of your Form I-590, Registration for Classification as Refugee, approval letter or a copy of a Form I-730, Refugee/Asylee Relative Petition, approval notice.

Paroled as a Refugee--(a)(4). File your EAD application with a copy of your Form I-94, Departure Record.

Asylee (granted asylum)--(a)(5). File your EAD application with a copy of the INS letter, or judge's decision, granting you asylum. It is not necessary to apply for an EAD as an asylee until 90 days before the expiration of your current EAD.

Asylum Applicant (with a pending asylum application) who Filed for Asylum on or after January 4, 1995--(c)(8). (For specific instructions for applicants with pending asylum claims, see page 5).

Nationality Categories.

Citizen of Micronesia, the Marshall Islands or Palau--(a)(8). File your EAD application if you were admitted to the United States as a citizen of the Federated States of Micronesia (CFA/FSM), the Marshall Islands (CFA/MIS), or Palau, pursuant to agreements between the United States and the former trust territories.

Deferred Enforced Departure (DED) / Extended Voluntary Departure--(a)(11). File your EAD application with evidence of your identity and nationality.

Temporary Protected Status (TPS)--(a)(12). File your EAD application with Form I-821, Application for Temporary Protected Status. If you are filing for an initial EAD based on your TPS status, include evidence of identity and nationality as required by the Form I-821 instructions.

Temporary treatment benefits --(c)(19). For an EAD based on 8 CFR 244.5. Include evidence of nationality and identity as required by the Form I-821 instructions.

- Extension of TPS status: Include a copy (front and back) of your last available TPS document: EAD, Form I-94 or approval notice.
- Registration for TPS only without employment authorization : File the Form I-765, Form I-821, and a letter indicating that this form is for registration purposes only. No fee is required for the Form I-765 filed as part of TPS registration. (Form I-821 has separate fee requirements.)

NACARA Section 203 Applicants who are eligible to apply for NACARA relief with INS--(c)(10). See the instructions to Form I-881, Application for Suspension of Deportation or Special Rule Cancellation of Removal, to determine if you are eligible to apply for NACARA 203 relief with USCIS.

If you are eligible, follow the instructions below and submit your Form I-765 at the same time you file your Form I-881 application with USCIS:

- If you are filing a Form I-881 with USCIS, file your EAD application at the same time and at the same filing location. Your response to **Question 16** on the Form I-765 should be **"(c)(10)."**
- If you have already filed your I-881 application at the service center specified on the Form I-881, and now wish to apply for employment authorization, your response to **Question 16** on Form I-765 should be **"(c)(10)."** You should file your EAD application at the Service Center designated in Part 5 of these instructions.
- If you are a NACARA Section 203 applicant who previously filed a Form I-881 with USCIS, and the application is still pending, you may renew your EAD. Your response to **Question 16** on Form I-765 should be **"(c)(10)."** Submit the required fee and the EAD application to the service center designated in Part 5 of these instructions.

Dependent of TECRO E-1 Nonimmigrant--(c)(2). File your EAD application with the required certification from the American Institute in Taiwan if you are the spouse, or unmarried dependent son or daughter of an E-1 employee of the Taipei Economic and Cultural Representative Office.

Foreign Students.

F-1 Student Seeking Optional Practical Training in an Occupation Directly Related to Studies--(c)(3)(i). File your EAD application with a Certificate of Eligibility of Nonimmigrant (F-1) Student Status (Form I-20 A-B/I-20 ID) endorsed by a Designated School Official within the past 30 days.

F-1 Student Offered Off-Campus Employment under the Sponsorship of a Qualifying International Organization-- (c)(3)(ii). File your EAD application with the international organization's letter of certification that the proposed employment is within the scope of its sponsorship, and a Certificate of Eligibility of Nonimmigrant (F-1) Student Status--For Academic and Language Students (Form I-20 A-B/I-20 ID) endorsed by the Designated School Official within the past 30 days.

F-1 Student Seeking Off-Campus Employment Due to Severe Economic Hardship--(c)(3)(iii). File your EAD application with Form I-20 A-B/I-20 ID, Certificate of Eligibility of Nonimmigrant (F-1) Student Status--For Academic and Language Students, and any evidence you wish to submit, such as affidavits, that detail the unforeseen economic circumstances that cause your request, and evidence you have tried to find off-campus employment with an employer who has filed a labor and wage attestation.

J-2 Spouse or Minor Child of an Exchange Visitor--(c)(5). File your EAD application with a copy of your J-1's (principal alien's) Certificate of Eligibility for Exchange Visitor (J-1) Status (Form IAP-66). You must submit a written statement, with any supporting evidence showing, that your employment is not necessary to support the J-1 but is for other purposes.

M-1 Student Seeking Practical Training after Completing Studies--(c)(6). File your EAD application with a completed Form I-539, Application to Change/Extend Nonimmigrant Status. Form I-20 M-N, Certificate of Eligibility for Nonimmigrant (M-1) Student Status--For Vocational Students endorsed by the Designated School Official within the past 30 days.

Eligible Dependents of Employees of Diplomatic Missions, International Organizations or NATO.

Dependent of A-1 or A-2 Foreign Government Officials--(c)(1). Submit your EAD application with Form I-566, Inter-Agency Record of Individual Requesting Change/Adjustment to, or from, A or G Status; or Requesting A, G, or NATO Dependent Employment Authorization, through your diplomatic mission to the Department of State (DOS). The DOS will forward all favorably endorsed applications directly to the Nebraska Service Center for adjudication.

Dependent of G-1, G-3 or G-4 Nonimmigrant--(c)(4). Submit your EAD application with a Form I-566, Inter-Agency Record of Individual Requesting Change/Adjustment to or from A or G Status; or Requesting A, G, or NATO Dependent Employment Authorization, through your international organization to the Department of State (DOS). [In New York City, the United Nations (UN) and UN missions should submit such applications to the United States Mission to the UN (USUN).] The DOS or USUN will forward all favorably endorsed applications directly to the Nebraska Service Center for adjudication.

Dependent of NATO-1 through NATO-6--(c)(7). Submit your EAD application with Form I-566, Inter-Agency Record of Individual Requesting Change/Adjustment to, or from, A or G Status; or Requesting A, G or NATO Dependent Employment Authorization, to NATO SACLANT, 7857 Blandy Road, C-027, Suite 100, Norfolk, VA 23551-2490. NATO/SACLANT will forward all favorably endorsed applications directly to the Nebraska Service Center for adjudication.

Employment-Based Nonimmigrant Categories.

B-1 Nonimmigrant who is the personal or domestic servant of a nonimmigrant employer--(c)(17)(i). File your EAD application with:

- Evidence from your employer that he or she is a B, E, F, H, I, J, L, M, O, P, R, or TN nonimmigrant and you were employed for at least one year by the employer before the employer entered the United States or your employer regularly employs personal and domestic servants and has done so for a period of years before coming to the United States; and
- Evidence that you have either worked for this employer as a personal or domestic servant for at least one year or, evidence that you have at least one year's experience as a personal or domestic servant; and
- Evidence establishing that you have a residence abroad which you have no intention of abandoning.

B-1 Nonimmigrant Domestic Servant of a U.S. Citizen-- (c)(17)(ii). File your EAD application with:

- Evidence from your employer that he or she is a U.S. citizen; and
- Evidence that your employer has a permanent home abroad or is stationed outside the United States and is temporarily visiting the United States or the citizen's current assignment in the United States will not be longer than four 4 years; and
- Evidence that he or she has employed you as a domestic servant abroad for at least six 6 months prior to your admission to the United States.

B-1 Nonimmigrant Employed by a Foreign Airline--(c)(17)(iii). File your EAD application with a letter from the airline fully describing your duties and indicating that your position would entitle you to E nonimmigrant status except for the fact that you are not a national of the same country as the airline or because there is no treaty of commerce and navigation in effect between the United States and that country.

Spouse of an E-1/E-2 Treaty Trader or Investor--(a)(17). File your EAD application with evidence of your lawful status and evidence you are a **spouse** of a principal E-1/E-2, such as your I-94. (Other relatives or dependents of E-1/E-2 aliens who are in E status are not eligible for employment authorization and may not file under this category.)

Spouse of an L-1 Intracompany Transferee--(a)(18). File your EAD application with evidence of your lawful status and evidence you are a **spouse** of a principal L-1, such as your I-94. (Other relatives or dependents of L-1 aliens who are in L status are not eligible for employment authorization and may not file under this category.)

Family-Based Nonimmigrant Categories.

K-1 Nonimmigrant Fiance(e) of U.S. Citizen or K-2 Dependent--(a)(6). File your EAD application if you are filing within 90 days from the date of entry. This EAD cannot be renewed. Any EAD application other than for a replacement must be based on your pending application for family-based adjustment under (c)(9).

K-3 Nonimmigrant Spouse of U.S. Citizen or K-4 Dependent--(a)(9). File your EAD application along with evidence of your admission such as copies of your Form I-94, passport, and K visa.

Family Unity Program--(a)(13). File your EAD application with a copy of the approval notice, if you have been granted status under this program. You may choose to file your EAD application concurrently with your Form I-817, Application for Voluntary Departure under the Family Unity Program. USCIS may take up to 90 days from the date upon which you are granted status under the Family Unity Program to adjudicate your EAD application. If you were denied Family Unity status solely because your legalized spouse or parent first applied under the Legalization/SAW programs after May 5, 1988, file your EAD application with a new Form I-817 application and a copy of the original denial. However, if your EAD application is based on continuing eligibility under (c)(12), please refer to **Deportable Alien Granted Voluntary Departure.**

LIFE Family Unity--(a)(14). If you are applying for initial employment authorization pursuant to the Family Unity provisions of section 1504 of the LIFE Act Amendments, or an extension of such authorization, you should not be using this form. Please obtain and complete a Form I-817, Application for Family Unity Benefits. If you are applying for a replacement EAD that was issued pursuant to the LIFE Act Amendments Family Unity provisions, file your EAD application with the required evidence listed in **Part 3**.

V-1, V-2 or V-3 Nonimmigrant--(a)(15). If you have been inspected and admitted to the United States with a valid V visa, file this application along with evidence of your admission, such as copies of your Form I-94, passport, and K visa. If you have been granted V status while in the United States, file this application along with evidence of your V status, such as an approval notice. If you are in the United States but you have not yet filed an application for V status, you may file this application at the same time as you file your application for V status. USCIS will adjudicate this application after adjudicating your application for V status.

EAD Applicants Who Have Filed for Adjustment of Status.

Employment-Based Adjustment Applicant--(c)(9). File your EAD application with a copy of the receipt notice or other evidence that your Form I-485, application for permanent residence, is pending. If you have not yet filed your Form I-485, you may submit Form I-765 together with your Form I-485.

Family-Based Adjustment Application --(c)(9). File your EAD application with a clpy of the receipt notice other evidence that your Form I-485, application for permanent residence, is pending. You may file Form I-765 together with your Form I-485 is.

Adjustment Applicant Based on Continuous Residence Since January 1, 1972--(c)(16). File your EAD application with your Form I-485, Application for Permanent Residence; a copy of your receipt notice; or other evidence that the Form I-485 is pending.

Others.

N-8 or N-9 Nonimmigrant--(a)(7). File your EAD application with the required evidence listed in **Part 3**.

Granted Withholding of Deportation or Removal --(a)(10). File your EAD application with a copy of the Immigration Judge's order. It is not necessary to apply for a new EAD until 90 days before the expiration of your current EAD.

Applicant for Suspension of Deportation--(c)(10). File your EAD application with evidence that your Form I-881, Application for Suspension of Deportation, or EOIR-40, is pending

Paroled in the Public Interest--(c)(11). File your EAD application if you were paroled into the United States for emergent reasons or reasons strictly in the public interest.

Deferred Action--(c)(14). File your EAD application with a copy of the order, notice or document placing you in deferred action and evidence establishing economic necessity for an EAD.

Final Order of Deportation--(c)(18). File your EAD application with a copy of the order of supervision and a request for employment authorization which may be based on, but not limited to the following:

- Existence of a dependent spouse and/or children in the United States who rely on you for support; and
- Existence of economic necessity to be employed;
- Anticipated length of time before you can be removed from the United States.

LIFE Legalization applicant--(c)(24). We encourage you to file your EAD application together with your Form I-485, Application to Regsiter Permanent Residence or Adjust Status, to facilitate processing. However, you may file Form I-765 at a later date with evidence that you were a CSS, LULAC, or Zambrano class member applicant before October 1, 2000 and with a copy of the receipt notice or other evidence that your Form I-485 is pending.

T-1 Nonimmigrant--(a)(16). If you are applying for initial employment authorization as a T-1 nonimmigrant, file this form only if you did not request an employment authorization document when you applied for T nonimmigrant status. If you have been granted T status and this is a request for a renewal or replacement of an employment authorization document, file this application along with evidence of your T status, such as an approval notice.

T-2, T-3, or T-4 Nonimmigrant--(c)(25). File this form with a copy of your T-1's (principal alien's) approval notice and proof of your relationship to the T-1 principal.

Part 3. Required Documentation.

All applications must be filed with the documents required below, in addition to the particular evidence required for the category listed in **Part 2**, **Eligibility Categories**, with fee, if required.

If you are required to show economic necessity for your category (See **Part 2**), submit a list of your assets, income and expenses.

Please assemble the documents in the following order:

Your application with the filing fee. See **Part 4**, **Fee** for details.

If you are mailing your application to the USCIS, you must also submit:

- A copy of Form I-94 Departure Record (front and back), if available.
- A copy of your last EAD (front and back).
- Two passport-style color photos with a white background taken no earlier than 30 days before submission to USCIS. They should be unmounted, glossy and unretouched. The photos should show a full-frontal facial position. Your head should be bare unless you are wearing a headdress as required by a religious order to which you belong. The photo should not be larger than 2 x 2 inches, with the distance from the top of the head to just below the chin about 1 1/4 inches. Lightly print our name and your A#, if known, on the back of each photo with a pencil.

Special Filing Instructions for Those With Pending Asylum Applications (c)(8).

Asylum applicant (with a pending asylum application) who filed for asylum on or after January 4, 1995. *You must wait at leat 150 days following the filing of your asylum claim before you are eligible to apply for an EAD. If you file your EAD application early, it will be denied. File your EAD application with:*

- A copy of the USCIS acknowledgement mailer which was mailed to you; or
- Other evidence that your Form I-589 was filed with USCIS; or
- Evidence that your Form I-589 was filed with an Immigration Judge at the Executive Office for Immigration Review (EOIR); or
- Evidence that your asylum application remains under administrative or judicial review.

Asylum applicant (with a pending asylum application) who filed for asylum and for withholding of deportation prior to January 4, 1995 and is *NOT* in exclusion or deportation proceedings.
You may file your EAD application at any time; however, it will only be granted if USCIS finds that your asylum application is not frivolous. File your EAD application with:

- A complete copy of your previously filed Form I-589; AND
- A copy of your USCIS receipt notice; or
- A copy of the USCIS acknowledgement mailer; or
- Evidence that your Form I-589 was filed with EOIR; or
- Evidence that your asylum application remains under administrative or judicial review; or
- Other evidence that you filed an asylum application.

Asylum applicant (with a pending asylum application) who filed an initial request for asylum prior to January 4, 1995, and *IS IN* exclusion or deportation proceedings. If you filed your Request for Asylum and Withholding of Deportation (Form I-589) prior to January 4, 1995 and you ARE IN exclusion or deportation proceedings, file your EAD application with:

- A date-stamped copy of your previously filed Form I-589; or
- A copy of Form I-221, Order to Show Cause and Notice of Hearing, or Form I-122, Notice to Applicant for Admission Detained for Hearing Before Immigration Judge; or
- A copy of EOIR-26, Notice of Appeal, date stamped by the Office of the Immigration Judge; or
- A date-stamped copy of a petition for judicial review or for *habeas corpus* issued to the asylum applicant; or
- Other evidence that you filed an asylum application with EOIR.

Asylum Application Under the ABC Settlement Agreement--(c)(8). If you are a Salvadoran or Guatemalan national eligible for benefits under the ABC settlement agreement, American Baptist Churches v. Thornburgh , 760 F. Supp. 976 (N.D. Cal. 1991), please follow the instructions contained in this section when filing your Form I-765.

You must have asylum application (Form I-589) on file either with USCIS or with an immigration judge in order to receive work authorization. Therefore, please submit evidence that you have previously filed an asylum application when you submit your EAD application. You are not required to submit this evidence when you apply, but it will help USCIS process your request efficiently.

If you are renewing or replacing your EAD, you must pay the filing fee.

Mark your application as follows:

- Write "ABC" in the top right corner of your EAD application. You must identify yourself as an ABC class member if you are applying for an EAD under the ABC settlement agreement.
- Write "(c)(8)" in **Section 16** of the application.

You are entitled to an EAD without regard to the merits of your asylum claim. Your application for an EAD will be decided within 60 days if: (1) you pay the filing fee, (2) you have a complete, pending asylum application on file, and (3) write "ABC" in the top right corner of your EAD application. If you do not pay the filing fee for an initial EAD request, your request may be denied if USCIS finds that your asylum application is frivolous. However, if you cannot pay the filing fee for an EAD, you may qualify for a fee waiver under 8 CFR 103.7(c). See **Part 4** concerning fee waivers.

Part 4. Fee.

What Is the Fee? Applicants must pay a fee of **$180.00** unless noted below.

If a fee is required, it will not be refunded. Pay in the exact amount. Checks and money orders must be payable in U.S. currency. Make check or money order payable to the **"Department of Homeland Security,"** unless:

If you live in Guam make your check or money order payable to **"Treasurer, Guam."** If you live in the U.S. Virgin Islands make your check or money order payable to **"Commissioner of Finance of the Virgin Islands."**

A charge of $30.00 will be imposed if a check in payment of a fee is not honored by the bank on which it is drawn. Please do **not** send cash in the mail.

Initial EAD: If this is your initial application and you are applying under one of the following categories, a filing fee is **not** required:

- (a)(3) Refugee;
- (a)(4) Paroled as Refugee;
- (a)(5) Asylee;
- (a)(7) N-8 or N-9 nonimmigrant;
- (a)(8) Citizen of Micronesia, Marshall Islands or Palau;
- (a)(10) Granted Withholding of Deportation;
- (a)(11) Deferred Enforced Departure;
- (a)(16) Victim of Severe Form of Trafficking (T-1);
- (c)(1), (c)(4), or (c)(7) Dependent of certain foreign government, international organization, or NATO personnel; or
- (c)(8) Applicant for asylum [an applicant filing under the special ABC procedures must pay the fee].

Renewal EAD: If this is a renewal application and you are applying under one of the following categories, a filing fee is **not** required:

- (a)(8) Citizen of Micronesia, Marshall Islands, or Palau;
- (a)(10) Granted Withholding of Deportation;
- (a)(11) Deferred Enforced Departure; or
- (c)(l), (c)(4), or (c)(7) Dependent of certain foreign government, international organization, or NATO personnel.

Replacement EAD: If this is your replacement application and you are applying under one of the following categories, *a* filing fee is **not** required:

- (c)(l), (c)(4), or (c)(7) Dependent of certain foreign government, international organization, or NATO personnel.

You may be eligible for a fee waiver under 8 CFR 103.7(c).

USCIS will use the Poverty Guidelines published annually by the Department of Health and Human Services as the basic criteria in determining the applicant's eligibility when economic necessity is identified as a factor.

The Poverty Guidelines will be used as a guide, but not as a conclusive standard, in adjudicating fee waiver requests for employment authorization applications requiring a fee.

How to Check If the Fee Is Correct: The fee on this form is current as of the edition date appearing in the lower right corner of this page. However, because USCIS fees change periodically, you can verify if the fee is correct by following one of the steps below:

- Visit our website at **www.uscis.gov** and scroll down to "Forms and E-Filing" to check the appropriate fee, or
- Review the Fee Schedule included in your form package, if you called us to request the form, or
- Telephone our National Customer Service Center at **1-800-375-5283** and ask for the fee information.

NOTE: If your application requires a biometric services fee for USCIS to take your fingerprints, photograph or signature, you can use the same procedure above to confirm the biometrics fee.

Part 5. Where to File.

If your response to **Question 16** is: **(a)(3), (a)(4), (a)(5), (a)(7)** or **(a)(8)** mail your application to:

USCIS Service Center
P.O. Box 87765
Lincoln, NE 68501-7765

If your response to **Question 16** is **(a)(9)**, mail your application to:

USCIS
P.O. Box 7218
Chicago, IL 60680-7218

If your response to **Question 16** is **(a)(15)**, mail your application to:

USCIS
P.O. Box 7216
Chicago, IL 60680-7216

If your response to **Question 16** is **(a)(14)** or **(c)(24)**, mail your application to:

USCIS
P.O. Box 7219
Chicago, IL 60680-7219

If your response to **Question 16** is: **(a)(16)** or **(c)(25)** mail your application to:

USCIS Service Center
75 Lower Welden St.
St. Albans, VT 05479-0001

If your response to **Question 16** is: **(a)(10), (c)(11), (c)(12), (c)(14), (c)(16) or (c)(18),** apply at the local USCIS office having jurisdiction over your place of residence.

If your response to **Question 16** is: **(a)(12)** or **(c)(19)**, file your EAD application according to the instructions in the Federal Register notice for your particular country's TPS designation.

If your response to **Question 16** is **(c)(1), (c)(4)** or **(c)(7)**, submit your application through your principal's sponsoring organization . Your application will be reviewed and forwarded by the DOS, USUN or NATO/SACLANT to the Nebraska Service Center following certification of your eligibility for an EAD.

If your response to **Question 16** is **(c)(8)** under the special ABC filing instructions and you are filing your asylum and EAD applications together, mail your application to the office where you are filing your asylum application.

If your response to **Question 16** is **(c)(9), employment-based adjustment**, file your application as follows:

Concurrent Forms I-765/I-140/I-485 Filings:

- If you are filing your Form I-765 together with a Forms I-140 (Petition for Alien Worker)/I-485 package, submit the entire package of the three forms to:

USCIS Service Center
P.O. Box 87485
Lincoln, NE 68501-7485

Concurrent Forms I-765/I-485 Fillings:

- If your Form I-140 petition is pending or has already been approved, file your Forms I-485/I-765 package with the service center where the Form I-140 is pending or approved. Include the Form I-140 receipt or approval notice.

Form I-765 Filed Alone:

- If your employment-based Form I-485 is pending, file your Form I-765 at the same Service Center currently processing your Form I-485. Include a copy of your receipt notice.
- In all other cases if your response to **Question 16** is **(c)(9),** file your Form I-765 according to the instructions noted on the "Direct Mail Instructions for Persons Filing Form I-765" that are included with the Form I-765 on our website at **www. uscis.gov** under "Forms and E-Filing."

If your response to **Question 16** is: **(a)(6), (a)(11), (a)(13), (a)(17), (a)(18), (c)(2), (c)(3)(i), (c)(3)(ii), (c)(3)(iii), (c)(5), (c)(6), (c)(8),(c)(17)(i), (c)(17)(ii) or (c)(17)(iii):** mail your application based on your address to the appropriate **Service Center**. The correct **Service Center** is based on the state or territory in which you live.

If you live in:		**Mail your application to:**
Connecticut D.C. Maryland New Hampshire New York Puerto Rico Vermont West Virginia	Delaware Maine Massachusetts New Jersey Pennsylvania Rhode Island Virginia U.S.V.I.	**USCIS Service Center** 75 Lower Welden Street St. Albans, VT 05479-0001
Arizona Guam Nevada	California Hawaii	**USCIS Service Center** P.O. Box 10765 Laguna Niguel, CA 92067-1076
Alabama Florida Kentucky Mississippi North Carolina South Carolina Texas	Arkansas Georgia Lousiana New Mexico Oklahoma Tennessee	**USCIS Service Center** P.O. Box 851041 Mesquite, TX 75185-1041
Alaska Idaho Indiana Kansas Minnesota Montana North Dakota Oregon Utah Wisconsin	Colorado Illinois Iowa Michigan Missouri Nebraska Ohio South Dakota Washington Wyoming	**USCIS Service Center** P.O. Box 87765 Lincoln, NE 68501-7765

- If your response to **Question 16** is **(c)(10)**, and you are a NACARA 203 applicant eligible to apply for relief with USCIS, or if your Form I-881 application is still pending with USCIS and you wish to renew your EAD, mail your EAD application with the required fee to the appropriate USCIS service center below:

If you live in Alabama, Arkansas, Colorado, Connecticut, Delaware, the District of Columbia, Florida, Georgia, Louisiana, Maine, Maryland, Massachusetts, Mississippi, New Hampshire, New Jersey, New Mexico, New York, North Carolina, Oklahoma, Pennsylvania, Puerto Rico, Rhode Island, South Carolina, Tennessee, Texas, Utah, the U.S. Virgin Islands, Vermont, Virginia, West Virginia or Wyoming, mail your application to:

USCIS Service Center
75 Lower Welden St.
St. Albans, VT 05479-0001

- If you live in Alaska, Arizona, California, the Commonwealth of Guam, Hawaii, Idaho, Illinois, Indiana, Iowa, Kansas, Kentucky, Michigan, Minnesota, Missouri, Montana, Nebraska, Nevada, North Dakota, Oregon, Ohio, South Dakota, Washington, or Wisconsin, mail your application to:

  USCIS Service Center
  P.O. Box 10765
  Laguna Niguel, CA 92067-1076

You should submit the fee for the EAD application on a separate check or money order. Do not combine your check or money order with the fee for the Form I-881.

If your response to **Question 16** is **(c)(10) and you are not eligible to apply for NACARA 203 relief with USCIS,** but you are eligible for other deportation or removal relief, apply at the local USCIS office having jurisdiction over your place of residence.

Part 6. Processing Information.

Acceptance. If your application is complete and filed at a USCIS Service Center, you will be mailed a Form I-797 receipt notice. However, an application filed without the required fee, evidence, signature or photographs (if required) will be returned to you as incomplete. You may correct the deficiency and resubmit the application; however, an application is not considered properly filed until USCIS accepts it.

Approval. If approved, your EAD will either be mailed to you or you may be required to appear at your local USCIS office to pick it up.

Request for Evidence. If additional information or documentation is required, a written request will be sent to you specifying the information or advising you of an interview.

Denial. If your application cannot be granted, you will receive a written notice explaining the basis of your denial.

Interim EAD. If you have not received a decision within 90 days of receipt by USCIS of a properly filed EAD application or within 30 days of a properly filed initial EAD application based on an asylum application filed on or after January 4, 1995, you may obtain interim work authorization by appearing in person at your local USCIS district office. You must bring proof of identity and any notices that you have received from USCIS in connection with your application for employment authorization.

Part 7. Other Information.

Penalties for Perjury. All statements contained in response to questions in this application are declared to be true and correct under penalty of perjury. Title 18, United States Code, Section 1546, provides in part:

. . . Whoever knowingly makes under oath, or as permitted under penalty of perjury under 1746 of Title 28, United States Code, knowingly subscribes as true, any false statement with respect to a material fact in any application, affidavit, or other document required by the immigration laws or regulations prescribed thereunder, or knowingly presents any such application, affidavit, or other document containing any such false statement-shall be fined in accordance with this title or imprisoned not more than five years, or both.

The knowing placement of false information on this application may subject you and/or the preparer of this application to criminal penalties under Title 18 of the United States Code. The knowing placement of false information on this application may also subject you and/or the preparer to civil penalties under Section 274C of the Immigration and Nationality Act (INA), 8 U.S.C. 1324c. Under 8 U.S.C. 1324c, a person subject to a final order for civil document fraud is deportable from the United States and may be subject to fines.

Authority for Collecting This Information. The authority to require you to file Form I-765, Application for Employment Authorization, when applying for employment authorization is found at sections 103(a) and 274A(h)(3) of the Immigration and Nationality Act. Information you provide on your Form I-765 is used to determine whether you are eligible for employment authorization and for the preparation of your Employment Authorization Document if you are found eligible. Failure to provide all information as requested may result in the denial or rejection of this application. The information you provide may also be disclosed to other federal, state, local and foreign law enforcement and regulatory agencies during the course of the USCIS investigations.

USCIS Forms and Information. To order USCIS forms, call our toll-free number at **1-800-870-3676.** You can also get USCIS forms and information on immigration laws, regulations and procedures by telephoning our **National Customer Service Center** at **1-800-375-5283** or visiting our internet website at **www.uscis.gov.**

Use InfoPass for an Appointments. As an alternative to waiting in line for assistance at your local USCIS office, you can now schedule an appointment through our internet-based system, **InfoPass**. To access the system, visit our website at **www.uscis.gov.** Use the **InfoPass** appointment scheduler and follow the screen prompts to set up your appoinment. **InfoPass** generates an electronic appointment notice that appears on the screen. Print the notice and take it with you to your appointment. The notice gives the time and date or your appoinment, along with the address of the USCIS office.

Paperwork Reduction Act. An agency may not conduct or sponsor an information collection and a person is not required to respond to a collection of information unless it displays a currently valid OMB control number.

U.S. Citizenship and Immigration Servies (USCIS) tries to create forms and instructions which are accurate and easily understood. Often this is difficult because immigration law can be very complex.

The public reporting burden for this form is estimated to average three 3 hours and 25 minutes per response, including the time for reviewing instructions, gathering and maintaining the data needed, and completing and reviewing the collection of information.

The USCIS welcomes your comments regarding this burden estimate or any other aspect of this form, including suggestions for reducing this burden to U.S. Citizenship and Immigration Services, Regulatory Management Division, 111 Massachusetts Avenue, N.W., Washington DC, 20529; OMB No. 1615-0040. **Do not mail your completed application to this Washington, D.C. address.**

OMB No. 1615-0040; Expires 08/31/08

Department of Homeland Security
U.S. Citizenship and Immigration Services

I-765, Application for Employment Authorization

Do not write in this block.

Remarks	Action Block	Fee Stamp
A#		
Applicant is filing under §274a.12 ______		

☐ Application Approved. Employment Authorized / Extended *(Circle One)* until ______________ (Date).
______________ (Date).

Subject to the following conditions: ______________

☐ Application Denied.

☐ Failed to establish eligibility under 8 CFR 274a.12 (a) or (c).

☐ Failed to establish economic necessity as required in 8 CFR 274a.12(c)(14), (18) and 8 CFR 214.2(f)

I am applying for:
☐ Permission to accept employment.
☐ Replacement of lost Employment Authorization Document.
☐ Renewal of my permission to accept employment *(attach previous Employment Authorization Document).*

1. Name (Family Name in CAPS) (First) (Middle)

2. Other Names Used (Include Maiden Name)

3. Address in the United States (Number and Street) (Apt. Number)

(Town or City) (State/Country) (ZIP Code)

4. Country of Citizenship/Nationality

5. Place of Birth (Town or City) (State/Province) (Country)

6. Date of Birth (mm/dd/yyyy)

7. Gender ☐ Male ☐ Female

8. Marital Status ☐ Married ☐ Single ☐ Widowed ☐ Divorced

9. U.S. Social Security Number (Include all numbers you have ever used, if any)

10. Alien Registration Number (A-Number) or I-94 Number (if any)

11. Have you ever before applied for employment authorization from USCIS?
☐ Yes (If yes, complete below) ☐ No
Which USCIS Office? Date(s)

Results (Granted or Denied - attach all documentation)

12. Date of Last Entry into the U.S. (mm/dd/yyyy)

13. Place of Last Entry into the U.S.

14. Manner of Last Entry (Visitor, Student, etc.)

15. Current Immigration Status (Visitor, Student, etc.)

16. Go to **Part 2** of the Instructions, Eligibility Categories. In the space below place the letter and number of the category you selected from the instructions. (For example, (a)(8); (c)(17)(iii); etc.)

Eligibility under 8 CFR 274a.12
( ) ( ) ( )

Certification.

Your Certification: I certify, under penalty of perjury under the laws of the United States of America, that the foregoing is true and correct. Furthermore, I authorize the release of any information that U.S. Citizenship and Immigration Services needs to determine eligibility for the benefit I am seeking. I have read the Instructions in **Part 2** and have identified the appropriate eligibility category in **Block 16**.

Signature Telephone Number Date

Signature of person preparing form, if other than above: I declare that this document was prepared by me at the request of the applicant and is based on all information of which I have any knowledge.

Print Name Address *Signature* Date

Remarks	Initial Receipt	Resubmitted	Relocated		Completed		
			Rec'd	Sent	Approved	Denied	Returned

f

OMB No. 1615-0001; Expires 06/30/06

Department of Homeland Security
U.S. Citizenship and Immigration Services

I-129F, Petition for Alien Fiancé(e)

Instructions

1. Who May File?

You may file this petition if:

A. You are a U.S. citizen, and

B. You and your fiancé(e) intend to marry within 90 days of your fiancé(e) entering the United States, and are both free to marry, and have met in person within two years before your filing of this petition unless:

(1) The requirement to meet your fiancé(e) in person would violate strict and long-established customs of your or your fiancé(e)'s foreign culture or social practice; or

(2) It is established that the requirement to personally meet your fiancé(e) would result in extreme hardship to you.

OR

C. You wish to have your alien spouse or child enter as a nonimmigrant. **See Question 11, How Do You Use This Form for Your Spouse or Child Seeking Entry Using a K-3/K-4 Visa.**

NOTE: Unmarried children of your fiancé(e) or spouse who are under 21 years of age and listed on this form will be eligible to apply to accompany your fiancé(e) or spouse.

2. General Filing Instructions.

A. Type or print legibly in black ink.

B. If extra space is needed to complete any item, attach a continuation sheet, indicate the item number, and date and sign each sheet.

C. Answer all questions fully and accurately. State that an item is not applicable with "N/A." If the answer is "none," write none.

D. ***Translations.*** Any foreign language document must be accompanied by a full English translation that the translator has certified as complete and correct, and by the translator's certification that he or she is competent to translate the foreign language into English.

E. ***Copies.*** If these instructions state that a copy of a document may be filed with this petition and you choose to send us the original, the U.S. Citizenship and Immigration Services (USCIS) may keep that original for our records. If USCIS requires the original, we will request it.

NOTE: USCIS is comprised of offices of the former Immigration and Naturalization Service (INS).

3. What Documents Do You Need to Show That You Are a U.S. Citizen?

A. If you were born in the United States, give USCIS a copy, front and back, of your birth certificate.

B. If you were naturalized, give USCIS a copy, front and back, of your original Certificate of Naturalization.

C. If you were born outside the United States and you are a U.S. citizen through your parents, give USCIS:

(1) Your original Certificate of Citizenship, or

(2) Your Form FS-240 (Report of Birth Abroad of a United States Citizen).

D. In place of any of the above, you may give USCIS a copy of your valid, unexpired U.S. passport that was issued for at least five years. You must submit copies of all pages in the passport.

E. If you do not have any of the above and were born in the United States, see instruction under **Number 4 below, "What If a Document Is Not Available?"**

4. What If a Document Is Not Available?

If the documents needed above are not available, you can instead give USCIS the following secondary evidence. However, USCIS may request in writing that you obtain a statement from the appropriate civil authority certifying that the needed document is not available. Any evidence submitted must contain enough information, such as a birth date, to establish the event you are trying to prove.

A. ***Baptismal certificate***. A copy, front and back, of the certificate under the seal of the church, synagogue or other religious entity showing where the baptism, dedication or comparable rite occurred, as well as the date and place of the child's birth, date of baptism and names of the child's parents. The baptism must have occurred within two months after the birth of the child.

B. ***School record***. A letter from the school authority (preferably from the first school attended), showing the date of admission to the school, child's date or age at that time, place of birth and the names of the parents.

C. ***Census record.*** State or Federal census record showing the name(s), date(s) and place(s) of birth or age(s) of the person(s) listed.

D. ***Affidavits***. Written statements sworn to or affirmed by two persons who were living at the time and who have personal knowledge of the event. For example, an event such as a birth, marriage or death. The persons making the affidavits may be relatives and do not have to be citizens of the United States. Each affidavit should contain the person's full name and address, date and place of birth, and relationship to you and must fully describe the event and explain how he or she acquired knowledge of the event.

5. What Documents Do You Need to Prove That You Can Legally Marry?

A. Provide copies of evidence that you and your fiancé (e) have personally met within the last two years; or if you have never met within the last two years, provide a detailed explanation and evidence of the extreme hardship or customary, cultural or social practices that have prohibited your meeting; and

B. Provide original statements from you and your fiancé (e) whom you plan to marry within 90 days of his or her admission, and copies of any evidence you wish to submit to establish your mutual intent; and

C. If either of you is of an age that requires special consent or permission for you to marry in the jurisdiction where your marriage will occur, give proof of that consent or permission; and

D. If either you or your fiancé(e) were married before, give copies of documents showing that each prior marriage was legally terminated.

6. What Other Documents Do You Need?

A. Give USCIS a passport-style color photograph of yourself and a passport-style color photograph of your fiancé(e), with both photos taken within 30 days of the date of filing this petition. The photos must have a white background, be glossy, unretouched and not mounted. The dimension of the full frontal facial image of you and your fiancé(e) in separate photos should be about one inch from your chin to the top of your hair in 3/4 frontal view. Using a pencil or felt pen, lightly print the name (and Alien Registration Number, if known) on the back of each photograph.

B. Submit a completed and signed Form G-325A (Biographic Information) for you and a completed and signed Form G-325A for your fiancé(e). Except for name and signature, you do not have to repeat on the Biographic Information form the information given on your Form I-129F.

C. If either you or the person you are filing for is using a name other than that shown on the relevant documents, you must give USCIS copies of the legal documents that made the change, such as a marriage certificate, adoption decree or court order.

7. Where Should You File This Form?

A. If you are filing for your fiancé(e), submit this application according to your place of residence, as listed below:

- If you live in Connecticut, Delaware, District of Columbia, Maine, Maryland, Massachusetts, New Hampshire, New Jersey, New York, Pennsylvania, Puerto Rico, Rhode Island, Vermont, U.S. Virgin Islands, Virginia or West Virginia, mail this petition to:

  USCIS Vermont Service Center
  75 Lower Welden Street
  St. Albans, VT 05479-0001

- If you live in Alabama, Arkansas, Florida, Georgia, Kentucky, Louisiana, Mississippi, New Mexico, North Carolina, Oklahoma, South Carolina, Tennessee or Texas, mail this petition to:

  USCIS Texas Service Center
  P.O. Box 850965
  Mesquite, TX 75185-0965

- If you live in Arizona, California, Guam, Hawaii or Nevada, mail this petition to:

  USCIS California Service Center
  P.O. Box 10130
  Laguna Niguel, CA 92607-1013

- If you live in Alaska, Colorado, Idaho, Illinois, Indiana, Iowa, Kansas, Michigan, Minnesota, Missouri, Montana, Nebraska, North Dakota, Ohio, Oregon, South Dakota, Utah, Washington, Wisconsin or Wyoming, mail the petition to:

  USCIS Nebraska Service Center
  P.O. Box 87130
  Lincoln, NE 68501-7130

- If you live outside the United States, mail your petition to USCIS Service Center listed above that has jurisdiction over the last place you lived in the United States. **NOTE:** Your petition cannot be adjudicated at a USCIS office abroad.

B. If you are filing for your spouse under the K nonimmigrant visa program, mail your application to:

USCIS
P.O. Box 7218
Chicago, IL 60680-7218

8. What Is the Fee?

The fee for filing this form is **$170.00**.

The fee will not be refunded, whether the petition is approved or not. Do not mail cash. All checks or money orders, whether U.S. or foreign, must be payable in U.S. currency at a financial institution in the United States. When a check is drawn on the account of a person other than yourself, write your name on the face of the check. If the check is not honored, USCIS will charge you $30.00.

Pay by check or money in the exact amount. Make the check or money order payable to the **Department of Homeland Security.**

How to Check If the Fee Is Correct.

The fee on this form is current as of the edition date appearing in the lower right corner of this page. However, because USCIS fees change periodically, you can verify if the fee is correct by following one of the steps below:

- Visit our website at **www.uscis.gov** and scroll down to "Forms and E-Filing" to check the appropriate fee, or
- Review the Fee Schedule included in your form package, if you called us to request the form, or
- Telephone our National Customer Service Center at **1-800-375-5283** and ask for the fee information.

9. How Does Your Alien Fiancé(e) Obtain Permanent Resident Status?

Your alien fiancé(e) may apply for conditional permanent resident status after you have entered into a valid marriage to each other within 90 days of your fiancé(e)'s entry into the United States. Your alien spouse should then apply promptly to UCIS for adjustment of status to conditional permanent resident, using Form I-485, Application to Register or Adjust Status.

10. How Does Your Spouse Become a Permanent Resident Without Conditions?

Both you and your conditional permanent resident spouse are required to file a petition, Form I-751, Petition to Remove the Conditions on Residence, during the 90-day period immediately before the second anniversary of the date your alien spouse was granted conditional permanent residence. Children who were admitted as conditional permanent residents with your spouse may be included in the joint petition to remove the conditions.

The rights, privileges, responsibilities and duties that apply to all other permanent residents apply equally to a conditional permanent resident to file petitions on behalf of qualifying relatives, or to reside permanently in the United States as an immigrant in accordance with the immigration laws.

Notice

Failure to file Form I-751, Petition to Remove the Conditions on Residence, will result in termination of permanent residence status and initiation of removal proceedings.

11. How Do You Use This Form for Your Spouse or Child Seeking Entry With a K-3/K-4 Visa?

This form may be used to obtain a K-3/K-4 visa for your alien spouse and her or his child. Fill out the form as directed, except assume that "fiancé" or "fiancé(e)" means "spouse." answer Questions **B.17** and **B.18** by stating "N/A." Note that filing this form is only necessary to facilitate the entry of your spouse and her or his child as a **nonimmigrant**.

You must submit the documents required in Questions **3**, **4** and **6** of the instructions, but may omit the documents required in Question **5**. In addition, U.S. citizens petitioning for K-3 visas for their alien spouses must also include evidence that they have filed Form I-130, Petition for Alien Relative, on behalf of the alien spouse listed on this form, and a marriage certificate evidencing the legal marriage between the citizen and alien.

The LIFE Act requires applicants to apply for a K-3/K-4 visa in the country where their marriage to the U.S. citizen petitioner occurred. Petitioners should make sure to identify the appropriate consulate, in the same country where they married the alien for whom they are petitioning, in block **19** to avoid lengthy delays. In the event the petitioner and alien were married in the United States, they should list the country of the alien's current residence. See U.S. Department of State regulations at 21 CFR 41.81.

12. Processing Information.

Any petition that is not signed or accompanied by the correct fee will be rejected with a notice that it is deficient. You may correct the deficiency and resubmit the petition. However, a petition is not considered properly filed until accepted by USCIS. Once the petition has been accepted, it will be checked for completeness, including submission of the required evidence. If you do not completely fill out the form or file it without required initial evidence, you will not establish a basis for eligibility and we may deny your petition.

We may request more information or evidence or we may request that you appear at a USCIS office for an interview.

13. What Are the Penalties for Marriage Fraud or Giving False Information?

We may request more information or evidence or we may request that you appear at a USCIS office for an interview.

Title 8, United States Code, Section 1325 states that any person who knowingly enters into a marriage contract for the purpose of evading any provision of the immigration laws shall be imprisoned for not more than five years or fined not more than $250,000, or both.

14. USCIS Forms and Information.

To order USCIS forms, call our toll-free forms line at **1-800-870-3676**. You can also get USCIS forms and information on immigration laws, regulations or procedures by calling our National Customer Service Center at **1-800-375-5283** or visiting our internet website at **www.uscis.gov.**

15. Use InfoPass to Make an Appointment.

As an alternative to waiting in line for assistance at your local USCIS office, you can now schedule an appointment through our internet-based system, **InfoPass.** To access the system, visit our website at **www.uscis.gov.** Use the **InfoPass** appointment scheduler and follow the screen prompts to set up your appointment. **InfoPass** generates an electronic appointment notice that appears on the screen. Print the notice and take it with you to your appointment. The notice gives the time and date of your appointment, along with the address of the USCIS office.

16. What Is Our Authority for Collecting This Information?

We request the information on this form to carry out the immigration laws contained in Title 8, United States Code 1184(d). We need this information to determine whether a person is eligible for immigration benefits. The information you provide may also be disclosed to other federal, state, local and foreign law enforcement and regulatory agencies during the course of the investigation required by USCIS. You do not have to give this information. However, if you refuse to give some or all of it, your petition may be denied.

17. What Is the Reporting Burden?

Under the Paperwork Reduction Act, a person is not required to respond to a collection of information unless it displays a currently valid OMB control number. We try to create forms and instructions that are accurate, can be easily understood and that impose the least possible burden on you to provide us with information. Often this is difficult because some immigration laws are very complex. The estimated time to file this application is 30 minutes per application.

If you have any comments regarding the accuracy of this estimate, or suggestions for making this form simpler, you can write to the U.S. Citizenship and Immigration Services, Regulatory Management Division, 111 Massachusetts Avenue, N.W., Washington, DC 20529, OMB No. 1615-0001 **Do not mail your completed application to this address.**

OMB No. 1615-0001; Expires 06/30/06

Department of Homeland Security
U.S. Citizenship and Immigration Services

I-129F, Petition for Alien Fiancé(e)

Do not write in this block. **For USCIS Use Only**

Case ID #	Action Block	Fee Stamp
A #		
G-28 #		AMCON:
The petition is approved for status under Section 101(a)(5)(k). It is valid for four months from the date of action. ______		☐ Personal Interview ☐ Previously Forwarded ☐ Document Check ☐ Field Investigation
Remarks:		

Part A. Information about you.

1. **Name** *(Family name in CAPS)* *(First)* *(Middle)*

2. **Address** *(Number and Street)* Apt. #

(Town or City) (State or Country) (Zip/Postal Code)

3. **Place of Birth** *(Town or City)* (State/Country)

4. **Date of Birth** *(mm/dd/yyyy)* 5. **Gender**
☐ Male ☐ Female

6. **Marital Status**
☐ Married ☐ Single ☐ Widowed ☐ Divorced

7. **Other Names Used** *(including maiden name)*

8a. **U.S. Social Security Number** 8b. **A#** *(if any)*

9. **Names of Prior Spouses** **Date(s) Marriage(s) Ended**

10. **My citizenship was acquired through** *(check one)*
☐ Birth in the U.S. ☐ Naturalization
Give number of certificate, date and place it was issued.

☐ Parents
Have you obtained a certificate of citizenship in your name?
☐ Yes ☐ No
If "Yes," give certificate number, date and place it was issued.

11. **Have you ever filed for this or any other alien fiancé(e) or husband/wife before?**
☐ Yes ☐ No
If "Yes," give name of alien, place and date of filing and result.

Part B. Information about your alien fiancé(e).

1. **Name** *(Family name in CAPS)* *(First)* *(Middle)*

2. **Address** *(Number and Street)* Apt. #

(Town or City) (State or Country) (Zip/Postal Code)

3a. **Place of Birth** *(Town or City)* (State/Country)

3b. **Country of Citizenship**

4. **Date of Birth** *(mm/dd/yyyy)* 5. **Gender**
☐ Male ☐ Female

6. **Marital Status**
☐ Married ☐ Single ☐ Widowed ☐ Divorced

7. **Other Names Used** *(including maiden name)*

8. **U.S. Social Security #** 9. **A#** *(if any)*

10. **Names of Prior Spouses** **Date(s) Marriage(s) Ended**

11. **Has your fiancé(e) ever been in the U.S.?**
☐ Yes ☐ No

12. **If your fiancé(e) is currently in the U.S., complete the following:**
He or she last arrived as a:*(visitor, student, exchange alien, crewman, stowaway, temporary worker, without inspection, etc.)*

Arrival/Departure Record (I-94) Number
☐☐☐ — ☐☐☐☐☐☐☐☐

Date of Arrival *(mm/dd/yy)* **Date authorized stay expired, or will expire as shown on I-94 or I-95**

INITIAL RECEIPT ______ RESUBMITTED ______ RELOCATED: Rec'd. ______ Sent ______ COMPLETED: Appv'd. ______ Denied ______ Ret'd. ______

13. List all children of your alien fiancé(e) *(if any)*

Name *(First/Middle/Last)*	Date of Birth *(mm/dd/yyyy)*	Country of Birth	Present Address

14. Address in the United States where your fiancé(e) intends to live.

(Number and Street) (Town or City) (State)

15. Your fiancé(e)'s address abroad.

(Number and Street) (Town or City) (State or Province)

(Country) (Phone Number; Include Country, City and Area Codes)

16. If your fiancé(e)'s native alphabet uses other than Roman letters, write his or her name and address abroad in the native alphabet.

(Name) (Number and Street)

(Town or City) (State or Province) (Country)

17. Is your fiancé(e) related to you? ☐ Yes ☐ No

If you are related, state the nature and degree of relationship, e.g., third cousin or maternal uncle, etc.

18. Has your fiancé(e) met and seen you within the two-year period immediately preceding the filing of this petition? ☐ Yes ☐ No

Describe the circumstances under which you met. If you have not personally met each other, explain how the relationship was established. Explain also in detail any reasons you may have for requesting that the requirement that you and your fiancé(e) must have met should not apply to you.

19. Your fiancé(e) will apply for a visa abroad at the American embassy or consulate at:

(City) (Country)

NOTE: (Designation of a U.S. embassy or consulate outside the country of your fiancé(e)'s last residence does not guarantee acceptance for processing by that foreign post. Acceptance is at the discretion of the designated embassy or consulate.)

C. Other information.

If you are serving overseas in the Armed Forces of the United States, please answer the following:

I presently reside or am stationed overseas and my current mailing address is: I plan to return to the United States on or about:

D. Penalties, certification and petitioner's signature.

PENALTIES: **You may by law be imprisoned for not more than five years, or fined $250,000, or both, for entering into a marriage contract for the purpose of evading any provision of the immigration laws, and you may be fined up to $10,000 or imprisoned up to five years, or both, for knowingly and willfully falsifying or concealing a material fact or using any false document in submitting this petition.**

YOUR CERTIFICATION: **I am legally able to and intend to marry my alien fiancé(e) within 90 days of his or her arrival in the United States. I certify, under penalty of perjury under the laws of the United States of America, that the foregoing is true and correct. Furthermore, I authorize the release of any information from my records that the U.S. Citizenship and Immigration Services needs to determine eligibility for the benefit that I am seeking.**

Signature **Date** *(mm/dd/yyyy)* **Daytime Telephone Number** *(with area code)*

E-Mail Address (if any)

E. Signature of person preparing form, if other than above. *(Sign below.)*

I declare that I prepared this application at the request of the applicant and it is based on all information of which I have knowledge.

Signature	Print or Type Your Name	G-28 ID Number	Date *(mm/dd/yyyy)*

Firm Name and Address	Daytime Telephone Number (*with area code*)
	E-Mail Address (if any)

OMB No. 1615-0003; Expires 11/30/07

Department of Homeland Security
U.S. Citizenship and Immigration Services

I-539, Application to Extend/ Change Nonimmigrant Status

Instructions

NOTE: You have the option of submitting this paper version of Form I-539 according to form's instructions or you may file the application electronically. To file electronically, visit our internet website at **www. uscis.gov** and follow the instructions on e-filing. Whether you submit this paper form or e-file, U.S. Citizenship and Immigration Services (USCIS) recommends that you retain a copy of your application and supporting documents for your records. USCIS is comprised of offices of the former Immigration and Naturalization Service (INS).

Purpose of This Form.

You should use this form if you are one of the nonimmigrants listed below and wish to apply to U.S. Citizenship and Immigration Services (USCIS) for an extension of stay or a change to another nonimmigrant status.

In certain situations, you may use this form to apply for an initial nonimmigrant status.

You may also use this form if you are a nonimmigrant F-1 or M-1 student applying for reinstatement.

Who May File/Initial Evidence.

Extension of Stay or Change of Status:

Nonimmigrants in the United States may apply for an extension of stay or a change of status on this form, except as noted in these instructions under the heading, "Who May Not File."

Multiple Applicants.

You may include your spouse and your unmarried children under age 21 years as co-applicants in your application for the same extension or change of status, if you are all now in the same status or they are all in derivative status.

Required Documentation - Form I-94, Nonimmigrant Arrival/ Departure Record.

You are required to submit with your Form I-539 application the original or copy, front and back, of Form I-94 of each person included in your application. If the original Form I-94 or required copy cannot be submitted with this application, include a Form I-102, Application for Replacement/Initial Nonimmigrant Arrival/Departure Document, with the required fee.

Valid Passport.

If you were required to have a passport to be admitted into the United States, you must maintain the validity of your passport during your nonimmigrant stay. If a required passport is not valid when you file the Form I-539 application, submit an explanation with your form.

Additional Evidence.

You may be required to submit additional evidence noted in these instructions.

Nonimmigrant Categories.

This form may be used by the following nonimmigrants listed in alphabetical order:

- **An A, Ambassador, Public Minister, or Career Diplomatic or Consular Officer and their immediate family members.**

You must submit a copy, front and back, of the Form I-94 of each person included in the application and a Form I-566, Interagency Record of Individual Requesting Change, Adjustment to, or from, A to G Status; or Requesting A, G or NATO Dependent Employment Authorization, certified by the U.S. Department of State to indicate your accredited status.

NOTE: An A-1 or A-2 nonimmigrant is not required to pay a fee with the Form I-539 application.

- **An A-3, Attendant or Servant of an A Nonimmigrant and the A-3's immediate family members.**

You must submit a copy, front and back, of the Form I-94 of each person included in the application.

The application must be filed with:

-- A copy of your employer's Form I-94 or approval notice demonstrating A status;

-- An original letter from your employer describing your duties and stating that he or she intends to personally employ you; and arrangements you have made to depart from the United States; and

-- An original Form I-566, certified by the Department of State, indicating your employer's continuing accredited status.

- **A B-1, Visitor for Business or B-2, Visitor for Pleasure.**

If you are filing for an extension/change, you must file your application with the original Form I-94 of each person included in your application. In addition, you must submit a written statement explaining in detail:

-- The reasons for your request;

-- Why your extended stay would be temporary, including what arrangements you have made to depart from the United States; and

-- Any effect the extended stay may have on your foreign employment or residency.

- **Dependents of an E, Treaty Trader or Investor.**

  If you are filing for an extension/change of status as the dependent of an E, this application must be submitted with:

  -- The Form I-129, Petition for Alien Worker, filed for that E or a copy of the filing receipt noting that the petition is pending with USCIS;

  -- A copy of the E's Form I-94 or approval notice showing that he or she has already been granted status to the period requested on your application; and

  -- Evidence of relationship (example: birth or marriage certificate).

- **NOTE:** An employer or investor should file Form I-129 to request an extension/change to E status for an employee, prospective employee, or the investor. Dependents of E employees should file for an extension/change of status on this form, not Form I-129.

- **An F-1, Academic Student.**

  To request a change to F-1 status or to apply for reinstatement as an F-1 student, you must submit your original Form I-94, as well as the original Form I-94 of each person included in the application.

  Your application must include your original Form I-20 (Certificate of Eligibility for Nonimmigrant Student) issued by the school where you will study. To request either a change or reinstatement, you must submit documentation that demonstrates your ability to pay for your studies and support yourself while you are in the United States.

F-1 Extensions:

Do not use this form to request an extension. For information concerning extensions, contact your designated school official at your institution.

F-1 Reinstatement:

You will only be considered for reinstatement as an F-1 student if you establish:

-- That the violation of status was due solely to circumstances beyond your control or that failure to reinstate you would result in extreme hardship;

-- You are pursuing or will pursue a full course of study;

-- You have not been employed without authorization; and

-- You are not in removal proceedings.

- **A G, Designated Principal Resident Representative of a Foreign Government and his or her immediate family members.**

  You must submit a copy, front and back, of the Form I-94, of each person included in the application, and a Form I-566, certified by the Department of State to indicate your accredited status.

  NOTE: A G-1 through G-4 nonimmigrant is not required to pay a fee with the I-539 application.

- **A G-5, Attendant or Servant of a G Nonimmigrant and the G-5's immediate family members.**

  You must submit a copy, front and back, of the Form I-94 of each person included in the application.

  The application must also be filed with:

  -- A copy of your employer's Form I-94 or approval notice demonstrating G status;

  -- An original letter from your employer describing your duties and stating that he or she intends to personally employ you; and arrangements you have made to depart from the United States; and

  -- An original Form I-566, certified by the Department of State, indicating your employer's continuing accredited status.

- **Dependents of an H, Temporary Worker.**

  If you are filing for an extension/change of status as the dependent of an employee who is an H temporary worker, this application must be submitted with:

  -- The Form I-129 filed for that employee or a copy of the filing receipt noting that the petition is pending with the USCIS;

  -- A copy of the employee's Form I-94 or approval notice showing that he or she has already been granted status to the period requested on your application; and

  -- Evidence of relationship (example: birth or marriage certificate).

  NOTE: An employer should file Form I-129 to request an extension/change to H status for an employee or prospective employee. Dependents of such employees should file for an extension/change of status on this form, not on Form I-129.

- **A J-1, Exchange Visitor.**

If you are requesting a change of status to J-1, your application must be filed with an original Form IAP-66, Certificate of Eligibility for Exchange Visitor Status, issued by your program sponsor. You must also submit your original Form I-94, as well as the original Form I-94 of each person included in the application.

NOTE: A J-1 exchange visitor whose status is for the purpose of receiving graduate medical education or training, who has not received the appropriate waiver, is ineligible for any change of status. Also, a J-1 subject to the foreign residence requirement, who has not received a waiver of that requirement, is only eligible for a change of status to A or G.

J-1 Extensions:

If you are seeking an extension, contact the responsible officer of your program for information about this procedure.

J-1 Reinstatement:

If you are a J-1 exchange visitor seeking reinstatement, you may need to apply for such approval by the Department of State's Office of Education and Cultural Affairs. Contact the responsible officer at your sponsoring program for information on the reinstatement filing procedure.

- **Dependents of an L, Intracompany Transferee.**

If you are filing for an extension/change of status as the dependent of an employee who is an L intracompany transferee, this application must be submitted with:

-- The Form I-129 filed for that employee or a copy of the filing receipt noting that the petition is pending with USCIS;

-- A copy of the employee's Form I-94 or approval notice showing that he or she has already been granted status to the period requested on your application; and

-- Evidence of relationship (example: birth or marriage certificate).

NOTE: An employer should file Form I-129 to request an extension/change to L status for an employee or prospective employee. Dependents of such employees should file for an extension/change of status on this form, not on Form I-129.

- **An M-1, Vocational or Non-Academic Student.**

To request a change to or extension of M-1 status, or apply for reinstatement as an M-1 student, you must submit your original Form I-94, as well as the original Form I-94 of each person included in the application.

Your application must include your original Form I-20 issued by the school where you will study. To request either extension/change or reinstatement, you must submit documentation that demonstrates your ability to pay for your studies and support yourself while you are in the United States.

M-1 Reinstatement:

You will only be considered for reinstatement as an M-1 student if you establish:

-- That the violation of status was due solely to circumstances beyond your control or that failure to reinstate you would result in extreme hardship;

-- You are pursuing or will pursue a full course of study;

-- You have not been employed without authorization; and

-- You are not in removal proceedings.

NOTE: If you are an M-1 student, you are not eligible for a change to F-1 status and you are not eligible for a change to any H status, if the training you received as an M-1 helps you qualify for the H status. Also, you may not be granted a change to M-1 status for training to qualify for H status.

- **An N-1 or N-2, Parent or Child of an Alien Admitted as a Special Immigrant Under Section 101(a)(27)(I) of the INA.**

You must file the application with a copy, front and back, of your Form I-94 and a copy of the special immigrant's permanent resident card and proof of the relationship (example: birth or marriage certificate).

- **Dependents of an O, Alien of Extraordinary Ability or Achievement.**

If you are filing for an extension/change of status as the dependent of an employee who is classified as an O nonimmigrant, this application must be submitted with:

-- The Form I-129 filed for that employee or a copy of the filing receipt noting that the petition is pending with USCIS;

-- A copy of the employee's Form I-94 or approval notice showing that he or she has already been granted status to the period requested on your application; and

-- Evidence of relationship (example: birth or marriage certificate).

NOTE: An employer should file Form I-129 to request an extension/change to an O status for an employee or prospective employee. Dependents of such employees should file for an extension/change of status on this form, not on Form I-129.

- **Dependents of a P, Artists, Athletes and Entertainers.**

If you are filing for an extension/change of status as the dependent of an employee who is classified as a P nonimmigrant, this application must be submitted with:

-- The Form I-129 filed for that employee or a copy of the filing receipt noting that the petition is pending with the USCIS;

-- A copy of the employee's Form I-94 or approval notice showing that he or she has already been granted status to the period requested on your application; and

-- Evidence of relationship (example: birth or marriage certificate).

NOTE: An employer should file Form I-129 to request an extension/change to P status for an employee or prospective employee. Dependents of such employees should file for an extension/change of status on this form, not on Form I-129.

- **Dependents of an R, Religious Worker.**

If you are filing for an extension/change of status as the dependent of an employee who is classified as an R nonimmigrant, this application must be submitted with:

-- The Form I-129 filed for that employee or a copy of the filing receipt noting that the petition is pending with USCIS;

-- A copy of the employee's Form I-94 or approval notice showing that he or she has already been granted status to the period requested on your application; and

-- Evidence of relationship (example: birth or marriage certificate).

- **TD Dependents of TN Nonimmigrants.**

TN nonimmigrants are citizens of Canada or Mexico who are coming as business persons to the United States to engage in business activities at a professional level, pursuant to the North American Free Trade Agreement (NAFTA). The dependents (spouse or unmarried minor children) of a TN nonimmigrant are designated as TD nonimmigrants. A TD nonimmigrant may accompany or follow to join the TN professional. TD nonimmigrants may not work in the United States.

The Form I-539 shall be used by a TD nonimmigrant to request an extension of stay or by an applicant to request a change of nonimmigrant status to TD classification.

If you are filing for an extension/change of status as the dependent of an employee who is classified as a TN nonimmigrant, this application must be submitted with:

-- The Form I-129 filed for that employee or a copy of the filing receipt noting that the petition is pending with USCIS;

-- A copy of the employee's Form I-94 or approval notice showing that he or she has already been granted status to the period requested on your application; and

-- Evidence of relationship (example: birth or marriage certificate).

- **A V, Spouse or Child of a Lawful Permanent Resident.**

Use this Form I-539 if you are physically present in the United States and wish to request initial status or change status to a V nonimmigrant, or to request an extension of your current V nonimmigrant status.

Applicants should follow the instructions on this form and the attached instructions to Supplement A to Form I-539, Filing Instructions for V Nonimmigrants. The supplement contains additional information and the location where V applicants must file their applications.

NOTE: In addition to the **$200.00** application fee required to file Form I-539, V applicants are required to pay a **$70.00** biometric services fee for USCIS to take their fingerprints.

If necessary, USCIS may also take the V applicant's photograph and signature as part of the biometric services.

Notice to V Nonimmigrants.

The Legal Immigration Family Equity Act (LIFE), signed into law on December 21, 2000, created a new V visa. This nonimmigrant status allows certain persons to reside legally in the United States and to travel to and from the United States while they wait to obtain lawful permanent residence.

In order to be eligible for a V visa, all of the following conditions must be met:

- You must be the spouse or the unmarried child of a lawful permanent resident;
- A Form I-130, Petition for Alien Relative, must have been filed for you by your permanent resident spouse on or before December 21, 2000; and
- You must have been waiting for at least three years after the Form I-130 was filed for you;

Or you must be the unmarried child (under 21 years of age) of a person who meets the three requirements listed above.

V visa holders will be eligible to adjust to lawful permanent resident status once an immigrant visa becomes available to them. While they are waiting, V visa holders may be authorized to work following their submission and USCIS approval of their Form I-765, Application for Employment Authorization.

WARNING: Be advised that persons in V status who have been in the United States illegally for more than 180 days may trigger the grounds of inadmissibility regarding unlawful presence (for the applicable 3-year or 10-year bar to admission) if they leave the United States. Their departure may prevent them from adjusting status as a permanent resident.

Who May Not File.

You may not be granted an extension or change of status if you were admitted under the Visa Waiver Program or if your current status is:

- An alien in transit (C) or in transit without a visa (TWOV);
- A crewman (D); or
- A fiance'(e) or dependent of a fiance'(e) (K)(1) or (K)(2).

A spouse (K-3) of a U.S. citizen and their children (K-4), accorded such status pursuant to the LIFE Act, may not change to another nonimmigrant status.

EXCEPTION: A K-3 and K-4 are eligible to apply for an extension of status. They should file for an extension during the processing of the Form I-130 filed on their behalf and up to completion of their adjustment of status application.

NOTE: Any nonimmigrant (A to V) may not change their status to K-3 or K-4.

General Filing Instructions.

Please answer all questions by typing or clearly printing in black ink. Indicate that an item is not applicable with "N/A." If the answer is "none," please so state. If you need extra space to answer any item, attach a sheet of paper with your name and your alien registration number (A#), if any, and indicate the number of the item to which the answer refers. Your application must be filed with the required initial evidence. Your application must be properly signed and filed with the correct fee. If you are under 14 years of age, your parent or guardian may sign your application.

Original and Copies.

If these instructions state that a copy of a document may be filed with this application and you choose to send us the original, we will keep that original document in our records.

Translations.

Any foreign language document must be accompanied by a full English translation that the translator has certified as complete and correct, and by the translator's certification that he or she is competent to translate the foreign language into English.

When and Where to File.

You must submit an application for extension of stay or change of status before your current authorized stay expires. We suggest you file at least 45 days before your stay expires, or as soon as you determine your need to change status. Failure to file before the expiration date may be excused if you demonstrate when you file the application that:

- The delay was due to extraordinary circumstances beyond your control;
- The length of the delay was reasonable;
- You have not otherwise violated your status;
- You are still a bona fide nonimmigrant; and
- You are not in removal proceedings.

If you are filing as a V applicant, follow the instructions on the Supplement A to Form I-539, Filing Instructions for V Nonimmigrants, on where to file your application.

If you are filing for reinstatement as an F-1 or M-1 student, submit this application at your local USCIS office. For information on how to use our InfoPass system to make an appointment at your local USCIS office, visit our website at **www.uscis.gov.**

If you are the dependent spouse or child of a principal E, H, L, O, P, R or TN nonimmigrant and you are seeking a change of status or extension of stay, and:

- If your Form I-539 is being filed together with the principal's Form I-129, send the entire Forms I-129/I-539 package to the Vermont Service Center at the address noted below:

  USCIS Vermont Service Center
  75 Lower Welden Street
  St. Albans, VT 05479

- If the principal's Form I-129 has already been approved, submit your Form I-539 to the Vermont Service Center at the address noted below. (Include a copy of the principal's Form I-129 approval notice.)

  USCIS Vermont Service Center
  75 Lower Welden Street
  St. Albans, VT 05479

- If the principal's Form I-129 is still pending, file your Form I-539 with the same service center where the Form I-129 is pending. (Include a copy of the receipt notice for the principal's pending Form I-129.)

In all other instances, mail your application to the USCIS Service Center listed below having jurisdiction over where you live in the United States.

If you live in Connecticut, Delaware, District of Columbia, Maine, Maryland, Massachusetts, New Hampshire, New Jersey, New York, Pennsylvania, Puerto Rico, Rhode Island, the U.S. Virgin Islands, Vermont, Virginia or West Virginia, mail your application to:

USCIS Vermont Service Center
75 Lower Welden Street
St. Albans, VT 05479-0001

If you live in Alabama, Arkansas, Florida, Georgia, Kentucky, Louisiana, Mississippi, New Mexico, North Carolina, Oklahoma, South Carolina, Tennessee or Texas, mail your application to:

USCIS Texas Service Center
P.O. Box 851182
Mesquite, TX 75185-1182

If you live in Arizona, California, Guam, Hawaii or Nevada, mail your application to:

USCIS California Service Center,
P.O. Box 10539
Laguna Niguel, CA 92607-1053

If you live elsewhere in the United States, mail your application to:

USCIS Nebraska Service Center
P.O. Box 87539
Lincoln, NE 68501-7539

What Is the Fee?

The fee for this application is **$200.00**, except for certain A and G nonimmigrants who are not required to pay a fee, as noted in these instructions.

The fee must be submitted in the exact amount. It cannot be refunded. **Do not mail cash.**

All checks and money orders must be drawn on a bank or other institution located in the United States and must be payable in U.S. currency.

The check or money order should be made payable to the **Department of Homeland Security**, except that:

-- If you live in Guam, make your check or money order payable to the "Treasurer, Guam."

-- If you live in the U.S. Virgin Islands, make your check or money order payable to the "Commissioner of Finance of the Virgin Islands."

Checks are accepted subject to collection. An uncollected check will render the application and any document issued invalid. A charge of $30.00 will be imposed if a check in payment of a fee is not honored by the bank on which it is drawn.

How to Check If the Fee Is Correct.

The fee on this form is current as of the edition date appearing in the lower right corner of this page. However, because USCIS fees change periodically, you can verify if the fee is correct by following one of the steps below:

- Visit our website at **www.uscis.gov** and scroll down to "Forms and E-Filing" to check the appropriate fee, or
- Review the Fee Schedule included in your form package, if you called us to request the form, or
- Telephone our National Customer Service Center at **1-800-375-5283** and ask for the fee information.

NOTE: If your petition or application requires a biometric services fee for USCIS to take your fingerprints, photograph or signature, use the same procedure above to confirm the biometrics fee.

Processing Information.

Acceptance.

Any application that is not signed or is not accompanied by the correct fee will be rejected with a notice that the application is deficient. You may correct the deficiency and resubmit the application. An application is not considered properly filed until accepted by USCIS.

Initial Processing.

Once the application has been accepted, it will be checked for completeness. If you do not completely fill out the form, or file it without the required initial evidence, you will not establish a basis for eligibility and we may deny your application.

Requests for More Information or Interview.

We may request more information or evidence or we may request that you appear at a USCIS office for an interview. We may also request that you submit the originals of any copy. We will return these originals when they are no longer required.

Decision.

An application for extension of stay, change of status, initial status or reinstatement, may be approved at the discretion of USCIS. You will be notified in writing of the decision on your application.

Penalties.

If you knowingly and willfully falsify or conceal a material fact or submit a false document with this application, we will deny the benefit you are seeking and may deny any other immigration benefit. In addition, you will face severe penalties provided by law and may be subject to criminal prosecution.

Privacy Act Notice.

We ask for the information on this form and associated evidence to determine if you have established eligibility for the immigration benefit you are seeking. Our legal right to ask for this information is in 8 U.S.C. 1184 and 1258. We may provide this information to other government agencies. Failure to provide this information and any requested evidence may delay a final decision or result in denial of your request.

USCIS Forms and Information.

To order USCIS forms, call our toll-free forms line at **1-800-870-3676**. If you need information on immigration laws, regulations or procedures call our National Customer Service Center at **1-800-375-5283** or visit our internet website at **www.uscis.gov.**

Use InfoPass for Appointments.

As an alternative to waiting in line for assistance at your local USCIS office, you can now schedule an appointment through our internet-based system, **InfoPass.** To access the system, visit our website at **www.uscis.gov.** Use the **InfoPass** appointment scheduler and follow the screen prompts to set up your appointment. **InfoPass** generates an electronic appointment notice that appears on the screen. Print the notice and take it with you to your appointment. The notice gives the time and date of your appointment, along with the address of USCIS office.

Paperwork Reduction Act Notice.

An agency may not conduct or sponsor an information collection and a person is not required to respond to a collection of information unless it displays a currently valid OMB control number.

We try to create forms and instructions that are accurate, can easily be understood and that impose the least possible burden on you to provide us with information. Often this is difficult because some immigration laws are very complex.

The estimate average time to complete and file this application is as follows: (1) 10 minutes to learn about the law and form; (2) 10 minutes to complete the form; and (3) 25 minutes to assemble and file the application; for a total estimated average of 45 minutes per application.

If you have comments regarding the accuracy of this estimate, or suggestions for making this form simpler, you can write to U.S. Citizenship and Immigration Services, Regulatory Management Division, 111 Massachusetts Avenue, N.W., Washington, D.C. 20529; OMB No. 1615-0003. **Do not mail your completed application to this Washington, D.C. address.**

Mailing Label - Complete the following mailing label and submit this page with your application if you are required to submit your original Form I-94.

Name and address of applicant.

Name

Street Number and Name

City, State and Zip Code

Your Form I-94, Arrival/Departure Record is attached. It has been amended to show the extension of stay/change of status granted.

OMB No. 1115-0093; Expires 11/30/07

Department of Homeland Security
U.S. Citizenship and Immigration Services

I-539, Application to Extend/ Change Nonimmigrant Status

START HERE - Please type or print in black ink.

For USCIS Use Only

Part 1. Information about you.

Family Name	Given Name	Middle Name

Address -
In care of -

Street Number and Name			Apt. #
City	State	Zip Code	Daytime Phone #

Country of Birth	Country of Citizenship	
Date of Birth (mm/dd/yyyy)	U. S. Social Security # (if any)	A # (if any)
Date of Last Arrival Into the U.S.	I-94 #	
Current Nonimmigrant Status	Expires on (mm/dd/yyyy)	

Part 2. Application type. *(See instructions for fee.)*

1. I am applying for: *(Check one.)*
   a. ☐ An extension of stay in my current status.
   b. ☐ A change of status. The new status I am requesting is: ______
   c. ☐ Other: *(Describe grounds of eligibility.)* ______
2. Number of people included in this application: *(Check one.)*
   a. ☐ I am the only applicant.
   b. ☐ Members of my family are filing this application with me.
   The total number of people (including me) in the application is: ______
   (Complete the supplement for each co-applicant.)

Part 3. Processing information.

1. I/We request that my/our current or requested status be extended until (mm/dd/yyyy): ______
2. Is this application based on an extension or change of status already granted to your spouse, child or parent?
   ☐ No ☐ Yes. USCIS Receipt # ______
3. Is this application based on a separate petition or application to give your spouse, child or parent an extension or change of status? ☐ No ☐ Yes, filed with this I-539.
   ☐ Yes, filed previously and pending with USCIS. Receipt #: ______
4. If you answered "Yes" to Question 3, give the name of the petitioner or applicant:

   If the petition or application is pending with USCIS, also give the following data:

   Office filed at ______ Filed on (mm/dd/yyyy) ______

Part 4. Additional information.

1. For applicant #1, provide passport information: Country of Issuance	Valid to: (mm/dd/yyyy)
2. Foreign Address: Street Number and Name	Apt. #
City or Town	State or Province
Country	Zip/Postal Code

Returned	Receipt
Date	
Resubmitted	
Date	
Reloc Sent	
Date	
Reloc Rec'd	
Date	
☐ Applicant Interviewed on ______ Date	

☐ *Extension Granted to (Date):* ______

Change of Status/Extension Granted
New Class: ______ From *(Date)*: ______ To *(Date)*: ______

If Denied:
☐ Still within period of stay
☐ S/D to: ______
☐ Place under docket control

Remarks:

Action Block

To Be Completed by *Attorney or Representative,* if any

☐ Fill in box if G-28 is attached to represent the applicant.

ATTY State License #

Form I-539 (Rev. 04/01/06)Y

Part 4. Additional information.

3. **Answer the following questions. If you answer "Yes" to any question, explain on separate sheet of paper.**	Yes	No
a. Are you, or any other person included on the application, an applicant for an immigrant visa?	☐	☐
b. Has an immigrant petition ever been filed for you or for any other person included in this application?	☐	☐
c. Has a Form I-485, Application to Register Permanent Residence or Adjust Status, ever been filed by you or by any other person included in this application?	☐	☐
d. Have you, or any other person included in this application, ever been arrested or convicted of any criminal offense since last entering the U.S.?	☐	☐
e. Have you, or any other person included in this application, done anything that violated the terms of the nonimmigrant status you now hold?	☐	☐
f. Are you, or any other person included in this application, now in removal proceedings?	☐	☐
g. Have you, or any other person included in this application, been employed in the U.S. since last admitted or granted an extension or change of status?	☐	☐

If you answered "Yes" to Question 3f, give the following information concerning the removal proceedings on the attached page entitled **"Part 4. Additional information. Page for answers to 3f and 3g."** Include the name of the person in removal proceedings and information on jurisdiction, date proceedings began and status of proceedings.

If you answered "No" to Question 3g, fully describe how you are supporting yourself on the attached page entitled **"Part 4. Additional information. Page for answers to 3f and 3g."** Include the source, amount and basis for any income.

If you answered "Yes" to Question 3g, fully describe the employment on the attached page entitled **"Part 4. Additional information. Page for answers to 3f and 3g."** Include the name of the person employed, name and address of the employer, weekly income and whether the employment was specifically authorized by USCIS.

Part 5. Signature. (*Read the information on penalties in the instructions before completing this section. You must file this application while in the United States.)*

I certify, under penalty of perjury under the laws of the United States of America, that this application and the evidence submitted with it is all true and correct. I authorize the release of any information from my records that U.S. Citizenship and Immigration Services needs to determine eligibility for the benefit I am seeking.

Signature	Print your Name	Date
Daytime Telephone Number	E-Mail Address	

NOTE: *If you do not completely fill out this form or fail to submit required documents listed in the instructions, you may not be found eligible for the requested benefit and this application may be denied.*

Part 6. Signature of person preparing form, if other than above. ***(Sign below.)***

I declare that I prepared this application at the request of the above person and it is based on all information of which I have knowledge.

Signature	Print your Name	Date
Firm Name and Address	Daytime Telephone Number *(Area Code and Number)*	
	Fax Number *(Area Code and Number)*	E-Mail Address

Part 4. Additional information. Page for answers to 3f and 3g.

If you answered "Yes" to Question 3f in Part 4 on Page 3 of this form, give the following information concerning the removal proceedings. Include the name of the person in removal proceedings and information on jurisdiction, date proceedings began and status of procedings.

If you answered "No" to Question 3g in Part 4 on Page 3 of this form, fully describe how you are supporting yourself. Include the source, amount and basis for any income.

If you answered "Yes" to Question 3g in Part 4 on Page 3 of this form, fully describe the employment. Include the name of the person employed, name and address of the employer, weekly income and whether the employment was specifically authorized by USCIS.

Supplement -1

Attach to Form I-539 when more than one person is included in the petition or application.

(List each person separately. Do not include the person named in the Form I-539.)

Family Name	Given Name	Middle Name	Date of Birth (mm/dd/yyyy)
Country of Birth	County of Citizenship	U.S. Social Security # (if any)	A # (if any)
Date of Arrival (mm/dd/yyyy)		I-94 #	
Current Nonimmigrant Status:		Expires on (mm/dd/yyyy)	
Country Where Passport Issued		Expiration Date (mm/dd/yyyy)	

Family Name	Given Name	Middle Name	Date of Birth (mm/dd/yyyy)
Country of Birth	Country of Citizenship	U.S. Social Security # (if any)	A # (if any)
Date of Arrival (mm/dd/yyyy)		I-94 #	
Current Nonimmigrant Status:		Expires on (mm/dd/yyyy)	
Country Where Passport Issued		Expiration Date (mm/dd/yyyy)	

Family Name	Given Name	Middle Name	Date of Birth (mm/dd/yyyy)
Country of Birth	Country of Citizenship	U.S. Social Security # (if any)	A # (if any)
Date of Arrival (mm/dd/yyyy)		I-94 #	
Current Nonimmigrant Status:		Expires on (mm/dd/yyyy)	
Country Where Passport Issued		Expiration Date (mm/dd/yyyy)	

Family Name	Given Name	Middle Name	Date of Birth (mm/dd/yyyy)
Country of Birth	Country of Citizenship	U.S. Social Security # (if any)	A # (if any)
Date of Arrival (mm/dd/yyyy)		I-94 #	
Current Nonimmigrant Status:		Expires on (mm/dd/yyyy)	
Country Where Passport Issued		Expiration Date (mm/dd/yyyy)	

Family Name	Given Name	Middle Name	Date of Birth (mm/dd/yyyy)
Country of Birth	Country of Citizenship	U.S. Social Security # (if any)	A # (if any)
Date of Arrival (mm/dd/yyyy)		I-94 #	
Current Nonimmigrant Status:		Expires on (mm/dd/yyyy)	
Country Where Passport Issued		Expiration Date (mm/dd/yyyy)	

If you need additional space, attach a separate sheet(s) of paper.

Place your name, A #, if any, date of birth, form number and application date at the top of the sheet(s) of paper.

FORMS FOR RELATIVE-BASED IMMIGRATION

In Chapter 3 we discussed various types of aliens who may qualify for LPR status because they are related to U.S. citizens or LPRs. Here are some of the essential forms that pertain to relative-based immigration.

I-130: Petition for Alien Relative

This form is filed by citizens or LPRs who wish to sponsor their relatives for LPR status.

G-325: Biographic Information

There are various G-325 forms, all of which are designed to provide biographic information about aliens. The most commonly-used is the G-325A, since most relative immigrants are required to use that one. Less commonly-used versions of the G-325 are included in this section as well.

I-864: Affidavit of Support under Section 213A of the Act

As we discussed in Chapter 3, it is essential for an alien seeking LPR status to be sponsored by someone who would be able to provide for the alien financially in case the alien cannot. That is designed to prevent the alien from becoming a public charge. Also included is the I-864A, which is a contract between the sponsor and any "household member" (applicable to certain relatives and/or dependents who live with the sponsor); the I-864P, which outlines poverty guidelines for the purpose of determining financial support; and the I-865, which requires the sponsor to notify DHS of any change of address.

I-134: Affidavit of Support

This form is completed by aliens applying for LPR status and those who sponsor them financially. The sponsor becomes obligated to financially support the alien so that the alien does not become a public charge.

I-600: Permission to Classify Orphan as an Immediate Relative

For immigration purposes, an "orphan" is an alien child under 16 who has either lost both parents or has lost one parent and the other parent has released the child for emigration and adoption, in writing. This form allows the adoptive parent to petition for the child to become his or her immediate relative (just as his or her biological child would be; see Chapter 3). The I-600A is to permit DHS to determine the adoptive parent's qualifications.

OMB # 1615-0012; Expires 01/31/07

Department of Homeland Security
U.S. Citizenship and Immigration Services

I-130, Petition for Alien Relative

Instructions

Read the instructions carefully. If you do not follow the instructions, U.S. Citizenship and Immigration Services (USCIS) may have to return your petition, which may delay final action. NOTE: USCIS is comprised of offices of the former Immigration and Naturalization Service.

1. Who May File?

A citizen or lawful permanent resident of the United States may file this form with U.S. Citizenship and Immigration Services (USCIS) to establish a relationship to certain alien relatives who wish to immigrate to the United States.

You must file a separate form for each eligible relative.

2. For Whom May You File?

A. If you are a citizen, you may file this form for:

(1) Your husband, wife or unmarried child under 21 years old
(2) Your parent if you are at least 21 years old;
(3) Your unmarried son or daughter over 21 years old;
(4) Your married son or daughter of any age;
(5) Your brother or sister if you are at least 21 years old.

B. If you are a lawful permanent resident, you may file this form for:

(1) Your husband or wife;
(2) Your unmarried child under 21 years of age;
(3) Your unmarried son or daughter over 21 years of age.

NOTE:

- If your relative qualifies under paragraph **A(3)**, **A(4)** or **A(5)** above, separate petitions are not required for his or her husband or wife or unmarried children under 21 years of age.
- If your relative qualifies under paragraph **B(2)** or **B(3)** above, separate petitions are not required for his or her unmarried children under 21 years of age.
- The persons described above under this **NOTE** will be able to apply for an immigrant visa along with your relative.

3. For Whom May You Not File?

You may not file for a person in the following categories:

A. An adoptive parent or adopted child, if the adoption took place after the child's 16th birthday, or if the child has not been in the legal custody and living with the parent(s) for at least two years.

B. A natural parent, if the United States citizen son or daughter gained permanent residence through adoption.

C. A stepparent or stepchild, if the marriage that created the relationship took place after the child's 18th birthday.

D. A husband or wife, if you and your spouse were not both physically present at the marriage ceremony, and the marriage was not consummated.

E. A husband or wife, if you gained lawful permanent resident status by virtue of a prior marriage to a United States citizen or lawful permanent resident, unless:

(1) A period of five years has elapsed since you became a lawful permanent resident; or

(2) You can establish by clear and convincing evidence that the prior marriage through which you gained your immigrant status was not entered into for the purpose of evading any provision of the immigration laws; or

(3) Your prior marriage through which you gained your immigrant status was terminated by the death of your former spouse.

F. A husband or wife, if he or she was in exclusion deportation, removal, rescission or judicial proceedings regarding his or her right to remain in the United States when the marriage took place, unless such spouse has resided outside the United States for a two-year period after the date of the marriage.

G. A husband or wife, if it has been legally determined that such an alien has attempted or conspired to enter into a marriage for the purpose of evading the immigration laws.

H. A grandparent, grandchild, nephew, niece, uncle, aunt cousin or in-law.

4. What Are the General Filing Instructions?

A. Type or print legibly in black ink.

B. If extra space is needed to complete any item, attach continuation sheet, indicate the item number, and date and sign each sheet.

C. Answer all questions fully and accurately. If any item does not apply, write "N/A."

D. **Translations**. Any foreign language document must be accompanied by a full English translation that the translator has certified as complete and correct, and by the translator's certification that he or she is competent to translate the foreign language into English.

E. **Copies.** If these instructions state that a copy of a document may be filed with this petition, submit a copy. If you choose to send the original, USCIS may keep that original for our records. If USCIS requires the original, it will be requested.

5. What Documents Do You Need to Show That You Are a United States Citizen?

A. If you were born in the United States, a copy of your birth certificate, issued by the civil registrar, vital statistics office, or other civil authority. If a birth certificate is not available, see **Section 9** on **Page 3** titled, **"What If a Document Is Not Available?"**

B. A copy of your naturalization certificate or certificate of citizenship issued by USCIS or the former INS.

C. A copy of Form FS-240, Report of Birth Abroad of a Citizen of the United States, issued by an American embassy or consulate.

D. A copy of your unexpired U.S. passport; or

E. An original statement from a U.S. consular officer verifying that you are a U.S. citizen with a valid passport.

F. If you do not have any of the above documents and you were born in the United States, see instructions under **Section 9 on Page 3, "What If a Document Is Not Available?"**

6. What Documents Do You Need to Show That You Are a Permanent Resident?

If you are a permanent resident, you must file your petition with a copy of the front and back of your permanent resident card. If you have not yet received your card, submit copies of your passport biographic page and the page showing admission as a permanent resident, or other evidence of permanent resident status issued by USCIS or the former INS.

7. What Documents Do You Need to Prove a Family Relationship?

You have to prove that there is a family relationship between you and your relative. If you are filing for:

A. A husband or wife, submit the following documentation:

(1) A copy of your marriage certificate.

(2) If either you or your spouse were previously married, submit copies of documents showing that all prior marriages were legally terminated.

(3) A passport-style color photo of yourself and a passport-style color photo of your husband or wife, taken within 30 days of the date of this petition. The photos must have a white background and be glossy, unretouched and not mounted. The dimensions of the full frontal facial image should be about 1 inch from the chin to top of the hair. Using pencil or felt pen, lightly print the name (and Alien Registration Number, if known) on the back of each photograph.

(4) A completed and signed Form G-325A, Biographic Information, for you and a Form G-325A for your husband or wife. Except for your name and signature you do not have to repeat on the Form G-325A the information given on your Form I-130 petition.

B. A child and you are the mother: Submit a copy of the child's birth certificate showing your name and the name of your child.

C. A child and you are the father: Submit a copy of the child's birth certificate showing both parents' names and your marriage certificate.

D. A child born out of wedlock and you are the father: If the child was not legitimated before reaching 18 years old, you must file your petition with copies of evidence that a bona fide parent-child relationship existed between the father and the child before the child reached 21 years This may include evidence that the father lived with the child, supported him or her, or otherwise showed continuing parental interest in the child's welfare.

E. A brother or sister: Submit a copy of your birth certificate and a copy of your brother's or sister's birth certificate showing that you have at least one common parent. If you and your brother or sister have a common father but different mothers, submit copies of the marriage certificates of the father to each mother and copies of documents showing that any prior marriages of either your father or mothers were legally terminated. If you and your brother or sister are related through adoption or through a stepparent, or if you have a common father and either of you were not legitimated before your 18th birthday, see also **H** and **I** below.

F. A mother: Submit a copy of your birth certificate showing your name and your mother's name.

G. A father: Submit a copy of your birth certificate showing the names of both parents. Also give a copy of your parents' marriage certificate establishing that your father was married to your mother before you were born, and copies of documents showing that any prior marriages of either your father or mother were legally terminated. If you are filing for a stepparent or adoptive parent, or if your are filing for your father and were not legitimated before your 18th birthday, also see, **D, H** and **I**.

H. Stepparent/stepchild: If your petition is based on a stepparent-stepchild relationship, you must file your petition with a copy of the marriage certificate of the stepparent to the child's natural parent showing that the marriage occurred before the child's 18th birthday, and copies of documents showing that any prior marriages were legally terminated.

I. Adoptive parent or adopted child: If you and the person you are filing for are related by adoption, you must submit a copy of the adoption decree(s) showing that the adoption took place before the child became 16 ready adopted, you must submit a copy of the adoption decree(s) showing that the adoption of the sibling occurred before that child's 18th birthday. In either case, you must also submit copies of evidence that each child was in the legal custody of and resided with the parent(s) who adopted him or her for at least two years before or after the adoption. Legal custody may only be granted by a court or recognized government entity and is usually granted at the time the adoption is finalized. However, if legal custody is granted by a court or recognized government agency prior to the adoption, that time may count to fulfill the two-year legal custody requirement.

8. What If Your Name Has Changed?

If either you or the person you are filing for is using a name other than shown on the relevant documents, you must file your petition with copies of the legal documents that effected the change, such as a marriage certificate, adoption decree or court order.

9. What If a Document Is Not Available?

In such situation, submit a statement from the appropriate civil authority certifying that the document or documents are not available. You must also submit secondary evidence, including:

A. **Church record:** A copy of a document bearing the seal of the church, showing the baptism, dedication or comparable rite occurred within two months after birth and showing the date and place of the child's birth, date of the religious ceremony and the names of the child's parents.

B. **School record:** A letter from the authority (preferably the first school attended) showing the date of admission to the school, the child's date of birth or age at that time place of birth, and names of the parents.

C. **Census record:** State or Federal census record showing the names, place of birth, date of birth or the age of the person listed.

D. **Affidavits:** Written statements sworn to or affirmed by two persons who were living at the time and who have personal knowledge of the event you are trying to prove. For example, the date and place of birth, marriage or death. The person making the affidavit does not have to be a U.S. citizen. Each affidavit should contain the following information regarding the person making the affidavit: his or her full name, address, date and place of birth and his or her relationship to you, if any, full information concerning the event, and complete details explaining how the person acquired knowledge of the event.

10. Where Should You File This Form?

If you reside in the United States, file this form at the USCIS Service Center having jurisdiction over your place of residence.

If you live in Connecticut, Delaware, District of Columbia, Maine, Maryland, Massachusetts, New Hampshire, New Jersey, New York, Pennsylvania, Puerto Rico, Rhode Island, Vermont, U.S. Virgin Islands, Virginia or West Virginia, mail this petition to:

USCIS Vermont Service Center
75 Lower Welden Street
St. Albans, VT 05479-0001

If you live in Alaska, Colorado, Idaho, Illinois, Indiana, Iowa, Kansas, Michigan, Minnesota, Missouri, Montana, Nebraska, North Dakota, Ohio, Oregon, South Dakota, Utah, Washington, Wisconsin or Wyoming, mail this petition to:

USCIS Nebraska Service Center
P.O. Box 87130,
Lincoln, NE 68501-7130

If you live in Alabama, Arkansas, Florida, Georgia, Kentucky, Louisiana, Mississippi, New Mexico, North Carolina, Oklahoma, South Carolina, Tennessee or Texas, mail this petition:

USCIS Texas Service Center
P.O. Box 850919
Mesquite, TX 75185-0919

If you live in Arizona, California, Guam, Hawaii or Nevada, mail this petition to:

USCIS California Service Center
P.O. Box 10130,
Laguna Niguel, CA 92607-0130

NOTE: If the Form I-130 petition is being filed concurrently with Form I-485, Application to Register Permanent Residence or Adjust Status, submit both forms at the local USCIS office having jurisdiction over the place where the Form I-485 applicant resides.

Applicants who reside in the jurisdiction of the Baltimore, MD, USCIS District Office should submit the Form I-130 petition and the Form I-485 concurrently to:

USCIS Vermont Service Center
75 Lower Welden Street
St. Albans, VT 05479-0001

Petitioners residing abroad: If you live in Canada, file your petition at the Vermont Service Center. **Exception:** If you are a U.S. citizen residing in Canada and you are petitioning for your spouse, child or parent, you may file the petition at the nearest American Embassy or Consulate, with the exception of the Consulate in Quebec City. If you reside elsewhere outside the United States, file your relative petition at the USCIS office overseas or the U.S. Embassy or Consulate having jurisdiction over the area where you live. For further information, contact the nearest American Embassy or Consulate.

11. What Is the Fee?

You must pay **$190.00** to file this form. **The fee will not be refunded, whether the petition is approved or not. Do not mail cash.** All checks or money orders, whether U.S. or foreign, must be payable in U.S. currency at a financial institution in the United States. When a check is drawn on the account of a person other than yourself, write your name on the face of the check. If the check is not honored, USCIS will charge you $30.00.

Pay by check or money order in the exact amount. Make the check or money order payable to the **Department of Homeland Security**, unless:

A. You live in Guam and are filing your petition there, make the check or money order payable to the "Treasurer, Guam" or

B. You live in the U.S. Virgin Islands and you are filing your petition there, make your check or money order payable to the "Commissioner of Finance of the Virgin Islands."

These provisions do not apply to the SSI, TANF or Food Stamp eligibility of aliens admitted as refugees, granted asylum or Cuban/ Haitian entrants as defined in section 501(e) of P.L. 96-422, and to dependent children of the sponsor or sponsor's spouse.

The provisions also do not apply to the SSI or Food Stamp eligibility of an alien who becomes blind or disabled after admission to the United States for permanent residency.

IV. Authority, Use and Penalties.

Authority for the collection of the information requested on this form is contained in 8 U.S.C. 1182(a)(15),1184(a) and 1258.

The information will be used principally by the CIS, or by any consular officer to whom it may be furnished, to support an alien's application for benefits under the Immigration and Nationality Act and specifically the assertion that he or she has adequate means of financial support and will not become a public charge. Submission of the information is voluntary.

It may also, as a matter of routine use, be disclosed to other federal, state, local and foreign law enforcement and regulatory agencies, including the Department of Health and Human Services, Department of Agriculture, Department of State, Department of Defense and any component thereof (if the deponent has served or is serving in the armed forces of the United States), Central Intelligence Agency, and individuals and organizations during the course of any investigation to elicit further information required to carry out CIS functions.

Failure to provide the information may result in the denial of the alien's application for a visa or his or her removal from the United States.

V. Information and CIS Forms.

For information on immigration laws, regulations and procedures or to order CIS forms, call our National Customer Service Center at **1-800-375-5283** or visit our website at **www.uscis.gov.**

VI. Privacy Act Notice.

We ask for the information on this form and associated evidence to determine if you have established eligibility for the immigration benefit you are seeking. Our legal right to ask for this information is in 8 U.S.C. 1203 and 1225. We may provide this information to other government agencies. Failure to provide this information and any requested evidence may delay a final decision or result in denial of your request.

VII. Paperwork Reduction Act Notice.

An agency may not conduct or sponsor a collection of information and a person is not required to respond to a collection of information unless it displays a currently valid OMB control number. We try to create forms and instructions that are accurate, can be easily understood and that impose the least possible burden on you to provide us with information. Often this is difficult because some immigration laws are very complex. The estimated average time to complete and file this application is 30 minutes per application, including the time to learn about the law and the form, complete the form, and assemble and submit the Affidavit. If you have comments regarding the accuracy of this estimate or suggestions for making this form simpler, write to the Bureau of Citizenship and Immigration Services, Regulations and Forms Services Division (HQRFS), 425 I Street, N.W., Room 4034, Washington, D.C. 20529; OMB No. 1615-0014. **Do not mail your completed application to this address.**

Department of Homeland Security
U.S. Citizenship and Immigration Services

OMB # 1615-0012; Expires 01/31/07

I-130, Petition for Alien Relative

DO NOT WRITE IN THIS BLOCK - FOR USCIS OFFICE ONLY..

A#	Action Stamp	Fee Stamp
Section of Law/Visa Category ☐ 201(b) Spouse - IR-1/CR-1 ☐ 201(b) Child - IR-2/CR-2 ☐ 201(b) Parent - IR-5 ☐ 203(a)(1) Unm. S or D - F1-1 ☐ 203(a)(2)(A)Spouse - F2-1 ☐ 203(a)(2)(A) Child - F2-2 ☐ 203(a)(2)(B) Unm. S or D - F2-4 ☐ 203(a)(3) Married S or D - F3-1 ☐ 203(a)(4) Brother/Sister - F4-1		Petition was filed on: ____________ (priority date) ☐ Personal Interview ☐ Previously Forwarded ☐ Pet. ☐ Ben. " A" File Reviewed ☐ I-485 Filed Simultaneously ☐ Field Investigation ☐ 204(g) Resolved ☐ 203(a)(2)(A) Resolved ☐ 203(g) Resolved

Remarks:

A. Relationship. You are the petitioner. Your relative is the beneficiary.

1. I am filing this petition for my: ☐ Husband/Wife ☐ Parent ☐ Brother/Sister ☐ Child

2. Are you related by adoption? ☐ Yes ☐ No

3. Did you gain permanent residence through adoption? ☐ Yes ☐ No

B. Information about you.

1. **Name** (Family name in CAPS) (First) (Middle)

2. **Address** (Number and Street) **(Apt.No.)**

(Town or City) (State/Country) (Zip/Postal Code)

3. **Place of Birth** (Town or City) (State/Country)

4. **Date of Birth** (mm/dd/yyyy)

5. **Gender** ☐ Male ☐ Female

6. **Marital Status** ☐ Married ☐ Single ☐ Widowed ☐ Divorced

7. **Other Names Used** (including maiden name)

8. **Date and Place of Present Marriage** (if married)

9. **U.S. Social Security Number** (if any)

10. **Alien Registration Number**

11. **Name(s) of Prior Husband(s)/Wive(s)**

12. **Date(s) Marriage(s) Ended**

13. **If you are a U.S. citizen, complete the following:**
My citizenship was acquired through (check one):
☐ Birth in the U.S.
☐ Naturalization. Give certificate number and date and place of issuance.
☐ Parents. Have you obtained a certificate of citizenship in your own name?
☐ Yes. Give certificate number, date and place of issuance. ☐ No

14a. If you are a lawful permanent resident alien, complete the following: Date and place of admission for or adjustment to lawful permanent residence and class of admission.

14b. Did you gain permanent resident status through marriage to a U.S. citizen or lawful permanent resident?
☐ Yes ☐ No

C. Information about your relative.

1. **Name** (Family name in CAPS) (First) (Middle)

2. **Address** (Number and Street) **(Apt. No.)**

(Town or City) (State/Country) (Zip/Postal Code)

3. **Place of Birth** (Town or City) (State/Country)

4. **Date of Birth** (mm/dd/yyyy)

5. **Gender** ☐ Male ☐ Female

6. **Marital Status** ☐ Married ☐ Single ☐ Widowed ☐ Divorced

7. **Other Names Used** (including maiden name)

8. **Date and Place of Present Marriage** (if married)

9. **U. S. Social Security Number** (if any)

10. **Alien Registration Number**

11. **Name(s) of Prior Husband(s)/Wive(s)**

12. **Date(s) Marriage(s) Ended**

13. **Has your relative ever been in the U.S.?** ☐ Yes ☐ No

14. **If your relative is currently in the U.S., complete the following:**
He or she arrived as a::
(visitor, student, stowaway, without inspection, etc.)

Arrival/Departure Record (I-94) **Date arrived** (mm/dd/yyyy)

Date authorized stay expired, or will expire, as shown on Form I-94 or I-95

15. **Name and address of present employer** (if any)

Date this employment began (mm/dd/yyyy)

16. **Has your relative ever been under immigration proceedings?**
☐ No ☐ Yes Where ________ When ________
☐ Removal ☐ Exclusion/Deportation ☐ Recission ☐ Judicial Proceedings

INITIAL RECEIPT ______ RESUBMITTED ______ RELOCATED: Rec'd ______ Sent ______ COMPLETED: Appv'd ______ Denied ______ Ret'd ______

Form I-130 (Rev. 10/26/05) Y

C. Information about your alien relative. (Continued.)

17. List husband/wife and all children of your relative.
(Name) (Relationship) (Date of Birth) (Country of Birth)

18. Address in the United States where your relative intends to live.
(Street Address) (Town or City) (State)

19. Your relative's address abroad. (Include street, city, province and country)
Phone Number (if any)

20. If your relative's native alphabet is other than Roman letters, write his or her name and foreign address in the native alphabet.
(Name) Address (Include street, city, province and country):

21. If filing for your husband/wife, give last address at which you lived together. (Include street, city, province, if any, and country):
From: (Month) (Year) **To:** (Month) (Year)

22. Complete the information below if your relative is in the United States and will apply for adjustment of status.
Your relative is in the United States and will apply for adjustment of status to that of a lawful permanent resident at USCIS office in:
_______________. If your relative is not eligible for adjustment of status, he or she
(City) (State)
will apply for a visa abroad at the American consular post in _______________ _______________
(City) (Country)

NOTE: Designation of an American embassy or consulate outside the country of your relative's last residence does not guarantee acceptance for processing by that post. Acceptance is at the discretion of the designated embassy or consulate.

D. Other information.

1. If separate petitions are also being submitted for other relatives, give names of each and relationship.

2. Have you ever before filed a petition for this or any other alien? ☐ Yes ☐ No
If "Yes," give name, place and date of filing and result.

WARNING: USCIS investigates claimed relationships and verifies the validity of documents. USCIS seeks criminal prosecutions when family relationships are falsified to obtain visas.

PENALTIES: By law, you may be imprisoned for not more than five years or fined $250,000, or both, for entering into a marriage contract for the purpose of evading any provision of the immigration laws. In addition, you may be fined up to $10,000 and imprisoned for up to five years, or both, for knowingly and willfully falsifying or concealing a material fact or using any false document in submitting this petition.

YOUR CERTIFICATION: I certify, under penalty of perjury under the laws of the United States of America, that the foregoing is true and correct. Furthermore, I authorize the release of any information from my records that U.S. Citizenship and Immigration Services needs to determine eligibility for the benefit that I am seeking.

E. Signature of petitioner.

Date Phone Number ( )

F. Signature of person preparing this form, if other than the petitioner.

I declare that I prepared this document at the request of the person above and that it is based on all information of which I have any knowledge.

Print Name _______________ Signature _______________ Date _______________

Address _______________ **G-28 ID or VOLAG Number, if any.** _______________

Form I-130 (Rev. 10/26/05) Y Page 2

U.S. Department of Justice
Immigration and Naturalization Service

OMB No. 1115-0066

BIOGRAPHIC INFORMATION

(Family name) (First name) (Middle name)	☐ MALE ☐ FEMALE	BIRTHDATE (Mo.-Day-Yr.)	NATIONALITY	FILE NUMBER A
ALL OTHER NAMES USED (Including names by previous marriages)	CITY AND COUNTRY OF BIRTH			SOCIAL SECURITY NO. (If any)

	FAMILY NAME	FIRST NAME	DATE, CITY AND COUNTRY OF BIRTH (If known)	CITY AND COUNTRY OF RESIDENCE.
FATHER				
MOTHER (Maiden name)				

HUSBAND (If none, so state) OR WIFE	FAMILY NAME (For wife, give maiden name)	FIRST NAME	BIRTHDATE	CITY & COUNTRY OF BIRTH	DATE OF MARRIAGE	PLACE OF MARRIAGE

FORMER HUSBANDS OR WIVES (if none, so state)

FAMILY NAME (For wife, give maiden name)	FIRST NAME	BIRTHDATE	DATE & PLACE OF MARRIAGE	DATE AND PLACE OF TERMINATION OF MARRIAGE

APPLICANT'S RESIDENCE LAST FIVE YEARS. LIST PRESENT ADDRESS FIRST.

STREETAND NUMBER	CITY	PROVINCE OR STATE	COUNTRY	FROM MONTH	FROM YEAR	TO MONTH	TO YEAR
						PRESENT TIME	

APPLICANT'S LAST ADDRESS OUTSIDE THE UNITED STATES OF MORE THAN ONE YEAR

STREETAND NUMBER	CITY	PROVINCE OR STATE	COUNTRY	FROM MONTH	FROM YEAR	TO MONTH	TO YEAR

APPLICANT'S EMPLOYMENT LAST FIVE YEARS. (IF NONE, SO STATE) LIST PRESENT EMPLOYMENT FIRST

FULL NAME AND ADDRESS OF EMPLOYER	OCCUPATION (SPECIFY)	FROM MONTH	FROM YEAR	TO MONTH	TO YEAR
				PRESENT TIME	

Show below last occupation abroad if not shown above. (Include all information requested above.)

THIS FORM IS SUBMITTED IN CONNECTION WITH APPLICATION FOR ☐ NATURALIZATION ☐ OTHER (SPECIFY): ☐ STATUS AS PERMANENT RESIDENT	SIGNATURE OF APPLICANT	DATE
Submit both copies of this form.	IF YOUR NATIVE ALPHABET IS IN OTHER THAN ROMAN LETTERS, WRITE YOUR NAME IN YOUR NATIVE ALPHABET IN THIS SPACE:	

PENALTIES: SEVERE PENALTIES ARE PROVIDED BY LAW FOR KNOWINGLY AND WILLFULLY FALSIFYING OR CONCEALING A MATERIAL FACT.

APPLICANT

BE SURE TO PUT YOUR NAME AND ALIEN REGISTRATION NUMBER IN THE BOX OUTLINED BY HEAVY BORDER BELOW.

COMPLETE THIS BOX (Family name)	(Given name)	(Middle name)	(Alien registration number)

Form G-325 (Rev. 09/11/00)Y

(1) Ident.

U.S. Department of Justice
Immigration and Naturalization Service

OMB No. 1115-0066

BIOGRAPHIC INFORMATION

(Family name) (First name) (Middle name)	☐ MALE ☐ FEMALE	BIRTHDATE (Mo.-Day-Yr.)	NATIONALITY	FILE NUMBER A
ALL OTHER NAMES USED (Including names by previous marriages)	CITY AND COUNTRY OF BIRTH			SOCIAL SECURITY NO. (If any)

	FAMILY NAME	FIRST NAME	DATE, CITY AND COUNTRY OF BIRTH (If known)	CITY AND COUNTRY OF RESIDENCE.
FATHER				
MOTHER (Maiden name)				

HUSBAND (If none, so state) OR WIFE	FAMILY NAME (For wife, give maiden name)	FIRST NAME	BIRTHDATE	CITY & COUNTRY OF BIRTH	DATE OF MARRIAGE	PLACE OF MARRIAGE

FORMER HUSBANDS OR WIVES (if none, so state)

FAMILY NAME (For wife, give maiden name)	FIRST NAME	BIRTHDATE	DATE & PLACE OF MARRIAGE	DATE AND PLACE OF TERMINATION OF MARRIAGE

APPLICANT'S RESIDENCE LAST FIVE YEARS. LIST PRESENT ADDRESS FIRST.

STREETAND NUMBER	CITY	PROVINCE OR STATE	COUNTRY	FROM MONTH	FROM YEAR	TO MONTH	TO YEAR
						PRESENT TIME	

APPLICANT'S LAST ADDRESS OUTSIDE THE UNITED STATES OF MORE THAN ONE YEAR

STREETAND NUMBER	CITY	PROVINCE OR STATE	COUNTRY	FROM MONTH	FROM YEAR	TO MONTH	TO YEAR

APPLICANT'S EMPLOYMENT LAST FIVE YEARS. (IF NONE, SO STATE) LIST PRESENT EMPLOYMENT FIRST

FULL NAME AND ADDRESS OF EMPLOYER	OCCUPATION (SPECIFY)	FROM MONTH	FROM YEAR	TO MONTH	TO YEAR
				PRESENT TIME	

Show below last occupation abroad if not shown above. (Include all information requested above.)

THIS FORM IS SUBMITTED IN CONNECTION WITH APPLICATION FOR ☐ NATURALIZATION ☐ OTHER (SPECIFY): ☐ STATUS AS PERMANENT RESIDENT	SIGNATURE OF APPLICANT	DATE
Submit both copies of this form.	IF YOUR NATIVE ALPHABET IS IN OTHER THAN ROMAN LETTERS, WRITE YOUR NAME IN YOUR NATIVE ALPHABET IN THIS SPACE:	

PENALTIES: SEVERE PENALTIES ARE PROVIDED BY LAW FOR KNOWINGLY AND WILLFULLY FALSIFYING OR CONCEALING A MATERIAL FACT.

APPLICANT **BE SURE TO PUT YOUR NAME AND ALIEN REGISTRATION NUMBER IN THE BOX OUTLINED BY HEAVY BORDER BELOW.**

COMPLETE THIS BOX (Family name)	(Given name)	(Middle name)	(Alien registration number)

(OTHER AGENCY USE)	INS USE (Office of Origin) OFFICE CODE: TYPE OF CASE: DATE:

Form G-325 (Rev. 09/11/00)Y Page 2

(2) Rec. BR.

OMB No. 1615-0008

Department of Homeland Security
U.S. Citizenship and Immigration Services

G-325A, Biographic Information

(Family name) (First name) (Middle name)	☐ Male ☐ Female	Birthdate (mm/dd/yyyy)	Citizenship/Nationality	File Number A
All Other Names Used (Including names by previous marriages)	City and Country of Birth			U.S. Social Security # *(If any)*

	Family Name	First Name	Date, City and Country of Birth (If Known)	City and Country of Residence
Father				
Mother (Maiden name)				

Husband (If none, so state) or Wife	Family Name (For wife, give maiden name)	First Name	Birthdate	City and Country of Birth	Date of Marriage	Place of Marriage

Former Husbands or Wives(if none, so state) Family Name (For wife, give maiden name)	First Name	Birthdate	Date and Place of Marriage	Date and Place of Termination of Marriage

Applicant's residence last five years. List present address first.

Street and Number	City	Province or State	Country	From Month	From Year	To Month	To Year
						Present Time	

Applicant's last address outside the United States of more than one year.

Street and Number	City	Province or State	Country	From Month	From Year	To Month	To Year

Applicant's employment last five years. (If none, so state.) List present employment first.

Full Name and Address of Employer	Occupation (Specify)	From Month	From Year	To Month	To Year
				Present Time	

Show below last occupation abroad if not shown above. (Include all information requested above.)

This form is submitted in connection with application for:
☐ Naturalization ☐ Status as Permanent Resident
☐ Other (Specify):

Signature of Applicant Date

Submit all copies of this form.

If your native alphabet is in other than Roman letters, write your name in your native alphabet below:

Penalties: Severe penalties are provided by law for knowingly and willfully falsifying or concealing a material fact.

Applicant: **Be sure to put your name and Alien Registration Number in the box outlined by heavy border below.**

Complete This Box (Family Name)	(Given Name)	(Middle Name)	(Alien Registration Number)

(1) Ident.

Form G-325A (Rev. 05/31/05)N (Prior editions may be used until 12/31/05)

Department of Homeland Security
U.S. Citizenship and Immigration Services

OMB No. 1615-0008

G-325A, Biographic Information

(Family name) (First name) (Middle name)	☐ Male ☐ Female	Birthdate (mm/dd/yyyy)	Citizenship/Nationality	File Number A
All Other Names Used (Including names by previous marriages)	City and Country of Birth			U.S. Social Security # *(If any)*

	Family Name	First Name	Date, City and Country of Birth (If Known)	City and Country of Residence
Father				
Mother (Maiden name)				

Husband (If none, so state) or Wife	Family Name (For wife, give maiden name)	First Name	Birthdate	City and Country of Birth	Date of Marriage	Place of Marriage

Former Husbands or Wives(if none, so state) Family Name (For wife, give maiden name)	First Name	Birthdate	Date and Place of Marriage	Date and Place of Termination of Marriage

Applicant's residence last five years. List present address first.

Street and Number	City	Province or State	Country	From Month	From Year	To Month	To Year
						Present Time	

Applicant's last address outside the United States of more than one year.

Street and Number	City	Province or State	Country	From Month	From Year	To Month	To Year

Applicant's employment last five years. (If none, so state.) List present employment first.

Full Name and Address of Employer	Occupation (Specify)	From Month	From Year	To Month	To Year
				Present Time	

Show below last occupation abroad if not shown above. (Include all information requested above.)

This form is submitted in connection with application for: ☐ Naturalization ☐ Status as Permanent Resident ☐ Other (Specify):	**Signature of Applicant**	Date
Submit all copies of this form.	If your native alphabet is in other than Roman letters, write your name in your native alphabet below:	

Penalties: Severe penalties are provided by law for knowingly and willfully falsifying or concealing a material fact.

Applicant: **Be sure to put your name and Alien Registration Number in the box outlined by heavy border below.**

Complete This Box (Family Name)	(Given Name)	(Middle Name)	(Alien Registration Number)

(OTHER AGENCY USE)	USCIS USE (Office of Origin)
	Office Code: Type Of Case: Date:

(2) Rec. Br.

Form G-325A (Rev. 05/31/05)N (Prior editions may be used until 12/31/05) Page 2

Department of Homeland Security
U.S. Citizenship and Immigration Services

OMB No. 1615-0008

G-325A, Biographic Information

(Family name) (First name) (Middle name)	☐ Male ☐ Female	Birthdate (mm/dd/yyyy)	Citizenship/Nationality	File Number A
All Other Names Used (Including names by previous marriages)	City and Country of Birth			U.S. Social Security # *(If any)*

	Family Name	First Name	Date, City and Country of Birth (If Known)	City and Country of Residence
Father				
Mother (Maiden name)				

Husband (If none, so state) or Wife	Family Name (For wife, give maiden name)	First Name	Birthdate	City and Country of Birth	Date of Marriage	Place of Marriage

Former Husbands or Wives(if none, so state) Family Name (For wife, give maiden name)	First Name	Birthdate	Date and Place of Marriage	Date and Place of Termination of Marriage

Applicant's residence last five years. List present address first.

Street and Number	City	Province or State	Country	From Month	From Year	To Month	To Year
						Present Time	

Applicant's last address outside the United States of more than one year.

Street and Number	City	Province or State	Country	From Month	From Year	To Month	To Year

Applicant's employment last five years. (If none, so state.) List present employment first.

Full Name and Address of Employer	Occupation (Specify)	From Month	From Year	To Month	To Year
				Present Time	

Show below last occupation abroad if not shown above. (Include all information requested above.)

This form is submitted in connection with application for: ☐ Naturalization ☐ Status as Permanent Resident ☐ Other (Specify):	**Signature of Applicant**	Date
Submit all copies of this form.	If your native alphabet is in other than Roman letters, write your name in your native alphabet below:	

Penalties: Severe penalties are provided by law for knowingly and willfully falsifying or concealing a material fact.

Applicant: **Be sure to put your name and Alien Registration Number in the box outlined by heavy border below.**

Complete This Box (Family Name)	(Given Name)	(Middle Name)	(Alien Registration Number)

(OTHER AGENCY USE)	USCIS USE (Office of Origin)
	Office Code: Type Of Code: DATE:

(3) C.

Department of Homeland Security
U.S. Citizenship and Immigration Services

OMB No. 1615-0008

G-325A, Biographic Information

(Family name) (First name) (Middle name)	Male / Female	Birthdate (mm/dd/yyyy)	Citizenship/Nationality	File Number A

All Other Names Used (Including names by previous marriages)	City and Country of Birth	U.S. Social Security # *(If any)*

	Family Name	First Name	Date, City and Country of Birth (If Known)	City and Country of Residence
Father				
Mother (Maiden name)				

Husband (If none, so state) or Wife	Family Name (For wife, give maiden name)	First Name	Birthdate	City and Country of Birth	Date of Marriage	Place of Marriage

Former Husbands or Wives(if none, so state) Family Name (For wife, give maiden name)	First Name	Birthdate	Date and Place of Marriage	Date and Place of Termination of Marriage

Applicant's residence last five years. List present address first.

Street and Number	City	Province or State	Country	From Month	From Year	To Month	To Year
						Present Time	

Applicant's last address outside the United States of more than one year.

Street and Number	City	Province or State	Country	From Month	From Year	To Month	To Year

Applicant's employment last five years. (If none, so state.) List present employment first.

Full Name and Address of Employer	Occupation (Specify)	From Month	From Year	To Month	To Year
				Present Time	

Show below last occupation abroad if not shown above. (Include all information requested above.)

This form is submitted in connection with application for:
☐ Naturalization ☐ Status as Permanent Resident
☐ Other (Specify):

Signature of Applicant Date

Submit all copies of this form.

If your native alphabet is in other than Roman letters, write your name in your native alphabet below:

Penalties: Severe penalties are provided by law for knowingly and willfully falsifying or concealing a material fact.

Applicant: **Be sure to put your name and Alien Registration Number in the box outlined by heavy border below.**

Complete This Box (Family Name)	**(Given Name)**	**(Middle Name)**	**(Alien Registration Number)**

(OTHER AGENCY USE)

USCIS USE (Office of Origin)

Office Code:

Type Of Case:

Date:

(4) Consulate

Form G-325A (Rev. 05/31/05)N (Prior editions may be used until 12/31/05) Page 4

U.S. Department of Justice
Immigration and Naturalization Service

BIOGRAPHIC INFORMATION

OMB No. 1115-0066

(Family name) (First name) (Middle name)	☐ MALE ☐ FEMALE	BIRTHDATE (Mo.-Day-Yr.)	NATIONALITY	FILE NUMBER A-
ALL OTHER NAMES USED (Including names by previous marriages)		CITY AND COUNTY OF BIRTH		SOCIAL SECURITY NO. (If any)

	FAMILY NAME	FIRST NAME	DATE, CITY AND COUNTRY OF BIRTH (If known)	CITY AND COUNTRY OF RESIDENCE
FATHER				
MOTHER (Maiden name)				

HUSBAND (If none, so state) OR WIFE	FAMILY NAME (For wife, give maiden name)	FIRST NAME	BIRTHDATE	CITY & COUNTRY OF BIRTH	DATE OF MARRIAGE	PLACE OF MARRIAGE

FORMER HUSBANDS OR WIVES (If none, so state)

FAMILY NAME (For wife, give maiden name)	FIRST NAME	BIRTHDATE	DATE AND PLACE OF MARRIAGE	DATE AND PLACE OF TERMINATION OF MARRIAGE

APPLICANTS RESIDENCE LAST FIVE YEARS. LIST PRESENT ADDRESS FIRST.

STREET AND NUMBER	CITY	PROVINCE OR STATE	COUNTRY	FROM MONTH	FROM YEAR	TO MONTH	TO YEAR
						PRESENT TIME	

APPLICANT'S LAST ADDRESS OUTSIDE THE UNITED STATES OF MORE THAN ONE YEAR.

				FROM		TO	

APPLICANT'S EMPLOYMENT LAST FIVE YEARS. (IF NONE, SO STATE.) LIST PRESENT EMPLOYMENT FIRST.

FULL NAME AND ADDRESS OF EMPLOYER	OCCUPATION (Specify)	FROM MONTH	FROM YEAR	TO MONTH	TO YEAR
				PRESENT TIME	

Show below last occupation abroad if not shown above. (Include all information requested above.)

THIS FORM IS SUBMITTED IN CONNECTION WITH APPLICATION FOR:

☐ NATURALIZATION ☐ OTHER (Specify)

☐ STATUS AS PERMANENT RESIDENT

If serving or ever served in the Armed Forces of the United States, complete the following:

Branch of Service | Rank | Service Number

To Other Agency: Please furnish on the reverse of this form, or by attachment hereto, any derogatory information that may be contained in your records concerning the above person, for use in connection with consideration of above application and return to U.S. Immigration and Naturalization Service.

INS USE (Office of Origin)

Office Code
Type of Case
Date

(OTHER AGENCY)

MIL PERS	AIR RESERVE
USAF PERS	ARMY PERS

SEE O.I. 328. 1 FOR MAILING ADDRESS

FORM G-325B
(Rev. 10-1-82)Y

☐ OSI (USAF)	☐ ONI (USN)
☐ MID G-2	☐ PROV. MAR.

(ALL DEFENSE CHECKS)

MAIL TO:

DIRECTOR,
UNITED STATES ARMY INVESTIGATIVE
RECORDS REPOSITORY
ATTN: ICIRR-A
FOR MEADE, MARYLAND 20755
ATTENTION: LIAISON OFFICE
IMMIGRATION AND NATURALIZATION SERVICE

STATE (P.P.)	STATE (S.Y.)	OTHER

SEE O.I. 105.4 FOR MAILING ADDRESS

FOR STATE DEPARTMENT USE

☐ SY
☐ RSC
☐ RMR
☐ C:Visa
☐ R:Visa
☐ ORM

Date ________________ 19 ___

Date of entry into service
Date of seperation
Service number

The records of this Department show the following with respect to the subject of your inquiry:

All organizations, clubs or societies in the United States, or in any other country, of which subject was a member at any time, and dates thereof. (If none, show "None".) ________________

____

____

____

All arrests, convictions, disciplinary actions, court martial proceedings, and illegal or immoral conduct in which subject involved, including dates and results thereof. (If none, show "None".)

____

____

____

____

Details of any oral or written statements, conduct, behavior or associations of the subject which may indicate belief in, advocacy of or preference or sympathy for Communism or any other foreign ideology inconsistent with loyalty to the United States or the form of government of the United States or attachment to the principles of the United States Constitution. (If none, show "None".)

____

____

____

____

Additional information or references.

____

____

____

____

I certify that the information here given concerning the person named is correct according to the records of the

____
(Name of Department or organization)

Official signature ________________

By ________________

U.S. Department of Justice
Immigration and Naturalization Service

BIOGRAPHIC INFORMATION

OMB No. 1115-0066

(Family name) (First name) (Middle name)	☐ MALE ☐ FEMALE	BIRTHDATE (Mo.-Day-Yr.)	NATIONALITY	FILE NUMBER A-
ALL OTHER NAMES USED (Including names by previous marriages)		CITY AND COUNTY OF BIRTH		SOCIAL SECURITY NO. (If any)

	FAMILY NAME	FIRST NAME	DATE, CITY AND COUNTRY OF BIRTH (If known)	CITY AND COUNTRY OF RESIDENCE
FATHER				
MOTHER (Maiden name)				

HUSBAND(If none, so state) OR WIFE	FAMILY NAME (For wife, give maiden name)	FIRST NAME	BIRTHDATE	CITY & COUNTRY OF BIRTH	DATE OF MARRIAGE	PLACE OF MARRIAGE

FORMER HUSBANDS OR WIVES (If none, so state)

FAMILY NAME (For wife, give maiden name)	FIRST NAME	BIRTHDATE	DATE AND PLACE OF MARRIAGE	DATE AND PLACE OF TERMINATION OF MARRIAGE

APPLICANTS RESIDENCE LAST FIVE YEARS. LIST PRESENT ADDRESS FIRST.

STREET AND NUMBER	CITY	PROVINCE OR STATE	COUNTRY	FROM MONTH	FROM YEAR	TO MONTH	TO YEAR
						PRESENT TIME	

APPLICANT'S LAST ADDRESS OUTSIDE THE UNITED STATES OF MORE THAN ONE YEAR.

				FROM		TO	

APPLICANT'S EMPLOYMENT LAST FIVE YEARS. (IF NONE, SO STATE.) LIST PRESENT EMPLOYMENT FIRST.

FULL NAME AND ADDRESS OF EMPLOYER	OCCUPATION (Specify)	FROM MONTH	FROM YEAR	TO MONTH	TO YEAR
				PRESENT TIME	
Show below last occupation abroad if not shown above. (Include all information requested above.)					

THIS FORM IS SUBMITTED IN CONNECTION WITH APPLICATION FOR:
☐ NATURALIZATION ☐ OTHER (Specify)
☐ STATUS AS PERMANENT RESIDENT

If serving or ever served in the Armed Forces of the United States, complete the following:
Branch of Service | Rank | Service Number

To Other Agency: Please furnish on the reverse of this form, or by attachment hereto, any derogatory information that may be contained in your records concerning the above person, for use in connection with consideration of above application and return to U.S. Immigration and Naturalization Service.

INS USE (Office of Origin)
Office Code
Type of Case
Date

(OTHER AGENCY)

FOR STATE DEPARTMENT USE

MIL PERS	AIR RESERVE
USAF PERS	ARMY PERS
SEE O.I. 328. 1 FOR MAILING ADDRESS	

☐ OSI (USAF)	☐ ONI (USN)
☐ MID G-2	☐ PROV. MAR.

(ALL DEFENSE CHECKS)
MAIL TO:
DIRECTOR,
UNITED STATES ARMY INVESTIGATIVE RECORDS REPOSITORY
ATTN: ICIRR-A
FOR MEADE, MARYLAND 20755
ATTENTION: LIAISON OFFICE
IMMIGRATION AND NATURALIZATION SERVICE

STATE (P.P.)	STATE (S.Y.)	OTHER
SEE O.I. 105.4 FOR MAILING ADDRESS		

☐ SY
☐ RSC
☐ RMR
☐ C:Visa
☐ R:Visa
☐ ORM

FORM G-325B
(Rev. 10-1-82)Y

Date ______________________ 19 ___

Date of entry into service
Date of seperation
Service number

The records of this Department show the following with respect to the subject of your inquiry:

All organizations, clubs or societies in the United States, or in any other country, of which subject was a member at any time, and dates thereof. (If none, show "None".) ______________________

____

____

____

All arrests, convictions, disciplinary actions, court martial proceedings, and illegal or immoral conduct in which subject involved, including dates and results thereof. (If none, show "None".)

____

____

____

____

Details of any oral or written statements, conduct, behavior or associations of the subject which may indicate belief in, advocacy of or preference or sympathy for Communism or any other foreign ideology inconsistent with loyalty to the United States or the form of government of the United States or attachment to the principles of the United States Constitution. (If none, show "None".)

____

____

____

____

Additional information or references.

____

____

____

____

I certify that the information here given concerning the person named is correct according to the records of the

____
(Name of Department or organization)

Official signature ______________________

By ______________________

U.S. Department of Justice
Immigration and Naturalization Service

FORM G-325C
BIOGRAPHIC INFORMATION

OMB No. 1115-0066
Approval expires 4-30-85

(FAMILY NAME)	(FIRST NAME)	(MIDDLE NAME)	☐ MALE ☐ FEMALE	BIRTHDATE (MO.-DAY-YR.)	NATIONALITY
ALL OTHER NAMES USED			CITY AND COUNTRY OF BIRTH		

	FAMILY NAME	FIRST NAME	DATE, CITY AND COUNTRY OF BIRTH (IF KNOWN)	CITY AND COUNTRY OF RESIDENCE
FATHER				
MOTHER (MAIDEN NAME)				

HUSBAND OR WIFE (IF NONE, SO STATE)	FAMILY NAME (FOR WIFE, GIVE MAIDEN NAME)	FIRST NAME	BIRTHDATE	CITY & COUNTRY OF BIRTH	DATE OF MARRIAGE	PLACE OF MARRIAGE

FORMER HUSBANDS OR WIVES (FILL IN THE BLOCKS BELOW. IF NONE, STATE "NONE".)

FAMILY NAME (FOR WIFE, GIVE MAIDEN NAME)	FIRST NAME	BIRTHDATE	DATE & PLACE OF MARRIAGE	DATE AND PLACE OF TERMINATION OF MARRIAGE

APPLICANT'S RESIDENCE LAST FIVE YEARS. LIST PRESENT ADDRESS FIRST.

STREET AND NUMBER	CITY	PROVINCE OR STATE	COUNTRY	FROM MONTH	FROM YEAR	TO MONTH	TO YEAR
						PRESENT TIME	

APPLICANT'S EMPLOYMENT LAST FIVE YEARS. (IF NONE, SO STATE) LIST PRESENT EMPLOYMENT FIRST.

FULL NAME AND ADDRESS OF EMPLOYER	OCCUPATION	FROM MONTH	FROM YEAR	TO MONTH	TO YEAR
				PRESENT TIME	

APPLICANT FOR REFUGEE STATUS	IF YOUR NATIVE ALPHABET IS IN OTHER THAN ROMAN LETTERS, WRITE YOUR NAME IN YOUR NATIVE ALPHABET BELOW:

DATE	(SIGNATURE OF APPLICANT)	PENALTIES: SEVERE PENALTIES ARE PROVIDED BY LAW FOR KNOWINGLY AND WILLFULLY FALSIFYING OR CONCEALING A MATERIAL FACT.

APPLICANT: BE SURE TO PUT YOUR NAME IN THE BOX OUTLINED BY HEAVY BORDER BELOW.

COMPLETE THIS BOX (FAMILY NAME)	(GIVEN NAME)	(MIDDLE NAME)

FORM G-325C (Rev 10-1-82)Y

U.S. Department of Justice
Immigration and Naturalization Service

OMB No. 1115-0214

Affidavit of Support Under Section 213A of the Act

INSTRUCTIONS

Purpose of this Form

This form is required to show that an intending immigrant has adequate means of financial support and is not likely to become a public charge.

Sponsor's Obligation

The person completing this affidavit is the sponsor. A sponsor's obligation continues until the sponsored immigrant becomes a U.S. citizen, can be credited with 40 qualifying quarters of work, departs the United States permanently, or dies. Divorce does not terminate the obligation. By signing this form, you, the sponsor, agree to support the intending immigrant and any spouse and/or children immigrating with him or her and to reimburse any government agency or private entity that provides these sponsored immigrants with Federal, State, or local means-tested public benefits.

General Filing Instructions

Please answer all questions by typing or clearly printing in black ink only. Indicate that an item is not applicable with "N/A". If an answer is "none," please so state. If you need extra space to answer any item, attach a sheet of paper with your name and Social Security number, and indicate the number of the item to which the answer refers.

You must submit an affidavit of support for each applicant for immigrant status. You may submit photocopies of this affidavit for any spouse or children immigrating with an immigrant you are sponsoring. For purposes of this form, a spouse or child is immigrating with an immigrant you are sponsoring if he or she is: 1) listed in Part 3 of this affidavit of support; and 2) applies for an immigrant visa or adjustment of status within 6 months of the date this affidavit of support is originally completed and signed. The signature on the affidavit must be notarized by a notary public or signed before an Immigration or a Consular officer.

You should give the completed affidavit of support with all required documentation to the sponsored immigrant for submission to either a Consular Officer with Form OF-230, Application for Immigrant Visa and Alien Registration, or an Immigration Officer with Form I-485, Application to Register Permanent Residence or Adjust Status. You may enclose the affidavit of support and accompanying documents in a sealed envelope to be opened only by the designated Government official. The sponsored immigrant must submit the affidavit of support to the Government within 6 months of its signature.

Who Needs an Affidavit of Support under Section 213A?

This affidavit must be filed at the time an intending immigrant is applying for an immigrant visa or adjustment of status. It is required for:

- All immediate relatives, including orphans, and family-based immigrants. (Self-petitioning widow/ers and battered spouses and children are exempt from this requirement); and
- Employment-based immigrants where a relative filed the immigrant visa petition or has a significant ownership interest (5 percent or more) in the entity that filed the petition.

Who Completes an Affidavit of Support under Section 213A?

- For immediate relatives and family-based immigrants, the family member petitioning for the intending immigrant must be the sponsor.
- For employment-based immigrants, the petitioning relative or a relative with a significant ownership interest (5 percent or more) in the petitioning entity must be the sponsor. The term "relative," for these purposes, is defined as husband, wife, father, mother, child, adult son or daughter, brother, or sister.
- If the petitioner cannot meet the income requirements, a joint sponsor may submit an additional affidavit of support.

A sponsor, or joint sponsor, must also be:

- A citizen or national of the United States or an alien lawfully admitted to the United States for permanent residence;
- At least 18 years of age; and
- Domiciled in the United States or its territories and possessions.

Sponsor's Income Requirement

As a sponsor, your household income must equal or exceed 125 percent of the Federal poverty line for your household size. For the purpose of the affidavit of support, household size includes yourself, all persons related to you by birth, marriage, or adoption living in your residence, your dependents, any immigrants you have previously sponsored using INS Form I-864 if that obligation has not terminated, and the intending immigrant(s) in Part 3 of this affidavit of support. The poverty guidelines are calculated and published annually by the Department of Health and Human Services. Sponsors who are on active duty in the U.S. Armed Forces other than for training need only demonstrate income at 100 percent of the poverty line *if* they are submitting this affidavit for the purpose of sponsoring their spouse or child.

If you are currently employed and have an *individual* income which meets or exceeds 125 percent of the Federal poverty line or (100 percent, if applicable) for your household size, you do not need to list the income of any other person. When determining your income, you may include the income generated by individuals related to you by birth, marriage, or adoption who are living in your residence, if they have lived in your residence for the previous 6 months, or who are listed as dependents on your most recent Federal income tax return whether or not they live in your residence. For their income to be considered, these household members or dependents must be willing to make their income available for the support of the sponsored immigrant(s) if necessary, and to complete and sign Form I-864A, Contract Between Sponsor and Household Member. However, a household member who is the immigrant you are sponsoring only need complete Form I-864A if his or her income will be used to determine your ability to support a spouse and/or children immigrating with him or her.

If in any of the most recent 3 tax years, you and your spouse each reported income on a joint income tax return, but you want to use only your own income to qualify (and your spouse is not submitting a Form I-864A), you may provide a separate breakout of your individual income for these years. Your individual income will be based on the earnings from your W 2 forms, Wage and Tax Statement, submitted to IRS for any such years. If necessary to meet the income requirement, you may also submit evidence of other income listed on your tax returns which can be attributed to you. You must provide documentation of such reported income, including Forms 1099 sent by the payer, which show your name and Social Security number.

You must calculate your household size and total household income as indicated in Parts 4.B. and 4.C. of this form. You must compare your total household income with the minimum income requirement for your household size using the poverty guidelines. For the purposes of the affidavit of support, determination of your ability to meet the income requirements will be based on the most recent poverty guidelines published in the Federal Register at the time the Consular or Immigration Officer makes a decision on the intending immigrant's application for an immigrant visa or adjustment of status. Immigration and Consular Officers will begin to use updated poverty guidelines on the first day of the second month after the date the guidelines are published in the Federal Register.

If your total household income is equal to or higher than the minimum income requirement for your household size, you do not need to provide information on your assets, and you may *not* have a joint sponsor unless you are requested to do so by a Consular or Immigration Officer. If your total household income does not meet the minimum income requirement, the intending immigrant will be ineligible for an immigrant visa or adjustment of status, unless:

- You provide evidence of assets that meet the requirements outlined under "Evidence of Assets" below; and/or
- The immigrant you are sponsoring provides evidence of assets that meet the requirements under "Evidence of Assets" below; or
- A joint sponsor assumes the liability of the intending immigrant with you. A joint sponsor must execute a separate affidavit of support on behalf of the intending immigrant and any accompanying family members. A joint sponsor must individually meet the minimum requirement of 125 percent of the poverty line based on his or her household size and income and/or assets, including any assets of the sponsored immigrant.

The Government may pursue verification of any information provided on or in support of this form, including employment, income, or assets with the employer, financial or other institutions, the Internal Revenue Service, or the Social Security Administration.

Evidence of Income

In order to complete this form you must submit the following evidence of income:

- A copy of your complete Federal income tax return, as filed with the Internal Revenue Service, for each of the most recent 3 tax years. If you were not required to file a tax return in any of the most recent 3 tax years, you must provide an explanation. If you filed a joint income tax return and are using only your own income to qualify, you must also submit copies of your W-2s for each of the most recent 3 tax years, and if necessary to meet the income requirement, evidence of other income reported on your tax returns, such as Forms 1099.

- If you rely on income of any members of your household or dependents in order to reach the minimum income requirement, copies of their Federal income tax returns for the most recent 3 tax years. These persons must each complete and sign a Form I-864A, Contract Between Sponsor and Household Member.

- Evidence of current employment or self-employment, such as a recent pay statement, or a statement from your employer on business stationery, showing beginning date of employment, type of work performed, and salary or wages paid. You must also provide evidence of current employment for any person whose income is used to qualify.

Evidence of Assets

If you want to use your assets, the assets of your household members or dependents, and/or the assets of the immigrant you are sponsoring to meet the minimum income requirement, you must provide evidence of assets with a cash value that equals at least five times the difference between your total household income and the minimum income requirement. For the assets of a household member, other than the immigrant(s) you are sponsoring, to be considered, the household member must complete and sign Form I-864A, Contract Between Sponsor and Household Member.

All assets must be supported with evidence to verify location, ownership, and value of each asset. Any liens and liabilities relating to the assets must be documented. List only assets that can be readily converted into cash within one year. Evidence of assets includes, but is not limited to the following:

- Bank statements covering the last 12 months, *or* a statement from an officer of the bank or other financial institution in which you have deposits, including deposit/withdrawal history for the last 12 months, and current balance;
- Evidence of ownership and value of stocks, bonds, and certificates of deposit, and date(s) acquired;
- Evidence of ownership and value of other personal property, and date(s) acquired; and
- Evidence of ownership and value of any real estate, and date(s) acquired.

Change of Sponsor's Address

You are required by 8 U.S.C. 1183a(d) and 8 CFR 213a.3 to report every change of address to the Immigration and Naturalization Service and the State(s) in which the sponsored immigrant(s) reside(s). You must report changes of address to INS on Form I-865, Sponsor's Notice of Change of Address, within 30 days of any change of address. You must also report any change in your address to the State(s) in which the sponsored immigrant(s) live.

Penalties

If you include in this affidavit of support any material information that you know to be false, you may be liable for criminal prosecution under the laws of the United States.

If you fail to give notice of your change of address, as required by 8 U.S.C. 1183a(d) and 8 CFR 213a.3, you may be liable for the civil penalty established by 8 U.S.C. 1183a(d)(2). The amount of the civil penalty will depend on whether you failed to give this notice because you were aware that the immigrant(s) you sponsored had received Federal, State, or local means-tested public benefits.

Privacy Act Notice

Authority for the collection of the information requested on this form is contained in 8 U.S.C. 1182(a)(4), 1183a, 1184(a), and 1258. The information will be used principally by the INS or by any Consular Officer to whom it is furnished, to support an alien's application for benefits under the Immigration and Nationality Act and specifically the assertion that he or she has adequate means of financial support and will not become a public charge. Submission of the information is voluntary. Failure to provide the information will result in denial of the application for an immigrant visa or adjustment of status.

The information may also, as a matter of routine use, be disclosed to other Federal, State, and local agencies or private entities providing means-tested public benefits for use in civil action against the sponsor for breach of contract. It may also be disclosed as a matter of routine use to other Federal, State, local, and foreign law enforcement and regulatory agencies to enable these entities to carry out their law enforcement responsibilites.

Reporting Burden

A person is not required to respond to a collection of information unless it displays a currently valid OMB control number. We try to create forms and instructions that are accurate, can be easily understood, and which impose the least possible burden on you to provide us with information. Often this is difficult because some immigration laws are very complex. The reporting burden for this collection of information on Form I-864 is computed as follows: 1) learning about the form, 63 minutes; 2) completing the form, 105 minutes; and 3) assembling and filing the form, 65 minutes, for an estimated average of 3 hours and 48 minutes minutes per response. The reporting burden for collection of information on Form I-864A is computed as: 1) learning about the form, 20 minutes; 2) completing the form, 55 minutes; 3) assembling and filing the form, 30 minutes, for an estimated average of 1 hour and 45 minutes per response. If you have comments regarding the accuracy of this estimates, or suggestions for making this form simpler, you can write to the Immigration and Naturalization Service, HQPDI, 425 I Street, N.W., Room 4034, Washington, DC 20536. **DO NOT MAIL YOUR COMPLETED AFFIDAVIT OF SUPPORT TO THIS ADDRESS.**

CHECK LIST

The following items must be submitted with Form I-864, Affidavit of Support Under Section 213A:

For *ALL* sponsors:

- ☐ This form, the **I-864, completed and signed** before a notary public or a Consular or Immigration Officer.
- ☐ Proof of **current employment** or self employment.
- ☐ Your individual Federal **income tax returns for the most recent 3 tax years,** or an explanation if fewer are submitted. Your **W-2s** for any of the most recent 3 tax years for which you filed a joint tax return but are using only your own income to qualify. Forms 1099 or evidence of other reported income *if* necessary to qualify.

For *SOME* sponsors:

- ☐ *If the immigrant you are sponsoring is bringing a spouse or children,* **photocopies of the immigrant's affidavit of support** for each spouse and/or child immigrating with the immigrant you are sponsoring.
- ☐ *If you are on active duty in the U.S. Armed Forces and are sponsoring a spouse or child using the 100 percent of poverty level exception,* **proof of your active military status.**

If you are using the income of ***persons in your household or dependents*** *to qualify,*

- ☐ A separate **Form I-864A** for each person whose income you will use. A sponsored immigrant/household member who is not immigrating with a spouse and/or child **does not need to complete Form I-864A.**
- ☐ Proof of their **residency and relationship** to you if they are not listed as dependents on your income tax return for the most recent tax year.
- ☐ Proof of their **current employment** or self-employment.

- [ ] Copies of their individual Federal **income tax returns for the 3 most recent tax years,** or an explanation if fewer are submitted.

If you use your assets or the assets of the sponsored immigrant to qualify,

- [ ] **Documentation of assets** establishing location, ownership, date of acquisition, and value. Evidence of any liens or liabilities against these assets.

- [ ] A separate **Form I-864A** for each household member other than the sponsored immigrant/household member.

If you are a joint sponsor or the relative of an employment-based immigrant requiring an affidavit of support, **proof of your citizenship status.**

- [ ] For U.S. citizens or nationals, a copy of your birth certificate, passport, or certificate of naturalization or citizenship.

- [ ] For lawful permanent residents, a copy of both sides of your I-551, Permanent Resident Card.

OMB No. 1115-0214

U.S. Department of Justice
Immigration and Naturalization Service

Affidavit of Support Under Section 213A of the Act

START HERE - Please Type or Print

Part 1. Information on Sponsor (You)

Last Name	First Name	Middle Name	
Mailing Address *(Street Number and Name)*		Apt/Suite Number	
City		State or Province	
Country		ZIP/Postal Code	Telephone Number

Place of Residence if different from above *(Street Number and Name)*		Apt/Suite Number
City		State or Province
Country	ZIP/Postal Code	Telephone Number
Date of Birth *(Month, Day, Year)*	Place of Birth *(City, State, Country)*	Are you a U.S. Citizen? ☐ Yes ☐ No
Social Security Number	A-Number *(If any)*	

FOR AGENCY USE ONLY

This Affidavit	Receipt
[ ] Meets [ ] Does not meet Requirements of Section 213A	
Officer or I.J. Signature	
Location	
Date	

Part 2. Basis for Filing Affidavit of Support

I am filing this affidavit of support because *(check one)*:

a. ☐ I filed/am filing the alien relative petition.

b. ☐ I filed/am filing an alien worker petition on behalf of the intending immigrant, who is related to me as my ______________________ *(relationship)*.

c. ☐ I have ownership interest of at least 5% ______________________ *(name of entity which filed visa petition)* which filed an alien worker petition on behalf of the intending immigrant, who is related to me as my ______________________ *(relationship)*.

d. ☐ I am a joint sponsor willing to accept the legal obligations with any other sponsor(s).

Part 3. Information on the Immigrant(s) You Are Sponsoring

Last Name	First Name	Middle Name
Date of Birth *(Month, Day, Year)*	Sex ☐ Male ☐ Female	Social Security Number *(If any)*

Country of Citizenship	A-Number *(If any)*	
Current Address *(Street Number and Name)*	Apt/Suite Number	City

State/Province	Country	ZIP/Postal Code	Telephone Number

List any spouse and/or children immigrating with the immigrant named above in this Part: *(Use additional sheet of paper if necessary.)*

Name	Relationship to Sponsored Immigrant			Date of Birth			A-Number *(If any)*	Social Security *(If any)*
	Spouse	Son	Daughter	Mo.	Day	Yr.		

Form I-864 (Rev. 11/05/01)Y

Part 4. Eligibility to Sponsor

To be a sponsor you must be a U.S. citizen or national or a lawful permanent resident. If you are not the petitioning relative, you must provide proof of status. To prove status, U.S. citizens or nationals must attach a copy of a document proving status, such as a U.S. passport, birth certificate, or certificate of naturalization, and lawful permanent residents must attach a copy of both sides of their Permanent Resident Card (Form I-551).

The determination of your eligibility to sponsor an immigrant will be based on an evaluation of your demonstrated ability to maintain an annual income at or above 125 percent of the Federal poverty line (100 percent if you are a petitioner sponsoring your spouse or child and you are on active duty in the U.S. Armed Forces). The assessment of your ability to maintain an adequate income will include your current employment, household size, and household income as shown on the Federal income tax returns for the 3 most recent tax years. Assets that are readily converted to cash and that can be made available for the support of sponsored immigrants if necessary, including any such assets of the immigrant(s) you are sponsoring, may also be considered.

The greatest weight in determining eligibility will be placed on current employment and household income. If a petitioner is unable to demonstrate ability to meet the stated income and asset requirements, a joint sponsor who *can* meet the income and asset requirements is needed. Failure to provide adequate evidence of income and/or assets or an affidavit of support completed by a joint sponsor will result in denial of the immigrant's application for an immigrant visa or adjustment to permanent resident status.

A. Sponsor's Employment

I am: 1. ☐ Employed by ______________________ *(Provide evidence of employment)*

Annual salary __________ or hourly wage $ __________ *(for* ______ *hours per week)*

2. ☐ Self employed ______________________ *(Name of business)*

Nature of employment or business ______________________

3. ☐ Unemployed or retired since ______________________

B. Sponsor's Household Size

Number

1. Number of persons (related to you by birth, marriage, or adoption) living in your residence, including yourself *(Do NOT include persons being sponsored in this affidavit.)* ________
2. Number of immigrants being sponsored in this affidavit *(Include all persons in Part 3.)* ________
3. Number of immigrants **NOT** living in your household whom you are obligated to support under a previously signed Form I-864. ________
4. Number of persons who are otherwise dependent on you, as claimed in your tax return for the most recent tax year. ________
5. Total household size. ***(Add lines 1 through 4.)*** **Total** ________

List persons below who are included in lines 1 or 3 for whom you previously have submitted INS Form I-864, *if your support obligation has not terminated.*

(If additional space is needed, use additional paper)

Name	A-Number	Date Affidavit of Support Signed	Relationship

Part 4. Eligibility to Sponsor ***(Continued)***

C. Sponsor's Annual Household Income

Enter total unadjusted income from your Federal income tax return for the most recent tax year below. If you last filed a joint income tax return but are using only your *own* income to qualify, list total earnings from your W-2 Forms, or, *if* necessary to reach the required income for your household size, include income from other sources listed on your tax return. If your *individual* income does not meet the income requirement for your household size, you may also list total income for anyone related to you by birth, marriage, or adoption currently living with you in your residence if they have lived in your residence for the previous 6 months, or any person shown as a dependent on your Federal income tax return for the most recent tax year, even if not living in the household. For their income to be considered, household members or dependents must be willing to make their income available for support of the sponsored immigrant(s) and to complete and sign Form I-864A, Contract Between Sponsor and Household Member. A sponsored immigrant/household member only need complete Form I-864A if his or her income will be used to determine your ability to support a spouse and/or children immigrating with him or her.

You must attach evidence of current employment and copies of income tax returns as filed with the IRS for the most recent 3 tax years for yourself and all persons whose income is listed below. See "Required Evidence " in Instructions. Income from all 3 years will be considered in determining your ability to support the immigrant(s) you are sponsoring.

- ☐ I filed a single/separate tax return for the most recent tax year.
- ☐ I filed a joint return for the most recent tax year which includes only my own income.
- ☐ I filed a joint return for the most recent tax year which includes income for my spouse and myself.
  - ☐ I am submitting documentation of my individual income (Forms W-2 and 1099).
  - ☐ I am qualifying using my spouse's income; my spouse is submitting a Form I-864A.

Indicate most recent tax year ________________
(tax year)

Sponsor's individual income $________________

or

Sponsor and spouse's combined income $________________
(If spouse's income is to be considered, spouse must submit Form I-864A.)

Income of other qualifying persons.
(List names; include spouse if applicable. Each person must complete Form I-864A.)

________________________________ $________________

________________________________ $________________

________________________________ $________________

Total Household Income $________________

Explain on separate sheet of paper if you or any of the above listed individuals were not required to file Federal income tax returns for the most recent 3 years, or if other explanation of income, employment, or evidence is necessary.

D. Determination of Eligibility Based on Income

1. ☐ I am subject to the 125 percent of poverty line requirement for sponsors.
   ☐ I am subject to the 100 percent of poverty line requirement for sponsors on active duty in the U.S. Armed Forces sponsoring their spouse or child.
2. Sponsor's total household size, from Part 4.B., line 5 ________________.
3. Minimum income requirement from the Poverty Guidelines chart for the year of ________________ *(year)* is $ __________ for this household size.

If you are currently employed and your household income for your household size is equal to or greater than the applicable poverty line requirement (from line D.3.), you do not need to list assets (Parts 4.E. and 5) or have a joint sponsor (Part 6) unless you are requested to do so by a Consular or Immigration Officer. You may skip to Part 7, Use of the Affidavit of Support to Overcome Public Charge Ground of Admissibility. **Otherwise, you should continue with Part 4.E.**

Part 4. Eligibility to Sponsor *(Continued)*

E. Sponsor's Assets and Liabilities

Your assets and those of your qualifying household members and dependents may be used to demonstrate ability to maintain an income at or above 125 percent (or 100 percent, if applicable) of the poverty line *if* they are available for the support of the sponsored immigrant(s) and can readily be converted into cash within 1 year. The household member, other than the immigrant(s) you are sponsoring, must complete and sign Form I-864A, Contract Between Sponsor and Household Member. List the cash value of each asset *after* any debts or liens are subtracted. Supporting evidence must be attached to establish location, ownership, date of acquisition, and value of each asset listed, including any liens and liabilities related to each asset listed. See "Evidence of Assets" in Instructions.

Type of Asset	Cash Value of Assets *(Subtract any debts)*
Savings deposits	$
Stocks, bonds, certificates of deposit	$
Life insurance cash value	$
Real estate	$
Other *(specify)*	$
Total Cash Value of Assets	$ ________________

Part 5. Immigrant's Assets and Offsetting Liabilities

The sponsored immigrant's assets may also be used in support of your ability to maintain income at or above 125 percent of the poverty line *if* the assets are or will be available in the United States for the support of the sponsored immigrant(s) and can readily be converted into cash within 1 year.

The sponsored immigrant should provide information on his or her assets in a format similar to part 4.E. above. Supporting evidence must be attached to establish location, ownership, and value of each asset listed, including any liens and liabilities for each asset listed. See "Evidence of Assets" in Instructions.

Part 6. Joint Sponsors

If household income and assets do not meet the appropriate poverty line for your household size, a joint sponsor is required. There may be more than one joint sponsor, but each joint sponsor must individually meet the 125 percent of poverty line requirement based on his or her household income and/or assets, including any assets of the sponsored immigrant. By submitting a separate Affidavit of Support under Section 213A of the Act (Form I-864), a joint sponsor accepts joint responsibility with the petitioner for the sponsored immigrant(s) until they become U.S. citizens, can be credited with 40 quarters of work, leave the United States permanently, or die.

Part 7. Use of the Affidavit of Support to Overcome Public Charge Ground of Inadmissibility

Section 212(a)(4)(C) of the Immigration and Nationality Act provides that an alien seeking permanent residence as an immediate relative (including an orphan), as a family-sponsored immigrant, or as an alien who will accompany or follow to join another alien is considered to be likely to become a public charge and is inadmissible to the United States unless a sponsor submits a legally enforceable affidavit of support on behalf of the alien. Section 212(a)(4)(D) imposes the same requirement on an employment-based immigrant, and those aliens who accompany or follow to join the employment- based immigrant, if the employment-based immigrant will be employed by a relative, or by a firm in which a relative owns a significant interest. Separate affidavits of support are required for family members at the time they immigrate if they are not included on this affidavit of support or do not apply for an immigrant visa or adjustment of status within 6 months of the date this affidavit of support is originally signed. The sponsor must provide the sponsored immigrant(s) whatever support is necessary to maintain them at an income that is at least 125 percent of the Federal poverty guidelines.

I submit this affidavit of support in consideration of the sponsored immigrant(s) not being found inadmissible to the United States under section 212(a)(4)(C) (or 212(a)(4)(D) for an employment-based immigrant) and to enable the sponsored immigrant(s) to overcome this ground of inadmissibility. I agree to provide the sponsored immigrant(s) whatever support is necessary to maintain the sponsored immigrant(s) at an income that is at least 125 percent of the Federal poverty guidelines. I understand that my obligation will continue until my death or the sponsored immigrant(s) have become U.S. citizens, can be credited with 40 quarters of work, depart the United States permanently, or die.

Part 7. Use of the Affidavit of Support to Overcome Public Charge Grounds *(Continued)*

Notice of Change of Address.

Sponsors are required to provide written notice of any change of address within 30 days of the change in address until the sponsored immigrant(s) have become U.S. citizens, can be credited with 40 quarters of work, depart the United States permanently, or die. To comply with this requirement, the sponsor must complete INS Form I-865. Failure to give this notice may subject the sponsor to the civil penalty established under section 213A(d)(2) which ranges from $250 to $2,000, unless the failure to report occurred with the knowledge that the sponsored immigrant(s) had received means-tested public benefits, in which case the penalty ranges from $2,000 to $5,000.

If my address changes for any reason before my obligations under this affidavit of support terminate, I will complete and file INS Form I-865, Sponsor's Notice of Change of Address, within 30 days of the change of address. I understand that failure to give this notice may subject me to civil penalties.

Means-tested Public Benefit Prohibitions and Exceptions.

Under section 403(a) of Public Law 104-193 (Welfare Reform Act), aliens lawfully admitted for permanent residence in the United States, with certain exceptions, are ineligible for most Federally-funded means-tested public benefits during their first 5 years in the United States. This provision does not apply to public benefits specified in section 403(c) of the Welfare Reform Act or to State public benefits, including emergency Medicaid; short-term, non-cash emergency relief; services provided under the National School Lunch and Child Nutrition Acts; immunizations and testing and treatment for communicable diseases; student assistance under the Higher Education Act and the Public Health Service Act; certain forms of foster-care or adoption assistance under the Social Security Act; Head Start programs; means-tested programs under the Elementary and Secondary Education Act; and Job Training Partnership Act programs.

Consideration of Sponsor's Income in Determining Eligibility for Benefits.

If a permanent resident alien is no longer statutorily barred from a Federally-funded means-tested public benefit program and applies for such a benefit, the income and resources of the sponsor and the sponsor's spouse will be considered (or deemed) to be the income and resources of the sponsored immigrant in determining the immigrant's eligibility for Federal means-tested public benefits. Any State or local government may also choose to consider (or deem) the income and resources of the sponsor and the sponsor's spouse to be the income and resources of the immigrant for the purposes of determining eligibility for their means-tested public benefits. The attribution of the income and resources of the sponsor and the sponsor's spouse to the immigrant will continue until the immigrant becomes a U.S. citizen or has worked or can be credited with 40 qualifying quarters of work, provided that the immigrant or the worker crediting the quarters to the immigrant has not received any Federal means-tested public benefit during any creditable quarter for any period after December 31, 1996.

I understand that, under section 213A of the Immigration and Nationality Act (the Act), as amended, this affidavit of support constitutes a contract between me and the U.S. Government. This contract is designed to protect the United States Government, and State and local government agencies or private entities that provide means-tested public benefits, from having to pay benefits to or on behalf of the sponsored immigrant(s), for as long as I am obligated to support them under this affidavit of support. I understand that the sponsored immigrants, or any Federal, State, local, or private entity that pays any means-tested benefit to or on behalf of the sponsored immigrant(s), are entitled to sue me if I fail to meet my obligations under this affidavit of support, as defined by section 213A and INS regulations.

Civil Action to Enforce.

If the immigrant on whose behalf this affidavit of support is executed receives any Federal, State, or local means-tested public benefit before this obligation terminates, the Federal, State, or local agency or private entity may request reimbursement from the sponsor who signed this affidavit. If the sponsor fails to honor the request for reimbursement, the agency may sue the sponsor in any U.S. District Court or any State court with jurisdiction of civil actions for breach of contract. INS will provide names, addresses, and Social Security account numbers of sponsors to benefit-providing agencies for this purpose. Sponsors may also be liable for paying the costs of collection, including legal fees.

Part 7. Use of the Affidavit of Support to Overcome Public Charge Grounds *(Continued)*

I acknowledge that section 213A(a)(1)(B) of the Act grants the sponsored immigrant(s) and any Federal, State, local, or private agency that pays any means-tested public benefit to or on behalf of the sponsored immigrant(s) standing to sue me for failing to meet my obligations under this affidavit of support. I agree to submit to the personal jurisdiction of any court of the United States or of any State, territory, or possession of the United States if the court has subject matter jurisdiction of a civil lawsuit to enforce this affidavit of support. I agree that no lawsuit to enforce this affidavit of support shall be barred by any statute of limitations that might otherwise apply, so long as the plaintiff initiates the civil lawsuit no later than ten (10) years after the date on which a sponsored immigrant last received any means-tested public benefits.

Collection of Judgment.

I acknowledge that a plaintiff may seek specific performance of my support obligation. Furthermore, any money judgment against me based on this affidavit of support may be collected through the use of a judgment lien under 28 U.S.C 3201, a writ of execution under 28 U.S.C 3203, a judicial installment payment order under 28 U.S.C 3204, garnishment under 28 U.S.C 3205, or through the use of any corresponding remedy under State law. I may also be held liable for costs of collection, including attorney fees.

Concluding Provisions.

I, ________________________________, certify under penalty of perjury under the laws of the United States that:

(a) I know the contents of this affidavit of support signed by me;
(b) All the statements in this affidavit of support are true and correct,
(c) I make this affidavit of support for the consideration stated in Part 7, freely, and without any mental reservation or purpose of evasion;
(d) Income tax returns submitted in support of this affidavit are true copies of the returns filed with the Internal Revenue Service; and
(e) Any other evidence submitted is true and correct.

________________________________ ________________________
(Sponsor's Signature) *(Date)*

Subscribed and sworn to (or affirmed) before me this

__________ day of ________________, ____________
(Month) *(Year)*

at ________________________________.

My commission expires on ____________________.

____
(Signature of Notary Public or Officer Administering Oath)

____
(Title)

Part 8. If someone other than the sponsor prepared this affidavit of support, that person must complete the following:

I certify under penalty of perjury under the laws of the United States that I prepared this affidavit of support at the sponsor's request, and that this affidavit of support is based on all information of which I have knowledge.

Signature	Print Your Name	Date	Daytime Telephone Number

Firm Name and Address

U.S. Department of Justice
Immigration and Naturalization Service

OMB No. 1115-0214

Contract Between Sponsor and Household Member

Sponsor's Name *(Last, First, Middle)*	Social Security Number	A-Number (If any)

General Filing Instruction

Form I-864A, Contract Between Sponsor and Household Member, is an attachment to Form I-864, Affidavit of Support Under Section 213A of the Immigration and Nationality Act (the Act). The sponsor enters the information above, complete Part 2 of this form, and signs in Part 5. The household member completes Parts 1 and 3 of this form and signs in Part 6. A household member who is also the sponsored immigrant completes Parts 1 and 4 (instead of Part 3) of this form and signs i Part 6. The Privacy Act Notice and information on penalties for misrepresentation or fraud are included on the instructions to Form I-864.

The signatures on the I-864A must be notarized by a notary public or signed before an immigration or consular officer. A separate form must be used for each household member whose income and/or assets are being used to qualify. This blank form may be photocopied for that purpose. A sponsored immigrant who qualifies as a household member is only required to complete this form if he or she has one or more family members immigrating with him or her and is making his or her *income* available for their support. Sponsored immigrants who are using their *assets* to qualify are not required to complete this form. This completed form is submitted with Form I-864 by the sponsored immigrant with an application for an immigrant visa or adjustment of status.

Purpose

This contract is intended to benefit the sponsored immigrant(s) and any agency of the Federal Government, any agency of a State or local government, or any private entity to which the sponsor has an obligation under the affidavit of support to reimburse for benefits granted to the sponsored immigrant, and these parties will have the right to enforce this contract in ai court with appropriate jurisdiction. Under Section 213A of Act, this contract must be completed and signed by the sponsoı and any household member, including the sponsor's spouse, whose income is included as household income by a person sponsoring one or more immigrants. The contract must also be completed if a sponsor is relying on the assets of a househo member who is not the sponsored immigrant to meet the income requirements. If the sponsored immigrant is a household member immigrating with a spouse or children, and is using his or her income to assist the sponsor in meeting the income requirement, he or she must complete and sign this contract as a "sponsored immigrant/household member."

By signing this form, a household member, who is not a sponsored immigrant, agrees to make his or her income and/or assets available to the sponsor to help support the immigrant(s) for whom the sponsor has filed an affidavit of support and to be responsible, along with the sponsor, to pay any debt incurred by the sponsor under the affidavit of support. A sponsored immigrant/household member who signs this contract agrees to make his or her income available to the sponsor to help support any spouse or children immigrating with him or her and to be responsible, along with the sponsor, to pay any debt incurred by the sponsor under the affidavit of support. The obligations of the household member and the sponsored immigrant/household member under this contract terminate when the obligations of the sponsor under the affidavit of support terminate. For additional information see section 213A of the Act, part 213a of title 8 of the Code of Federal Regulations, and Form I-864, Affidavit of Support Under Section 213A of the Act.

Definitions:

1) An "affidavit of support" refers to Form I-864, Affidavit of Support Under Section 213A of the Act, which is complete and filed by the sponsor.
2) A "sponsor" is a person, either the petitioning relative, the relative with a significant ownership interest in the petitionin entity, or another person accepting joint and several liability with the sponsor, who completes and files the Affidavit of Support under Section 213A of the Act on behalf of a sponsored immigrant.
3) A "household member" is any person (a) sharing a residence with the sponsor for at least the last 6 months who is related to the sponsor by birth, marriage, or adoption, *or* (b) whom the sponsor has lawfully claimed as a dependent or the sponsor's most recent federal income tax return even if that person does not live at the same residence as the sponsor, *and* whose income and/or assets will be used to demonstrate the sponsor's ability to maintain the sponsored immigrant(s) at an annual income at the level specified in section 213A(f)(1)(E) or 213A(f)(3) of the Act.
4) A "sponsored immigrant" is a person listed on this form on whose behalf an affidavit of support will be completed anc filed.
5) A "sponsored immigrant/household member" is a sponsored immigrant who is also a household member.

Part 1. Information on Sponsor's Household Member or Sponsored Immigrant/Household Member

Last Name	First Name	Middle Name

Date of Birth *(Month,Day, Year)*	Social Security Number *(Mandatory for non-citizens; voluntary for U.S. citizens)*	A-Number *(If any)*

Address *(Street Number and Name)* Apt Number	City	State/Province	ZIP/Postal Code

Telephone Number ( )	Relationship to Sponsor: ______ I am: ☐ The sponsor's household member. *(Complete Part 3.)* ☐ The sponsored immigrant/household member. *(Complete Part*	Length of residence with sponsor ____ years, ____ months)

Part 2. Sponsor's Promise

I, THE SPONSOR, ______________ *(Print name of sponsor)*, in consideration of the household member's promise to support the sponsored immigrant(s) and to be jointly and severally liable for any obligations I incur under the affidavit of support, promise to complete and file an affidavit of support on behalf of the following ________ *(Indicate number)* sponsored immigrant(s):

Name of Sponsored Immigrant *(First, Middle, Last)*	Date of Birth *(Month, Day, Year)*	Social Security Number *(If any)*	A-Number *(If any)*

Part 3. Household Member's Promise

I, THE HOUSEHOLD ______________ *(Print name of household member)*, in consideration of the sponsor's promise to complete and file the affidavit of support on behalf of the sponsored immigrant(s):

1) Promise to provide any and all financial support necessary to assist the sponsor in maintaining the sponsored immigrant(s) at or above the minimum income provided for in section 213A(a)(1)(A) of the Act (not less than 125 percent of the Federal Poverty Guidelines) during the period in which the affidavit of support is enforceable;

2) Agree to be jointly and severally liable for payment of any and all obligations owed by the sponsor under the affidavit of support to the sponsored immigrant(s), to any agency of the Federal Government, to any agency of a state or local government, or to any private entity;

3) Agree to submit to the personal jurisdiction of any court of the United States or of any state, territory, or possession of the United States if the court has subject matter jurisdiction of a civil lawsuit to enforce this contract or the affidavit of support; and

4) Certify under penalty of perjury under the laws of the United States that all the information provided on this form is true and correct to the best of my knowledge and belief and that the income tax returns I submitted in support of the sponsor affidavit are true copies of the returns filed with the Internal Revenue Service.

Part 4. Sponsored Immigrant/Household Member's Promise

I, THE SPONSORED IMMIGRANT/HOUSEHOLD ______________________________
(Print name o f sponsored immigrant)

in consideration of the sponsor's promise to complete and file the affidavit of support on behalf of the sponsored immigrant(s) accompanying me:

1) Promise to provide any and all financial support necessary to assist the sponsor in maintaining any sponsored immigrant(s) immigrating with me at or above the minimum income provided for in section 213A(a)(1)(A) of the Act (not less than 125 percent of the Federal Poverty Guidelines) during the period in which the affidavit of support is enforceable;

2) Agree to be jointly and severally liable for payment of any and all obligations owed by the sponsor under the affidavit of support to any sponsored immigrant(s) immigrating with me, to any agency of the Federal Government, to any agency of a state or local government, or to any private entity;

3) Agree to submit to the personal jurisdiction of any court of the United States or of any state, territory, or possession of the United States if the court has subject matter jurisdiction of a civil lawsuit to enforce this contract or the affidavit of support; and

4) Certify under penalty of perjury under the laws of the United States that all the information provided on this form is tru and correct to the best of my knowledge and belief and that the income tax returns I submitted in support of the sponsor's affidavit of support are true copies of the returns filed with the Internal Revenue Service.

Part 5. Sponsor's Signature

______________________________ Date: ______________________________
Sponsor's Signature

Subscribed and sworn to *(or affirmed)* before me this________ day of ________________, __________
(Month) *(Year)*

at ______________________________. My commission expires on________________.

______________________________ ______________________________
Signature of Notary Public or Officer Administering Oath *Title*

Part 6. Household Member's or Sponsored Immigrant/Household Member's Signature

______________________________ Date: ______________________________
Household Member's or Sponsored Immigrant/Household Member's Signature

Subscribed and sworn to *(or affirmed)* before me this________ day of ________________, __________
(Month) *(Year)*

at ______________________________. My commission expires on________________.

______________________________ ______________________________
Signature of Notary Public or Officer Administering Oath *Title*

Department of Homeland Security
U.S.Citizenship and Immigration Services

OMB# 1615-0075; Expires 09/30/06

I-864P, Poverty Guidelines

2006 Poverty Guidelines*
Minimum Income Requirement For Use in Completing Form I-864

For the 48 Contiguous States, the District of Columbia, Puerto Rico, the U.S. Virgin Islands, and Guam:

Sponsor's Household Size	100% of Poverty Line For sponsors on active duty in the U.S. Armed Forces who are petitioning for their spouse or child.	**125% of Poverty Line** **For all other sponsors**
2	$13,200	**$16,500**
3	16,600	**20,750**
4	20,000	**25,000**
5	23,400	**29,250**
6	26,800	**33,500**
7	30,200	**37,750**
8	33,600	**42,000**
	Add $3,400 for each additional person.	**Add $4,250 for each additional person.**

	For Alaska		For Hawaii	
Sponsor's Household Size	100% of Poverty Line For sponsors on active duty in the U.S. Armed Forces who are petitioning for their spouse or child	**125% of Poverty Line** **For all other sponsors**	100% of Poverty Line For sponsors on active duty in the U.S. Armed Forces who are petitioning for their spouse or child	**125% of Poverty Line** **For all other sponsors**
2	$16,500	**$20,625**	$15,180	**$18,975**
3	20,750	**25,937**	19,090	**23,862**
4	25,000	**31,250**	23,000	**28,750**
5	29,250	**36,562**	26,910	**33,637**
6	33,500	**41,875**	30,820	**38,525**
7	37,750	**47,187**	34,730	**43,412**
8	42,000	**52,500**	38,640	**48,300**
	Add $4,250 for each additional person.	**Add $5,112 for each additional person.**	Add $3,910 for each additional person.	**Add $4,887 for each additional person.**

Means-Tested Public Benefits

Federal Means-Tested Public Benefits. To date, Federal agencies administering benefit programs have determined that Federal means-tested public benefits include Food Stamps, Medicaid, Supplemental Security Income (SSI), Temporary Assistance for Needy Families (TANF), and the State Child Health Insurance Program (SCHIP).

State Means-Tested Public Benefits. Each State will determine which, if any, of its public benefits are means-tested. If a State determines that it has programs which meet this definition, it is encouraged to provide notice to the public on which programs are included. Check with the State public assistance office to determine which, if any, State assistance programs have been determined to be State means-tested public benefits.

Programs Not Included: The following Federal and State programs are ***not*** included as means-tested benefits: emergency Medicaid; short-term, non-cash emergency relief; services provided under the National School Lunch and Child Nutrition Acts; immunizations and testing and treatment for communicable diseases; student assistance under the Higher Education Act and the Public Health Service Act; certain forms of foster-care or adoption assistance under the Social Security Act; Head Start Programs; means-tested programs under the Elementary and Secondary Education Act; and Job Training Partnership Act programs.

*** These poverty guidelines remain in effect for use with Form I-864, Affidavit of Support, from March 1, 2006 until new poverty guidelines go into effect in the spring of 2007.**

Form I-864P (Rev. 02/21/06)N

OMB No. 1615-0076; Expires 6/30/2006

Department of Homeland Security
U.S. Citizenship and Immigration Services

I-865, Sponsor's Notice of Change of Address

Instructions

Please read these instructions carefully to properly complete this form. If you need more space to complete an answer, use a separate sheet(s) of paper. Write your name and Alien Registration Number (A#), if any, at the top of each sheet and indicate the number of the item that refers to your answer. Include the Part and letter or number of the item on the form relating to the additional information you are providing (example: Part 2, Z). NOTE: U.S. Citizenship and Immigration Services (USCIS is comprised of offices of the former Immigration and Naturalization Service (INS).

Use Form I-865, Sponsor's Notice of Change of Address, to report a sponsor's new address.

You will need to give us a completed and signed Form I-865.

To file this notice see Step 2 for specific instructions.

When Should I Use Form I-865?

If at any time in the past you completed a Form I-864, Affidavit of Support, to sponsor an immigrant, you are required to report your change of address within 30 days of the change if the sponsorship agreement is still in force.

The sponsorship agreement remains in force until the sponsored immigrant:

- Becomes a U.S. citizen;
- Can be credited with 40 quarters of work;
- Departs the United States permanently and either formally abandons lawful permanent resident status (by filing Form I-407) or is formally held in a removal proceeding to have abandoned that status;
- In a removal proceeding, loses the lawful permanent resident status that the sponsored immigrant obtained based on your Form I-864; or
- Dies.

How Do I File Form I-865?

A separate Form I-865 must be submitted for each person who is filing a notice of address change. Follow the steps below to complete the form:

Step 1 - Fill Out fhe Form I-865.

Step 2 - Submit Your Notice.

If you give us false documents, misrepresent facts or otherwise engage in fraud, USCIS will take appropriate action. This means you may lose current and future immigration benefits. You may also face penalties, including criminal and/or civil prosecution leading to fines and/or imprisonment.

Step 1. Fill Out Form I-865.

Use **black ink**. Type or print clearly using capital letters. If an item does not apply to you, write "N/A". If the answer is none, write "NONE".

This form is divided into **Parts 1** through **4**. The following information should help you fill out the form.

Part 1 - Information about you, the sponsor.

- **Family Name** (Last name) - Give your legal name. If you have two last names, include both and use a hyphen (-) between the names, if appropriate.
- **Date of Birth** - Use eight numbers to show your date of birth (example: May 1, 1979, should be written 05/01/1979).
- **Place of Birth** - Give the name of the country where you were born. Include also the city and state or province.
- **A #** - This is your USCIS (or former INS) file number. If you do not have an Alien Registration Number (A#) or do not know it, leave this blank or write "None".
- **U.S. Social Security #** - This is your U.S. Social Security number. If you do not have a U.S. Social Security number, leave this blank.
- **U.S. Citizen** - Check the appropriate box if you are a U.S. citizen and provide proof of your citizenship if you became a U.S. citizen following the filing of your Form I-864, Affidavit of Support, or submission of a prior Form I-865 address change.
- **Lawful Permanent Resident** - Check the appropriate box if you are a permanent resident.
- **New Home Address** - Give your new physical street address. This must include a street number and name or a rural route number. Do not put a post office box (P.O. Box) number here.
- **New Mailing Address** - Give your mailing address, if different from your home address.
- **Telephone Number** - Give a telephone number with area code where you can be reached during the day.

Part 2 - Information on sponsored immigrant(s).

- Give the requested information about the sponsored immigrant(s). If there is more than one immigrant, use a separate sheet(s) of paper to provide complete information.

Part 3 - Signature.

- You, the sponsor, must sign and date the notice. If you do not sign the form, the notice will be returned as incomplete.

Part 4 - Signature of person preparing form, if other than the sponsor.

- If you, the sponsor, did not fill out the Form I-865, the preparer must also sign, date and give his or her address.

Step 3. Submit Your Notice.

You must include the following items:

- **Your signed and completed Form I-865.**
- **Filing Fee.** There is no filing fee for Form I-865.
- **Retain a copy of your completed form.** You should retain in your records (1) a copy of the completed Form I-865, and (2) evidence that you sent the original Form I-865 to the correct USCIS office and the USCIS received the original Form I-865.

  USCIS will accept this documentation as proof that you compiled with the requirement to file Form I-865. For example, if you send Form I-865 using the U.S. Postal Service, you should keep with your file copy of Form I-865, the U.S. Postal Service certified mail receipt or Express Mail shipping label along with a return receipt, both bearing postmarks and the address where you mailed Form I-865.

  If you send Form I-865 by a commercial delivery service, you should keep with your file copy of Form I-865 a photocopy of the shipping label and signature proof of delivery.

- **Submit your Form I-865.** Where the notice should be sent depends on where you now live. See below to determine where to mail your notice.

  If your new address is in Connecticut, Delaware, District of Columbia, Maine, Maryland, Massachusetts, New Jersey, New Hampshire, New York, Pennsylvania, Puerto Rico, Rhode Island, Vermont, Virginia, West Virginia or the U.S. Virgin Islands, mail the notice to:

  USCIS - Vermont Service Center
  75 Lower Weldon Street
  St. Albans, VT 05479-0001

  If your new address is in Alabama, Arkansas, Florida, Georgia, Kentucky, Louisiana, Mississippi, New Mexico, North Carolina, Oklahoma, South Carolina, Tennessee or Texas, mail the notice to:

  USCIS - Texas Service Center
  P.O. Box 851804
  Irvin, TX. 75185-1804

  If your new address is in Arizona, California, Guam, Hawaii or Nevada, mail the notice to:

  USCIS - California Service Center
  P.O. Box 10485
  Laguna Niguel, CA 92607-0485

  If you live anywhere else in the United States, mail the notice to:

  USCIS - Nebraska Service Center
  P.O. Box 87485
  Lincoln, NE 68501-7485

Processing Information.

If the sponsor fails to give notice of a **change in his or her address,** as required in 8 U.S.C. 1183a(d) and 8 CFR 213a.3, **the sponsor may be liable for the civil penalty** established by 8 U.S.C. 1183a(d). The amount of the civil penalty will depend on whether the sponsor failed to give this notice knowing that the sponsored immigrant(s) has received means-tested public benefits.

NOTE: If the sponsor is a permanent resident, he or she must file a Form AR-11, Alien Change of Address Card, to comply with the change of address requirement in 8 CFR 265.1, as well as filing this Form I-865.

USCIS Forms and Information. To request USCIS forms, call our toll-free forms line at **1-800-870-3676**. You may also get USCIS forms and information about immigration laws and regulations by calling our National Customer Service Center at **1-800-375-5283** or visiting our internet website at **www.uscis.gov.**

Use InfoPass for Appointments. As an alternative to waiting in line for assistance at your local USCIS office, you can now schedule an appointment through our internet-based system, InfoPass. To access the system, visit our website at www.uscis.gov. Use the InfoPass appointment scheduler and follow the screen prompts to set up your appointment. InfoPass generates an electronic appointment notice that appears on the screen. Print the notice and take it with you to your appointment. The notice gives the time and date of your appointment, along with the address of the USCIS office.

Privacy Act Notice. As a sponsor, you are required by statute to provide us with your change of address. The information requested on the form will be used principally by the USCIS to verify your compliance with the change of address requirement, and to notify agencies that furnish means-tested public benefits of your address change, if requested.

The information may also, as a matter of routine use, be disclosed to other Federal, State and local agencies providing means-tested public benefits for use in civil action against you for breach of contract. It may also be disclosed as a matter of routine use to other Federal, State, local or foreign law enforcement and regulatory agencies to enable these entities to carry out their law enforcement responsibilities. Failure to provide the information may result in the imposition of the penalty established in 8 U.S.C. 1183a(d).

Paperwork Reduction Act Notice. You are not required to respond to this form unless it displays a currently valid OMB control number.

We try to create forms and instructions that are accurate, can be easily understood and impose the least possible burden on you to provide us with information. Often this is difficult because some immigration laws are very complex.

The estimated average time to complete and file this notice is 15 minutes.

If you have comments regarding the accuracy of this estimate, or suggestions for making this form simpler, you may write to: U.S. Citizenship and Immigration Services, Regulatory Management Division, 111 Massachusetts Avenue, N.W., Washington, DC 20529. **Do not mail your completed notice to this address.**

OMB No. 1615-0076; Expires 06/30/2006

Department of Homeland Security
U.S. Citizenship and Immigration Services

I-865, Sponsor's Notice of Change of Address

START HERE- Please type or print in black ink.

For USCIS Use Only

Returned	Receipt
Date	
Resubmitted	
Date	
Date	

Action Block

Remarks

Part 1. Information about you, the sponsor.

Family Name | Given Name | Middle Name

Date of Birth *(mm/dd/yyyy)* | Place of Birth *(City, State/Province /Country)*

A Number *(if any)* | U.S. Social Security Number

Your current status- (*check one*)

I am a ☐ U.S. Citizen ☐ Lawful Permanent Resident

NOTE: If you became a U.S. citizen following the filing of your Form I-864, Affidavit of Support, or submission of a prior Form I-865 address change, include a copy of proof of your U.S. citizenship (example: naturalization certificate, certificate of citizenship, U.S. passport) with this notice.

Your New Home Address - Street Number and Name; include apt. # if applicable.

City | State or Province

Zip/Postal Code | Country

Effective Date of Change of Address | Daytime Telephone *(Area/Country Code)*

E-Mail Address *(if any)*

Your New Mailing Address - NOTE: You do not need to complete this section if your new mailing address is the same as your new home address above.

Street Number and Name; include apt.#, if applicable.

C/O (*in care of*): | City | State or Province | Zip/Postal Code

Effective Date of Change of Address | Daytime Telephone *(Area/Country Code)* | E-Mail Address *(if any)*

Part 2. Information on sponsored immigrant(s). *(If more than one person, continue this part on a separate sheet(s) of paper.)*

Provide the requested information on the person(s) your are sponsoring:.

Family Name | Given Name | Middle Name | A #

Form I-865 (Rev. 01/23/06)Y

Part 3. Sponsor's Signature. *(Read the information on penalties in the instructions before completing this part.)*

I certify, under penalty of perjury under the laws of the United States of America, that all the information provided on this notice is true and correct.

Signature	**Date** *(mm/dd/yyyy)*

Part 4. Signature of person preparing form, if other than above. *(Sign below.)*

I declare that I prepared this request at the request of the above person and it is based on all information of which I have knowledge.

Preparer's Signature	**Preparer's Printed Name**	**Date** *(mm/dd/yyyy)*

Preparer's Firm Name *(if applicable)*	**Preparer's Address**

Daytime Phone Number *(with area code)*	Fax Number *(if any)*	E-Mail Address *(if any)*
( )	( )	

OMB No. 1615-0014; Exp. 04-30-07

U.S. Department of Homeland Security
Bureau of Citizenship and Immigration Services

I-134, Affidavit of Support

(Answer All Items: Type or Print in Black Ink.)

I, ______________________ residing at ______________________
(Name) (Street and Number)

____
(City) (State) (Zip Code if in U.S.) (Country)

BEING DULY SWORN DEPOSE AND SAY:

1. I was born on __________ at ______________________
(Date-mm/dd/yyyy) (City) (Country)

If you are **not** a native born United States citizen, answer the following as appropriate:

a. If a United States citizen through naturalization, give certificate of naturalization number __________

b. If a United States citizen through parent(s) or marriage, give citizenship certificate number __________

c. If United States citizenship was derived by some other method, attach a statement of explanation.

d. If a lawfully admitted permanent resident of the United States, give "A" number __________

2. That I am ______ years of age and have resided in the United States since (date) __________

3. That this affidavit is executed on behalf of the following person:

Name (Family Name)	(First Name)	(Middle Name)	Gender	Age

Citizen of (Country)	Marital Status	Relationship to Sponsor

Presently resides at (Street and Number)	(City)	(State)	(Country)

Name of spouse and children accompanying or following to join person:

Spouse	Gender	Age	Child	Gender	Age
Child	Gender	Age	Child	Gender	Age
Child	Gender	Age	Child	Gender	Age

4. That this affidavit is made by me for the purpose of assuring the United States Government that the person(s) named in item **3** will not become a public charge in the United States.

5. That I am willing and able to receive, maintain and support the person(s) named in item **3**. That I am ready and willing to deposit a bond, if necessary, to guarantee that such person(s) will not become a public charge during his or her stay in the United States, or to guarantee that the above named person(s) will maintain his or her nonimmigrant status, if admitted temporarily and will depart prior to the expiration of his or her authorized stay in the United States.

6. That I understand this affidavit will be binding upon me for a period of three (3) years after entry of the person(s) named in item **3** and that the information and documentation provided by me may be made available to the Secretary of Health and Human Services and the Secretary of Agriculture, who may make it available to a public assistance agency.

7. That I am employed as or engaged in the business of ______________ with ______________
(Type of Business) (Name of Concern)

at ______________________
(Street and Number) (City) (State) (Zip Code)

I derive an annual income of *(if self-employed, I have attached a copy of my last income tax return or report of commercial rating concern which I certify to be true and correct to the best of my knowledge and belief. See instructions for nature of evidence of net worth to be submitted.)* $__________

I have on deposit in savings banks in the United States $__________

I have other personal property, the reasonable value which is $__________

I have stocks and bonds with the following market value, as indicated on the attached list, which I certify to be true and correct to the best of my knowledge and belief. $______

I have life insurance in the sum of $______

With a cash surrender value of $______

I own real estate valued at $______

With mortgage(s) or other encumbrance(s) thereon amounting to $ ______

Which is located at ______
(Street and Number) (City) (State) (Zip Code)

8. That the following persons are dependent upon me for support: *(Place an "x" in the appropriate column to indicate whether the person named is* ***wholly*** *or* ***partially*** *dependent upon you for support.)*

Name of Person	Wholly Dependent	Partially Dependent	Age	Relationship to Me

9. That I have previously submitted affidavit(s) of support for the following person(s). If none, state ***"None."***

Name Date submitted

______

______

10. That I have submitted visa petition(s) to the Bureau of Citizenship and Immigration Services (CIS) on behalf of the following person(s). If none, state none.

Name Relationship Date submitted

______

______

11. That I ☐ intend ☐ do not intend to make specific contributions to the support of the person(s) named in item **3**. *(If you check "intend," indicate the exact nature and duration of the contributions. For example, if you intend to furnish room and board, state for how long and, if money, state the amount in United States dollars and state whether it is to be given in a lump sum, weekly or monthly, or for how long.)*

______

______

______

Oath or Affirmation of Sponsor

I acknowledge that I have read Part III of the Instructions, Sponsor and Alien Liability, and am aware of my responsibilities as an immigrant sponsor under the Social Security Act, as amended, and the Food Stamp Act, as amended.

I swear (affirm) that I know the contents of this affidavit signed by me and that the statements are true and correct.

Signature of sponsor ______

Subscribed and sworn to (affirmed) before me this ______ **day of** ______, ______

at ______. **My commission expires on** ______

Signature of Officer Administering Oath ______ **Title** ______

If the affidavit is prepared by someone other than the sponsor, please complete the following: I declare that this document was prepared by me at the request of the sponsor and is based on all information of which I have knowledge.

______

(Signature) **(Address)** **(Date)**

U.S. Department of Homeland Security
Bureau of Citizenship and Immigration Services

OMB No. 1615-0014; Exp. 04-30-07

I-134, Affidavit of Support

Instructions

I. Execution of Affidavit.

A separate affidavit must be submitted for each person. As the sponsor, you must sign the affidavit in your full, true and correct name and affirm or make it under oath.

- If you are **in the United States**, the affidavit may be sworn to or affirmed before an officer of the Bureau of Citizenship and Immigration Services (CIS) without the payment of fee, or before a notary public or other officers authorized to administer oaths for general purposes, in which case the official seal or certificate of authority to administer oaths must be affixed.

- If you are **outside the United States,** the affidavit must be sworn to or affirmed before a U.S. consular or immigration officer.

II. Supporting Evidence.

As the sponsor, you must show you have sufficient income and/or financial resources to assure that the alien you are sponsoring will not become a public charge while in the United States.

Evidence should consist of copies of any or all of the following documentation listed below that are applicable to your situation.

Failure to provide evidence of sufficient income and/or financial resources may result in the denial of the alien's application for a visa or his or her removal from the United States.

The sponsor must submit in duplicate evidence of income and resources, as appropriate:

A. Statement from an officer of the bank or other financial institution where you have deposits, giving the following details regarding your account:
 1. Date account opened;
 2. Total amount deposited for the past year;
 3. Present balance.

B. Statement of your employer on business stationery, showing:
 1. Date and nature of employment;
 2. Salary paid;
 3. Whether the position is temporary or permanent.

C. If self-employed:
 1. Copy of last income tax return filed; or
 2. Report of commercial rating concern.

D. List containing serial numbers and denominations of bonds and name of record owner(s).

III. Sponsor and Alien Liability.

Effective October 1, 1980, amendments to section 1614(f) of the Social Security Act and Part A of Title XVI of the Social Security Act establish certain requirements for determining the eligibility of aliens who apply for the first time for Supplemental Security Income (SSI) benefits.

Effective October 1, 1981, amendments to section 415 of the Social Security Act establish similar requirements for determining the eligibility of aliens who apply for the first time for Aid to Families with Dependent Children (AFDC), currently administered under Temporary Assistance for Needy Families (TANF). Effective December 22, 1981, amendments to the Food Stamp Act of 1977 affect the eligibility of alien participation in the Food Stamp Program.

These amendments require that the income and resources of any person, who as the sponsor of an alien's entry into the United States, executes an affidavit of support or similar agreement on behalf of the alien, and the income and resources of the sponsor's spouse (if living with the sponsor) shall be deemed to be the income and resources of the alien under formulas for determining eligibility for SSI, TANF and Food Stamp benefits during the three years following the alien's entry into the United States.

Documentation on Income and Resources.

An alien applying for SSI must make available to the Social Security Administration documentation concerning his or her income and resources and those of the sponsor, including information that was provided in support of the application for an immigrant visa or adjustment of status.

An alien applying for TANF or Food Stamps must make similar information available to the State public assistance agency.

The Secretary of Health and Human Services and the Secretary of Agriculture are authorized to obtain copies of any such documentation submitted to the CIS or the U.S. Department of State and to release such documentation to a State public assistance agency.

Joint and Several Liability Issues.

Sections 1621(e) and 415(d) of the Social Security Act and subsection 5(i) of the Food Stamp Act also provide that an alien and his or her sponsor shall be jointly and severally liable to repay any SSI, TANF or Food Stamp benefits that are incorrectly paid because of misinformation provided by a sponsor or because of a sponsor's failure to provide information.

Incorrect payments that are not repaid will be withheld from any subsequent payments for which the alien or sponsor are otherwise eligible under the Social Security Act or Food Stamp Act, except that the sponsor was without fault or where good cause existed.

These provisions do not apply to the SSI, TANF or Food Stamp eligibility of aliens admitted as refugees, granted asylum or Cuban/ Haitian entrants as defined in section 501(e) of P.L. 96-422, and to dependent children of the sponsor or sponsor's spouse.

The provisions also do not apply to the SSI or Food Stamp eligibility of an alien who becomes blind or disabled after admission to the United States for permanent residency.

IV. Authority, Use and Penalties.

Authority for the collection of the information requested on this form is contained in 8 U.S.C. 1182(a)(15),1184(a) and 1258.

The information will be used principally by the CIS, or by any consular officer to whom it may be furnished, to support an alien's application for benefits under the Immigration and Nationality Act and specifically the assertion that he or she has adequate means of financial support and will not become a public charge. Submission of the information is voluntary.

It may also, as a matter of routine use, be disclosed to other federal, state, local and foreign law enforcement and regulatory agencies, including the Department of Health and Human Services, Department of Agriculture, Department of State, Department of Defense and any component thereof (if the deponent has served or is serving in the armed forces of the United States), Central Intelligence Agency, and individuals and organizations during the course of any investigation to elicit further information required to carry out CIS functions.

Failure to provide the information may result in the denial of the alien's application for a visa or his or her removal from the United States.

V. Information and CIS Forms.

For information on immigration laws, regulations and procedures or to order CIS forms, call our National Customer Service Center at **1-800-375-5283** or visit our website at **www.uscis.gov.**

VI. Privacy Act Notice.

We ask for the information on this form and associated evidence to determine if you have established eligibility for the immigration benefit you are seeking. Our legal right to ask for this information is in 8 U.S.C. 1203 and 1225. We may provide this information to other government agencies. Failure to provide this information and any requested evidence may delay a final decision or result in denial of your request.

VII. Paperwork Reduction Act Notice.

An agency may not conduct or sponsor a collection of information and a person is not required to respond to a collection of information unless it displays a currently valid OMB control number. We try to create forms and instructions that are accurate, can be easily understood and that impose the least possible burden on you to provide us with information. Often this is difficult because some immigration laws are very complex. The estimated average time to complete and file this application is 30 minutes per application, including the time to learn about the law and the form, complete the form, and assemble and submit the Affidavit. If you have comments regarding the accuracy of this estimate or suggestions for making this form simpler, write to the Bureau of Citizenship and Immigration Services, Regulations and Forms Services Division (HQRFS), 425 I Street, N.W., Room 4034, Washington, D.C. 20529; OMB No. 1615-0014. **Do not mail your completed application to this address.**

OMB No. 1615-0028; Expires 08/31/08

Department of Homeland Security
U.S. Citizenship and Immigration Services

I-600, Petition to Classify Orphan as an Immediate Relative

Instructions

1. Eligibility.

A. Child.

Under immigration law, an orphan is an alien child who has no parents because of the death or disappearance of abandonment or desertion by, or separation or loss from both parents.

An orphan is also an alien child who has only one parent who is not capable of taking care of the orphan and who has in writing irrevocably released the alien for emigration and adoption.

A petition to classify an alien as an orphan may not be filed on behalf of a child in the United States, unless that child is in parole status and has not been adopted in the United States.

The petition must be filed before the child's 16th birthday.

B. Parent(s).

The petition may be filed by a married U.S. citizen and spouse or unmarried U.S. citizen at least 25 years of age. The spouse does not need to be a U.S. citizen, but must be in lawful immigration status.

C. Adoption abroad.

If the orphan was adopted abroad, it must be established that both the married petitioner and spouse or the unmarried petitioner personally saw and observed the child prior to or during the adoption proceedings. The adoption decree must show that a married petitioner and spouse adopted the child jointly or that an unmarried petitioner was at least 25 years of age at the time of the adoption.

D. Proxy adoption abroad.

If both the petitioner and spouse or the unmarried petitioner did not personally see and observe the child prior to or during the adoption proceedings abroad, the petitioner (and spouse, if married) must submit a statement indicating the petitioner's (and, if married, the spouse's) willingness and intent to readopt the child in the United States.

If requested by USCIS, the petitioner must submit a statement by an official of the State in which the child will reside that readoption is permissible in that State In addition, evidence of compliance with the preadoption requirements, if any, of that State must be submitted.

E. Preadoption requirements.

If the orphan has not been adopted abroad, the petitioner and spouse or the unmarried petitioner must establish that:

- The child will be adopted in the United States by the petitioner and spouse jointly or by the unmarried petitioner, and that
- The preadoption requirements, if any, of the State of the orphan's proposed residence have been met.

2. Filing Petition for Known Child.

An orphan petition for a child who has been identified must be submitted on a completed Form I-600 with the certification of the petitioner executed and required fee. If the petitioner is married, the Form I-600 must also be signed by the petitioner's spouse.

The petition must be accompanied by the following:

A. Proof of U.S. citizenship of the petitioner.

If a U.S. citizen by birth in the United States, submit a copy of the birth certificate, issued by the civil registrar, vital statistics office or other civil authority. If a birth certificate is not available, submit a statement from the appropriate civil authority certifying that a birth certificate is not available. In such a situation, secondary evidence must be submitted, including:

- **Church records** bearing the seal of the church showing the baptism, dedication or comparable rite occurred within two months after birth and showing the date and place of the petitioner's birth, date of the religious ceremony and the names of the parents;
- **School records** issued by the authority (preferably the first school attended) showing the date of admission to the school, the petitioner's birth date or age at the time, the place of birth and the names of the parents;
- **Census records** (state or federal) showing the name, place of birth, date of birth or age of the petitioner listed;
- **Affidavits** sworn to or affirmed by two persons who were living at the time and who have personal knowledge of the date and place of birth in the United States of the petitioner. Each affidavit should contain the following information regarding the person making the affidavit: his or her full name, address, date and place of birth and relationship to the petitioner, if any, and full information concerning the event and complete details of how the affiant acquired knowledge of petitioner's birth; or
- An unexpired **U.S. passport**, initially issued for ten years may also be submitted as proof of U.S. citizenship.

If the petitioner was born outside the United States, submit a copy of one of the following:

- Certificate of Naturalization or Certificate of Citizenship issued by the U.S. Citizenship and Immigration Services (USCIS) or former Immigration and Naturalization Service (INS);
- Form FS-240, Report of Birth Abroad of a Citizen of the United States, issued by an American embassy;

- An unexpired U.S. passport initially issued for ten years, or
- An original statement from a U.S. consular officer verifying the applicant's U.S. citizenship with a valid passport.

NOTE: Proof of the lawful immigration status of the petitioner's spouse, if applicable, must be submitted. If the spouse is not a U.S. citizen, proof of the spouse's lawful immigration status, such as Form I-551, Permanent Resident Card; Form I-94, Arrival-Departure Record; or a copy of the biographic pages of the spouse's passport and the nonimmigrant visa pages showing an admission stamp may be submitted.

B. Proof of marriage of petitioner and spouse.

The married petitioner must submit a copy of the certificate of marriage and proof of termination of all prior marriages of himself or herself and spouse. In the case of an unmarried petitioner who was previously married, submit proof of termination of all prior marriages.

NOTE: If any change occurs in the petitioner's marital status while the case is pending, immediately notify the USCIS office where the petition was filed.

C. Proof of age of orphan.

The petitioner should submit a copy of the orphan's birth certificate if obtainable; if not obtainable, submit an explanation together with the best available evidence of birth.

D. Copies of the death certificate(s) of the child's parent(s) if applicable.

E. A certified copy of adoption decree together with certified translation, if the orphan has been lawfully adopted abroad.

F. Evidence that the sole or surviving parent is incapable of providing for the orphan's care and has in writing irrevocably released the orphan for immigration and adoption, if the orphan has only one parent.

G. Evidence that the orphan has been unconditionally abandoned to an orphanage, if the orphan has been placed in an orphanage by his or her parent or parents.

H. Evidence that the preadoption requirements, if any, of the state of the orphan's proposed residence have been met, if the child is to be adopted in the United States.

If is not possible to submit this evidence upon initial filing of the petition under the laws of the State of proposed residence, it may be submitted later. The petition, however, will not be approved without it.

I. Home Study.

The home study must include a statement or attachment recommending or approving the adoption or proposed adoption and be signed by an official of the responsible State agency in the State of the proposed residence or of an agency authorized by that State. In the case of a child adopted abroad, the statement or attachment must be signed by an official of an appropriate public or private adoption agency that is licensed in the United States.

The home study must be prepared by an entity (individual or organization) licensed or otherwise authorized under the law of the State of the orphan's proposed residence to conduct research and preparation for a home study, including the required personal interviews.

If the recommending entity is licensed, the recommendation must state that it is licensed, where it is licensed, its license number, if any, and the period of validity of the license.

However, the research, including the interview and the preparation of the home study, may be done by an individual or group in the United States or abroad that is satisfactory to the recommending entity.

A responsible State agency or licensed agency may accept a home study made by an unlicensed or foreign agency and use that home study as a basis for a favorable recommendation.

The home study must provide an assessment of the capabilities of the prospective adoptive parent(s) to properly parent the orphan and must include a discussion of the following areas:

- An explanation regarding any history of abuse or violence or any complaints, charges, citations, arrests, convictions, prison terms, pardons rehabilitation decrees for breaking or violating any law or ordinance by the petitioner(s) or any additional adult member of the household over age 18.

  NOTE: Having committed any crime of moral turpitude or a drug-related offense does not necessarily mean that a petitioner or petitioner's spouse will be found ineligible to adopt an orphan. However, failure to disclose such information may result in denial of this application and/or any subsequent petition for an orphan.

- An assessment of the financial ability of the petitioner and petitioner's spouse, if applicable.
- A detailed description of the living accommodations where the petitioner and petitioner's spouse currently reside(s).
- If the petitioner and petitioner's spouse are residing abroad at the time of the home study, a description of the living accommodations where the child will reside in the United States with the petitioner and petitioner's spouse, if known.
- An assessment of the physical, mental and emotional capabilities of the petitioner and petitioner's spouse in relation to rearing and educating the child.

J. Biometric services.

As part of the USCIS biometric services requirements, the following persons must be fingerprinted in connection with this petition:

- The petitioner and petitioner's spouse, if applicable, and
- Each additional adult member the petitioner's household, 18 years of age or older. **NOTE:** Submit a copy of the birth certificate of each household member over 18.

If necessary, USCIS may also take a photograph and signature of those named above as part of the biometric services.

Petitioners residing in the United States. After filing this petition, USCIS will notify each person in writing of the time and location where they must go to be fingerprinted. Failure to appear to be fingerprinted or for other biometric services may result in denial of the petition.

Petitioners residing abroad. Completed fingerprint cards (Forms FD-258) must be submitted with the petition. Do not, bend, fold or crease completed fingerprint cards. Fingerprint cards must be prepared by a U.S. embassy or consulate, USCIS office or military installation.

3. Filing Petition for Known Child Without Full Documentation on Child or Home Study.

When a child has been identified but the documentary evidence relating to the child or the home study is not yet available, an orphan petition may be filed without that evidence or home study.

The evidence outlined in Instructions **2A** and **2B** (proof of petitioner's U.S. citizenship and documentation of marriage of petitioner and spouse), however, must be submitted.

If the necessary evidence relating to the child or the home study is not submitted within one year from the date of submission of the petition, the petition will be considered abandoned and the fee will not be refunded. Any further proceeding will require the filing of a new petition.

4. Submitting Advance Processing Application for Orphan Child Not Yet Identified.

A prospective petitioner may request advance processing when the child has not been identified or when the prospective petitioner and/or spouse is or are going abroad to locate or adopt a child.

If unmarried, the prospective petitioner must be at least 24 years of age, provided that he or she will be at least 25 at the time of the adoption and the completed petition on behalf of a child is filed.

The request must be on Form I-600A, Application for Advance Processing of Orphan Petition, and accompanied by the evidence requested on that form.

After a child or children are located and/or identified, a separate Form I-600 must be filed for each child. If only one Form I-600 is filed, a new fee is not required, provided the form is filed while the advance processing application (Form I-600A) application is pending or within 18 months of the approval of the advance processing application.

5. When Child/Children Are Located and/or Identified.

A separate Form I-600, Petition to Classify Orphan as an Immediate Relative, must be filed for each child.

Generally, Form I-600 should be submitted at the USCIS office where the advance processing application was filed.

If a prospective petitioner goes abroad to adopt or locate a child in one of the countries noted below, he or she should file Form I-600 at the USCIS office having jurisdiction over the place where the child is residing or will be located, unless the case is retained at the stateside office.

USCIS has offices in the following countries: Austria, China, Cuba, the Dominican Republic, El Salvador, Germany, Ghana, Great Britain, Greece, Guatemala, Haiti Honduras, India, Italy, Jamaica, Kenya, Korea, Mexico, Pakistan, Panama, Peru, the Philippines, Russia, South Africa, Thailand and Vietnam.

If a prospective petitioner goes abroad to any country not listed above to adopt or locate a child he or she should file Form I-600 at the American embassy or consulate having jurisdiction over the place where the child is residing or will be located, unless the case is retained at the Stateside office.

6. General Filing Instructions.

A. Type or print legibly in black ink.

B. If extra space is needed to complete any item, attach a continuation sheet, indicate the item number, and date and sign each sheet.

C. Translations.

Any foreign language document must be accompanied by a full English translation, that the translator has certified as complete and correct, and by the translator's certification that he or she is competent to translate the foreign language.

D. Copies.

If these instructions tell you to submit a copy of a particular document, you do not have to send the original document. However, if there are stamps, remarks, notations, etc., on the back of the original documents, also submit copies of the back of the document(s). You do not have to submit the original document unless USCIS requests it.

There are times when USCIS must request an original copy of a document. In that case, the original is generally returned after it has been reviewed.

7. Filing the Petition.

A petitioner residing in the United States should send the completed petition to the USCIS office having jurisdiction over his or her place of residence. A petitioner residing outside the United States should consult the nearest American embassy or consulate designated to act on the petition.

8. What Is the Fee?

A fee of **$545.00** must be submitted for filing this petition. However, a fee is not required for this petition if you filed an advance processing application (Form I-600A) within the previous 18 months and it was approved or is still pending.

In addition to the fee for the application, there is a **$70.00** biometric services fee for fingerprinting every adult person living in the household in the United States where the child will reside.

For example, if a petition is filed by a married people residing in the United States with one additional adult member in their household, the total fee that must be submitted would be **$755.00** (**$545.00** for the petition and **$210.00** for biometric services for fingerprinting the three adults).

NOTE: If the prospective adoptive parents and any other adult members of the household reside abroad at the time of filing, they are exempt from paying the USCIS biometric services fee. However, they may have to pay the fingerprinting fee charged by the U.S. consular office or military installation.

When more than one petition is submitted by the same petitioner on behalf of orphans who are siblings, only one Form I-600 petition and fee for biometric services is required, unless re-fingerprinting is ordered. If the orphans are not siblings, a separate filing fee must be submitted for each additional Form I-600 petition.

The fee will not be refunded, whether the petition is approved or not. **Do not mail cash**. All checks or money orders, whether U.S. or foreign, must be payable in U.S. currency at a financial institution in the United States. When a check is drawn on the account of a person other than yourself, write your name on the face of the check. If the check is not honored, USCIS will charge you $30.00.

Pay by check or money order in the exact amount. Make the check or money order payable to the **Department of Homeland Security**, unless:

A. You live in Guam, make the check or money order payable to the "Treasurer, Guam" or ;

B. You live in the U.S. Virgin Islands, make your check or money order payable to the "Commissioner of Finance of the Virgin Islands."

How to Check If the Fee Is Correct.

The fee on this form is current as of the edition date appearing in the lower right corner of this page. However, because USCIS fees change periodically, you can verify if the fee is correct by following one of the steps below:

- Visit our website at **www.uscis.gov** and scroll down to "Forms and E-Filing" to check the appropriate fee, or
- Review the Fee Schedule included in your form package, if you called us to request the form, or
- Telephone our National Customer Service Center at **1-800-375-5283** and ask for the fee information.

NOTE: If your petition or application requires a biometric services fee for USCIS to take your fingerprints, photograph or signature, you can use the same procedure above to confirm the biometrics fee.

9. Penalties.

Willful false statements on this form or supporting documents may be punished by fine or imprisonment. U.S. Code, Title 18, Sec. 1001 (formerly Sec. 80.)

10. Authority to Collect Information.

8 USC 1154(a). Routine uses for disclosure under the Privacy Act of 1974 have been published in the Federal Register and are available upon request. USCIS will use the information to determine immigrant eligibility. Submission of the information is voluntary, but failure to provide any or all of the information may result in denial of the petition.

11. USCIS Forms and Information.

To order USCIS forms, call our toll-free number at **1-800-870-3676**. You can also get USCIS forms and information on laws, regulations and procedures by telephoning our National Customer Service Center at **1-800-375-5283** or visiting our internet website at, **www.uscis.gov**.

12. Use InfoPass for Appointments.

As an alternative to waiting in line for assistance at your local USCIS office, you can now schedule an appointment through our internet-based system, **InfoPass**. To access the system, visit our website at **www.uscis.gov**. Use the **InfoPass** appointment scheduler and follow the screen prompts to set up your appointment. **InfoPass** generates an electronic appointment notice that appears on the screen. Print the notice and take it with you to your appointment. The notice gives the time and date of your appointment, along with the address of the USCIS office.

13. Reporting Burden.

A person is not required to respond to a collection of information unless it displays a currently valid OMB control number.

Public reporting burden for this collection of information is estimated to average 30 minutes per response, including the time for reviewing instructions, searching existing data sources, gathering and maintaining the data needed, and completing and reviewing the collection of information.

Send comments regarding this burden estimate or any other aspect of this collection of information, including suggestions for reducing this burden, to the: U.S. Citizenship and Immigration Services, Regulatory Management Division, 111 Massachusetts Avenue, North West, Washington, DC 20529; OMB No. 1615-0028. **Do not mail your completed petition.**

Form I-600 Instructions (Rev. 10/26/05)Y Page 4

OMB No. 1615-0028; Expires 08/31/08

Department of Homeland Security
U.S. Citizenship and Immigration Services

I-600, Petition to Classify Orphan as an Immediate Relative

Do not write in this block. **(For USCIS Use Only.)**

TO THE SECRETARY OF STATE:
The petition was filed by:
☐ Married petitioner ☐ Unmarried petitioner

The petition is approved for orphan:
☐ Adopted abroad ☐ Coming to U.S. for adoption. Preadoption requirements have been met.

Remarks:

Fee Stamp

File number

DATE OF ACTION
DD
DISTRICT

Type or print legibly in black ink. Complete a separate petition for each child.
Petition is being made to classify the named orphan as an immediate relative

Block I - Information about petitioner.

1. My name is: (Last) (First) (Middle)

2. Other names used (including maiden name if appropriate):

3. I reside in the U.S. at: (C/O if appropriate) (Apt. No.)
(Number and Street) (Town or City) (State) (Zip Code)

4. Address Abroad (if any): (Number and Street) (Apt. No.)
(Town or city) (Province) (Country)

5. I was born on: *(mm/dd/yyyy)*
In: (Town or City) (State or Province) (Country)

6. My telephone number is: (Include Area Code)

7. My marital status is:
☐ Married
☐ Widowed
☐ Divorced
☐ Single
☐ I have never been married.
☐ I have been previously married _______ time(s).

8. If you are now married, give the following information:
Date and place of present marriage *(mm/dd/yyyy)*

Name of present spouse (include maiden name of wife)

Date of birth of spouse *(mm/dd/yyyy)* Place of birth of spouse

Number of prior marriages of spouse

My spouse resides ☐ With me ☐ Apart from me (provide address below)
(Apt. No.) (No. and Street) (City) (State) (Country)

9. I am a citizen of the United States through:
☐ Birth ☐ Parents ☐ Naturalization

If acquired through naturalization, give name under which naturalized, number of naturalization certificate, and date and place of naturalization:

If not, submit evidence of citizenship. See Instruction **2.a(2).**

If acquired through parentage, have you obtained a certificate in your own name based on that acquisition?
☐ No ☐ Yes

Have you or any person through whom you claimed citizenship ever lost U.S. citizenship?
☐ No ☐ Yes (If Yes, attach detailed explanation.)

Received	Trans. In	Ret'd Trans. Out	Completed

Block II - Information about orphan beneficiary.

10. Name at Birth (First) (Middle) (Last)

11. Name at Present (First) (Middle) (Last)

12. Any other names by which orphan is or was known.

13. Gender ☐ Male ☐ Female

14. Date of birth *(mm/dd/yyyy)*

15. Place of Birth (City) (State or Province) (Country)

16. The beneficiary is an orphan because (check one):
☐ He or she has no parents.
☐ He or she has only one parent who is the sole or surviving parent.

17. If the orphan has only one parent, answer the following:
a. State what has become of the other parent:

b. Is the remaining parent capable of providing for the orphan's support? ☐ Yes ☐ No

c. Has the remaining parent in writing irrevocably released the orphan for emigration and adoption? ☐ Yes ☐ No

18. Has the orphan been adopted abroad by the petitioner and spouse jointly or the unmarried petitioner? ☐ Yes ☐ No

If yes, did the petitioner and spouse or unmarried petitioner personally see and observe the child prior to or during the adoption proceedings? ☐ Yes ☐ No

Date of adoption *(mm/dd/yyyy)*

Place of adoption

19. If either answer in Question **18** is "No," answer the following:

a. Do petitioner and spouse jointly or does the unmarried petitioner intend to adopt the orphan in the United States? ☐ Yes ☐ No

b. Have the preadoption requirements, if any, of the orphan's proposed State of residence been met? ☐ Yes ☐ No

c. If **b** is answered "No," will they be met later? ☐ Yes ☐ No

20. To petitioner's knowledge, does the orphan have any physical or mental affliction? ☐ Yes ☐ No

If "Yes," name the affliction.

21. Who has legal custody of the child?

22. Name of child welfare agency, if any, assisting in this case:

23. Name of attorney abroad, if any, representing petitioner in this case.

Address of above.

24. Address in the United States where orphan will reside.

25. Present address of orphan.

25. If orphan is residing in an institution, give full name of institution.

26. If orphan is not residing in an institution, give full name of person with with whom residing.

27. Give any additional information necessary to locate orphan, such as name of district, section, zone or locality in which orphan resides.

28. Location of American embassy or consulate where application for visa will be made.

(City in Foreign Country) (Foreign Country)

Certification of petitioner.
I certify, under penalty of perjury under the laws of the United States of America, that the foregoing is true and correct and that I will care for an orphan or orphans properly if admitted to the United States.

(Signature of Petitioner)

Executed on (Date)

Certification of married prospective petitioner's spouse.
I certify, under penalty of perjury under the laws of the United States of America, that the foregoing is true and correct and that my spouse and I will care for an orphan or orphans properly if admitted to the United States.

(Signature of Petitioner)

Executed on (Date)

Signature of person preparing form, if other than petitioner.
I declare that this document was prepared by me at the request of the petitioner and is based entirely on information of which I have knowledge.

(Signature)

Street Address and Room or Suite No./City/State/Zip Code

Executed on (Date)

OMB No. 1615-0028; Expires 08/31/08

Department of Homeland Security
U.S. Citizenship and Immigration Services

I-600A, Application for Advance Processing of Orphan Petition

Instructions

What Is the Purpose of This Form?

This form is used by a U.S. citizen who plans to adopt a foreign-born orphan but does not have a specific child in mind. "Advance Processing" enables USCIS to first adjudicate the application that relates to the qualifications of the applicant(s) as a prospective adoptive parent(s).

Additionally, this form may be used in cases where the child is known and the prospective adoptive parent(s) are traveling to the country where the child is located. However, it is important that prospective adoptive parent(s) be aware that the child must remain in the foreign country where he or she is located until the processing is completed.

NOTE: This Form I-600A application is not a petition to classify an orphan as an immediate relative. Form I-600, Petition to Classify Orphan as an Immediate Relative, is used for that purpose.

1. What Are the Eligibility Requirements?

A. Eligibility for advance processing application (Form I-600A).

An application for advance processing may be filed by a married U.S. citizen and spouse. The spouse of the applicant does not need to be a U.S. citizen; however, he or she must be in a lawful immigration status. An application for advance processing may also be filed by an unmarried U.S citizen who is at least 24 years of age provided that he or she will be at least 25 at the time of adoption and the filing of an orphan petition on behalf of a child.

B. Eligibility for orphan petition (Form I-600).

In addition to the requirements concerning the citizenship and age of the applicant described above in Instruction **1. A.** when a child is located and identified the following eligibility requirements will apply:

(1) Child.

Under U.S. immigration law, an orphan is an alien child who has no parents because of the death or disappearance of, abandonment or desertion by, or separation or loss from both parents.

An orphan is also a child who has only one parent who is not capable of taking care of the orphan and who has, in writing, irrevocably released the orphan for emigration and adoption.

A petition to classify an alien as an orphan (Form I-600) may not be filed on behalf of a child who is present in the United States, unless that child is in parole status and has not been adopted in the United States.

The petition must be filed before the child's 16th birthday.

(2) Adoption abroad.

If the orphan was adopted abroad, it must be established that both the married applicant and spouse or the unmarried applicant personally saw and observed the child prior to or during the adoption proceedings. The adoption decree must show that a married prospective adoptive parent and spouse adopted the child jointly or that an unmarried prospective parent was at least 25 years of age at the time of the adoption and filing of Form I-600.

(3) Proxy adoption abroad.

If both the applicant and spouse or the unmarried applicant did not personally see and observe the child prior to or during the adoption proceedings abroad the applicant (and spouse, if married) must submit a statement indicating the applicant's (and, if married the spouse's) willingness and intent to readopt the child in the United States. If requested, the applicant must submit a statement by an official of the state in which the child will reside that readoption is permissible in that State. In addition, evidence must be submitted to show compliance with the preadoption requirements, if any, of that State.

(4) Preadoption requirements.

If the orphan has not been adopted abroad, the applicant and spouse or the unmarried applicant must establish that the child will be adopted in the United States by the prospective applicant and spouse jointly or by the unmarried prospective applicant, and that the preadoption requirements, if any, of the State of the orphan's proposed residence have been met.

2. What Are the Requirements to File?

A. Proof of U. S. citizenship of the prospective adoptive parent(s).

(1) If a U.S. citizen by birth in the United States, submit a copy of the birth certificate issued by the civil registrar, vital statistics office or other civil authority. If a birth certificate is not available, submit a statement from the appropriate civil authority certifying that a birth certificate is not available. In such a situation secondary evidence must be submitted, including:

- **Church records** bearing the seal of the church showing the baptism, dedication or comparable rite occurred within two months after birth and showing the date and place of the prospective adoptive parent's birth, date of the religious ceremony and the names of the parents;
- School Records issued by the authority (preferably the first school attended) showing the date of admission to the school, prospective adoptive parent's date of birth or age at the time, the place of birth and the names of the parents;

- **Census records** (state or federal) showing the name place of birth, date of birth or age of the prospective adoptive parent listed;
- **Affidavits** sworn to or affirmed by two persons who were living at the time and who have personal knowledge of the date and place of birth in the United States of the prospective adoptive parent. Each affidavit should contain the following information regarding the person making the affidavit: his or her full name, address, date and place of birth and relationship to the prospective adoptive parent, if any and full information concerning the event and complete details of how the affiant acquired knowledge of the birth; or
- An unexpired **U.S. passport**, initially issued for ten years, may also be submitted as proof of U.S citizenship.

(2) If the prospective adoptive parent was born outside the United States, submit a copy of one of the following:

- Certificate of Naturalization or Certificate of Citizenship issued the by U.S. Citizenship and Immigration Services (USCIS) or the former Immigration and Naturalization Service (INS);
- Form FS-240, Report of Birth Abroad of a Citizen of the United States, issued by an American embassy;
- An unexpired U.S. passport initially issued for ten years; or
- An original statement from a U.S. consular officer verifying the applicant's U.S. citizenship with a valid passport.

NOTE: Proof of the lawful immigration status of the applicant's spouse, if applicable, must be submitted. If the spouse is not a U.S. citizen, proof of her or his lawful immigration status, such as Form I-551, Permanent Resident Card; Form I-94, Arrival-Departure Record; or a copy of the biographic pages of the spouse's passport and the nonimmigrant visa pages showing an admission stamp may be submitted.

B. Proof of marriage of applicant and spouse.

The married applicant must submit a copy of the certificate of marriage and proof of termination of all prior marriages of himself or herself and spouse. In the case of an unmarried applicant who was previously married, submit proof of termination of all prior marriages.

NOTE: If any change occurs in the applicant'(s) marital status while the application is pending, immediately notify the USCIS office where the application was filed.

C. Home Study.

The home study must include a statement or attachment recommending or approving the adoption or proposed adoption, and be signed by an official of the responsible State agency in the State of the proposed residence or of an agency authorized by that State.

In the case of a child adopted abroad, the statement or attachment must be signed by an official of an appropriate public or private adoption agency which is licensed in the U.S.

The home study must be prepared by an entity (individual or organization) licensed or otherwise authorized under the laws of the State of the orphan's proposed residence to conduct research and preparation for a home study, including the required personal interviews.

If the recommending agency is licensed, the recommendation must specify that it is licensed, the State in which it is licensed, its license number, if any, and the period of validity of the license.

However, the research, including the interview and the preparation of the home study may be done by an individual or group in the United States or abroad that is satisfactory to the recommending entity.

A responsible State agency or licensed agency may accept a home study made by an unlicensed or foreign agency and use that home study as a basis for a favorable recommendation.

The home study must provide an assessment of the capabilities of the prospective adoptive parent(s) to properly parent the orphan and must include a discussion of the following areas:

(1) An assessment of the financial ability of the adoptive or prospective adoptive parents or parent.

(2) A detailed description of the accommodations where the adoptive or prospective adoptive parents or parent currently reside(s).

(3) If the prospective adoptive parent or parents residing abroad at the time of the home study, a description of the living accommodations where the child will reside in the United States, with the prospective adoptive parent or parents, if known.

(4) An assessment of the physical, mental and emotional capabilities of the adoptive or prospective adoptive parent or parents in relation to rearing and educating the child.

(5) An explanation regarding any history of abuse or violence or any complaints, charges, arrests, citations convictions, prison terms, pardons, rehabilitation decrees for breaking or violating any law or ordinance by the prospective adoptive parent(s) or any additional adult member of the household over age 18 years.

NOTE: Having committed any crime of moral turpitude or a drug-related offense does not necessarily mean that the prospective adoptive parent(s) will be found not qualified to adopt an orphan. However, failure to disclose such information may result in denial of this application and/or any subsequent petition for an orphan.

D. Biometric services.

As part of the USCIS biometric services requirement, the following persons must be fingerprinted in connection with this application:

- The married prospective adoptive parent and spouse, if applicable, and
- Each additional adult member 18 years of age or older, of the prospective adoptive parent(s)' household. **NOTE:** Submit a copy of the birth certificate of each qualifying household member over 18.

If necessary, USCIS may also take each person's photograph and signature as part of the biometric services.

(1) Petitioners residing in the United States. After filing this petition, USCIS will notify each person in writing of the time and location where they must go to be fingerprinted. Failure to appear to be fingerprinted or for other biometric services may result in denial of this application.

(2) Petitioners residing abroad. Completed fingerprint cards (Forms FD-258) must be submitted with this application. Do not bend, fold or crease the completed fingerprint cards. The fingerprint cards must be prepared by a U.S. embassy or consulate, USCIS office or U.S. military installation.

3. General Filing Instructions.

A. Type or print legibly in black ink.

B. If extra space is needed to complete any item, attach a continuation sheet, indicate the item number, and date and sign each sheet.

C. Translations.

Any foreign language document must be accompanied by a full English translation that the translator has certified as complete and correct. The translator must also certify that he or she is competent to translate the foreign language into English.

D. Copies.

If these instructions tell you to submit a copy of document, you do not have to send the original document. However, if there are stamps, remarks, notations, etc., on the back of the original documents, also submit copies of the back of each document(s). You will not have to submit the original document unless USCIS requests it.

There are times when USCIS must request an original copy of a document. In that case, the original document is generally returned after it has been reviewed.

E. Certification.

The "Certification of Prospective Adoptive Parent" block of Form I-600A must be executed by the prospective adoptive parent. The spouse, if applicable, must execute the **"Certification of Married Prospective Adoptive Parent Spouse"** block on **Page 2** of the form. Failure to do so will result in the rejection of the Form I-600A.

F. Submission of the Application.

A prospective adoptive parent residing in the United States should send the completed application to the USCIS office having jurisdiction over his or her place of residence. A prospective adoptive parent residing outside the United States should consult the nearest American consulate for the overseas or stateside USCIS office designated to act on the application.

4. What Is the Fee.

A fee of **$545.00** must be submitted for filing this application.

In addition to the fee for the application, there is a **$70.00** biometric services fee for fingerprinting every adult person living in the household in the United States where the child will reside.

For example, if an application is filed by a married couple residing in the United States with one additional adult member in their household, the total fees that must be submitted would be **$755.00** (**$545.00** for the petition and **$210.00** for the biometric services fees for fingerprinting the three adults).

NOTE: If the prospective adoptive parent(s) and any other adult members of the household are residing abroad at the time of filing, they are exempt from paying the biometric services fee for fingerprinting. However, they may have to pay fingerprinting fees charged by the U.S. Department of State or military installation.

The fee will not be refunded, whether the application is approved or not. Do not mail cash. All checks or money orders, whether U.S. or foreign, must be payable in U.S.currency at a financial institution in the United States.When a check is drawn on the account of a person other than yourself, write your name on the face of the check. If the check is not honored, USCIS will charge you $30.00.

Pay by check or money order in the exact amount. Make the check or money order payable to the **Department of Homeland Security**, unless:

A. You live in Guam, make the check or money order payable to the "Treasurer, Guam" or

B. You live in the U.S. Virgin Islands, make your check or money order payable to the "Commissioner of Finance of the Virgin Islands."

How to Check If the Fee Is Correct.

The fee on this form is current as of the edition date appearing in the lower right corner of this page. However, because USCIS fees change periodically, you can verify if the fee is correct by following one of the steps below:

- Visit our website at **www.uscis.gov** and scroll down to "Forms and E-Filing" to check the appropriate fee, or
- Review the Fee Schedule included in your form package, if you called us to request the form, or
- Telephone our National Customer Service Center at **1-800-375-5283** and ask for the fee information.

NOTE: If your petition or application requires a biometric services fee for USCIS to take your fingerprints, photograph or signature, you can use the same procedure above to confirm the biometrics fee.

5. What Should You Do After Locating and/or Identifying a Child or Children?

Form I-600, Petition to Classify Orphan as an Immediate Relative, is filed when a child has been located and/or identified for the prospective adoptive parent(s). A new fee is not required if Form I-600 is filed within 18 months from the approval date of the Form I-600A application. If approved in the home study for more than one orphan, the prospective adoptive parent(s) may file a petition for each of the additional children to the maximum number approved. If the orphans are siblings, no additional filing fee is required. However, if the orphans are not siblings, an additional filing fee is required for each orphan beyond the first orphan.

NOTE: Approval of an advance processing application does not guarantee that the orphan petition(s) will be approved.

Form I-600 must be accompanied by all the evidence required by the instructions of that form, except where provided previously with Form I-600A.

Generally, Form I-600 should be submitted at the USCIS office where the advance processing application, Form I-600A, was filed. Prospective adoptive parent(s) going abroad to adopt or locate a child may file Form I-600 with either the USCIS office or American consulate or embassy having jurisdiction over the place where the child is residing or will be located, unless the case is being retained at the USCIS office stateside.

USCIS has offices in the following countries: Austria, China, Cuba, the Dominican Republic, El Salvador, Germany, Ghana, Great Britain, Greece, Guatemala, Haiti, Honduras, India, Italy, Jamaica, Kenya, Korea, Mexico, Pakistan, Panama, Peru, the Philippines, Russia, South Africa, Thailand and Vietnam.

6. Penalties.

Willful false statements on this form or supporting documents may be punished by fine or imprisonment. U. S. Code, Title 18, Sec. 1001 (Formerly Sec. 80.)

7. Authority for Collecting Information.

8 U.S.C 1154 (a). Routine uses for disclosure under the Privacy Act of 1974 have been published in the Federal Register and are available upon request. USCIS will use the information to determine immigrant eligibility Submission of the information is voluntary, but failure to provide any or all of the information may result in denial of the application.

8. USCIS Forms and Information.

To order USCIS forms, call our toll-free number at **1-800-870-3676**. You can also get USCIS forms and information on laws, regulations and procedures by telephoning our **National Customer Service Center** at **1-800-375-5283** or visiting our internet website at **www.uscis.gov.**

9. Use InfoPass for Appointments.

As an alternative to waiting in line for assistance at your local USCIS office, you can now schedule an appointment through our internet-based system, **InfoPass**. To access the system, visit our website at **www.uscis.gov**. Use the **InfoPass** appointment scheduler and follow the screen prompts to set up your appointment. **InfoPass** generates an electronic appointment notice that appears on the screen. Print the notice and take it with you to your appointment. The notice gives the time and date of your appointment, along with the address of the USCIS office.

10. Reporting Burden.

A person is not required to respond to a collection of information unless it displays a currently valid OMB control number. Public reporting burden for this collection of information is estimated to average 30 minutes per response including the time for reviewing instructions, searching existing data sources, gathering and maintaining the data needed, and completing and reviewing the collection of information. Send comments regarding this burden estimate or any other aspect of this collection of information, including suggestions for reducing this burden, to U.S. Citizenship and Immigration Services, Regulatory Management Division, 111 Massachusetts Avenue, N.W., Washington, DC 20529; OMB No. 1615-0028 **Do not mail your completed application to this address.**

OMB No. 1615-0028; Expires 08/31/08

Department of Homeland Security
U.S. Citizenship and Immigration Services

I-600A, Application for Advance Processing of Orphan Petition

Do not write in this block. **For USCIS Use Only.**

It has been determined that the:

☐ Married ☐ Unmarried

prospective adoptive parent will furnish proper care to a beneficiary orphan if admitted to the United States.

There:

☐ are ☐ are not

preadoptive requirements in the State of the child's proposed residence.

The following is a description of the preadoption requirements, if any, of the State of the child's proposed residence:

The preadoption requirements, if any,:

☐ have been met. ☐ have not been met.

Fee Stamp

DATE OF FAVORABLE DETERMINATION

DD

DISTRICT

File number of applicant, if applicable.

Please type or print legibly in black ink.

This application is made by the named prospective adoptive parent for advance processing of an orphan petition.

BLOCK I - Information about the prospective adoptive parent.

1. My name is: (Last) (First) (Middle)

2. Other names used (including maiden name if appropriate):

3. I reside in the U.S. at: (C/O if appropriate) (Apt. No.)

(Number and Street) (Town or City) (State) (Zip Code)

4. Address abroad (If any): (Number and Street) (Apt. No.)

(Town or City) (Province) (Country)

5. I was born on: *(mm/dd/yyyy)*

In: (Town or City) (State or Province) (Country)

6. My telephone number is: (Include Area Code)

7. My marital status is:

☐ Married
☐ Widowed
☐ Divorced
☐ Single
 ☐ I have never been married.
 ☐ I have been previously married __________ time(s).

8. If you are now married, give the following information:

Date and place of present marriage *(mm/dd/yyyy)*

Name of present spouse (include maiden name of wife)

Date of birth of spouse *(mm/dd/yyyy)* Place of birth of spouse

Number of prior marriages of spouse

My spouse resides ☐ With me ☐ Apart from me (provide address below)

(Apt. No.) (No. and Street) (City) (State) (Country)

9. I am a citizen of the United States through:

☐ Birth ☐ Parents ☐ Naturalization

If acquired through naturalization, give name under which naturalized, number of naturalization certificate, and date and place of naturalization.

If not, submit evidence of citizenship. See Instruction 2.a(2).

If acquired through parentage, have you obtained a certificate in your own name based on that acquisition?

☐ No ☐ Yes

Have you or any person through whom you claimed citizenship ever lost United States citizenship?

☐ No ☐ Yes (If Yes, attach detailed explanation.)

Received	Trans. In	Ret'd Trans. Out	Completed

BLOCK II - General information.

10. Name and address of organization or individual assisting you in locating or identifying an orphan
(Name)

(Address)

11. Do you plan to travel abroad to locate or adopt a child?
☐ Yes ☐ No

12. Does your spouse, if any, plan to travel abroad to locate or adopt a child?
☐ Yes ☐ No

13. If the answer to Question **11** or **12** is "Yes," give the following information:
a. Your date of intended departure
b. Your spouse's date of intended departure
c. City, province

14. Will the child come to the United States for adoption after compliance with the preadoption requirements, if any, of the State of proposed residence?
☐ Yes ☐ No

15. If the answer to Question **14** is "No," will the child be adopted abroad after having been personally seen and observed by you and your spouse, if married?
☐ Yes ☐ No

16. Where do you wish to file your orphan petition?
The USCIS office located at

The American Embassy or Consulate at

17. Do you plan to adopt more than one child?
☐ Yes ☐ No
If "Yes," how many children do you plan to adopt?

Certification of prospective adoptive parent.
I certify, under penalty of perjury under the laws of the United States of America, that the foregoing is true and correct and that I will care for an orphan/orphans properly if admitted to the United States.

(Signature of Prospective Adoptive Parent)

Executed on (Date)

Certification of married prospective adoptive parent spouse.
I certify, under penalty of perjury under the laws of the United States of America, that the foregoing is true and correct and that my spouse and I will care for an orphan/orphans properly if admitted to the United States.

(Signature of Prospective Adoptive Parent Spouse)

Executed on (Date)

Signature of person preparing form, if other than petitioner.
I declare that this document was prepared by me at the request of the petitioner and is based entirely on information of which I have knowledge.

(Signature)

Street Address and Room or Suite No./City/State/Zip Code

Executed on (Date)

FORMS FOR EMPLOYMENT-BASED IMMIGRATION

As we discussed in Chapter 4, some aliens may qualify for LPR status based on employment in the United States. These are the most common forms pertaining to employment-based immigration.

ETA 750: Application for Alien Employment Certification

This form is required by the U.S. Department of Labor (DOL) for certain aliens seeking employment-based immigration. The DOL becomes involved in immigration matters regarding second and third preference aliens (see Chapter 4).

If the DOL approves the application, then it has to go to DHS.

I-140: Immigrant Petition for Alien Worker

This is the form used by DHS regarding employment-based immigration. All aliens seeking that status must file this form; second and third preference aliens must file the ETA 750 with the U.S. Department of Labor first.

OMB Approval No. 1205-0015

U.S. DEPARTMENT OF LABOR
Employment and Training Administration

APPLICATION FOR ALIEN EMPLOYMENT CERTIFICATION

IMPORTANT: READ CAREFULLY BEFORE COMPLETING THIS FORM

PRINT legibly in ink or use a typewriter. If you need more space to answer questions in this form, use a separate sheet. Identify each answer with the number of the corresponding question. SIGN AND DATE each sheet in original signature.

To knowingly furnish any false information in the preparation of this form and any supplement thereto or to aid, abet, or counsel another to do so is a felony punishable by $10,000 fine or 5 years in the penitentiary, or both (18 U.S.C. 1001)

PART A. OFFER OF EMPLOYMENT

1. Name of Alien (Family name in capital letter, First, Middle, Maiden)

2. Present Address of Alien (Number, Street, City and Town, State ZIP code or Province, Country)

3. Type of Visa (If in U.S.)

The following information is submitted as an offer of employment.

4. Name of Employer (Full name of Organization)

5. Telephone

6. Address (Number, Street, City and Town, State ZIP code)

7. Address Where Alien Will Work (if different from item 6)

8. Nature of Employer's Business Activity	9. Name of Job Title	10. Total Hours Per Week		11. Work Schedule (Hourly)	12. Rate of Pay	
		a. Basic	b. Overtime	a.m. p.m.	a. Basic $ per ______	b. Overtime $ per hour

13. Describe Fully the job to be Performed (Duties)

14. State in detail the MINIMUM education, training, and experience for a worker to perform satisfactorily the job duties described in item 13 above.

EDU-CATION (Enter number of years)	Grade School	High School	College	College Degree Required (specify)
				Major Field of Study
TRAIN-ING	No. Yrs.		No. Mos.	Type of Training
EXPERI-ENCE	Job Offered		Related Occupation	Related Occupation (specify)
	Number			
	Yrs.	Mos.	Yrs. / Mos.	

15. Other Special Requirements

16. Occupational Title of Person Who Will Be Alien's Immediate Supervisor

17. Number of Employees Alien Will Supervise

ENDORSEMENTS (Make no entry in section - for Government use only)

Date Forms Received	
L.O.	S.O.
R.O.	N.O.
Ind. Code	Occ. Code
Occ. Title	

Replaces MA 7-50A, B and C (Apr. 1970 edition) which is obsolete.

ETA 750 (Oct. 1979)

18. COMPLETE ITEMS ONLY IF JOB IS TEMPORARY			19. IF JOB IS UNIONIZED (Complete)	
a. No. of Openings To Be Filled By Aliens Under Job Offer	b. Exact Dates You Expect To Employ Alien		a. Number of Local	b. Name of Local
	From	To		c. City and State

20. STATEMENT FOR LIVE-AT-WORK JOB OFFERS (Complete for Private Household ONLY)						
a. Description of Residence		b. No. Persons residing at Place of Employment				c. Will free board and private room not shared with anyone be provided? ("X" one)
("X" one)	Number of Rooms	Adults		Children	Ages	
☐ House			BOYS			☐ YES ☐ NO
☐ Apartment			GIRLS			

21. DESCRIBE EFFORTS TO RECRUIT U.S. WORKERS AND THE RESULTS. (Specify Sources of Recruitment by Name)

22. Applications require various types of documentation. Please read Part II of the instructions to assure that appropriate supporting documentation is included with your application.

23. EMPLOYER CERTIFICATIONS

By virtue of my signature below, I HEREBY CERTIFY the following conditions of employment.

a. I have enough funds available to pay the wage or salary offered the alien.

b. The wage offered equals or exceeds the prevailing wage and I guarantee that, if a labor certification is granted, the wage paid to the alien when the alien begins work will equal or exceed the prevailing wage which is applicable at the time the alien begins work.

c. The wage offered is not based on commissions, bonuses, or other incentives, unless I guarantee a wage paid on a weekly, bi-weekly, or monthly basis.

d. I will be able to place the alien on the payroll on or before the date of the alien's proposed entrance into the United States.

e. The job opportunity does not involve unlawful discrimination by race, creed, color, national origin, age, sex, religion, handicap, or citizenship.

f. The job opportunity is not:

(1) Vacant because the former occupant is on strike or is being locked out in the course of a labor dispute involving a work stoppage.

(2) At issue in a labor dispute involving a work stoppage.

g. The job opportunity's terms, conditions and occupational environment are not contrary to Federal, State or local law.

h. The job opportunity has been and is clearly open to any qualified U.S. worker.

24. DECLARATIONS

DECLARATION OF EMPLOYER ➤ Pursuant to 28 U.S.C. 1746, I declare under penalty of perjury the foregoing is true and correct.

SIGNATURE	DATE
NAME (Type or Print)	TITLE

AUTHORIZATION OF AGENT OF EMPLOYER ➤ I HEREBY DESIGNATE the agent below to represent me for the purposes of labor certification and I TAKE FULL RESPONSIBILITY for accuracy of any representations made by my agent.

SIGNATURE OF EMPLOYER	DATE
NAME OF AGENT (Type or Print)	ADDRESS OF AGENT (Number, Street, City, State, ZIP code)

PRIVACY ACT STATEMENT

In accordance with the Privacy Act of 1974, as amended (5 U.S.C. 552a), you are hereby notified that the information provided herein is protected under the Privacy Act. The Department of Labor (Department) is maintaining a System of Records titled Employer Application and Attestation File for Permanent and Temporary Alien Workers (DOL/ETA-7).

Case files developed in processing labor certification applications, labor condition applications, or labor attestations, may be released to the employers which filed such applications, their representatives, and to named alien beneficiaries or their representatives, if requested, to review Employment and Training Administration (ETA) actions in connection with appeals of denials before the DOL Office of Administrative Law Judges and federal courts; to participating agencies such as the DOL Office of Inspector General, Employment Standards Administration, Department of Homeland Security's U.S. Citizenship and Immigration Services and Bureau of Immigration and Customs Enforcement, and Department of State in connection with administering and enforcing related immigration laws and regulations; and to the DOL Office of Administrative Law Judges and Federal Courts in connection with appeals of denials of labor certification requests, labor condition applications, and labor attestations.

Further disclosures may be made under the following circumstances: in connection with federal litigation; for law enforcement purposes; to authorized parent locator persons under Pub. L. 93-647; to an information source in connection with personnel, procurement, or benefit-related matters, to a contractor or their employees, consultants, grantees or their employees, or volunteers who have been engaged to assist the agency in the performance of a contract; for Federal debt collection purposes; the Office of Management and Budget in connection with its legislative review, coordination, and clearance activities; if a person about whom this record is maintained submits a written request to a Member of Congress or their staff and that request is forwarded to the Department, we may release the information to the Member of Congress or Congressional staff in response to the inquiry made on behalf of the subject of the record; and to the news media and the public when a matter under investigation becomes public knowledge, the Solicitor of Labor determines the disclosure is necessary to preserve confidence or integrity of the Department, or the Solicitor of Labor determines that a legitimate public interest exists in the disclosure of information unless the disclosure would constitute an unwarranted invasion of personal privacy.

PART B. STATEMENT OF QUALIFICATIONS OF ALIEN

FOR ADVICE CONCERNING REQUIREMENTS FOR ALIEN EMPLOYMENT CERTIFICATION: If alien is in the U.S., contact nearest office of Immigration and Naturalization Service. If alien is outside U.S., contact nearest U.S. Consulate.

IMPORTANT: READ ATTACHED INSTRUCTIONS BEFORE COMPLETING THIS FORM.

Print legibly in ink or use a typewriter. If you need more space to fully answer any questions on this form, use a separate sheet. Identify each answer with the number of the corresponding question. Sign and date each sheet.

1. Name of Alien (Family name in capital letters)	First name	Middle name	Maiden name

2. Present Address (No., Street, City or Town, State or Province and ZIP code)	Country	3. Type of Visa (If in U.S.)

4. Alien's Birthdate (Month, Day, Year)	5. Birthplace (City or Town, State or Province)	Country	6. Present Nationality or Citizenship (Country)

7. Address in United States Where Alien Will Reside

8. Name and Address of Prospective Employer if Alien has job offer in U.S.	9. Occupation in which Alien is Seeking Work

10. "X" the appropriate box below and furnish the information required for the box marked

a. ☐ Alien will apply for a visa abroad at the American Consulate in →	City in Foreign Country	Foreign Country
b. ☐ Alien is in the United States and will apply for adjustment of status to that of a lawful permanent resident in the office of the Immigration and Naturalization Service at →	City	State

11. Names and Addresses of Schools, Colleges and Universities Attended (Include trade or vocational training facilities)	Field of Study	FROM		TO		Degrees or Certificates Received
		Month	Year	Month	Year	

SPECIAL QUALIFICATIONS AND SKILLS

12. Additional Qualifications and Skills Alien Possesses and Proficiency in the use of Tools, Machines or Equipment Which Would Help Establish if Alien Meets Requirements for Occupation in Item 9.

13. List Licenses (Professional, journeyman, etc.)

14. List Documents Attached Which are Submitted as Evidence that Alien Possesses the Education, Training, Experience, and Abilities Represented

Endorsements	DATE REC. DOL
(Make no entry in this section - FOR Government Agency USE ONLY)	O.T. & C.

(Items continued on next page)

15. WORK EXPERIENCE. List all jobs held during the last three (3) years. Also, list any other jobs related to the occupation for which the alien is seeking certification as indicated in item 9.			
a. NAME AND ADDRESS OF EMPLOYER			
NAME OF JOB	DATE STARTED Month Year	DATE LEFT Month Year	KIND OF BUSINESS
DESCRIBE IN DETAIL THE DUTIES PERFORMED, INCLUDING THE USE OF TOOLS, MACHINES OR EQUIPMENT			NO. OF HOURS PER WEEK
b. NAME AND ADDRESS OF EMPLOYER			
NAME OF JOB	DATE STARTED Month Year	DATE LEFT Month Year	KIND OF BUSINESS
DESCRIBE IN DETAIL THE DUTIES PERFORMED, INCLUDING THE USE OF TOOLS, MACHINES OR EQUIPMENT			NO. OF HOURS PER WEEK
c. NAME AND ADDRESS OF EMPLOYER			
NAME OF JOB	DATE STARTED Month Year	DATE LEFT Month Year	KIND OF BUSINESS
DESCRIBE IN DETAIL THE DUTIES PERFORMED, INCLUDING THE USE OF TOOLS, MACHINES OR EQUIPMENT			NO. OF HOURS PER WEEK

16. DECLARATIONS

DECLARATION OF ALIEN ➤ ➤	Pursuant to 28 U.S.C. 1746, I declare under penalty of perjury the foregoing is true and correct.
SIGNATURE OF ALIEN	DATE
AUTHORIZATION OF AGENT OF ALIEN ➤ ➤	I hereby designate the agent below to represent me for the purposes of labor certification and I take full responsibility for accuracy of any representations made by my agent.
SIGNATURE OF ALIEN	DATE
NAME OF AGENT (Type or print)	ADDRESS OF AGENT (No., Street, City, State, ZIP code)

PRIVACY ACT STATEMENT

In accordance with the Privacy Act of 1974, as amended (5 U.S.C. 552a), you are hereby notified that the information provided herein is protected under the Privacy Act. The Department of Labor (Department) is maintaining a System of Records titled Employer Application and Attestation File for Permanent and Temporary Alien Workers (DOL/ETA-7).

Case files developed in processing labor certification applications, labor condition applications, or labor attestations, may be released to the employers which filed such applications, their representatives, and to named alien beneficiaries or their representatives, if requested, to review Employment and Training Administration (ETA) actions in connection with appeals of denials before the DOL Office of Administrative Law Judges and federal courts; to participating agencies such as the DOL Office of Inspector General, Employment Standards Administration, Department of Homeland Security's U.S. Citizenship and Immigration Services and Bureau of Immigration and Customs Enforcement, and Department of State in connection with administering and enforcing related immigration laws and regulations; and to the DOL Office of Administrative Law Judges and Federal Courts in connection with appeals of denials of labor certification requests, labor condition applications, and labor attestations.

Further disclosures may be made under the following circumstances: in connection with federal litigation; for law enforcement purposes; to authorized parent locator persons under Pub. L. 93-647; to an information source in connection with personnel, procurement, or benefit-related matters, to a contractor or their employees, consultants, grantees or their employees, or volunteers who have been engaged to assist the agency in the performance of a contract; for Federal debt collection purposes; the Office of Management and Budget in connection with its legislative review, coordination, and clearance activities; if a person about whom this record is maintained submits a written request to a Member of Congress or their staff and that request is forwarded to the Department, we may release the information to the Member of Congress or Congressional staff in response to the inquiry made on behalf of the subject of the record; and to the news media and the public when a matter under investigation becomes public knowledge, the Solicitor of Labor determines the disclosure is necessary to preserve confidence or integrity of the Department, or the Solicitor of Labor determines that a legitimate public interest exists in the disclosure of information unless the disclosure would constitute an unwarranted invasion of personal privacy.

OMB No. 1615-0015; Exp. 06-30-06

Department of Homeland Security
U.S.Citizenship and Immigration Services

I-140, Immigrant Petition for Alien Worker

Purpose of This Form.

This form is used to petition U.S. Citizenship and Immigration Services (USCIS) for an immigrant visa based on employment. USCIS is comprised of offices of former Immigration and Naturalization Service (INS).

Who May File?

A U.S. employer may file this petition for:

- An outstanding professor or researcher, with at least three years of experience in teaching or research in the academic area, who is recognized internationally as outstanding:
  - -- In a tenured or tenure-track position at a university or institution of higher education to teach in the academic area; or
  - -- In a comparable position at a university or institution of higher education to conduct research in the area; or
  - -- In a comparable position to conduct research for a private employer that employs at least three persons in full-time research activities and which achieved documented accomplishments in an academic field.
- An alien who, in the three years preceding the filing of this petition, has been employed for at least one year by a firm or corporation or other legal entity and who seeks to enter the United States to continue to render services to the same employer, or to a subsidiary or affiliate, in a capacity that is managerial or executive.
- A member of the professions holding an advanced degree or an alien with exceptional ability in the sciences, arts, or business who will substantially benefit the national economy, cultural or educational interests, or welfare of the United States.
- A skilled worker (requiring at least two years of specialized training or experience in the skill) to perform labor for which qualified workers are not available in the United States.
- A member of the professions with a baccalaureate degree.
- An unskilled worker (requiring less than two years of specialized training or experience) to perform labor for which qualified workers are not available in the United States.

In addition, a person may file this petition on his or her own behalf if he or she:

- has extraordinary ability in the sciences, arts, education, business, or athletics demonstrated by sustained national or international acclaim, whose achievements have been recognized in the field; or
- is a member of the profession holding an advanced degree or is claiming exceptional ability in the sciences, arts, or business, and is seeking an exemption of the requirement of a job offer in the national interest (NIW).

General Filing Instructions.

Please answer all questions by typing or clearly printing in black ink. Indicate that an item is not applicable with "N/A." If an answer to a question is "none," write "none." If you need extra space to answer any item, attach a sheet of paper with your name and your A#, if any, and indicate the number of the item . You must file your petition with the required initial evidence. Your petition must be properly signed and filed with the correct fee.

Initial Evidence.

If you are filing for an alien of extraordinary ability in the sciences, arts, education, business or athletics:

You must file your petition with evidence that the alien has sustained national or international acclaim and that the achievements have been recognized in the field of expertise.

- Evidence of a one-time achievement (i.e., a major, internationally recognized award); or
- At least three of the following:
  - -- Receipt of lesser nationally or internationally recognized prizes or awards for excellence in the field of endeavor,
  - -- Membership in associations in the field which require outstanding achievements as judged by recognized national or international experts,
  - -- Published material about the alien in professional or major trade publications or other major media,
  - -- Participation on a panel or individually as a judge of the work of others in the field or an allied field,
  - -- Original scientific, scholarly, artistic, athletic, or business-related contributions of major significance in the field,
  - -- Authorship of scholarly articles in the field, in professional or major trade publications or other major media,
  - -- Display of the alien's work at artistic exhibitions or showcases,
  - -- Evidence that the alien has performed in a leading or critical role for organizations or establishments that have distinguished reputations,
  - -- Evidence that the alien has commanded a high salary or other high remuneration for services,
  - -- Evidence of commercial successes in the performing arts, as shown by box office receipts or record, casette, compact disk, or video sales.
- If the above standards do not readily apply to the alien's occupation, you may submit comparable evidence to establish the alien's eligibility; and

- Evidence that the alien is coming to the United States to continue work in the area of expertise. Such evidence may include letter(s) from prospective employer(s), evidence of prearranged commitments such as contracts, or a statement from the alien detailing plans on how he or she intends to continue work in the United States.

A U.S. employer filing for an outstanding professor or researcher must file the petition with:

- Evidence that the professor or researcher is recognized internationally as outstanding in the academic field specified in the petition. Such evidence shall consist of at least two of the following:
  -- Receipt of major prizes or awards for outstanding achievement in the academic field,
  -- Membership in associations in the academic field, which require outstanding achievements of their members,
  -- Published material in professional publications written by others about the alien's work in the academic field,
  -- Participation on a panel, or individually, as the judge of the work of others in the same or an allied academic field,
  -- Original scientific or scholarly research contributions to the academic field, or
  -- Authorship of scholarly books or articles, in scholarly journals with international circulation, in the academic field.
- Evidence the beneficiary has at least three years of experience in teaching and/or research in the academic field; and
- If you are a university or other institution of higher education, a letter indicating that you intend to employ the beneficiary in a tenured or tenure-track position as a teacher or in a permanent position as a researcher in the academic field; or
- If you are a private employer, a letter indicating that you intend to employ the beneficiary in a permanent research position in the academic field, and evidence that you employ at least three full-time researchers and have achieved documented accomplishments in the field.

A U.S. employer filing for a multinational executive or manager must file the petition with a statement which demonstrates that:

- If the worker is now employed outside the United States, that he or she has been employed outside the United States for at least one year in the past three years in an executive or managerial capacity by the petitioner or by its parent, branch, subsidiary or affiliate; or, if the worker is already employed in the United States, that he or she was employed outside the United States for at least one year in the three years preceding admission as a nonimmigrant in an executive or managerial capacity by the petitioner or by its parent, branch, subsidiary or affiliate;
- The prospective employer in the United States is the same employer or a subsidiary or affiliate of the firm or corporation or other legal entity by which the alien was employed abroad;
- The prospective United States employer has been doing business for at least one year; and
- The alien is to be employed in the United States in a managerial or executive capacity. A description of the duties to be performed should be included.

A U.S. employer filing for a member of the professions with an advanced degree or a person with exceptional ability in the sciences, arts or business must file the petition with:

- A labor certification (see **General Evidence**), or a request for a waiver of a job offer because the employment is deemed to be in the national interest, with documentation provided to show that the beneficiary's presence in the United States would be in the national interest; and either:

-- An official academic record showing that the alien has a U.S. advanced degree or an equivalent foreign degree, or an official academic record showing that the alien has a U.S. baccalaureate degree or an equivalent foreign degree and letters from current or former employers showing that the alien has at least five years of progressive post- baccalaureate experience in the specialty; or

  -- At least three of the following:
    - An official academic record showing that the alien has a degree, diploma, certificate, or similar award from an institution of learning relating to the area of exceptional ability;
    - Letters from current or former employers showing that the alien has at least ten years of full-time experience in the occupation for which he or she is being sought;
    - A license to practice the profession or certification for a particular profession or occupation;
    - Evidence that the alien has commanded a salary, or other remuneration for services, which demonstrates exceptional ability;
    - Evidence of membership in professional associations; or
    - Evidence of recognition for achievements and significant contributions to the industry or field by peers, governmental entities, or professional or business organizations.
- If the above standards do not readily apply to the alien's occupation, you may submit comparable evidence to establish the alien's eligibility.

A U.S. employer filing for a skilled worker must file the petition with:

- A labor certification (see **General Evidence**);
- Evidence that the alien meets the educational, training, or experience and any other requirements of the labor certification (the minimum requirement is two years of training or experience).

A U.S. employer filing for a professional must file the petition with:

- A labor certification (see **General Evidence**);
- Evidence that the alien holds a U.S. baccalaureate degree or equivalent foreign degree; and
- Evidence that a baccalaureate degree is required for entry into the occupation.

A U.S. employer filing for an unskilled worker must file the petition with:

- A labor certification (see **General Evidence**); and
- Evidence that the beneficiary meets any education, training, or experience requirements required in the labor certification.

General Evidence.

Labor certification.

Petitions for certain classifications must be filed with a certification from the U.S. Department of Labor or with documentation to establish that the alien qualifies for one of the shortage occupations in the Department of Labor's Labor Market Information Pilot Program or for an occupation in Group I or II of the Department of Labor's Schedule A.

A certification establishes that there are not sufficient workers who are able, willing, qualified, and available at the time and place where the alien is to be employed and that employment of the alien, if qualified, will not adversely affect the wages and working conditions of similarly employed U.S. workers. Application for certification is made on Form ETA-750 and is filed at the local office of the State Employment Service. If the alien is in a shortage occupation, or for a Schedule A/Group I or II occupation, you may file a fully completed, uncertified Form ETA-750 in duplicate with your petition for determination by the USCIS that the alien belongs to the shortage occupation.

NOTE: When filing for a Schedule A/Group I or II occupation, the petitioner must include evidence of having complied with the Department of Labor regulations at 20 CFR 656.222(b)(2), which require that the position or positions be properly posted for a minimum of ten consecutive days.

Ability to pay wage.

Petitions which require job offers must be accompanied by evidence that the prospective U.S. employer has the ability to pay the proffered wage. Such evidence shall be in the form of copies of annual reports, federal tax returns, or audited financial statements. In a case where the prospective U.S. employer employs 100 or more workers, a statement from a financial officer of the organization which establishes ability to pay the wage may be submitted. In appropriate cases, additional evidence, such as profit/loss statements, bank account records, or personnel records, may be submitted.

Translations.

Any foreign language document must be accompanied by a full English translation, which the translator has certified as complete and correct, and by the translator's certification that he or she is competent to translate the foreign language into English.

Copies.

If these instructions state that a copy of a document may be filed with this petition and you choose to send us the original, we may keep that original for our records. Copies may be submitted of all documentation with the exception of the Labor Certification which **must** be submitted in the original.

Where to File.

File this petition at the Nebraska Service Center, following the instructions noted above in the next column.

For Form I-140 **filed concurrently** with Form I-485, Application to Register or Adjust Status, mail your forms package to:

USCIS Nebraska Service Center
P.O. Box 87485
Lincoln, NE 68501-7485

For Form I-140 **filed alone,** mail the form to:

USCIS Nebraska Service Center
P.O. Box 87140
Lincoln, NE 68501-7140

Prior to submitting your form(s), note the different addresses. Make sure you send your form package to the appropriate address to avoid processing delays.

What Is the Fee?

The fee for this petition is **$195.00**.

The fee must be submitted in the exact amount. It cannot be refunded. **Do not mail cash.**

All checks and money orders must be drawn on a bank or other financial institution located in the United States and must be payable in United States currency. The check or money order should be made payable to the **Department of Homeland Security**, unless:

- If you live in Guam, make your check or money order payable to the "Treasurer, Guam."
- If you live in the U.S. Virgin Islands , make your check or money order payable to the "Commissioner of Finance of the Virgin Islands."

Checks are accepted subject to collection. An uncollected check will render the petition and any document issued invalid. A charge of $30.00 will be imposed if a check in payment of a fee is not honored by the bank on which it is drawn.

How to Check If the Fee Is Correct.

The fee on this form is current as of the edition date appearing in the lower right corner of this page. However, because USCIS fees change periodically, you can verify if the fee is correct by following one of the steps below:

- Visit our website at **www.uscis.gov** and scroll down to "Forms and E-Filing" to check the appropriate fee, or
- Review the Fee Schedule included in your form package, if you called us to request the form, or
- Telephone our National Customer Service Center at **1-800-375-5283** and ask for the fee information.

Processing Information.

Acceptance.
Any petition that is not signed or is not accompanied by the correct fee will be rejected with a notice that it is deficient. You may correct the deficiency and resubmit the petition. However, a petition is not considered properly filed until accepted by the USCIS. A priority date will not be assigned until the petition is properly filed.

Initial processing.
Once the petition has been accepted, it will be checked for completeness, including submission of the required initial evidence. If you do not completely fill out the form, or file it without the required initial evidence, you will not establish a basis for eligibility, and we may deny your petition.

Requests for more information or interview.
We may request more information or evidence, or we may request that you appear at a USCIS office for an interview. We may also request that you submit the originals of any copy. We will return these originals when they are no longer required.

Decision.
If you have established eligibility for the benefit requested, your petition will be approved. If you have not established eligibility, your petition will be denied. You will be notified in writing of the decision on your petition.

Meaning of petition approval.
Approval of a petition means you have established that the person you are filling for is eligible for the requested classification.

This is the first step towards permanent residence. However, this does not in itself grant permanent residence or employment authorization. You will be given information about the requirements for the person to receive an immigrant visa or to adjust status after your petition is approved.

Instructions for Industry and Occupation Codes.

NAICS Code.
The North American Industry Classification System (NAICS) code can be obtained from the U.S. Department of Commerce, U.S. Census Bureau at (www.census.gov/epcd/www/naics.html). Enter the code from left to right, one digit in each of the six boxes. If you use a code which is less than six digits, enter the code left to right and then add zeros in the remaining unoccupied boxes.

The code sequence 33466 would be entered as:

3	3	4	6	6	0

The code sequence 5133 would be entered as:

5	1	3	3	0	0

SOC Code.
The Standard Occupational Classification (SOC) System codes can be obtained from the Department of Labor, U.S. Bureau of Labor Statistics (http://stats.bls.gov/soc/socguide.htm). Enter the code from left to right, one digit in each of the six boxes. If you use a code which is less than six digits, enter the code left to right and then add zeros in the remaining unoccupied boxes.

The code sequence 19-1021 would be entered as:

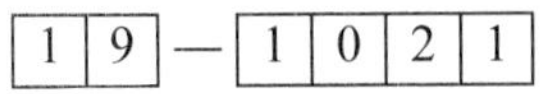

The code sequence 15-100 would be entered as:

1 5 — 1 0 0 0

Penalties.

If you knowingly and willfully falsify or conceal a material fact or submit a false document with this petition, we will deny the benefit your are seeking and may deny any other immigration benefit. In addition, you will face severe penalties provided by law and may be subject to criminal prosecution.

Privacy Act Notice.

We ask for the information on this form and associated evidence to determine if you have established eligibility for the immigration benefit you are seeking. Our legal right to ask for this information is in 8 U.S.C. 1154. We may provide this information to other government agencies. Failure to provide this information and any requested evidence may delay a final decision or result in denial of your request.

USCIS Forms and Information.

To order USCIS forms, call our toll-free forms line at **1-800-870-3676**. You can also obtain USCIS forms and information on immigration laws, regulations or procedures by calling our National Customer Service Center at **1-800-375-5283** or visiting our internet website at **www.uscis.gov.**

Use InfoPass to Make an Appointment.

As an alternative to waiting in line for assistance at your local USCIS office, you can now schedule an appointment through our internet-based system, **InfoPass.** To access the system, visit our website at **www.uscis.gov.** Use the **InfoPass** appointment scheduler and follow the screen prompts to set up your appointment. **InfoPass** generates an electronic appointment notice that appears on the screen. Print the notice and take it with you to your appointment. The notice gives the time and date of your appointment, along with the address of USCIS office.

Paperwork Reduction Act Notice.

An agency may not conduct or sponsor an information collection and a person is not required to respond to a collection of information unless it displays a currently valid OMB control number.

We try to create forms and instructions that are accurate, can easily be understood, and which impose the least possible burden on you to provide us with information. Often this is difficult because some immigration laws are very complex.

The estimate average time to complete and file this application is as follows: (1) 20 minutes to learn about the law and form; (2) 15 minutes to complete the form; and (3) 25 minutes to assemble and file the petition; for a total estimated average of 1 hour per petition.

If you have comments regarding the accuracy of this estimate, or suggestions for making this form simpler, you can write to U.S. Citizenship and Immigration Services, Regulatory Management Division, 111 Massachusetts Avenue, N.W., Washington, D.C. 20529; OMB No. 1615-0015. **Do not mail your completed petition to this Washington, D.C. address.**

Department of Homeland Security
U.S. Citizenship and Immigration Services

OMB No. 1615-0015; Exp. 06-30-06

I-140, Immigrant Petition for Alien Worker

START HERE - Please type or print in black ink.

For USCIS Use Only

Returned	Receipt
Date	
Date	
Resubmitted	
Date	
Date	
Reloc Sent	
Date	
Date	
Reloc Rec'd	
Date	
Date	

Part 1. Information about the person or organization filing this petition. If an individual is filing, use the top name line. Organizations should use the second line.

Family Name (Last Name) | Given Name (First Name) | Full Middle Name

Company or Organization Name

Address: (Street Number and Name) | Suite #

Attn:

City | State/Province

Country | Zip/Postal Code

IRS Tax # | U.S. Social Security # *(if any)* | E-Mail Address *(if any)*

Part 2. Petition type.

This petition is being filed for: *(Check one.)*

- **a.** ☐ An alien of extraordinary ability.
- **b.** ☐ An outstanding professor or researcher.
- **c.** ☐ A multinational executive or manager.
- **d.** ☐ A member of the professions holding an advanced degree or an alien of exceptional ability (who is NOT seeking a National Interest Waiver).
- **e.** ☐ A professional (at a minimum, possessing a bachelor's degree or a foreign degree equivalent to a U.S. bachelor's degree) or a skilled worker (requiring at least two years of specialized training or experience).
- **f.** ☐ (Reserved.)
- **g.** ☐ Any other worker (requiring less than two years of training or experience).
- **h.** ☐ Soviet Scientist.
- **i.** ☐ An alien applying for a National Interest Waiver (who **IS** a member of the professions holding an advanced degree or an alien of exceptional ability).

Classification:

- ☐ 203(b)(1)(A) Alien of Extraordinary Ability
- ☐ 203(b)(1)(B) Outstanding Professor or Researcher
- ☐ 203(b)(1)(C) Multi-National Executive or Manager
- ☐ 203(b)(2) Member of Professions w/Adv. Degree or Exceptional Ability
- ☐ 203(b)(3)(A)(i) Skilled Worker
- ☐ 203(b)(3)(A)(ii) Professional
- ☐ 203(b)(3)(A)(iii) Other Worker

Certification:

- ☐ National Interest Waiver (NIW)
- ☐ Schedule A, Group I
- ☐ Schedule A, Group II

Part 3. Information about the person you are filing for.

Family Name (Last Name) | Given Name (First Name) | Full Middle Name

Address: (Street Number and Name) | Apt. #

C/O: (In Care Of)

City | State/Province

Country | Zip/Postal Code | E-Mail Address *(if any)*

Daytime Phone # *(with area/country codes)* | Date of Birth *(mm/dd/yyyy)*

City/Town/Village of Birth | State/Province of Birth | Country of Birth

Country of Nationality/Citizenship | A # *(if any)* | U.S. Social Security # *(if any)*

If in the U.S.

Date of Arrival *(mm/dd/yyyy)* | I-94 # *(Arrival/Departure Document)*

Current Nonimmigrant Status | Date Status Expires *(mm/dd/yyyy)*

Priority Date | **Consulate**

Concurrent Filing:

☐ **I-485 filed concurrently.**

Remarks

Action Block

To Be Completed by *Attorney or Representative*, if any.
☐ Fill in box if G-28 is attached to represent the applicant.

ATTY State License #

Form I-140 (Rev. 04/01/06)Y

Part 4. Processing Information.

1. Please complete the following for the person named in **Part 3**: *(Check one)*

☐ Alien will apply for a visa abroad at the American Embassy or Consulate at:

City | Foreign Country

☐ Alien is in the United States and will apply for adjustment of status to that of lawful permanent resident.
Alien's country of current residence or, if now in the U.S., last permanent residence abroad.

2. If you provided a U.S. address in **Part 3**, print the person's foreign address:

3. If the person's native alphabet is other than Roman letters, write the person's foreign name and address in the native alphabet:

4. Are any other petition(s) or application(s) being filed with this Form I-140?
☐ No ☐ Yes-(check all that apply)
☐ Form I-485 ☐ Form I-765
☐ Form I-131 ☐ Other - Attach an explanation.

5. Is the person you are filing for in removal proceedings? ☐ No ☐ Yes-Attach an explanation.

6. Has any immigrant visa petition ever been filed by or on behalf of this person? ☐ No ☐ Yes-Attach an explanation.

If you answered yes to any of these questions, please provide the case number, office location, date of decision and disposition of the decision on a separate sheet(s) of paper.

Part 5. Additional information about the petitioner.

1. Type of petitioner *(Check one.)*
☐ Employer ☐ Self ☐ Other (Explain, e.g., Permanent Resident, U.S. citizen or any other person filing on behalf of the alien.)

2. If a company, give the following:

Type of Business | Date Established *(mm/dd/yyyy)* | Current Number of Employees

Gross Annual Income | Net Annual Income | NAICS Code

DOL/ETA Case Number

3. If an individual, give the following:

Occupation | Annual Income

Part 6. Basic information about the proposed employment.

1. Job Title
2. SOC Code

3. Nontechnical Description of Job

4. Address where the person will work if different from address in **Part 1**.

5. Is this a full-time position?
☐ Yes ☐ No

6. If the answer to **Number 5** is "No," how many hours per week for the position?

7. Is this a permanent position?
☐ Yes ☐ No

8. Is this a new position?
☐ Yes ☐ No

9. Wages per week
$

Part 7. Information on spouse and all children of the person for whom you are filing.

List husband/wife and all children related to the individual for whom the petition is being filed. Provide an attachment of additional family members, if needed.

Name *(First/Middle/Last)*	Relationship	Date of Birth *(mm/dd/yyyy)*	Country of Birth

Part 8. Signature. *Read the information on penalties in the instructions before completing this section. If someone helped you prepare this petition, he or she must complete **Part 9.***

I certify, under penalty of perjury under the laws of the United States of America, that this petition and the evidence submitted with it are all true and correct. I authorize U.S. Citizenship and Immigration Services to release to other government agencies any information from my USCIS (or former INS) records, if USCIS determines that such action is necessary to determine eligibility for the benefit sought.

Petitioner's Signature | **Daytime Phone Number** *(Area/Country Codes)* | **E-Mail Address**

Print Name | **Date** *(mm/dd/yyyy)*

NOTE: *If you do not fully complete this form or fail to submit the required documents listed in the instructions, a final decision on your petition may be delayed or the petition may be denied.*

Part 9. Signature of person preparing form, if other than above. ***(Sign below.)***

I declare that I prepared this petition at the request of the above person and it is based on all information of which I have knowledge.

Attorney or Representative: In the event of a Request for Evidence (RFE), may the USCIS contact you by Fax or E-mail? ☐ Yes ☐ No

Signature | **Print Name** | **Date** *(mm/dd/yyyy)*

Firm Name and Address

Daytime Phone Number *(Area/Country Codes)* | **Fax Number** *(Area/Country Codes)* | **E-Mail Address**

FORMS FOR ADJUSTMENT OF STATUS

In addition to the actual forms necessary to obtain a certain status, there are forms that are necessary for the adjustment process itself. For instance, if a temporary worker adjusts his or her status to LPR based on marrying an American citizen, then that person must submit all of the forms necessary for relative-based immigration and the forms for adjustment of status (provided that the alien chooses that path toward LPR status; see Chapter 5 for other options that might be available).

Here are the essential forms pertaining to adjustment of status.

I-485: Application to Register Permanent Residence or Adjust Status

This is the form used to adjust status. It is also used by those seeking LPR status through registry (see Chapter 5), that is, those aliens who have resided in the United States continuously since before January 1, 1972. Some aliens must complete the Supplement A version of the form because of the conditions of their entry and stay in the United States. The I-485 Supplement D is for aliens eligible for immigration under the LIFE Act, as discussed in Chapter 3.

I-693: Medical Examination of Aliens Seeking Adjustment of Status

Remember the discussion in Chapter 1 about the "immigration door"? One of the reasons for keeping the door closed is to make sure that aliens with dangerous, communicable diseases do not enter the United States. Consistent with that requirement, aliens seeking to adjust their status must undergo a medical examination, to be completed by the examining doctor on Form I-693.

OMB No. 1615-0023; Expires 09/30/08

Department of Homeland Security
U.S. Citizenship and Immigration Services

I-485, Application to Register Permanent Residence or Adjust Status

What Is the Purpose of This Form?

This form is used by a person who is in the United States to apply to U.S. Citizenship and Immigration Services (USCIS) to adjust to permanent resident status or register for permanent residence.

This form may also be used by certain Cuban nationals to request a change in the date that their permanent residence began.

NOTE: USCIS is comprised of offices of the former Immigration and Naturalization Service (INS).

Who May File?

Based on an immigrant petition.

You may apply to adjust your status if:

- An immigrant visa number is immediately available to you based on an approved immigrant petition; or
- You are filing this application with a completed relative petition, special immigrant juvenile petition or special immigrant military petition which if approved would make an immigrant visa number immediately available to you.

Based on being the spouse or child (derivative) - at the time another adjustment applicant (principal) files to adjust status or at the time a person is granted permanent resident status in an immigrant category that allows derivative status for spouses and children.

- **If the spouse or child is in the United States,** the individual derivatives may file their Form I-485 adjustment of status applications concurrently with the Form I-485 for the principal applicant, or file the Form I-485 at anytime after the principal is approved, if a visa number is available.
- **If the spouse or child is residing abroad,** the person adjusting status in the United States should file the **Form I-824, Application for Action on an Approved Application or Petition, concurrently** with the principal's adjustment of status application to allow the derivatives to immigrate to the United States without delay if the principal's adjustment of status application is approved. **The fee submitted with the Form I-824 will not be refunded if the principal's adjustment is not granted.**

Based on admission as the fiancé(e) of a U. S. citizen and subsequent marriage to that citizen.

You may apply to adjust status if you were admitted to the United States as the K-1 fiancé(e) of a United States citizen and you married that citizen within 90 days of your entry.

If you were admitted as the K-2 child of such a fiancé(e), you may apply to adjust status based on your parent's adjustment application.

Based on asylum status.

You may apply to adjust status after you have been granted asylum in the United States if you have been physically present in the United States for one year after the grant of asylum, provided you still qualify as an asylee or as the spouse or child of a refugee.

Based on refugee status.

You may apply to adjust status after you have been admitted as a refugee and have been physically present in the United States for one year following your admission, provided that your status has not been terminated.

Based on Cuban citizenship or nationality.

You may apply to adjust status if:

- You are a native or citizen of Cuba, were admitted or paroled into the United States after January 1, 1959, and thereafter have been physically present in the United States for at least one year; or
- You are the spouse or unmarried child of a Cuban described above and regardless of your nationality, you were admitted or paroled after January 1, 1959, and thereafter have been physically present in the United States for at least one year.

Applying to change the date on which your permanent residence began.

If you were granted permanent residence in the United States prior to November 6, 1966, and are a native or citizen of Cuba, or you are the spouse or unmarried child of such an individual, you may ask to change the date your lawful permanent residence began to your date of arrival in the United States or May 2, 1964, whichever is later.

Based on continuous residence since before January 1, 1972.

You may apply for permanent residence if you have continuously resided in the United States since before January 1, 1972. This is known as "Registry."

Other basis of eligibility.

If you are not included in the above categories, but believe you may be eligible for adjustment or creation of record of permanent residence, contact our National Customer Service Center at **1-800-375-5283** for information on how to use the internet to make an application at your local USCIS office.

Who Is Not Eligible to Adjust Status?

Unless you are applying for creation of record based on continuous residence since before January 1, 1972, or adjustment of status under a category in which special rules apply (such as 245(i) adjustment, asylum adjustment, Cuban adjustment, special immigrant juvenile adjustment, or special immigrant military personnel adjustment), **you are not eligible for adjustment of status if any of the following apply to you:**

- You entered the United States in transit without a visa;
- You entered the United States as a nonimmigrant crewman;
- You were not admitted or paroled following inspection by an immigration officer;
- Your authorized stay expired before you filed this application;
- You were employed in the United States, without USCIS authorization, prior to filing this application;
- You failed to maintain your nonimmigrant status, other than through no fault of your own or for technical reasons; unless you are applying because you are:
  - -- An immediate relative of a United States citizen (parent, spouse, widow, widower or unmarried child under 21 years old);
  - -- A K-1 fiancé(e) or a K-2 fiancé(e) dependent who married the United States petitioner within 90 days of admission; or
  - -- An H or I nonimmigrant or special immigrant (foreign medical graduates, international organization employees or their derivative family members);
- You were admitted as a K-1 fiancé(e), but did not marry the U.S. citizen who filed the petition for you, or you were admitted as the K-2 child of a fiancé(e) and your parent did not marry the United States citizen who filed the petition;
- You are or were a J-1 or J-2 exchange visitor and are subject to the two-year foreign residence requirement and you have not complied with or been granted a waiver of the requirement;
- You have A, E or G nonimmigrant status or have an occupation that would allow you to have this status, unless you complete Form I-508 (I-508F for French nationals) to waive diplomatic rights, privileges and immunities and, if you are an A or G nonimmigrant, unless you submit a completed Form I-566;
- You were admitted to Guam as a visitor under the Guam visa waiver program;
- You were admitted to the United States as a visitor under the Visa Waiver Program, unless you are applying because you are an immediate relative of a U.S. citizen (parent, spouse, widow, widower or unmarried child under 21 years old); or
- You are already a conditional permanent resident.

What Are the General Filing Instructions?

Please answer all questions by typing or clearly printing in black ink. Indicate that an item is not applicable with **"N/A."** If the answer is **"none,"** write **"none."** If you need extra space to answer any item, attach a sheet of paper with your name and your alien registration number (A#), if any, and indicate the number of the item to which the answer refers. You must file your application with the required **Initial Evidence** described below. Your application must be properly signed and filed with the correct fee. If you are under 14 years of age, your parent or guardian may sign your application.

Translations.

Any foreign language document must be accompanied by a full English translation that the translator has certified as complete and correct and by the translator's certification that he or she is competent to translate the foreign language into English.

Copies.

If these instructions state that a copy of a document may be filed with this application, and you choose to send us the original, we may keep the original for our records.

Initial Evidence.

You must file your application with the following evidence:

- ***Birth certificate.***

  Submit a copy of your foreign birth certificate or other record of your birth that meets the provisions of secondary evidence found in Title 8, Code of Federal Regulations (CFR), 103.2(b)(2).

- ***Copy of passport page with nonimmigrant visa.***

  If you have obtained a nonimmigrant visa(s) from an American embassy or consulate abroad within the last year, submit a photocopy(ies) of the page(s) of your passport containing the visa(s).

- ***Photos.***

  Submit two identical, natural color passport-style photographs of yourself, taken within 30 days of the application. The photos must have a white background, be unmounted, printed on thin paper, and be glossy and unretouched. They must show your full-frontal facial position with your head bare. You may wear a headdress, if required by a religious order of which you are a member.

  The photos must be no larger than 2 x 2 inches, with the distance from the top of the head to just below the chin about 1 and 1/4 inches. Using a pencil, lightly print your Alien Registration Number (A#), or your name, if you do not have an A#, on the back of each photo.

- ***Biometric services.***

  If you are between the ages of 14 and 79, you must be fingerprinted as part of the USCIS biometric services requirement. After you have filed this application, USCIS will notify you in writing of the time and location where you must go to be fingerprinted. If necessary, USCIS may also take your photograph and signature. Failure to appear to be fingerprinted or for other biometric services may result in a denial of your application.

- ***Police clearances.***

  If you are filing for adjustment of status as a member of a special class described in an I-485 supplement form, please read the instructions on the supplement form to see if you need to obtain and submit police clearances, in addition to the required fingerprints, with your application.

- ***Medical examination.***

  When required, submit a medical examination report on the form you have obtained from USCIS.

  -- **Individuals applying for adjustment of status through a USCIS service center.**

  (1) General:
  If you are filing your adjustment of status application with a USCIS service center, include your medical examination report with the application, unless you are a refugee.

  (2) Refugees:
  If you are applying for adjustment of status one year after you were admitted as a refugee, you only need to submit a vaccination supplement with your adjustment of status application, not the entire medical report, **unless** there were medical grounds of inadmissibility that arose during the initial examination that you had overseas.

  -- **Individuals applying for adjustment of status through a local USCIS office.**

  If you are filing your adjustment of status application with a local USCIS office include your medical examination report with the application.

  -- **Fiancé(e)s.**

  If you are a K-1 fiancé(e) or K-2 dependent who had a medical examination within the past year as required for the nonimmigrant fiancé(e) visa, you only need to submit a vaccination supplement, not the entire medical report. You may include the vaccination supplement with your adjustment of status application.

  Persons not required to have a medical examination.

  -- The medical report is not required if you are applying for creation of a record for admission as a lawful permanent resident under section 249 of the INA as someone who has continuously resided in the United States since January 1, 1972 (registry applicant).

- ***Form G-325A, Biographic Information Sheet.***

  You must submit a completed Form G-325A if you are between 14 and 79 years of age.

- ***Evidence of status.***

  Submit a copy of your Form I-94, Nonimmigrant Arrival/ Departure Record, showing your admission to the United States and current status, or other evidence of your status.

- ***Affidavit of Support/Employment Letter.***

  -- **Affidavit of Support.**

  Submit an Affidavit of Support (Form I-864) if your adjustment of status application is based on your entry as a fiancé(e), a relative visa petition (Form I-130) filed by your relative, or an employment based visa petition (Form I-140) related to a business that is five percent or more owned by your family.

-- **Employment Letter.**

If your adjustment of status application is related to an employment based visa petition (Form I-140), you must submit a letter on the letterhead of the petitioning employer which confirms that the job on which the visa petition is based is still available to you. The letter must also state the salary that will be paid.

NOTE: The affidavit of support and/or employment letter are not required if you are applying for creation of a record based on continuous residence since before January 1, 1972, asylum or refugee adjustment, or a Cuban citizen or a spouse or unmarried child of a Cuban citzen who was admitted after January 1, 1959.

- ***Evidence of eligibility.***

-- **Based on an immigrant petition.**

Attach a copy of the approval notice for an immigrant petition that makes a visa number immediately available to you, or submit a complete relative, special immigrant juvenile, or special immigrant military petition which, if approved, will make a visa number immediately available to you.

-- **Based on admission as the K-1 fiancé(e) of a U. S. citizen and subsequent marriage to that citizen.**

Attach a copy of the fiancé(e) petition approval notice, a copy of your marriage certificate and your Form 1-94.

-- **Based on asylum status.**

Attach a copy of the letter or Form 1-94 that shows the date you were granted asylum.

-- **Based on continuous residence in the United States since before January 1, 1972.**

Attach copies of evidence that shows continuous residence since before January 1, 1972.

-- **Based on Cuban citizenship or nationality.**

Attach evidence of your citizenship or nationality, such as a copy of your passport, birth certificate or travel document.

-- **Based on derivative status as the spouse or child of another adjustment applicant or person granted permanent residence based on issuance of an immigrant visa.**

File your application with the application of the other applicant, or with evidence that the application is pending with USCIS or was approved, or with evidence that your spouse or parent was granted permanent residence based on an immigrant visa, and:

If you are applying as the spouse of that person, also attach a copy of your marriage certificate and copies of documents showing the legal termination of all other marriages by you and your spouse;

If you are applying as the child of that person, attach also a copy of your birth certificate and, if the other person is not your parent, submit copies of evidence (such as a marriage certificate and documents showing the legal termination of all other marriages and an adoption decree) to demonstrate that you qualify as his or her child.

- ***Other basis for eligibility.***

Attach copies of documents proving that you are eligible for the classification.

Where Should You File Form I-485?

Employment-based adjustment of status.

- ***Form I-485 without Form I-140.***

If you have already filed Form I-140, Immigrant Petition for Alien Worker, submit your employment-based Form I-485 to the service center that approved or is currently responsible for adjudicating your Form I-140 petition. (See addresses of service centers listed below.) Include a copy of your Form I-140 filing receipt and/or transfer notice, as applicable.

USCIS Nebraska Service Center
P.O. Box 87485
Lincoln, NE 68501-7485

USCIS California Service Center
P.O. Box 10485
Laguna Niguel, CA 92607-1048

USCIS Texas Service Center
P.O. Box 851804
Mesquite, TX 75185-1804

USCIS Vermont Service Center
75 Lower Welden Street
St. Albans, VT 05479

- ***Concurrent Forms I-140/I-485 filings.***

  If you are filing your employment based Form I-485 concurrently with your Form I-140 petition, file the entire Form I-140/I-485 package at the:

  USCIS Nebraska Service Center
  P.O. Box 87485
  Lincoln, NE 68501-7485

In all other instances.

File this application at the USCIS service center or local office that has jurisdiction over your place of residence, or submit the form to the USCIS Lockbox Facility. For details on where to file your application, read the additional instructions that may be included with this form, call our National Customer Service Center at **1-800-375-5283** or visit our website at **www.uscis.gov.**

What Is the Fee?

The base fee for this application is **$325.00,** or **$225.00** if you are under 14 years of age.

There is no application fee if you are filing as a refugee under section 209(a) of the INA.

If you are between the ages of 14 and 79 years, there is also a **$70.00** biometric services fee for USCIS to take your fingerprints. If necessary, USCIS may also take your photograph and signature as part of the biometric services. Following submission of your application, USCIS will notify you when to go to an Application Support Center to be fingerprinted.

Submit both application and the biometric service fees with your Form I-485.

For example, if your application fee is **$325.00** and you are between the age of 14 and 79 (which means you must be fingerprinted), the total fee you must pay is **$395.00**.

You may submit one check or money order for both the application and biometric services fees.

Fees must be submitted in the exact amount. **Do not mail cash.** Fees cannot be refunded. All checks and money orders must be drawn on a bank or other institution located in the United States and must be payable in United States currency. The check or money order should be made payable to the **Department of Homeland Security except:**

-- If you live in Guam, make your check or money order payable to the "Treasurer, Guam."

-- If you live in the U.S. Virgin Islands, make your check or money order payable to the "Commissioner of Finance of the Virgin Islands."

Checks are accepted subject to collection. An uncollected check in payment of an application fee will render the application and any document issued invalid. A charge of $30.00 will be imposed if a check for payment of a fee is not honored by the bank on which it is drawn.

How to Check If the Fees Are Correct.

The fees on this page are current as of the edition date appearing in the lower right corner of this page. However, because USCIS fees change periodically, you can verify if the fees are correct by following one of the steps below:

- Visit our website at **www.uscis.gov** and scroll down to "Forms and E-Filing" to check the appropriate fee, or
- Review the Fee Schedule included in your form package, if you called us to request the form, or
- Telephone our National Customer Service Center at **1-800-375-5283** and ask for the fee information.

NOTE: If your application requires a biometric services fee for USCIS to take your fingerprints, photograph or signature, you can use the same procedure above to confirm the biometrics fee.

Processing Information.

Acceptance.

Any application that is not signed or is not accompanied by the correct application fee will be rejected with a notice that the application is deficient. You may correct the deficiency and resubmit the application. An application is not considered properly filed until accepted by USCIS.

Initial processing.

Once an application has been accepted, it will be checked for completeness, including submission of the required initial evidence. If you do not completely fill out the form or file it without required initial evidence, you will not establish a basis for eligibility and we may deny your application.

Requests for more information.

We may request more information or evidence. We may also request that you submit the originals of any copy. **Originals may be returned to you, if requested.**

Interview.

After you file your application, you may be notified to appear at a USCIS office to answer questions about the application. You will be required to answer these questions under oath or affirmation. You must bring your Arrival-Departure Record (Form I-94) and any passport or official travel document you have to the interview.

Decision.

You will be notified in writing of the decision on your application.

Selective Service Registration.

If you are a male at least 18 years old, but not yet 26 years old, and required according to the Military Selective Service Act to register with the Selective Service System, USCIS will help you register.

When your signed application is filed and accepted by USCIS, we will transmit to the Selective Service System your name, current address, Social Security number, date of birth and the date you filed the application. This action will enable the Selective Service System to record your registration as of the filing date of your application.

If USCIS does not accept your application and, if still so required, you are responsible to register with the Selective Service System by using other means, provided you are under 26 years of age. If you have already registered, the Selective Service System will check its records to avoid any duplication.

(NOTE: Men 18 through 25 years old who are applying for student financial aid, government employment or job training benefits should register directly with the Selective Service System or such benefits may be denied. Men can register at a local post office or on the internet at http://www.sss.gov).

Travel outside the United States for adjustment of status applicants under sections 209 and 245 of the Act, and Registry applicants under section 249 of the Act.

Your departure from the United States (including brief visits to Canada or Mexico) constitutes an abandonment of your adjustment of status application, unless you are granted permission to depart and you are inspected upon your return to the United States. Such permission to travel is called "advance parole." To request advance parole, you must file Form I-131, Application for Travel Document, with the appropriate fee at the USCIS office where you applied for adjustment of status.

-- **Exceptions.**

A. H, L, V or K3/K4 nonimmigrants:

If you are an H, L,V, or K3/K4 nonimmigrant who continues to maintain his or her status, you may travel on a valid H, L, V or K3/K4 visa without obtaining advance parole.

B. Refugees and Asylees:

If you are applying for adjustment of status one year after you were admitted as a refugee or one year after you were granted asylum, you may travel outside the United States on your valid refugee travel document, if you have one, without the need to obtain advance parole.

-- **Warning:**

Travel outside of the United States may trigger the three and ten year bar to admission under section 212(a)(9)(B)(i) of the Act for adjustment applicants, but not registry applicants. This ground of inadmissibility is triggered if you were unlawfully present in the United States (i.e., you remained in the United States beyond the period of authorized stay) for more than 180 days before you applied for adjustment of status and you travel outside of the United States while your adjustment of status application is pending.

NOTE: Only unlawful presence that was accrued on or after April 1, 1997, counts towards the three and ten year bar under section 212(a)(9)(B)(i) of the Act.)

If you become inadmissible under section 212(a)(9)(B)(i) of the Act while your adjustment of status application is pending, you will need a waiver of inadmissibility under section 212(a)(9)(B)(v) of the Act before your adjustment of status application can be approved. This waiver, however, is granted on a case-by-case basis and in the exercise of discretion. It requires a showing of extreme hardship to your United States citizen or lawful permanent resident spouse or parent, unless you are a refugee or asylee. For refugees and asylees, the waiver may be granted for humanitarian reasons, to assure family unity or if it is otherwise in the public interest.

Penalties.

If you knowingly and willfully falsify or conceal a material fact or submit a false document with this request, we will deny the benefit you are seeking and may deny any other immigration benefit. In addition, you will face severe penalties provided by law and may be subject to criminal prosecution.

Privacy Act Notice.

We ask for the information on this form and associated evidence to determine if you have established eligibility for the immigration benefit you are seeking. Our legal right to ask for this information is in 8 U.S.C. 1255 and 1259. We may provide this information to other government agencies, including the Selective Service System. Your failure to provide information on this form and any requested evidence may delay a final decision or result in denial of your application.

USCIS Forms and Information.

To order USCIS forms, call our toll-free forms line at **1-800-870-3676.** You can also obtain forms and information on immigration laws, regulations and procedures by telephoning our National Customer Service Center at **1-800-375-5283** or visiting our internet website at **www.uscis.gov**.

Use InfoPass for Appointments.

As an alternative to waiting in line for assistance at your local USCIS office, you can now schedule an appointment through our internet-based system, **InfoPass**. To access the system, visit our website at **www.uscis.gov**. Use the **InfoPass** appointment scheduler and follow the screen prompts to set up your appointment. **InfoPass** generates an electronic appointment notice that appears on the screen. Print the notice and take it with you to your appointment. The notice gives the time and date of your appointment, along with the address of the USCIS office.

Paperwork Reduction Act Notice.

An agency may not conduct or sponsor an information collection and a person is not required to respond to a collection of information unless it displays a current valid OMB number.

We try to create forms and instructions that are accurate, can be easily understood and that impose the least possible burden on you to provide us with information. Often this is difficult because some immigration laws are very complex.

The estimated average time to complete and file this application is computed as follows: (1) 20 minutes to learn about the law and form; (2) 25 minutes to complete the form and (3) 270 minutes to assemble and file the application, including the required interview and travel time, for a total estimated average of 5 hours and 15 minutes per application.

If you have comments regarding the accuracy of this estimate or suggestions to make this form simpler, you should write to the U.S. Citizenship and Immigration Services, Regulatory Management Division, 111 Masschuetts Avenue, N.W., Washington, DC 20529; OMB No. 1615-0023. **Do not mail your completed application to this address.**

OMB No. 1615-0023; Expires 09/30/08

Department of Homeland Security
U.S. Citizenship and Immigration Services

I-485, Application to Register Permanent Residence or Adjust Status

START HERE - Please type or print in black ink.

Part 1. Information about you.

Family Name	Given Name	Middle Name
Address- C/O		
Street Number and Name		Apt. #
City		
State	Zip Code	
Date of Birth *(mm/dd/yyyy)*	Country of Birth:	
	Country of Citizenship/Nationality:	
U.S. Social Security #	A # *(if any)*	
Date of Last Arrival *(mm/dd/yyyy)*	I-94 #	
Current USCIS Status	Expires on *(mm/dd/yyyy)*	

Part 2. Application type. *(Check one.)*

I am applying for an adjustment to permanent resident status because:

a. ☐ an immigrant petition giving me an immediately available immigrant visa number has been approved. (Attach a copy of the approval notice, or a relative, special immigrant juvenile or special immigrant military visa petition filed with this application that will give you an immediately available visa number, if approved.)

b. ☐ my spouse or parent applied for adjustment of status or was granted lawful permanent residence in an immigrant visa category that allows derivative status for spouses and children.

c. ☐ I entered as a K-1 fiancé(e) of a United States citizen whom I married within 90 days of entry, or I am the K-2 child of such a fiancé(e). (Attach a copy of the fiancé(e) petition approval notice and the marriage certificate).

d. ☐ I was granted asylum or derivative asylum status as the spouse or child of a person granted asylum and am eligible for adjustment.

e. ☐ I am a native or citizen of Cuba admitted or paroled into the United States after January 1, 1959, and thereafter have been physically present in the United States for at least one year.

f. ☐ I am the husband, wife or minor unmarried child of a Cuban described above in (e) and I am residing with that person, and was admitted or paroled into the United States after January 1, 1959, and thereafter have been physically present in the United States for at least one year.

g. ☐ I have continuously resided in the United States since before January 1, 1972.

h. ☐ Other basis of eligibility. Explain. If additional space is needed, use a separate piece of paper.

____

I am already a permanent resident and am applying to have the date I was granted permanent residence adjusted to the date I originally arrived in the United States as a nonimmigrant or parolee, or as of May 2, 1964, whichever date is later, and: *(Check one.)*

i. ☐ I am a native or citizen of Cuba and meet the description in (e) above.

j. ☐ I am the husband, wife or minor unmarried child of a Cuban, and meet the description in (f) above.

For USCIS Use Only

Returned	Receipt
Resubmitted	
Reloc Sent	
Reloc Rec'd	
Applicant Interviewed	

Section of Law

☐ Sec. 209(b), INA
☐ Sec. 13, Act of 9/11/57
☐ Sec. 245, INA
☐ Sec. 249, INA
☐ Sec. 1 Act of 11/2/66
☐ Sec. 2 Act of 11/2/66
☐ Other ____________

Country Chargeable

Eligibility Under Sec. 245

☐ Approved Visa Petition
☐ Dependent of Principal Alien
☐ Special Immigrant
☐ Other ____________

Preference

Action Block

To be Completed by ***Attorney or Representative,*** **if any**

☐ Fill in box if G-28 is attached to represent the applicant.

VOLAG #

ATTY State License #

Form I-485 (Rev. 04/01/06)Y

Part 3. Processing information.

A. City/Town/Village of Birth	Current Occupation
Your Mother's First Name	Your Father's First Name
Give your name exactly as it appears on your Arrival/Departure Record (Form I-94)	
Place of Last Entry Into the United States *(City/State)*	In what status did you last enter? *(Visitor, student, exchange alien, crewman, temporary worker, without inspection, etc.)*
Were you inspected by a U.S. Immigration Officer? ☐ Yes ☐ No	
Nonimmigrant Visa Number	Consulate Where Visa Was Issued
Date Visa Was Issued (mm/dd/yyyy) — Gender: ☐ Male ☐ Female	Marital Status: ☐ Married ☐ Single ☐ Divorced ☐ Widowed
Have you ever before applied for permanent resident status in the U.S.?	☐ No ☐ Yes. If you checked "Yes," give date and place of filing and final disposition.

B. List your present husband/wife, all of your sons and daughters (If you have none, write "none." If additional space is needed, use separate paper).

Family Name	Given Name	Middle Initial	Date of Birth *(mm/dd/yyyy)*
Country of Birth	Relationship	A #	Applying with you? ☐ Yes ☐ No
Family Name	Given Name	Middle Initial	Date of Birth *(mm/dd/yyyy)*
Country of Birth	Relationship	A #	Applying with you? ☐ Yes ☐ No
Family Name	Given Name	Middle Initial	Date of Birth *(mm/dd/yyyy)*
Country of Birth	Relationship	A #	Applying with you? ☐ Yes ☐ No
Family Name	Given Name	Middle Initial	Date of Birth *(mm/dd/yyyy)*
Country of Birth	Relationship	A #	Applying with you? ☐ Yes ☐ No
Family Name	Given Name	Middle Initial	Date of Birth *(mm/dd/yyyy)*
Country of Birth	Relationship	A #	Applying with you? ☐ Yes ☐ No

C. List your present and past membership in or affiliation with every organization, association, fund, foundation, party, club, society or similar group in the United States or in other places since your 16th birthday. Include any foreign military service in this part. If none, write "none." Include the name(s) of organization(s), location(s), dates of membership, from and to, and the nature of the organization(s). If additional space is needed, use a separate piece of paper.

____

____

____

____

____

____

Part 3. Processing information. *(Continued)*

Please answer the following questions. (If your answer is **"Yes"** on any one of these questions, explain on a separate piece of paper. Answering **"Yes"** does not necessarily mean that you are not entitled to adjust status or register for permanent residence.)

1. Have you ever, in or outside the United States:

   a. knowingly committed any crime of moral turpitude or a drug-related offense for which you have not been arrested? ☐ Yes ☐ No

   b. been arrested, cited, charged, indicted, fined or imprisoned for breaking or violating any law or ordinance, excluding traffic violations? ☐ Yes ☐ No

   c. been the beneficiary of a pardon, amnesty, rehabilitation decree, other act of clemency or similar action? ☐ Yes ☐ No

   d. exercised diplomatic immunity to avoid prosecution for a criminal offense in the United States? ☐ Yes ☐ No

2. Have you received public assistance in the United States from any source, including the United States government or any state, county, city or municipality (other than emergency medical treatment), or are you likely to receive public assistance in the future? ☐ Yes ☐ No

3. Have you ever:

   a. within the past ten years been a prostitute or procured anyone for prostitution, or intend to engage in such activities in the future? ☐ Yes ☐ No

   b. engaged in any unlawful commercialized vice, including, but not limited to, illegal gambling? ☐ Yes ☐ No

   c. knowingly encouraged, induced, assisted, abetted or aided any alien to try to enter the United States illegally? ☐ Yes ☐ No

   d. illicitly trafficked in any controlled substance, or knowingly assisted, abetted or colluded in the illicit trafficking of any controlled substance? ☐ Yes ☐ No

4. Have you ever engaged in, conspired to engage in, or do you intend to engage in, or have you ever solicited membership or funds for, or have you through any means ever assisted or provided any type of material support to any person or organization that has ever engaged or conspired to engage in sabotage, kidnapping, political assassination, hijacking or any other form of terrorist activity? ☐ Yes ☐ No

5. Do you intend to engage in the United States in:

   a. espionage? ☐ Yes ☐ No

   b. any activity a purpose of which is opposition to, or the control or overthrow of, the government of the United States, by force, violence or other unlawful means? ☐ Yes ☐ No

   c. any activity to violate or evade any law prohibiting the export from the United States of goods, technology or sensitive information? ☐ Yes ☐ No

6. Have you ever been a member of, or in any way affiliated with, the Communist Party or any other totalitarian party? ☐ Yes ☐ No

7. Did you, during the period from March 23, 1933 to May 8, 1945, in association with either the Nazi Government of Germany or any organization or government associated or allied with the Nazi Government of Germany, ever order, incite, assist or otherwise participate in the persecution of any person because of race, religion, national orgin or political opinion? ☐ Yes ☐ No

8. Have you ever engaged in genocide, or otherwise ordered, incited, assisted or otherwise participated in the killing of any person because of race, religion, nationality, ethnic origin or political opinion? ☐ Yes ☐ No

9. Have you ever been deported from the United States, or removed from the United States at government expense, excluded within the past year, or are you now in exclusion, deportation, removal or recission proceedings? ☐ Yes ☐ No

10. Are you under a final order of civil penalty for violating section 274C of the Immigration and Nationality Act for use of fraudulent documents or have you, by fraud or willful misrepresentation of a material fact, ever sought to procure, or procured, a visa, other documentation, entry into the United States or any immigration benefit? ☐ Yes ☐ No

11. Have you ever left the United States to avoid being drafted into the U.S. Armed Forces? ☐ Yes ☐ No

12. Have you ever been a J nonimmigrant exchange visitor who was subject to the two-year foreign residence requirement and have not yet complied with that requirement or obtained a waiver? ☐ Yes ☐ No

13. Are you now withholding custody of a U.S. citizen child outside the United States from a person granted custody of the child? ☐ Yes ☐ No

14. Do you plan to practice polygamy in the United States? ☐ Yes ☐ No

Part 4. Signature. *(Read the information on penalties in the instructions before completing this section. You must file this application while in the United States.)*

Your registration with U.S. Citizenship and Immigration Services.

"I understand and acknowledge that, under section 262 of the Immigration and Nationality Act (Act), as an alien who has been or will be in the United States for more than 30 days, I am required to register with U.S. Citizenship and Immigration Services. I understand and acknowledge that, under section 265 of the Act, I am required to provide USCIS with my current address and written notice of any change of address within **ten** days of the change. I understand and acknowledge that USCIS will use the most recent address that I provide to USCIS, on any form containing these acknowledgements, for all purposes, including the service of a Notice to Appear should it be necessary for USCIS to initiate removal proceedings against me. I understand and acknowledge that if I change my address without providing written notice to USCIS, I will be held responsible for any communications sent to me at the most recent address that I provided to USCIS. I further understand and acknowledge that, if removal proceedings are initiated against me and I fail to attend any hearing, including an initial hearing based on service of the Notice to Appear at the most recent address that I provided to USCIS or as otherwise provided by law, I may be ordered removed in my absence, arrested and removed from the United States."

Selective Service Registration.

The following applies to you if you are a male at least 18 years old, but not yet 26 years old, who is required to register with the Selective Service System: "I understand that my filing this adjustment of status application with U.S. Citizenship and Immigration Services authorizes USCIS to provide certain registration information to the Selective Service System in accordance with the Military Selective Service Act. Upon USCIS acceptance of my application, I authorize USCIS to transmit to the Selective Service System my name, current address, Social Security Number, date of birth and the date I filed the application for the purpose of recording my Selective Service registration as of the filing date. If, however, USCIS does not accept my application, I further understand that, if so required, I am responsible for registering with the Selective Service by other means, provided I have not yet reached age 26."

Applicant's Certification.

I certify, under penalty of perjury under the laws of the United States of America, that this application and the evidence submitted with it is all true and correct. I authorize the release of any information from my records that U.S. Citizenship and Immigration Services (USCIS) needs to determine eligibility for the benefit I am seeking.

Signature	*Print Your Name*	*Date*	*Daytime Phone Number*
			( )

NOTE: *If you do not completely fill out this form or fail to submit required documents listed in the instructions, you may not be found eligible for the requested document and this application may be denied.*

Part 5. Signature of person preparing form, if other than above. (sign below)

I declare that I prepared this application at the request of the above person and it is based on all information of which I have knowledge.

Signature	*Print Your Full Name*	*Date*	**Phone Number** *(Include Area Code)*
			( )
Firm Name and Address		*E-Mail Address (if any)*	

Form I-485 (Rev. 04/01/06)Y Page 4

OMB No. 1615-0023; Expires 09/30/08

Department of Homeland Security
U.S. Citizenship and Immigration Services

Supplement A to Form I-485
Adjustment of Status Under Section 245(i)

Instructions

NOTE: Use this form only if you are applying to the U.S. Citizenship and Immigration Services (USCIS) to adjust status to that of a lawful permanent resident under section 245(i) of the Immigration and Nationality Act. USCIS is comprised of offices of the former Immigration and Naturalization Service (INS).

What Is the Purpose of This Form?

Section 245 of the Immigration and Nationality Act (the Act) allows the Attorney General in his or her discretion to adjust the status of an alien to that of a lawful permanent resident (LPR), in lieu of consular visa processing, while the alien remains in the United States. In order to be eligible, the alien must have been inspected and admitted or paroled, be eligible for an immigrant visa and admissible for permanent residence, have an immigrant visa immediately available and, with some exceptions, have maintained lawful nonimmigrant status. The alien must also not have engaged in unauthorized employment and must not be ineligible to adjust status under section 245(c) of the Act. **If you meet all of these requirements, you do not have to submit this form when applying for adjustment of status to that of LPR.**

Section 245(i) of the Act allows certain aliens to file for adjustment of status upon payment of a penalty fee of **$1,000**, even though some of the conditions required by section 245(a) and (c) of the Act are not met. **Aliens in the United States who have an immigrant visa immediately available, but who entered the United States without inspection, remained in the United States past the period of admission, worked unlawfully, or are otherwise ineligible for adjustment of status under section 245(c) of the Act must submit this form along with Form I-485, Application to Register Permanent Residence or Adjust Status.**

NOTE: If you are applying to adjust as the spouse or unmarried minor child of a U.S. citizen or the parent of a U.S. citizen child at least 21 years of age, and if you were inspected and lawfully admitted to the United States other than in C-1 or S nonimmigrant status, you do not need to file this form.

Who May Use Supplement A to Adjust Status to That of LPR Under Section 245(i)?

You may apply for adjustment of status to that of LPR under section 245(i) if you:

- Are physically present in the United States when the application is submitted; and
- Have an immigrant visa number immediately available; and
- Are admissible to the United States for permanent residence; and
- Are the beneficiary of an approvable-when-filed visa petition, or an application for labor certification filed on or before April 30, 2001; and
- Pay a **$1,000.00** penalty fee (unless exempted).

In addition, the alien must fall within one of the categories noted below:

- Alien crewmen;
- Aliens who work without authorization;
- Aliens in unlawful immigrant status;
- Aliens who fail to continuously maintain a lawful status since entry into the United States;
- Aliens who were admitted in transit without visa;
- Aliens admitted as nonimmigrant visitors under section 212(l) of the Act or under the Visa Waiver Program;
- Aliens admitted as a nonimmigrant described in section 101(a)(15)(S) of the Act; or
- Aliens seeking employment-based adjustment of status who are not in lawful nonimmigrant status.

What Documentation Must You Include If You Are Submitting This Form With Form I-485?

You do not need to submit documentation in addition to the documentation required by the instructions on Form I-485 unless you are the beneficiary of a visa petition or application for labor certification properly filed on your behalf after January 14, 1998, and on or before April 30, 2001. **Aliens using section 245(i) because they are beneficiaries of a visa petition or application for labor certification filed after January 14, 1998, and on or before April 30, 2001, should submit documentation along with this form that demonstrates physical presence in the United States on December 21, 2000.**

What Documentation Demonstrates Your Physical Presence on December 21, 2000?

Documentation of your physical presence in the United States on December 21, 2000, can consist of Federal, state or local government-issued documents or other documents establishing your physical presence on that date. If one document does not establish your physical presence, you should submit documentation establishing your physical presence in the United States prior to and after December 21, 2000. In some cases, a single document may suffice to establish the applicant's physical presence on December 21, 2000. In most cases, however, the alien may need to submit several documents, because most applicants may not possess documentation that contains the exact date of December 21, 2000. In such instances, the applicant should submit sufficient documentation establishing the applicant's physical presence in the United States prior to and after December 21, 2000. If you submit affidavits, they should be accompanied by supporting documentation. USCIS will evaluate all documentation on a case-by-case basis.

Who Does Not Need to Use Supplement A to Form I-485?

You do not have to submit Supplement A to Form I-485 if you:

- Are already an LPR; or
- Have continuously maintained lawful immigration status in the United States since November 5, 1986; or
- Are applying to adjust status as the spouse or unmarried minor child of a U.S. citizen or the parent of a U.S. citizen child at least 21 years of age, and you were inspected and lawfully admitted to the United States other than in C-1 or S nonimmigrant status.

In addition, you do not have to submit Supplement A to Form I-485, if you are filing for an immigration benefit other than adjustment of status to that of LPR or if you are applying for adjustment of status to that of LPR because you:

- Were granted asylum in the United States; or
- Have continuously resided in the United States since January 1, 1972; or
- Entered as a K-1 fiancé(e) of a U.S. citizen; or
- Have an approved Form I-360, Petition for Amerasian, Widow(er), Battered or Abused Spouse or Child, or Special Immigrant, and are applying for adjustment as a special immigrant juvenile court dependent, or as a special immigrant who has served in the U.S. armed forces, or as a battered or abused spouse or child; or
- Are a special immigrant retired international organization employee or family member; or
- Are a special immigrant physician; or
- Are a public interest parolee, who was denied refugee status, and are from the former Soviet Union, Vietnam, Laos or Cambodia (a "Lautenberg Parolee" under Public Law 101-167); or
- Are eligible under the Immigration Nursing Relief Act.

What Are the Filing Fees for the Supplement A to Form I-485 and Form I-485 Filed Together?

The fees for this form when filed along with Form I-485 are:

- A base fee of **$325.00** is required with Form I-485 for applicants over the age of 14 years and **$225.00** for applicants under 14.
- A **$70.00** biometric services fee for having your fingerprints taken. If required, USCIS may also take your photograph and signature as part of the biometric services. Applicants younger than 14 years or older than 79 do not have to pay the biometric services fee.
- A **$1,000.00** penalty fee is required with the Supplement A Form.

If you filed Form I-485 separately, attach a copy of your filing receipt and pay only the additional sum of **$1,000.00**.

There are two categories of applicants who do not need to pay the **$1,000.00** fee associated with Supplement A to Form I-485:

1. Applicants under the age of 17 years; and
2. Applicants who are an unmarried son or daughter of a legalized alien and less than 21 years of age, or the spouse of a legalized alien, and have attached a copy of a USCIS (or former INS) receipt or approval notice for a properly filed Form I-817, Application for Family Unity Benefits.

How Can You Check If the Fees Are Correct.

The fees on this form are current as of the edition date appearing in the lower right corner of this page. However, because USCIS fees change periodically, you can verify if the fees are correct by following one of the steps below:

- Visit our website at **www.uscis.gov** and scroll down to "Forms and E-Filing" to check the appropriate fees, or
- Review the Fee Schedule included in your form package, if you called us to request the form, or

- Telephone our National Customer Service Center at **1-800-375-5283** and ask for the fee information.

NOTE: If your petition or application requires a biometric services fee for USCIS to take your fingerprints, photograph or signature, you can use the same procedure above to confirm the biometrics fee.

Where Should You File This Form?

You must file this form at the same USCIS office or location where you must submit the related Form I-485.

What Are the Penalties for Perjury?

All statements contained in response to questions in this application are declared to be true and correct under penalty of perjury. Title 18 of the United States Code, Section 1546, provides in part:

> Whoever knowingly makes under oath, or as permitted under penalty of perjury under 1746 of Title 28 of the United States Code, knowingly subscribes as true, any false statement with respect to a material fact in any application, affidavit, or other document required by the immigration laws or regulations prescribed thereunder, or knowlingly presents any such application, affidavit or other document containing any such false statement--shall be fined in accordance with this title or imprisoned not more than five years, or both.

What Is Our Authority for Collecting This Information?

We request the information on the form to carry out the immigration laws contained in Title 8 of the United States Code, section 1154(a). We need this information to determine whether you are eligible for immigration benefits. The information you provide may also be disclosed to other Federal, state, local and foreign law enforcement and regulatory agencies. Furnishing this information on this form is voluntary. However, if you do not give us some or all of the information, your application may be denied.

USCIS Forms and Information.

To order USCIS forms, telephone our toll-free forms line at **1-800-870-3676.** You can also obtain USCIS forms and information on immigration laws, regulations and procedures, by calling our National Customer Service Center at **1-800-375-5283** or visiting our internet website at **www.uscis.gov**.

Use InfoPass to Make an Appointment.

As an alternative to waiting in line for assistance at your local USCIS office, you can now schedule an appointment through our internet-based system, **InfoPass.** To access the system, visit our website at **www.uscis.gov.** Use the **InfoPass** appointment scheduler and follow the screen prompts to set up your appointment. **InfoPass** generates an electronic appointment notice that appears on the screen. Print the notice and take it wih you to your appointment. The notice gives the time and date of your appointment, along with the address of the USCIS office.

Paperwork Reduction Act Notice.

An agency may not conduct or sponsor an information collection and a person is not required to respond to an information collection unless it contains a currently valid OMB control number. We try to create forms that are accurate, can easily be understood and that impose the least possible burden on you to provide us with the information. Often this is difficult because some immigration laws are very complex. The public reporting burden for this information collection beyond the time to complete the parent form is estimated to average 13 minutes which includes learning about the form and understanding the instructions; collecting the necessary supporting documents; completing the form; and traveling to and waiting at a preparer's office (e.g., attorney or voluntary agency). If you have comments regarding the accuracy of this estimate or suggestions for making this form simpler, you can write to the U.S. Citizenship and Immigration Services, Regulatory Management Division, 111 Massachusetts Avenue, N.W., Washington, DC 20529; OMB No. 1615-0023. **Do not mail your completed application to this address.**

Checklist.

- ☐ I signed the form at **Part D**.
- ☐ I included the appropriate fees (if any).
- ☐ If I checked **box b** or **d** in **Question 1, Part B,** I included evidence of my physical presence in the United States on December 21, 2000.

OMB No. 1615-0023; Expires 09/30/08

Department of Homeland Security
U.S. Citizenship Immigration and Service

Supplement A to Form I-485
Adjustment of Status Under Section 245(i)

NOTE: Use this form only if you are applying to adjust status to that of a lawful permanent resident under section 245(i) of the Immigration and Nationality Act.

Part A. Information about you.	**For USCIS Use Only**
Last Name / First Name / Middle Name	Action Block
Address: In Care Of	
Street Number and Name / Apt. #	
City / State / Zip Code	
Alien Registration Number (A #) if any / Date of Birth *(mm/dd/yyyy)*	
Country of Birth / Country of Citizenship/Nationality	
Telephone Number ( ) / E-Mail Address, if any	

Part B. Eligibility. *(Check the correct response.)*

1. I am filing Supplement A to Form I-485 because:

a. ☐ I am the beneficiary of a visa petition filed on or before January 14, 1998.
b. ☐ I am the beneficiary of a visa petition filed on or after January 15, 1998, and on or before April 30, 2001.
c. ☐ I am the beneficiary of an application for a labor certification filed on or before January 14, 1998.
d. ☐ I am the beneficiary of an application for a labor certification filed on or after January 15, 1998, and on or before April 30, 2001.

If you checked box b or d in Question 1, you must submit evidence demonstrating that you were physically present in the United States on December 21, 2000.

2. And I fall into one or more of these categories: ***(Check all that apply to you.)***

a. ☐ I entered the United States as an alien crewman;
b. ☐ I have accepted employment without authorization;
c. ☐ I am in unlawful immigration status because I entered the United States without inspection or I remained in the United States past the expiration of the period of my lawful admission;
d. ☐ I have failed (except through no fault of my own or for technical reasons) to maintain, continuously, lawful status;
e. ☐ I was admitted to the United States in transit without a visa;
f. ☐ I was admitted as a nonimmigrant visitor without a visa;
g. ☐ I was admitted to the United States as a nonimmigrant in the S classification; or
h. ☐ I am seeking employment-based adjustment of status and am not in lawful nonimmigrant status.

Part C. Additional eligibility information.

1. Are you applying to adjust status based on any of the below reasons?

a. You were granted asylum in the United States;
b. You have continuously resided in the United States since January 1, 1972;
c. You entered as a K-1 fiancé(e) of a U.S. citizen;
d. You have an approved Form I-360, Petition for Amerasian, Widow(er), Battered or Abused Spouse or Child, or Special Immigrant, and are applying for adjustment as a special immigrant juvenile court dependent or a special immigrant who has served in the U.S. armed forces, or a battered or abused spouse or child;
e. You are a native or citizen of Cuba, or the spouse or child of such alien, who was not lawfully inspected or admitted to the United States;
f. You are a special immigrant retired international organization employee or family member;
g. You are a special immigrant physician;

Part C. Additional eligibility information. ***(Continued.)***

h. You are a public interest parolee, who was denied refugee status, and are from the former Soviet Union, Vietnam, Laos or Cambodia (a "Lautenberg Parolee" under Public Law 101-167); or

i. You are eligible under the Immigration Nursing Relief Act.

☐ **No.** I am not applying for adjustment of status for any of these reasons. *(Go to next question.)*

☐ **Yes.** I am applying for adjustment of status for any one of these reasons. **(If you answered "Yes," do not file this form.)**

2. Do any of the following conditions describe you?

a. You are already a lawful permanent resident of the United States.

b. You have continuously maintained lawful immigration status in the United States since November 5, 1986.

c. You are applying to adjust status as the spouse or unmarried minor child of a U.S. citizen or the parent of a U.S. citizen child at least 21 years of age, and you were inspected and lawfully admitted to the United States.

☐ **No.** None of these conditions describe me. *(Go to next question.)*

☐ **Yes. If you answered "Yes," do not file this form.**

Part D. Signature. *Read the information on penalties in the instructions before completing this section.*

I certify, under penalty of perjury under the laws of the United States of America, that this application and the evidence submitted with it is all true and correct. I authorize the release of any information from my records that the U.S. Citizenship and Immigration Services needs to determine eligibility for the benefit being sought.

Signature	Print Name	Date

Part E. Signature of person preparing form, if other than above. *Read the information on penalties in the instructions before completing this section.*

I certify, under penalty of perjury under the laws of the United States of America, that I prepared this form at the request of the above person and that to the best of my knowledge the contents of this application are all true and correct.

Signature	Print Name	Date

Firm Name and Address	Daytime Phone Number *(Area Code and Number)*
	( )
	E-Mail Address, if any

U.S. Department of Justice
Immigration and Naturalization Service

OMB No. 1115-0239; Expires 11/30/04

LIFE Legalization Supplement to Form I-485 Instructions

EXCEPT AS NOTED BELOW, THE INSTRUCTIONS CONTAINED ON THE FORM I-485 PERTAIN TO APPLICATIONS FOR ADJUSTMENT OF STATUS UNDER THE PROVISIONS OF SECTION 1104 OF PUBLIC LAW 106-553, LEGAL IMMIGRATION FAMILY EQUITY ACT (LIFE ACT), AND PUBLIC LAW 106-554, LIFE ACT AMENDMENTS.

What is the purpose of Form I-485?

In addition to the other purposes of the form listed in the instructions, Form I-485 may be used by certain class action participants applying to the Immigration and Naturalization Service (INS) for adjustment of status pursuant to section 1104 of the LIFE Act and section 1503 of the LIFE Act Amendments (LIFE Legalization), and Title 8 of the Code of Federal Regulations, sections 245a.10-245a.22.

Who may file this application?

You may file this application, either from within or outside the United States, if you:

- Before October 1, 2000, filed with the Attorney General a written claim for class membership in one of the following three class action lawsuits: Catholic Social Services, Inc., v. Meese, vacated sub nom. Reno v. Catholic Social Services, Inc., 509 U.S. 43 (1993) (CSS); League of United Latin American Citizens v. INS, vacated sub nom. Reno v. Catholic Social Services, Inc., 509 U.S. 43 (1993) (LULAC); or Zambrano v. INS, vacated, 509 U.S. 918 (1993) (Zambrano);
- Entered the United States before January 1, 1982, and resided continuously in the United States in an unlawful status since that date through May 4, 1988;
- Were continuously physically present in the United States from November 6, 1986, through May 4, 1988;
- Are admissible to the United States; and
- Have not been convicted of a felony or of three or more misdemeanors in the United States.

IMPORTANT NOTE: When completing the application for adjustment under LIFE Legalization, you MUST indicate, in Part 2, the classification you are seeking. **Check Block H and write "LIFE Legalization."**

What is meant by "admissible to the United States?"

You must be admissible to the United States pursuant to section 212(a) of the Immigration and Nationality Act (INA); however, there are some exceptions for LIFE Legalization applicants:

- Section 212(a)(5) of the INA (an alien without a labor certification or proper qualifications for certain occupations) and Section 212(a)(7)(A) of the INA (an alien not in possession of a valid immigrant visa) do not apply to LIFE Legalization applicants;
- If you are inadmissible under Section 212(a)(9)(A) of the INA (an alien previously removed) or Section 212(a)(9)(C) of the INA (an alien unlawfully present after previous immigration violations), the LIFE Act allows you to apply for a waiver from within the United States;
- If you are inadmissible under Section 212(a)(4) of the INA (an alien likely to become a public charge), you may still be admissible under the Special Rule. The Special Rule is discussed at 8 CFR 245a.18(d); in short, the Special rule allows the INS to look at an alien's employment history when determining whether he or she is likely to become a public charge. You will not be required to file a waiver application in order to apply for the Special Rule.

If you are inadmissible under any section of the INA for which a waiver is available, you will be required to file a Form I-690, Application for Waiver of Grounds of Excludability under sections 245A or 210 of the INA with the INS Service Center Director or District Director having jurisdiction over your case.

What evidence should be submitted with the adjustment application?

Each Form I-485 must be accompanied by:

- Proof of identity, e.g., passport or birth certificate;
- A completed Form G-325A, Biographic Information Sheet, if you are between 14 and 79 years of age;
- A completed Form I-693, Medical Examination of Aliens Seeking Adjustment of Status;
- Two photographs as described in the instructions that accompany the Form I-485;
- Evidence that, prior to October 1, 2000, you filed with the Attorney General a written claim for class membership in the CSS, LULAC, or Zambrano lawsuit;
- Evidence that you entered the United States before January 1, 1982, and resided continuously in the United States in an unlawful status since that date through May 4, 1988; and
- Evidence that you were continuously physically present in the United States from November 6, 1986, through May 4, 1988.

Upon receipt of your application, the INS will instruct you regarding the procedure for obtaining fingerprints through one of the INS's Application Support Centers (ASCs) or authorized Designated Law Enforcement Agencies (DLEAs) chosen specifically for that purpose. **You should not submit a fingerprint card when you file the Form I-485.**

Evidence -- General.

You must attach evidence that establishes your eligibility for adjustment under the provisions of LIFE Legalization. Further clarification and examples of evidence that may be submitted to establish your eligibility for adjustment of status under LIFE Legalization can be found at 8 CFR 245a.14 - 245a.17.

What evidence should be submitted to establish class membership application in the CSS, LULAC, or Zambrano lawsuit?

Examples of evidence that may establish that you applied for class membership in the CSS, LULAC, or Zambrano case before October 1, 2000, include, but are not limited to: Employment Authorization Document or other employment document issued by the INS pursuant to your class membership in CSS, LULAC or Zambrano; INS document(s) addressed to you, or your representative, granting or denying your class membership in CSS, LULAC, or Zambrano; Questionnaire for class member applicants in CSS, LULAC, or Zambrano submitted with the class membership application; INS doucment(s) addressed to you, or your representative, pursuant to your CSS, LULAC, or Zambrano class membership application (e.g., Form I-512 (Parole Authorization), or denial of such; Form I-221 (Order to Show Cause); Form I-862 (Notice to Appear); Final order of removal or deportation; Request for Evidence letter; Form I-687 (Application for Status as a Temporary Resident-Applicants under Section 245A of the INA) submitted with the CSS, LULAC, or Zambrano class membership application); Form I-765, Application for Employment Authorization, submitted pursuant to a court's order granting interim refief; an application for a stay of deportation, exclusion or removal pursant to a court's order granting interim relief; or any other relevant document(s).

What evidence should be submitted to establish continuous unlawful residence since before January 1, 1982, through May 4, 1988?

Examples of evidence that may establish that you entered the United States before January 1, 1982, include, but are not limited to: Form I-94 (Arrival-Departure Record); Form I-20A-B (Certificate of Eligibility for Nonimmigrant (F-1) Student Status -- For Academic and Language Students); Form IAP-66 (Certificate of Eligibility for Exchange Visitor Status); your passport; or the nonimmigrant visa issued to you.

Examples of evidence that may establish your continuous residence include, but are not limited to: past employment records; Forms W-2; certification of the filing of tax returns; letters from employers; utility bills, receipts, or letters from companies from which you received services; school records; hospital or medical records; rental receipts; personal checks bearing a dated bank cancellation stamp; credit card statements; deeds, mortgages, contracts to which you were a party; or insurance policies.

What evidence should be submitted to establish continuous physical presence from November 6, 1986, through May 4, 1988?

Examples of evidence that may establish your continuous physical presence include, but are not limited to: any documentation issued by any governmental or nongovernmental authority, provided such evidence bears the name of the applicant, was dated at the time it was issued, and bears the signature, seal, or other authenticating instrument of the authorized representative of the issuing authority, if the document would normally contain such authenticating instrument. For example: past employment records; Forms W-2; certification of the filing of tax returns; letters from employers; utility bills, receipts, or letters from companies from which you received services; school records; hospital or medical records; rental receipts; personal checks bearing a dated bank cancellation stamp; credit card statements; deeds, mortgages, contracts to which you were a party; or insurance policies.

Since you must establish **continuous residence** and **physical presence** in the United States, you are also required to submit a separate statement listing the dates of departure and return of **all absences** from the United States since your entry into the United States before January 1, 1982, through May 4, 1988. If you were not absent from the United States during the period in question, write "I was not outside the United States since my arrival before January 1, 1982, through May 4, 1988."

When can the application be filed?

The application period begins on **June 1, 2001**, and ends on **June 4, 2003**. All applications, whether filed in the United States or filed from abroad, must be **postmarked on or before June 4, 2003,** to be considered timely filed. Applications postmarked after **June 4, 2003**, will be denied.

What is the application fee?

The fee for filing a Form I-485 for adjustment of status under LIFE Legalization is $255. If you are between the ages of 14 and 79 years, there is a $50 fingerprinting fee in addition to the application fee. In other words, if you are between the ages of 14 and 79, and you are filing a Form I-485 for adjustment of status under LIFE Legalization, the total fee you must pay is $305.

You may submit one check or money order for both the application and fingerprinting fees. Fees must be submitted in the exact amount. **DO NOT MAIL CASH.** Fees cannot be refunded. Payment by check or money order must be drawn on a bank or other institution located in the United States and be payable in United States currency. If you reside in Guam and are filing your application there, the check or money order must be payable to the "Treasurer, Guam." If you reside in the Virgin Islands and are filing your application there, the check or money order must be payable to the "Commissioner of Finance of the Virgin Islands." All other applicants must make the check or money order payable to the "Immigration and Naturalization Service."

NOTE: If the Form I-485 is submitted from outside the United States, remittance may be made by bank international money order or foreign draft drawn on a financial institution in the United States and payable to the "Immigration and Naturalization Service" in United States currency.

Personal checks are accepted subject to collection. An uncollected check in payment of an application fee will render the application and any document issued invalid. A charge of $30 will be imposed if a check in payment of a fee is not honored by the bank on which it is

Where should the application be filed?

The application should be mailed to:

U.S. Immigration and Naturalization Service
Post Office Box 7219
Chicago, IL 60680-7219

Interview.

If necessary, interviews will take place at selected INS offices throughout the United States. If you filed your application from within the United States, you will receive notice in the mail concerning the time and place of your interview. If you filed your application from outside the United States, you will receive detailed insructions from the INS concerning the interview process. At your interview you must be able to demonstrate a minimal understanding of ordinary English and a knowledge and understanding of the history and government of the United States as required under Section 312 of the INA.

In lieu of this, you may instead present: (1) A high school diploma; (2) A general educational development diploma (GED); or (3) A certification on letterhead stationary from a state recognized, accredited learning institution in the United States that you are attending or have attended such institution. The course of study at such learning institution must be for a period of one academic year (or the equivalent thereof according to the standards of the learning institution) and the curriculum must include at least 40 hours of instruction in English and United States history and government. You may submit any of these documents either at the time of filing Form I-485, subsequent to filing the application but prior to the interview, or at the time of the interview (please make sure that your name and A-number appear on any such evidence submitted).

Can an applicant receive employment authorization while the adjustment application is pending?

If you are filing your application from within the United States, and would like work authorization, you may request authorization to work in the United States while your application for adjustment of status under LIFE Legalization is pending by filing Form I-765, Application for Employment Authorization, with fee. You may submit the Form I-765 either concurrently with or subsequent to the filing of this Form I-485. Once the INS has verified through INS indices, a review of your administrative file with the INS, and by all evidence filed by you, that you are/were a CSS, LULAC or Zambrano class member applicant during the specified time period, you will be eligible for work authorization while your Form I-485 is pending. **If you are/were not a CSS, LULAC, or Zambrano class member applicant, you are not entitled to, and will not receive, work authorization.** If you have already received work authorization under any other provision of the INA, that work authorization will not be affected by the filing of this Form I-485.

Can an applicant travel outside of the United States while the adjustment application is pending?

If you wish to travel outside the United States while your LIFE Legalization application is pending, you should apply for "advance parole" on Form I-131, Application for Travel Document. The Form I-131 must be mailed to the address provided on this Form I-485 Supplement D.

If you travel abroad and return to the United States with a grant of advance parole, the INS will presume that you are entitled to return to the United States. However, if you travel abroad and return to the United States **without a grant of advance parole**, you may be subject to removal proceedings and may have to process and/or await the processing of your application from outside the United States.

Penalties.

If you knowingly and willfully falsify or conceal a material fact or submit a false document with this request, we will deny the benefit you are seeking and may deny any other immigration benefit. In addition, you will face severe penalties provided by law and may be subject to criminal prosecution.

Privacy Act Notice.

We ask for the information on this form and associated evidence to determine if you have established eligibility for the immigration benefit you are seeking. Our legal right to ask for this information is in 8 U.S.C. 1203 and 1225. We may provide this information to other government agencies. Failure to provide this information and any requested evidence may delay a final decision or result in denial of your request.

Paperwork Reduction Act Notice.

An agency may not conduct or sponsor an information collection and a person is not required to respond to a collection of information unless it contains a currently valid OMB approval number. We try to create forms and instructions that are accurate, can be easily understood and which impose the least possible burden on you. Often this is difficult because some immigration laws are very complex. The estimated average time to complete and file this application (above and beyond the time necessary to complete and file Form I-485, to which this form is a supplement) is as follows: (1) 10 additional minutes to learn about the law and form; (2) 5 additional minutes to complete the form; (3) 15 additional minutes to assemble and file the application; and (4) 30 additional minutes to complete the interview; for a total estimated average response of 60 minutes per application. If you have comments regarding the accuracy of this estimate, or suggestions for making this form simpler, you can write to the Immigration and Naturalization Service, HQPDI, 425 I Street, N.W., Room 4034, Washington, DC 20536; OMB No. 1115-0239. **(DO NOT MAIL YOUR COMPLETED APPLICANTON TO THIS ADDRESS.)**

OMB No. 1615-0033; Expires 03/31/06

Department of Homeland Security
U.S. Citizenship and Immigration Services

I-693, Medical Examination of Aliens Seeking Adjustment of Status

I. Instructions for Aliens Applying for Adjustment of Status.

A medical examination is necessary as part of your application for adjustment of status.

Please communicate immediately with one of the physicians on the attached list to arrange for your medical examination, which must be completed before your status can be adjusted.

The purpose of the medical examination is to determine if you have certain health conditions which may need further follow-up. The information requested is required in order for a proper evaluation to be made of your health status.

The results of your examination will be provided to an Immigration officer and may be shared with health departments and other public health or cooperating medical authorities. All expenses in connection with this examination must be paid by you.

The examining physician may refer you to your personal physician or a local public health department and you must comply with some health follow-up or treatment recommendations for certain health conditions before your status will be adjusted.

This form should be presented to the examining physician. You must sign the form in the presence of the examining physician. **The law provides severe penalties for knowingly and willfully falsifying or concealing a material fact or using any false documents in connection with this medical examination. The medical examination must be completed in order for us to process your application.**

Medical Examination and Health Information.

A medical examination is necessary as part of your application for adjustment of status.

You should go for your medical examination as soon as possible. You will have to choose a doctor from a list you will be given. The list will have the names of doctors or clinics in your area that have been approved by the U.S. Citizenship and Immigration Services (USCIS) for this examination.

NOTE: USCIS is comprised of offices of the former Immigration and Naturalization Service (INS). You must pay for the examination.

If you become a temporary legal resident and later apply to become a permanent resident, you may need to have another medical examination at that time.

The purpose of the medical examination is to find out if you have certain health conditions which may need further follow-up. The doctor will examine you for certain physical and mental health conditions. You will have to remove your clothes for the medical procedures.

If you need more tests because of a condition found during your medical examination, the doctor may send you to your own doctor or to the local public health department. For some conditions, before you can become a temporary or permanent resident, you will have to show that you have followed the doctor's advice to get more tests or take treatment.

If you have any records of immunizations (vaccinations), you should bring them to show to the doctor. This is especially important for pre-school and school-age children. The doctor will tell you if any more immunizations are needed, and where you can get them (usually at your local public health department). It is important for your health that you follow the doctor's advice and go to get any immunizations.

One of the conditions you will be tested for is tuberculosis (TB). Applicants two years old or older will be required to have a tuberculin skin test. A civil surgeon may require an applicant younger than two to have a skin test if the child has a history of contact with a known TB case, or if there is any other reason to suspect TB disease.

You will be required to return to the civil surgeon in 2 - 3 days to have the skin test checked. If you do not have any reaction to the skin test you will not need any more tests for tuberculosis.

If you have any reaction to the skin test, you will also need to have a chest X-ray examination. If the doctor thinks you are infected with tuberculosis, you may have to go to the local health department and more tests may have to be done. The doctor will explain these medical matters to you.

Exceptions: If you are applying for adjustment of status under the Immigration Reform and Control Act of 1986, you may choose to have either a chest x-ray or a skin test.

You must also have a blood test for syphilis if you are 15 years of age or older.

You will also be tested to see if you have the human immuno-deficiency virus (HIV) infection. This virus is the cause of AIDS. If you have this virus, it may damage your body's ability to fight off other disease. The blood test you will take will tell if you have been exposed to this virus.

II. Instructions for the Physician Performing the Examination.

Please medically examine for adjustment of status the individual presenting this form. The medical examination should be performed according to the U.S. Public Health Service "Guidelines for Medical Examination of Aliens in the United States" and Supplements, which have been provided to you separately.

If the applicant is free of medical defects listed in Section 212(a) of the Immigration and Nationality Act, endorse the form in the space provided. While in your presence, the applicant must also sign the form in the space provided. You should retain one copy for your files and return all other copies in a sealed envelope to the applicant for presentation at the immigration interview.

If the applicant has a health condition that requires follow-up as specified in the "Guidelines for Medical Examination of Aliens in the United States" and Supplements, complete the referral information on the appropriate copy of the medical examination form, and advise the applicant that certain follow-up procedures must be done before the medical clearance can be granted.

Retain a copy of the form for your files and return all other copies to the applicant in a sealed envelope.

The applicant should return to you when the necessary follow-up has been completed for your final verification and signature.

Do not sign the form until the applicant has met the health follow-up requirements. All medical documents, including chest X-ray films if a chest X-ray examination was performed, should be returned to the applicant upon final medical clearance.

Instructions for Physician Providing Health Follow-Up Services.

The person presenting this form has been found to have a medical condition(s) requiring resolution before a medical clearance for adjustment of status can be granted. Please evaluate the applicant for the condition(s) identified.

The requirements for clearance are outlined on the second page of the form. When the person has completed clearance requirements, please sign the form in the space provided and return the medical examination form to the applicant.

Do You Need Forms or Information?

To order USCIS forms, call our toll-free forms line at **1-800-870-3676.** You can also order USCIS forms and obtain information on immigration laws, regulations and procedures by telephoning our **National Customer Service Center** toll-free at **1-800-375-5283** or visiting our internet web site at **www.uscis.gov.**

Use InfoPass for Appointments.

As an alternative to waiting in line for assistance at your local USCIS office, you can now schedule an appointment through our internet-based system, **InfoPass**. To access the system, visit our website at **www.uscis.gov**. Use the **InfoPass** appointment scheduler and follow the screen prompts to set up your appointment. **InfoPass** generates an electronic appointment notice that appears on the screen. Print the notice and take it with you to your appointment. The notice gives the time and date of your appointment, along with the address of the USCIS office.

Privacy Act Notice.

The authority for collection of the information requested on this form is contained in 8 U.S.C. 1182, 1183A, 1184(a), 1252, 1255, and 1258. The information will be used principally by USCIS to whom it may be furnished to support an individual's application for adjustment of status under the Immigration and Nationality Act. Submission of the information is voluntary. It may also, as a matter of routine use, be disclosed to other federal, state, local, and foreign law enforcement and regulatory agencies. Failure to provide the necessary information may result in the denial of the applicant's request.

Paperwork Reduction Act Notice.

An agency may not conduct or sponsor an information collection and a person is not required to respond to an information collection unless it displays a currently valid OMB control number. We try to create forms and instructions that are accurate, can be easily understood, and that impose the least possible burden on you to provide us with information. Often this is difficult because some immigraiton laws are very complex. The estimated average time to complete and file this application is 90 minutes per application. If you have comments regarding the accuracy of this estimate or suggestions for making this form simpler, write to the U.S. Citizenship and Immigration Services, Regulatory Management Division, 111 Massachuetts Avenue, N.W., Washington, DC 20529; OMB No. 1615-0033. **Do not mail your completed application to this address.**

OMB No. 1615-0033; Expires 03/31/06

Department of Homeland Security
U.S. Citizenship and Immigration Services

I-693, Medical Examination of Aliens Seeking Adjustment of Status

(Please type or print clearly in black ink.)

I certify that on the date shown I examined:

1. Name (Last Name in CAPS)

(First Name) (Middle Name)

2. Address (Street Number and Name) (Apt. Number)

(City) (State) (Zip Code)

3. File Number (A Number)

4. Gender
☐ Male ☐ Female

5. Date of Birth (mm/dd/yyyy)

6. Country of Birth

7. Date of Examination (mm/dd/yyyy)

General Physical Examination: I examined specifically for evidence of the conditions listed below. My examination revealed:

☐ No apparent defect, disease, or disability. ☐ The conditions listed below were found (check all boxes that apply).

Class A Conditions

☐ Chancroid
☐ Chronic alcoholism
☐ Gonorrhea
☐ Granuloma inguinal
☐ Hansen's disease, infectious
☐ HIV infection
☐ Insanity
☐ Lymphogranuloma venereum
☐ Mental defect
☐ Mental retardation
☐ Narcotic drug addiction
☐ Previous occurrence of one or more attacks of insanity
☐ Psychopathic personality
☐ Sexual deviation
☐ Syphilis, infectious
☐ Tuberculosis, active

Class B Conditions

☐ Hansen's disease, not infectious ☐ Tuberculosis, not active

☐ Other physical defect, disease or disability (specify below).

Examination for Tuberculosis - Tuberculin Skin Test

☐ Reaction ______mm ☐ No reaction ☐ Not Done

Doctor's name (please print) Date read

Examination for Tuberculosis - Chest X-Ray Report

☐ Abnormal ☐ Normal ☐ Not done

Doctor's name (please print) Date read

Serologic Test for Syphilis

☐ Reactive Titer (confirmatory test performed) ☐ Nonreactive

Test Type

Doctor's name (please print) Date read

Serologic Test for HIV Antibody

☐ Positive (confirmed by Western biot) ☐ Negative

Test Type

Doctor's name (please print) Date read

Immunization Determination (DTP, OPV, MMR, Td-Refer to ***PHS Guidelines*** for recommendations.)

☐ Applicant is current for recommended age-specific immunizations.

☐ Applicant is not current for recommended age-specific immunizations and I have encouraged that appropriate immunizations be obtained.

REMARKS:

Civil Surgeon Referral for Follow-up of Medical Condition

☐ The alien named above has applied for adjustment of status. A medical examination conducted by me identified the conditions above which require resolution before medical clearance is granted or for which the alien may seek medical advice. Please provide follow-up services or refer the alien to an appropriate health care provider. The actions necessary for medical clearance are detailed on the reverse of this form.

Follow-up Information:

The alien named above has complied with the recommended health follow-up.

Doctor's name and address (please type or print clearly) Doctor's signature Date

Application Certification

I certify that I understand the purpose of the medical examination, I authorize the required tests to be completed, and the information on this form refers to me.

Signature Date

Civil Surgeon Certification:

My examination showed the applicant to have met the medical examination and health follow-up requirements for adjustment of status.

Doctor's name address (please type or print clearly) Doctor's signature Date

I-693

ORIGINAL: USCIS A-FILE Form I-693 (Rev. 09/16/05) Y

Medical Clearance Requirements
for Aliens Seeking Adjustment of Status

Medical Condition	Estimated Time for Clearance	Action Required
**Suspected Mental Conditions*	5 - 30 Days	The applicant must provide to a civil surgeon a psychological or psychiatric evaluation from a specialist or medical facility for final classification and clearance.
Tuberculin Skin Test Reaction and Normal Chest X-Ray or Abnormal Chest X-Ray	Immediate	The applicant should be encouraged to seek further medical evaluation for possible preventive treatment.
Tuberculin Skin Test Reaction and Abnormal Chest X-Ray (Inactive/Class B)	10 - 30 Days	The applicant should be referred to a physician or local health department for further evaluation. Medical clearance may not be granted until the application returns to the civil surgeon with documentation of medical evaluation for tuberculosis.
Tuberculin Skin Test Reaction and Abnormal Chest X-Ray or Abnormal Chest X-Ray (Active of Suspected Active/Class A)	10 - 300 Days	The applicant should obtain an appointment with physical or local health department. If treatment for active disease is started, it must be completed (usually nine months) before a medical clearance may be granted. At the completion of treatment, the applicant must present to the civil surgeon documentation of completion. If treatment is not started, the applicant must present to the civil surgeon documentation of medical evaluation for tuberculosis.
Hansen's Disease	30 - 210 Days	Obtain an evaluation from a specialist or Hansen's disease clinic. If the disease is indeterminate or Tuberculoid, the applicant must present to the civil surgeon documentation of medical evaluation. If disease is Lepromotous of Borderline (dimorphous) and treatment is started, the applicant must complete at least six months and present documentation to the civil surgeon showing adequate supervision, treatment, and clinical response before a medical clearance is granted.
***Venereal Diseases*	1 - 30 Days	Obtain an appointment with a physician or local public health department. An applicant with a reactive serologic test for syphilis must provide to the civil surgeon documentation of evaluation for treatment. If any of the venereal diseases are infectious, the applicant must present to the civil surgeon documentation of completion of treatment.
Immunizations Incomplete	Immediate	Immunizations are not required, but the applicant should be encouraged to go to a physician or local health department for appropriate immunizations.
HIV Infection	Immediate	Post-test counseling is not required, but the applicant should be encouraged to seek appropriate post-test counseling.

*Mental retardation; insanity; previous attack of insanity; psychopathic personality, sexual deviation or mental defect; narcotic drug addition; and chronic alcoholism.

**Chancroid; gonorrhea; granuloma inguinal; lymphogranuloma venereum; and syphilis.

Form I-693 (Rev. 09/16/05) Y Page 2

OMB No. 1615-0033; Expires 03/31/06

Department of Homeland Security
U.S. Citizenship and Immigration Services

I-693, Medical Examination of Aliens Seeking Adjustment of Status

(Please type or print clearly in black ink.)
I certify that on the date shown I examined:

1. Name (Last Name in CAPS)

(First Name) (Middle Name)

2. Address (Street Number and Name) (Apt. Number)

(City) (State) (Zip Code)

3. File Number (A Number)

4. Gender
☐ Male ☐ Female

5. Date of Birth (mm/dd/yyyy)

6. Country of Birth

7. Date of Examination (mm/dd/yyyy)

General Physical Examination: I examined specifically for evidence of the conditions listed below. My examination revealed:

☐ No apparent defect, disease, or disability. ☐ The conditions listed below were found (check all boxes that apply).

Class A Conditions

☐ Chancroid
☐ Chronic alcoholism
☐ Gonorrhea
☐ Granuloma inguinal
☐ Hansen's disease, infectious
☐ HIV infection
☐ Insanity
☐ Lymphogranuloma venereum
☐ Mental defect
☐ Mental retardation
☐ Narcotic drug addiction
☐ Previous occurrence of one or more attacks of insanity
☐ Psychopathic personality
☐ Sexual deviation
☐ Syphilis, infectious
☐ Tuberculosis, active

Class B Conditions

☐ Hansen's disease, not infectious ☐ Tuberculosis, not active
☐ Other physical defect, disease or disability (specify below).

Examination for Tuberculosis - Tuberculin Skin Test

☐ Reaction ______mm ☐ No reaction ☐ Not Done

Doctor's name (please print) Date read

Examination for Tuberculosis - Chest X-Ray Report

☐ Abnormal ☐ Normal ☐ Not done

Doctor's name (please print) Date read

Serologic Test for Syphilis

☐ Reactive Titer (confirmatory test performed) ☐ Nonreactive

Test Type

Doctor's name (please print) Date read

Serologic Test for HIV Antibody

☐ Positive (confirmed by Western biot) ☐ Negative

Test Type

Doctor's name (please print) Date read

Immunization Determination (DTP, OPV, MMR, Td-Refer to ***PHS Guidelines*** for recommendations.)

☐ Applicant is current for recommended age-specific immunizations.

☐ Applicant is not current for recommended age-specific immunizations and I have encouraged that appropriate immunizations be obtained.

REMARKS:

Civil Surgeon Referral for Follow-up of Medical Condition

☐ The alien named above has applied for adjustment of status. A medical examination conducted by me identified the conditions above which require resolution before medical clearance is granted or for which the alien may seek medical advice. Please provide follow-up services or refer the alien to an appropriate health care provider. The actions necessary for medical clearance are detailed on the reverse of this form.

Follow-up Information:

The alien named above has complied with the recommended health follow-up.

Doctor's name and address (please type or print clearly) Doctor's signature Date

Application Certification

I certify that I understand the purpose of the medical examination, I authorize the required tests to be completed, and the information on this form refers to me.

Signature Date

Civil Surgeon Certification:

My examination showed the applicant to have met the medical examination and health follow-up requirements for adjustment of status.

Doctor's name address (please type or print clearly) Doctor's signature Date

I-693

CIVIL SURGEON

Form I-693 (Rev. 09/16/05) Y Page 3

Medical Clearance Requirements for Aliens Seeking Adjustment of Status

Medical Condition	Estimated Time for Clearance	Action Required
**Suspected Mental Conditions*	5 - 30 Days	The applicant must provide to a civil surgeon a psychological or psychiatric evaluation from a specialist or medical facility for final classification and clearance.
Tuberculin Skin Test Reaction and Normal Chest X-Ray or Abnormal Chest X-Ray	Immediate	The applicant should be encouraged to seek further medical evaluation for possible preventive treatment.
Tuberculin Skin Test Reaction and Abnormal Chest X-Ray (Inactive/Class B)	10 - 30 Days	The applicant should be referred to a physician or local health department for further evaluation. Medical clearance may not be granted until the application returns to the civil surgeon with documentation of medical evaluation for tuberculosis.
Tuberculin Skin Test Reaction and Abnormal Chest X-Ray or Abnormal Chest X-Ray (Active of Suspected Active/Class A)	10 - 300 Days	The applicant should obtain an appointment with physical or local health department. If treatment for active disease is started, it must be completed (usually nine months) before a medical clearance may be granted. At the completion of treatment, the applicant must present to the civil surgeon documentation of completion. If treatment is not started, the applicant must present to the civil surgeon documentation of medical evaluation for tuberculosis.
Hansen's Disease	30 - 210 Days	Obtain an evaluation from a specialist or Hansen's disease clinic. If the disease is indeterminate or Tuberculoid, the applicant must present to the civil surgeon documentation of medical evaluation. If disease is Lepromotous of Borderline (dimorphous) and treatment is started, the applicant must complete at least six months and present documentation to the civil surgeon showing adequate supervision, treatment, and clinical response before a medical clearance is granted.
***Venereal Diseases*	1 - 30 Days	Obtain an appointment with a physician or local public health department. An applicant with a reactive serologic test for syphilis must provide to the civil surgeon documentation of evaluation for treatment. If any of the venereal diseases are infectious, the applicant must present to the civil surgeon documentation of completion of treatment.
Immunizations Incomplete	Immediate	Immunizations are not required, but the applicant should be encouraged to go to a physician or local health department for appropriate immunizations.
HIV Infection	Immediate	Post-test counseling is not required, but the applicant should be encouraged to seek appropriate post-test counseling.

*Mental retardation; insanity; previous attack of insanity; psychopathic personality, sexual deviation or mental defect; narcotic drug addition; and chronic alcoholism.

**Chancroid; gonorrhea; granuloma inguinal; lymphogranuloma venereum; and syphilis.

Form I-693 (Rev. 09/16/05) Y Page 4

OMB No. 1615-0033; Expires 03/31/06

Department of Homeland Security
U.S. Citizenship and Immigration Services

I-693, Medical Examination of Aliens Seeking Adjustment of Status

(Please type or print clearly in black ink.)

I certify that on the date shown I examined:

1. Name (Last Name in CAPS)

(First Name) (Middle Name)

2. Address (Street Number and Name) (Apt. Number)

(City) (State) (Zip Code)

3. File Number (A Number)

4. Gender
☐ Male ☐ Female

5. Date of Birth (mm/dd/yyyy)

6. Country of Birth

7. Date of Examination (mm/dd/yyyy)

General Physical Examination: I examined specifically for evidence of the conditions listed below. My examination revealed:

☐ No apparent defect, disease, or disability. ☐ The conditions listed below were found (check all boxes that apply).

Class A Conditions

☐ Chancroid
☐ Chronic alcoholism
☐ Gonorrhea
☐ Granuloma inguinal
☐ Hansen's disease, infectious
☐ HIV infection
☐ Insanity
☐ Lymphogranuloma venereum
☐ Mental defect
☐ Mental retardation
☐ Narcotic drug addiction
☐ Previous occurrence of one or more attacks of insanity
☐ Psychopathic personality
☐ Sexual deviation
☐ Syphilis, infectious
☐ Tuberculosis, active

Class B Conditions

☐ Hansen's disease, not infectious ☐ Tuberculosis, not active

☐ Other physical defect, disease or disability (specify below).

Examination for Tuberculosis - Tuberculin Skin Test

☐ Reaction ______mm ☐ No reaction ☐ Not Done

Doctor's name (please print) Date read

Examination for Tuberculosis - Chest X-Ray Report

☐ Abnormal ☐ Normal ☐ Not done

Doctor's name (please print) Date read

Serologic Test for Syphilis

☐ Reactive Titer (confirmatory test performed) ☐ Nonreactive

Test Type

Doctor's name (please print) Date read

Serologic Test for HIV Antibody

☐ Positive (confirmed by Western biot) ☐ Negative

Test Type

Doctor's name (please print) Date read

Immunization Determination (DTP, OPV, MMR, Td-Refer to ***PHS Guidelines*** for recommendations.)

☐ Applicant is current for recommended age-specific immunizations.

☐ Applicant is not current for recommended age-specific immunizations and I have encouraged that appropriate immunizations be obtained.

REMARKS:

Civil Surgeon Referral for Follow-up of Medical Condition

☐ The alien named above has applied for adjustment of status. A medical examination conducted by me identified the conditions above which require resolution before medical clearance is granted or for which the alien may seek medical advice. Please provide follow-up services or refer the alien to an appropriate health care provider. The actions necessary for medical clearance are detailed on the reverse of this form.

Follow-up Information:

The alien named above has complied with the recommended health follow-up.

Doctor's name and address (please type or print clearly) Doctor's signature Date

Application Certification

I certify that I understand the purpose of the medical examination, I authorize the required tests to be completed, and the information on this form refers to me.

Signature Date

Civil Surgeon Certification:

My examination showed the applicant to have met the medical examination and health follow-up requirements for adjustment of status.

Doctor's name address (please type or print clearly) Doctor's signature Date

I-693

APPLICANT

Form I-693 (Rev. 09/16/05) Y Page 5

Medical Clearance Requirements for Aliens Seeking Adjustment of Status

Medical Condition	Estimated Time for Clearance	Action Required
**Suspected Mental Conditions*	5 - 30 Days	The applicant must provide to a civil surgeon a psychological or psychiatric evaluation from a specialist or medical facility for final classification and clearance.
Tuberculin Skin Test Reaction and Normal Chest X-Ray or Abnormal Chest X-Ray	Immediate	The applicant should be encouraged to seek further medical evaluation for possible preventive treatment.
Tuberculin Skin Test Reaction and Abnormal Chest X-Ray (Inactive/Class B)	10 - 30 Days	The applicant should be referred to a physician or local health department for further evaluation. Medical clearance may not be granted until the application returns to the civil surgeon with documentation of medical evaluation for tuberculosis.
Tuberculin Skin Test Reaction and Abnormal Chest X-Ray or Abnormal Chest X-Ray (Active of Suspected Active/Class A)	10 - 300 Days	The applicant should obtain an appointment with physical or local health department. If treatment for active disease is started, it must be completed (usually nine months) before a medical clearance may be granted. At the completion of treatment, the applicant must present to the civil surgeon documentation of completion. If treatment is not started, the applicant must present to the civil surgeon documentation of medical evaluation for tuberculosis.
Hansen's Disease	30 - 210 Days	Obtain an evaluation from a specialist or Hansen's disease clinic. If the disease is indeterminate or Tuberculoid, the applicant must present to the civil surgeon documentation of medical evaluation. If disease is Lepromotous of Borderline (dimorphous) and treatment is started, the applicant must complete at least six months and present documentation to the civil surgeon showing adequate supervision, treatment, and clinical response before a medical clearance is granted.
***Venereal Diseases*	1 - 30 Days	Obtain an appointment with a physician or local public health department. An applicant with a reactive serologic test for syphilis must provide to the civil surgeon documentation of evaluation for treatment. If any of the venereal diseases are infectious, the applicant must present to the civil surgeon documentation of completion of treatment.
Immunizations Incomplete	Immediate	Immunizations are not required, but the applicant should be encouraged to go to a physician or local health department for appropriate immunizations.
HIV Infection	Immediate	Post-test counseling is not required, but the applicant should be encouraged to seek appropriate post-test counseling.

*Mental retardation; insanity; previous attack of insanity; psychopathic personality, sexual deviation or mental defect; narcotic drug addition; and chronic alcoholism.

**Chancroid; gonorrhea; granuloma inguinal; lymphogranuloma venereum; and syphilis.

Form I-693 (Rev. 09/16/05) Y Page 6

OMB No. 1615-0033; Expires 03/31/06

Department of Homeland Security
U.S. Citizenship and Immigration Services

I-693, Medical Examination of Aliens Seeking Adjustment of Status

(Please type or print clearly in black ink.)

I certify that on the date shown I examined:

1. Name (Last Name in CAPS)

(First Name) (Middle Name)

2. Address (Street Number and Name) (Apt. Number)

(City) (State) (Zip Code)

3. File Number (A Number)

4. Gender
☐ Male ☐ Female

5. Date of Birth (mm/dd/yyyy)

6. Country of Birth

7. Date of Examination (mm/dd/yyyy)

General Physical Examination: I examined specifically for evidence of the conditions listed below. My examination revealed:

☐ No apparent defect, disease, or disability. ☐ The conditions listed below were found (check all boxes that apply).

Class A Conditions

☐ Chancroid
☐ Chronic alcoholism
☐ Gonorrhea
☐ Granuloma inguinal
☐ Hansen's disease, infectious
☐ HIV infection
☐ Insanity
☐ Lymphogranuloma venereum
☐ Mental defect
☐ Mental retardation
☐ Narcotic drug addiction
☐ Previous occurrence of one or more attacks of insanity
☐ Psychopathic personality
☐ Sexual deviation
☐ Syphilis, infectious
☐ Tuberculosis, active

Class B Conditions

☐ Hansen's disease, not infectious ☐ Tuberculosis, not active

☐ Other physical defect, disease or disability (specify below).

Examination for Tuberculosis - Tuberculin Skin Test

☐ Reaction ______mm ☐ No reaction ☐ Not Done

Doctor's name (please print) Date read

Examination for Tuberculosis - Chest X-Ray Report

☐ Abnormal ☐ Normal ☐ Not done

Doctor's name (please print) Date read

Serologic Test for Syphilis

☐ Reactive Titer (confirmatory test performed) ☐ Nonreactive

Test Type

Doctor's name (please print) Date read

Serologic Test for HIV Antibody

☐ Positive (confirmed by Western biot) ☐ Negative

Test Type

Doctor's name (please print) Date read

Immunization Determination (DTP, OPV, MMR, Td-Refer to ***PHS Guidelines*** for recommendations.)

☐ Applicant is current for recommended age-specific immunizations.

☐ Applicant is not current for recommended age-specific immunizations and I have encouraged that appropriate immunizations be obtained.

REMARKS:

Civil Surgeon Referral for Follow-up of Medical Condition

☐ The alien named above has applied for adjustment of status. A medical examination conducted by me identified the conditions above which require resolution before medical clearance is granted or for which the alien may seek medical advice. Please provide follow-up services or refer the alien to an appropriate health care provider. The actions necessary for medical clearance are detailed on the reverse of this form.

Follow-up Information:

The alien named above has complied with the recommended health follow-up.

Doctor's name and address (please type or print clearly) Doctor's signature Date

Application Certification

I certify that I understand the purpose of the medical examination, I authorize the required tests to be completed, and the information on this form refers to me.

Signature Date

Civil Surgeon Certification:

My examination showed the applicant to have met the medical examination and health follow-up requirements for adjustment of status.

Doctor's name address (please type or print clearly) Doctor's signature Date

I-693

PHYSICAN OR HEALTH DEPARTMENT

Form I-693 (Rev. 09/16/05) Y Page 7

Medical Clearance Requirements for Aliens Seeking Adjustment of Status

Medical Condition	Estimated Time for Clearance	Action Required
**Suspected Mental Conditions*	5 - 30 Days	The applicant must provide to a civil surgeon a psychological or psychiatric evaluation from a specialist or medical facility for final classification and clearance.
Tuberculin Skin Test Reaction and Normal Chest X-Ray or Abnormal Chest X-Ray	Immediate	The applicant should be encouraged to seek further medical evaluation for possible preventive treatment.
Tuberculin Skin Test Reaction and Abnormal Chest X-Ray (Inactive/Class B)	10 - 30 Days	The applicant should be referred to a physician or local health department for further evaluation. Medical clearance may not be granted until the application returns to the civil surgeon with documentation of medical evaluation for tuberculosis.
Tuberculin Skin Test Reaction and Abnormal Chest X-Ray or Abnormal Chest X-Ray (Active of Suspected Active/Class A)	10 - 300 Days	The applicant should obtain an appointment with physical or local health department. If treatment for active disease is started, it must be completed (usually nine months) before a medical clearance may be granted. At the completion of treatment, the applicant must present to the civil surgeon documentation of completion. If treatment is not started, the applicant must present to the civil surgeon documentation of medical evaluation for tuberculosis.
Hansen's Disease	30 - 210 Days	Obtain an evaluation from a specialist or Hansen's disease clinic. If the disease is indeterminate or Tuberculoid, the applicant must present to the civil surgeon documentation of medical evaluation. If disease is Lepromotous of Borderline (dimorphous) and treatment is started, the applicant must complete at least six months and present documentation to the civil surgeon showing adequate supervision, treatment, and clinical response before a medical clearance is granted.
***Venereal Diseases*	1 - 30 Days	Obtain an appointment with a physician or local public health department. An applicant with a reactive serologic test for syphilis must provide to the civil surgeon documentation of evaluation for treatment. If any of the venereal diseases are infectious, the applicant must present to the civil surgeon documentation of completion of treatment.
Immunizations Incomplete	Immediate	Immunizations are not required, but the applicant should be encouraged to go to a physician or local health department for appropriate immunizations.
HIV Infection	Immediate	Post-test counseling is not required, but the applicant should be encouraged to seek appropriate post-test counseling.

*Mental retardation; insanity; previous attack of insanity; psychopathic personality, sexual deviation or mental defect; narcotic drug addition; and chronic alcoholism.

**Chancroid; gonorrhea; granuloma inguinal; lymphogranuloma venereum; and syphilis.

Form I-693 (Rev. 09/16/05) Y Page 8

FORMS FOR CITIZENSHIP

N-400: Application for Naturalization

LPRs who want to become U.S. citizens apply for naturalization by using this form. At the present time, this is one of the forms that has not changed since DHS took over immigration responsibilities from INS. Accordingly, the form refers to INS, though it remains the form of record.

N-600: Application for Certificate of Citizenship

Foreign-born children, sons, and daughters (remember the difference as discussed in Chapter 3) of U.S. citizens may certify their citizenship using the N-600 if they are adults or the N-600K if they are minors (in the case of the latter, the citizen parent will file for them). Note that these people receive a Certificate of Citizenship, whereas naturalized citizens receive a Certificate of Naturalization. Recipients of either certificate are U.S. citizens.

N-565: Application for Replacement Naturalization/Citizenship Document

If you've lost your naturalization or citizenship certificate, this is the form that you would use to replace it.

N-644: Application for Posthumous Citizenship

This form enables the families of veterans who died during military service to the U.S. to apply for posthumous citizenship on their behalf.

OMB No. 1615-0052; Expires 11/30/06

Department of Homeland Security
U.S. Citizenship and Immigration Services

N-400, Application for Naturalization

Instructions

What Is the Purpose of This Form?

Form N-400 is an application for U.S. citizenship (naturalization). For more information about the naturalization process and eligibility requirements, please read *A Guide to Naturalization* (M-476). If you do not already have a copy of the *Guide*, you can get a copy from:

- The USCIS website **(www.uscis.gov)**;
- The USCIS toll-free forms line at **1-800-870-3676** or
- The USCIS National Customer Service Center (NCSC) at **1-800-375-5283 (TTY:1-800-767-1833)**.

Who Should Use This Form?

To use this form you must be **ONE** of the following:

(1) A Lawful Permanent Resident for at least five years and at least 18 years old;

(2) A Lawful Permanent Resident for at least three years and at least 18 years old,

AND

- You have been married to and living with the same U.S. citizen for the last three years,

AND

- Your spouse has been a U.S. citizen for the last three years;

(3) A member of one of several other groups eligible to apply for naturalization (for example, persons who are nationals but not citizens of the United States) and at least 18 years old. For more information about these groups, please see the *Guide*.

(4) A person who has served honorably in the U.S. Armed Forces,

AND

- If you are at least 18 years old, a Lawful Permanent Resident with at least one year of U.S. Armed Forces service, and you are filing your application for naturalization while still in the service or within six months after the termination of such service.

OR

- You served honorably as a member of the Selected Reserve of the Ready Reserve or in active-duty status during a designated period of hostilities. You then may apply for naturalization without having been physically present in the United States for any specified period.

For more information, please see "Military Naturalization" under "Hot Topics" at **www.uscis.gov**.

NOTE: If you are married to a U.S. citizen who is employed or deployed abroad, you may in some circumstances be eligible for expedited naturalization under section 319(b) of the Immigration and Nationality Act (INA). For further assistance, please refer to our "Eligibility Worksheet" at **www.uscis.gov/graphics/services/natz/wsinstruct.html**.

Who Should Not Use This Form?

In certain cases, a person who was born outside of the United States to U.S. citizen parents is already a citizen and does not need to apply for naturalization. To find out more information about this type of citizenship and whether you should file a Form N-600, "Application for Certificate of Citizenship," read the *Guide.*

Other permanent residents under 18 years of age may be eligible for U.S. citizenship if their U.S. citizen parent or parents file a Form N-600 application in their behalf. For more information, see "Frequently Asked Questions" in the *Guide.*

When Am I Eligible to Apply?

You may apply for naturalization when you meet **all** the requirements to become a U.S. citizen. The section of the *Guide* called "Who is Eligible for Naturalization" and the Eligibility Worksheet found in the back of the *Guide* are tools to help you determine whether you are eligible to apply for naturalization. You should complete the Worksheet before filling out this Form N-400 application.

If you are applying based on five years as a Lawful Permanent Resident or based on three years as a Lawful Permanent Resident married to a U.S. citizen, you may apply for naturalization up to 90 days before you meet the "continuous residence" requirement. You must meet all other requirements at the time that you file your application with us.

Certain applicants have different English and civics testing requirements based on their age and length of lawful permanent residence **at the time of filing**. If you are over 50 years of age and have lived in the United States as a lawful permanent resident for periods totaling at least 20 years, or if you are over 55 years of age and have lived in the United States as a lawful permanent resident for periods totaling at least 15 years, you do not have to take the English test but you have to take the civics test in the language of your choice.

If you are over 65 years of age and have lived in the United States as a lawful permanent resident for periods totaling at least 20 years, you do not have to take the English test but you have to take a simpler version of the civics test in the language of your choice.

What Does It Cost to Apply for Naturalization and How Do I Pay?

The fee for this application is **$330.00**. A **$70.00** biometric services fee for fingerprinting is also required. You should submit both fees with your Form N-400.

For military applicants filing under Section 328 and Section 329 of the INA, no fee is required.

For more information on fees and form of payment, call the NCSC at **1-800-375-5283 (TTY: 1-800-767-1833)** or visit our website at **www.uscis.gov** and click on "Immigration Forms, Fees and Fingerprints."

Your fee is not refundable, even if you withdraw your application or it is denied. If you are unable to pay the naturalization application fee, you may apply in writing for a fee waiver. For information about the fee waiver process, telephone the NCSC at **1-800-375-5283 (TTY: 1-800-767- 1833)** or visit our website at **www.uscis.gov** and click on "Immigration Forms, Fees and Fingerprints."

What Do I Send With My Application?

All applicants must send certain documents with their application.

For example, if you have been arrested or convicted of a crime, you must send a certified copy of the arrest report, court disposition, sentencing and any other relevant documents, including any countervailing evidence concerning the circumstances of your arrest and/or conviction that you would like USCIS to consider. Note that unless a traffic incident was alcohol or drug related, you do not need to submit documentation for traffic fines and incidents that did not involve an actual arrest if the only penalty was a fine of less than **$500** and/or points on your driver's license.

For more information on the documents you must send with your application, see the Document Checklist in the *Guide.*

Where Do I Send My Application?

You must send your Form N-400 application and supporting documents to a USCIS Service Center.

To find the Service Center address you should use, read the section in the Guide called "Completing Your Application and Getting Photographed" or call the NCSC at **1-800-375-5283 (TTY: 1-800-767-1833)** or visit our website at **www.uscis.gov** and click on "Immigration Forms, Fees and Fingerprints."

All naturalization applicants filing under the military provisions, Section 328 or 329 of the INA, should file their application at the Nebraska Service Center regardless of geographic location or jurisdiction. Please send your application to:

Nebraska Service Center
P.O. Box 87426
Lincoln, NE 68501-7426

How Do I Complete This Application?

- Please print clearly or type your answers using CAPITAL letters in each box.
- Use black ink.
- **Write your USCIS (or former INS) "A"- number on the top right hand corner of each page.** Use your "A"- number on your Permanent Resident Card (formerly known as the Alien Registration or "Green" Card). To locate your "A"- number, see the sample Permanent Resident Cards in the *Guide.* The "A" number on your card consists of seven to nine numbers, depending on when your record was created. If the "A"- number on your card has fewer than nine numbers, place enough zeros before the first number to make a *total of nine numbers* on the application. For example, write card number A1234567 as A001234567, but write card number A12345678 as A012345678.
- If a question does not apply to you, write **N/A** (meaning "Not Applicable") in the space provided.
- If you need extra space to answer any item:
  - -- Attach a separate sheet of paper (or more sheets if needed);
  - -- Write your name, your "A"- number, and "N-400" on the top right corner of the sheet; and
  - -- Write the number of each question for which you are providing additional information.

Step-by-Step Instructions.

This form is divided into 14 parts. The information below will help you fill out the form.

Part 1. Your Name *(the Person Applying for Naturalization).*

A. **Your current legal name** - Your current legal name is the name on your birth certificate, unless it has been changed after birth by a legal action such as a marriage or court order.

B. **Your name exactly as it appears on your Permanent Resident Card** *(if different from above)*-- Write your name exactly as it appears on your card, even if it is misspelled.

C. **Other names you have used** - If you have used any other names in your life, write them in this section. If you need more space, use a separate sheet of paper.

If you have **never** used a different name, write "N/A" in the space for "Family Name *(Last Name).*"

D. **Name change *(optional)*** - A court can allow a change in your name when you are being naturalized. A name change does not become final until a court naturalizes you. For more information regarding a name change, see the *Guide.*

If you want a court to change your name at a naturalization oath ceremony, check "Yes" and complete this section. If you do not want to change your name, check "No" and go to Part 2.

Part 2. Information About Your Eligibility.

Check the box that shows why you are eligible to apply for naturalization. If the basis for your eligibility is not described in one of the first three boxes, check "Other" and briefly write the basis for your application on the lines provided.

Part 3. Information About You.

A. **U.S. Social Security number** - Print your U.S. Social Security number. If you do not have one, write "N/A" in the space provided.

B. **Date of birth** - Always use eight numbers to show your date of birth. Write the date in this order: Month, Day, Year. For example, write May 1, 1958 as 05/01/1958.

C. **Date you became a Permanent Resident** - Write the official date when your lawful permanent residence began, as shown on your Permanent Resident Card. To help locate the date on your card, see the sample Permanent Resident Cards in the *Guide.* Write the date in this order: Month, Day,Year. For example, write August 9, 1988 as 08/09/1988.

D. Country of birth - Write the name of the country where you were born. Write the name of the country even if it no longer exists.

E. Country of nationality - Write the name of the country (or countries) where you are currently a citizen or national.

- If you are stateless, write the name of the country where you were last a citizen or national.
- If you are a citizen or national of more than one country, write the name of the foreign country that issued your last passport.

F. Citizenship of parents - Check "Yes" if either of your parents is a U.S. citizen. If you answer "Yes," you may already be a citizen. For more information, see "Frequently Asked Questions" in the *Guide*.

G. Current marital status - Check the marital status you have on the date you are filing this application. If you are currently not married, but had a prior marriage that was annulled, or otherwise legally terminated, check "Other" and explain it.

H. Request for disability waiver - If you have a medical disability or impairment that you believe qualifies you for a waiver of the tests of English and/ or U.S. government and history, check "Yes" and attach a properly completed Form N-648, Medical Certification for Disability Exceptions. If you ask for this waiver it does not guarantee that you will be excused from the testing requirements. For more information about this waiver, see the *Guide*.

I. Request for disability accommodations - We will make every reasonable effort to help applicants with disabilities complete the naturalization process. For example, if you use a wheelchair, we will make sure that you can be fingerprinted and interviewed, and can attend a naturalization ceremony at a location that is wheelchair accessible. If you are deaf or hearing impaired and need a sign language interpreter, we will make arrangements with you to have one at your interview.

If you believe you will need us to modify or change the naturalization process for you, check the box or write in the space the kind of accommodation you need. If you need more space, use a separate sheet of paper. You do not need to send us a Form N-648 to request an accommodation. You only need to send a Form N-648 to request a waiver of the test of English and/or civics.

We consider requests for accommodations on a case-by-case basis. Asking for an accommodation will not affect your eligibility for citizenship.

Part 4. Addresses and Telephone Numbers.

A. Home address - Give the address where you now live. Do **not** put post office (P.O.) box numbers here.

B. Mailing address - If your mailing address is the same as your home address, write "same." If your mailing address is different from your home address, write it in this part.

C. Telephone numbers - By giving us your telephone numbers and e-mail address, we can contact you about your application more quickly. If you are hearing impaired and use a TTY telephone connection, please indicate this by writing "(TTY)" after the telephone number.

Part 5. Information for Criminal Records Search.

The Federal Bureau of Investigation (FBI) will use the information in this section, together with your fingerprints, to search for criminal records. Although the results of this search may affect your eligibility, we do **not** make naturalization decisions based on your gender, race or physical description.

For each item, check the box or boxes that best describes you. The categories are those used by the FBI. You can select one or more.

NOTE: As part of the USCIS biometric services requirement, you must be fingerprinted after you file this application. If necessary, USCIS may also take your photograph and signature. Check our website at **www.uscis.gov** or call our National Customer Service Center at **1-800-375-5253** to determine the fee for the biometric services.

Part 6. Information About Your Residence and Employment.

A. Write every address where you have lived during the last five years (including in other countries).

Begin with where you live now. Include the dates you lived in those places. For example, write May 1998 to June 1999 as 05/1998 to 06/1999.

If you need separate sheets of paper to complete section A or B or any other questions on this application, be sure to follow the Instructions in **"How Do I Complete This Application?"** on **Page 2.**

B. List where you have worked (or, if you were a student, the schools you have attended) during the last five years. Include military service. If you worked for yourself, write "self employed." Begin with your most recent job. Also, write the dates when you worked or studied in each place.

Part 7. Time Outside the United States *(Including Trips to Canada, Mexico and the Caribbean).*

A. Write the total number of days you spent outside of the United States (including on military service) during the last five years. Count the days of every trip that lasted 24 hours or longer.

B. Write the number of trips you have taken outside the United States during the last five years. Count every trip that lasted 24 hours or longer.

C. Provide the requested information for every trip that you have taken outside the United States since you became a Lawful Permanent Resident. Begin with your most recent trip.

Part 8. Information About Your Marital History.

A. Write the number of times you have been married. Include any annulled marriages. If you were married to the same spouse more than one time, count each time as a separate marriage.

B. If you are now married, provide information about your current spouse.

C. Check the box to indicate whether your current spouse is a U.S. citizen.

D. If your spouse is a citizen through naturalization, give the date and place of naturalization. If your spouse regained U.S. citizenship, write the date and place the citizenship was regained.

E. If your spouse is not a U.S. citizen, complete this section.

F. If you were married before, give information about your former spouse or spouses. In question F.2, check the box showing the immigration status your former spouse had during your marriage. If the spouse was not a U.S. citizen or a Lawful Permanent Resident at that time check "Other" and explain. For question F.5, if your marriage was annulled, check "Other" and explain. If you were married to the same spouse more than one time, write about each marriage separately.

G. For any prior marriages of your current spouse, follow the instructions in section F above.

NOTE: If you or your present spouse had more than one prior marriage, provide the same information required by section F and section G about every additional marriage on a separate sheet of paper.

Part 9. Information About Your Children.

A. Write the total number of sons and daughters you have had. Count **all** of your children, regardless of whether they are:

- Alive, missing, or dead;
- Born in other countries or in the United States;
- Under 18 years old or adults;
- Married or unmarried;
- Living with you or elsewhere;
- Stepsons or stepdaughters or legally adopted; or
- Born when you were not married.

B. Write information about all your sons and daughters. In the last column ("Location"), write:

- "With me" - if the son or daughter is currently living with you;
- The street address and state or country where the son or daughter lives - if the son or daughter is **not** currently living with you; or
- "Missing" or "dead" - if that son or daughter is missing or dead.

If you need space to list information about additional sons and daughters, attach a separate sheet of paper.

Part 10. Additional Questions.

Answer each question by checking "Yes" or "No." If **any** part of a question applies to you, you must answer "Yes." For example, if you were never arrested but *were* once detained by a police officer, check "Yes" to the question "Have you ever been arrested or detained by a law enforcement officer?" and attach a written explanation.

We will use this information to determine your eligibility for citizenship. Answer every question honestly and accurately. If you do not, we may deny your application for lack of good moral character. Answering "Yes" to one of these questions does not always cause an application to be denied. For more information on eligibility, please see the *Guide*.

Part 11. Your Signature.

After reading the statement in Part 11, you must sign and date it. You should sign your full name without abbreviating it or using initials. The signature must be legible. Your application may be returned to you if it is not signed.

If you cannot sign your name in English, sign in your native language. If you are unable to write in any language, sign your name with an "X."

NOTE: A designated representative may sign this section on behalf an applicant who qualifies for a waiver of the Oath of Allegiance because of a development or physical impairment (see the *Guide* for more information). In such a case the designated representative should write the name of the applicant and then sign his or her own name followed by the words "Designated Representative." The information attested to by the Designated Representative is subject to the same penalties discussed on **Page 6** of these Instructions.

Part 12. Signature of Person Who Prepared the Form for You.

If someone filled out this form for you, he or she must complete this section.

Part 13. Signature at Interview.

Do not complete this part. You will be asked to complete this part at your interview.

Part 14. Oath of Allegiance.

Do not complete this part. You will be asked to complete this part at your interview.

If we approve your application, you must take this Oath of Allegiance to become a citizen. In limited cases you can take a modified Oath. The Oath requirement cannot be waived unless you are unable to understand its meaning because of a physical or developmental disability or mental impairment. For more information, see the *Guide*. Your signature on this form only indicates that you have no objections to taking the Oath of Allegiance. **It does not mean that you have taken the Oath or that you are naturalized**. If USCIS approves your application for naturalization, you must attend an oath ceremony and take the Oath of Allegiance to the United States.

Penalties.

If you knowingly and willfully falsify or conceal a material fact or submit a false document with this request, we will deny your application for naturalization and may deny any other immigration benefit. In addition, you will face severe penalties provided by law and may be subject to a removal proceeding or criminal prosecution.

If we grant you citizenship after you falsify or conceal a material fact or submit a false document with this request, your naturalization may be revoked.

Privacy Act Notice.

We ask for the information on this form and for other documents to determine your eligibility for naturalization. Form N-400 processes are generally covered in 8 U.S.C. 1421 through 1430 and 1436 through 1449. We may provide information from your application to other government agencies.

Use InfoPass for Appointments.

As an alternative to waiting in line for assistance at your local USCIS office, you can now schedule an appointment through our internet-based system, **InfoPass**. To access the system, visit our website at **www.uscis.gov**. Use the **InfoPass** appointment scheduler and follow the screen prompts to set up your appointment. **InfoPass** generates an electronic appointment notice that appears on the screen. Print the notice and take it with you to your appointment. The notice gives the time and date of your appointment, along with the address of USCIS office.

Paperwork Reduction Act Notice.

A person is not required to respond to a collection of information unless it displays a valid OMB control number.

We try to create forms and instructions that are accurate, can be easily understood and that impose the least possible burden on you to provide us with the information. Often this is difficult because some immigration laws are very complex.

The estimated average time to complete and file this form is computed as follows: (1) 2 hours and 8 minutes to learn about and complete the form; (2) 4 hours to assemble and file the information - for a total estimated average of 6 hours and 8 minutes per application.

If you have comments about the accuracy of this estimate or suggestions to make this form simpler, you may write to U.S. Citizenship and Immigration Services, Regulatory Management Division, 111 Massachusetts Avenue N.W., Washington, DC 20529; OMB No. 1615-0052. **Do not mail your completed application to this address.**

OMB No. 1615-0052

Department of Homeland Security
U.S Citizenship and Immigration Services

N-400 Application for Naturalization

Print clearly or type your answers using CAPITAL letters. Failure to print clearly may delay your application. Use black ink.

Part 1. Your Name. *(The Person Applying for Naturalization)*

Write your USCIS "A"- number here:
A

For USCIS Use Only

Bar Code	Date Stamp
	Remarks
Action Block	

A. Your current legal name.

Family Name *(Last Name)*

Given Name *(First Name)* Full Middle Name *(If applicable)*

B. Your name **exactly** as it appears on your Permanent Resident Card.

Family Name *(Last Name)*

Given Name *(First Name)* Full Middle Name *(If applicable)*

C. If you have ever used other names, provide them below.

Family Name *(Last Name)*	Given Name *(First Name)*	Middle Name

D. Name change *(optional)*

Please read the Instructions before you decide whether to change your name.

1. Would you like to legally change your name? ☐ Yes ☐ No

2. If "Yes," print the new name you would like to use. Do not use initials or abbreviations when writing your new name.

Family Name *(Last Name)*

Given Name *(First Name)* Full Middle Name

Part 2. Information About Your Eligibility. *(Check Only One)*

I am at least 18 years old **AND**

A. ☐ I have been a Lawful Permanent Resident of the United States for at least five years.

B. ☐ I have been a Lawful Permanent Resident of the United States for at least three years, **and** I have been married to and living with the same U.S. citizen for the last three years, **and** my spouse has been a U.S. citizen for the last three years.

C. ☐ I am applying on the basis of qualifying military service.

D. ☐ Other *(Please explain)* ______________________

Part 3. Information About You.

Write your USCIS "A"- number here:
A

A. U.S. Social Security Number

B. Date of Birth *(mm/dd/yyyy)*

C. Date You Became a Permanent Resident *(mm/dd/yyyy)*

D. Country of Birth

E. Country of Nationality

F. Are either of your parents U.S. citizens? *(if yes, see Instructions)* ☐ Yes ☐ No

G. What is your current marital status? ☐ Single, Never Married ☐ Married ☐ Divorced ☐ Widowed

☐ Marriage Annulled or Other *(Explain)* ______

H. Are you requesting a waiver of the English and/or U.S. History and Government requirements based on a disability or impairment and attaching a Form N-648 with your application? ☐ Yes ☐ No

I. Are you requesting an accommodation to the naturalization process because of a disability or impairment? *(See Instructions for some examples of accommodations.)* ☐ Yes ☐ No

If you answered "Yes," check the box below that applies:

☐ I am deaf or hearing impaired and need a sign language interpreter who uses the following language: ______

☐ I use a wheelchair.

☐ I am blind or sight impaired.

☐ I will need another type of accommodation. Please explain: ______

Part 4. Addresses and Telephone Numbers.

A. Home Address - Street Number and Name *(Do **not** write a P.O. Box in this space)* | Apartment Number

City | County | State | ZIP Code | Country

B. Care of | Mailing Address - Street Number and Name *(If different from home address)* | Apartment Number

City | State | ZIP Code | Country

C. Daytime Phone Number *(If any)* ( ) | Evening Phone Number *(If any)* ( ) | E-mail Address *(If any)*

Part 5. Information for Criminal Records Search.

Write your USCIS "A"- number here:
A

NOTE: The categories below are those required by the FBI. See Instructions for more information.

A. Gender

☐ Male ☐ Female

B. Height

Feet Inches

C. Weight

Pounds

D. Are you Hispanic or Latino? ☐ Yes ☐ No

E. Race *(Select one or more.)*

☐ White ☐ Asian ☐ Black or African American ☐ American Indian or Alaskan Native ☐ Native Hawaiian or Other Pacific Islander

F. Hair color

☐ Black ☐ Brown ☐ Blonde ☐ Gray ☐ White ☐ Red ☐ Sandy ☐ Bald (No Hair)

G. Eye color

☐ Brown ☐ Blue ☐ Green ☐ Hazel ☐ Gray ☐ Black ☐ Pink ☐ Maroon ☐ Other

Part 6. Information About Your Residence and Employment.

A. Where have you lived during the last five years? Begin with where you live now and then list every place you lived for the last five years. If you need more space, use a separate sheet(s) of paper.

Street Number and Name, Apartment Number, City, State, Zip Code and Country	Dates *(mm/dd/yyyy)*	
	From	To
Current Home Address - Same as Part 4.A		Present

B. Where have you worked (or, if you were a student, what schools did you attend) during the last five years? Include military service. Begin with your current or latest employer and then list every place you have worked or studied for the last five years. If you need more space, use a separate sheet of paper.

Employer or School Name	Employer or School Address *(Street, City and State)*	Dates *(mm/dd/yyyy)*		Your Occupation
		From	To	

Part 7. Time Outside the United States.
(Including Trips to Canada, Mexico and the Caribbean Islands)

Write your USCIS "A"- number here:
A

A. How many total days did you spend outside of the United States during the past five years? ______ days

B. How many trips of 24 hours or more have you taken outside of the United States during the past five years? ______ trips

C. List below all the trips of 24 hours or more that you have taken outside of the United States since becoming a Lawful Permanent Resident. Begin with your most recent trip. If you need more space, use a separate sheet(s) of paper.

Date You Left the United States *(mm/dd/yyyy)*	Date You Returned to the United States *(mm/dd/yyyy)*	Did Trip Last Six Months or More?	Countries to Which You Traveled	Total Days Out of the United States
		☐ Yes ☐ No		
		☐ Yes ☐ No		
		☐ Yes ☐ No		
		☐ Yes ☐ No		
		☐ Yes ☐ No		
		☐ Yes ☐ No		
		☐ Yes ☐ No		
		☐ Yes ☐ No		
		☐ Yes ☐ No		
		☐ Yes ☐ No		

Part 8. Information About Your Marital History.

A. How many times have you been married (including annulled marriages)? ______ If you have **never** been married, go to Part 9.

B. If you are now married, give the following information about your spouse:

1. Spouse's Family Name *(Last Name)* Given Name *(First Name)* Full Middle Name *(If applicable)*

2. Date of Birth *(mm/dd/yyyy)* 3. Date of Marriage *(mm/dd/yyyy)* 4. Spouse's U.S. Social Security #

5. Home Address - Street Number and Name Apartment Number

City State Zip Code

Part 8. Information About Your Marital History. ***(Continued)***

Write your USCIS "A"- number here:
A

C. Is your spouse a U.S. citizen? ☐ Yes ☐ No

D. If your spouse is a U.S. citizen, give the following information:

1. When did your spouse become a U.S. citizen? ☐ At Birth ☐ Other

If "Other," give the following information:

2. Date your spouse became a U.S. citizen

3. Place your spouse became a U.S. citizen *(Please see Instructions)*

City and State

E. If your spouse is **not** a U.S. citizen, give the following information :

1. Spouse's Country of Citizenship

2. Spouse's USCIS "A"- Number *(If applicable)*

A

3. Spouse's Immigration Status

☐ Lawful Permanent Resident ☐ Other ______

F. If you were married before, provide the following information about your prior spouse. If you have more than one previous marriage, use a separate sheet(s) of paper to provide the information requested in Questions 1-5 below.

1. Prior Spouse's Family Name *(Last Name)* Given Name *(First Name)* Full Middle Name *(If applicable)*

2. Prior Spouse's Immigration Status

☐ U.S. Citizen

☐ Lawful Permanent Resident

☐ Other ______

3. Date of Marriage *(mm/dd/yyyy)*

4. Date Marriage Ended *(mm/dd/yyyy)*

5. How Marriage Ended

☐ Divorce ☐ Spouse Died ☐ Other ______

G. How many times has your current spouse been married (including annulled marriages)?

If your spouse has **ever** been married before, give the following information about **your spouse's** prior marriage.
If your spouse has more than one previous marriage, use a separate sheet(s) of paper to provide the information requested in Questions 1 - 5 below.

1. Prior Spouse's Family Name *(Last Name)* Given Name *(First Name)* Full Middle Name *(If applicable)*

2. Prior Spouse's Immigration Status

☐ U.S. Citizen

☐ Lawful Permanent Resident

☐ Other ______

3. Date of Marriage *(mm/dd/yyyy)*

4. Date Marriage Ended *(mm/dd/yyyy)*

5. How Marriage Ended

☐ Divorce ☐ Spouse Died ☐ Other ______

Part 9. Information About Your Children.

Write your USCIS "A"- number here:
A

A. How many sons and daughters have you had? For more information on which sons and daughters you should include and how to complete this section, see the Instructions.

B. Provide the following information about all of your sons and daughters. If you need more space, use a separate sheet(s) of paper.

Full Name of Son or Daughter	Date of Birth *(mm/dd/yyyy)*	USCIS "A"- number *(if child has one)*	Country of Birth	Current Address *(Street, City, State and Country)*
		A		
		A		
		A		
		A		
		A		
		A		
		A		
		A		

Add Children

Go to continuation page

Part 10. Additional Questions.

Please answer Questions 1 through 14. If you answer "Yes" to any of these questions, include a written explanation with this form. Your written explanation should (1) explain why your answer was "Yes" and (2) provide any additional information that helps to explain your answer.

A. General Questions.

1. Have you **ever** claimed to be a U.S. citizen *(in writing or any other way)*? ☐ Yes ☐ No
2. Have you **ever** registered to vote in any Federal, state or local election in the United States? ☐ Yes ☐ No
3. Have you **ever** voted in any Federal, state or local election in the United States? ☐ Yes ☐ No
4. Since becoming a Lawful Permanent Resident, have you **ever** failed to file a required Federal state or local tax return? ☐ Yes ☐ No
5. Do you owe any Federal, state or local taxes that are overdue? ☐ Yes ☐ No
6. Do you have any title of nobility in any foreign country? ☐ Yes ☐ No
7. Have you ever been declared legally incompetent or been confined to a mental institution within the last five years? ☐ Yes ☐ No

Part 10. Additional Questions. (Continued)

Write your USCIS "A"- number here:
A

B. Affiliations.

8. a Have you **ever** been a member of or associated with any organization, association, fund foundation, party, club, society or similar group in the United States or in any other place? ☐ Yes ☐ No

b. If you answered "Yes," list the name of each group below. If you need more space, attach the names of the other group(s) on a separate sheet(s) of paper.

Name of Group	Name of Group
1.	6.
2.	7.
3.	8.
4.	9.
5.	10.

9. Have you **ever** been a member of or in any way associated *(either directly or indirectly)* with:

a. The Communist Party? ☐ Yes ☐ No

b. Any other totalitarian party? ☐ Yes ☐ No

c. A terrorist organization? ☐ Yes ☐ No

10. Have you **ever** advocated *(either directly or indirectly)* the overthrow of any government by force or violence? ☐ Yes ☐ No

11. Have you **ever** persecuted *(either directly or indirectly)* any person because of race, religion, national origin, membership in a particular social group or political opinion? ☐ Yes ☐ No

12. Between March 23, 1933 and May 8, 1945, did you work for or associate in any way *(either directly or indirectly)* with:

a. The Nazi government of Germany? ☐ Yes ☐ No

b. Any government in any area (1) occupied by, (2) allied with, or (3) established with the help of the Nazi government of Germany? ☐ Yes ☐ No

c. Any German, Nazi, or S.S. military unit, paramilitary unit, self-defense unit, vigilante unit, citizen unit, police unit, government agency or office, extermination camp, concentration camp, prisoner of war camp, prison, labor camp or transit camp? ☐ Yes ☐ No

C. Continuous Residence.

Since becoming a Lawful Permanent Resident of the United States:

13. Have you **ever** called yourself a "nonresident" on a Federal, state or local tax return? ☐ Yes ☐ No

14. Have you **ever** failed to file a Federal, state or local tax return because you considered yourself to be a "nonresident"? ☐ Yes ☐ No

Part 10. Additional Questions. (Continued)

Write your USCIS "A"- number here:
A

D. Good Moral Character.

For the purposes of this application, you must answer "Yes" to the following questions, if applicable, even if your records were sealed or otherwise cleared or if anyone, including a judge, law enforcement officer or attorney, told you that you no longer have a record.

15. Have you **ever** committed a crime or offense for which you were **not** arrested? ☐ Yes ☐ No

16. Have you **ever** been arrested, cited or detained by any law enforcement officer (including USCIS or former INS and military officers) for any reason? ☐ Yes ☐ No

17. Have you **ever** been charged with committing any crime or offense? ☐ Yes ☐ No

18. Have you **ever** been convicted of a crime or offense? ☐ Yes ☐ No

19. Have you **ever** been placed in an alternative sentencing or a rehabilitative program (for example: diversion, deferred prosecution, withheld adjudication, deferred adjudication)? ☐ Yes ☐ No

20. Have you **ever** received a suspended sentence, been placed on probation or been paroled? ☐ Yes ☐ No

21. Have you **ever** been in jail or prison? ☐ Yes ☐ No

If you answered "Yes" to any of Questions 15 through 21, complete the following table. If you need more space, use a separate sheet (s) of paper to give the same information.

Why were you arrested, cited, detained or charged?	Date arrested, cited, detained or charged? *(mm/dd/yyyy)*	Where were you arrested, cited, detained or charged? *(City, State, Country)*	Outcome or disposition of the arrest, citation, detention or charge *(No charges filed, charges dismissed, jail, probation, etc.)*

Answer Questions 22 through 33. If you answer "Yes" to any of these questions, attach (1) your written explanation why your answer was "Yes" and (2) any additional information or documentation that helps explain your answer.

22. Have you **ever:**

a. Been a habitual drunkard? ☐ Yes ☐ No

b. Been a prostitute, or procured anyone for prostitution? ☐ Yes ☐ No

c. Sold or smuggled controlled substances, illegal drugs or narcotics? ☐ Yes ☐ No

d. Been married to more than one person at the same time? ☐ Yes ☐ No

e. Helped anyone enter or try to enter the United States illegally? ☐ Yes ☐ No

f. Gambled illegally or received income from illegal gambling? ☐ Yes ☐ No

g. Failed to support your dependents or to pay alimony? ☐ Yes ☐ No

23. Have you **ever** given false or misleading information to any U.S. government official while applying for any immigration benefit or to prevent deportation, exclusion or removal? ☐ Yes ☐ No

24. Have you **ever** lied to any U.S. government official to gain entry or admission into the United States? ☐ Yes ☐ No

Part 10. Additional Questions. (Continued)

Write your USCIS "A"- number here:
A

E. Removal, Exclusion and Deportation Proceedings.

25. Are removal, exclusion, rescission or deportation proceedings pending against you? ☐ Yes ☐ No

26. Have you **ever** been removed, excluded or deported from the United States? ☐ Yes ☐ No

27. Have you **ever** been ordered to be removed, excluded or deported from the United States? ☐ Yes ☐ No

28. Have you **ever** applied for any kind of relief from removal, exclusion or deportation? ☐ Yes ☐ No

F. Military Service.

29. Have you **ever** served in the U.S. Armed Forces? ☐ Yes ☐ No

30. Have you **ever** left the United States to avoid being drafted into the U.S. Armed Forces? ☐ Yes ☐ No

31. Have you **ever** applied for any kind of exemption from military service in the U.S. Armed Forces? ☐ Yes ☐ No

32. Have you **ever** deserted from the U.S. Armed Forces? ☐ Yes ☐ No

G. Selective Service Registration.

33. Are you a male who lived in the United States at any time between your 18th and 26th birthdays in any status except as a lawful nonimmigrant? ☐ Yes ☐ No

If you answered "NO," go on to question 34.

If you answered "YES," provide the information below.

If you answered "YES," but you did not register with the Selective Service System and are still under 26 years of age, you must register before you apply for naturalization, so that you can complete the information below:

Date Registered (mm/dd/yyyy) ______ Selective Service Number ______

If you answered "YES," but you did not register with the Selective Service and you are now 26 years old or older, attach a statement explaining why you did not register.

H. Oath Requirements. *(See Part 14 for the Text of the Oath)*

Answer Questions 34 through 39. If you answer "No" to any of these questions, attach (1) your written explanation why the answer was "No" and (2) any additional information or documentation that helps to explain your answer.

34. Do you support the Constitution and form of government of the United States? ☐ Yes ☐ No

35. Do you understand the full Oath of Allegiance to the United States? ☐ Yes ☐ No

36. Are you willing to take the full Oath of Allegiance to the United States? ☐ Yes ☐ No

37. If the law requires it, are you willing to bear arms on behalf of the United States? ☐ Yes ☐ No

38. If the law requires it, are you willing to perform noncombatant services in the U.S. Armed Forces? ☐ Yes ☐ No

39. If the law requires it, are you willing to perform work of national importance under civilian direction? ☐ Yes ☐ No

Part 11. Your Signature.

Write your USCIS "A"- number here:
A

I certify, under penalty of perjury under the laws of the United States of America, that this application, and the evidence submitted with it, are all true and correct. I authorize the release of any information that the USCIS needs to determine my eligibility for naturalization.

Your Signature

Date *(mm/dd/yyyy)*

Part 12. Signature of Person Who Prepared This Application for You. ***(If Applicable)***

I declare under penalty of perjury that I prepared this application at the request of the above person. The answers provided are based on information of which I have personal knowledge and/or were provided to me by the above named person in response to the *exact questions* contained on this form.

Preparer's Printed Name

Preparer's Signature

Date *(mm/dd/yyyy)*

Preparer's Firm or Organization Name *(If applicable)*

Preparer's Daytime Phone Number

Preparer's Address - Street Number and Name

City

State

Zip Code

NOTE: Do not complete Parts 13 and 14 until a USCIS Officer instructs you to do so.

Part 13. Signature at Interview.

I swear (affirm) and certify under penalty of perjury under the laws of the United States of America that I know that the contents of this application for naturalization subscribed by me, including corrections numbered 1 through _____ and the evidence submitted by me numbered pages 1 through _____ , are true and correct to the best of my knowledge and belief.

Subscribed to and sworn to (affirmed) before me

Officer's Printed Name or Stamp

Date *(mm/dd/yyyy)*

Complete Signature of Applicant

Officer's Signature

Part 14. Oath of Allegiance.

If your application is approved, you will be scheduled for a public oath ceremony at which time you will be required to take the following oath of allegiance immediately prior to becoming a naturalized citizen. By signing, you acknowledge your willingness and ability to take this oath:

I hereby declare, on oath, that I absolutely and entirely renounce and abjure all allegiance and fidelity to any foreign prince, potentate, state, or sovereignty, of whom or which I have heretofore been a subject or citizen;

that I will support and defend the Constitution and laws of the United States of America against all enemies, foreign and domestic;

that I will bear true faith and allegiance to the same;

that I will bear arms on behalf of the United States when required by the law;

that I will perform noncombatant service in the Armed Forces of the United States when required by the law;

that I will perform work of national importance under civilian direction when required by the law; and

that I take this obligation freely, without any mental reservation or purpose of evasion; so help me God.

Printed Name of Applicant

Complete Signature of Applicant

OMB No. 1615-0057; Expires 11/30/06

Department of Homeland Security
U.S. Citizenship and Immigration Services

N-600, Application for Certificate of Citizenship

Instructions

What Is the Purpose of This Form?

This Form N-600 is an application for a Certificate of Citizenship.

To request forms from the U.S. Citizenship and Immigration Services (USCIS), call our toll-free forms line at **1-800-870-3676**. You may also get USCIS forms and information about immigration laws and regulations by calling our **National Customer Service Center** at **1-800-375-5283** or visiting our internet website at **http://www.uscis.gov.**

NOTE: USCIS is comprised of offices of the former Immigration and Naturalization (INS).

Who Should Use This Form?

You may use this form if you claim U.S. citizenship either by action of law while residing in the United States or by having been born outside the United States to U.S. citizen parent(s).

If you are the biological or adopted child of a U.S. citizen, you were born outside the United States and you are claiming citizenship by action of law, you automatically become a U.S. citizen if:

- You have at least one parent who is a U.S. citizen, whether by birth or naturalization; **and**
- You regularly reside in the United States in the legal and physical custody of your U.S. citizen parent; **and**
- You have been lawfully admitted for permanent residence (**NOTE:** If you entered the United States as an adopted child, you must have been admitted as an IR-3 (child adopted outside the United States). If you entered as an IR-4 (child coming to the United States to be adopted), a final adoption must take place for this section of law to apply to you.); **and**
- You have not yet reached your 18th birthday; **and**
- You are a biological child, you were legitimate or you were legitimated while in the legal custody of your legitimating parent(s) prior to reaching your 16th birthday; **or**
- You are a biological child born out of wedlock and you have not been legitimated and your **mother** naturalizes as a U.S. citizen.

NOTE: If you are now over the age of 18 years but all of the above conditions applied to you before your 18th birthday **and** you were under the age of 18 on February 27, 2001 (the date the law took effect), you may file this form to obtain a certificate of citizenship.

If you were under the age of 18 on February 27, 2001, but not all of the conditions noted above were met prior to your 18th birthday, you must qualify for U.S. citizenship in your own right.

You may also file for a certificate of citizenship if all of the following actions occurred before your 18th birthday and prior to February 27, 2001:

- You regularly resided in the United States after admission as a lawful permanent resident; **and**
- Both of your parents, the parent having legal and physical custody of you or your sole surviving parent naturalized as a U.S. citizen.

If you are the biological child of a U.S. citizen, you were born outside the United States and you are claiming citizenship by having been born to U.S. citizen parent(s), you automatically become a U.S. citizen at birth if:

- You were born to two U.S. citizen parents and at least one of your parents had a residence in the United States or one if its outlying possessions. This residence had to have taken place prior to your birth; **or**
- You were born to parents, one of whom is an alien and the other a U.S. citizen who, prior to your birth, had been physically present in the United States or one of its outlying possessions for a period or periods totaling not less than five years, at least two of which were after the age of 14 years.

NOTE: To determine if you were born a U.S. citizen, USCIS must look at the law that was in effect at the time of your birth. The current law was enacted on November 14, 1986 and was last amended on February 27, 2001. If you were born before November 14, 1986, and believe you may be a U.S. citizen, you should contact USCIS by calling our National Customer Service Center **1-800-375-5283** or visiting our internet website at **http://www.uscis.gov.**

Who Should Not Use This Form?

- Persons who do not have a claim to citizenship either at the time of birth or by action of law.
- Stepchildren.
- Children who are not legitimate or who were not legitimated prior to their 16th birthday. (Except for children who were born abroad to an eligible U.S. citizen mother or eligible children who became citizens through the naturalization of their mother.)

- U.S. citizen parents of children who regularly reside outside the United States. They should use Form N-600K, Application for Citizenship and Issuance of Certificate Under Section 322.

When May This Form Be Filed?

Any person who was born a U.S. citizen outside the United States or who fulfilled the requirements for becoming a U.S. citizen prior to their 18th birthday may file this form at any time during his or her lifetime.

Who May File This Form?

This Form N-600 may be filed by any person claiming to have acquired (at birth) or derived (after birth) U.S. citizenship through a U.S. citizen parent.

In the case of minor adopted or biological children (under 18 years) qualifying for citizenship under section 320 of the Immigration and Nationality Act (INA), the application must be filed by the U.S. citizen parent or legal guardian with legal and physical custody of the child.

In the case of an adult applicant with a disability, an immediate relative or legal guardian may file the application.

What Is the Fee ?

The fee for this Form N-600 is **$255.00**, except for U.S. citizen parents requesting a Certificate of Citizenship for an adopted chid.

For U.S. citizen parents filing on behalf of an adopted minor child under section 320 of the INA (checking **Part 2, Box C on the Form**), the fee for the Form N-600 is **$215.00**.

The fee must be paid at the time of filing the application. The fee is not refundable, even if the application is subsequently withdrawn.

Use the following guidelines when you prepare your check or money order:

- The check or money order must be drawn on a bank or other financial institution located in the United States and must be payable in U.S. currency. **Do not mail cash**.
- Make the check or money order payable to the **Department of Homeland Security**, unless:

  -- You live in Guam and are filing your application there, make it payable to the Treasurer, Guam; or

  -- You live in the U.S. Virgin Islands and are filing your application there, make it payable to the Commissioner of Finance of the Virgin Islands.

Do not use the initials "USDHS" or "DHS" on your check or money order.

How to Check If the Fees Are Correct.

The fees on this form are current as of the edition date appearing in the lower right corner of this page. However, because USCIS fees change periodically, you can verify if the fees are correct by following one of the steps below:

- Visit our website at **www.uscis.gov** and scroll down to "Forms and E-Filing" to check the appropriate fees, or
- Review the Fee Schedule included in your form package, if you called us to request the form, or
- Telephone our National Customer Service Center at **1-800-375-5283** and ask for the fee information.

Where Do You Send the Application?

The completed Form N-600 and accompanying documentation must be filed with the appropriate USCIS office in the United States with jurisdiction over your place of residence. Form N-600 may be filed at any USCIS office or suboffice in the United States or its outlying possessions, including San Juan, Puerto Rico; the U.S. Virgin Islands and Guam. The address of each USCIS office can be found at: **http://www.uscis.gov/graphics/fieldoffices/alphaa.htm.**

What Documents Must You Submit?

You do not need to submit documents that were provided in connection with:

- An application for an immigrant visa and retained by the American embassy or consulate for inclusion in the immigrant visa package, or
- An immigrant petition or application and included in a USCIS administrative file. You should indicate that you want USCIS to rely on such documents and identify the administrative file(s) by name and A-number. USCIS will only request the required documentation again if necessary.

The following is a list of documents that must be submitted with the Form N-600, if the USCIS does not already have the document or if the you would rather resubmit the document than wait for the retrieval of the USCIS file. Unless specifically noted otherwise, you must submit each of the documents listed below for yourself and/or your child and the U.S. citizen parent(s) through whom you are claiming U.S. citizenship.

NOTE: Any document in a foreign language must be accompanied by a translation in English. The translator must certify that he or she is competent to translate and that the translation is true and accurate. For each document needed, you may submit a clear, readable copy or the originals. Do not send an original Certificate of Citizenship or Certificate of Naturalization. USCIS may request that you present original documents at the interview.

- **Photographs** - *(Only required of the person to whom the Certificate of Citizenship will be issued).*

  You must include three identical, natural color passport-style photographs of you alone, taken within 30 days of submission of the application. The photographs must be clear, showing a full frontal view of your face. The photos should be unglazed and have a white or off-white background and be unmounted, glossy and unretouched. The photos should be taken without any headdress (unless the applicant is wearing a headdress as required by a religious order of which he or she is a member). **Do not submit digital photographs.**

  The photos should be 2 x 2 inches in size, with the distance from the top of the head to just below the chin about 1and 3/8 inches.

  The photographs must be on thin paper with a light background and not mounted in any way.

  The photographs must not be signed. Using a soft lead pencil, print your name (or if a U.S. citizen parent applying on behalf of a minor child, the child's name) and Alien Registration Number (if applicable) in the center of the back of each photograph.

- **Birth certificate or record** - A certified birth certificate or record issued by a civil authority in the country of birth.
- **Marriage certificate(s)** - Certified marriage certificate(s) issued by a civil authority in the state or country of marriage.
- **Documents showing the termination of a marriage** - Examples include a divorce decree, death certificate or annulment document.
- **Proof of U.S. citizenship** - Examples of this are birth certificates showing birth in the United States; an N-550, Certificate of Naturalization; an N-560, Certificate of Citizenship; an FS-240, Report of Birth Abroad of United States Citizen; or a valid unexpired U.S passport.
- **Proof of status as National of United States** - *(Only required for applicants claiming U.S. citizenship through a national of the United States, such as a person born in American Samoa or Swains Islands.*

  A person is born a citizen if born outside of the United States and its outlying possessions of parents, one of whom is a citizen of the United States who has been physically present in the United States or one of its outlying possessions for a continuous period of one year prior to the birth of such person, and the other of whom is a national but not a citizen of the United States. If the non-citizen parent is an alien but not a national, the citizen parent would need to meet the physical presence requirement, depending on the date of birth, prior to the child's birth.)

- **Proof of legitimation** - *(Only required for applicants who were born out of wedlock).*

  Documents must establish legitimation according to the laws of the child's residence or domicile or father's residence or domicile (if applicable). Legitimation for INA benefits requires that the child be in the legal custody of the legitimating parent(s) at the time of legitimation.

- **Proof of legal custody** - *(Only required for applicants whose U.S. citizen parent(s) divorced and/or separated and for applicants who are adopted or legitimated).*
- **Copy of Permanent Resident Card or other evidence of Lawful Permanent Resident status** - *(Only required for applicants claiming U.S. citizenship through alien parent(s) who naturalized or claiming automatic acquisition of U.S. citizenship while under the age of 18 under section 320 of INA.)*
- **Proof of required residence or physical presence in the United States** - Any document that proves the U.S citizen parent(s)' residence or physical presence in the United States. This proof may include but is not limited to the following:
  - -- School, employment, military records;
  - -- Deeds, mortgages, leases showing residence;
  - -- Attestations by churches, unions or other organizations;
  - -- U.S. Social Security quarterly reports;
  - -- Affidavits of third parties having knowledge of the residence and physical presence.
- **Copy of full, final adoption decree** - *(Only required for adopted applicants).*
- **Evidence of all legal name changes.**

What If a Document Is Not Available?

If it is not possible to obtain any one of the above-required documents, you must establish why the evidence is not available. You may be required to submit an original written statement from the relevant government or other authority explaining the reason for the unavailability of the document(s).

- **Baptismal certificate:** A certificate under the seal of the church where the baptism occurred, showing the date and place of the child's birth, date of baptism, the names of the godparents, if known.
- **Church records:** A certificate under the church seal issued within two months of birth.
- **School record:** A letter from authorities of the school attended (preferably the first school), showing the date of admission to the school, the child's date of birth or age at that time, place of birth, and the names and places of birth of parents, if shown in the school records.
- **Census records:** State or federal census records showing the name(s) and place(s) of birth, and the date(s) of birth or age(s) of the person(s) listed.
- **Affidavits:** Written statements sworn (or affirmed) to by two persons who have personal knowledge of the claimed event (i.e., the date and place of a birth, marriage or death). The persons may be relatives and need not be citizens of the United States. Each affidavit should contain the following information regarding the person making the affidavit: his or her full name and address; date and place of birth; relationship to the applicant, if any; full information concerning the event; and complete details concerning how he or she acquired knowledge of the event.

How Do You Complete the Application?

- Please print clearly in black ink or type your answers using CAPITAL letters in each box.
- **If you are the applicant or you are filing for a child and you or the child have an A-number, write that A-number in the place indicated on the top right hand corner of the first page.** If there is no A-number, leave this blank. The A-number can be found on you or the child's Permanent Resident Card, if applicable, or on DHS issued travel documents or letters.
- If the A-number has fewer than nine numbers, place enough zeros before the first number to make a *total of nine numbers* on the application. For example, A 12 345 678 as A 012 345 678.
- Individuals can become citizens under several very different sections of law and can use this form to obtain a certificate of citizenship. You only need to complete those sections of the form that relate to you or the child's eligibility.
- If a question does not apply to you, write N/A (Not Applicable) in the space provided.
- If you need extra space to answer any item:
  - -- Attach a separate sheet of paper (or more sheets if needed);
  - -- Write your name, your "A" number (if any) and "N-600" on the top right corner of the sheet; and
  - -- Write the number of each question for which you are providing additional information.

Step-by-Step Instructions.

This form is divided into ten parts. The information below will help you fill out the form.

Part 1. Information About Your Child.

The person seeking the Certificate of Citizenship should complete information in this section.

NOTE: If you are a U.S. citizen parent applying for a certificate of citizenship on behalf of your minor biological or adopted child, provide information relating to your **minor child**.

A. Current legal name - Your current legal name is the name on the birth certificate, unless it has been changed after birth by a legal action such as a marriage, adoption or court order.

B. Name exactly as it appears on your Permanent Resident Card (if different from above) - Write your name exactly as it appears on the card, even if it is misspelled.

C. Other names used since birth - If you have ever used any other names since birth, write them in this section. If you need more space, use a separate sheet of paper.

D. U.S. Social Security number - Print your U.S. Social Security number. If the child does not have a U.S. Social Security number, write "N/A" in the space provided.

E. Date of birth - Use eight numbers to show your date of birth (example: May 1, 1979, should be written 05/01/1979).

F. Country of birth - Give the name of the country where you were born. Write the name of the country even if it no longer exists. If the name of the country has changed, write the name of the country as it was at the time of your birth.

G. Country of prior nationality - If you were a citizen of a different country before becoming a U. S. citizen, write the name of the country of your prior nationality.

- If the country no longer exists and/or the child is stateless, write the name of the country where the child was last a citizen or national.
- If you were a citizen or national of more than one country, write the name of the foreign country that issued your last passport.

H. Gender - Indicate whether male or female.

I. Height - Give your height in feet and inches.

Part 2. Information About Your Eligibility.

Check the box in **Section A** that best indicates why you are eligible for a Certificate of Citizenship.

If you are a U.S. citizen parent applying for a Certificate of Citizenship on behalf of a minor child, check the box in either **Section B or C,** indicating whether you are applying for a biological or adopted child.

If the basis for your eligibility is not described in any of the categories, check **Box D "Other"** and briefly write the basis for your application on the lines provided.

Part 3. Additional Information About You.

Complete information must be provided about the person seeking a Certificate of Citizenship.

NOTE: If you are a U.S. citizen parent applying for a Certificate of Citizenship on behalf of your minor biological or adopted child, submit information relating to your **minor child**.

A. Home address - Give the address where you now live. Do not put post office (P.O.) box numbers here.

B. Mailing address - If your mailing address is the same as the home address, write "same." If the mailing address is different from your home address, write it in this part. Provide "Care Of" information if applicable.

C. Telephone numbers (optional) - Telephone numbers and e-mail addresses allow USCIS to contact you more quickly about the application. If you are hearing impaired and use a TTY telephone connection, please indicate this by writing "(TTY)" after the telephone number.

D. Current marital status - Check the marital status you have on the date you are filing this application. If you are currently not married but had a prior marriage that was annulled (declared by a court to be invalid), check "Other" and provide an explanation.

E. Information about your child's entry into the United States and current immigration status-

1. Provide information about where you entered the United States and what name you used when you entered.
2. Provide information about what documents you presented to enter the United States. Provide your passport number and date of issuance, if known.
3. Provide information about your immigration status on entry into the United States.
4. If you adjusted to lawful permanent resident status while in the United States, provide the date you became a lawful permanent resident and place where such status was granted.

F. Previous application for Certificate of Citizenship or U.S. passport - If you previously applied for a Certificate of Citizenship or a U.S. passport (or you are a U.S. citizen parent who previously applied for a Certificate of Citizenship or U.S. passport for your minor child), indicate on a separate piece of paper what happened with the application and whether a Certificate of Citizenship or U.S. passport was or was not issued.

G. Information on adoption - If you were adopted, provide information as to the place and date of the adoption.

H. Re-adoption in the United States - Children who are admitted to the United States under section 101 (b)(1)(F) of the INA as IR-4s (orphans coming to the United States to be adopted by U.S. citizen parent(s)) do not automatically acquire citizenship on entry, even though admitted as lawful permanent residents. Children admitted as IR-4s must have been finally adopted in the United States or had the foreign adoption recognized by the state where the child is permanently residing. If you or your child had to be re-adopted in the United States, provide the information requested. If the appropriate authority in your current place of residence recognizes the validity of a full, final foreign adoption, submit evidence of this.

I. Marital status of parents at time of birth (or adoption) - Indicate whether the child's parents were married to each other at the time of the child's birth. If the child was born out-of- wedlock, indicate "No," even if the parents subsequently married. If the child was adopted, indicate whether the adoptive parents were married to each other at the time of the adoption.

If you are a U.S. citizen parent applying on behalf of a minor biological or adopted child, indicate whether you were married to the child's natural (or adoptive mother) at the time of your minor child's birth (or adoption). If your minor child was born out of wedlock, indicate "No," even if you subsequently married the child's other parent.

J. Absences from the United States - Provide the requested information for every trip that you have taken since you first arrived in the United States. Begin with the most recent trip. This information is needed only for persons born before October 10, 1952, who are claiming U. S. citizenship at the time of birth.

Part 4. Information About the U.S. Citizen Father (or Adoptive Father).

Information in this section should be completed if you are claiming citizenship through a U.S. citizen father (or adoptive father). If you are claiming citizenship solely through a U.S. citizen mother (or adoptive mother), **see Part 5.**

NOTE: If you are a U.S. citizen father (or adoptive father) applying for a certificate of citizenship on behalf of your minor child, where information is requested about the U.S. citizen, **provide information about YOURSELF in the sections noted.**

A. Current legal name - Give the U.S. citizen father's current legal name. It is the name on the birth certificate unless it was changed after birth by a legal action (marriage, adoption or court order).

B. Date of birth - Use eight numbers to show the U.S. citizen father's date of birth (example: May 1, 1969, should be written 05/01/1969).

C. Country of birth - Give the name of the country where the U.S. citizen father was born. Write the name of the country even if it no longer exists. If the name of the country has changed, write the name of the country as it was at the time of the U. S. citizen father's birth.

D. Country of nationality - Write the name of the country where the U.S. citizen father is currently a citizen or national. If the country no longer exists and/or you are stateless, write the name of the country where the U.S. citizen father was last a citizen or national.

E. Home address - Give the address where the U.S. citizen father now lives. Do not put post office (P. O.) box numbers here. If deceased, write "deceased" and provide the date of death.

F. U. S. citizenship - Indicate how the U.S. citizen father became a U.S. citizen. Provide all the requested information.

G. Loss of U. S. citizenship - Indicate whether the U. S. citizen father ever lost his U.S. citizenship. Provide this information even if the U.S. citizen father regained citizenship at a later date.

H. Residence and/or physical presence - Only applicants born outside the United States who are claiming to have been born United States citizens are required to provide all the dates when their U. S. citizen father was in the United States. Dates should include all time immediately after birth as well as after the age of 14 years and older.

I. Marital history-

1. Write the number of times the U.S. citizen father was married. Include any annulled marriages. If he was married more than one time to the same spouse, count each time as a separate marriage.

2. If now married, provide information about the U.S. citizen father's current spouse. Check the appropriate box to indicate his immigration status.

3. Indicate whether the U.S. citizen father's current spouse is also your parent. If "No," you will be asked to provide information about your father's previous spouse or spouses.

Part 5. Information About Your U.S. Citizen Mother (or Adoptive Mother).

Information in this section should be completed if you are claiming citizenship through a U.S. citizen mother (or adoptive mother). If you are claiming citizenship solely through a U.S. citizen father (or adoptive father), **see Part 4**.

NOTE: If you are a U.S. citizen mother (or adoptive mother) applying on behalf of your minor child, where information is requested about "the U.S. citizen mother," **provide information about YOURSELF in the sections noted**.

A. Current legal name - Give current legal name of the U.S. citizen mother. It is the name on her birth certificate unless it was changed after birth by a legal action such as a marriage, adoption or court order.

B. Date of birth - Use eight numbers to show the U.S. citizen mother's date of birth (example: May 1, 1969, should be written 05/01/1969).

C. Country of birth - Give the name of the country where the U.S. citizen mother was born. Write the name of the country even if it no longer exists. If the name of the country has changed, write the name of the country as it was at the time of the U.S. citizen mother's birth.

D. Country of nationality - Write the name of the country where the U.S. citizen mother is currently a citizen or national. If the country no longer exists and/or you are stateless, write the name of the country where the U.S. citizen mother was last a citizen or national.

E. Home address - Give the address where the U.S. citizen mother now lives. Do not put post office (P. O.) box numbers here. If the U.S. citizen mother is deceased, write "deceased" and provide the date of death.

F. U. S. citizenship - Indicate how the U.S. citizen mother became a U.S. citizen. Provide all the requested information.

G. Loss of U. S. citizenship - Indicate whether the U. S. citizen mother ever lost her U.S. citizenship. Provide this information even if the U.S. citizen mother regained citizenship at a later date.

H. Residence and/or physical presence - Only applicants who are claiming to have been born U. S. citizens outside of the United States are required to provide all the dates when the U.S. citizen mother was in the United States. Dates should include all time immediately after birth as well as after the age of 14 years and older.

I. Marital history-

1. Write the number of times the U.S. citizen mother was married. Include any annulled marriages. If she was married more than one time to the same spouse, count each time as a separate marriage.

2. If now married, provide information about the U.S. citizen mother's current spouse. Check the appropriate box to indicate his immigration status.

3. Indicate whether the U.S. citizen mother's current spouse is also your parent. If "No," you will be asked to provide information about your mother's previous spouse or spouses.

Part 6. Information About Military Service of U.S. Citizen Parent -- *(Applicable only for applications filed under section 301(g)*

Provide requested information if either U.S. citizen parent served in the U.S. Armed Forces. Also indicate whether he or she was honorably discharged from service.

Part 7. Your Signature.

If you are over the age of 18 years and you are filing this application for yourself, you must sign and date the application. If you do not sign the application, USCIS will return the application to you.

If you are under the age of 18 years and your U.S. citizen parent or legal guardian is filing the application on your behalf, your U.S. citizen parent or legal guardian must sign and date the application. If your U. S. citizen parent or legal guardian does not sign the application, the application will be returned.

Part 8. Signature of Person Preparing Form, If Other Than Applicant.

If you do not fill out this Form N-600, the preparer must also sign, date and give his or her address. If the preparer is a business or organization, it is name must be included on the form.

Part 9. Affidavit.

Do not complete this part.

Part 10. Officer Report and Recommendation.

Do not complete this part.

Penalties.

USCIS wants to make sure that you receive the requested immigration benefit if you are eligible for it. To do this, we may ask for more evidence, interview you, and/or conduct an investigation. **If you give us false documents, misrepresent facts or otherwise engage in fraud, USCIS will take appropriate action.** This means we may not only deny your application, you may lose current and future immigration benefits. You may also face penalties, including criminal and/or civil prosecution leading to fines and/or imprisonment.

Privacy Act Notice.

USCIS will use the information and evidence requested on Form N-600 to determine your eligibility for the requested immigration benefit. We may provide information from your application to other government agencies.

Use InfoPass for Appointments.

As an alternative to waiting in line for assistance at your local USCIS office, you can now schedule an appointment through our internet-based system, **InfoPass**. To access the system, visit our website at **www.uscis.gov**. Use the **InfoPass** appointment scheduler and follow the screen prompts to set up your appointment. **InfoPass** generates an electronic appointment notice that appears on the screen. Print the notice and take it with you to your appointment. The notice gives the time and date of your appointment, along with the address of the USCIS office.

Paperwork Reduction Act Notice.

You are not required to respond to this form unless it displays a currently valid OMB control number. USCIS strives to create forms and instructions that are accurate, easy to understand and impose the least possible burden on you to provide the information and evidence needed to process your application.

For this application we estimate that it takes 15 minutes to learn about the law, form and process. The time it takes to complete the form is estimated at 20 minutes and 1 hour to assemble and file the application, including average travel time. The total preparation time is estimated at 1 hour and 35 minutes. If you have comments about this estimate or suggestions for simplifying this form, write to the: U.S. Citizenship and Immigration Services, Regulatory Management Division, 111 Massachusetts Avenue N.W.,Washington, D.C. 20529; OMB No. 1615-0057.

Do not mail your completed application to this address.

OMB No. 1615-0057; Expires 10/31/05
You may continue to use this form after expiration date.

Department of Homeland Security
U.S. Citizenship and Immigration Services

N-600, Application for Certificate of Citizenship

Print clearly or type your answers, using CAPITAL letters in black ink. Failure to print clearly may delay processing of your application.

Part I. Information About You.

(Provide information about yourself, if you are a person applying for the Certificate of Citizenship. If you are a U.S. citizen parent applying for a Certificate of Citizenship for your minor child, ***provide information about your child).***

A. Current legal name

Family Name *(Last Name)*

Given Name *(First Name)* | Full Middle Name *(If applicable)*

B. Name exactly as it appears on your Permanent Resident Card *(If applicable).*

Family Name *(Last Name)*

Given Name *(First Name)* | Full Middle Name *(If applicable)*

C. Other names used since birth

Family Name *(Last Name)*	Given Name *(First Name)*	Middle Name *(If applicable)*

D. U.S. Social Security # *(If applicable)*

E. Date of Birth *(mm/dd/yyyy)*

F. Country of Birth

G. Country of Prior Nationality

H. Gender

☐ Male ☐ Female

I. Height

Part 2. Information About Your Eligibility. *(Check only one).*

A. I am claiming U.S. citizenship through:

☐ A U.S. citizen father or a U.S. citizen mother.

☐ Both U.S. citizen parents.

☐ A U.S. citizen adoptive parent(s).

☐ An alien parent(s) who naturalized.

B. ☐ **I am a U.S. citizen parent applying for a certificate of citizenship on behalf of my minor (under 18 years) BIOLOGICAL child.**

C. ☐ **I am a U.S. citizen parent applying for a certificate of citizenship on behalf of my minor (less than 18 years) ADOPTED child.**

D. ☐ **Other** *(Please explain fully)* ____________________

____

If your child has an "A" Number, write it here:

A

For USCIS Use Only

Returned	Receipt
Date	
Date	
Resubmitted	
Date	
Date	
Reloc Sent	
Date	
Date	
Reloc Rec'd	
Date	
Date	

Remarks

Action Block

To Be Completed by
☐ ***Attorney or Representative,*** if any.
Fill in box if G-28 is attached to represent the applicant.

ATTY State License #

Part 3. Additional Information About You. *(Provide additional information about **yourself**, if you are the person applying for the Certificate of Citizenship. If you are a U.S. citizen parent applying for a Certificate of Citizenship for your **minor child**, provide the additional information about your **minor child**).*

A. Home Address - Street Number and Name *(Do not write a P.O. Box in this space)* Apartment Number

City County State/Province Country Zip/Postal Code

B. Mailing Address - Street Number and Name *(If different from home address)* Apartment Number

City County State/Province Country Zip/Postal Code

C. Daytime Phone Number *(If any)* Evening Phone Number *(If any)* E-Mail Address *(If any)*

( ) ( )

D. Marital Status

☐ Single, Never Married ☐ Married ☐ Divorced ☐ Widowed

☐ Marriage Annulled or Other *(Explain)*

E. Information about entry into the United States and current immigration status

1. I arrived in the following manner:

   Port of Entry *(City/State)* Date of Entry *(mm/dd/yyyy)* Exact Name Used at Time of Entry:

2. I used the following travel document to enter:

   ☐ Passport

   ☐ Passport Number Country Issuing Passport Date Passport Issued *(mm/dd/yyyy)*

   Other *(Please Specify Name of Document and Dates of Issuance)*

3. I entered as:

   ☐ An immigrant (lawful permanent resident) using an immigrant visa

   ☐ A nonimmigrant

   ☐ A refugee

   ☐ Other *(Explain)* ____________________

4. I obtained lawful permanent resident status through adjustment of status *(If applicable)*:

   Date you became a Permanent Resident *(mm/dd/yyyy)* USCIS (or former INS) Office where granted adjustment of status

F. Have you previously applied for a certificate of citizenship or U.S. passport? ☐ No ☐ Yes *(Attach Explanation)*

Part 3. Additional Information About You. *(Provide additional information about **yourself**, if you are the person applying for the Certificate of Citizenship. If you are a U.S. citizen parent applying for a Certificate of Citizenship for your **minor child**, provide the additional information about your **minor child**). **Continued.***

G. Were you adopted? ☐ No ☐ Yes *(Please complete the following information):*

Date of Adoption *(mm/dd/yyyy)* | Place of Final Adoption *(City/State or Country)*

Date Legal Custody Began *(mm/dd/yyyy)* | Date Physical Custody Began *(mm/dd/yyyy)*

H. Did you have to be re-adopted in the United States? ☐ No ☐ Yes *(Please complete the following information):*

Date of Final Adoption *(mm/dd/yyyy)* | Place of Final Adoption *(City/State)*

Date Legal Custody Began *(mm/dd/yyyy)* | Date Physical Custody Began *(mm/dd/yyyy)*

I. Were your parents married to each other when you were born (or adopted)? ☐ No ☐ Yes

J. Have you been absent from the United States since you first arrived? *(Only for persons born before October 10, 1952, who are claiming U.S. citizenship at time of birth; otherwise, do not complete this section.)* ☐ No ☐ Yes

If yes, complete the following information about all absences, beginning with your most recent trip. If you need more space, use a separate sheet of paper.

Date You Left the United States *(mm/dd/yyyy)*	Date You Returned to the United States *(mm/dd/yyyy)*	Place of Entry Upon Return to the United States

Part 4. Information About U.S. Citizen Father (or Adoptive Father). *(Complete this section if you are claiming citizenship through a U.S. citizen father. If you are a U.S. citizen father applying for a Certificate of Citizenship on behalf of your minor biological or adopted child, provide information about **yourself** below.)*

A. Current legal name of U.S. citizen father.

Family Name *(Last Name)* | Given Name *(First Name)* | Full Middle Name *(If applicable)*

B. Date of Birth *(mm/dd/yyyy)* | **C. Country of Birth** | **D. Country of Nationality**

E. Home Address - Street Number and Name *(If deceased, so state and enter date of death)* | Apartment Number

City | County | State/Province | Country | Zip/Postal Code

Part 4. Information About U.S. Citizen Father (or Adoptive Father). *(Complete this section if you are claiming citizenship through a U.S. citizen father. If you are a U.S. citizen father applying for a Certificate of Citizenship on behalf of your minor biological or adopted child, provide information about* ***yourself*** *below.)* ***Continued.***

F. U.S. citizen by:

☐ Birth in the United States

☐ Birth abroad to U.S. citizen parent(s)

☐ Acquisition after birth through naturalization of alien parent(s)

☐ Naturalization

Date of Naturalization *(mm/dd/yyyy)* Place of Naturalization *(Name of Court and City/State or USCIS or Former INS Office Location)*

Certificate of Naturalization Number Former "A" Number *(If known)*

G. Has your father ever lost U.S. citizenship or taken any action that would cause loss of U.S. citizenship?

☐ No ☐ Yes *(Provide full explanation on a separate sheet(s) of paper.)*

H. Dates of Residence and/or Physical Presence in the United States *(Complete this only if you are an applicant claiming U.S. citizenship at time of birth abroad)*

Provide the dates your U.S. citizen father resided in or was physically present in the United States. If you need more space, use a separate sheet(s) of paper.

From *(mm/dd/yyyy)*	**To** *(mm/dd/yyyy)*

I. Marital History

1. How many times has your U.S. citizen father been married (including annulled marriages)?

2. Information about U.S. citizen father's **current spouse:**

Family Name *(Last Name)* Given Name *(First Name)* Full Middle Name *(If applicable)*

Date of Birth *(mm/dd/yyyy)* Country of Birth Country of Nationality

Home Address - Street Number and Name Apartment Number

City County State or Province Country Zip/Postal Code

Date of Marriage *(mm/dd/yyyy)* Place of Marriage *(City/State or Country)*

Spouse's Immigration Status:

☐ U.S. Citizen ☐ Lawful Permanent Resident ☐ Other *(Explain)*

3. Is your U.S. citizen father's current spouse also your mother? ☐ No ☐ Yes

Part 5. Information About Your U.S. Citizen Mother (or Adoptive Mother). *(Complete this section if you are claiming citizenship through a U.S. citizen mother (or adoptive mother). If you are a U.S. citizen mother applying for a Certificate of Citizenship on behalf of your minor biological or adopted child, provide information about **yourself** below).*

A. Current legal name of U.S. citizen mother.

Family Name *(Last Name)* | Given Name *(First Name)* | Full Middle Name *(If applicable)*

B. Date of Birth *(mm/dd/yyyy)* | **C. Country of Birth** | **D. Country of Nationality**

E. Home Address - Street Number and Name *(If deceased, so state and enter date of death)* | Apartment Number

City | County | State/Province | Country | Zip/Postal Code

F. U.S. citizen by:

- ☐ Birth in the United States
- ☐ Birth abroad to U.S. citizen parent(s)
- ☐ Acquisition after birth through naturalization of alien parent(s)
- ☐ Naturalization

Date of Naturalization *(mm/dd/yyyy)* | Place of Naturalization *(Name of Court and City/State or USCIS or Former INS Office Location)*

Certificate of Naturalization Number | Former "A" Number *(If known)*

G. Has your mother ever lost U.S. citizenship or taken any action that would cause loss of U.S. citizenship?

☐ No ☐ Yes *(Provide full explanation on a separate sheet(s) of paper.)*

H. Dates of Residence and/or Physical Presence in the United States *(Complete this only if you are an applicant claiming U.S. citizenship at time of birth abroad)*

Provide the dates your U.S. citizen father resided in or was physically present in the United States. If you need more space, use a separate sheet(s) of paper.

From *(mm/dd/yyyy)*	**To** *(mm/dd/yyyy)*

I. Marital History

1. How many times has your U.S. citizen mother been married (including annulled marriages)?
2. Information about U.S. citizen mother's **current spouse:**

Family Name *(Last Name)* | Given Name *(First Name)* | Full Middle Name *(If applicable)*

Date of Birth *(mm/dd/yyyy)* | Country of Birth | Country of Nationality

Part 5. Information About Your U.S. Citizen Mother (or Adoptive Mother). *(Complete this section if you are claiming citizenship through a U.S. citizen mother (or adoptive mother). If you are a U.S. citizen mother applying for a Certificate of Citizenship on behalf of your minor biological or adopted child, provide information about* ***yourself*** *below).* ***Continued.***

2. Information about U.S. citizen mother's **current spouse**: *(Continued.)*

Home Address - Street Number and Name | Apartment Number

City | County | State or Province | Country | Zip/Postal Code

Date of Marriage *(mm/dd/yyyy)* | Place of Marriage *(City/State or Country)*

Spouse's Immigration Status:

☐ U.S. Citizen ☐ Lawful Permanent Resident ☐ Other *(Explain)*

3. Is your U.S. citizen mother's current spouse also your father? ☐ No ☐ Yes

Part 6. Information About Military Service of U. S. Citizen Parent(s). *(Complete this only if you are an applicant claiming U.S. citizenship at time of birth abroad)*

1. Has your U. S. citizen parent(s) served in the armed forces? ☐ No ☐ Yes

2. If "Yes," which parent? ☐ U.S. Citizen Father ☐ U.S. Citizen Mother

3. Dates of Service. *(If time of service fulfills any of required physical presence, submit evidence of service.)*

From *(mm/dd/yyyy)* | To *(mm/dd/yyyy)* | From *(mm/dd/yyyy)* | To *(mm/dd/yyyy)*

4. Type of discharge. ☐ Honorable ☐ Other than Honorable ☐ Dishonorable

Part 7. Signature.

I certify, under penalty of perjury under the laws of the United States, that this application and the evidence submitted with it is all true and correct. I authorize the release of any information from my records, or my minor child's records, that U.S. Citizenship and Immigration Services needs to determine eligibility for the benefit I am seeking.

Applicant's Signature | Printed Name | Date *(mm/dd/yyyy)*

Part 8. Signature of Person Preparing This Form, If Other Than Applicant.

I declare that I prepared this application at the request of the above person. The answers provided are based on information of which I have personal knowledge and/or were provided to me by the above-named person in response to the questions contained on this form.

Preparer's Signature | Preparer's Printed Name | Date *(mm/dd/yyyy)*

Name of Business/Organization *(If applicable)* | Preparer's Daytime Phone Number ( )

Preparer's Address - Street Number and Name

City | County | State | Zip Code

NOTE: Do not complete the following parts unless a USCIS officer instructs you to do so at the interview.

Part 9. Affidavit.

I, the (applicant, parent or legal guardian) ______________________ do swear or affirm, under penalty of perjury laws of the United States, that I know and understand the contents of this application signed by me, and the attached supplementary pages number (___) to (___) inclusive, that the same are true and correct to the best of my knowledge, and that corrections number (___) to (___) were made by me or at my request.

Signature of parent, guardian or applicant

Date *(mm/dd/yyyy)*

Subscribed and sworn or affirmed before me upon examination of the applicant (parent, guardian) on ______________________ at ____.

Signature of Interviewing Officer

Title

Part 10. Officer Report and Recommendation on Application for Certificate of Citizenship.

On the basis of the documents, records and the testimony of persons examined, and the identification upon personal appearance of the underage beneficiary, I find that all the facts and conclusions set forth under oath in this application are ☐ true and correct; that the applicant did ☐ derive or acquire U.S. citizenship on ______________________ *(mm/dd/yyyy)*, through *(mark "X" in appropriate section of law or, if section of law not reflected, insert applicable section of law in "Other" block):* ☐ **section 301 of the INA** ☐ **section 309 of the INA** ☐ **section 320 of the INA** ☐ **section 321 of the INA** ☐ **Other** ______________________

and that (s)he ☐ *has* ☐ *has not* been expatriated since that time. I recommend that this application be ☐ *granted* ☐ *denied* and that ☐ *A or* ☐ *AA* Certificate of Citizenship be issued in the name of ______________________________________.

District Adjudication Officer's Name and Title

District Adjudication Officer's Signature

I do ☐ do not ☐ concur in recommendation of the application.

District Director or Officer-in-Charge Signature

Date *(mm/dd/yyyy)*

OMB No. 1615-0087; Expires 04/30/06

Department of Homeland Security
U.S. Citizenship and Immigration Services

N-600K, Application for Citizenship and Issuance of Certificate Under Section 322

Instructions

What Is This Form?

This form, the N-600K is an application for the naturalization of a child **who regularly resides outside the United States** and for the issuance of a certificate of citizenship to the child.

To request U.S. Citizenship and Immigration Services (USCIS) forms, call our toll-free forms line at **1-800-870-3676**. You may also get USCIS forms and information about the immigration laws and regulations by calling **1-800-375-5283** or from the USCIS internet website at **http://www.uscis. gov.**

Who Should Use This Form?

The following individuals may use this form:

- A U.S. citizen parent seeking citizenship on behalf of a minor adopted or biological child under section 322 of the Immigration and Nationality Act (INA) (providing for citizenship through an application process for biological and adopted children who regularly reside outside of the United States and meet certain conditions while under the age of 18 years).
- If a U.S. citizen parent of a child who otherwise meets the eligibility requirements of INA 322 has died, a U.S. citizen parent of the U.S. citizen parent or a U.S. legal guardian can file this application at any time within five years of the U. S. citizen parent's death.

Who Can File This Form?

In the case of minor adopted or biological children (under 18 years) qualifying for citizenship under section 322 of the INA, the application must be filed by the U.S. citizen parent with legal and physical custody of the child.

In the case of an application filed by a U.S. citizen parent of a deceased citizen parent or of an application filed by a U.S. citizen legal guardian, the child does **not** have to be residing in the legal and physical custody of the applicant. The application can be filed and approved if the child is residing in the legal and physical custody of a person who does not object to the application.

This form should be filed only if the child:

- Will not yet have reached their 18th birthday at the time of fulfilling all of the requirements for citizenship, including the required interview of United States citizen parent and the child, and
- Is a biological child who is a legitimate child or is a child who was legitimated, while in the legal custody of the legitimating parent(s), prior to reaching the 16th birthday **or**
- Is an adopted child who has a full and final adoption **and** the child either is the beneficiary of an approved I-600 or fulfilled the two-years legal custody, two-years joint residence requirements of INA section 101(b)(1)(E).

Who Should Not Use This Form?

Therefore this form should not be used for stepchildren, children who are not legitimate and children who were not legitimated prior to their 16th birthday. Such children are not eligible for benefits under section 322 of the INA. Any person other than a citizen parent should not use this form except in cases in which a U.S. citizen parent has died.

What Is the Fee to Apply for a Certificate of Citizenship?

Except for a person who is requesting a certificate of citizenship for an adopted child, (checking **Part 2, Box A or C on the Form**), all applicants must pay the fee for this Form N-600K, Application for Citizenship and Issuance of Certificate, under section 322 of the INA - **$255.00**.

For U.S. citizen parents, or a U.S. citizen grandparent or U.S. citizen legal guardian filing in lieu of a deceased U.S. citizen parent, filing on behalf of an adopted minor child under section 322 of the INA (checking **Part 2, Box B on the form**), the fee for this is **$215.00**.

The fee must be paid at the time of filing the application. The fee is not refundable, even if the application is subsequently withdrawn.

Use the following guidelines when you prepare your check or money order:

- The check or money order must be drawn on a bank or other financial institution located in the United States and must be payable in U.S. currency. **Do not mail cash.**

- Make the check or money order payable to: **Department of Homeland Security**, unless:
  -- If you live in Guam and are filing your application there, make it payable to **Treasurer, Guam;** or
  -- If you live in the U.S. Virgin Islands and are filing your application there, make it payable to **Commissioner of Finance of the Virgin Islands.**

Do not use the initials "USDHS" or "DHS" on your check or money order.

How to Check If the Fees Are Correct.

The fees on this form are current as of the edition date appearing in the lower right corner of this page. However, because USCIS fees change periodically, you can verify if the fees are correct by following one of the steps below:

- Visit our website at **www.uscis.gov** and scroll down to "Forms and E-Filing" to check the appropriate fees, or
- Review the Fee Schedule included in your form package, if you called us to request the form, or
- Telephone our National Customer Service Center at **1-800-375-5283** and ask for the fee information.

Where Do I Send the Application?

For all applicants seeking a U.S. citizenship and the issuance of a certificate of citizenship for a minor adopted or biological child who resides outside of the United States and qualifies for citizenship under section 322 of the INA, the Form N-600K may be filed at any USCIS office or suboffice in the United States or its outlying possessions (including San Juan, Puerto Rico; the U.S. Virgin Islands; and Guam). The address of USCIS offices can be found at:

http://www.uscis.gov/graphics/fieldoffices/alphaa.htm.

What Documents or Evidence Must I Send With the Application?

The following is a list of documents that must be submitted with the Form N-600K. **Unless specifically noted otherwise, every applicant must submit each of the documents listed below for himself/herself and the U.S. citizen parent(s) (or grandparent(s) if applicable) through whom the applicant is claiming U.S. citizenship.**

Any document in a foreign language must be accompanied by a translation in English. The translator must certify that he/she is competent to translate and that the translation is true and accurate. For each document needed, you may submit a clear, readable copy or the originals. Do not send an original Certificate of Citizenship or Certificate of Naturalization. USCIS may request that you present original documents at the interview.

- **Photographs** - *(Only required of the person to whom the Certificate of Citizenship will be issued)*

  You must submit three identical, unglazed passport-style photographs in color taken within 30 days of the date of filing of this application. The photographs should be 2" x 2", and must be in natural color and taken without any headdress (unless the applicant is wearing a headdress as required by a religious order of which he or she is a member). The dimensions of the full-frontal facial position should be about 1 inch from the top of the hair to the chin. The photographs must be on thin paper with a light background and not mounted in any way. The photographs must not be signed but you should print your name (or if a U.S. citizen parent applying on behalf of a minor child, the child's name) and Alien Registration Number in the center of the back of each photograph with a soft lead pencil.

- **Birth Certificate or Record of the Child** - A certified birth certificate or record issued by a civil authority in the country of birth.

- **Birth Certificate or Record of the Citizen Parent** - A certified birth certificate or record issued by a civil authority in the country of birth is required for applications filed by a citizen parent of a citizen parent.

- **Marriage Certificate(s)** - Certified marriage certificate(s) issued by a civil authority in the state or country of marriage.

- **Documents Showing the Termination of a Marriage** - Examples include a divorce decree, death certificate, or annulment document.

- **Proof of U.S. Citizenship** - Examples of this are birth certificates showing birth in the United States; an N-550, Certificate of Naturalization; an N-560, Certificate of Citizenship; an FS-240, Report of Birth Abroad of United States Citizen; or a valid unexpired U.S passport.

- **Proof of Legitimation** - *(Only required for applicants who were born out of wedlock).*

  Documents must establish legitimation according to the laws of the child's residence or domicile or father's residence or domicile (if applicable).

Legitimation for INA benefits requires that the child is in the legal custody of the legitimating parent(s) at the time of legitimation.

- **Proof of Legal Guardianship** - Proof of legal guardianship issued by competent authority in the place of residence of the legal guardian must be submitted for any application filed by a legal guardian in lieu of a deceased citizen parent.

- **Proof of Legal Custody** - *(Only required for applicants whose U.S. citizen parent(s) divorced and/or separated and for applicants who are adopted or legitimated).*

- **Evidence of Lawful Admission and Maintenance of Such Lawful Status** (e.g. Form I-94, Arrival/ Departure Record) - *(Required at time of interview for all applicants seeking citizenship under section 322 of the INA).*

- **Proof of Required Residence or Physical Presence in the United States** - Any document that proves the U.S citizen parent(s)' residence or physical presence in the United States. This proof may include but is not limited to the following:
  - -- School, employment, military records;
  - -- Deeds, mortgages, leases showing residence;
  - -- Attestations by churches, unions, or other organizations;
  - -- U.S. Social Security quarterly reports;
  - -- Affidavits of third parties having knowledge of the residence and physical presence.

- **Proof of U.S. Citizen Grandparent(s)' Required Physical Presence in the United States** - *(Only required for applicants seeking citizenship under section 322 of the Act whose U.S. citizen parent(s) does not meet the physical presence requirement of five years in the United States, two years of which were after the age of 14).*

  Documentation establishing that the U.S. citizen grandparent(s) met the required physical presence requirements.

- **Current Status of Citizen Grandparent.**

  An application filed by a citizen parent that relies on the physical presence in the United States of a citizen grandparent cannot be approved unless the citizen grandparent is a U.S. citizen, if living, or if deceased, was at the time of his or her death a U.S. citizen.

  An application filed by any grandparent or legal guardian in lieu of a deceased citizen parent that relies on the physical presence of a citizen grandparent cannot be approved unless evidence is submitted that the citizen grandparent was a U.S. citizen and still alive at the time of the death of the citizen parent.

- **Copy of Notice of Approval of a Form I-600, Petition to Classify Orphan as an Immediate Relative, and Supporting Documentation for Such Form (Except Home Study)** - *(All adopted orphans applying under section 322 of the INA must either have this form or have complied with the two years legal custody and two years of joint residence requirement of INA 101(b)(1)(E)).*

- **Copy of Full, Final Adoption Decree** - *(Only required for adopted applicants).*

- **Evidence of All Legal Name Changes.**

What If a Document Is Not Available?

If it is not possible to obtain any one of the above-required documents, you must establish why the evidence is not available. You may be required to submit an original written statement from the relevant government or other authority explaining the reason for the unavailability of the document(s). You may submit the following **secondary evidence** for consideration. However, secondary documents that do not overcome the availability of primary documents may result in denial of the application:

- **Baptismal Certificate:** A certificate under the seal of the church where the baptism occurred, showing the date and place of the child's birth, date of baptism, the names of the godparents, if known.

- **Church Records:** A certificate under the church seal issued within two months of birth.

- **School Record:** A letter from authorities of the school attended (preferably the first school), showing the date of admission to the school, the child's date of birth or age at that time, place of birth, and the names and places of birth of parents, if shown in the school records.

- **Census Records:** State or federal census records showing the name(s) and place(s) of birth, and the date(s) of birth or age(s) of the person(s) listed.

- **Affidavits:** Written statements sworn to (or affirmed) by two persons who have personal knowledge of the claimed event (i.e., the date and place of a birth, marriage, or death). The persons may be relatives and need not be citizens of the United States. Each affidavit should contain the following information regarding the person making the affidavit: his (her) full name and address; date and place of birth; relationship to the applicant, if any; full information concerning the event; and complete details concerning how he (she) acquired knowledge of the event.

How Do I Complete This Application?

- Please print clearly or type your answers using CAPITAL letters in each box.
- Use black ink.
- **If the child has a USCIS "A" number, write the "A" number in the place indicated on the top right hand corner of the first page.** Use the "A" number on the Permanent Resident Card (formerly known as the Alien Registration Receipt or "Green" Card), if the child has one. Otherwise, use the "A" number shown on the USCIS or former INS-issued correspondence about the child.
- If a question does not apply to you, write N/A (meaning "Not Applicable") in the space provided.
- If you need extra space to answer any item:
  - -- Attach a separate sheet of paper (or more sheets if needed);
  - -- Write your name, your "A" number (if available), and "N-600K" on the top right corner of the sheet; and
  - -- Write the number of each question for which you are providing additional information.

Step-By-Step Instructions.

This form is divided into ten parts. The information below will help you fill out the form.

Part 1. Information About Your Child.

NOTE: If you are a U.S. citizen parent, grandparent or legal guardian applying for a certificate of citizenship on behalf of your minor biological or adopted child, give information for your **minor child**.

A. **Current Legal Name** - The child's current legal name is the name on the birth certificate unless it has been changed after birth by a legal action such as a marriage, adoption, or court order.

B. **Name Exactly as It Appears on Your Permanent Resident Card** (if applicable and if different from above) - Write the child's name exactly as it appears on the card, even if it is misspelled.

C. **Other Names Used Since Birth** - If the child has ever used any other names since birth, write them in this section. If you need more space, use a separate sheet of paper.

D. **U.S. Social Security Number** - Print the child's U. S. Social Security number. If the child does not have a Social Security number, write "N/A" in the space provided.

E. **Date of Birth** - Use eight numbers to show the child's date of birth (example: May 1, 1992, should be written 05/01/1992).

F. **Country of Birth** - Give the name of the country where the child was born. Write the name of the country even if it no longer exists. If the name of the country has changed, write the name of the country as it was at the time of your birth.

G. **Country of Citizenship/Nationality** - Write the name of the country of the child's citizenship/ nationality.

- If the country no longer exists and/or the child is stateless, write the name of the country where the child was last a citizen or national.
- If the child is a citizen or national of more than one country, write the name of the foreign country that issued the last passport.

H. **Gender** - Indicate whether male or female.

I. **Height** - Give the child's height in feet and inches.

Part 2. Information About the Child's Eligibility.

Check the box that indicates why the child is eligible to apply for a certificate of citizenship.

If you are a U.S. citizen parent applying for a certificate of citizenship on behalf of a minor biological child, check the box in **Section A**. If you are a U.S. citizen parent applying for a certificate of citizenship on behalf of a minor adopted child, check the box in **Section B**. If you are the U.S. citizen parent of a deceased U.S. citizen parent applying for your grandchild, check the box in **Section C**. If you are the U.S. citizen legal guardian of an eligible child, check the box in **Section C**.

Part 3. Additional Information About the Child.

The information in this section should be about the child who will be issued the certificate of citizenship.

NOTE: If you are a U.S. citizen parent, grandparent or legal guardian applying for a certificate of citizenship on behalf of a minor biological or adopted child, give information for your **minor child**.

A. Home Address - Give the address where the child now lives. Do not put post office (P.O.) box numbers here.

B. Mailing Address - If the mailing address is the same as the home address, write "same." If the mailing address is different from the home address, write it in this part. Provide "Care Of" information if applicable.

C. Telephone Numbers - Telephone numbers and e-mail addresses allow USCIS to contact you more quickly about the application. If you are hearing impaired and use a TTY telephone connection, please indicate this by writing "(TTY)" after the telephone number.

D. Current Marital Status - Check the marital status the child has on the date you are filing this application.

E. Information About the Child's Entry Into the U.S. and Current Immigration Status -

Do not complete this section. The USCIS Adjudicator will complete this during the interview.

F. Previous Application for Certificate of Citizenship or U.S. Passport - If you know of any prior application for a certificate of citizenship or a U.S. passport (or you are a U.S. citizen parent who previously applied for a certificate of citizenship or U.S. passport for your minor child), indicate on a separate piece of paper what happened with the application and whether a certificate of citizenship or U.S. passport was or was not issued.

G. Information on Adoption - If the child was adopted, provide information as to the place and date of adoption.

H. Marital Status of Parents at Time of Birth (or Adoption) - Indicate whether the child's parents were married to each other at the time of the child's birth. If the child was born out-of-wedlock, indicate "No," even if the parents subsequently married. If the child was adopted, indicate whether the adoptive parents were married to each other at the time of the adoption.

Part 4. Information on Child's U.S. Citizen Father or Mother (or Adoptive Father or Mother).

NOTE: If **you are a U.S. citizen father** or **mother** (or **adoptive father** or **mother**) applying for citizenship and a certificate of citizenship on behalf of your minor child, where information is requested about in this section, provide **information about YOURSELF** in the sections noted. If **you are a U.S. citizen grandparent** or **legal guardian**, provide **information about the child's U.S. citizen PARENT** in the sections noted.

A. Current Legal Name - Give current legal name, or name at time of death, of the U.S. citizen father or mother. It is the name on the birth certificate unless it was changed after birth by a legal action such as a marriage, adoption, or court order.

B. Date of Birth - Use eight numbers to show the U. S. citizen father or mother's date of birth (example: May 1, 1969, should be written 05/01/1969).

C. Country of Birth - Give the name of the country where the U.S. citizen father or mother was born. Write the name of the country even if it no longer exists. If the name of the country has changed, write the name of the country as it was at the time of your U.S. citizen father or mother's birth.

D. **Home Address** - Give the address where the U.S. citizen father or mother now lives. Do not put post office (P.O.) box numbers here.

E. **U.S. Citizenship** - Indicate how the U.S. citizen father or mother became a U.S. citizen. Provide all the requested information.

F. **Loss of U.S. Citizenship** - Indicate whether the U. S. citizen father or mother ever lost U.S. citizenship. Provide this information even if the U.S. citizen father or mother regained citizenship at a later date.

G. **Residence and/or Physical Presence** - Provide all the dates when the U.S. citizen father or mother was in United States. Dates should include all time immediately after birth as well as after the age of 14 years and older.

H. **Marital History.**

1. Write the number of times the U.S. citizen father or mother was married. Include any annulled marriages. If there were more than one marriage to the same spouse, count each time as a separate marriage.

2. If now married, provide information about the U.S. citizen father or mother's current spouse. Check appropriate box to indicate immigration status.

3. Indicate whether the U.S. citizen father or mother's current spouse is also your parent. If "No," you will be asked to provide information about your father or mother's previous spouse or spouses.

Part 5. Information About the U.S. Citizen Grandfather or Grandmother.

Complete This Section Only If:

1. You are a U.S. citizen parent, grandparent or legal guardian applying for citizenship on behalf of a United States citizen's adopted or biological child who regularly resides outside the United States;

2. The U.S. citizen parent, **has not** been physically present in the United States for five years, two years of which were after the age of 14 years; and

3. If the eligible application is relying on the physical presence in the United States of the U.S citizen father or mother of the United States citizen parent (the child's grandfather or grandmother) to get citizenship for the adopted or biological child.

The applicant should provide information about the U. S. citizen parent (the grandparent of the child) of the U. S. citizen father or mother in the sections noted.

A. **Current Legal Name** - Give current legal name of the U.S. citizen grandfather or grandmother. It is the name on his or her birth certificate unless it was changed after birth by a legal action such as a marriage, adoption or court order.

B. **Date of Birth** - Use eight numbers to show the U. S. citizen grandfather or grandmother's date of birth (example: May 1, 1949, should be written 05/01/1949).

C. **Country of Birth** - Give the name of the country where the U.S. citizen grandfather or grandmother was born. Write the name of the country even if it no longer exists. If the name of the country has changed, write the name of the country as it was at the time of the U.S. citizen grandfather or grandmother's birth.

D. **Home Address** - Give the address where the U.S. citizen grandfather or grandmother now lives. Do not put post office (P.O.) box numbers here.

E. **U.S. Citizenship** - Indicate how the U.S. citizen grandfather or grandmother became a U.S. citizen. Provide all the requested information.

F. **Loss of U.S. Citizenship** - Indicate whether the U. S. citizen grandfather or grandmother ever lost U. S. citizenship. Provide this information even if the U.S. citizen grandfather or grandmother regained citizenship at a later date.

G. **Residence and/or Physical Presence** - Provide all the dates when the U.S. citizen grandfather or grandmother was in United States. Dates should include all time immediately after birth as well as after the age of 14 years and older.

Part 6. Legal Guardian.

Complete this part only for applications filed by a legal guardian in lieu of a deceased U.S. citizen parent.

Part 7. Your Signature.

Except in cases in which a U.S. citizen parent of the child has died, only a U.S. citizen parent may file this application on their child's behalf. In cases in which a U.S. citizen parent has died, a U.S. citizen grandparent or U.S. citizen legal guardian can file the application. The applicant must sign and date the application. If the applicant does not sign the application, the application will be returned.

Part 8. Signature of Person Preparing Form, If Other Than Applicant.

If you do not fill out the Form N-600K yourself, the preparer must also sign, date and give his or her address. If the preparer is a business or organization, its' name must be included on the form.

Part 9. Affidavit.

Do not complete this part. You will be asked to complete this part at the interview.

Part 10. Officer Report and Recommendation.

Do not complete this part. This part is for USCIS use only.

Penalties.

USCIS wants to make sure that you receive the requested immigration benefit if you are eligible for it. To do this, we may ask for more evidence, interview you, and/or conduct an investigation. **If you give us false documents, misrepresent facts, or otherwise engage in fraud, USCIS will take appropriate action.** This means we will not only deny your application, but you may lose current and future immigration benefits and you may face penalties including criminal and/or civil prosecution leading to fines and/or imprisonment.

Privacy Act Notice

USCIS will use the information and evidence requested on Form N-600K to determine your eligibility for the requested immigration benefit. We may provide information from your application to other government agencies.

Use InfoPass for Appointments.

As an alternative to waiting in line for assistance at your local USCIS office, you can now schedule an appointment through our internet-based system, **InfoPass.** To access the system, visit our website at **www.uscis.gov.** Use the **InfoPass** appointment scheduler and follow the screen prompts to set up your appointment. **InfoPass** generates an electronic appointment notice that appears on the screen. Print the notice and take it with you to your appointment. The notice gives the time and date of your appointment, along with the address of the USCIS office.

Paperwork Reduction Act Notice.

You are not required to respond to this form unless it displays a currently valid OMB control number. The USCIS strives to create forms and instructions that are accurate, easy to understand and impose the least possible burden on you to provide the information and evidence needed to process your application.

For this application we estimate that it takes 15 minutes to learn about the law, form, and process. The time it takes to complete the form is estimated at 20 minutes and 1 hour to assemble and file the application, including average travel time. The total preparation time is estimated at 1 hour and 35 minutes. If you have comments about this estimate or suggestions for simplifying this form, write to: U.S. Citizenship and Immigration, Regulatory Management Division, 111 Massachusetts Avenue, N.W., Washington, DC 20529, OMB No. 1615-0087. **Do not mail your completed application to this address.**

OMB No. 1615-0087; Expires 04/30/06

Department of Homeland Security
U.S. Citizenship and Immigration Services

N-600K, Application for Citizenship and Issuance of Certificate Under Section 322

Print clearly or type your answers in black ink, using CAPITAL letters. Failure to print clearly may delay your application.

Part 1. Information About Your Child. *(Provide information about the child on whose behalf this application for citizenship and a Certificate of Citizenship is being filed.)*

If your child has an "A" Number, write it here:

___-___-___

For USCIS Use Only

Bar Code	Date Stamp
Remarks	
Action	

A. Current legal name.

Family Name *(Last Name)*

Given Name *(First Name)* Full Middle Name *(If Applicable)*

B. Name exactly as it appears on your Permanent Resident Card *(If Applicable)*.

Family Name *(Last Name)*

Given Name *(First Name)* Full Middle Name *(If Applicable)*

C. Other names used since birth.

Family Name *(Last Name)*	Given Name *(First Name)*	Middle Name *(If Applicable)*

D. U.S. Social Security # *(If Applicable)*

E. Date of Birth *(mm/dd/yyyy)*

F. Country of Birth

G. Country of Citizenship/Nationality

H. Gender

Male ☐ Female ☐

I. Height

Part 2. Information About the Child's Eligibility. *(Check only one)*

This application is being filed on my behalf based on the fact that:

A. ☐ I am a BIOLOGICAL child (under 18 years) of a United States citizen parent who is applying for citizenship on my behalf.

B. ☐ I am an ADOPTED child (under 18 years) of a United States citizen parent who is applying for citizenship on my behalf.

C. ☐ I am a child (under 18 years) of a United States citizen parent who died during the five years preceding the filing of this application. A United States citizen grandparent or a United States citizen legal guardian is applying for citizenship on my behalf.

Part 3. Additional Information About the Child. *(Provide information about the child on whose behalf this application for citizenship and a Certificate of Citizenship is being filed.)*

A. Home Address - Street Number and Name *(Do **not** write a P.O. Box in this space.)* Apartment Number

City County

State or Province Country Zip Code

Part 3. Additional Information About the Child. *(Provide information about the child on whose behalf this application for citizenship and a Certificate of Citizenship is being filed.)* - ***Continued.***

B. Mailing Address - Street Number and Name *(If Different From Home Address)* Apartment Number

City County State or Province Country Zip Code

C. Daytime Phone Number *(If Any)* Evening Phone Number *(If Any)* E-Mail Address *(If Any)*

D. Marital Status

☐ Single, Never Married ☐ Married ☐ Divorced ☐ Widowed

☐ Marriage Annulled or Other *(Explain)* ________

E. Information about entry into the United States and current immigration status.
*(Do **not** complete this section. The Adjudicator will complete it with you during the interview.)*

I arrived in the following manner:

Port of Entry *(City/State)* Date of Entry *(mm/dd/yyyy)* Current Immigration Status

Exact Name Used at Time of Entry:

F. Do you know of any prior application for a certificate of citizenship or U.S. passport for this child? ☐ No ☐ Yes

G. Was the child adopted? ☐ No ☐ Yes *(Please complete the following information):*

Date of Adoption *(mm/dd/yyyy)* Date Legal Custody Began *(mm/dd/yyyy)* Date Physical Custody Began *(mm/dd/yyyy)*

H. Were the child's parents married to each other when the child was born (or adopted)? ☐ No ☐ Yes

Part 4. Information About the Child's U.S. Citizen Father or Mother (or Adoptive Father or Mother). *(If you are a United States citizen father or mother applying for citizenship and a Certificate of Citizenship on behalf of your eligible child, provide information about* ***yourself*** *below). If you are a U.S. citizen grandparent or legal guardian, provide information about the child's U.S. citizen* ***parent in the sections noted.***

A. Current legal name of U.S. citizen father or mother.

Family Name *(Last Name)* Given Name *(First Name)* Full Middle Name *(If Applicable)*

B. Date of Birth *(mm/dd/yyyy)* **C. Country of Birth**

D. Home Address - Street Number and Name Apartment Number

City County State or Province Country Zip Code

Part 4. Information About the Child's U.S. Citizen Father or Mother (or Adoptive Father or Mother). *(If you are a United States citizen father or mother applying for citizenship and a Certificate of Citizenship on behalf of your eligible child, provide information about* ***yourself*** *below). If you are a U.S. citizen grandparent or legal guardian, provide information about the child's U.S. citizen* **parent in the sections noted.- (Continued).**

E. U.S. citizen by:

☐ Birth in the United States

☐ Naturalization

Date of Naturalization *(mm/dd/yyyy)*

Place of Naturalization *(Name of Court and City/State or USCIS (or former INS) Office Location)*

Certificate of Naturalization Number

Former "A" Number *(If Known)*

☐ Through birth abroad to U.S. citizen parent(s)

☐ Acquired after birth through naturalization of alien parent(s)

F. Has the U.S. citizen father or mother ever lost U.S. citizenship or taken any action that would cause loss of United States citizenship?

☐ No ☐ Yes *(Please Provide Full Explanation.)*

G. Dates of Residence and/or Physical Presence in the United States.

Provide the dates the U.S. citizen father or mother resided in or was physically present in the United States. If you need more space, use a separate sheet of paper.

From *(Month/Day/Year - mm/dd/yyyy)*	**To** *(Month/Day/Year - mm/dd/yyyy)*

H. Marital History.

1. How many times has the U.S. citizen father or mother been married (including annulled marriages)?
2. Information about the U.S. citizen father or mother's **current spouse:**

Family Name *(Last Name)* | Given Name *(First Name)* | Full Middle Name *(If Applicable)*

Date of Birth *(mm/dd/yyyy)* | Country of Birth | Country of Citizenship/Nationality

Home Address - Street Number and Name | Apartment Number

City | County | State or Province | Country | Zip Code

Date of Marriage *(mm/dd/yyyy)* | Place of Marriage *(City/State or Country)*

Spouse's Immigration Status:

☐ U.S. Citizen ☐ Lawful Permanent Resident ☐ Other *(Explain)*

3. Is the U.S. citizen Father or Mother's current spouse listed in **Question 2** above also the parent of the child (biological or adoptive) for whom this application is being submitted? ☐ No ☐ Yes

Part 5. Information About the U.S. Citizen Grandfather or Grandmother. *(Complete this section **only** if you are a U.S. citizen parent (or adoptive parent) grandparent or legal guardian applying for a Certificate of Citizenship for your biological or adopted child and the citizen parent **has not** been physically present in the United States for five years, two years of which were after the age of 14. The information provided here should describe, the U.S. citizen grandfather or U.S. grandmother of the minor child.)*

A. **Current legal name of U.S. citizen grandfather or grandmother.**

Family Name *(Last Name)* | Given Name *(First Name)* | Full Middle Name *(If Applicable)*

B. **Date of Birth** *(mm/dd/yyyy)*

C. **Country of Birth**

D. **Home Address** - Street Number and Name | Apartment Number

City | County | State or Province | Country | Zip Code

E. **U.S. citizen by:**

☐ Birth in the United States

☐ Naturalization

Date of Naturalization *(mm/dd/yyyy)*

Place of Naturalization *(Name of Court and City/State or (USCIS or former INS) Office Location)*

Certificate of Naturalization Number

Former "A" Number *(If Known)*

☐ Through birth abroad to U.S. citizen parent(s)

☐ Acquired after birth through naturalization of alien parent(s)

F. **Has your father or mother *(your child's grandfather or grandmother)* ever lost U.S. citizenship or taken any action that would cause loss of U.S. citizenship?**

☐ No ☐ Yes *(Please provide full explanation)* ______________________

G. **Dates of Residence and/or Physical Presence in the United States**

Provide the dates that your U.S. citizen father or mother *(your child's grandfather or grandmother)* lived in the United States. If you need more space, use a separate sheet of paper.

From *(Month/Day/Year - mm/dd/yyyy)*	**To** *(Month/Day/Year - mm/dd/yyyy)*

Part 4. Information About U.S. Citizen Father (or Adoptive Father). *(Complete this section if you are claiming citizenship through a U.S. citizen father. If you are a U.S. citizen father applying for a Certificate of Citizenship on behalf of your minor biological or adopted child, provide information about* ***yourself*** *below.)* ***Continued.***

F. U.S. citizen by:

☐ Birth in the United States

☐ Birth abroad to U.S. citizen parent(s)

☐ Acquisition after birth through naturalization of alien parent(s)

☐ Naturalization

Date of Naturalization *(mm/dd/yyyy)* | Place of Naturalization *(Name of Court and City/State or USCIS or Former INS Office Location)*

Certificate of Naturalization Number | Former "A" Number *(If known)*

G. Has your father ever lost U.S. citizenship or taken any action that would cause loss of U.S. citizenship?

☐ No ☐ Yes *(Provide full explanation on a separate sheet(s) of paper.)*

H. Dates of Residence and/or Physical Presence in the United States *(Complete this only if you are an applicant claiming U.S. citizenship at time of birth abroad)*

Provide the dates your U.S. citizen father resided in or was physically present in the United States. If you need more space, use a separate sheet(s) of paper.

From *(mm/dd/yyyy)*	**To** *(mm/dd/yyyy)*

I. Marital History

1. How many times has your U.S. citizen father been married (including annulled marriages)?

2. Information about U.S. citizen father's **current spouse:**

Family Name *(Last Name)* | Given Name *(First Name)* | Full Middle Name *(If applicable)*

Date of Birth *(mm/dd/yyyy)* | Country of Birth | Country of Nationality

Home Address - Street Number and Name | Apartment Number

City | County | State or Province | Country | Zip/Postal Code

Date of Marriage *(mm/dd/yyyy)* | Place of Marriage *(City/State or Country)*

Spouse's Immigration Status:

☐ U.S. Citizen ☐ Lawful Permanent Resident ☐ Other *(Explain)*

3. Is your U.S. citizen father's current spouse also your mother? ☐ No ☐ Yes

Part 8. Signature of Person Preparing This Form, If Other Than Above.

I declare that I prepared this application at the request of the above person. The answers provided are based on information of which I have personal knowledge and/or were provided to me by the above-named person in response to the questions contained on this form.

Preparer's Printed Name

Preparer's Signature

Name of Business/Organization *(If Applicable)*

Preparer's Daytime Phone Number

Date *(mm/dd/yyyy)*

Preparer's Address - Street Number and Name

City

County

State

Zip Code

NOTE: Do not complete the following parts below unless the USCIS officer instructs you to do so at the interview.

Part 9. Affidavit.

I, the parent/grandparent/legal guardian, ______________________ do swear or affirm, under penalty of perjury laws of the United States, that I know and understand the contents of this application signed by me, and the attached supplementary pages number (   ) to (   ) inclusive, that the same are true and correct to the best of my knowledge, and that corrections number (   ) to (   ) were made by me or at my request.

Signature of U.S. citizen parent/grandparent/legal guardian

Date *(mm/dd/yyyy)*

Subscribed and sworn or affirmed before me upon examination of the applicant and U.S. citizen parent/grandparent/legal guardian on

________________ at ________________ .

Signature of Interviewing Officer

Title

Part 10. Officer Report and Recommendation.

On the basis of the documents, records, and the testimony of persons examined, and the identification upon personal appearance of the underage beneficiary, I find that all the facts and conclusions set forth under oath in this application are ______ true and correct; that the applicant is eligible to be naturalized on ______________ *(month/day/year)*, through **section 322 of the INA** ______ ; **section 322 of the INA (grandparent residence)** ______ **section 322 of the INA (grandparent or legal guardian application)** ______ .

and I recommend that this application be ______________ *(granted or denied)* and that a Certificate of Citizenship be issued in the name of

______________________________ .

District Adjudications Officer's Name and Title

District Adjudications Officer's Signature

I do ______ concur in recommendation of the application.

Date: ______________
(mm/dd/yyyy)

District Director or Officer-in-Charge Signature:

OMB No. 1615-0091; Expires 01/31/07

Department of Homeland Security
U.S. Citizenship and Immigration Services

N-565, Application for Replacement Naturalization/Citizenship Document

Instructions

Purpose of This Form.

This form is used to apply to the U.S. Citizenship and Immigration Services (USCIS) for a replacement:

- Declaration of Intention, or
- Naturalization Certificate, or
- Certificate of Citizenship, or
- Repatriation Certificate, or to
- Apply for a special certificate of naturalization as a U.S. citizen to be recognized by a foreign country.

NOTE: USCIS is comprised of offices of the former Immigration and Naturalization Service (INS).

Who May File?

You may apply for a replacement:

- If you have been issued a Naturalization Certificate, Certificate of Citizenship, Declaration of Intention or Repatriation Certificate which has been lost, mutilated, or destroyed, or;
- If your name has been changed by marriage or by court order after the document was issued and you seek a document in the new name.
- If you are a naturalized citizen desiring to obtain recognition as a citizen of the United States by a foreign country, you may apply for a special certificate for that purpose.

General Filing Instructions.

Please answer all questions by typing or clearly printing in black ink. Indicate that an item is not applicable with "N/A." If an answer is "none," so state. If you need extra space to answer any item, attach a sheet of paper with your name and your A#, if any, and indicate the number of the item.

Every application must be properly signed and filed with the correct fee. If you are under 14 years of age, your parent or guardian may sign the application in your behalf.

Initial Evidence Requirements.

You must file your application with the following evidence:

- You must submit two standard passport-style photographs in color of yourself taken within 30 days of this application. These photos must be glossy, unretouched and unmounted, and have a white background. The dimension of your full frontal facial position should be about 1 inch from your chin to the top of your hair. Using pencil or felt pen, lightly print your name and A# if any, on the back of each photo. This requirement may be waived by USCIS if you can establish that you are confined because of age or physical infirmity.
- If you are applying for replacement of a mutilated document, you must attach the mutilated document.
- If you are applying for a new document because your name has been changed, you must submit the original USCIS (or former INS) document and a copy of the marriage certificate or court order showing the name change.
- If you are applying for a special certificate of naturalization, you must attach a copy of your naturalization certificate.

Copies.

If these instructions state that a copy of a document may be filed with this application, and you choose to send us the original, we may keep that original for our records.

Where to File.

File this application at the local USCIS office having jurisdiction over your place of residence.

What Is the Fee?

The fee for this petition is **$220.00**, except there is no fee if you check **block 2 (d)** of **Part 2** of the form.

The fee must be submitted in the exact amount. It cannot be refunded. **Do not mail cash.**

All checks and money orders must be drawn on a bank or other institution located in the United States and must be payable in United States currency. The check or money order should be made payable to the **Department of Homeland Security**, except that:

- If you live in Guam, and are filing this application in Guam, make your check or money order payable to the "Treasurer, Guam."
- If you live in the U.S. Virgin Islands, and are filing this application in the U.S. Virgin Islands, make your check or money order payable to the "Commissioner of Finance of the Virgin Islands."

Check are accepted subject to collection. An uncollected check will render the application and any document issued invalid. A charge of $30.00 will be imposed if a check in payment of a fee is not honored by the bank on which it is drawn.

How to Check If the Fee Is Correct.

The fee on this form is current as of the edition date appearing in the lower right corner of this page. However, because USCIS fees change periodically, you can verify if the fee is correct by following one of the steps below:

- Visit our website at **www.uscis.gov** and scroll down to "Forms and E-Filing " to check the appropriate fee, or
- Review the Fee Schedule included in your form package, if you called us to request the form, or
- Telephone our National Customer Service Center at **1-800-375-5283** and ask for the fee information.

Processing Information.

Rejection. Any application that is not signed or not accompanied by the correct fee will be rejected with a notice that the application is deficient. You may correct the deficiency and resubmit the application. However, an application is not considered properly filed until accepted by USCIS.

Initial processing. Once the application has been accepted, it will be checked for completeness, including submission of the required initial evidence. If you do not completely fill out the form, or file it without required initial evidence, you will not establish a basis for eligibility and we may deny your application.

Requests for more information or interview. We may request more information or evidence or we may request that you appear at a USCIS office for an interview. We may also request that you submit the originals of any copy. We will return these originals when they are no longer required.

Decision. If you establish eligibility for the document, your application will be approved and the document issued. A special certificate of naturalization will be forwarded to the U.S. Department of State for delivery to a foreign government official. If your application is denied, you will be notified in writing of the reasons for the denial.

USCIS Forms and Information.

To order USCIS forms, call our toll-free forms line at **1-800-870-3676**. You can also get USCIS forms and information on immigration laws, regulations or procedures by telephoning our National Customer Service Center at **1-800-375-5283** or visiting our USCIS internet website at **www.uscis.gov.**

Use InfoPass for Appointments.

As an alternative to waiting in line for assistance at your local USCIS office, you can now schedule an appointment through our internet-based system, **InfoPass.** To access the system, visit our website at **www.uscis.gov.** Use the **InfoPass** appointment scheduler and follow the screen prompts to set up your appointment. **InfoPass** generates an electronic appointment notice that appears on the screen. Print the notice and take it with you to your appointment. The notice gives the time and date of your appointment, along with the address of the USCIS office.

Penalties.

If you knowingly and willfully falsify or conceal a material fact or submit a false document with this request, we will deny the benefit you are filing for, and may deny any other immigration benefit. In addition, you will face severe penalties provided by law, and may be subject to criminal prosecution.

Privacy Act Notice.

We ask for the information on this form, and associated evidence, to determine if you have established eligibility for the immigration benefit you are seeking. Our legal right to ask for this information is in 8 USC 1439, 1440, 1443, 1445, 1446, and 1452. We may provide this information to other government agencies. Failure to provide this information, and any requested evidence, may delay a final decision or result in denial of your request.

Paperwork Reduction Act Notice.

A person is not required to respond to a collection of information unless it displays a currently valid OMB control number.

We try to create forms and instructions that are accurate, can be easily understood and which impose the least possible burden on you to provide us with information. Often this is difficult because some immigration laws are very complex.

Accordingly, the reporting burden for this collection of information is computed as follows: (1) learning about the law and form, 10 minutes; (2) completing the form, 10 minutes; and (3) assembling and filing the application, 35 minutes, for an estimated average of 55 minutes per response.

If you have comments regarding the accuracy of this estimate, or suggestions for making this form simpler, you can write to the U.S. Citizenship and Immigration Services, Regulatory Management Division, 111 Massachusetts Avenue, N.W., Washington, D.C. 20536; OMB No. 1615-0091. **Do not mail your completed application to this address.**

OMB No. 1615-0091; Expires 01/31/07

Department of Homeland Security
U.S. Citizenship and Immigration Services

N-565, Application for Replacement Naturalization/Citizenship Document

START HERE - Please type or print in black ink.

For USCIS Use Only

Part 1. Information about you.

Family Name | Given Name | Middle Name

Address - In care of:

Street Number and Name | Apt #

City or town | State or Province

Country | Zip or Postal Code

Date of Birth *(mm/dd/yyyy)* | Country of Birth

Certificate Number | A #

Telephone # (with area/country codes) | E-Mail Address (if any)

Part 2. Type of application.

1. I hereby apply for: (check one)

a. ☐ New Certificate of Citizenship.
b. ☐ New Certificate of Naturalization.
c. ☐ New Certificate of Repatriation.
d. ☐ New Declaration of Intention.
e. ☐ Special Certificate of Naturalization to obtain recognition of my U.S. citizenship by a foreign country.

2. Basis for application: (If you checked other than **"e"** in **Part 1**, check one)

a. ☐ My certificate is/was lost, stolen or destroyed (attach a copy of the certificate if you have one). Explain when, where and how.

____

____

b. ☐ My certificate is mutilated (attach the certificate).
c. ☐ My name has been changed (attach the certificate).
d. ☐ My certificate or declaration is incorrect (attach the documents).

Part 3. Processing information.

Gender ☐ Male ☐ Female | Height | Marital Status ☐ Single ☐ Married ☐ Widowed ☐ Divorced

My last certificate or Declaration of Intention was issued to me by:

USCIS Office or Name of Court | Date *(mm/dd/yyyy)*

Name in which the document was issued:

Other names I have used (if none, so indicate):

Since becoming a citizen, have you lost your citizenship in any manner?

☐ No ☐ Yes (attach an explanation)

Part 4. Complete if applying for a new document because of a name change.

Name changed to present name by: (check one)

☐ Marriage or divorce on (month/day/year) __________ (Attach a copy of marriage or divorce certificate).

☐ Court Decree (month/day/year) __________ (Attach a copy of the court decree).

Returned	Receipt
Resubmitted	
Reloc Sent	
Reloc Rec'd	
☐ Applicant Interviewed	

☐ Declaration of Intention verified by

☐ Citizenship verified by

Remarks

Action Block

To Be Completed by *Attorney or Representative*, if any

☐ Fill in box if G-28 is attached to represent the applicant

VOLAG#

ATTY State License #

Part 5. Complete if applying to correct your document.

If you are applying for a new certificate or Declaration of Intention because your current one is incorrect, explain why it is incorrect and attach copies of the documents supporting your request.

Part 6. Complete if applying for a special certificate of recognition as a citizen of the U.S. by the Government of a foreign country.

Name of Foreign Country

Information about official of the country who has requested this certificate (if known)

Name		Official Title	
Government Agency			
Address: Street # and Name			Room #
City	State/ Province		
Country			Zip or Postal Code

Part 7. Signature.

Read the information on penalties in the instructions before completing this part. If you are going to file this application at an USCIS office in the United States sign below. If you are going to file this application at a USCIS office abroad, sign it in front of a USCIS or Consular Official.

I certify, or if outside the United States, I swear or affirm, under penalty of perjury under the laws of the United States of America, that this application and the evidence submitted with it is all true and correct. I authorize the release of any information from my records which the U.S. Citizenship and Immigration Services needs to determine eligibility for the benefit I am seeking.

Signature		**Date**
Signature of USCIS or Consular Official	Print Name	Date

NOTE: *If you do not completely fill out this form or fail to submit required documents listed in the instructions, you may not be found eligible for a certificate and this application may be denied.*

Part 8. Signature of person preparing form, if other than above. (Sign below.)

I declare that I prepared this application at the request of the above person and it is based on all information of which I have knowledge.

Signature	**Print Your Name**	**Date**
Firm Name and Address		Telephone Number (with area code)
		E-Mail Address (if any)

U.S. Department of Homeland Security
Bureau of Citizenship and Immigration Services

OMB No.1115-0173

N-644, Application for Posthumous Citizenship

Instructions

Complete only Part I of this application. Do not write In Parts II, III or IV.

General Information

Public Law 101-249, as amended, provides that an alien or non-citizen national of the United States who dies as a result of injury or disease incurred by active duty with the U.S. Armed Forces during specified periods of military hostilities may be granted United States citizenship. If the application is approved, a Certificate of Citizenship (N-645) will be issued in the name of the decedent (the deceased veteran). The certificate establishes that the decedent is considered a citizen of the United States as of the date of his or her death. Posthumous citizenship is an honorary status commemorating the bravery and sacrifices of the veteran; it conveys no benefit under the immigration and nationality laws to any relative of the decedent.

Who Is Eligible for Posthumous Citizenship?

To qualify for Posthumous Citizenship, the decedent must have been an alien or non-citizen national of the United States who:

(1) served honorably in an active-duty status in the military, air or naval forces of the United States during:

(a) 04/06/1917 - 11/11/1918 (World War I); or

(b) 09/01/1939 - 12/31/1946 (World War II); or

(c) 06/25/1950 - 07/01/1955 (Korean Hostilities); or

(d) 02/28/1961 - 10/15/1978 (Vietnam Hostilities); or

(e) 08/02/1990 - 04/11/1991 (Persian Gulf Conflict); or

(f) from 09/11/2001 until terminated by Executive Order of the President; or

(g) any other period of military hostilities designated by Executive Order of the President for the purpose of naturalization benefits; or

(h) a period of at least five years following enlistment or reenlistment in the U.S. Army under the Lodge Act of June 30, 1950; and who:

(2) died because of injury or disease incurred in or aggravated by that service; and

(3) met one of the following enlistment requirements:

(a) was enlisted, reenlisted, or inducted in the United States, Panama Canal Zone, American Samoa, or Swain's Island; or

(b) was admitted to the United States as a lawful permanent resident at any time; or

(c) if a person described in (1)(f) above, entered the United States, Panama Canal Zone, American Samoa, or Swain's Island pursuant to military orders at some time during such service.

When Must the Application Be Filed?

The application must be filed no later than:

(a) November 2, 2004; or

(b) two years after the date of the decedent's death, whichever is later.

Who Can File?

You may file this form only if your relationship to the decedent was:

(a) Spouse; or

(b) Father/Mother; or

(c) Son/Daughter; or

(d) Brother/Sister; or

You are the decedent's representative, defined as:

(e) Executor or Administrator of decedent's estate; or

(f) Guardian, Conservator, or Committee of decedent's next-of-kin; or

(g) Service organization recognized by the Department of Veterans Affairs.

NOTE: Once a certificate of Posthumous Citizenship has been issued for a veteran, the Service will **not** approve any later application on his or her behalf, except in the case of an application to replace a certificate that was lost, mutilated, or destroyed.

What Documents Need to Be Submitted?

Authorization documents:

(a) Unless you are the spouse of the decedent or the executor or administrator of the decedent's estate, you must obtain authorization from all living next-of-kin above you in the order of succession. For example, if you are the decedent's brother, you would have to obtain authorization all living relatives in classes (a), (b) and (c) in the **Who Can File?** section above. The authorization must be in the form of an affidavit stating the affiant's name, address and relationship to the decedent and authorizing you to apply for posthumous U.S. citizenship on behalf of the decedent. If the affidavit is in a language other than English, it must be accompanied by a certified English translation.

(b) If you are in category (e) or (f) of the section, **Who Can File?**, you must submit a certified copy of your letter of appointment as the executor or administrator of the decedent's estate, or as the guardian, conservator, or committee of the decedent's next-of-kin.

(c) If you are in group (g) of the section, **Who Can File?**, you must submit evidence of recognition of your organization by the Department of Veterans Affairs.

Documentation of the decedent's service and death: To facilitate certification of the decedent's military service and service-connected death by the executive departments, you should submit a legible copy of each of the following documents, if available:

(d) Form DD 214, Certificate of Release or Discharge from Active Duty; or

(e) Form DD 1300, Report of Casualty/Military Death Certificate; or

(f) Any other military or state issued certificate of the decedent's death.

Failure to submit any of these documents may not automatically result in the denial of your application, but will delay the certification process.

How Should You Prepare This Form?

(a) **Complete only Part I** of this application. **Do not write in Parts II, III, or IV**, which are reserved for the use of the executive departments.

(b) Type or print legibly in ink.

(c) Please read and follow all instructions carefully, so that it will not be necessary to return your application.

(d) Answer all questions fully and accurately. If any item does not apply to the decedent, write "N/A" (meaning "Not Applicable") or "None," as the case requires.

What Is the Fee?

You must pay $80.00 to file this form. *The fee will not be refunded, whether the application is approved or not.* All checks or money orders, whether U.S. or foreign, must be payable in U.S. currency at a financial institution in the United States. *Do not mail cash.* When a check is drawn on the account of a person other than yourself, write your name on the face of the check. For any check you submit that is not honored there is an additional charge of $30.00. Pay by check or money order in the exact amount. Make the check or money order payable to "Bureau of Citizenship and Immigration Services."

Will You Have to Appear For an Interview?

No. However, if the application is approved, and you reside outside the United States, you will be required to appear at the nearest American Embassy or Consulate to sign for the Certificate of Citizenship (N-645).

Where Should You File the Application?

Mail this form with supporting documents, if required, to the Bureau of Citizenship and Immigration Services (BCIS) Service Center having jurisdiction over your place of residence. The address and the respective areas of jurisdiction to the appropriate center are as follows:

- If you currently live in Connecticut, Delaware, District of Columbia, Maine, Maryland, Massachusetts, New Jersey, New Hampshire, New York, Pennsylvania, Puerto Rico, Rhode Island, Vermont, Virginia, West Virginia or the U.S. Virgin Islands, mail the petition to:

  Vermont Service Center
  75 Lower Welden Street
  St. Albans, VT 05479-0001

- If you currently live in Alabama, Arkansas, Florida, Georgia, Kentucky, Louisiana, Mississippi, New Mexico, North Carolina, Oklahoma, South Carolina, Tennessee or Texas, mail the petition to:

  Texas Service Center
  P.O. Box 852135
  Irving, TX 75185-2135

- If you currently live in Arizona, California, Guam, Hawaii or Nevada, mail the petition to:

  California Service Center
  P.O. Box 10360
  Laguna Niguel, CA 92607-1036

- If you currently live anywhere else in the United States, mail the application to:

  Nebraska Service Center
  P.O. Box 87360
  Lincoln, NE 68501-7360

- If you currently live outside the United States, mail your application to any one of above listed Service Centers.

What Are the Penalties for Submitting False Information?

Title 18, United States Code, Section 1001, states whoever willfully and knowingly falsifies a material fact, makes a false statement, or makes use of a false document will be fined up to $10,000 or imprisoned up to five (5) years or both.

What Is the Authority for Collecting This Information?

We request information on this form to carry out the immigration laws contained in Title 8, United States Code 1225. We need this information to determine your eligibility to file this application, and the decedent's eligibility for Posthumous citizenship. The information you provide may also be disclosed to other federal agencies as part of the adjudication of this application. You do not have to give this information; however, if you refuse, your application may be denied.

What Is the Reporting Burden?

A person is not required to respond to a collection of information unless it displays a currently valid OMB control number. This collection of information is estimated to average one hour and fifty minutes per response, including the time for reviewing instructions, searching existing data sources, gathering and maintaining the data needed, and completing and reviewing the collection of information. Send comments regarding this burden estimate or any other aspect of this collection of information, including suggestions for reducing this burden to, Bureau of Citizenship and Immigration Services, HQRFS, 425 I Street, N.W., Room 4034, Washington, DC 20536; OMB No. 1115-0173. **DO NOT MAIL YOUR COMPLETED APPLICATION TO THIS ADDRESS.**

U.S. Department of Homeland Security
Bureau of Citizenship and Immigration Services

OMB No.1115-0173

N-644, Application for Posthumous Citizenship

Space to the right for the use of the Bueau of Citizenship and Immigration Services ONLY

Fee Stamp

PART I - To Be Completed by the Applicant

A. Information about you, the Applicant

1. Name (Last/First/Middle)
2. Address (Street Name and Number)
   (Town/City, State/Country, ZIP/Postal Code)
3. If abroad, city/country of nearest American Embassy or Consulate
4. Telephone number (include Area Code)
5. Total Number of Authorization Affidavits Attached (see instructions)

6. Your Relationship to Decedent at time of his/her death (check one)

Next-of-Kin

a. ☐ Spouse
b. ☐ Parent
c. ☐ Son/Daughter
d. ☐ Brother/Sister

Representative

e. ☐ Executor or Administrator of Decedent's Estate
f ☐ Guardian, Conservator, or Committee of Decedent's Next-of-Kin
g. ☐ VA Recognized Service Organization (Name below)
(Name of Service Organization)

B. Information about the Decedent

1. Name Used During Active Service (Last/First/Middle)
2. Other Names Used
3. Date of Birth (MM/DD/YYYY) 4. Place of Birth (City/State/Country)
5. Date of Death (MM/DD/YYYY) 6. Place of Death (City/State/Country)
7. Immigration Status at Time of Death (Permanent Resident, Student, Visitor, etc.)
8. Alien Registration Number or Other INS File Number
9. Social Security Number (if any)
10. Father's Full Name a. ☐ Living b. ☐ Deceased
11. Mother's Maiden Name a. ☐ Living b. ☐ Deceased
12. Marital Status at Time of death a. ☐ Married b. ☐ Widowed c. ☐ Divorced d. ☐ Single
13. Military Service Serial Number (If different from Social Security #)
14. Date Entered Active Duty Service (MM/DD/YYYY)
15. Place Entered Active Duty Service (City/State/Country)
16. Date Released From Active Duty Service (MM/DD/YYYY)
17. Branch of Service 18. Type of Discharge
19. Military Rank at Time of Discharge 20. Retired From military? ☐ Yes ☐ No

21. VA Claim Number (if any)
22. Total Number of Children (if none, write None)
23. Complete the Following for Each Child.

Name (Last/First/Middle)	Date of Birth (MM/DD/YYYY)
	☐ Living ☐ Deceased
	☐ Living ☐ Deceased
	☐ Living ☐ Deceased

24. Total Number of Brothers and Sisters (if none, write None)
25. Complete the Following for Each Brother and Sister.

Name (Last/First/Middle)	Date of Birth (MM/DD/YYYY)
	☐ Living ☐ Deceased
	☐ Living ☐ Deceased
	☐ Living ☐ Deceased

Certification of Applicant

I certify, under penalty of perjury under the laws of the United States of America, that the information in Part I is true and correct.

Signature Date

Declaration of person preparing form, if other than above.

I declare that I prepared this document at the request of the person above and that it is based on all information of which I have any knowledge.

Signature Date

Name (print or type)

Address

Form N-644 (Rev. 02/25/03)N

PART II -
To Be Completed by the Applicable Executive Department

1. ☐ No Active Duty Records Found for This Individual
2. ☐ No Casualty Records Found for This Individual
3. ☐ Name of Decedent Correctly Shown
4. ☐ Name of Decedent Different in Records

(List name shown in records)

5. ☐ Active Duty Service Records Found (complete a through f)

a. Branch of Service

b. Date Entered Active Duty

c. Place Entered Active Duty Service (City/State/Country)

d. Service Number

e. Date Released From Service (MM/DD/YYYY)

f. Honorable Service During a Period of Hostilities by ☐ Yes ☐ No

6. Individual Entered Service Under the Lodge Act? ☐ Yes ☐ No ☐ Unable to Determine

7. ☐ Record of Death Found (Complete a and b)

a. Date of Death

b. Death resulted from injury or disease incurred in or aggravated by active duty service during a period of military hostilities specified by law?
☐ Yes ☐ No ☐ Unable to Determine

8. Certification

I certify the information given here concerning the (check one or both, as appropriate)
☐ Service ☐ Death
of the individual named on this form is correct according to the records of the (Name below)

(Specify Executive Department)

Signature Date

Title

PART III - To Be Completed by the Department of Defense, Washington Headquarters Services, Directorate for Information Operations and Reports

A. Certification

Based on the information received from the Department of Veterans Affairs concerning the death of the individual named on this form, I certify that the individual died on

Date (MM/DD/YYYY)

as a result of injury or disease incurred in or aggravated by service during a period of hostilities specified by law.

Signature Date

Title

B. Unable to Certify

Based on the information received from the Department of Veterans Affairs concerning the death of the individual named on this form, I am unable to certify that the individual died as a result of injury or disease incurred in or aggravated by service during a period of hostilities specified by law.

Signature Date

Title

Space below (Part IV) for use of the Bureau of Citizenship and Immigration Services ONLY

Part IV -
To Be Completed by Bureau of Citizenship and Immigration Services

Applicant Authorized Next-of-Kin or Representative
Positive Certification Military Service
Positive Certification Service Connected Death
Place of Enlistment Qualifies Under INA Section 329(a)(1)
Decedent Admitted for Lawful Permanent Residence

Action Stamp

Cert. #	Date Mailed
A #	Reg. Mail #

Initial Receipt	Resubmitted	Relocated		Completed		
		Rec'd	Sent	App'd	Denied	Ret'd

FORMS FOR RELIEF FROM INADMISSIBILITY OR REMOVAL

In Chapter 7 we discussed conditions known as "inadmissibility" and "removal." Those terms were referred to as "exclusion" and "deportation" in the past. Although the terms and many of the forms have changed, some of the forms contained here use the old terms in some places.

I-690: Application for Waiver of Grounds of Excludability

This form is for aliens seeking a waiver of inadmissibility. Though the form was established after the term "exclusion" was replaced by "inadmissibility," the words on the form itself have not been fully updated. The I-601 is for aliens applying for this waiver who are outside of the United States at the time of the application.

I-246: Application for Stay of Deportation or Removal

As discussed in Chapter 7, certain aliens may apply for a temporary stay of removal. They must submit this form in order to do so.

I-881: Application for Suspension of Deportation or Special Rule Cancellation of Removal

Aliens who seek cancellation of removal use this form to apply. Again, the phrase "suspension of deportation" has not been changed on the form, though the words "cancellation of removal" have been added.

OMB No. 1615-0032; Expires 10/31/05
You may continue to use this form after expiration date.

Department of Homeland Security
U. S. Citizenship and Immigration Services

I-690, Application for Waiver of Grounds of Inadmissibility

Instructions

1. What Is the Purpose of This Form?

This form is used to apply for a waiver of inadmissibility by an applicant for adjustment of status under section 245A or 210 of the Immigration and Nationality Act (INA).

A separate waiver application must be filed by each applicant who is inadmissible. All applications must be typed or clearly printed in black ink and completed in full. If extra space is needed to answer an item, attach a continuation sheet and indicate your name, "A" file number and item number.

2. Special Instructions for Individuals Applying for a Waiver of One or More of the Medical Grounds Under Section 212(a)(1)(A) of the INA.

A. Applicants who Require a Waiver for Human Immunodeficiency Virus (HIV) or Tuberculosis (TB).

The physician or medical facility that will provide the required treatment to you must fill out **Part C** of the accompanying TB/HIVsupplement. If that physician or health care facility is not part of the state or local health department, then the local health department in the jurisdiction where you will reside must also complete and sign **Part D**. If you are outside of the United States, a relative in the United States must complete this process for you.

After the TB/HIV supplement has been completed, attach the supporting documents and file your waiver application. If you are inadmissible because of HIV and/or TB and your waiver application does not include a properly completed HIV/TB supplement, your waiver application will be returned to you.

B. Applicants Requesting a Waiver of the Vaccination Requirements of INA 212(a)(1)(A)(ii)

If your waiver application is based on religious or moral objections to vaccinations, you must establish that:

- You object to vaccinations in any form; and
- You object because of your religious beliefs or moral convictions (you do not need to be a member of a "mainstream" or recognized religion); and
- Your beliefs are sincere.

At a minimum, you must submit a personal statement describing the basis of your objection.

You can apply for a waiver of the vaccination requirements without filing this form and without paying a fee, if:

- You initially did not submit proof that you have received the required vaccines, but you are vaccinated now; or
- It is not medically appropriate for you to have one or more of the missing vaccines. The physician will make this certification according to the applicable regulations published by the Department of Health and Human Services (HHS) and the accompanying technical instructions for physicians designated to perform the required medical examination. These instructions are published by the Centers for Disease Control and Prevention (CDC). According to these technical instructions, "not medically appropriate" covers the following situations:
  - -- The vaccination is not recommended by the Advisory Committee for Immunization Practices (ACIP) for your age group; or
  - -- The vaccination is medically contraindicated; or
  - -- There is an insufficient interval between doses for vaccines requiring a series of doses; or
  - -- It is not the flu season (for the flu vaccine only).

C. Applicants Who Have a Physical or Mental Disorder With Associated Harmful Behavior - INA 212(a)(1)(A)(iii)(I) or (II).

If the examining physician determines that you have a physical or mental disorder with associated harmful behavior, or a past history of a physical or mental disorder with harmful behavior that is likely to recur, the medical examination report completed by the designated physician will, at a minimum, contain the following information, as required by HHS regulations at 42 CFR part 34 and the accompanying technical instructions published by the CDC:

- A complete medical history, including the details of any prior or current hospitalization, treatment, or care;
- The current findings, diagnosis, and prognosis; and
- Any other information necessary for USCIS to determine, in consultation with HHS, the terms and conditions that should be imposed on the waiver, if it is granted.

D. Applicants Who Are Inadmissible because of Substance or Drug Abuse or Substance or Drug Addiction - INA 212(a)(1)(A)(iv)

The designated physician will determine whether you are currently using, or have used in the past, any controlled or psychoactive substance. The examining physician will make this determination during the required medical exam, according to the applicable HHS regulations at 42 CFR part 34 and the accompanying technical instructions published by the CDC.

If you are inadmissible under INA 212(a)(1)(A)(iv) due to drug abuse or drug addiction, you may apply for a waiver.

USCIS will exercise discretion in determining whether to grant this waiver, after consulting with HHS, and if you are not inadmissible on any other grounds that cannot be waived.

You are not inadmissible under INA 212(a)(1)(A)(iv) if the designated physician that performed the required medical exam determined that you are in remission for prior drug use or abuse or that your prior drug use was strictly experimental. The designated physician will determine whether any prior drug use is in remission, or whether it was strictly experimental, based on the applicable HHS regulations and the accompanying technical instructions published by the CDC.

Note the following key items:

- If you engaged in the use of any controlled substance, and such use was illegal at the place where it occurred, your admission to the examining physician may be sufficient to make you inadmissible on criminal grounds under INA 212(a)(2)(A)(i)(II) relating to any controlled substance violation (U.S. or foreign).
- The USCIS officer reviewing your primary benefit application (Form I-687, Form I-698, Form I-700, and/or Form I-485) will determine whether this admission to the designated physician makes you inadmissible under INA 212(a)(2)(A)(i)(II).
- The only drug offense under INA 212(a)(2)(A)(i)(II) that can be waived is one offense of simple possession of marijuana (30 grams or less).
- Any willful concealment or misrepresentation of any material fact made to procure an immigration benefit (including any willful concealments or misrepresentations made to avoid being found inadmissible under any provision), will result in the denial of this waiver application and your primary benefit application. You may also become subject to additional penalties under the law.

3. What Is the Fee?

You must pay **$95.00** to file this application. The fee is not refundable, whether the application is approved or denied.

Do not mail cash. A separate check or money order must be submitted for each application. All checks or money orders, whether U.S. or foreign, must be payable in U.S. currency at a financial institution in the United States. When a check is drawn on the account of a person other than yourself, write your name on the face of the check. If the check is not honored, USCIS will charge you $30.00.The check or money order must be in the exact amount payable to the **U.S. Department of Homeland Security,** unless:

- If you live in Guam, make the check or money order payable to the "Treasurer, Guam" or
- If you live in the U.S. Virgin Islands, make your check or money order payable to the "Commissioner of Finance of the Virgin Islands."

How to Check if the Fee is Correct?

The fee on this form is current as of the edition date appearing in the lower right corner of this page. However, because USCIS fees change periodically, you can verify if the fee is correct by following one of the steps below:

- Visit our website at **www.uscis**.gov and scroll down to "Forms and E-Filing" to check the appropriate fee, or
- Review the Fee Schedule included in your form package, if you called us to request the form, or
- Telephone our National Customer Service Center at **1-800-375-5283** and ask for the fee information.

4. Where Must the Application Be Filed?

You must file this waiver application with the USCIS office that has jurisdiction over your primary benefit application -- Form I-687, Form I-698 and/or Form I-485.

5. Do You Need Forms or Information?

To order USCIS forms, call our toll-free forms line at **1-800-870-3676**. You can also order USCIS forms and obtain information on immigration laws, regulations and procedures by telephoning our National Customer Service Center toll-free at **1-800-375-5283** or visiting our internet website at **www.uscis.gov**.

6. Use InfoPass for Appointments.

As an alternative to waiting in line for assistance at your local USCIS office, you can now schedule an appointment through our internet-based system, **InfoPass**. To access the system, visit our website at **www.uscis.gov**. Use the **InfoPass** appointment scheduler and follow the screen prompts to set up your appointment. **InfoPass** generates an electronic appointment notice that appears on the screen. Print the notice and take it with you to your appointment. The notice gives the time and date of your appointment, along with the address of the USCIS office.

7. Paperwork Reduction Act Information.

An agency may not conduct or sponsor an information collection and a person is not required to respond to this collection of information unless it displays a currently valid OMB control number.

The estimated average time to complete and file this application is 15 minutes per application.

If you have comments regarding this form you can write to U.S. Citizenship and Immigration Services, Regulatory Management Division, 111 Massachusetts Avenue, N.W., Washington, DC 20529; OMB No. 1615-0032. **Do not mail your completed application to this address.**

OMB No. 1615-0032; Expires 10/31/05
You may continue to use this form after expiration date.

Department of Homeland Security
U.S. Citizenship and Immigration Services

I-690, Application for Waiver of Grounds of Inadmissibility

For Government Use Only.

Fee Receipt Number (This application):	Fee Stamp
Alien Registration Number (A# of This Applicant):	

APPLICANT: See instructions before filling in this application. If you need more space to answer fully any question on this form, use a separate sheet and identify each answer with the number of the corresponding question. Type or print in black ink.

1. Family Name *(Last Name in CAPITAL letters)* *(First Name)* *(Middle Name)*

2. Date of Birth *(mm/dd/yyyy)*

3. Address *(No. and Street)* *(Apt. No.)* *(City/Town)* *(State/Country)* *(Zip/Postal Code)*

4. Place of Birth *(City or Town and County, Province or State)* *(Country)*

5. U.S. Social Security Number

6. Date of Visa Application *(mm/dd/yyyy)* **for:** ☐ Permanent Residence ☐ Temporary Residence

7. Visa applied for at:

8. I am applying for a waiver of: ☐ 212 (a) (1)(A)(i), (ii), (iii) or (iv) ☐ 212 (a)(2)(C)(i)(II) - possession of marijuana, 30 gms or less

☐ 212 (a)(6)(A)(i) ☐ 212(a)(6)(C)(i) or (ii) ☐ 212(a)(6)(D) and/or (E) ☐ 212(a)(8)(A) and/or (B) ☐ 212(a)(9)(A)(i) or (ii)

☐ 212(a)(9)(B)(i)(I) or (i)(II) ☐ 212(a)(9)(C)(i)(I) or (i)(II) ☐ 212 (a)(10)(A), (B), (C), (D), and/or (E) - Please specify: ________

9. List reasons of inadmissibility:

10. List all immediate relatives in the United States *(parents, spouse and children):*

Name	Address	Relationship	Immigration Status

11. I should be granted a waiver because: *(Describe family unity considerations or humanitarian or public interest reasons for granting a waiver). If more space is needed attach an additional sheet.*

12. Applicant's Signature

13. Date

FOR USCIS USE ONLY. Recommended by:

*(Print Name and Title)*________________________ Date ____________

Signature ____________ *Stamp #* ________ Director ____________

f

Supplement for Applicants With Human Immunodeficiency Virus (HIV) Infection or Tuberculosis (TB)

Part A. Applicant's Sponsor in the U.S.

1. Make arrangements for the applicant's medical care and have the attending physician or facility complete **Part C**.
2. Obtain the necessary endorsements.
   a. **Treatment is being provided by a state or local health department:** If a state or local health department will provide the necessary care and/or treatment to the applicant, that facility should check block (a) in Number 4 under **Part C**. The health department is not required to complete anything else on this form.
   b. **Treatment is being provided by a private physician or by any other private or public facility:** If a private physician, a private medical facility or a public medical facility (other than a state or local health department) will provide the applicant's medical care and/or treatment, that facility should check block (b) or (c) under Number 4 of **Part C**, as applicable. In that case, the state or local health department in the jurisdiction where the applicant will reside must complete **Part D**.
3. Address in the United States where the applicant plans to reside:

Address *(Number and Street)* *(Apartment No.)*

City, State and Zip Code

Part B. Applicant's Statement:

Upon admission to the United States I will:

1. Go directly to the physician or health facility named in Number 5 of **Part C**;
2. Present copies of diagnostic tests used on the visa examination to substantiate diagnosis;
3. Submit to counseling and such examinations, treatment and medical regimen as may be required; and
4. Remain under prescribed treatment or observation whether on inpatient or outpatient basis, until discharged.

Part C. *Statement by Physician or Health Facility:*

1. I agree to supply counseling and any treatment or observation necessary for the proper management of the applicant's condition. *(Check applicable box(es):*

   ☐ HIV Infection ☐ Tuberculosis

2. I agree to submit a copy of my evaluation to the Division of Global Migration and Quarantine (E03), Centers for Disease Control and Prevention, Atlanta, Georgia 30333, and certify the following:
   a. I will submit a copy of my evaluation within 30 days of the date the applicant is required to appear for evaluation and/or care; and
   b. If at the end of the 30-day period the applicant fails to appear for evaluation and/or care as required, I will submit a report to that effect to the CDC.
3. Satisfactory financial arrangements have been made for the applicant's medical care and treatment. (This statement does not relieve the applicant from submitting evidence, as required by the consular officer or USCIS, to establish that he or she is not likely to become a public charge (another ground of inadmissibility under section 212(a)(4) of the Immigration and Nationality Act).
4. I represent: *(Check the appropriate box and provide the information requested below)*
   a. ☐ Local Health Department
   b. ☐ Other Public Health Facility
   c. ☐ Private Medical Practice
5. ☐ I agree to submit a copy of my evaluation to the health officer indicated in **Part D**. *(Required if you checked block (b) or (c) in Number 4 directly above.)*

Name of Physician or Facility *(Please type or print)*

Address *(Number and Street)*

City, State and Zip Code

Signature of Physician Date

Part D. Endorsement of Local or State Health Officer :

Endorsement signifies recognition of the physician or facility for the purpose of providing care for HIV infection or tuberculosis. If the facility physician who signed in **Part C** is not in your health jurisdiction or is not familiar to you, you may wish to contact the health officer responsible for the jurisdiction, and/or the physician, before you sign this endorsement.

Official Name of Department *(Please type or print)*

Signature Date

Name of Health Department to receive the required notice from the CDC following the Applicant's arrival in the U.S./adjustment of status. *(Please type or print)*

Address *(Number and Street)*

City, State and Zip Code

OMB No. 1615-0029; Expires 01/31/07

Department of Homeland Security
U.S. Citizenship and Immigration Services

I-601, Application for Waiver of Grounds of Inadmissibility

Instructions

NOTE: Please read instructions carefully. Fee will not be refunded. Type or print legibly in black ink.

1. Filing the Application.

The application and supporting documents should be taken or mailed to:

- The American Embassy or Consulate where the applicant is applying for a visa, if the applicant is not in the United States; or
- The office of the U.S. Citizenship and Immigration Services (USCIS) having jurisdiction over the applicant's place of residence, if the applicant is in the United States and applying for status as a permanent resident.

2. What is the Fee?

No fee is required if this application is filed for an alien who:

- Is afflicted with tuberculosis;
- Is mentally retarded; or
- Has a history of mental illness.

All other applications must be accompanied by a fee of **$265.00.** The fee cannot be refunded, regardless of the action taken on the application. **Do not mail cash.**

NOTE: Only a single application and fee is required when an alien is applying simultaneously for a waiver both sections 212 (h) and (i) of the Immigration and Nationality Act.

Payment must be made by a check or money order:

- Drawn on a bank or other institution located in the United States;
- Payable in U.S. currency; and
- **Payable in the exact amount.**

If the check is drawn on an account of a person other than the applicant, the name of the applicant must be entered on the face of the check.

Personal checks are accepted subject to collectibility. An uncollectible check will void the application and any documents issued pursuant to the application. A charge of $30.00 will be imposed if the check is not honored by the bank on which it is drawn.

Unless the applicant resides in the U.S. Virgin Islands or Guam, the check or money order must be made payable to the **Department of Homeland Security.**

- If the applicant resides in Guam, make the check or money order payable to the "Treasurer, Guam."
- If the applicant resides in the U.S. Virgin Islands, make the check or money order payable to the "Commissioner of Finance of the Virgin Islands."

How to Check If the Fee Is Correct.

The fee on this form is current as of the edition date appearing in the lower right corner of this page. However, because USCIS fees change periodically, you can verify if the fee is correct by following one of the steps below:

- Visit our website at **www.uscis.gov** and scroll down to "Forms and E-Filing" to check the appropriate fee, or
- Review the Fee Schedule included in your form package, if you called us to request the form, or
- Telephone our National Customer Service Center at **1-800-375-5283** and ask for the fee information.

3. Applicants With Tuberculosis.

An applicant with active tuberculosis or suspected tuberculosis must complete **Statement A** on **Page 2** of this form. The applicant and his or her sponsor is also responsible for having:

- **Statement B** completed by the physician or health facility which has agreed to provide treatment or observation, and **Statement D**, if required, completed by the appropriate local or state health officer.

This form should then be returned to the applicant for presentation to the consular office or appropriate USCIS office.

Submission of the application without the required fully executed statements will result in the return of the application to the applicant without further action.

4. Applicants With Mental Conditions.

An alien who is mentally retarded or who has a history of mental illness shall attach a statement that arrangements have been made for the submission of a medical report, as follows, to the office where this form is filed:

The medical report shall contain:

- A complete medical history of the alien, including details of any hospitalization or institutional care or treatment for any physical or mental condition;
- Findings as to the current physical condition of the alien, including reports of chest X-rays and a serologic test if the alien is 15 years of age or older, and other pertinent diagnostic tests; and
- Findings as to the current mental condition of the alien, with information as to prognosis and life expectancy and with a report of a psychiatric examination conducted by a psychiatrist who shall, in the case of mental retardation, also provide an evaluation of intelligence.

For an alien with a past history of mental illness, the medical report shall also contain available information on which the U.S. Public Health Service can base a finding as to whether the alien has been free of such mental illness for a period of time, sufficient in the light of such history, to demonstrate recovery.

The medical report will be referred to the U.S. Public Health Service for review and, if found acceptable, the alien will be required to submit such additional assurances as the U.S. Public Health Service may deem necessary in his or her particular case.

5. USCIS Forms and Information.

To order USCIS forms, telephone our toll-free forms line at **1-800-870-3676.** You can also get USCIS forms and information on immigration laws, regulations and procedures, by calling our National Customer Service Center at **1-800-375-5283** or visiting our website at **www.uscis.gov.**

6. Use InfoPass to Make an Appointment.

As an alternative to waiting in line for assistance at your local USCIS office, you can now schedule an appointment through our internet-based system, **InfoPass.** To access the system, visit our website at **www.uscis.gov.** Use the **InfoPass** appointment scheduler and follow the screen prompts to set up your appointment. **InfoPass** generates an electronic appointment notice that appears on the screen. Print the notice and take it with you to your appointment. The notice gives the time and date of your appointment, along with the address of the USCIS office.

7. Public Reporting Burden.

A person is not required to respond to a collection of information unless it displays a currently valid OMB control number. Public reporting burden for this collection of information is estimated to average 30 minutes per response, including the time for reviewing instructions, searching existing data sources, gathering and maintaining the data needed, and completing and reviewing the collection of information. Send comments regarding this burden estimate or any other aspect of this collection of information, including suggestions for reducing this burden, to the U.S. Citizenship and Immigration Services, Regulatory Management Division, 111 Massachusetts Avenue, N.W., Washington, D. C. 20529; OMB No. 1615-0029. **Do not mail your completed application to this address.**

OMB No. 1615-0029; Expires 01/31/07

Department of Homeland Security
U.S. Citizenship and Immigration Services

I-601, Application for Waiver of Grounds of Inadmissibility

Do not write in this block. For Government use only.

☐ 212 (a) (1)	☐ 212 (a) (10)	Fee Stamp
☐ 212 (a) (3)	☐ 212 (a) (12)	
☐ 212 (a) (6)	☐ 212 (a) (19)	
☐ 212 (a) (9)	☐ 212 (a) (23)	

A. Information about applicant.

1. Family Name (Surname In CAPS) (First) (Middle)

2. Address (Number and Street) (Apartment Number)

3. (Town or City) (State/Country) (Zip/Postal Code)

Telephone Number E-Mail Address

4. Date of Birth *(mm/dd/yyyy)* **5.** USCIS File Number

A-

6. City/Province-State of Birth

7a. Country of Birth **7b.** Country of Citizenship/Nationality

8. Date of Visa Application **9.** Visa Applied for at:

10. Applicant was declared inadmissible to the United States for the following reasons: (List acts, convictions, or physical or mental conditions. If applicant has active or suspected tuberculosis, **Page 2** of this form must be fully completed.)

11. Applicant was previously in the United States, as follows:

City and State	From (Date)	To (Date)	Immigration Status

12. Applicant's U.S. Social Security Number (if any)

B. Information about relative, through whom applicant claims eligibility for a waiver.

1. Family Name (Surname in CAPS) (First) (Middle)

2. Address (Number and Street) (Apartment Number)

3. (Town or City) (State) (Zip/Postal Code)

Telephone Number E-Mail Address

4. Relationship to Applicant **5.** Immigration Status

FOR USCIS USE ONLY. DO NOT WRITE IN THIS AREA.

Initial receipt	Resubmitted	Relocated		Completed		
		Received	Sent	Approved	Denied	Returned

Form I-601 (Rev. 10/26/05)Y

C. Information about applicant's other relatives in the United States. *(List only U.S. citizens and permanent residents)*

1. Family Name (Surname in CAPS) (First) (Middle)

2. Address (Number and Street) (Apartment Number)

3. (Town or City) (State) (Zip/Postal Code)

4. Relationship to Applicant 5. Immigration Status

1. Family Name (Surname in CAPS) (First) (Middle)

2. Address (Number and Street) (Apartment Number)

3. (Town or City) (State) (Zip/Postal Code)

4. Relationship to Applicant 5. Immigration Status

1. Family Name (Surname in CAPS) (First) (Middle)

2. Address (Number and Street) (Apartment Number)

3. (Town or City) (State) (Zip/Postal Code)

4. Relationship to Applicant 5. Immigration Status

CERTIFICATION: Signature (of applicant or petitioning relative)

Relationship to Applicant Date

PREPARER OF APPLICATION: Signature (of person preparing application, if not the applicant or petitioning relative). I declare that this document was prepared by me at the request of the applicant or petitioning relative, and is based on all information of which I have any knowledge.

Signature

Address Date

To Be Completed for Applicants With Active Tuberculosis or Suspected Tuberculosis

A. Statement by Applicant.

Upon admission to the United States I will:

- Go directly to the physician or health facility named in **Section B**;
- Present all X-rays used in the visa medical examination to substantiate diagnosis;
- Submit to such examinations, treatment, isolation and medical regimen as may be required; and
- Remain under the prescribed treatment or observation whether on inpatient or outpatient basis, until discharged.

Signature of Applicant

Date

B. Statement by Physician or Health Facility.

(May be executed by a private physician, health department, other public or private health facility or military hospital.)

I agree to supply any treatment or observation necessary for the proper management of the alien's tuberculosis condition.

I agree to submit Form CDC 75.18, "Report on Alien with Tuberculosis Waiver," to the health officer named in **Section D**:

- Within 30 days of the alien's reporting for care, indicating presumptive diagnosis, test results and plans for future care of the alien; or
- 30 days after receiving Form CDC 75.18, if the alien has not reported.

Satisfactory financial arrangements have been made. (This statement does not relieve the alien from submitting evidence, as required by consul, to establish that the alien is not likely to become a public charge.)

I represent (enter an "X" in the appropriate box and give the complete name and address of the facility below.)

- ☐ **1.** Local Health Department
- ☐ **2.** Other Public or Private Facility
- ☐ **3.** Private Practice
- ☐ **4.** Military Hospital

Name of Facility (Please type or print in black ink)

Address (Number and Street) **(Room/Suite Number)**

City, State and Zip Code

Signature of Physician **Date**

C. Applicant's Sponsor in the United States.

Arrange for medical care of the applicant and have the physician complete **Section B**.

If medical care will be provided by a physician who checked **Box 2** or **3**, in **Section B**, have **Section D** completed by the local or State Health Officer who has jurisdiction in the United States area where the applicant plans to reside.

If medical care will be provided by a physician who checked **Box 4**, in **Section B**, forward this form directly to the military facility at the address provided in **Section B**.

Address in the United States where the alien plans to reside:

Address (Number and Street) (Apt #)

City, State and Zip Code

D. Endorsement of Local or State Health Officer.

Endorsement signifies recognition of the physician or facility for the purpose of providing care for tuberculosis. If the facility or physician who signed his or her name in **Section B** is not in your health jurisdiction and not familiar to you, you may want to contact the health officer responsible for the jurisdiction of the facility or physician prior to endorsing.

Endorsed by: **Signature of Health Officer**

Date

Enter below the name and address of the Local Health Department where the "Notice of Arrival of Alien with Tuberculosis Waiver" should be sent when the alien arrives in the United States.

Official Name of Department

Address (Number and Street) (Room/Suite Number)

City, State and Zip Code

NOTE: If further assistance is needed, contact the USCIS office with jurisdiction over the intended place of United States residence of the applicant.

OMB No. 1615-0029; Expires 01/31/07

Department of Homeland Security
U.S. Citizenship and Immigration Services

I-601, Application for Waiver of Grounds of Inadmissibility

Do not write in this block. For Government use only.

☐ 212 (a) (1)	☐ 212 (a) (10)	Fee Stamp
☐ 212 (a) (3)	☐ 212 (a) (12)	
☐ 212 (a) (6)	☐ 212 (a) (19)	
☐ 212 (a) (9)	☐ 212 (a) (23)	

A. Information about applicant.

1. Family Name (Surname In CAPS) (First) (Middle)

2. Address (Number and Street) (Apartment Number)

3. (Town or City) (State/Country) (Zip/Postal Code)

Telephone Number E-Mail Address

4. Date of Birth *(mm/dd/yyyy)* **5.** USCIS File Number A-

6. City/Province-State of Birth

7a. Country of Birth **7b.** Country of Citizenship/Nationality

8. Date of Visa Application **9.** Visa Applied for at:

10. Applicant was declared inadmissible to the United States for the following reasons: (List acts, convictions, or physical or mental conditions. If applicant has active or suspected tuberculosis, **Page 2** of this form must be fully completed.)

11. Applicant was previously in the United States, as follows:

City and State	From (Date)	To (Date)	Immigration Status

12. Applicant's U.S. Social Security Number (if any)

B. Information about relative, through whom applicant claims eligibility for a waiver.

1. Family Name (Surname in CAPS) (First) (Middle)

2. Address (Number and Street) (Apartment Number)

3. (Town or City) (State) (Zip/Postal Code)

Telephone Number E-Mail Address

4. Relationship to Applicant **5.** Immigration Status

FOR USCIS USE ONLY. DO NOT WRITE IN THIS AREA.	Initial receipt	Resubmitted	Relocated		Completed		
			Received	Sent	Approved	Denied	Returned

C. Information about applicant's other relatives in the United States. *(List only U.S. citizens and permanent residents)*

1. Family Name (Surname in CAPS) (First) (Middle)

2. Address (Number and Street) (Apartment Number)

3. (Town or City) (State) (Zip/Postal Code)

4. Relationship to Applicant 5. Immigration Status

1. Family Name (Surname in CAPS) (First) (Middle)

2. Address (Number and Street) (Apartment Number)

3. (Town or City) (State) (Zip/Postal Code)

4. Relationship to Applicant 5. Immigration Status

1. Family Name (Surname in CAPS) (First) (Middle)

2. Address (Number and Street) (Apartment Number)

3. (Town or City) (State) (Zip/Postal Code)

4. Relationship to Applicant 5. Immigration Status

USCIS Use Only: Additional Information and Instructions

Signature and Title of Requesting Officer

Address Date

This office will maintain only a folder relating to the applicant pursuant to A.M. 2712.01

AGENCY COPY

OMB APPROVAL NO. 1115-0055

U.S. Department of Justice
Immigration and Naturalization Service

Application for Stay of Deportation or Removal

Fee Stamp

SUBMIT IN DUPLICATE

Read instructions on reverse before filling out application

File No.
Date

1. Name (Family Name in CAPITAL letters, First, Middle)	
2. Present Address (Apt. No.) (Number and Street) (Town or City) (State) (Zip Code)	
3. Country of Citizenship	4. Date to which passport is valid (Attach passport)
5. Country to which deportation or removal has been ordered	6. Date to which stay of deportation or removal is requested
7. Reasons for requesting stay of deportation or removal	

8. I certify that the statements I have made in this application are true and correct to the best of my knowledge and belief.

(Signature) (Location) (Date)

9. Signature of person preparing form, if other than applicant.
I declare that this document was prepared by me at the request of the applicant and is based on all information of which I have knowledge. Failure by a preparer to complete this block may result in criminal prosecution and, upon conviction, a fine or imprisonment.

(Signature) (Printed Name) (Date)

APPLICANT: DO NOT WRITE BELOW THIS LINE

Stay ☐ Denied ☐ Granted ______ at ______
(Date) (Place Where Granted)

By ______ ______ ______
(Signature) (Title) (Date)

Form I-246 (Rev. 09/19/00)Y

INSTRUCTIONS

1. May I file this application? - You may file this application if you have been ordered deported or removed from the United States and you wish to obtain a stay of deportation or removal under the provisions of 8 CFR 241.6.

2. Where should I submit the application? - Submit this application to the local office of the Immigration and Naturalization Service (INS) having jurisdiction over the place you are currently located. If you are unsure of the address of that office, you may either check the listing in your local telephone book or call 1-800-375-5283 and receive the address based on your telephonic area code.

3. What additional documents or evidence should I submit with this application? - PASSPORT. You must submit a passport valid for at least 60 days beyond the expiration of the requested stay with this application, or explain why this is not possible to do so. ADDITIONAL EVIDENCE. You may submit any additional evidence in support of your application which you want considered by INS.

4. If the application is denied, may I file an appeal from that decision? - No. The denial of an application for a stay of deportation or removal may not be appealed.

5. What fee should I submit with the application? - A fee of $155.00 must be paid for filing this application. It cannot be refunded regardless of the action taken on the application. DO NOT MAIL CASH. ALL FEES MUST BE SUBMITTED IN THE EXACT AMOUNT. Payment by check or money order must be drawn on a bank or other institution located in the United States and be payable in United States currency. If the applicant resides in Guam, check or money order must be payable to the "Treasurer, Guam." If the applicant resides in the Virgin Islands, check or money order must be payable to the "Commissioner of Finance, Virgin Islands." All other applicants must make the check or money order payable to the "Immigration and Naturalization Service." When the check is drawn on the account of a person other than the applicant, the name of the applicant must be entered on the face of the check. If the application is submitted from outside the United States, remittance may be made by bank international money order of foreign draft drawn on a financial institution in the United States and payable to the Immigration and Naturalization Service in United States currency. Personal checks are accepted subject to collectibility. An uncollectible check will render the application and any document issued pursuant thereto invalid. A charge of $30.00 will be imposed if a check in payment of a fee is not honored by the bank on which it is drawn.

6. Under what authority is the information requested? - The authority to prescribe this form is contained in 8 U.S.C. 1203(a). Submission of the information requested on this form is voluntary. The solicited information will be used by INS principally to determine whether the applicant is eligible for a stay of deportation or removal under the provisions of 8 CFR 241.6. The information may also, as a matter of routine, be used by or disclosed to other federal, state, local and foreign law enforcement and regulatory agencies. All applicants are subject to a check of criminal information databases in order to determine eligibility.

7. What can happen if I submit false information? - All statements made in response to questions in this application are declared to be true and correct and under penalty of perjury. Title 18, United States Code, Section 1546, provides, in part:

> ...Whoever knowingly makes under oath, or as permitted under penalty of perjury under section 1746 of Title 28, United States Code, knowingly subscribes as true, any false statement with respect to a material fact in any application, affidavit, or other document required by the immigration laws or regulations prescribed thereunder, or knowingly presents any such application, affidavit, or other document containing any such false statement - shall be fined in accordance with this title or imprisoned not more than five years, or both.

The knowing placement of false information on the application may subject you, or the preparer of this application, to criminal penalties under 18 U.S.C., and you and the preparer to civil penalties under section 274C of the INA, 8 U.S.C. 1324c.

Paperwork Reduction Act Notice.
Under the paperwork Reduction Act, a person is not required to respond to a collection of information unless it displays a currently valid OMB control number. We try to create forms and instructions that are easily understood and which impose the least possible burden on you to provide us with information. Often this is difficult because some immigration laws are very complex. The estimated average time to complete and file this application is 30 minutes. If you have comments regarding the accuracy of this estimate or suggestions for making this form simpler, you can write to the Immigration and Naturalization Service, HQPDI, 425 I Street N.W., Room 4034, Washington, DC 20536; OMB No. 1115-0055. **Do not mail your completed application to this address.**

NOTICE

Neither the filing of this application, nor the failure to receive a notice of decision thereon shall relieve or excuse the applicant from presenting himself or herself for deportation or removal at the time and place designated for deportation or removal.

Form I-246 (Rev. 09/19/00) Y

OMB No. 1615-0072; Exp. 02-28-06

Department of Homeland Security
U.S. Citizenship and Immigration Services
Department of Justice
U.S. Executive Office for Immigration Review

I-881, Application for Suspension of Deportation or Special Rule Cancellation of Removal

(Pursuant to Section 203 of Public Law 105-100, NACARA)

Instructions

Application for Suspension of Deportation or Special Rule Cancellation of Removal Pursuant to Section 203 of Public Law 105-100, the Nicaraguan Adjustment and Central American Relief Act (NACARA)

What Is the Purpose of This Form?

This form is to be used by any alien eligible to apply for suspension of deportation or special rule cancellation of removal under section 203 of Public Law 105-100, the Nicaraguan Adjustment and Central American Relief Act (NACARA 203).

You may use this form only if:

(1) You are a national of El Salvador or Guatemala, or

(2) You were, on December 31, 1991, a national of the Soviet Union, Russia, any Republic of the former Soviet Union (including Armenia, Azerbaijan, Belarus, Georgia, Kazakstan, Kyrgyzstan, Moldova, Tajikistan, Turkmenistan, Ukraine, and Uzebekistan), Latvia, Estonia, Lithuania, Poland, Czechoslovakia, Romania, Hungary, Bulgaria, Albania, East Germany (German Democratic Republic), Yugoslavia, or any state of the former Yugoslavia (including Bosnia, Croatia, Macedonia, Slovenia, and Serbia and Montenegro), or

(3) You are the spouse, child or unmarried son or unmarried daughter of one of the above described nationals. In addition, you must meet the other requirments explained in these instructions. Certain individuals who have been battered or subjected to extreme cruelty, or whose child has been battered or subjected to extreme cruelty, may also use this form, if they meet the criteria outlined in Part I of this form.

If you are in immigration proceedings before the Executive Office for Immigration Review (EOIR) and are not eligible to apply for suspension of deportation or special rule cancellation of removal under section 203 of NACARA, you must use a Form EOIR-40 Application for Suspension of Deportation (if you are in deportation proceedings) or a Form EOIR-42B Application for Cancellation of Removal and Adjustment of Status for Certain Nonpermanent Residents (if you are in removal proceedings).

These instructions are presented in eight parts:

- **Part I** explains who is eligible to apply for suspension of deportation or special rule cancellation of removal under section 203 of NACARA.
- **Part II** explains eligibility to be granted NACARA relief.
- **Part III** explains how to complete this application.
- **Part IV** explains how to apply before the Department of Homeland Security (DHS), U.S. Citizenship and Immigration Services (USCIS). USCIS is comprised of offices of the former Immigration and Naturalization Service (INS).
- **Part V** explains how to apply before the Immigration Court.
- **Part VI** contains information regarding the types of supporting documents you may wish to submit with your application to show that you are eligible for NACARA relief.
- **Part VII** contains information about employment authorization.
- **Part VIII** contains information about change of address notification requirements.

Please read these instructions carefully. The instructions will help you complete your application and understand how it will be processed.

WARNING: Applicants who are in the United States illegally are subject to deportation or removal if their suspension of deportation or special rule cancellation of removal claims are not granted by an asylum officer or an Immigration Judge. Any information provided in completing this application may be used as a basis for the institution of, or as evidence in, deportation or removal proceedings, even if the application is later withdrawn. If you have any concerns about this, you should consult with an attorney or representative before you submit this application to the USCIS.

INDEX

PART I: WHO IS ELIGIBLE TO APPLY FOR SUSPENSION OF DEPORTATION OR SPECIAL RULE CANCELLATION OF REMOVAL UNDER SECTION 203 OF NACARA?

If you have not been convicted of an aggravated felony and you are described in one of the following five categories, you are eligible to apply for suspension of deportation or special rule cancellation of removal under section 203 of NACARA.

You **must** be described in one of these categories to use this form:

A.i. A **Salvadoran** national who:

- First entered the United States on or before September 19, 1990;
- Registered for benefits under the ABC settlement agreement (*American Baptist Churches v. Thornburgh,* 760 F. Supp. 796 (N.D. Cal. 1991)) on or before October 31, 1991 (either by submitting an ABC registration form or by applying for temporary protected status - TPS); and
- Was not apprehended at the time of entry after December 19, 1990.

You may apply with USCIS only if you have also applied for asylum on or before February 16, 1996, and USCIS has not issued a final decision on your asylum application. Even if you have been placed in deportation or removal proceedings, you may still be eligible to apply with USCIS, if those proceedings have been administratively closed under the ABC settlement agreement.

To make an initial application before the Immigration Court, you must be in deportation or removal proceedings.

If you are described in this category, check (a) in Part 2 of the attached form.

A.ii. A **Guatemalan** national who:

- First entered the United States on or before October 1, 1990;
- Registered for benefits under the ABC settlement agreement (*American Baptist Churches v. Thornburgh,* 760 F. Supp. 796 (N.D. Cal. 1991)) on or before December 31, 1991; and
- Was not apprehended at the time of entry after December 19, 1990.

You may apply with USCIS only if you have also applied for asylum on or before January 3, 1995, and USCIS has not issued a final decision on your asylum application. Even if you have been placed in deportation or removal proceedings, you may still be eligible to apply with USCIS, if those proceedings have been administratively closed under the ABC settlement agreement.

To make an initial application before the Immigration Court, you must be in deportation or removal proceedings.

If you are described in this category, check (a) in Part 2 of the attached form.

B. A **Guatemalan** or **Salvadoran** national who filed an application for asylum on or before April 1, 1990.

You may apply with USCIS only if USCIS has not issued a final decision on your asylum application.

To make an initial application before the Immigration Court, you must be in deportation or removal proceedings.

If you are described in this category, check (b) in Part 2 of the attached form.

C. An alien who:

- Entered the United States on or before December 31, 1990;
- Filed an application for asylum on or before December 31, 1991; and
- At the time of filing the application was a national of the **Soviet Union, Russia, any republic of the former Soviet Union, Albania, Bulgaria, Czechoslovakia, East Germany, Estonia, Hungary, Latvia, Lithuania, Poland, Romania, Yugoslavia, or any state of the former Yugoslavia.**

You may apply with USCIS only if USCIS has not issued a final decision on your asylum application.

To make an initial application before the Immigration Court, you must be in deportation or removal proceedings.

If you are described in this category, check (c) in Part 2 of the attached form.

D. The **spouse, child, unmarried son, or unmarried daughter** of an individual described in Part I (A), (B), or (C) above, who has been granted suspension of deportation or cancellation of removal. The relationship to your spouse or parent must exist at the time that your spouse or parent is granted suspension of deportation or cancellation of removal. If you are an unmarried son or unmarried daughter at least 21 years of age at the time your parent is granted the benefit, you must have entered the United States on or before October 1, 1990.

You may apply with USCIS only if USCIS has granted your parent or spouse suspension of deportation or special rule cancellation of removal, or your parent or spouse has a Form I-881 **pending** with USCIS. You may submit your application at the same time as your parent or spouse, while your parent's or spouse's application is still pending with USCIS or after your parent or spouse has already been granted suspension of deportation or special rule cancellation of removal by USCIS. You may also apply with USCIS if you were in deportation or removal proceedings and those proceedings have been closed to give you the opportunity to apply for suspension of deportation or special rule cancellation of removal with USCIS because your parent or spouse has applied with USCIS.

If USCIS does not grant suspension of deportation or special rule cancellation of removal to your spouse or parent and you appear to be inadmissible or deportable, USCIS will refer your application to the Immigration Court to be decided in removal proceedings.

To make an initial application before the Immigration Court, you must be in deportation or removal proceedings.

If you are described in this category, check (d) in Part 2 of the attached form.

E. **An alien who has been battered or subjected to extreme cruelty** by an individual described in Part 1(A), (B), or (C), and who was the spouse or child of that individual at the time that individual:

- Was granted suspension of deportation or cancellation of removal;
- Filed an application for suspension of deportation or cancellation of removal;
- Registered for ABC benefits;
- Applied for temporary protected status (TPS); or
- Applied for asylum.

An alien whose child has been battered or subjected to extreme cruelty by an individual described in Part 1(A), (B), or (C), and who was the spouse of that individual at any of the times described in the bullets above is also eligible to apply.

USCIS does not have authority to decide eligibility for NACARA 203 relief for individuals described only in paragraph (E). Special provisions for individuals described in that paragraph are applied only to cases decided in Immigration Court. Therefore, if you are applying as a spouse or child who has been battered or subjected to extreme cruelty, you must make your initial application before the Immigration Court.

To make an initial application before the Immigration Court, you must be in deportation or removal proceedings.

If you are described in this category, check (e) in Part 2 of the attached form.

PART II: ELIGIBILITY TO BE GRANTED RELIEF.

You may be eligible for NACARA 203 relief if you fall into category (a), (b), (c), or (d) of Part 2 of the form **and** you have established seven years of continuous physical presence in the United States, good moral character for that time period, and that you or your spouse, parent or child who is a United States citizen or lawful permanent resident will experience extreme hardship if you are returned to your country.

You may be eligible for NACARA 203 relief if you fall into category (e) of Part 2 of the form **and** you have established three years continuous physical presence, good moral character for that time period, and you or your spouse, parent or child who is a United States citizen or lawful permanent resident will experience extreme hardship if you are returned to your country.

Other requirements may apply, including ten years physical presence and a showing of exceptional and extremely unusual hardship upon your return to your country, if you are deportable or removable from the United States based on certain provisions in the immigration law. There are also special provisions for individuals who have served in the U.S. Military.

PART III: HOW TO COMPLETE THE APPLICATION.

A. General Instructions.

Submit a separate application for each applicant. A separate application must be prepared and submitted for each person applying for suspension of deportation or special rule cancellation of removal. An application on behalf of a person who is mentally incompetent or is a child under 14 years of age must be signed by a parent or guardian. Applicants who check category (d) only in Part 2 on the first page of the form must submit proof of relationship to the parent or spouse who is applying or has applied for suspension of deportation or special rule cancellation of removal.

Applicants who check category (e) of Part 2 on the first page of the form should also submit evidence of the past relationship with the individual described in Part 1 (A), (B), or (C) of these instructions. If you checked category (e) of Part 2 of the form you will also be asked to submit evidence of the battery or extreme cruelty.

Answer in English. You must fully and accurately answer all questions, providing explanations as required on the attached Form I-881. **Your answers must be in English.** Your responses must be typed or printed legibly in ink. Do not leave any questions unanswered or blank. If any question does not apply to you, write 'None" or "N/A" in the appropriate space. **An incomplete form may be returned to you for completion.**

Attach additional sheets and documents where necessary. Answer questions directly on the form, where possible. However, if you do not have enough space on the form to respond to a question fully, please continue your answer on an additional sheet. You may use page 8 of the form for this purpose. **You are strongly urged to attach additional written statements and documents that support your claim.** ABC class members who check category (a) or (b) in Part 2 of the attached form do not need to submit documentation to support a claim that removal would result in extreme hardship. (See Part VI of these instructions.)

If you need more than one additional sheet, please photocopy page 8 or attach additional sheets that show your Alien Registration Number (A#), name (exactly as it appears in Part I of the form), signature, date and the number of the question being answered.

You may amend and supplement your application. You will be permitted to amend or supplement your application at the time of your hearing in Immigration Court or at your interview with a USCIS asylum officer, by providing additional information and explanations about your claim.

B. Translation of Documents.

Any document you submit that is in a language other than English must be accompanied by an English language translation and a certificate signed by the translator stating that he or she is competent to translate the document and that the translation is true and accurate to the best of the translator's abilities. The certification must be printed legibly or typed.

C. Fees.

Fees required. To apply for suspension of deportation or special rule cancellation of removal, you must pay the filing fee of **$285.00** per individual application submitted, with the exception that all immediate family members (spouse, child, unmarried son or unmarried daughter) who submit their applications together in a single package are eligible for the family filing fee of **$570.00. Note that the fees you must pay if you are applying in Immigration Court are different from the fees you must pay if you are applying with USCIS.**

In addition, each person applying must pay a biometric services fee of **$70.00** for USCIS to take their fingerprints and photograph, and if also required, their signature. There is no family discount for the biometric services fee.

If you are unable to pay the fees, you may ask permission to file your Form I-881 without fees, pursuant to 8 CFR § 103.7(c).

These fees will not be refunded, regardless of the action taken on your application. Therefore, it is important that you read the instructions and application carefully before applying.

Form of payment. All fees must be submitted in the exact amount. Payment may be made by cash, personal check, cashier's check, certified bank check, bank international money order, or foreign draft drawn on a financial institution in the United States. Remittances must be payable in United States currency and made payable to the **Department of Homeland Security**. If the check is drawn on an account of a person other than yourself, you must write your name and Alien Registration Number (A#) on the front of the check. An uncollectible check will make your application invalid, and any receipt issued by USCIS for the remittance shall not be binding on USCIS. A charge of $30.00 will be imposed if the check in payment of a fee is not honored by the bank on which it is drawn.

How to pay when applying with USCIS. You must include the required fees with your application when you send it to USCIS. You may use one check to cover the application fee and the fingerprint fee. All immediate family members (spouse, child, unmarried son or unmarried daughter) who wish to take advantage of a family discount for filing fees must send their applications in a single package.

How to pay when applying in Immigration Court. If you are in deportation or removal proceedings and you are applying for suspension of deportation or special rule cancellation of removal with the Immigration Court, you must first pay the fee to the USCIS District Director. After you pay the fee, USCIS will return the Form I-881 to you for submission to the Immigration Court.

Evidence of payment of this fee, in the form of a fee stamp or receipt, must accompany your Form I-881 when you submit it to the Immigration Court.

If you are filing your application with the Immigration Court, you must pay a **$165.00** fee to the **U.S. Department of Justice,** not the Department of Homeland Security. A single fee of $165.00 will be charged by the court whenever applications are filed by two or more aliens in the same proceedings. The $165.00 is not required if USCIS refers the application to the Immigration Court.

How to Check If the Fees Are Correct.

The fees on this form are current as of the edition date appearing in the lower right corner of this page. However, because USCIS fees change periodically, you can verify if the fees are correct by following one of the steps below:

- Visit our website at **www.uscis.gov** and scroll down to "Forms and E-Filing" to check the appropriate fees, or
- Review the Fee Schedule included in your form package, if you called us to request the form, or
- Telephone our National Customer Service Center at **1-800-375-5283** and ask for the fee information.

NOTE: If your petition aplication requires a biometric services fee for USCIS to take your fingerprints, photograph or signature, you can use the same procedure above to confirm the biometrics fee.

D. Biometric Services for Fingerprints, Photograph and Signature.

Each applicant 14 years or older must be fingerprinted and photographed as part of USCIS biometric services. Your fingerprints and photograph must be taken at a designated Application Support Center or Law Enforcement Agency. You will be notified in writing of your appointment date and exact location where you must go for the biometric services. If required, USCIS may also take your signature.

In addition, you must submit with your application, **four adit-style** glossy, unretouched, standard passport-style photographs in color of yourself taken within 30 days of the date you file this application. The photos must have a white background and must not be mounted. The dimension of your full frontal facial position in the photograph should be about 1 inch from chin to top of hair. Using a pencil or felt pen, you should lightly print your name and Alien Registration Number (A#) on the back of each photograph.

PART IV: HOW TO APPLY BEFORE USCIS.

A. Are you eligible to apply before USCIS?

Not everyone who is eligible to apply for suspension of deportation or special rule cancellation of removal is eligible to submit an application for decision by USCIS. Some persons who are eligible to apply may ask for the benefit only in proceedings in Immigration Court. Please see Part I of these instructions to determine whether you are eligible to apply with USCIS.

B. ABC Class Members Who Have Received a Final Order of Deportation.

If you are an ABC class member who is eligible for a new asylum interview with USCIS under the ABC settlement agreement and you are under a final order of deportation that has not been executed, you cannot apply for suspension of deportation with USCIS unless you have filed and been granted a motion to reopen your deportation proceedings, pursuant to 8 CFR §3.43. Once the deportation proceedings have been reopened, you may ask the Immigration Judge to administratively close the proceedings so that you may proceed with your suspension of deportation application with USCIS. To apply with USCIS, you will need to submit to USCIS the fees and documents described in paragraph C below.

C. What to Include With Your Application.

You must send to the appropriate USCIS Service Center the following documents (see section D below for addresses):

- An original completed Form I-881 with all attachments and supporting documents;
- One copy of a completed Form I-881 with all attachments and supporting documents;
- **Four adit-style** photographs of you that meet the requirements described in Part III.D of these instructions;
- Payment for the fees as explained in Part III.C of these instructions or a request for a waiver of the fees pursuant to 8 CFR § 103.7(c);
- Proof of relationship to the spouse or parent who is applying for or has applied for suspension of deportation or special rule cancellation of removal under NACARA 203, if you check only box (d) in Part 2 on the first page of the Form I-881.

Please submit **two copies** of supporting documents and bring the originals with you to your interview with an asylum officer. Any original documents you submit will not be returned to you.

The EOIR-40 form will not be accepted when applying for Section 203 NACARA relief after June 21, 1999, except in the following limited circumstance. If you filed an EOIR-40 before June 21, 1999, and are eligible to apply with USCIS, then you may apply with USCIS by submitting the EOIR-40 attached to a completed first page of the I-881. If you are filing an I-881 or EOIR-40 (with page 1 of the I-881 attached) with USCIS and you have an order to administratively close the proceedings issued by an Immigration Judge or Board of Immigration Appeals, you should attach a copy of the order to your application.

D. Where to File the Application.

If you are eligible to apply for suspension of deportation or special rule cancellation of removal with USCIS, mail your completed application and all supporting documents with the required fees to USCIS Service Center indicated below:

If you live in Alabama, Arkansas, Colorado, Connecticut, Delaware, the District of Columbia, Florida, Georgia, Louisiana, Maine, Maryland, Massachusetts, Mississippi, New Hampshire, New Jersey, New Mexico, New York, North Carolina, Oklahoma, Pennsylvania, the Commonwealth of Puerto Rico, Rhode Island, South Carolina, Tennessee, Texas, Utah, the United States Virgin Islands, Vermont, Virginia, West Virginia or Wyoming, mail your application to:

USCIS Vermont Service Center
Attn: I-881
75 Lower Welden St.
St. Albans, VT 05479-0881

If you live in Alaska, Arizona, California, the Commonwealth of Guam, Hawaii, Idaho, Illinois, Indiana, Iowa, Kansas, Kentucky, Michigan, Minnesota, Missouri, Montana, Nebraska, Nevada, North Dakota, Oregon, Ohio, South Dakota, Washington or Wisconsin, mail your application to:

USCIS California Service Center
P.O. Box 10881
Laguna Niguel, CA 92607-0881

E. Interview Process

You will be notified by USCIS Asylum Office of the date, time and place (address) of a scheduled interview. You should bring a copy of your application and originals of your supporting documents with you when you have your interview. You should also bring some form of identification to your interview, including any passport(s), other travel or identification documents, or Form I-94 Arrival/Departure Record. You have the right to legal representation at your interview, at no cost to the U. S. Government.

If you are unable to proceed with the interview in fluent English, you must provide at no expense to USCIS a competent interpreter fluent in both English and a language that you speak fluently.

Your interpreter must be at least 18 years of age. The following persons cannot serve as your interpreter: your attorney or representative of record, a witness testifying on your behalf at the interview or, if you have an asylum application pending, a representative or employee of your country. Quality interpretation may be crucial to your claim. Such assistance must be obtained, at your expense, prior to the interview.

Failure without good cause to bring a competent interpreter to your interview may be considered an unexcused failure to appear for the interview. Any unexcused failure to appear for an interview may result in dismissal of your application, or it may be referred directly to the Immigration Court.

If you cannot attend the interview, you should send a written request to reschedule your interview, as soon as you know that you cannot attend. You should send your request to USCIS Asylum Office that sent you the interview notice.

F. Decision Process and Admission of Deportability or Inadmissibility.

USCIS cannot grant suspension of deportation or special rule cancellation of removal unless you admit that you are inadmissible to or deportable from the United States. If USCIS determines that you are eligible for suspension of deportation or special rule cancellation of removal, you will be notified that USCIS has found you eligible for the benefit. At that time, you will be asked to sign an admission of deportability or inadmissibility. If you have any concerns about this, you should consult with an attorney or representative before you submit this application to USCIS.

If USCIS grants you suspension of deportation or special rule cancellation of removal, your status will be adjusted to that of a lawful permanent resident. If USCIS determines that you are not eligible for suspension of deportation or special rule cancellation of removal, and you appear to be inadmissible or deportable from the United States, you may be placed in removal proceedings or, if you previously were in proceedings before an Immigration Judge or the Board of Immigration Appeals which were administratively closed, USCIS will move to recalendar those proceedings. At the same time, USCIS will refer your application to EOIR for adjudication in deportation or removal proceedings.

Certain applicants not eligible for a grant by USCIS. USCIS will not be able to grant your application for suspension of deportation if you are deportable under paragraph (2) (criminal grounds), paragraph (3) (failure to register and falsification of documents), or paragraph (4) (security and related grounds) of former section 241(a) of the Immigration and Nationality Act (INA) as it existed prior to April 1, 1997. The CIS will not be able to grant your application for special rule cancellation of removal if you are inadmissible under paragraph (2) (criminal and related grounds) of section 212(a), or deportable under paragraph (2) (criminal offenses other than (A)(iii), relating to aggravated felonies), paragraph (3) (failure to register and falsification of documents), or paragraph (4) (security and related grounds) of section 237 (a) the INA.

However, if you are deportable or inadmissible under these provisions (other than those related to security concerns), you may still be eligible for relief from deportation or removal by an Immigration Judge under certain higher eligibility standards.

USCIS is not able to grant your Form I-881 application if you are eligible to apply only as someone described in Part I (E) of these instructions. Instead, if you are someone described in Part I (E), you may be eligible to apply with the Immigration Court as provided for in Part V below.

PART V: HOW TO APPLY WITH THE IMMIGRATION COURT.

If you are in deportation or removal proceedings, you may apply for suspension of deportation or special rule cancellation of removal only with the Immigration Court, unless proceedings have been administratively closed because 1) you are eligible for an asylum interview with USCIS under the terms of the ABC settlement agreement; or 2) you are a spouse, child, unmarried son or unmarried daughter whose proceedings have been administratively closed because your spouse or parent has a Form I-881 pending with USCIS.

To apply with the Immigration Court, you must serve the following documents on the DHS District Counsel:

- One copy of a completed Form I-881 with all attachments and supporting documents;
- An adit-style photograph of you that meets the requirements explained in Part III(D) of these instructions.

In addition, you must file the following documents with the appropriate Immigration Court:

- An original completed Form I-881 with all attachments and supporting documents;
- Evidence of payment of the filing fee as explained in Part III(C) of these instructions or a request for a waiver of the fee by an Immigration Judge;
- An adit-style photograph of you that meets the requirements explained in Part III(D) of these instructions;
- A certificate showing service of these documents on the DHS District Counsel, unless service is made on the record at the hearing;
- Biographic Information Sheet, G-325A, if you are between 14 and 79 years of age.

Please submit **copies** of supporting documents and bring the originals with you to your hearing with an Immigration Judge. Any original documents you submit will not be returned to you.

The EOIR-40 will not be accepted when applying for NACARA 203 relief after June 21, 1999, except under the following limited circumstance. If you have filed an EOIR-40 before June 21, 1999, you do not need to file the I-881.

PART VI: SUPPORTING DOCUMENTS TO SHOW ELIGIBILITY FOR RELIEF.

Your answers to the questions on this form and your testimony before an asylum officer or Immigration Judge may help you establish that you meet the requirements for this benefit. However, it is also recommended that you submit documents to help support your claim.

Below is a list of documents that you may wish to submit in support of your claim. The list is not exclusive, and you may submit other documents you believe will help support your claim.

Continuous physical presence. Documents that may support your claim of continuous physical presence include, but are not limited to, the following:

- Bankbooks;
- Leases, deeds;
- Licenses;
- Receipts;
- Letters;
- Birth, church, school or employment records;
- Evidence of tax payments, which may include IRS computer printouts;
- Employment Authorization Documents (EAD) or other documents issued by USCIS (or former INS).

Good moral character. Documents that may support your claim of good moral character include, but are not limited to, the following:

- Affidavits, declarations, or letters of at least two witnesses, preferably United States citizens;
- Affidavits, declarations, or letters of your employer, if employed;
- Evidence of tax payments, which may include IRS computer printouts.

Extreme hardship. If you meet the eligibility requirements listed in (a) or (b) in Part 2 on Page 1 of the form, you are an ABC class member eligible to apply for NACARA relief. If you are an ABC class member described in either category (a) or (b) in Part 2 on the form, you will be presumed to meet the extreme hardship requirement unless evidence in the record establishes that neither you nor any qualified relative would experience extreme hardship if you are removed from the United States. As an ABC class member you do not need to initially submit documents that support your claim that your removal would result in extreme hardship.

If you are unsure if you qualify for a presumption of extreme hardship, you should submit documents that support your claim that removal would result in extreme hardship. All individuals who cannot check box (a) or (b) in Part 2 on Page 1 of the form are strongly urged to submit documents to support their claim that removal would result in extreme hardship.

Documents that may support your claim for extreme hardship include, but are not limited to, the following:

- School records of your children;
- Medical records, where relevant;
- Records of your participation in community organizations or a church (for example, letters from others involved in the same organization or church);
- Records of any volunteer work you have done;
- If you are self-employed, documents showing the number of people you employ, if any, and balance sheets;
- Copies of permanent resident alien cards ("Green Cards") of any relatives who may suffer extreme hardship if you are deported or removed.

In addition to the documents described above as examples of support of continuous physical presence, good moral character, and extreme hardship, you should submit with your application copies of any documents that USCIS (or former INS) has issued to you. The Immigration Judge or USCIS asylum officer may require you to submit additional records relating to your request for suspension of deportation or special rule cancellation of removal. These documents may include, but are not limited to, court convictions, payment of child support during the time you have been physically present in the United States, or documents relevant to extreme hardship for ABC class members.

PART VII: EMPLOYMENT AUTHORIZATION.

Applicants for suspension of deportation or special rule cancellation of removal under NACARA 203 are eligible to apply for and be granted employment authorization under 8 CFR 274a.12(c)(10). Applicants who wish to apply for employment authorization under this provision should submit a completed Form I-765, Application for Employment Authorization, following the instructions on that form.

If you are applying for employment authorization with your Form I-881, you should submit the fee for the EAD Form I-765 application on a separate check or money order from the check or money order submitted for the Form I-881 application.

PART VIII: ADDRESS NOTIFICATION REQUIREMENTS, PENALTIES AND PAPERWORK REDUCTION.

A. CHANGE OF ADDRESS.

If you change your address, you must inform the DHS in writing of your new address within ten (10) days of moving.

You must notify the the DHS of any change of address by submitting Form AR-11 (Change of Address Form) to the DHS address listed on the Form within ten (10) days after you change your address. While your application is pending with USCIS Asylum Office, you must also notify USCIS Asylum Office by submitting a copy of the completed Form AR-11, or a signed and dated letter containing the change of address within ten (10) days after you change your address. The address that you provide on the application, or the last change of address notification you submitted, will be used by the DHS for mailing. Any notices mailed to that address will constitute adequate service, except where personal service is required.

If you are already in proceedings in Immigration Court, you MUST notify the Immigration Court on Form EOIR-33/IC (Change of Address Form) of any changes of address within five (5) days of the change of address. You must send the notification to the Immigration Court having jurisdiction over your case.

If you are already in proceedings before the Board of Immigration Appeals, you MUST notify the Board on Form EOIR-33/BIA (Change of Address Form) of any changes of address within five (5) days of the change of address.

B. PENALTIES.

You must answer all questions on Form I-881 truthfully and submit only genuine documents in support of your application. You will be required to swear or affirm that the contents of your application and the supporting documents are true to the best of your knowledge. Your answer to the questions on this form and the supporting documents you present will be used to determine whether your deportation should be suspended or your removal should be canceled. Any answer you give and any supporting documents you present may also be used as evidence in any proceeding to determine your right to be admitted, be readmitted, pass through, or reside in the United States. Your application may be denied if any of your answers or supporting documents are found to be false.

Presenting false answers or false documents may also subject you to criminal prosecution under 18 U.S.C. 1546 and/or subject you to civil penalties under 8 U.S.C. 1324c if you submit your application knowing that the application or any supporting document contains any false statement with respect to a material fact, or if you swear or affirm that the contents of your application and the supporting documents are true, knowing that the application or any supporting document contains any false statement with respect to a material fact.

If convicted, you could be fined up to $250,000, imprisoned for up to five years, or both, according to 18 U.S.C. 1546(a), 3559 (a)(4), 357(b)(3). If it is determined that you have violated the prohibition against document fraud and a final order is entered against you, you could be subject to a civil penalty up to $2,000 for each document used or created for the first offense and up to $5,000 for any second or subsequent offense. In addition, if you are the subject of a final order for violating 8 U.S.C. 1324c, relating to civil penalties for document fraud, you will be removable from the United States.

C. USCIS FORMS AND INFORMATION.

To order USCIS forms, call our toll-free forms line at **1-800-870-3676**. You can also get USCIS forms and information on immigration laws, regulations and procedures by telephoning our National Customer Service Center at **1-800-375-5283** or visit our internet website at **www.uscis.gov.**

D. NEED TO MAKE AN APPOINTMENT AT A USCIS OFFICE? USE INFO PASS.

As an alternative to waiting in line for assistance at your local USCIS office, you can now schedule an appointment through our internet-based system, **InfoPass.** To access the system, visit our website at **www.uscis.gov.** Use the **InfoPass** appointment scheduler and follow the screen prompts to set up your appointment. **InfoPass** generates an electronic appointment notice that appears on the screen. Print the notice and take it with you to your appointment. The notice gives the time and date of your appointment, along with the address of USCIS office.

E. PAPERWORK REDUCTION ACT NOTICE.

An agency may not conduct or sponsor an information collection and a person is not required to respond to an information collection unless it displays a currently valid OMB control number.

We try to create forms and instructions that are accurate, can easily be understood and which impose the least possible burden on you to provide us with information. Often this is difficult because some immigration laws are complex. The reporting burden for this collection of information is computed as follows: (1) learning about the form, 2 hours; (2) completing the form, 5 hours, 3) assembling and filing the form, 5 hours, for an estimated average of 12 hours per application.

If you have comments regarding the accuracy of this estimate, or suggestions for making the form simpler you can write to the U.S. Citizenship and Immigration Services, Regulatory Management Division, 111 Massachusetts Avenue, N.W., Washington, DC 20529. **Do not mail your application to this address.**

OMB No. 1615-0072; Exp. 02-28-06

Department of Homeland Security
U.S. Citizenship and Immigration Services
Department of Justice
U.S. Executive Office for Immigration Review

I-881, Application for Suspension of Deportation or Special Rule Cancellation of Removal

(Pursuant to Section 203 of Public Law 105-100, NACARA)

START HERE - Please type or print in black ink. If any question does not apply to you, write "None" or "N/A" in the appropriate space.

Part 1. Background information about YOU.

Alien Registration Number(s), if any (List every "A-number" you have been given)

Family Name(s)	Given Name	Middle Name

What other names have you used? (Include maiden name and aliases)

Address - Street Number and Name (or P.O. Box) Apt #

City	State Zip Code
Date of Birth (mm/dd/yyyy)	Place of Birth (City or Town and Country)
U.S. Social Security #	Gender ☐ Male ☐ Female
Present Nationality (Citizenship)	Home Phone #

Part 2. Application type (check all that apply to you).

I am eligible to apply for suspension of deportation or special rule cancellation of removal under the Nicaraguan Adjustment and Central American Relief Act (NACARA) because I have not been convicted of an aggravated felony and:

☐ **(a)** I am a national of El Salvador who first entered the United States on or before September 19, 1990, or a national of Guatemala who first entered the United States on or before October 1, 1990. I also timely registered for benefits under the settlement agreement in *American Baptist Churches v. Thornburgh (ABC)*, 760 F. Supp. 796 (N.D. Cal. 1991), either directly or, if Salvadoran, by applying for Temporary Protected Status (TPS), and I have not been apprehended at time of entry after December 19, 1990.

☐ **(b)** I am a national of Guatemala or El Salvador who filed an application for asylum on or before April 1, 1990.

☐ **(c)** I entered the United States on or before December 31, 1990; filed an application for asylum on or before December 31, 1991; and at the time of filing was a national of the Soviet Union (USSR), Russia, any republic of the former Soviet Union, Latvia, Estonia, Lithuania, Poland, Czechoslovakia, Romania, Hungary, Bulgaria, Albania, East Germany, Yugoslavia, or any state of the former Yugoslavia.

☐ **(d)** I am the spouse, child (unmarried and under 21 years of age), unmarried son or unmarried daughter of someone who has already applied, or is presently filing with me, for suspension of deportation or special rule cancellation of removal under NACARA. If I am an unmarried son or unmarried daughter, I entered the United States on or before October 1, 1990, or my parent was granted suspension of deportation or special rule cancellation of removal when I was less than 21 years of age. Attach proof of relationship and provide the following information about that spouse or parent:

Name:
A-number(s):
The person who has applied for suspension of deportation or special rule cancellation of removal is your: ☐ **Spouse** ☐ **Parent**

☐ **(e)** I am or was the ☐ spouse or ☐ child of an individual described in Part 2 (a), (b) or (c) above, and I or my child has been battered or subjected to extreme cruelty by that individual described in Part 2 (a), (b), or (c) above.

For USCIS Use Only

Returned	**Receipt**
Resubmitted	
Reloc. Sent	
Reloc. Received	

Decision

☐ Suspension of Deportation or Special Rule Cancellation of Removal and Adjustment of Status granted

☐ Referred to Immigration Judge in accordance with 8 CFR Section 240.70

(Adjudicating Officer's Signature)

(Date of Action) (Office Location)

EOIR Actions

Attorney or Representative, if any

☐ Check box if G-28 is attached.

VOLAG#

Atty. State License #

Part 3. Information about your presence in the United States.

1. Provide information about the places where you have resided in the United States during the last ten years: *(List PRESENT ADDRESS FIRST and work back in time. List only places where you resided 60 days or more. Attach additional sheets of paper as needed.)*

Street and Number	Apt. or Room #	City or Town	State	ZIP Code	Resided From: (Month/Year)	Resided To: (Month/Year)
						Present

2. Provide information about your **first** entry into the United States:

Name used when first entered the United States: *(Family Name, First, Middle)*	Place of first entry into the United States: *(City and State)*	
Your status when you first entered the United States:	Date of first entry into the United States: *(mm/dd/yyyy)*	Period for which admitted: *(mm/dd/yyyy)* From: To:
If you changed nonimmigrant status after entry, list status you changed to:	Date you changed status: *(mm/dd/yyyy)*	Last Extension of Stay expired on: *(mm/dd/yyyy)*

3. Provide information about any departure from and return to the United States you have made since your first entry: *(Please list all departures, including brief ones. Attach additional sheets of paper as needed.)*

If you have not departed the United States since your first date of entry, please mark an X in this box: ☐

Port of Departure: *(Place or Port, City, State)*	Departure Date: *(mm/dd/yyyy)*	Purpose of Travel:	Destination:
Port of Return: *(Place or Port, City, State)*	Return Date: *(mm/dd/yyyy)*	Status at Entry:	Inspected and Admitted? ☐ Yes ☐ No
Port of Departure: *(Place or Port, City, State)*	Departure Date: *(mm/dd/yyyy)*	Purpose of Travel:	Destination:
Port of Return: *(Place or Port, City, State)*	Return Date: *(mm/dd/yyyy)*	Status at Entry:	Inspected and Admitted? ☐ Yes ☐ No

4. Have you ever:

(a) been ordered deported or removed? ☐ Yes ☐ No

(b) departed the United States under an order of deportation or removal? ☐ Yes ☐ No

(c) overstayed a grant of voluntary departure from an Immigration Judge or the DHS (or former INS)? ☐ Yes ☐ No

(d) departed the United States pursuant to a grant of voluntary departure? ☐ Yes ☐ No

(e) failed to appear for deportation or removal? ☐ Yes ☐ No

If you responded "Yes" to any of the above, please indicate the name and Alien Registration Number (A#) you were using at that time, along with the date you left the United States, if applicable: ____________________

If you are unsure about any of your answers to questions 4(a)-(e) above, please indicate which question(s) and explain why you are unsure about the response(s) you have given: *(Attach additional sheets of paper as needed.)*

Part 4. Information about your financial status and employment.

1. Provide information about the places where you have been employed for the last ten years: *(List PRESENT EMPLOYMENT FIRST and work back in time. Include all employment, even if less than full-time. If you did the same type of work for three or more employers during any six-month period and you do not know the names and addresses of those employers, you may state "multiple employers." Indicate the city or region where you did the work, list the type of work you did, and estimate your earnings during that period. Any periods of unemployment, unpaid work (as a homemaker or intern, for example), or school attendance should be specified. Attach additional sheets of paper as needed.)*

Full Name and Address of Employer or School: *(If self-employed, give name and address of business.)*	**Earnings per Week** *(approximate)*	**Type of Work Performed:**	**Employed From:** *(Month/Year)*	**Employed To:** *(Month/Year)*
				Present

2. Provide information about your assets in the United States and other countries, including those held jointly with your spouse, if you are married, or with others. Do not include the value of clothing and household necessities. If married, provide information about your spouse's assets that he or she does not hold jointly with you:

Self *(Including assets jointly owned with Spouse or others)*		Spouse	
Cash, Checking or Savings Accounts:	$	Cash, Checking or Savings Accounts:	$
Motor Vehicle(s): *(Minus any amount owed)*	$	Motor Vehicle(s): *(Minus any amount owed)*	$
Real Estate: *(Minus any amount owed)*	$	Real Estate: *(Minus any amount owed)*	$
Other: *(Describe below, e.g., stocks, bonds)*	$	Other: (*Describe below, e.g., stocks, bonds)*	$
Total:	$	**Total:**	$

3. Have you filed a federal income tax return while in the United States? ☐ Yes ☐ No If "Yes," indicate the years you filed and attach evidence that you filed the returns. If you did not file a tax return during any particular year(s), please explain why you did not file. *(Attach additional sheets of paper as needed):*

Part 5. Information about your marital status and spouse.

Marital status: ☐ Married ☐ Single *(If single, skip this Part and go to Part 6)* ☐ Divorced ☐ Separated ☐ Widower

1. Information about Spouse:		
Name: *(Family Name(s), First, Middle)*	Date of Marriage: *(mm/dd/yyyy)*	Place of Marriage: *(City and Country)*
Place of Birth: *(City and Country)*	Date of Birth: *(mm/dd/yyyy)*	Citizenship:

Your spouse currently resides at: *(Indicate "with me" if spouse resides with you)*

Number and Street *Apt. #* *City or Town* *State/Country* *Zip Code*

If presently residing in the United States, your spouse's present status is: ☐ U.S. Citizen ☐ Lawful Permanent Resident ☐ Asylee ☐ Asylum Applicant ☐ Other *(Please describe):*

His/her alien registration number(s) is *(List all A#s your spouse has been given): A #*

Your spouse ☐ is ☐ is not employed. If employed, please give salary and the name and address of the place(s) of employment.

Full Name and Address of Employer:	Earnings Per Week: *(Approx)*	Type of Work:	Employed from: *(mm/dd/yyyy)*	Employed to: *(mm/dd/yyyy)*

2. Information about Previous Spouse(s):

I ☐ have ☐ have not been previously married: *(If previously married, list the names of each prior spouse, the dates on which each marriage began and ended, the place where the marriage ended, and describe how each marriage ended. Attach additional sheets of paper as needed.)*

Name of Prior Spouse: *(FamilyName(s), First, Middle)*	Date married: *(mm/dd/yyyy)*	Date marriage ended: *(mm/dd/yyyy)*	Place marriage ended: *(City and Country)*	Manner in which marriage was terminated or ended: *(e.g., death of spouse, divorce)*

3. Have you been ordered by any court, or are you otherwise under any legal obligation to provide child support and/or spousal maintenance? ☐ Yes ☐ No If "Yes," on a separate sheet of paper please explain what type of obligation you have, to whom it is owed, and whether you are fulfilling that obligation.

Part 6. Information about your child/children.

1. Do you have children? ☐ Yes ☐ No *(If "No," then skip this Part and go to Part 7)*
2. Please list all your children below, regardless of their age, giving the requested information about each of them. *(In the address box, indicate "with me" if the child currently resides with you, or if the child does not live with you, provide his or her address and relationship to the person with whom he or she lives. Attach additional sheets of paper as needed.)*

Name of Child: *(Family Name(s), First, Middle)*	**A#**	**Place of Birth** *(City and Country)*	**Date of Birth** *(mm/dd/yyyy)*	**Immigration Status**
(1)				
Current Address:			Citizenship:	
(2)				
Current Address:			Citizenship:	
(3)				
Current Address:			Citizenship:	
(4)				
Current Address:			Citizenship:	

Part 7. Information about your parent(s).

You do not need to provide information about your parents' assets and earnings unless you believe that your removal would result in extreme hardship to your parent or parents.

Name of Parent: *(Family Name(s), First, Middle)*	A#	Place of Birth *(City and Country)*	Date of Birth *(mm/dd/yyyy)*	Immigration Status
Father:				
Current Address: *(Number and Street, City, State or Country)*			Citizenship:	
Estimated total assets: $		Weekly earnings: $		
Mother:				
Current Address: *(Number and Street, City, State or Country)*			Citizenship:	
Estimated total assets: $		Weekly earnings: $		

Part 8. Miscellaneous information.

Please respond to the following questions. If you answer "Yes" to any of these questions, please provide an explanation on an attached sheet of paper.

1. Have you ever (either in the United States or in a foreign country) been arrested, summoned into court as a defendant, convicted, fined, imprisoned, placed on probation, or forfeited collateral for an act involving a felony, misdemeanor, or breach of any public law or ordinance (including, but not limited to, driving violations involving alcohol)? ☐ Yes ☐ No
(If you answered "Yes," your explanation should include a brief description of each offense, including the name and location of the offense, date of conviction, any penalty imposed, any sentence imposed and the time actually served.)

2. Have you ever been:		
☐ Yes	☐ No	A habitual drunkard?
☐ Yes	☐ No	One who has derived income principally from illegal gambling?
☐ Yes	☐ No	One who has given false testimony for the purpose of obtaining immigration benefits?
☐ Yes	☐ No	One who has engaged in prostitution or unlawful commercialized vice?
☐ Yes	☐ No	Involved in a serious criminal offense and asserted immunity from prosecution?
☐ Yes	☐ No	One who has aided and/or abetted another to enter the United States illegally?
☐ Yes	☐ No	A trafficker of a controlled substance, or one who knowingly assisted, abetted, conspired, or colluded with others in any such trafficking (not including a single offense of simple possession of 30 grams or less of marijuana)?
☐ Yes	☐ No	A practicing polygamist?
☐ Yes	☐ No	Admitted into the United States as a crewman after June 30, 1964?
☐ Yes	☐ No	Admitted into the United States as, or after arrival acquired the status of, an exchange visitor?
☐ Yes	☐ No	Inadmissible or deportable on security related grounds under sections 212(a)(3) or 237(a)(4) (for cancellation applicants), or under pre-IIRIRA section 241(a)(4) (for suspension applicants) of the Immigration and Nationality Act (INA)?
☐ Yes	☐ No	One who has ordered, incited, assisted, or otherwise participated in the persecution of an individual on account of his or her race, religion, nationality, membership in a particular social group, or political opinion?
☐ Yes	☐ No	A person previously granted relief under section 212(c) (waiver for certain grounds of admissibility) or 244 (a) (suspension of deportation) of the INA or whose removal has previously been canceled under section 240A (cancellation of removal) of the INA?

Part 9. Information about hardship you and/or your family will face if you are deported or removed from the United States.

Please answer the following questions by checking "Yes," "No", or "Not applicable" in the boxes provided. Where required, please provide an explanation of your answer on an attached sheet of paper. You should reference the number of each question for which you are providing an explanation. Your responses in this Part should be about you and/or your qualifying family member(s), except for your response to question 11. A qualifying family member is a parent, spouse, or child who is a United States citizen (USC) or lawful permanent resident (LPR) of the United States. When providing responses about a family member, please provide the family member's name and his or her relationship to you. **Please attach any documents you have to support the responses you give below.** *(See the instructions for types of documents that you may wish to submit.)*

IMPORTANT: *If you meet the eligibility requirements for NACARA suspension of deportation or special rule cancellation of removal listed in (a) or (b), under* ***Part 2, Application type*** *on Page 1 of this form and you complete this form, you will be presumed to meet the extreme hardship requirement, unless evidence in the record establishes that neither you nor your qualified relative are likely to experience extreme hardship if you are deported or removed from the United States. If you qualify for a presumption of extreme hardship, you do not need to submit documents that support your answers below regarding your claim to extreme hardship,* ***but you need to provide explanations to your answers below.***

1. ☐ Yes ☐ No ☐ Not applicable - If you have (USC/LPR) children, do your children speak, read, and write English?

2. ☐ Yes ☐ No ☐ Not applicable - If you have (USC/LPR) children, do your children speak, read and write the native language of the country you would be returned to if deported or removed?

3. ☐ Yes ☐ No - Do you or any of your qualified family members suffer or have suffered any illness, health problem, or disability that required medical attention? If yes, please provide information about the health problem, the name of the qualified family member who suffers or suffered from it, and any care the person receives in the United States that would not be available in the country to which you would be deported or removed.

4. ☐ Yes ☐ No - Would you be able to obtain employment in the country to which you would be deported or removed? If yes, explain the type of employment you would be able to obtain. If no, explain why you would be unable to find employment.

5. ☐ Yes ☐ No ☐ Not applicable - If you or a qualified family member are currently pursuing educational opportunities in the United States, would you or the qualified family member continue to pursue the educational opportunities if deported or removed from the United States? If no, explain why not.

6. ☐ Yes ☐ No ☐ Not applicable - If you are deported or removed from the United States, would all qualified family member(s) accompany you? If no, list which qualified family member(s) would not accompany you. Also, explain why the qualified family member(s) would not accompany you and how that affects you and your family member(s).

7. ☐ Yes ☐ No - Would you or qualified members of your family experience any emotional or psychological impact if you were deported or removed from the United States? If yes, please explain.

8. ☐ Yes ☐ No - Would the current conditions in the country to which you would be deported or removed cause you or your qualified family members extreme hardship if you were returned? If yes, please explain.

9. ☐ Yes ☐ No - Do you presently have any other way, besides this application for suspension of deportation or special rule cancellation of removal, to adjust status to that of a permanent resident in the United States? If yes, please explain.

10. ☐ Yes ☐ No ☐ Not applicable - If you belong to any civic, political, religious, community, or social organization, association, foundation, club, or similar group or participate in volunteer activities, would your separation from these community ties and activities affect you if you are deported or removed from the United States? If yes, please explain.

11. ☐ Yes ☐ No - Is there any other type of hardship that you or your family would face if you are deported or removed from the United States? Include any hardship to your non USC/LPR children, spouse or parents and any hardship to brothers, sisters, grandparents or other extended family members. If yes, please explain.

Part 10. Signature.

After reading the information on penalties in the instructions, complete and sign below. If someone helped you prepare this application, he or she must complete **Part 11.**

I certify, under penalty of perjury under the laws of the United States of America, that this application and the evidence submitted with it are all true and correct. Title 18, United States Code, Section 1546, provides in part: "Whoever knowingly makes under oath, or as permitted under penalty of perjury under Section 1746 of Title 28, United States Code, knowingly subscribes as true, any false statement with respect to a material fact in any application, affidavit, or other document required by the immigration laws or regulations prescribed thereunder, or knowingly presents any such application, affidavit, or other document containing any such false information or which fails to contain any reasonable basis in law or fact shall be fined in accordance with this title or imprisoned not more than five years, or both."

Staple your photographs here

I authorize the release of any information from my record that the U.S. Citizenship and Immigration Services needs to determine eligibility for the benefit I am seeking.

WARNING: Applicants who are in the United States illegally are subject to deportation or removal if their applications are not granted by an Asylum Officer or an Immigration Judge. Any information provided in completing this application may be used as a basis for the institution of, or as evidence in, deportation or removal proceedings, even if the application is later withdrawn.

Signature of Applicant: ______________________ **Date:** ______________ *(mm/dd/yyyy)*

Print Name:	Write your name in your native alphabet:

Part 11. Signature of person preparing form, if other than above. *(Read the following information and sign below.)*

I declare that I have prepared this application at the request of the person named in Part 10, that the responses provided are based on all information of which I have knowledge, or which was provided to me by the applicant, and that the completed application was read to the applicant in a language the applicant speaks fluently for verification before he or she signed the application in my presence. I am aware that the knowing placement of false information on the Form I-881 may subject me to civil penalties under 8 U.S.C. 1324 (c).

Signature of Preparer:	Print Name:	Date: *(mm/dd/yyyy)*

Daytime Telephone #:	Address of Preparer: *(Street Number and Name, City or Town, State, Zip Code)*

Part 12. To be completed at interview or hearing.

You will be asked to complete this Part when you are before an Asylum Officer of the U.S. Citizenship and Immigration Services or an Immigration Judge of the Executive Office for Immigration Review (EOIR) for examination.

I swear (affirm) that I know the contents of this application that I am signing, including the attached documents and supplements, are ☐ all true or ☐ not all true to the best of my knowledge and that the corrections numbered ______ to ______ were made by me or at my request.

Signed and sworn to before me by the above-named applicant on:

______________________ **Signature of Applicant**

______________________ **Date** *(mm/dd/yyyy)*

______________________ Write your Name in your Native Alphabet

______________________ **Signature of Asylum Officer or Immigration Judge**

FORMS FOR ASYLUM AND TEMPORARY PROTECTED STATUS

In Chapter 8 we discussed that some aliens who would otherwise have to leave the United States might be able to become LPRs by being granted asylum. Others might be able to stay temporarily under Temporary Protected Status (TPS). The forms central to obtaining these statuses are included here.

I-589: Application for Asylum and for Withholding of Removal

Aliens seeking asylum complete this form. In turn, if their request is approved, then their removal is withheld, and they may adjust their status to LPR after one year. Supplements A and B, which are part of the main I-589 form, refer to the applicant's children (Supplement A) and request additional information (Supplement B), if applicable.

I-821: Application for Temporary Protected Status

Aliens seeking Temporary Protected Status apply for that status by completing this form. It provides information about how aliens may find out if they qualify for TPS, based on whether DHS has designated their country's residents as eligible.

U.S. Department of Justice
Immigration and Naturalization Service

OMB Approval No. 1115-0060

Certification by Designated School

SECTION A. This section must be completed by the student, as appropriate. *(Please print or type):*

1. Name: *(Family in CAPS)* *(First)* *(Middle)*	2. Date of birth:
3. Student admission number:	4. Date first granted F-1 or M-1 status:
5. Level of education being sought:	6. Student's major field of study:

7. Describe the proposed employment for practical training:

Beginning date: ______ Ending date: ______ Number of hours per week: ______

8. List all periods of previously authorized employment for practical training:

A. Curricular or work/study:	B. Post completion of studies

Signature of student: ______ Date: ______

SECTION B. This section must be completed by the designated school official (DSO) of the school the student is attending or was last authorized to attend:

9. I hereby certify that:

The student named above:

☐ Is taking a full course of study at this school, and the expected date of completion is: ______

☐ Is taking less than a full course of study at this school because: ______

☐ Completed the course of study at this school on (date): ______

☐ Did not complete the course of study. Terminated attendance on (date): ______

Check one:

☐ A. The employment is for practical training in the student's field of study. The student has been in the educational program for at least nine (9) months, is in good academic standing, and is eligible for the requested practical training in accordance with INS regulations at 8 CFR 214.2(f)(10). The training that the student will participate in is an integral part of an established curriculum.

☐ B. The employment is for an internship with a recognized international organization and is within the scope of the organization's sponsorship. The student is in good academic standing.

10. Name and title of DSO:	Signature:	Date:
11. Name of school:	School file number:	Telephone Number:

For Official Use Only
Microfilm Index Number:

(See instructions on reverse)

Form I-538 (Rev. 08/12/02)Y

TABLE OF CONTENTS

PART 1: FILING INSTRUCTIONS

I. Who May Apply and Filing Deadlines

You may apply for asylum irrespective of your immigration status, and even if you are in the United States unlawfully.

You MUST file this application within one (1) year after you arrived in the United States, unless you can show that there are changed circumstances that materially affect your eligibility for asylum or extraordinary circumstances directly related to your failure to file within one (1) year. (See Instructions, Part 1: Filing Instructions, Section V, "Completing the Form," Part C, for further explanation of this requirement.)

If you have previously been denied asylum by an Immigration Judge or the Board of Immigration Appeals, you must show that there are changed circumstances that affect your eligibility for asylum.

The determination of whether you are permitted to apply for asylum will be made once you have had an asylum interview with an Asylum Officer or a hearing before an Immigration Judge. Even if you are not eligible to apply for asylum for the reasons stated above, you may still be eligible to apply for withholding of removal under section 241(b)(3) of the Immigration and Nationality Act (Act) or the Convention Against Torture before the Immigration Court.

II. Basis of Eligibility

A. Asylum

In order to qualify for asylum, you must establish that you are a refugee. A refugee is a person who is unable or unwilling to return to his or her country of nationality, or last habitual residence in the case of a person having no nationality, because of persecution or a well-founded fear of persecution on account of race, religion, nationality, membership in a particular social group, or political opinion.

If you are granted asylum, you and any eligible dependents included in your application will be permitted to remain and work in the United States and may eventually adjust to lawful permanent resident status. **If you are not granted asylum, the Department of Homeland Security (DHS) may use the information you provide in this application to establish that you are removable from the United States.**

B. Withholding of Removal

Your asylum application is also considered to be an application for withholding of removal under section 241(b)(3) of the Act, as amended. It may also be considered an application for withholding of removal under the Convention Against Torture if you checked the box at the top of page 1 of this application. If asylum is not granted, you may still be eligible for withholding of removal. Regardless of the basis for the withholding application, you will not be eligible for withholding if you 1) assisted in Nazi persecution or engaged in genocide, 2) have persecuted another person, 3) have been convicted by a final judgment of a particularly serious crime and therefore represent a danger to the community of the United States, 4) are considered for serious reasons to have committed a serious non-political crime outside the United States, or 5) represent a danger to the security of the United States. (See section 241(b)(3) of the Act; 8 CFR 208.16.)

i. Withholding of Removal under Section 241 (b)(3) of the Act

In order to qualify for withholding of removal under section 241(b)(3) of the Act, you must establish that it is more likely than not that your life or freedom would be threatened on account of race, religion, nationality, membership in a particular social group, or political opinion, in the proposed country of removal.

If you obtain an order withholding your removal, you cannot be returned to the country in which your life or freedom would be threatened. This means that you may be removed to a third country in which your life or freedom would not be threatened. Withholding of removal does not apply to any spouse or child included in the application. They would have to apply for such protection on their own. If you are granted withholding of removal, this would not give you the right to bring dependents to the United States. It also would not give you the right to become a lawful permanent resident of the United States.

ii. Withholding of Removal under the Convention Against Torture

The Convention Against Torture refers to the United Nations Convention Against Torture and other Cruel, Inhuman or Degrading Treatment or Punishment.

To be granted withholding of removal to a country under the Convention Against Torture, you must show that it is more likely than not that you would be tortured in that country.

"Torture" is defined in Article 1 of the Convention Against Torture and at 8 CFR 208.18(a). For an act to be considered torture, it must be an extreme form of cruel and inhuman treatment; it must cause severe physical or mental pain and suffering; and it must be intended to cause severe pain and suffering. Torture is an act inflicted for such purposes as obtaining from the victim or a third person information or a confession, punishing the victim for an act he or she or a third person has committed or is suspected of having committed, or intimidating or coercing the victim or a third person, or for any reason based on discrimination of any kind. Torture must be inflicted by or at the instigation of a public official or someone acting in an official capacity, or it must be inflicted with the consent or acquiescence of a public official or person acting in an official capacity. The victim must be in the custody or physical control of the torturer. Torture does not include pain or suffering that arises from or is incidental to lawful sanctions.

Form I-589, Application for Asylum and for Withholding of Removal, will be considered an application for withholding of removal under the Convention Against Torture if you tell the Immigration Judge that you would like to be considered for withholding of removal under the Convention Against Torture or if it is determined that the evidence you present indicates you may be tortured in the country of removal. To apply for withholding of removal under the Convention Against Torture, you must check the box at the top of page one (1) of the application and fully complete the Form I-589. You should include a detailed explanation of why you fear torture in response to Part B, Question 4 of the application. In your response you should write about any mistreatment you experienced or any threats made against you by a government or somebody connected to a government.

Only Immigration Judges and the Board of Immigration Appeals may grant withholding of removal or deferral of removal under the Convention Against Torture. If you have applied for asylum, the Immigration Judge will first determine whether you are eligible for asylum under section 208 of the Act and for withholding of removal under section 241(b)(3) of the Act. If you are not eligible for either asylum or withholding of removal under section 241(b)(3) of the Act, the Immigration Judge will determine whether the Convention Against Torture prohibits your removal to a country in which you fear torture.

Article 3 of the Convention Against Torture prohibits the United States from removing you to a country in which it is more likely than not that you would be subject to torture. The Convention Against Torture does not prohibit the United States from returning you to any other country where you would not be tortured. This means that you may be removed to a third country, in which you would not be tortured. Withholding of removal does not allow you to adjust to lawful permanent resident status or to petition to bring family members to come to, or remain in, the United States.

C. Deferral of Removal under the Convention Against Torture.

If it is more likely than not that you will be tortured in a country but you are ineligible for withholding of removal, your removal will be deferred under 8 CFR 208.17(a). Deferral of removal does not confer any lawful or permanent immigration status in the United States and does not necessarily result in release from detention. Deferral of removal is effective only until it is terminated. Deferral of removal is subject to review and termination if it is determined that it is no longer more likely than not that you would be tortured in the country to which your removal is deferred or if you request that your deferral be terminated.

D. Legal Sources Relating to Eligibility

The documents listed below are some of the legal sources relating to asylum, withholding of removal under section 241(b)(3) of the Act, and withholding of removal or deferral of removal under the Convention Against Torture. These sources are provided for reference only. You do not need to refer to them in order to complete your application.

- Section 101(a)(42) of the Act, 8 U.S.C. 1101(a)(42) (defining "refugee");
- Section 208 of the Act, 8 U.S.C. 1158 (regarding eligibility for asylum);
- Section 241(b)(3) of the Act, 8 U.S.C. 1231 (b)(3) (regarding eligibility for withholding of removal);
- Title 8 of the Code of Federal Regulations, section 208, et seq.;
- Article 3 of the Convention Against Torture and Other Cruel, Inhuman or Degrading Treatment or Punishment as ratified by Sec. 2242(b) of the Foreign Affairs Reform and Restructuring Act of 1998 and 8 CFR 208 as amended by the Regulations Concerning the Convention Against Torture: Interim Rule, 64 FR 8478-8492 (February 19, 1999) (effective March 22, 1999); 64 FR 13881 (March 23, 1999);
- The 1967 United Nations Protocol Relating to the Status of Refugees;
- The 1951 Convention Relating to the Status of Refugees; and
- Office of the United Nations High Commissioner for Refugees, Handbook on Procedures and Criteria for Determining Refugee Status (Geneva, 1992).

III. Confidentiality

The information collected will be used to make a determination on your application. It may also be provided to other government agencies (federal, state, local and/or foreign) for purposes of investigation or legal action on criminal and/or civil matters and for issues arising from the adjudication of benefits. However, no information indicating that you have applied for asylum will be provided to any government or country from which you claim a fear of persecution. Regulations at 8 CFR 208.6 protect the confidentiality of asylum claims.

IV. Right to Counsel

Immigration law concerning asylum and withholding of removal or deferral of removal is complex. You have a right to provide your own legal representation at an asylum interview and during immigration proceedings before the Immigration Court, at no cost to the United States Government. If you need, or would like, help in completing this form and preparing your written statements, assistance from pro bono (free) attorneys and/or voluntary agencies may be available. Voluntary agencies may help you for no fee or for a reduced fee and attorneys on the list may take your case for no fee. If you have not already received from DHS or the Immigration Court a list of attorneys and accredited representatives, you may obtain a list by calling 1-800-870-FORM (3676) or visiting the United States Department of Justice, Executive Office for Immigration Review (EOIR) website at: http://www.usdoj.gov/eoir/probono/states.htm.

Representatives of the United Nations High Commissioner for Refugees (UNHCR) may be able to assist you in identifying persons to help you complete the application. The UNHCR website provides useful country conditions information and also has links to other reliable sources. You may also, if you wish, forward a copy of your application and other supporting documents to the UNHCR. (For instructions on where to file the original, please see Instructions, Part 1: Filing Instructions, Section XII. "Where to File.") The current address of the UNHCR is:

United Nations High Commissioner for Refugees
1775 K Street, NW, Suite 300
Washington, DC 20006
Telephone: (202) 296-5191
Website: http://www.unhcr.ch

Calls from Detention Centers and Jails: Between the hours of 2:00 and 5:00 p.m. (Eastern Standard Time), Monday through Friday, asylum-seekers in detention centers and jails may call UNHCR collect at (202) 296-5191 or may call UNHCR's toll-free number at (888) 272-1913.

V. Completing the Form

Type or print all of your answers in black ink on the Form I-589. Your answers must be completed in English. Forms completed in a language other than English will be returned to you.

Provide the specific information requested about you and your family. **Answer ALL of the questions asked.** If any question does not apply to you or you do not know the information requested, answer "none," "not applicable," or "unknown." Provide detailed information and answer the questions as completely as possible. If you need more space, attach the Supplement A or B Forms (included in the application package) and/or an additional sheet(s) indicating the question number(s) you are answering. You are strongly urged to attach additional written statements and documents that support your claim. Your written statements should include events, dates, and details of your experiences that relate to your claim for asylum.

NOTE: Please put your Alien Registration Number (A#), (if any), name (exactly as it appears in Part A.I. of the form), signature, and date on each supplemental sheet and on the cover page of any supporting documents.

You will be permitted to amend or supplement your application at the time of your asylum interview before an Asylum Officer and at your hearing in Immigration Court by providing additional information and explanations about your asylum claim.

Part A. I. Information about You

This part asks for basic information about you. Alien Registration Number (A#) refers to your DHS file number. If you do not already have an A#, the DHS will assign one to you. You must provide your residential street address in the United States in Part A. I., Question 7, of the asylum application. You may also provide a mailing address, if different from the address where you reside, in Question 8. In Question 12, use the current name of the country. Do not use historical, ethnic, provincial, or other local names.

If you entered the country with inspection, the I-94#, referred to in Question 18b, is the number on Form I-94, Arrival-Departure Record, OMB No. 1653-0011, given to you when you entered the United States. In Question 18c, enter the date and status as it appears on the Form I-94. If you did not receive a Form I-94, write "None." If you entered without being inspected by an immigration officer, write "No Inspection" in Question 18c in the current status or status section.

Part A. II. Spouse and Children

You should list your spouse and all your children in this application regardless of their age, marital status, whether they are in the United States, or whether or not they are included in this application or filing a separate asylum application.

You may ask to have included in your asylum application your spouse and/or any children who are under the age of 21 and unmarried, if they are in the United States. Children who are married and/or children who are 21 years of age or older must file separately for asylum by submitting their own asylum application (Form I-589).

If you apply for asylum while in proceedings before the Immigration Court, the Immigration Judge may not have authority to grant asylum to any spouse or child included in your application who is not also in proceedings.

When including family members in your asylum application, you MUST submit one additional copy of your completed asylum application and primary documentary evidence establishing your family relationship, for each family member, as described below.

- If you are including your spouse in your application, submit three (3) copies of your marriage certificate, and three (3) copies of proof of termination of any prior marriages.

- If you are including any unmarried children under 21 years of age in your application, submit three (3) copies of each child's birth certificate.

If you do not have and are unable to obtain these documents, you must submit secondary evidence. Secondary evidence includes, but is not limited to, medical records, religious records, and school records. You may also submit an affidavit from at least one (1) person for each event you are trying to prove. Affidavits may be provided by relatives or others. Persons providing affidavits need not be United States citizens or lawful permanent residents.

Affidavits must:

- fully describe the circumstances or event(s) in question and fully explain how the person acquired knowledge of the event(s);

- be sworn to, or affirmed by, persons who were alive at the time of the event(s) and have personal knowledge of the event(s) (date and place of birth, marriage, etc.) that you are trying to prove; and

- show the full name, address, date, and place of birth of each person giving the affidavit, and indicate any relationship between you and the person giving the affidavit.

If you submit secondary evidence or affidavits, you must explain why primary evidence (e.g., birth or marriage certificate) is unavailable. You may explain the reasons primary evidence is unavailable using the Supplement B Form or additional sheets of paper. Attach this explanation to your secondary evidence or affidavits.

If you have more than four (4) children, complete the Supplement A Form for each additional child, or attach additional pages and documentation providing the same information asked in Part A. II. of the Form I-589.

Part A. III. Information about Your Background

Please answer questions 1 through 5, providing details as requested for each question. Your responses to the questions concerning the places you have lived, your education, and employment histories should be in reverse chronological order starting with your current residence, education, and employment, working back in time.

Part B. Information about Your Application

This part asks specific questions relevant to eligibility for asylum, for withholding of removal under section 241(b)(3) of the Act, or for withholding of removal under the Convention Against Torture. At question 1, please check the box(es) next to the reason(s) that you are completing this application. For all other questions, please check "Yes"or "No" in the box provided. If you answer "Yes" to any question, explain in detail using the Supplement B Form or additional sheets of paper as needed. You should clearly describe any of your experiences, or those of family members or others who have had similar experiences, that may show that you are a refugee.

If you have experienced harm that is difficult for you to write down and express, you should be aware that these experiences may be very important to the decision-making process regarding your request to remain in the United States. At your interview with an Asylum Officer or hearing with an Immigration Judge, you will need to be prepared to discuss the harm you have suffered. If you are having trouble remembering or talking about past events, it is suggested that you talk to a lawyer, an accredited representative, or a health professional who may be able to help you explain your experiences and current situation.

Part C. Additional Information about Your Application

Check "Yes" or "No" in the box provided for each question. If you answer "Yes" to any question, explain in detail using the Supplement B Form or additional sheets of paper as needed.

If you answer "Yes" to question 5, you must explain why you did not apply for asylum within the first year after you arrived in the United States. The government will accept as an explanation certain changes in the conditions in your country, certain changes in your own circumstances, and certain other events that may have prevented you from applying earlier. For example, some of the events the government might consider as valid explanations include, but are not limited to, the following:

- You have learned that human rights conditions in your country have worsened since you left;
- Because of your health, you were not able to submit this application within a year after you arrived;
- You previously submitted an application, but it was returned to you because it was not complete, and you submitted a complete application within a reasonable amount of time.

Federal regulations specify some of the other types of events that may also qualify as valid explanations for why you filed late. These regulations are found at 8 CFR 208.4. The list in the regulations is not all-inclusive, and the government recognizes that there are many other circumstances that might be acceptable reasons for filing more than one year after arrival.

If you are unable to explain why you did not apply for asylum within the first year after you arrived in the United States, or your explanation is not accepted by the government, you may not be eligible to apply for asylum, but you could still be eligible for withholding of removal.

Part D. Your Signature

You must sign your application in Part D and respond to the questions concerning any assistance you received to complete your application, providing the information requested. Sign after you have completed and reviewed the application.

If it is determined that you have knowingly made a frivolous application for asylum, you can be permanently ineligible for any benefits under the Immigration and Nationality Act. According to regulations at 8 CFR 208.20, an application is frivolous if any of its material elements is deliberately fabricated. (See Instructions, Part 1: Filing Instructions, Section IV, "Right to Counsel," in the event that you have any questions.)

Part E. Signature of Person Preparing Form If Other than You

Any person, other than an immediate family member (your spouse, parent(s), or children) who helped prepare your application must sign the application in Part E and provide the information requested.

Penalty for Perjury. All statements in response to questions contained in this application are declared to be true and correct under penalty of perjury. You and anyone, other than an immediate family member, who assists you in preparing the application must sign the application under penalty of perjury. Your signature is evidence that you are aware of the contents of this application. Any person assisting you in preparing this form, other than an immediate family member, must include his or her name, address, telephone number, and sign the application where indicated in Part E. Failure of the preparer to sign will result in the application being returned to you as an incomplete application. If the BCIS or EOIR later learns that you received assistance from someone other than an immediate family member and the person who assisted you **willfully** failed to sign the application, this may result in an adverse ruling against you.

Title 18, United States Code, Section 1546, provides in part:

> Whoever knowingly makes under oath, or as permitted under penalty of perjury under Section 1746 of Title 28, United States Code, knowingly subscribes as true, any false statement with respect to a material fact in any application, affidavit, or other document required by the immigration laws or regulations prescribed thereunder, or knowingly presents any such application, affidavit, or other document containing any such false statement shall be fined in accordance with this title or imprisoned not more than five years, or both.

If you knowingly provide false information on this application, you or the preparer of this application may be subject to criminal penalties under Title 18 of the United States Code and to civil penalties under Section 274C of the Immigration and Nationality Act, 8 U.S.C. 1324c.

Part F. To Be Completed at Interview or Hearing

Do not sign your application in Part F before filing this form. You will be asked to sign your application in this space at the conclusion of the interview regarding your claim.

NOTE: You must, however, sign Part D of the application.

VI. Required Documents and Required Number of Copies that You Must Submit with Your Application

You must submit the following documents to apply for asylum and withholding of removal:

- **The completed, signed original and two (2) copies of your completed application** Form I-589, and the original and two (2) copies of any supplementary sheets and supplementary statements. If you choose to submit additional supporting material (See Instructions, Part 1: Filing Instructions, Section VII, "Additional Documents that You Should Submit," page 9), you MUST include three (3) copies of each document. You should make and keep one (1) additional copy of the completed application for your own records.

- **One (1) color passport-style photo** of yourself and each family member listed in Part A. II. who is included in your application. These photos should be taken no more than 30 days before submission of your application to the BCIS or EOIR.

  Using a pencil, lightly write each person's complete name and DHS A number, if known, on the the back of his or her photo. Each photo must:

  - be taken with a white background, be un-mounted, be printed on thin paper, have a glossy finish, and not be retouched;

  - not be larger than 1 1/2 x 1 1/2 inches, with the distance from the top of the head to just below each person's chin about 1 1/4 inches.

- **Three (3) copies of all passports or other travel documents** (cover to cover) in your possession, and three (3) copies of any U.S. immigration documents, such as an I-94 Arrival-Departure Record, for you and each family member who you want included in your application, if you have such documents.

- If you have **other identification documents** (for example, birth certificate, military or national identification card, driver's license, etc.), it is recommended that you submit three (3) copies with your application and bring the original(s) with you to the interview.

- **Three (3) copies of primary or secondary evidence of relationship**, such as birth or school records of your children, marriage certificate, or proof of termination of marriage, for each family member listed in Part A. II. who you want to have included in your application.

  NOTE: If you submit an affidavit, you must submit the original and two (2) copies. (For affidavit requirements, see Instructions, Part 1: Filing Instructions, Section V, "Completing the Form," Part A. II., page 6.)

- **One additional copy of your completed application** Form I-589, with supplementary sheets and supplementary statements, for each family member listed in Part A. II. who you want to have included in your application.

It is recommended that any documents filed with this application be photocopies but, please be advised, if you choose to send an original document, the DHS or Immigration Court may keep that original document for its records.

Translation of documents not in English is required. Any document in a language other than English must be accompanied by an adequate English translation that the translator has certified as complete and correct, and by the translator's certification that he or she is competent to translate into English the language used in the document.

VII. Additional Documents that You Should Submit

If they are available to you, you should submit documents evidencing (1) the general conditions in the country from which you are seeking asylum, and (2) the specific facts on which you are relying to support your claim. If documents supporting your claim are not available or you are not providing them at this time, you must explain why using the Supplement B Form or additional sheets of paper. Supporting documents may include, but are not limited to, country condition reports, newspaper articles, affidavits of witnesses or experts, medical and/or psychological records, doctors' statements, periodicals, journals, books, photographs, official documents, or personal statements.

If you have difficulty discussing harm you have suffered in the past, you may wish to submit a health professional's report explaining this difficulty.

VIII. Fee

There is no fee for filing this application.

IX. Fingerprints

Applicants for asylum are subject to a check of all appropriate records and other information databases maintained by the Attorney General, Secretary of Homeland Security and by the Secretary of State. You and all of your dependents fourteen (14) years of age or older listed on your asylum application must be fingerprinted and photographed. You and your dependents will be given instructions on how to complete this requirement.

You will be notified in writing of the time and location of the Application Support Center or the designated Law Enforcement Agency where you must go to be fingerprinted and photographed. Failure to appear for a scheduled fingerprinting may delay eligibility for work authorization and/or result in an Asylum Officer dismissing your asylum application or referring it to an Immigration Judge. For applicants before an Immigration Judge, such failure will make the applicant ineligible for asylum and may delay eligibility for work authorization.

X. Organizing Your Application

Put your application together in the following order, forming one (1) complete package (if possible, secure with binder clips and rubber bands so that material may be easily separated):

- Your original Form I-589, with all questions completed, and the application signed by you in Part D, and signed by any preparer, in Part E; and
- One (1) passport-style photograph of you stapled to the form at Part D, page 9.

Behind your original Form I-589, attach in the following order:

- One (1) Form G-28 Notice of Entry of Appearance as Attorney or Representative, or EOIR 28 Notice of Entry of Appearance as Attorney or Representative Before an Immigration Judge, signed by you and the attorney/representative if you are represented by an attorney or other representative;
- The original of all supplemental sheets and supplementary statements submitted with your application;
- All passports, other travel or identification documents;
- One (1) copy of the evidence of your relationship to your spouse and unmarried children under 21 years of age who you want included in your application, if any; and
- Supporting documents, if available, such as but not limited to, country condition reports, newspaper articles, affidavits of witnesses or experts, medical and/or psychological records, doctors' statements, etc.

Behind this original complete package include two (2) additional copies of all the items listed above except for your photograph.

If you are including family members in your application, attach one (1) additional package as specified below for each family member. Arrange each family member's package as follows:

- One (1) copy of pages 1, 2, 3 and 9 of the principal's Form I-589 application (including Supplement A Form I-589 as needed);
- On Part D, page 9 of your family member's copy of the Form I-589 staple in the upper right corner one (1) passport-style photo of the family member to be included.
- One (1) copy of the proof of relationship to the principal applicant; and
- One (1) copy of the Form G-28, if any.

For example, if you include your spouse and two (2) children, you should submit your original package, plus two (2) duplicates for you, plus one (1) package for your spouse, plus one (1) package for each child, for a total of six (6) packages. Be sure each has the appropriate documentation.

NOTE: Any additional pages submitted should include your printed name (exactly as it appears in Part A.I. of the form), A# (if any), signature and date.

XI. Incomplete Asylum Applications

An asylum application that is incomplete will be returned to you by mail within thirty (30) days of receipt of the application by the BCIS. An application that has not been returned to you within thirty (30) days of having been received by the BCIS will be considered complete and you will receive written acknowledgement of receipt from the BCIS.

The filing of a complete application starts the 150-day period you must wait before you may apply for employment authorization. If your application is not complete and is returned to you, the 150-day period will not begin until you resubmit a complete application. (See Instructions, Part 2: Information Regarding Post-Filing Requirements, Section V, "Employment Authorization while Your Application is Pending," for further information regarding eligibility for employment authorization.) The starting date of the 150-day waiting period is listed at the end of the first sentence in the I-589 Acknowledgement of Receipt Notice sent to you by the BCIS.

This notice informs you that your application was received by the BCIS and is pending as of that date.

An application will be considered incomplete in each of the following cases:

- The application does not include a response to each of the questions contained in the Form I-589;
- The application is unsigned;
- The application is submitted without the required photographs;
- The application is sent without the appropriate number of copies for any supporting materials submitted; or
- You indicated in Part D that someone prepared the application other than yourself or an immediate family member and the preparer failed to complete Part E of the asylum application.

XII. Where to File

Although the BCIS will confirm in writing its receipt of your application, you may wish to send the completed forms by registered mail (return receipt requested) for your own records.

If you are in proceedings in Immigration Court:

If you are currently in proceedings in Immigration Court (that is, if you have been served with Form I-221, Order to Show Cause and Notice of Hearing; Form I-122, Notice to Applicant for Admission Detained for Hearing Before an Immigration Judge; Form I-862, Notice to Appear; or Form I-863, Notice of Referral to Immigration Judge), you are required to file your Form I-589, Application for Asylum and for Withholding of Removal, with the Immigration Court having jurisdiction over your case with your accompanying G-28 or EOIR-28.

If you are NOT in proceedings in Immigration Court:

You are to mail your completed application for Asylum and for Withholding of Removal, Form I-589, and any other additional information, to the BCIS Service Center as indicated below.

If you live in Alabama, Arkansas, Colorado, Commonwealth of Puerto Rico, District of Columbia, Florida, Georgia, Louisiana, Maryland, Mississippi, New Mexico, North Carolina, Oklahoma, western Pennsylvania in the jurisdiction of the Pittsburgh Suboffice*, South Carolina, Tennessee, Texas, United States Virgin Islands, Utah, Virginia, West Virginia, or Wyoming, mail your application to:

BCIS Texas Service Center
Attn: Asylum
P.O. Box 851892
Mesquite, TX 75185-1892

If you live in Alaska, northern California*, Idaho, Illinois, Indiana, Iowa, Kansas, Kentucky, Michigan, Minnesota, Missouri, Montana, Nebraska, northern Nevada in the jurisdiction of the Reno Suboffice*, North Dakota, Ohio, Oregon, South Dakota, Washington, or Wisconsin, mail your application to:

BCIS Nebraska Service Center
P.O. Box 87589
Lincoln, NE 68501-7589

If you live in Arizona, southern California*, Hawaii, southern Nevada in the jurisdiction of the Las Vegas Suboffice*, or the Territory of Guam, mail your application to:

BCIS California Service Center
P.O. Box 10589
Laguna Niguel, CA 92607-0589

If you live in Connecticut, Delaware, Maine, Massachusetts, New Hampshire, New Jersey, New York, eastern Pennsylvania excluding the jurisdiction of the Pittsburgh Suboffice*, Rhode Island, or Vermont, mail your application to:

BCIS Vermont Service Center
Attn: Asylum
75 Lower Welden Street
St. Albans, VT 05479-0589

*For applicants in the states of California, Nevada and Pennsylvania who may be unsure of which Service Center to use for mailing applications, you may call the National Customer Service Center or your local asylum office for more specific information. The National Customer Service Center and the asylum offices serving those states are listed below with their public information numbers:

The National Customer Service Center:

Toll Free Number	800-375-5283
TDD Hearing Impaired	800-767-1833

For California or Nevada:

Los Angeles Asylum Office	714-808-8199
San Francisco Asylum Office	415-744-8419

For Pennsylvania:

Newark Asylum Office	201-531-0555
Arlington Asylum Office	703-525-8141

Information concerning asylum offices and where to file asylum applications is also available on the BCIS website at: http://www.bcis.gov.

PART 2: INFORMATION REGARDING POST-FILING REQUIREMENTS

I. Notification Requirements when Your Address Changes

If you change your address you must inform the DHS in writing within ten (10) days of moving.

While your asylum application is pending before the asylum office, you MUST notify the asylum office on Form AR-11 (Change of Address Form) or by a signed and dated letter of any changes of address within ten (10) days after you change your address. The address that you provide on the application, or the last change of address notification you submitted, will be used by the DHS for mailing. Any notices mailed to that address will constitute adequate service, except that personal service may be required for the following: Notice to Alien Detained for Hearing by an Immigration Judge (Form I-122), Notice to Appear (Form I-862), Notice of Referral to Immigration Judge (Form I-863), and a Notice and Order of Expedited Removal (Form I- 860).

If you are already in proceedings in Immigration Court, you MUST notify the Immigration Court on Form EOIR 33 (Change of Address Form) or by a signed and dated letter of any changes of address within five (5) days of the change in address. You must send the notification to the Immigration Court having jurisdiction over your case.

II. Asylum Interview Process

If you are not in proceedings in Immigration Court, you will be notified by the BCIS asylum office of the date, time and place (address) of a scheduled interview. The BCIS suggests that you bring a copy of your Form I-589, asylum application, with you when you have your asylum interview. An Asylum Officer will interview you under oath and make a determination concerning your claim. In most cases, you will not be notified of the decision in your case until a date after your interview. You have the right to legal representation at your interview, at no cost to the United States Government. (See Instructions, Part 1: Filing Instructions, Section IV, "Right to Counsel.") You also may bring witnesses with you to the interview to testify on your behalf.

If you are unable to proceed with the asylum interview in fluent English, you must provide at no expense to the BCIS, a competent interpreter fluent in both English and a language that you speak fluently. Your interpreter must be at least 18 years of age. The following persons cannot serve as your interpreter: your attorney or representative of record; a witness testifying on your behalf at the interview; or a representative or employee of your country. Quality interpretation may be crucial to your claim. Such assistance must be obtained, at your expense, prior to the interview.

Failure without good cause to bring a competent interpreter to your interview may be considered an unexcused failure to appear for the interview. Any unexcused failure to appear for an interview may prevent you from receiving work authorization, and your asylum application may be dismissed or referred directly to the Immigration Court.

If available, you must bring some form of identification to your interview, including any passport(s), other travel or identification documents, or Form I-94 Arrival-Departure Record. You may bring to the interview any additional available items documenting your claim that you have not already submitted with your application.

If members of your family are included in your application for asylum, they must also appear for the interview and bring any identity or travel documents they have in their possession.

III. Status while Your Claim Is Pending

While your case is pending, you will be permitted to remain in the United States. After your asylum interview, if you have not been granted asylum and appear to be deportable under Section 237 of the Act, 8 U.S.C. 1227, or inadmissible under Section 212 of the Act, 8 U.S.C. 1182, your application will be filed with the Immigration Court upon referral by the asylum office.

IV. Travel Outside the United States

If you leave the United States without first obtaining advance parole from the DHS using Form I-131, Application for a Travel Document, OMB No. 1615-0013, it will be presumed that you have abandoned your application. If you obtain advance parole and return to the country of claimed persecution, it will be presumed that you abandoned your application, unless you can show that there were compelling reasons for your return.

NOTE: The application process for advance parole varies depending on your personal circumstances. Check with your local BCIS District Office for application instructions.

V. Employment Authorization while Your Application is Pending

You will be granted permission to work if your asylum application is granted.

Simply filing an application for asylum does not entitle you to work authorization. You may request permission to work if your asylum application is pending and 150 days have lapsed since your application was accepted by the BCIS or the Immigration Court. See 8 CFR 208.7(a)(1). Any delay in the processing of your asylum application that you request or cause shall not be counted as part of the 150-day period. If your asylum application has not been denied within 180 days from the date of filing a complete asylum application, you may be granted permission to work by filing an Application for Employment Authorization, Form I-765 (OMB No. 1615-0040), with the BCIS. Follow the instructions on that application and submit it with a copy of evidence as specified in the instructions that you have a pending asylum application. Each family member you have asked to have included in your application who also wants permission to work must submit a separate Form I-765. You may obtain a Form I-765 by calling 1- 800-870-FORM (3676), or from the BCIS website at http://www.bcis.gov.

VI. Privacy Act Notice

The authority to collect this information is contained in Title 8 of the United States Code. Furnishing the information on this form is voluntary; however, failure to provide all of the requested information may result in the delay of a final decision or denial of your request.

VII. Paperwork Reduction Act Notice

Under the Paperwork Reduction Act an agency may not conduct or sponsor an information collection and a person is not required to respond to a collection of information unless it displays a currently valid OMB control number. We try to create forms and instructions that are accurate, can be easily understood, and which impose the least possible burden on you to provide us with information. Often this is difficult because some immigration laws are very complex. The estimated average time to complete and file this application is as follows: (1) 2 hours to learn about the form; (2) 5 hours to complete the form; and (3) 5 hours to assemble and file the application; for the total estimated average burden hours of 12 hours per application. The estimated time to complete the form will vary depending on the complexity of your individual circumstances. If you have comments regarding the accuracy of this estimate or suggestions for making this form simpler, you can write to the Regulations and Forms Services Division, Department of Homeland Security, 425 I Street, N.W., Room 4034, Washington, DC 20536, OMB No. 1615-0067. **DO NOT MAIL YOUR COMPLETED APPLICATION TO THIS ADDRESS.**

SUPPLEMENTS TO THE FORM I-589

Form I-589, Supplement A - for use in completing Part A. II.

Form I-589, Supplement B - for use in completing Parts B, C, and to provide additional information for any other part of the application.

U.S. Department of Homeland Security
Bureau of Citizenship and Immigration Services

U.S. Department of Justice
Executive Office for Immigration Review

OMB No. 1615-0067; Expires 11/30/06

Application for Asylum and for Withholding of Removal

Start Here - Please Type or Print. **USE BLACK INK. SEE THE SEPARATE INSTRUCTION PAMPHLET FOR INFORMATION ABOUT ELIGIBILITY AND HOW TO COMPLETE AND FILE THIS APPLICATION.** (Note: There is NO filing fee for this application.)

Please check the box if you also want to apply for withholding of removal under the Convention Against Torture. ☐

PART A. I. INFORMATION ABOUT YOU

1. Alien Registration Number(s)(A#'s)*(If any)*		2. Social Security No. *(If any)*
3. Complete Last Name	4. First Name	5. Middle Name
6. What other names have you used? *(Include maiden name and aliases.)*		
7. Residence in the U.S. C/O		Telephone Number
Street Number and Name		Apt. No.
City	State	ZIP Code
8. Mailing Address in the U.S., if other than above		Telephone Number
Street Number and Name		Apt. No.
City	State	ZIP Code

9. Sex ☐ Male ☐ Female

10. Marital Status: ☐ Single ☐ Married ☐ Divorced ☐ Widowed

11. Date of Birth *(Mo/Day/Yr)*

12. City and Country of Birth

13. Present Nationality *(Citizenship)*

14. Nationality at Birth

15. Race, Ethnic or Tribal Group

16. Religion

17. *Check the box, a through c that applies:*
a. ☐ I have never been in immigration court proceedings.
b. ☐ I am now in immigration court proceedings.
c. ☐ I am **not** now in immigration court proceedings, but I have been in the past.

18. *Complete 18 a through c.*
a. When did you last leave your country? *(Mo/Day/Yr)* ______________
b. What is your current I-94 Number, if any? ______________

c. Please list each entry to the U.S. beginning with your most recent entry.
List date (Mo/Day/Yr), place, and your status for each entry. (Attach additional sheets as needed.)

Date __________ Place ______________________ Status ________ Date Status Expires ____________
Date __________ Place ______________________ Status ________
Date __________ Place ______________________ Status ________
Date __________ Place ______________________ Status ________

19. What country issued your last passport or travel document?

20. Passport #
Travel Document #

21. Expiration Date *(Mo/Day/Yr)*

22. What is your native language?

23. Are you fluent in English? ☐ Yes ☐ No

24. What other languages do you speak fluently?

FOR EOIR USE ONLY	FOR BCIS USE
	Action: Interview Date: ____________ **Decision:** __ Approval Date: ____________ — Denial Date: ____________ — Referral Date: ____________ Asylum Officer ID# ____________

PART A. II. INFORMATION ABOUT YOUR SPOUSE AND CHILDREN

Your Spouse. ☐ I am not married. (Skip to ***Your Children***, *below.)*

1. Alien Registration Number (A#) *(If any)*	2. Passport/ID Card No. *(If any)*	3. Date of Birth *(Mo/Day/Yr)*	4. Social Security No. *(If any)*
5. Complete Last Name	6. First Name	7. Middle Name	8. Maiden Name
9. Date of Marriage *(Mo/Day/Yr)*	10. Place of Marriage	11. City and Country of Birth	
12. Nationality *(Citizenship)*	13. Race, Ethnic or Tribal Group	14. Sex ☐ Male ☐ Female	
15. Is this person in the U.S.? ☐ Yes *(Complete blocks 16 to 24.)* ☐ No *(Specify location)*			
16. Place of last entry in the U.S. ?	17. Date of last entry in the U.S. *(Mo/Day/Yr)*	18. I-94 No. *(If any)*	19. Status when last admitted *(Visa type, if any)*
20. What is your spouse's current status?	21. What is the expiration date of his/her authorized stay, if any? *(Mo/Day/Yr)*	22. Is your spouse in immigration court proceedings? ☐ Yes ☐ No	23. If previously in the U.S., date of previous arrival *(Mo/Day/Yr)*
24. If in the U.S., is your spouse to be included in this application? *(Check the appropriate box.)* ☐ Yes *(Attach one (1) photograph of your spouse in the upper right hand corner of page 9 on the extra copy of the application submitted for this person.)* ☐ No			

Your Children. Please list **ALL** of your children, regardless of age, location, or marital status.

☐ I do not have any children. *(Skip to Part A. III.,* ***Information about Your Background.)***
☐ I do have children. Total number of children __________

(Use Supplement A Form I-589 or attach additional pages and documentation if you have more than four (4) children.)

1. Alien Registration Number (A#) *(If any)*	2. Passport/ID Card No. *(If any)*	3. Marital Status *(Married, Single, Divorced, Widowed)*	4. Social Security No. *(If any)*
5. Complete Last Name	6. First Name	7. Middle Name	8. Date of Birth *(Mo/Day/Yr)*
9. City and Country of Birth	10. Nationality *(Citizenship)*	11. Race, Ethnic or Tribal Group	12. Sex ☐ Male ☐ Female
13. Is this child in the U.S.? ☐ Yes *(Complete blocks 14 to 21.)* ☐ No *(Specify Location)*			
14. Place of last entry in the U.S.?	15. Date of last entry in the U.S.? *(Mo/Day/Yr)*	16. I-94 No. *(If any)*	17. Status when last admitted *(Visa type, if any)*
18. What is your child's current status?	19. What is the expiration date of his/her authorized stay, if any? *(Mo/Day/Yr)*	20. Is your child in immigration court proceedings? ☐ Yes ☐ No	
21. If in the U.S., is this child to be included in this application? *(Check the appropriate box.)* ☐ Yes *(Attach one (1) photograph of your child in the upper right hand corner of page 9 on the extra copy of the application submitted for this person.)* ☐ No			

PART A. II. INFORMATION ABOUT YOUR SPOUSE AND CHILDREN Continued

1. Alien Registration Number (A#) *(If any)*	2. Passport/IDCard No. *(If any)*	3. Marital Status *(Married, Single, Divorced, Widowed)*	4. Social Security No. *(If any)*
5. Complete Last Name	6. First Name	7. Middle Name	8. Date of Birth *(Mo/Day/Yr)*
9. City and Country of Birth	10. Nationality *(Citizenship)*	11. Race, Ethnic or Tribal Group	12. Sex ☐ Male ☐ Female
13. Is this child in the U.S.? ☐ Yes *(Complete blocks 14 to 21.)* ☐ No *(Specify Location)*			
14. Place of last entry in the U.S.?	15. Date of last entry in the U.S. ? *(Mo/Day/Yr)*	16. I-94 No. *(If any)*	17. Status when last admitted *(Visa type, if any)*
18. What is your child's current status?	19. What is the expiration date of his/her authorized stay,*(if any)? (Mo/Day/Yr)*	20. Is your child in immigration court proceedings? ☐ Yes ☐ No	
21. If in the U.S., is this child to be included in this application? *(Check the appropriate box.)* ☐ Yes *(Attach one (1) photograph of your child in the upper right hand corner of page 9 on the extra copy of the application submitted for this person.)* ☐ No			

1. Alien Registration Number *(A#) (If any)*	2. Passport/ID Card No.*(If any)*	3. Marital Status *(Married, Single, Divorced, Widowed)*	4. Social Security No. *(If any)*
5. Complete Last Name	6. First Name	7. Middle Name	8. Date of Birth *(Mo/Day/Yr)*
9. City and Country of Birth	10. Nationality *(Citizenship)*	11. Race, Ethnic or Tribal Group	12. Sex ☐ Male ☐ Female
13. Is this child in the U.S. ? ☐ Yes *(Complete blocks 14 to 21.)* ☐ No *(Specify Location)*			
14. Place of last entry in the U.S.?	15. Date of last entry in the U.S.? *(Mo/Day/Yr)*	16. I-94 No. *(If any)*	17. Status when last admitted *(Visa type, if any)*
18. What is your child's current status?	19. What is the expiration date of his/her authorized stay, if any? *(Mo/Day/Yr)*	20. Is your child in immigration court proceedings? ☐ Yes ☐ No	
21. If in the U.S., is this child to be included in this application? *(Check the appropriate box.)* ☐ Yes *(Attach one (1) photograph of your child in the upper right hand corner of page 9 on the extra copy of the application submitted for this person.)* ☐ No			

1. Alien Registration Number (A#) *(If any)*	2. Passport/ID Card No. *(If any)*	3. Marital Status *(Married, Single, Divorced, Widowed)*	4. Social Security No. *(If any)*
5. Complete Last Name	6. First Name	7. Middle Name	8. Date of Birth *(Mo/Day/Yr)*
9. City and Country of Birth	10. Nationality *(Citizenship)*	11. Race, Ethnic or Tribal Group	12. Sex ☐ Male ☐ Female
13. Is this child in the U.S.? ☐ Yes *(Complete blocks 14 to 21.)* ☐ No *(Specify Location)*			
14. Place of last entry in the U.S.?	15. Date of last entry in the U.S.? *(Mo/Day/Yr)*	16. I-94 No. (If *any)*	17. Status when last admitted *(Visa type, if any)*
18. What is your child's current status?	19. What is the expiration date of his/her authorized stay, if any? *(Mo/Day/Yr)*	20. Is your child in immigration court proceedings? ☐ Yes ☐ No	
21. If in the U.S., is this child to be included in this application? *(Check the appropriate box.)* ☐ Yes *(Attach one (1) photograph of your child in the upper right hand corner of page 9 on the extra copy of the application submitted for this person.)* ☐ No			

PART A. III. INFORMATION ABOUT YOUR BACKGROUND

1. Please list your last address where you lived before coming to the U.S. If this is not the country where you fear persecution, also list the last address in the country where you fear persecution. *(List Address, City/Town, Department, Province, or State, and Country.) (Use Supplement B Form I-589 or additional sheets of paper if necessary.)*

Number and Street *(Provide if available)*	City/Town	Department, Province or State	Country	Dates From *(Mo/Yr)*	To *(Mo/Yr)*

2. Provide the following information about your residences during the last five years. List your present address first. *(Use Supplement Form B or additional sheets of paper if necessary.)*

Number and Street	City/Town	Department, Province or State	Country	Dates From *(Mo/Yr)*	To *(Mo/Yr)*

3. Provide the following information about your education, beginning with the most recent. *(Use Supplement B Form I-589 or additional sheets of paper if necessary.)*

Name of School	Type of School	Location (Address)	Attended From *(Mo/Yr)*	To *(Mo/Yr)*

4. Provide the following information about your employment during the last five years. List your present employment first. *(Use Supplement Form B or additional sheets of paper if necessary.)*

Name and Address of Employer	Your Occupation	Dates From *(Mo/Yr)*	To *(Mo/Yr)*

5. Provide the following information about your parents and siblings (brother and sisters). Check box if the person is deceased. *(Use Supplement B Form I-589 or additional sheets of paper if necessary.)*

Name	City/Town and Country of Birth	Current Location
Mother		☐ Deceased
Father		☐ Deceased
Siblings		☐ Deceased
		☐ Deceased

PART B. INFORMATION ABOUT YOUR APPLICATION

(Use Supplement B Form I-589 or attach additional sheets of paper as needed to complete your responses to the questions contained in PART B.)

When answering the following questions about your asylum or other protection claim (withholding of removal under 241(b)(3) of the Act or withholding of removal under the Convention Against Torture) you should provide a detailed and specific account of the basis of your claim to asylum or other protection. To the best of your ability, provide specific dates, places, and descriptions about each event or action described. You should attach documents evidencing the general conditions in the country from which you are seeking asylum or other protection and the specific facts on which you are relying to support your claim. If this documentation is unavailable or you are not providing this documentation with your application, please explain why in your responses to the following questions. Refer to Instructions, Part 1: Filing Instructions, Section II, "Basis of Eligibility," Parts A - D, Section V, "Completing the Form," Part B, and Section VII, "Additional Documents that You Should Submit" for more information on completing this section of the form.

1. Why are you applying for asylum or withholding of removal under section 241(b)(3) of the Act, or for withholding of removal under the Convention Against Torture? Check the appropriate box (es) below and then provide detailed answers to questions A and B below:

   I am seeking asylum or withholding of removal based on

   ☐ Race
   ☐ Religion
   ☐ Nationality
   ☐ Political opinion
   ☐ Membership in a particular social group
   ☐ Torture Convention

   A. Have you, your family, or close friends or colleagues ever experienced harm or mistreatment or threats in the past by anyone?

   ☐ No ☐ Yes If your answer is "Yes," explain in detail:

   1) What happened;
   2) When the harm or mistreatment or threats occurred;
   3) Who caused the harm or mistreatment or threats; and
   4) Why you believe the harm or mistreatment or threats occurred.

   B. Do you fear harm or mistreatment if you return to your home country?

   ☐ No ☐ Yes If your answer is "Yes," explain in detail:

   1) What harm or mistreatment you fear;
   2) Who you believe would harm or mistreat you; and
   3) Why you believe you would or could be harmed or mistreated.

PART B. INFORMATION ABOUT YOUR APPLICATION Continued

2. Have you or your family members ever been accused, charged, arrested, detained, interrogated, convicted and sentenced, or imprisoned in any country other than the United States?

☐ No ☐ Yes If "Yes," explain the circumstances and reasons for the action.

3. A. Have you or your family members ever belonged to or been associated with any organizations or groups in your home country, such as, but not limited to, a political party, student group, labor union, religious organization, military or paramilitary group, civil patrol, guerrilla organization, ethnic group, human rights group, or the press or media?

☐ No ☐ Yes If "Yes," describe for each person the level of participation, any leadership or other positions held, and the length of time you or your family members were involved in each organization or activity.

B. Do you or your family members continue to participate in any way in these organizations or groups?

☐ No ☐ Yes If "Yes," describe for each person, your or your family members' current level of participation, any leadership or other positions currently held, and the length of time you or your family members have been involved in each organization or group.

4. Are you afraid of being subjected to torture in your home country or any other country to which you may be returned?

☐ No ☐ Yes If "Yes," explain why you are afraid and describe the nature of the torture you fear, by whom, and why it would be inflicted.

PART C. ADDITIONAL INFORMATION ABOUT YOUR APPLICATION

(Use Supplement B Form I-589 or attach additional sheets of paper as needed to complete your responses to the questions contained in Part C.)

1. Have you, your spouse, your child(ren), your parents, or your siblings ever applied to the United States Government for refugee status, asylum, or withholding of removal? ☐ No ☐ Yes

   If "Yes" explain the decision and what happened to any status you, your spouse, your child(ren), your parents, or your siblings received as a result of that decision. Please indicate whether or not you were included in a parent or spouse's application. If so, please include your parent or spouse's A- number in your response. If you have been denied asylum by an Immigration Judge or the Board of Immigration Appeals, please describe any change(s) in conditions in your country or your own personal circumstances since the date of the denial that may affect your eligibility for asylum.

2. A. After leaving the country from which you are claiming asylum, did you or your spouse or child(ren), who are now in the United States, travel through or reside in any other country before entering the United States? ☐ No ☐ Yes

   B. Have you, your spouse, your child(ren), or other family members such as your parents or siblings ever applied for or received any lawful status in any country other than the one from which you are now claiming asylum? ☐ No ☐ Yes

   If "Yes" to either or both questions (2A and/or 2B), provide for each person the following: the name of each country and the length of stay; the person's status while there; the reasons for leaving; whether the person is entitled to return for lawful residence purposes; and whether the person applied for refugee status or for asylum while there, and, if not, why he or she did not do so.

3. Have you, your spouse, or child(ren) ever ordered, incited, assisted, or otherwise participated in causing harm or suffering to any person because of his or her race, religion, nationality, membership in a particular social group or belief in a particular political opinion?

   ☐ No ☐ Yes If "Yes," describe in detail each such incident and your own or your spouse's or child(ren)'s involvement.

PART C. ADDITIONAL INFORMATION ABOUT YOUR APPLICATION Continued

4. After you left the country where you were harmed or fear harm, did you return to that country?

☐ No ☐ Yes If "Yes," describe in detail the circumstances of your visit (for example, the date(s) of the trip(s), the purpose(s) of the trip(s), and the length of time you remained in that country for the visit(s)).

5. Are you filing the application more than one year after your last arrival in the United States?

☐ No ☐ Yes If "Yes," explain why you did not file within the first year after you arrived. You should be prepared to explain at your interview or hearing why you did not file your asylum application within the first year after you arrived. For guidance in answering this question, see Instructions, Part 1: Filing Instructions, Section V. "Completing the Form," Part C.

6. Have you or any member of your family included in the application ever committed any crime and/or been arrested, charged, convicted and sentenced for any crimes in the United States?

☐ No ☐ Yes If "Yes," for each instance, specify in your response what occurred and the circumstances; dates; length of sentence received; location; the duration of the detention or imprisonment; the reason(s) for the detention or conviction; any formal charges that were lodged against you or your relatives included in your application; the reason(s) for release. Attach documents referring to these incidents, if they are available, or an explanation of why documents are not available.

PART D. YOUR SIGNATURE

After reading the information regarding penalties in the instructions, complete and sign below. If someone helped you prepare this application, he or she must complete Part E.

I certify, under penalty of perjury under the laws of the United States of America, that this application and the evidence submitted with it are all true and correct. Title 18, United States Code, Section 1546, provides in part: "Whoever knowingly makes under oath, or as permitted under penalty of perjury under Section 1746 of Title 28, United States Code, knowingly subscribes as true, any false statement with respect to a material fact in any application, affidavit, or knowingly presents any such application, affidavit, or other document required by the immigration laws or regulations prescribed thereunder, or knowingly presents any such application, affidavit, or other document containing any such false statement or which fails to contain any reasonable basis in law or fact - shall be fined in accordance with this title or imprisoned not more than five years, or both." I authorize the release of any information from my record which the Bureau of Citizenship and Immigration Services needs to determine eligibility for the benefit I am seeking.	Staple your photograph here or the photograph of the family member to be included on the extra copy of the application submitted for that person.

WARNING: **Applicants who are in the United States illegally are subject to removal if their asylum or withholding claims are not granted by an Asylum Officer or an Immigration Judge. Any information provided in completing this application may be used as a basis for the institution of, or as evidence in, removal proceedings even if the application is later withdrawn. Applicants determined to have knowingly made a frivolous application for asylum will be permanently ineligible for any benefits under the Immigration and Nationality Act. See 208(d)(6) of the Act and 8 CFR 208.20.**

Print Complete Name	Write your name in your native alphabet

Did your spouse, parent, or child(ren) assist you in completing this application? ☐ No ☐ Yes *(If "Yes," list the name and relationship.)*

_______________ _______________ _______________ _______________
(Name) *(Relationship)* *(Name)* *(Relationship)*

Did someone other than your spouse, parent, or child(ren) prepare this application? ☐ No ☐ Yes *(If "Yes," complete Part E)*

Asylum applicants may be represented by counsel. Have you been provided with a list of persons who may be available to assist you, at little or no cost, with your asylum claim? ☐ No ☐ Yes

Signature of Applicant *(The person in Part A. I.)*

[______________________________] _______________

Sign your name so it all appears within the brackets Date *(Mo/Day/Yr)*

PART E. DECLARATION OF PERSON PREPARING FORM IF OTHER THAN APPLICANT, SPOUSE, PARENT OR CHILD

I declare that I have prepared this application at the request of the person named in Part D, that the responses provided are based on all information of which I have knowledge, or which was provided to me by the applicant and that the completed application was read to the applicant in his or her native language or a language he or she understands for verification before he or she signed the application in my presence. I am aware that the knowing placement of false information on the Form I-589 may also subject me to civil penalties under 8 U.S.C. 1324(c).

Signature of Preparer		Print Complete Name	
Daytime Telephone Number ( )		Address of Preparer: Street Number and Name	
Apt. No.	City	State	ZIP Code

PART F. TO BE COMPLETED AT INTERVIEW OR HEARING

You will be asked to complete this Part when you appear before an Asylum Officer of theU.S. Department of Homeland Security, Bureau of Citizenship and Immigration Services (BCIS), or an Immigration Judge of the U.S. Department of Justice, Executive Office for Immigration Review (EOIR) for examination.

I swear (affirm) that I know the contents of this application that I am signing, including the attached documents and supplements, that they are all true to the best of my knowledge taking into account correction(s) numbered __________ to __________ that were made by me or at my request.

Signed and sworn to before me by the above named applicant on:

_______________ _______________

Signature of Applicant Date *(Mo/Day/Yr)*

_______________ _______________

Write Your Name in Your Native Alphabet Signature of Asylum Officer or Immigration Judge

SUPPLEMENT A FORM I-589

A # *(If available)*	Date
Applicant's Name	Applicant's Signature

LIST ALL OF YOUR CHILDREN, REGARDLESS OF AGE OR MARITAL STATUS.

(Use this form and attach additional pages and documentation as needed to your application if you have more than four (4) children.)

1. Alien Registration Number (A#)*(If any)*	2. Passport/ID Card No. *(If any)*	3. Marital Status *(Married, Single, Divorced, Widowed)*	4. Social Security No. *(If any)*
5. Complete Last Name	6. First Name	7. Middle Name	8. Date of Birth *(Mo/Day/Yr)*
9. City and Country of Birth	10. Nationality *(Citizenship)*	11. Race, Ethnic or Tribal Group	12. Sex ☐ Male ☐ Female
13. Is this child in the U.S.? ☐ Yes *(Complete blocks 14 to 21.)* ☐ No *(Specify Location)*			
14. Place of last entry in the U.S.?	15. Date of last entry in the U.S.? *(Mo/Day/Yr)*	16. I-94 No. *(If any)*	17. Status when last admitted *(Visa type, if any)*
18. What is your child's current status?	19. What is the expiration date of his/her authorized stay, if any? *(Mo/Day/Yr)*		20. Is your child in immigration court proceedings? ☐ Yes ☐ No
21. If in the U.S., is this child to be included in this application? *(Check the appropriate box.)* ☐ Yes *(Attach one (1) photograph of your child in the upper right hand corner of page 9 on the extra copy of the application submitted for this person.)* ☐ No			

1. Alien Registration Number (A#)*(If any)*	2. Passport/ID Card No. *(If any)*	3. Marital Status *(Married, Single, Divorced, Widowed)*	4. Social Security No. *(If any)*
5. Complete Last Name	6. First Name	7. Middle Name	8. Date of Birth *(Mo/Day/Yr)*
9. City and Country of Birth	10. Nationality *(Citizenship)*	11. Race, Ethnic or Tribal Group	12. Sex ☐ Male ☐ Female
13. Is this child in the U.S.? ☐ Yes *(Complete blocks 14 to 21.)* ☐ No *(Specify Location)*			
14. Place of last entry in the U.S.?	15. Date of last entry in the U.S.? *(Mo/Day/Yr)*	16. I-94 No. *(If any)*	17. Status when last admitted *(Visa type, if any)*
18. What is your child's current status?	19. What is the expiration date of his/her authorized stay, if any? *(Mo/Day/Yr)*		20. Is your child in immigration court proceedings? ☐ Yes ☐ No
21. If in the U.S., is this child to be included in this application? *(Check the appropriate box.)* ☐ Yes *(Attach one (1) photograph of your child in the upper right hand corner of page 9 on the extra copy of the application submitted for this person.)* ☐ No			

Form I-589 Supplement A (Rev. 07/03/03)Y

SUPPLEMENT B FORM I-589

ADDITIONAL INFORMATION ABOUT YOUR CLAIM TO ASYLUM.

A # *(If available)*	Date
Applicant's Name	Applicant's Signature

Use this as a continuation page for any information requested. Please copy and complete as needed.

PART _____

QUESTION _____

OMB No. 1615-0043; Exp. 07/31/07

Department of Homeland Security
U.S. Citizenship and Immigration Services

I-821, Application for Temporary Protected Status

Instructions

NOTE: This revision of Form I-821 updates instructions required for TPS registration and re-registration at questions 7 and 10(B) on Page 2. This revision also combines instructions in questions 7 and 13 from prior editions of this form into a new question 7 on Page 2. The new question 7 updates instructions on biometric services.

Please read these instructions carefully to properly complete this form. If you need more space to answer a question, use a separate sheet(s) of paper. Write your name and Alien Registration Number (A#) at the top of each sheet and indicate the number of the item to which the answer refers. An incomplete application may be returned to you, causing a delay in the processing of your application. The U.S.Citizenship and Immigration Services (USCIS) is comprised of offices of the former Immigration and Naturalization Service (INS).

1. Who May File for TPS?

You must be an eligible national of a foreign state (or parts thereof) or an alien having no nationality who last habitually resided in a foreign state that has been designated for Temporary Protected Status (TPS) by the Secretary of the Department of Homeland Security pursuant to section 244A of the Immigration and Nationality Act. You should check with the nearest office of USCIS for designations currently in force or visit our website at **www.uscis.gov**.

2. What Documents Should You Submit?

You do not need to provide original documents with this application.

You must give USCIS copies of documents to prove you are a national of the country designated for TPS, your date of entry into the United States, and your U.S. residence. In addition:

A. In certain circumstances, USCIS may ask you to submit original documents.

B. Copies of documents in a foreign language must be accompanied by an English translation. The translator must certify that the translation is accurate and that he or she is competent to translate the foreign language into English.

C. **Documentation exception:** If you are filing this application for annual registration, re-registration, or renewal of temporary treatment benefits (**Parts 1** and **2** on Form I-821), you do not have to submit any copies of documentation. You may, however, be asked for additional information and/or documentation in certain circumstances.

3. What Documents Do You Need to Prove Identity and Nationality?

Submit any of the following:

A. Passport;

B. Birth certificate accompanied by photo identification; or

C. Any national identity document from your country of origin bearing your photo and/or fingerprint.

4. What Documents Do You Need to Prove Date of Entry Into the United States?

Submit any of the following documents:

A. Passport;

B. I-94 Arrival/Departure Record; or

C. Copies of documents specified in item **Number 5** below.

5. What Documents Do You Need to Prove Residence in the United States?

Submit any relevant documents such as:

A. Employment records (e.g., pay stubs, W-2 Forms, certification of the filing of Federal income tax returns, state verification of the filing of state income tax returns, letters from employer(s) or, if you are self employed, letters from banks and other firms with whom you have done business.

NOTE: In all of these documents, your name and the name of the employer or other interested organization must appear on the form or letter, as well as relevant dates. Letters from employers must be in affidavit form and shall be signed and attested to by the employer under penalty of perjury.

Such letters must include: **(1)** your address(es) at the time of employment; **(2)** exact period(s) of employment; **(3)** period(s) of layoff; **(4)** duties with the company. If the employment records are unavailable, submit an affidavit form-letter explaining why these records cannot be obtained. This affidavit form-letter shall be signed and attested to by the employer under penalty of perjury.

B. Rent receipts, utility bills (gas, electric, phone, etc.), receipts, or letters from companies showing the dates during which you received service.

C. School records (letters, report cards, etc.) from the schools that you or your children have attended in the United States, showing the name(s) of the schools and periods of school attendance.

D. Hospital or medical records concerning treatment or hospitalization of you or your children, showing the name of the medical facility or physician and the date(s) of the treatment or hospitalization.

E. Attestations by churches, unions or other organizations to your residence identifying you by name. The attestation must be signed by an official (whose title is shown); show inclusive dates of membership; state the address where you resided during membership period(s); include the seal of the organization impressed on the letter or the letterhead of the organization, if the organization has letterhead stationery; establish how the author knows you; and establish the origin of the information being attested to.

F. Additional documents may include money order receipts for money sent in or out of the country; passport entries; birth certificates of children born in the United States; dated bank transactions; correspondence between you and another person or organization; U.S. Social Security card; Selective Service card; automobile license receipts, title, vehicle registration, etc.; deeds, mortgages, contracts to which you have been a party; tax receipts; insurance policies; receipts; letters; or

G. Any other relevant document.

6. What If Documents Are Not Available?

If documents are not available, you may give USCIS an affidavit showing proof of unsuccessful efforts to obtain the documents, explaining why the consular process is unavailable (for identity documents), and affirming that you are a national of the designated state. (USCIS may require a statement from the appropriate issuing authority, certifying that the document is not available.) Affidavits may also be used to help prove your date of entry into the United States and residence in the United States.

7. Will TPS Applicants Need to Provide Fingerprints and Photographs?

- Except as noted below, all applicants for initial registration, re-registration or renewal of temporary treatment benefits will have a full set of biometrics (fingerprints, photograph, and a signature) collected at an Application Support Center (ASC), and must submit the **$70.00** biometrics services fee.
- TPS applicants under 14 years of age who are not filing for an EAD are exempt from biometrics collection and the associated biometrics fee.
- USCIS may, in its discretion, waive the collection of certain biometrics such as fingerprints and signatures.

If the Federal Register notice announcing the designation or extension of a particular country requires photos to be submitted with the application, attach two standard passport-style color photos of you taken within 30 days of submission of this application. The photos should be 2x2 inches in size and have a white background. The photos should be glossy and not retouched or mounted. The dimension of the facial image should be about 1 inch to 1 3/8 inches from the chin to the top of the hair in a full frontal view. Using a pencil or felt pen, lightly print your name and Alien Registration Number (A#), if any, on the back of the photographs.

8. How Should You Prepare This Form?

A. Type or print legibly in black ink.

B. If you need extra space to complete any item, attach a continuation sheet, indicate the item number and date and sign each sheet.

C. Answer all questions fully and accurately. If any item does not apply, please write "N/A."

9. Where Should You File This Form?

The USCIS office having jurisdiction over your place of residence will accept this application, either in person or through the mail, or both. For filing instructions, please inquire by calling the USCIS National Customer Service Center at **1-800-375-5283.**

10. What Is the Fee?

A. An initial (i.e.,) first-time) applicant must submit:

1. A **$50.00** application fee for the Form I-821; and
2. A **$70.00** fee for biometric services, including fingerprints, photograph and signature, if required. (See **No. 7**, Will TPS Applicants Need to Provide Fingerprints and Photographs?); and
3. A **$180.00** fee for the Form I-765, Application for Employment Authorization, if you are between the ages of 14 and 64 years and seeking employment.

B. An applicant for TPS re-registration or renewal of temporary treatment benefits must submit:

1. A **$70.00** fee for biometric services, including fingerprints, photograph and signature, if required. (See **No. 7**, Will TPS Applicants Need to Provide Fingerprints and Photographs?); and
2. A **$180.00** fee for the Form I-765, Application for Employment Authorization, if you wish to apply for employment authorization.

C. The fee must be submitted in the exact amount. It cannot be refunded. **Do Not Mail Cash**. All checks and money orders must be drawn on a bank or other institution located in the United States and must be payable in United States currency. Please assure that if a check or money order is drawn on the account of a person other than yourself, your name appears in the lower left corner on the face of the check or money order. If the check is not honored, USCIS will charge you $30.00.

Make the check or money order payable to the **Department of Homeland Security**, except:

1. If you live in Guam and are filing your application there, make the check or money order payable to "Treasurer, Guam" or;
2. If you live in the U.S. Virgin Islands and you are filing your application there, make the check or money order payable to "Commissioner of Finance of the Virgin Islands."

NOTE: When preparing a check or money order, spell out Department of Homeland Security. Do not use the initials "USDHS" or "DHS."

How to Check If the Fees Are Correct.

The fees on this form are current as of the edition date appearing in the lower right corner of this page. However, because USCIS fees change periodically, you can verify if the fees are correct by following one of the steps below:

- Visit our website at **www.uscis.gov** and scroll down to "Forms and E-Filing" to check the appropriate fees, or
- Review the Fee Schedule included in your form package, if you called us to request the form, or
- Telephone our National Customer Service Center at **1-800-375-5283** and ask for the fee information.

NOTE: If your petition or application requires a biometric services fee for USCIS to take your fingerprints, photograph or signature, you can use the same procedure above to confirm the biometrics fee.

11. Are You Also Required to File Form I-765, Application for Employment Authorization?

A. Yes. Each applicant, regardless of age, must also submit a completed Form I-765, even if employment authorization is not being requested.

If your application for TPS is granted and you want to travel outside the United States and return, you must request advance parole from USCIS by filing a Form I-131, Application for Travel Document, with the appropriate USCIS office. A Form I-512 travel document will be issued to you if your request is granted.

B. As noted in **No. 10**, What Is the Fee?, only those applicants requesting employment authorization must pay the fee for Form I-765.

12. May the Filing Fees for Forms I-821 and I-765 Be Waived?

Yes. If you are unable to pay the filing fees, 8 CFR 103.7(c) states that you may apply for a waiver of the filing fees. In order to obtain a fee waiver, you must submit with these forms a written statement, made under oath, affirmation, or pursuant to 28 USC 1746, under penalty of perjury. In the written statement you must state that you believe you are eligible for TPS and that you want the filing fees waived. You must also explain why you are unable to pay the required fees.

13. What If I Change My Address?

If you change your address after filing for TPS, you must complete and mail us a Form AR-11, Alien's Change of Address Card. Enclose the AR-11 in an envelope addressed to the office having jurisdiction over your residence. Include copies of your application and any USCIS documents or correspondence relating to your case.

NOTE: If you informed your U.S. Post Office but not USCIS about your address change, please be advised that the Postal Service will not forward USCIS mail to you. The mail will be returned to USCIS as undeliverable.

14. What Is Our Authority for Collecting This Information?

We request the information on the form to carry out the immigration laws contained in Title 8, United States Code, Section 1154(a). We need this information to determine whether you are eligible for immigration benefits.

The information you provide may also be disclosed to other federal, state, local, and foreign law enforcement and regulatory agencies. You do not have to give this information. However, if you do not give some or all of the requested information, your application may be denied.

15. Do You Need USCIS Forms or Information?

To order USCIS forms, call our toll-free forms line at **1-800-870-3676**. You can also get USCIS forms and information on immigration laws, regulations or procedures by calling our National Customer Service Center at **1-800-375-5283** or visiting our internet website at **www.uscis.gov.**

16. Need to Make an Appointment at a USCIS Office? Use InfoPass.

As an alternative to waiting in line for assistance at your local USCIS office, you can now schedule an appointment through our internet-based system, **InfoPass.** To access the system, visit our website at **www.uscis.gov.** Use the **InfoPass** appointment scheduler and follow the screen prompts to set up your appointment. **InfoPass** generates an electronic appointment notice that appears on the screen. Print the notice and take it with you to your appointment. The notice gives the time and date of your appointment, along with the address of the USCIS office.

17. Reporting Burden.

Under the Paperwork Reduction Act, an agency may not conduct or sponsor an information collection. A person is not required to respond to an information collection unless it displays a currently valid OMB control number.

We try to create forms and instructions that are accurate, can easily be understood and impose the least possible burden on you to provide us with information. Often this is difficult because some immigration laws are very complex.

The estimated average time to complete this application is 1 hour and 30 minutes computed as follows: 1) learning about the form and understanding the instructions, 30 minutes; 2) collecting the necessary supporting documents 15 minutes; 3) completing the form, 15 minutes; and 4) traveling to and waiting at a preparer's office (e.g. attorney or voluntary agency), 30 minutes.

If you have comments regarding the accuracy of this estimate, or suggestions for making this form simpler, you can write to the U.S. Citizenship and Immigration Services, Regulatory Management Division 111 Massachusetts Avenue N.W., Washington, DC 20529; OMB No. 1615-0043. **Do not mail your completed application to this address.**

OMB No. 1615-0043; Exp. 07/31/07

Department of Homeland Security
U.S. Citizenship and Immigration Services

I-821, Application for Temporary Protected Status

START HERE - Please type or print in black ink.

Part 1. Type of application. *(check one)*

a. ☐ This is my first application to register for Temporary Protected Status (TPS).

b. ☐ This is my application for re-registration or renewal of temporary treatment benefits. I have previously been granted TPS or temporary treatment benefits. I have maintained and continue to maintain eligibility for TPS.

Part 2. Information about you.

Family Name (Last Name) | Given Name (First Name) | Full Middle Name

U.S. Mailing Address: (Street Number and Name) | Apt. #

C/O: (In Care Of)

Town/City | State

County | Zip Code

Date of Birth *(mm/dd/yyyy)* | Gender ☐ Male ☐ Female

Place of Birth (Town or City) | State/Country

Country of Residence | Country of Citizenship/Nationality

Marital Status
☐ Single ☐ Married ☐ Divorced ☐ Widowed

Other Names Used *(including maiden name)*

Date of Entry Into the U.S. *(mm/dd/yyyy)* | Place of Entry Into the U.S.

Manner of Arrival *(Visitor, student, stowaway, without inspection, etc.)*

Arrival/Departure Record (I-94) Number | Date authorized stay expired/or will expire, as shown on Form I-94 or I-95 *(mm/dd/yyyy)*

Your Current Immigration Status:
In Status *(state nonimmigrant classification, e.g. F-1, etc.)* | Out of Status *(state nonimmigrant violation, e.g., overstay student, EWI etc.)*

Alien Registration Number (A#) *(if any)* | U.S. Social Security Number *(if any)*

Are you now or have you ever been under immigration proceedings?
☐ Yes ☐ No

If you answered "Yes" to the above question, provide the following information.
Type of proceedings:
☐ Exclusion ☐ Removal/Deportation ☐ Recission ☐ Judicial Proceedings

Location of Proceedings | Date of Proceedings *(mm/dd/yyyy)*

For USCIS Use Only

Returned	Receipt
Date	
Date	
Resubmitted	
Date	
Date	
Reloc Sent	
Date	
Date	
Reloc Rec'd	
Date	
Date	
☐ Applicant Interviewed on ________	

Case ID #:

A #:

Remarks

Action Block

To Be Completed by
Attorney or Representative, if any.
☐ Fill in box if G-28 is attached to represent the applicant.

ATTY State License #

Part 3. Information about your spouse and children. *(if any)*

1. **Provide the following information about your spouse** *(if married).*

Last Name of Spouse | First Name | Middle Name

Address (Street Number and Name) | Apt #

Town/City | State/Province | Country | Zip/Postal Code

Your Spouse's Birth Date *(mm/dd/yyyy)* | Date and Place of Present Marriage

Name of Prior Husbands/Wives | Date(s) Marriage(s) Ended *(mm/dd/yyyy)*

2. **List the names, ages and current residence of children** *(if any).*

Name *(First/Middle/Last)*	Date of Birth (mm/dd/yyyy	Residence

Part 4. Eligibility standards.

1. **Provide the following information:**

I am a national of, or an alien having no nationality, who last habitually resided in the foreign state of:

I entered the United States on the following date (provide month/day/year), and have resided in the United States since that time.

2. To be eligible for Temporary Protected Status, you must be admissible as an immigrant to the United States, with certain exceptions.

If any of the questions beginning below on this page and continuing on **Page 3** apply to you, number which one(s) in the box(es): (for example, 2k for Have you entered the United States as a stowaway;) and include a full explanation on a separate sheet(s) of paper. Use the number **2** before each letter referring to the specific question (2a, 2b, etc.).

If you were ever arrested, provide the disposition (outcome) of the arrest. For example, "case dismissed" from the appropriate authority.

NOTE: For information about waivers concerning the grounds of inadmissibility, see **Page 3.**

2a. Have you been convicted of any felony or two or more misdemeanors committed in the United States;

2b. (i) Have you ordered, incited, assisted or otherwise participated in the persecution of any person on account of race, religion, nationality, membership in a particular social group or political opinion;

(ii) Have you been convicted by a final judgment of a particularly serious crime, constituting a danger to the community of the United States (an alien convicted of an aggravated felony is considered to have committed a particularly serious crime);

(iii) Have you committed a serious nonpolitical crime outside of the United States prior to your arrival in the United States; or

(iv) Have you engaged in or are you still engaged in activities that could be reasonable grounds for concluding that you are a danger to the security of the United States?

Part 4. Eligibility standards. *(Continued)*

2c. (i) Have you been convicted of, or have you committed acts which constitute the essential elements of a crime (other than a purely political offense) or a violation of or a conspiracy to violate any law relating to a controlled substance as defined in Section 102 of the Controlled Substance Act;

(ii) Have you been convicted of two or more offenses (other than purely political offenses) for which the aggregate sentences to confinement actually imposed were five years or more;

(iii) Have you trafficked in or do you continue to traffic in any controlled substance or are or have been a knowing assister, abettor, conspirator, or colluder with others in the illicit trafficking of any controlled substance;

(iv) Have you engaged or do you continue to engage solely, principally, or incidentally in any activity related to espionage or sabotage or violate any law involving the export of goods, technology, or sensitive information, any other unlawful activity, or any activity the purpose of which is in opposition, or the control, or overthrow of the government of the United States;

(v) Have you engaged in or do you continue to engage in terrorist activities;

(vi) Have you engaged in or do you continue to engage or plan to engage in activities in the United States that would have potentially serious adverse foreign policy consequences for the United States;

(vii) Have you been or do you continue to be a member of the Communist or other totalitarian party, except when membership was involuntary; and

(viii) Have you participated in Nazi persecution or genocide;

2d. Have you been arrested, cited, charged, indicted, fined, or imprisoned for breaking or violating any law or ordinance, excluding traffic violations, or been the beneficiary of a pardon, amnesty, rehabilitation decree, other act of clemency or similar action;

2e. Have you committed a serious criminal offense in the United States and asserted immunity from prosecution;

2f. Have you within the past ten years engaged in prostitution or procurement of prostitution or do you continue to engage in prostitution or procurement of prostitution;

2g. Have you been or do you intend to be involved in any other commercial vice;

2h. Have you been excluded and deported from the United States within the past year, or have you been deported or removed from the United States at government expense within the last five years (20 years if you have been convicted of an aggravated felony);

2i. Have you ever assisted any other person to enter the United States in violation of the law;

2j. (i) Do you have a communicable disease of public health significance.

(ii) Do you have or have you had a physical or mental disorder and behavior (or a history of behavior that is likely to recur) associated with the disorder which has posed or may pose a threat to the property, safety or welfare of yourself or others;

(iii) Are you now or have you been a drug abuser or drug addict;

2k. Have you entered the United States as a stowaway;

2l. Are you subject to a final order for violation of section 274C (producing and/or using false documentation to unlawfully satisfy a requirement of the Immigration and Nationality Act);

2m. Do you practice polygamy;

2n. Were you the guardian of, and did you accompany another alien who was ordered excluded and deported (or removed) from the United States;

2o. Have you detained, retained, or withheld the custody of a child, having a lawful claim to United States citizenship, outside the United States from a United States citizen granted custody?

NOTE ABOUT WAIVERS: If you placed any of the following numbered references in the boxes on Page **2**, you may be eligible for a waiver of the grounds described in the questions: 2e; 2f; 2g; 2h; 2i; 2j; 2k; 2l; 2m; 2n or 2o. The Form I-601 is the USCIS application used to request a waiver. The form is available at local USCIS offices, on our website at **www.uscis.gov** or by calling the USCIS toll-free forms line at **1-800-870-3676.**

Part 5. Signature. *Read the information on penalties in the instructions before completing this section. If someone helped you prepare this petition, he or she must complete **Part 6.***

YOUR CERTIFICATION: I certify, under penalty of perjury under the laws of the United States of America, that the foregoing is true and correct. Copies of documents submitted are exact photocopies of unaltered original documents and I understand that I may be required to submit original documents to USCIS at a later date. Furthermore, I authorize the release of any information from my records that the U.S. Citizenship and Immigration Services needs to determine eligibility for the benefit that I am seeking.

Signature	**Daytime Phone Number** *(Area/Country Codes)*	**Date** *(mm/dd/yyyy)*

NOTE: If you do not completely fill out this form or fail to submit required documents listed in the instructions, you may not be found eligible for the requested benefit and this petition may be denied.

Part 6. Signature of person preparing form, if other than above.

I declare that I prepared this petition at the request of the above person and it is based on all information of which I have knowledge.

Attorney or Representative: In the event of a Request for Evidence (RFE), may USCIS contact you by Fax or E-Mail? ☐ Yes ☐ No

Signature	**Print Your Name**	**Date** *(mm/dd/yyyy)*

Firm Name and Address

Daytime Phone Number *(Area/Country Codes)*	**Fax Number** *(Area/Country Codes)*	**E-Mail Address**

Part 7. Checklist.

- ☐ Did you answer each question?
- ☐ Did you sign the Form I-821 application?
- ☐ Did you submit the required application and biometric services (fingerprinting) fees?
- ☐ Did you submit the necessary documents and photos, if so required?
- ☐ Did you also submit the Form I-765 with the filing fee or a written request for a waiver of the filing fee (See instructions, items **10, 11** and **12**)?

Have you submitted:

- ☐ The filing fee for this application or a written request for a waiver of the filing fee (see instructions, items **10** and **12**)?
- ☐ Supporting evidence to prove identity, nationality, date of entry and residence?
- ☐ Other required supporting documents (photos, etc.) for each application?

GLOSSARY

admission: For immigration purposes, physical presence and freedom from official restraint in the United States.

advanced degree: For immigration purposes, an academic degree beyond the baccalaureate.

alien: A person in the United States who is not a U.S. citizen.

Alien Registration Card: A card which identifies an alien's LPR status; informally known as a green card.

ambassador: A diplomat who heads the diplomatic mission at an embassy.

amnesty: The process by which legal or illegal aliens were permitted to become LPRs if they arrived in the United States before 1982. This provision of the INA has expired.

asylee: A person who has been granted asylum.

asylum: A process available to aliens who qualify as refugees, permitting such aliens to lawfully remain in the United States and to become LPRs.

baccalaureate: A bachelor's degree.

bigamist: For immigration purposes, a person who is married to more than one person at the same time.

Black Letter law: A clearly measurable law, such as "The maximum speed limit is 55 miles per hour."

Board of Immigration Appeals (BIA): The court of appeals within the administrative branch of immigration law. Decisions from the lower immigration court are appealed to the BIA.

Bureau of Citizenship and Immigration Services (BCIS): This is the DHS subagency responsible for immigration services and benefits, such as obtaining permission to visit the United States or to gain U.S. citizenship.

Bureau of Customs and Border Protection (BCBP): This is the DHS subagency responsible for aspects of border patrol and inspections.

Bureau of Immigration and Customs Enforcement (BICE): This is the DHS subagency responsible for dealing with immigration investigations and illegal aliens.

cancellation of removal: A term in the INA essentially replacing suspension of deportation, although some of the requirements may differ.

case law: Law determined by judicial decisions.

child: For immigration purposes, unmarried minor (under 21 years old) offspring.

confidentiality: The requirement that a lawyer, or anyone working for a lawyer, not disclose information received from a client.

consulate: A branch of the U.S. embassy that typically grants visas to eligible persons who want to travel to the United States.

curricular practical training: Permission for alien nonimmigrant students who have not yet completed their course of study to work in a certain capacity and for a certain period of time.

daughter: For immigration purposes, a female offspring who is married, at least 21 years old, or both.

democracy: Government by the people, either directly or indirectly through representatives; ideally, as a basis for a system highly protective of individual liberties.

denaturalization: The process by which a naturalized citizen loses his or her U.S. citizenship.

Department of Homeland Security (DHS): In order to maximize our national security, President George W. Bush established a new government agency, the Department of Homeland Security. Includes three subagencies, called bureaus, that now handle immigration matters once handled by INS. The three bureaus are the BCBP, BCIS, and BICE.

deportation: Term referring to expulsion from the United States as ordered by the immigration court; now called removal.

discretionary relief: Relief that may be granted to aliens at the discretion of the DHS, BIA, or federal court under the judicial system.

diversity-based immigration: A process providing immigrant visas for persons from countries which have been adversely affected in the immigration process.

dual citizenship: Simultaneously holding citizenship in two countries. This can occur because a person was born in one country to parents who are citizens of another or because a country of which a person is a citizen still recognizes that citizenship after the person becomes a citizen of another country.

embassy: The residence and place of business of an ambassador. An embassy, or where applicable through its consulate, typically grants visas to eligible persons who want to travel to the United States.

emigrant: A person who leaves his or her country with the intent to permanently settle in another country.

entry with inspection: Applies to aliens who entered the United States with DHS knowledge.

entry without inspection: Applies to aliens who entered the United States without DHS knowledge. Such aliens are also referred to as "border jumpers."

ethics: A set of values about what is good, right, and just. Various professions, including law, have their own set of ethical codes.

exceptional ability: For immigration purposes, a person who has achieved excellence in a particular field but is not uniquely outstanding.

exchange visitor: An alien who enters the United States as a nonimmigrant in order to teach or learn in a particular academic course or program similar to the course of study in the alien's own country.

exclusionable: Denial of an alien to enter the United States at the point of DHS inspection. Now called inadmissibility.

executive branch: The branch of government that executes the law.

expatriation: The process by which both natural-born and naturalized citizens lose their U.S. citizenship.

extraordinary ability: A person who is uniquely outstanding in a particular field.

green card: Formally, an Alien Registration Card, which identifies an alien's LPR status.

House of Representatives: Along with the Senate, a body of legislators that comprises the United States Congress, that is, the legislative branch.

illegal alien: An alien in the United States who either entered illegally or became illegal because his or her lawful status expired.

immediate relative: For immigration purposes, a spouse, parent, or child of a U.S. citizen.

immigrant: A person who has arrived into another country with the intent to permanently settle there.

Immigration and Nationality Act of 1990 (INA): The United States immigration law, as established by Congress.

Immigration and Naturalization Service (INS): Formerly the administrative agency under the United States executive branch that was primarily responsible for executing the INA. The INS has been replaced by the Department of Homeland Security (DHS) and its subagencies.

Immigration Marriage Fraud: The act of an alien and a citizen entering into a marriage for the primary purpose of benefiting the alien's immigration status.

Immigration Marriage Fraud amendments: A set of laws established as a method to combat immigration marriage fraud.

inadmissible: Denial of an alien to enter the United States at the point of DHS inspection. Formerly called exclusion.

intracompany transferee: An alien who enters the United States as a nonimmigrant because he works for a foreign company which has (or will open) affiliated sites in the United States and who will work at one or more of those affiliated sites.

Judicial branch: The branch of government responsible for enforcing the law.

labor certification: Approval by the U.S. Department of Labor to permit an alien to become an LPR through employment-based immigration. The alien then must apply to DHS to become an LPR.

legal alien: An alien who is legally in the United States.

Legal Permanent Resident (LPR): A legal U.S immigrant who is not a U.S. citizen.

Legislative branch: The branch of government responsible for enforcing the law.

lottery: An actual lottery by which aliens eligible for diversity immigration may receive LPR status if their names are selected from the drawing.

natural-born citizen: Persons born in the United States or, in many cases, its territories and are subject to the jurisdiction of the United States.

naturalized citizen: An alien who has become a U.S. citizen through the process of naturalization (i.e., by the DHS, in compliance with the INA).

9/11: September 11, 2001. The day on which terrorists flew airplanes into New York City's World Trade Center and the Pentagon Building in Washington, DC, killing thousands. A third airplane, purportedly headed toward Washington, DC, was thwarted in its attempt by passengers; the plane crashed in Pennsylvania, killing all on board.

nonattorney: A legal professional who is not an attorney (lawyer). One type of nonattorney is a paralegal.

nonimmigrant: A person who is in another country without the intent to permanently settle there.

numerical limitations: Restrictions in the number of applications made to DHS during a particular period of time, often creating long waiting lists for applicants.

opinion: A judicial decision about a case.

paralegal: A type of nonattorney; paralegals arguably are more formally recognized than any other type of nonattorney.

parole: Permission granted to an alien who is found to be excludable to leave the United States border without being placed in custody, with the promise that he will be present at his removal hearing.

polygamist: A person who is married to two or more people at the same time; for immigration purposes, such person is a bigamist (which traditionally means a person married to two people at the same time).

postcompletion practical training: Permission for alien nonimmigrant students who have completed their course of study to work in a certain capacity and for a certain period of time.

prevailing wage: The wage which the U.S. Department of Labor determines to be the competitive rate in a particular occupation.

priority date: A date used to measure when an approved application to DHS has been received.

priority worker: For immigration purposes, persons of extraordinary ability in the sciences, arts, education, business, or athletics; outstanding professors and researchers; or certain multinational managers and executives.

refugee: A person outside his or her native country or country where he or she last resided who is unable or unwilling to return there because of persecution or a well-founded fear of persecution.

registry : For immigration purposes, a status which provides for legal or illegal aliens to become LPRs because they have continuously resided in the United States since before 1972.

religious worker: An alien who enters the United States either as a nonimmigrant or an immigrant, who is permitted to enter based on the religious work he or she have done in his own country and such work which he or she plans to do in the United States.

removal: Expulsion from the United States as ordered by the immigration court; formerly called deportation.

removal hearing: A formal hearing to determine whether an alien should be inadmissible or removed. Formerly called exclusion hearing (to determine inadmissibility) or deportation hearing (to determine removability).

Senate: Along with the House of Representatives, a body of legislators that comprises the United States Congress, that is, the legislative branch.

skilled worker: For immigration purposes, a person who has two years of training or experience in a particular field or occupation.

son: For immigration purposes, a male offspring who is married, at least 21 years old, or both.

statute: A law created by the legislative branch of government.

stay of removal: A temporary waiver of removal granted to aliens who have secured some other method of remaining in the United States lawfully.

supremacy clause: A clause in the U.S. Constitution which states that federal law prevails over state law where there is a conflict of the two.

Temporary Protected Status (TPS): A provision permitting aliens to enter or remain in the United States because their countries are in the middle of war, political turmoil, or environmental disaster.

treason: The act or overthrowing (or attempting to overthrow) the government or betraying the country into the hands of the enemy.

treaty investor: An alien who may enter the United States as a nonimmigrant in order to invest money in goods and services involved in the trade of commerce of navigation based on treaties between the United States and their country.

treaty trader: An alien who may enter the United States as a nonimmigrant in order to engage in trade of commerce or navigation based on treaties between the United States and their country.

United States Constitution: The document on which our two-tier, three-branch system of government was founded.

U.S. citizen: A person who is either a natural-born or naturalized citizen of the United States.

visa: Written official approval permitting a person to enter the United States as an immigrant or nonimmigrant.

visitor: An alien who may enter the United States as a nonimmigrant in order to visit the United States for a specific period of time for purposes of either business or pleasure.

voluntary departure: A process permitting an alien ordered removed to leave the United States voluntarily at his or her own expense, thus avoiding some of the consequences of removal.

waiver: A form of discretionary relief, whereby a condition requiring an alien to be removed or to face another penalty is removed.

well-founded fear of persecution: Along with actual persecution, the basis for granting refugee status or asylum. Generally, the alien must have a well-founded fear of persecution based on race, religion, nationality, membership in a particular social group, or political opinion.

with inspection: The process of an alien being lawfully admitted into the United States.

withholding of removal: A waiver of removal typically granted to aliens seeking asylum.

without inspection: The act of an alien entering the United States without being lawfully admitted.

xenophobia: Fear of strangers. For immigration purposes, a fear of immigrants, often resulting in resentment or mistreatment of immigrants.

zealous representation within the bounds of the law: An ethical rule by which attorneys and other legal professionals must use their best efforts to represent their clients within the bounds of the law in order to achieve the best possible result.

INDEX

References are to pages.

H

I

J

K

L

M

N

O